world
CHEESE
BOOK

world
CHEESE
BOOK

EDITOR-IN-CHIEF
JULIET HARBUTT

CONTRIBUTORS

ANDROUET • MARTIN ASPINWALL • VINCENZO BOZZETTI • KEVIN JOHN BROOME
RAN BUCK • SAGI COOPER • DIANNE CURTIN • JIM DAVIES • SHEANA DAVIS • ANGELA GRAY
RIE HIJIKATA • RUMIKO HONMA • KATIE JARVIS • MONIKA LINTON • GURTH PRETTY
HANSUELI RENZ • RICHARD SUTTON • WILL STUDD • JOE WARWICK • AAD VERNOOIJ

LONDON, NEW YORK, MELBOURNE,
MUNICH, AND DELHI

Project Editor Danielle Di Michiel
Senior Art Editor Elly King
Editorial Assistants Shashwati Tia Sarkar, Erin Boeck Motum
Designer William Hicks
Managing Editor Dawn Henderson
Managing Art Editor Christine Keilty
Senior Jacket Creative Nicola Powling
Senior Production Editor Jennifer Murray
Production Controller Alice Holloway
Creative Technical Support Sonia Charbonnier

US Editors Rebecca Warren, Christy Lusiak

DK India
DTP Designers Dheeraj Arora, Preetam Singh, Jagtar Singh
Senior Designer Tannishtha Chakraborty
Design Manager Romi Chakraborty
Head of Publishing Aparna Sharma

First American Edition, 2009

Published in the United States by
DK Publishing
375 Hudson Street
New York, New York 10014

10 11 12   10 9 8 7 6 5 4 3 2

WD205—October 2008

Published in Great Britain by Dorling Kindersley Limited.

A catalog record for this book is available from the Library of Congress.

ISBN 978-0-7566-5442-9

DK books are available at special discounts when purchased in bulk for sales promotions,
premiums, fund-raising, or educational use. For details, contact: DK Publishing Special
Markets, 375 Hudson Street, New York, New York 10014 or SpecialSales@dk.com.

Printed and bound in Singapore by Star Standard

**Discover more at
www.dk.com**

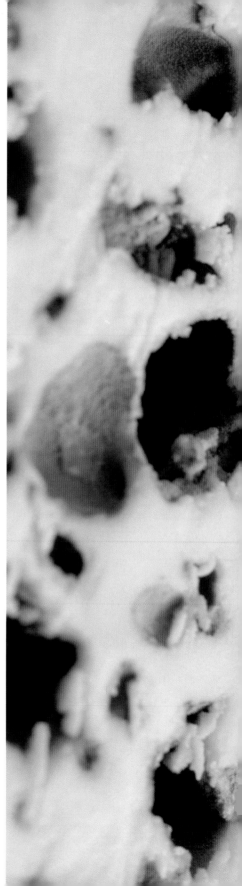

CONTENTS

Introduction 6
Understanding Cheese 8
Using this Book 9
Fresh Cheeses 10
Aged Fresh Cheeses 12
Soft White Cheeses 14
Semi-soft Cheeses 16
Hard Cheeses 18
Blue Cheeses 20
Flavor-added Cheeses 22
The Perfect Cheeseboard 24

France 26
Special Features
  Beaufort 38
  Brie de Meaux 46
  Comté 56
  Epoisses de Bourgogne 64
  Reblochon de Savoie 74
  Roquefort 82
  Sainte-Maure de Touraine 92

Italy 102
Special Features
  Gorgonzola 110
  Mozzarella di Bufala 120
  Parmigiano-Reggiano 130
  Taleggio 138

Spain and Portugal 146
Spain 148
Portugal 167
Special Features
  Mahòn 154
  Manchego 162

**Great Britain and
Ireland 170**
England 172
Scotland 207
Wales 213
Ireland 219
Special Features
  Cheddar 180
  Stilton 192
  Yarg Cornish Cheese 200
  Caboc 210
  Caerphilly 216

Low Countries 226
Belgium 227
The Netherlands 230
Special Features
  Gouda 232

**Germany, Austria,
and Switzerland 234**
Germany 235
Austria 238
Switzerland 240
Special Features
  Emmentaler 242

Scandinavia 246
Denmark 247
Norway 249
Sweden 250
Finland 253

**Eastern Europe and
the Near East 254**
Greece 256
Hungary 260
Slovakia 260
Turkey 261
Cyprus 261
Lebanon 264
Israel 264
Special Features
  Feta 258
  Halloumi 262

The Americas 266
USA 270
Canada 312
Mexico 320
Brazil 321
Argentina 321
Special Features
  Monterey Jack 286

Japan 322

**Australia and
New Zealand 326**
Australia 328
New Zealand 335

Glossary 342
Resources 344
Index 346
Contributors 351
Acknowledgments 352

Introduction

Evidence of cheesemaking has been found dating back to 2800 BCE, but the discovery of cheese would have come about as a happy accident. Any milk left to warm by a fire or stored in a sack made from the stomach of an animal would have soured, causing the milk solids (the curds) and liquid (the whey) to coagulate and separate, allowing humans to learn that their most precious commodity, milk, could be preserved in the form of cheese and, eventually, that rennet found in the stomach of the milk-producing animal was the coagulant.

The Story of Cheese

Now, some 5,000 years later, cheese is made all over the world with all kinds of milk, from reindeer's milk in Lapland, to buffalo's milk in Australia, and yak's milk in the Kingdom of Bhutan. The miracle of cheese is that, although milk tastes virtually the same the world over, the diversity of textures, tastes, and aromas is almost infinite, and virtually any cheese can be made anywhere in the world. The size, shape, and milk of a cheese, however, has been determined by such diverse external forces as historical events, centuries of experimentation, religious orders, and the terrain, while the nuances of texture and taste are influenced by the raw materials—the type and breed of animal, the soil, the grazing, the climate, microclimate, and ingenuity of the cheesemaker.

European cheeses owe much to the Greeks' knowledge and, later, the Romans, who built on that knowledge and took their recipes for making cheese across Europe to feed their legions as their Empire spread—a legacy clearly seen throughout Europe to this day. The Middle Ages saw the proliferation of monastic orders across Europe and into Britain and Ireland, particularly the Benedictine and, later, the Cistercian monks, who developed the cheeses we

The ancient art of cheesemaking is lovingly depicted in this colorful Swiss wood engraving.

know today as Trappist or monastery cheeses, of which Maroilles of Northern France was probably the first.

Historically, a cheese's size was determined by the amount of milk available and the proximity to the nearest market; hence, mountain cheese tended to be large, with the farmers combining their milk to make slow-ripening cheeses they could sell at the end of the summer months when the cows returned to the valleys. Those made in the valleys and near large markets would have been smaller, quicker to ripen, and sold at weekly markets. Shape was determined by the sophistication of the maker and the raw materials available to make the molds—whether woven grass, fired clay, or wood.

Today, Europe's traditional cheeses are typically made in designated areas by various artisan producers whose combined volume is sufficiently high that the cheese can be found around the world. Classic examples include raw milk Camembert de Normandie (see p44), made by only five producers and Parmigiano-Reggiano (see p130), made by around 830 small producers. Artisan cheeses developed in the last 30 years or so, however, tend to be invented by individual cheesemakers and are often hard to find outside their region or country of origin, even if made in large volumes.

The Raw Materials

The individual identity and personality of a cheese is determined by a number of facts of nature.

The climate and landscape, including the minerals in the soil, affect what flora grows, and therefore what a milk-producing animal eats, thereby influencing the subtle flavors of the milk. Even the most unobservant cannot fail to see and smell the difference between fresh grass, wild clover, and meadow flowers compared with compacted feed, silage, or turnips. Minerals also affect the speed of ripening, the texture, and flavor of the cheese.

The animal and its grazing habits add another dimension. The comfort-loving cow is largely found on rich plains, lush valleys, and sunny mountain pastures. Goats, unlike cows and sheep, are browsers, tearing sparse but aromatic flora from hedges, craggy peaks, rock-strewn valleys or, when the opportunity arises, from the farmers' carefully manicured garden. The resulting milk is herbaceous, like a crisp, white wine infused with herbs, becoming like marzipan or ground almonds with age.

The sweet, almost caramel, taste of ewe's milk has been valued in Europe and the Middle East for thousands of years. The numerous breeds adapt to almost any climate, some surviving on seemingly nothing, yielding but a few liters of milk a day imbued with the essence of the wild, aromatic herbs, grasses, and flora that form their diet.

The breed of animal can also be a factor. Compared with the high volume yield of the Friesian, for example, milk from Jersey or Guernsey cows has large fat globules that produce a richer, smoother deep Monet-yellow cheese, and the sweet, mellifluous milk of the Montbéliarde cow is renowned throughout the Savoy region of France.

The microclimate of both the milk and the cheese room provide the finishing touch. Tiny colorful, wind-born molds and yeasts treat each new batch of protein-rich curd as a canvas on which to create their daily masterpiece, while a multitude of naturally occurring bacteria prefer the seclusion and warmth of the interior to work their magic. These convert the sweet milk sugars, or lactose, into lactic acid and so begins the fermentation process. Once an accident of nature, most have been harnessed by cheesemakers to ensure the end result is more predictable. These microflora, along with the subtleties inherent in milk, are lost when the milk is pasteurized and must be re-introduced in the form of a cocktail of bacteria known as a starter culture. Regrettably, these laboratory-produced cultures cannot emulate the complexity provided by Mother Nature.

How Cheese is Made

Cheesemaking equipment and methods vary from cheesemaker to cheesemaker, but the basic principles involved have remained unchanged for thousands of years.

1 The milk Ideally, milk is pumped straight from the milking parlor to the dairy where it is checked and tested to ensure it is pure and clean. It may then be pasteurized, typically at 165°F (73°C) for 15 seconds. The milk is transferred to a vat and heated until it reaches the acidity level required for the type of cheese being made.

2 Coagulation or curdling Once the acidity reaches the desired level, a special cocktail of lactic bacteria or starter culture is added. This both converts the lactose to lactic acid and contributes to the flavor, aroma, and texture of the cheese. (Too much or not enough acidity results in imperfect cheeses.) Most cheeses are made by adding rennet (derived from the stomach of a milk-fed animal) or another coagulant to make sure the protein and fat in the milk bond and are not lost in the whey.

Curdling is the fundamental step in cheesemaking, as the degree of coagulation determines the final moisture content of the cheese, and this in turn affects the speed of the fermentation process.

3 Separation of curds and whey The freshly formed curd looks like white jelly, while the whey is a yellow-green color. Gently separating the curds from the whey creates soft, high-moisture cheeses, while cutting the curds expels more whey and produces harder cheeses. The finer the curd is cut, the harder and finer-grained the final cheese. The whey is drained off once it reaches the desired acidity.

4 Shaping and salting The curds are then piled into molds or hoops and may be pressed before being turned out of their molds. Once out of the mold, the cheese is rubbed or sprinkled with salt or soaked in brine before being placed in a cold room or cellar to age.

5 Aging and the *affineur* The aging process is the art and science of cheesemaking, as it brings out the character of the milk and the unique flavors attributed to the grazing. A good *affineur*, someone who ripens cheeses, can nurture the simplest cheese to yield up every nuance of flavor. Artisan cheeses vary from day to day, depending on the grazing, the season, the conditions in the cheese room, and the cheesemaker; so, unlike wine, cheese has a vintage every day, which is what makes it so extraordinary and wonderful.

FRESH CHEESES
(See pp10–11)

AGED FRESH CHEESES
(See pp12–13)

SOFT WHITE CHEESES
(See pp14–15)

Understanding Cheese

There is no universal system for identifying cheeses. Instead, every cheese-producing country has its own system using technical terms such as semi-hard, semi-cooked, pressed uncooked, smear-ripened, or washed-curd that are all but meaningless, and confusing, to cheese lovers.

By contrast, this book uses the Editor-in-Chief's easy-to-grasp system of identifying cheese types, based on the type of rind a cheese grows and its texture.

The way it works is that the amount of moisture, or whey, that is left in the cheese determines not only the texture of the interior, or paste as it is often called, but also the type of rind and molds the cheese will grow. There is the odd exception that crosses two of these categories, but most are very obvious.

The Editor-in-Chief's system (see pp10–23) identifies seven different types of cheese:
Fresh, Aged Fresh, Soft White, Semi-soft, Hard, Blue, and Flavor-added.

Using this system, with just a glance and a gentle squeeze you can categorize 99 percent of the cheeses you meet, whether from a French market, a New York cheese shop, or elsewhere. With a little practice, you can assess a cheese's basic character, strength of flavor, how it will behave when cooked, and even its ripeness and quality.

HARD CHEESES
(See pp18–19)

BLUE CHEESES
(See pp20–21)

**FLAVOR-ADDED
CHEESES (See pp22–23)**

SEMI-SOFT CHEESES
(See pp16–17)

Denomination and Designation of Origin

Some cheeses have legally protected names linked to their provenance. Certifying the origin of a cheese recognizes its *terroir* (French) or *tipicità* (Italian), acknowledging that the unique character of each traditionally made food is a result of a complex interaction of soil, plant life, and climate combined with traditional production methods and raw materials—a combination that cannot be replicated elsewhere. There are various national systems, such as the French AOC (Appellation d'Origine Contrôlée) and the Italian DOC (Denominazione d'Origine Controlata), as well as the European Community-created PDO (Protected Designation of Origin) for traditional regional wines and food made throughout the EC.

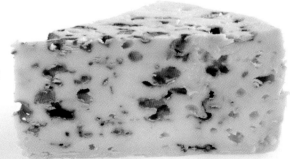

In 1666, Roquefort was the first cheese to be protected by law, the forerunner for the AOC system in France.

Using this Book

This book will open up a world of exciting cheeses for cheese fans. The core of the book is formed by chapters cataloging cheeses from each country, detailing their origins, tasting notes, and how best to enjoy them, with prominent and important cheeses explored in greater depth. The information box included with each cheese entry, explained here, contains information that is key to understanding the identity of the cheese.

Region
Some cheeses are made all over a country, while others are made by various producers in specific regions. Where three or fewer producers make the cheese in a specific location, a city or town is also listed. The region can reveal much about the *terroir* of a cheese, which dictates the type of animal found there and its grazing environment.

Age
This gives the age or range of ages in which a cheese is at its best.

Weight and Shape
Some cheeses are made in one weight and shape only, but most are produced in a range of sizes, which we have listed wherever possible.

Size
This gives the dimensions of a cheese, usually measurements such as diameter (D), height (H), length (L), or width (W), depending on its shape. Where there is a range of sizes, a range of dimensions is given. In some cases, where the range is not known, the dimensions of the pictured cheese are given.

Milk
This gives the type of animal whose milk is used to make the cheese. In some cases, a cheese may be made from a mix of milk from different animals, depending on the season and availability.

Classification
Each cheese is categorized as one of the seven types described in the Editor-in-Chief's system (see pp10–23).

Producer
Up to three producers are listed for artisan cheesemakers. "Various" indicates that the cheese is made by more than three producers.

Pecorino Siciliano PDO

This cheese is documented as far back as 900 BCE, when Odysseus meets the Cyclops Polyphemus in Homer's *Odyssey*. As in ancient times, this cheese is still hand-made using lamb's rennet.

TASTING NOTES Yellow and sometimes studded with whole black peppercorns, it is firm and friable with a pungent, salty, full, and long-lasting flavor.

HOW TO ENJOY Serve young cheeses with vegetables; aged ones with bread and olives or grated over pasta.

ITALY Sicily		
Age 4–12 months		
Weight and Shape 9–26½lb (4–12kg), wheel		
Size D. 5½–15in (14–38cm), H. 4–7in (10–18cm)		
Milk Ewe		
Classification Hard		
Producer Various		

Name
The name of a cheese is always given in the language of the cheese's origin, followed by any designation of origin status if it applies.

Introduction
This describes cheese in terms of its identity, giving useful information about its makers and origins.

Tasting Notes
These describe the aroma, flavor, texture, and finish of the cheese.

How to Enjoy
This offers suggestions on how best to enjoy the cheese, including cooking ideas and wine accompaniments.

Map
A quick reference to the country that produces the cheese. The red dot indicates the general location or region of the cheesemaker. Where there is no red dot, the cheese is produced all over the country.

Photograph
For ease of recognition, this shows a cheese as it is sold. Generally, this shows both the exterior and the interior of the cheese.

Scale
This symbol provides an at-a-glance visual guide to the approximate size of the cheese in relation to an averaged-sized hand. When a cheese has its size listed as "various," the symbol indicates the size of the cheese photographed. Where the symbol is missing, the sizing information was unavailable, or the cheese is soft and sold in tubs or pots.

Fresh Cheeses

NO RIND · HIGH MOISTURE CONTENT · MILD · FRESH · LEMONY

Ready to eat within a few days, or even hours, of being made, fresh cheeses are so young that they barely have time to develop any more than a whisper of the milk's potential flavor, so the taste is typically described as lactic or milky, sweet, lemony, refreshing, citrus, or acidic. This does not mean they are bland. On the contrary, the skill of the true craftsman can coax the subtle flavors from the milk; the sweet, grassy notes of cow's milk; the aromatic, herbaceous character of goat's milk, with its hints of white wine and crushed almonds; the richness of ewe's milk that suggests Brazil nuts, caramelized onions, and roast lamb; the leathery, earthy undertones of buffalo's milk.

HALLOUMI

Defining Features

Fresh cheeses are easy to recognize because they are very white, usually shiny, and have no rind. Beyond their defining features shown below, however, there is much variety among them, particularly in terms of texture (see Excellent Examples, opposite).

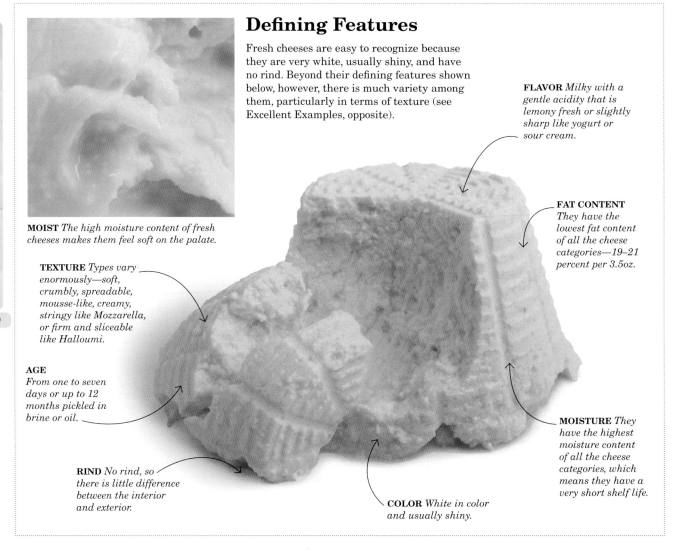

MOIST *The high moisture content of fresh cheeses makes them feel soft on the palate.*

FLAVOR *Milky with a gentle acidity that is lemony fresh or slightly sharp like yogurt or sour cream.*

FAT CONTENT *They have the lowest fat content of all the cheese categories—19–21 percent per 3.5oz.*

TEXTURE *Types vary enormously—soft, crumbly, spreadable, mousse-like, creamy, stringy like Mozzarella, or firm and sliceable like Halloumi.*

AGE *From one to seven days or up to 12 months pickled in brine or oil.*

RIND *No rind, so there is little difference between the interior and exterior.*

COLOR *White in color and usually shiny.*

MOISTURE *They have the highest moisture content of all the cheese categories, which means they have a very short shelf life.*

How They're Made

The most common fresh cheeses such as fromage frais or cottage cheese are made by heating the milk then adding a starter culture of bacteria that will cause the milk to curdle. Excess whey is then drained off and the loose curd is put into cheesecloth or small molds for a few hours before being turned out and salted. A similar process, shown here, is used to produce fresh cheeses from whey, such as Ricotta.

Firstly, the whey, *left over from making hard cheese, is heated with a little vinegar to raise its acidity and cause the protein to rise to the surface in tiny lumps.*

2 **Once firm,** *the curd lumps are scooped into open-weave basket molds.*

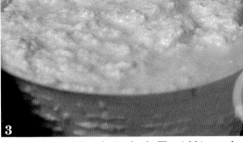

3 **The curds** *are left to drain slowly. The yield is very low, only a few ounces from a gallon of whey.*

4 **The fragile curds** *are turned over once in the basket and when removed will bear the imprint of the mold.*

Excellent Examples

Halloumi
A harder, denser texture than other fresh cheeses because the curd has been "kneaded".The brine it is preserved in gives it a salty tang. (See p262–63).

Ricotta
A soft, moist, fragile whey cheese. (See p135).

Feta
Dense, creamy, and crumbly in texture, it is preserved in brine, giving it a salty taste and texture. (See pp.258–59).

Mozzarella
Because the fresh curd is placed in hot water, this cheese is very elastic and can be stretched and formed into different shapes. (See pp120–21).

Mascarpone
Sweet in flavor, it is made by heating cream rather than milk. (See p122).

How to enjoy

UNCOOKED The microscopic fat globules trapped in fresh cheeses absorb and concentrate the flavors of the other ingredients, transforming the simplest dishes into classics like Feta in a Greek salad, cream cheese with smoked salmon or Mascarpone in tiramasu. Consequently, fresh cheese is used to add texture to a recipe rather than to give it additional flavor. Fresh cheeses destined for the cheeseboard are often decorated, rolled, or dusted in ash, herbs, or spices to enhance their appearance and flavor.

COOKED Fresh cheeses are at their best when melted or baked in classic dishes, such as Feta in spanakopita, Ricotta in ravioli, or Mozzarella on pizza. However, their high moisture content and loose texture means they fall apart in sauces and become tough when broiled too long.

WITH DRINKS With their high acidity, fresh cheeses are best with crisp, white wines or cider. For a non-alcoholic alternative try apple juice or elderflower cordial. However, when fresh cheeses are combined with other ingredients choose a wine that complements the more dominant flavors.

Aged Fresh Cheeses

THIN, WRINKLED RIND · GRAINY TO CREAMY · WHITE, GRAY, AND BLUE MOLD

As the name implies, these are fresh cheeses that have been allowed to age and dry out in special temperature- and humidity-controlled caves or cellars, where a multitude of molds and yeasts are encouraged to grow on the rind. The best-known are made in the Loire in France; they are the small rounds, pyramids, cones, bells, and logs you see in small, straw-lined, wooden boxes on rickety tables in French markets, but are increasingly made around the world. These creamy and aromatic cheeses are mostly goat's cheeses and often covered in ash, herbs, or spices, or wrapped in vine or chestnut leaves over which the molds grow. When made with cow's or ewe's milk the texture is softer, the molds less aggressive, and the taste creamier and sweeter.

CLOCHETTE

12

Defining Features

Their distinctive thin, wrinkled rinds are coated with a myriad of molds and yeasts (the most dominant of which are splashes of steely gray or blue molds called *Penicillium glaucum*) and dusted with a thin layer of *Penicillium candidum* or *Geometricium candidum*. Thinner cheeses develop a softer rind with less mold and become almost runny just beneath the rind. As it ages the cheese develops a texture some call "claggy", and coats the roof of the mouth.

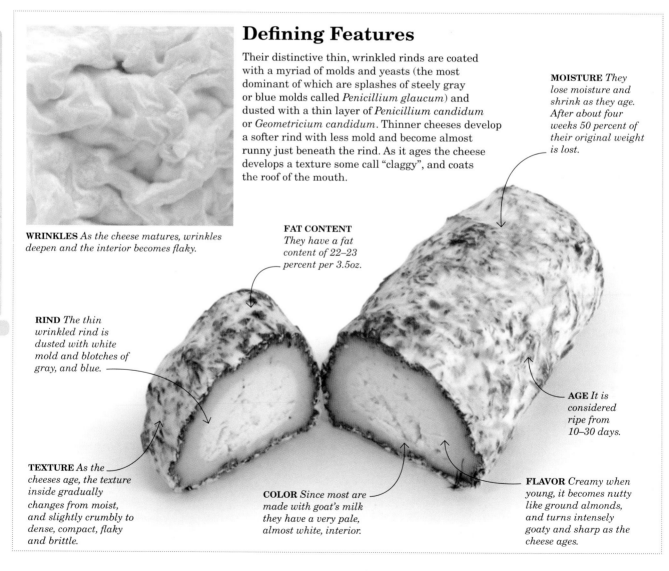

WRINKLES *As the cheese matures, wrinkles deepen and the interior becomes flaky.*

MOISTURE *They lose moisture and shrink as they age. After about four weeks 50 percent of their original weight is lost.*

FAT CONTENT *They have a fat content of 22–23 percent per 3.5oz.*

RIND *The thin wrinkled rind is dusted with white mold and blotches of gray, and blue.*

TEXTURE *As the cheeses age, the texture inside gradually changes from moist, and slightly crumbly to dense, compact, flaky and brittle.*

COLOR *Since most are made with goat's milk they have a very pale, almost white, interior.*

AGE *It is considered ripe from 10–30 days.*

FLAVOR *Creamy when young, it becomes nutty like ground almonds, and turns intensely goaty and sharp as the cheese ages.*

How They're Made

When left to age naturally, usually in cool cellars, the protein-rich surface of fresh cheese attracts a range of natural microflora, each contributing to the ripening process. In the hands of a competent *affineur,* they will age gracefully and be sold at varying stages of ripeness depending on the tastes of the clientèle. Each will develop its own individual character that is influenced by the cheesemaker, animals, grazing, season, and microclimate in which they are made and ripened. The following is a general outline of the stages through which these cheeses pass.

1

The delicate, *pure-white curd is carefully hand ladled into individual molds and then topped up until they are almost overflowing. The weight of the curd gradually forces the expulsion of the excess whey.*

2

Once the level *of the curd has dropped, the base of each cheese is sprinkled with salt to speed up the expulsion of the remaining whey.*

3

After a few hours, *the cheeses are firm enough to retain their shape and are turned out onto draining trays. At this stage it is a fresh cheese.*

4

Gradually *over the next few days the cheese develops a soft, thin almost opaque rind that gradually shrinks and becomes wrinkled.*

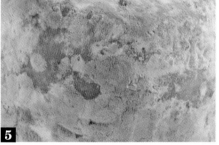

5

Within 9–12 days *a layer of white* Penicillium candidum *develops followed by a pale-blue mold that darkens and covers the cheese.*

How to enjoy

UNCOOKED The texture and rind of the various aged fresh cheeses do not lend themselves to spreads or dips but no cheeseboard is truly complete without one of these attractive, rustic-looking cheeses.

COOKED Chèvre Salad is ubiquitous throughout France, but is not, as so many chefs think, simply a "goat's cheese salad". In fact it is made with an aged fresh cheese, typically Crottin de Chavignol (see p54),

sliced, drizzled with olive oil and broiled on rounds of baguette. To use any other type of goat's cheese is a travesty since you will not get that wonderful nutty, aromatic flavor characteristic of these cheeses when broiled or baked.

WITH DRINKS A crisp, white Sauvignon Blanc, Viognier, or Rosé is perfect, especially if it is from the same area as the cheese. Alternatively, a light ale or beer brings out the nutty side of the cheese and the taste of the hops.

Excellent Examples

Valençay
A rind of this truncated pyramid is encrusted with a dusty blue-gray mold. The goat's milk interior is a bright white. (See p97).

Clochette
This bell-shaped example from France has a rind that is dusted with a fine white mold. (See p52).

Vicky's Spring Splendour
This Canadian log has a creamy texture that is softer and more yielding just under the rind. (See p319).

Ketem
Based on French-style aged fresh cheeses, Israel's Ketem illustrates the growing popularity of this cheese type. (See p264).

St. Tola
This Irish cheese is produced in a large log shape and has a silky, creamy texture. (See p225).

Soft White Cheeses

VELVETY WHITE RIND · CREAMY INTERIOR · MUSHROOMY TASTE

Camembert de Normandie and Brie de Meaux are the best-known examples and the inspiration behind the variations produced around the world. Soft white cheeses typically have a white crust, a slightly grainy to almost runny texture, and a wonderful aroma of mushrooms. The mildest cheeses hint of sweet hay and button mushrooms; the strongest taste like creamy, wild mushroom soup and finish with the peppery bite of dandelions, and have an earthy aroma reminiscent of cool cellars and mushrooms warmed in butter. Those made with ewe's milk have a subtle sweetness with just a hint of roast lamb or lanolin, while those made with goat's milk taste of almonds or even marzipan.

CAPRICORN GOAT

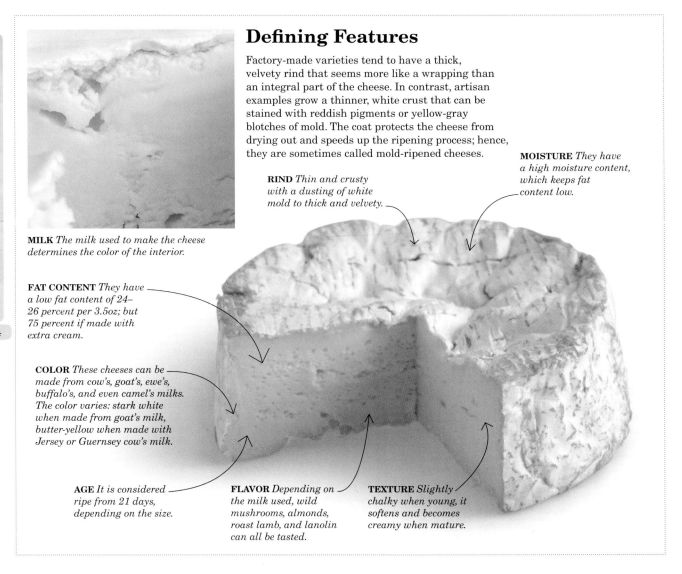

MILK *The milk used to make the cheese determines the color of the interior.*

Defining Features

Factory-made varieties tend to have a thick, velvety rind that seems more like a wrapping than an integral part of the cheese. In contrast, artisan examples grow a thinner, white crust that can be stained with reddish pigments or yellow-gray blotches of mold. The coat protects the cheese from drying out and speeds up the ripening process; hence, they are sometimes called mold-ripened cheeses.

RIND *Thin and crusty with a dusting of white mold to thick and velvety.*

MOISTURE *They have a high moisture content, which keeps fat content low.*

FAT CONTENT *They have a low fat content of 24–26 percent per 3.5oz; but 75 percent if made with extra cream.*

COLOR *These cheeses can be made from cow's, goat's, ewe's, buffalo's, and even camel's milks. The color varies: stark white when made from goat's milk, butter-yellow when made with Jersey or Guernsey cow's milk.*

AGE *It is considered ripe from 21 days, depending on the size.*

FLAVOR *Depending on the milk used, wild mushrooms, almonds, roast lamb, and lanolin can all be tasted.*

TEXTURE *Slightly chalky when young, it softens and becomes creamy when mature.*

How They're Made

To achieve their almost-liquid texture, soft white cheeses must retain a high percentage of whey. This means that the curds must be scooped gently into the molds. During this part of the process only the weight of the curd is used to lightly press out the excess whey. The surface of the cheese is then enveloped in a white, velvety *Penicillium candidum* coat that is made up of millions of microscopic mushrooms of the penicillin family. This is where the mushroomy aroma and taste originate.

1

The floppy, jelly-like *curd is gently scooped from the vat and put layer upon layer into the round, high-sided hoops, or molds, until full.*

2

Once firm, *the cheese is turned out of the molds and a disc is placed on top of each one, gently pressing out any remaining whey.*

3

After receiving *a sprinkling of salt, they are moved to a room where the white mold, and sometimes others, is introduced.*

4

The mold is naturally *attracted to the moist, protein-rich surface, and gradually spreads over the entire the cheese.*

5

After two weeks *its velvety white coat has formed. Colorful molds may appear but most cheesemakers encourage only the purest white.*

How to Enjoy

UNCOOKED These wonderful cheeses are at their very best when served at room temperature with crusty bread and a glass of wine.

COOKED A popular recipe involves baking a small soft white cheese in the oven for about 15 minutes and scooping out the molten interior with chunks of bread or raw vegetables. These cheeses also broil well; try it on a croissant layered with roasted peppers or sweet chutney, but cut off the rind around the sides, because it will become dry and a little bitter.

WITH DRINKS The French serve cider or calvados with Camembert, Chardonnay with Brie de Meaux, and Champagne with Chaource. As a general rule, goat's or ewe's milk variations work very well with similar wines. Alternatively, try a tawny Port with a strong soft white. A hoppy pale ale (rather than a bitter beer) works with the milder, sweeter cheeses.

Excellent Examples

Brie de Melun
Like most Bries, Brie de Melun has a strong mushroom flavor, but is less well known than Brie de Meaux. (See p42).

Camembert de Normandie
France's other famous soft white comes packed in wooden boxes. Ripe examples have pink or brown-tinged rinds. (See p44).

Sharpham
Its buttercup-yellow interior is a result of the high carotene content of the Jersey cow's milk it is made with. (See p195).

Brillat-Savarin
Extra cream added to the milk triples its fat content to 75 percent per 3.5oz and gives this cheese a wickedly rich feel. (See p42).

Capricorn Goat
One of England's first soft white goat cheeses, it has a stark white interior typical of goat's milk cheeses. (See p175).

Semi-Soft Cheeses

THIN AND DRY TO ORANGE AND STICKY RIND · MILD TO PUNGENT · RUBBERY TO RUNNY

Semi-soft cheeses vary in appearance and texture more than any other cheese type, but can be divided into two styles. Dry rind cheeses ripen slowly and range from springy, mild, sweet, and nutty with barely formed rinds, to rubbery, floral, and pungent with thick leathery rinds. When made with goat's milk, they are mild and nutty, with a hint of marzipan. Those with a sticky orange rind are called washed-rind cheeses and are softer and have a pungent, savory, farm-yardy, smoky, and even meaty taste and aroma. They tend to be grainy, with a softening just under the rind when young, and become soft and supple with age. The washed-rind type includes those known as Trappist or monastery-style.

LANGRES

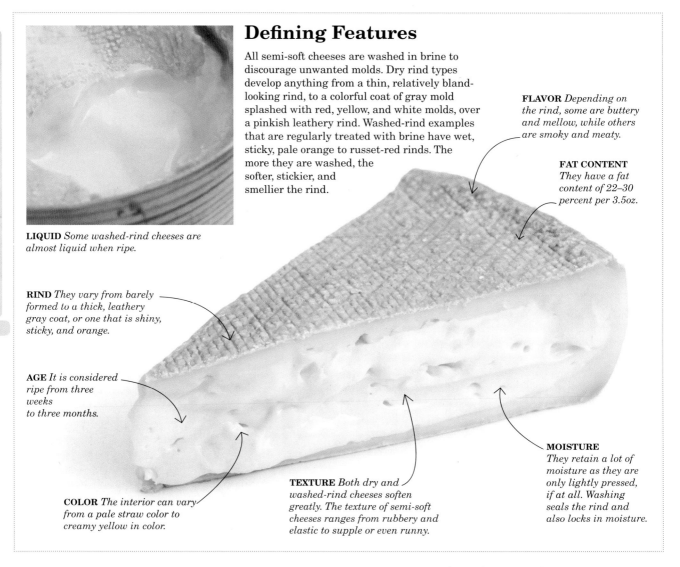

Defining Features

All semi-soft cheeses are washed in brine to discourage unwanted molds. Dry rind types develop anything from a thin, relatively bland-looking rind, to a colorful coat of gray mold splashed with red, yellow, and white molds, over a pinkish leathery rind. Washed-rind examples that are regularly treated with brine have wet, sticky, pale orange to russet-red rinds. The more they are washed, the softer, stickier, and smellier the rind.

LIQUID *Some washed-rind cheeses are almost liquid when ripe.*

RIND *They vary from barely formed to a thick, leathery gray coat, or one that is shiny, sticky, and orange.*

AGE *It is considered ripe from three weeks to three months.*

COLOR *The interior can vary from a pale straw color to creamy yellow in color.*

TEXTURE *Both dry and washed-rind cheeses soften greatly. The texture of semi-soft cheeses ranges from rubbery and elastic to supple or even runny.*

FLAVOR *Depending on the rind, some are buttery and mellow, while others are smoky and meaty.*

FAT CONTENT *They have a fat content of 22–30 percent per 3.5oz.*

MOISTURE *They retain a lot of moisture as they are only lightly pressed, if at all. Washing seals the rind and also locks in moisture.*

How They're Made

Semi-soft cheeses are washed in numerous ways, each creating a different style of rind. Those soaked in brine for a few hours or days and then left to dry out develop a pale, barely formed to thin pink-tinged leathery rind. Splashing or spraying the cheese creates a thin, sticky, pale orange rind, like the Stinking Bishop example shown here, but they become stickier and brighter with more frequent washing. Those dipped in, or wiped with, brine by hand are called smear-ripened.

Perforated molds *let the whey drain from the curd, although some semi-soft cheeses may be lightly pressed.*

Any white mold *that grows is knocked out by the washing process and, after five to six weeks, the rind becomes very soft.*

1

Rennet is added *to the milk to coagulate it. Along with the starter culture, this separates the curds from the whey.*

3

Once removed *from its mold, it is bound with a thin strip of wood and hand washed with a mix of brine and perry (or fermented pear juice).*

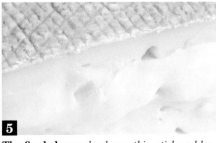

5

The final cheese *develops a thin, sticky golden rind, and the texture is so soft that it literally oozes out when it is cut.*

Excellent Examples

Taleggio
The fine, dry rind, feels gritty and has patches of gray and white molds. A stamp of quality and authenticity marks its rind. (See pp138–39).

Stinking Bishop
This washed-rind cheese is splashed or rubbed in brine mixed with perry. It is named after the pear variety used to make the perry. (See p198).

Langres
Frequent washing and ripening in very humid cellars creates the bright color. The rind shrinks and wrinkles as it ages, and can also be finely dusted with mold. (See p63).

Edam
Edam is a washed-curd cheese (see p19) and has a sweet flavor, a rubbery texture, and a very thin, barely formed rind dipped in a protective coat of red wax. (See p230).

Vacherin Mont d'Or
The thick rind of this cheese protects the moisture in the interior, and as a result the interior is a runny liquid. (See p245).

How to Enjoy

UNCOOKED Mild semi-soft cheeses such as Edam or Havarti are classic breakfast cheeses, while the stronger varieties are essential on any cheeseboard.

COOKED The dry rind cheeses are superb when broiled since their rubbery texture stretches but holds its shape—but for the same reason they do not work well in sauces. Washed-rind cheeses, however, melt superbly in sauces, although a little goes a long way. When they are baked whole, they become sweeter and more savory, which makes them an amazing starter.

WITH DRINKS The milder cheeses need a Chardonnay, a light red like Merlot, or beer, but more acidic wines will make the cheese taste sour. The pungent washed-rind cheeses are superb with beers, ciders, and sweeter grape varieties such as Riesling or Gewürztraminer. These wines highlight the fruity, sweet meadow-flower character that is usually hidden beneath their farm-yardy aroma and taste.

Hard Cheeses

ROUGH OR POLISHED RIND · CRUMBLY TO BRITTLE · COMPLEX FLAVORS

The large wheels, cylinders, and drums of hard cheese found in all traditional cheesemaking countries are typically made with cow's, goat's, or ewe's milks. Their rinds range across the spectrum from smooth with polished rinds to rough and pockmarked like the moon's surface. Flavors grow complex as they mature; very old hard cheeses such as Parmigiano-Reggiano and Dry Jack become granular, giving the cheese a crunchy feel in the mouth. Classic ewe's milk hard cheeses, such as Manchego and Pecorino, have a dense, slightly grainy texture with an oily-yet-dry feel in the mouth, a characteristic sweet, caramelized onion flavor, and an aroma reminiscent of roast lamb or wet wool. Hard goat's milk cheeses have a subtle almond taste.

MANCHEGO

Defining Features

Hard cheeses can vary greatly in appearance. Traditional hard British cheeses are clothbound drums or tall cylinders. The Dutch and Swiss tend to make large boulders or wheels with polished or waxed rinds. Spanish cheeses usually bear the imprint of plaited reeds or the wooden molds in which they were drained. Producers in France and Italy make hundreds of different hard cheeses, from smooth barrel-shaped Pecorino to enormous wheels of Beaufort, with its thin, tough rind.

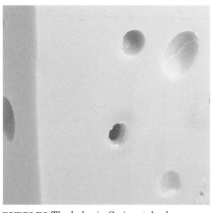

BUBBLES *The holes in Swiss-style cheeses are formed by gas bubbles created when the cheese is moved to a warm room for secondary ripening, activating the starter culture.*

FLAVOR *When young they are slightly sharp or buttery; with age they dry out and the intensity increases, becoming fruity and tangy.*

COLOR *This varies with the seasons— pale when animals are hay-fed in winter, but brighter yellows come with fresh summer grazing.*

MOISTURE *The amount of whey expelled determines the texture. The more moisture removed, the longer the maturation, and more complex the final flavors.*

TEXTURE *This category ranges from textures that are creamy, to flexible, through to brittle.*

FAT CONTENT *They have a fat content of 28–34 percent per 3.5oz.*

AGE *Considered ripe from a few weeks old to three years.*

RIND *This varies enormously from thin and leathery to very hard and thick. Some types are waxed, polished or bound in cloth.*

How They're Made

Hard cheeses fall into one of two categories. Pressed uncooked cheeses are lightly pressed for a few hours and eaten from one week old when still mild and springy. Cooked and pressed cheeses are heated in the whey and then pressed. Different temperatures give various results. Other methods include milling the curds between cutting and pressing to expel extra whey and create a finer texture; soaking in brine to achieve a thick rind; or washing the curds in hot water to scald them, creating a supple texture.

1

After the coagulation process, *the cheese curd is sliced using different-sized giant combs with knife-sharp wires.*

2

When making washed-curd *cheeses such as Gouda, hot water is added to the vat of curd, which gives the cheese a sweeter taste.*

3

Some cheeses, *such as Parmigiano-Reggiano, are placed in brine baths for up to 21 days, where the salt draws out more of the whey.*

4

Pressing is often *carried out by hand. The pressure is gradually increased to avoid loosing too much whey too quickly.*

5

To prevent moisture loss *as they ripen, some cheeses are sealed with wax, wrapped in cloth, or sometimes rubbed with lard.*

How to Enjoy

UNCOOKED The most versatile of any cheese type, hard cheeses are ideal for cheeseboards. They can also be shaved or grated into salads, dips, and dressings, for instance Parmigiano-Reggiano in pesto.

COOKED Hard cheeses play an integral role in the culinary history of the country where they are made. Thermized cheeses (see Emmentaler, right) such as Gruyère and Beaufort become stretchy when heated, making them perfect for broiling or fondues rather than in sauces. Others

melt completely, while very hard cheeses such as Parmigiano-Reggiano simply dissolve, adding a subtle taste but not texture; both these styles are excellent when added to sauces, pasta, and soups.

WITH DRINKS Their high fat content and stronger, more intense taste marries best with red wines. They absorb the rough edges of young wines or soften the tannin in wines such as Cabernet Sauvignon or Barolo. White wines bring out the fruitier nature of the cheese, while beer and cider, with their natural acidity, make equally good companions.

Excellent Examples

Manchego
The interior has tiny eyeholes, and an oily sheen typical of hard ewe's milk cheeses. The wooden board on which it is drained makes the ridges on the base. (See pp162–63).

Emmentaler
The milk is heated to 129°F (54°C), a process known as thermizing, resulting in sweet, fruity flavors and an elastic texture. (See p242–43).

Grana Padano
Curds cut into rice-sized pieces give this cheese a brittle texture. It has a thick, hard rind from soaking in brine for 21 days and tastes sweet, like ripe pineapple. (See p119).

Cheddar
Cheddar curds are cooked at 104°F (40°C), then milled before being pressed to create a smooth, very creamy, texture and a savory, raw-onion tang. (See pp180–181).

Mimolette
This cheese has a dry crust that is often attacked by harmless cheese mites, creating a rind like a rusty cannonball. (See p68).

Blue Cheeses

STICKY TO CRUSTY RIND · STREAKED WITH BLUE MOLD · SPICY TANG

Blue molds are members of the penicillin family but, unlike white molds, they grow inside a cheese. They create a seemingly endless array of wonderful cheeses from dense, buttery Stilton to sweet Gorgonzola with its luscious, gooey texture and spicy tang. Ewe's milk blue cheeses such as Roquefort retain the sweet, burnt-caramel taste of the milk that offsets the sharp, salty, steely blue finish. Most European blues are wrapped in tin foil, ensuring their rinds remain damp and sticky and develop a multitude of molds layered on them, while traditional British blues have rough, dry, crusty, orange-brown rinds, often splashed with blue and gray molds.

STILTON

STREAKS *Erratic lines and intense pockets of mold typify these cheeses.*

Defining Features

There is extraordinary variety in taste and texture, but blues all have a spicy, slightly metallic tang, often taste saltier than other cheeses, and attract a rainbow of colorful molds that exude a powerful aroma. The moist interiors of wet rind blues develop wide uneven streaks and pockets of blue, whereas dry rind blues have a dense, compact texture that develops thinner, longer streaks and looks like shattered porcelain when cut. There are also soft white blues, which have white rinds and patches of blue.

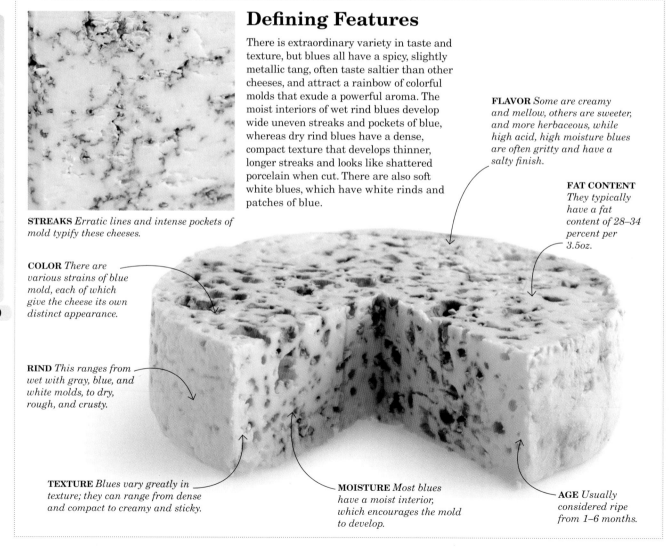

FLAVOR *Some are creamy and mellow, others are sweeter, and more herbaceous, while high acid, high moisture blues are often gritty and have a salty finish.*

FAT CONTENT *They typically have a fat content of 28–34 percent per 3.5oz.*

COLOR *There are various strains of blue mold, each of which give the cheese its own distinct appearance.*

RIND *This ranges from wet with gray, blue, and white molds, to dry, rough, and crusty.*

TEXTURE *Blues vary greatly in texture; they can range from dense and compact to creamy and sticky.*

MOISTURE *Most blues have a moist interior, which encourages the mold to develop.*

AGE *Usually considered ripe from 1–6 months.*

How They're Made

Cheeses were once ripened in caves, stone cellars, or barns, which were havens for blue molds in particular. They made their way into the warm interior through cracks in the rind and grew in the gaps in the fresh curd. Today, the blue mold is added to the milk in powder form, then the young cheese is pierced to allow air to enter and the mold to turn blue. Soft white cheeses must be injected with molds, as they are too creamy and dense for the mold to spread naturally.

1

Along with *the starter culture, penicillin mold is added to the warm milk or sometimes, as shown here, to the freshly formed curd.*

2

Blue cheeses *are never pressed. The curd must remain loosely packed, leaving space for the blue mold to grow and spread.*

3

After two or three weeks, *the sides of most types of blue cheese are scraped smooth to cover any cracks before being rubbed with salt.*

4

After a few weeks *the young cheese is pierced with rods to create tunnels in the curd. Exposed to air, the blue mold flourishes in these gaps.*

5

To check the texture *and the even spread of the blue mold, a grader will remove a plug of cheese with a cheese "iron" and then replace it.*

How to Enjoy

UNCOOKED Blue cheeses are essential on any cheese platter and, with the exception of the brie-style blues, also add another dimension to salads especially when crumbled over flageolet beans, walnuts, and peppery arugula dressed with a honey vinaigrette. Walnut bread is especially good with blue cheeses, and a drizzle of honey brings out the subtlety of the cheese.

COOKED Stir small amounts into pasta, soups, and sauces to elevate dishes into classics like celery and Stilton soup; pasta with pinenuts and Gorgonzola; or grilled steak with blue cheese sauce.

WITH DRINKS Try a vintage or late-bottled-vintage (LBV) Port rather than the sweeter, less complex tawny or ruby Ports, as they tend to overpower the majority of blue cheeses. If Port is not to your taste, a sweet or dry Riesling can make a perfect partner. Match the dessert wine Sauternes only with the very sharp, salty, steely blues, such as Roquefort, with its sweet undertones.

Excellent Examples

Stilton
This cheese has the dry rind typical of many British blue cheeses. The dense buttery interior forces the blue mold to develop as thin broken streaks. (See pp192–193).

Roquefort
The famous ewe's milk blue has a loose, moist interior, allowing *Penicillium roqueforti* to grow *en masse* as thin streaks and large scattered pockets. (See pp82–83).

Gorgonzola
Thick, blue-green streaks and scattered patches fill the interior. Its thin wet, sticky rind, finely dusted with mold, typifies traditional European blues. (See pp110–11).

Bavaria Blu
This is a soft white-style blue. Pockets (rather than streaks) of blue result from injecting blue mold directly into this creamy, dense cheese. (See p236).

Flavor-added Cheeses

COLORFUL AND EXOTIC RINDS · HARD OR SEMI-SOFT · SAVORY OR SWEET

With their bright colors, the vast array of flavor-added cheeses stands out on deli counters across the world. Smoked cheeses have existed since humans learned to make hard cheeses and stored them near their wood fires, while in the 16th century, Dutch cheesemakers were quick to incorporate the exotic spices brought back from the East Indies into Edam and Gouda, producing a tantalizing mélange of flavors. Today, most flavor-added cheeses are well-known hard or semi-soft cheeses combined with fruit, spices, and herbs.

HEREFORD HOP *Its rind is encrusted with toasted hops*

UNDERSTANDING CHEESE

22

Defining Features

Flavor-added cheeses can be divided into four distinct types. Natural smoked cheeses have a golden brown to caramel-colored rind but the internal color is not affected. Traditional-style examples (based on the original Dutch method where the ingredients are matured with the fresh curds) absorb and intensify the aroma and essence of the added ingredients. Rind-flavored cheeses have various ingredients, such as vine leaves, toasted hops, or grape-must, pressed into the rind. The majority, however, are re-formed cheeses, where a young cheese is broken up, blended with added ingredients, then re-formed.

A fine gray-white mold grows across the cheese, emphasizing the nettles.

Yarg Cornish Cheese
Probably the best-known British example of a rind-flavored cheese, its elegant rind of interwoven forest-green nettles imparts a subtle flavor. (See pp200–201).

Wensleydale with Cranberries
The most successful re-formed flavor-added cheeses blend young, low-acid cheeses with sweet, dried fruit. Here, the young hard cheese Wensleydale has been crumbled up with cranberries. (See Wensleydale, p204).

Taramundi
This traditional-style Spanish cheese has a semi-soft texture and is made by adding local crushed walnuts and hazelnuts. (See p164).

One of only a few cheeses with nuts added.

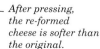

After pressing, the re-formed cheese is softer than the original.

How to Enjoy

UNCOOKED The choice of flavors to add to cheese is limited only by the imagination of the cheesemaker. Flavor-added cheeses with dried fruit are typical served in place of dessert, while only those with garlic, herbs, chives or that are smoked work in salads. Weird combinations such as those with chocolate, pickles, or fruitcake are curiosities best left to those who enjoy experimenting with unconventional flavors.

COOKED Traditionally-made semi-soft or hard flavored cheeses behave like their unflavored counterparts when cooked and can add character to basics like baked potatoes or pasta—smoked cheeses work especially well for this. Additional ideas can be found under the entries for individual cheeses.

WITH DRINKS Beers nicely complement savory-flavored cheeses with onion, chives, garlic, oak smoke, and chiles, while the sweet dessert cheeses are better with cider or Chardonnay. The tannin and red berry flavor of red wines tends to clash with all but the hard cheeses like Cheddar with garlic or Gouda with peppercorns.

Nagelkaas means "nail cheese." This refers to the shape of the cloves studded in its interior.

Nagelkaas
This traditional-style flavor-added cheese from the Netherlands is based on a Gouda recipe and uses cloves. The orange color comes from adding annatto (a natural dye derived from the *Bixa orellana* seed), and provides an attractive contrast to the dark cloves. (See p231).

Wonderful smoky bacon taste, and nut-brown rind.

Idiazabal
A great example of a natural smoked cheese, Idiazabal was traditionally stored in the rafters of shepherds' huts in Northern Spain, where the young cheeses would absorb the smoke from the wood fires. Today, they are cold-smoked in special rooms over a few days. (See p157).

How They're Made

Smoked cheeses are matured over natural fires. Traditional flavor-added cheeses are made by adding the flavor ingredients to the curd of semi-soft and hard cheeses. Rind-flavored cheeses are covered with the flavor ingredient after the cheese has been pressed. Re-formed cheeses are made by breaking up the curd of a young hard cheese, blending it with different flavors, then re-forming and pressing it.

Herbs & Garlic
Fresh herbs can deteriorate within a cheese's damp interior, so they are mostly used dried. Examples include sage, nettles, basil, rosemary, and lavender. Garlic and chives are also popular.

Nuts
Nuts are not commonly used, but walnuts are sometimes added to fresh cheeses because they have a high acidity and ripen quickly.

Spices
Cumin, caraway seeds, black or red peppercorns, paprika, and cloves are widely used as they make natural partners with the savory tang of hard cheeses.

Dried Fruit
Adding fruit is a modern trend. The most popular are candied citrus, dried berries, apple flakes, figs, and apricots.

The Perfect Cheeseboard

There are no hard and fast rules to determining a cheese category or type, but some guidance can enable you to create an amazing and memorable cheeseboard. If you're having your cheeseboard with a meal, make sure you enjoy it after the main meal but before dessert.

ACCOMPANIMENTS

Grilled vegetables, **dried fruit**, **apples**, and **toasted walnuts** work well with almost all cheeses.

Celery and **grapes** can be enjoyed with blues and strong hard cheeses.

Crusty or **fruity bread**, rather than crackers, allow you to experience the texture and feel of the cheeses in your mouth.

THE BASICS

Buy the cheeses as near to the time you want to eat them as possible—they will not improve in a refrigerator.

Shop somewhere that encourages you to taste before purchasing.

Support your local cheesemakers.

Search for medal winners and the AOC, DOC, or PDO label on European cheeses.

Remove cheeses from the refrigerator at least an hour before serving so that they come to room temperature.

THE BOARD

An elegant **wooden board**, **chunk of driftwood**, or **wicker basket** lined with linen cloth gives the cheese a fresh and natural appearance.

Slate looks great; **marble** or **granite** is marvelous, but is often very heavy!

Decorate the board with some wild flowers, herbs, or seasonal leaves.

Alternatively, prepare individual plates with small chunks and wedges of cheese.

FLAVOR-ADDED
Yarg Cornish Cheese pp200–201

QUINCE

SEMI-SOFT
Taleggio pp138–139

AGED FRESH
Sainte-Maure de Touraine pp92–93

DRIED FIGS

THE CHEESES

One superb large cheese is better than three or four small wedges, which can be in danger of drying out quickly.

Color and shape should come from an interesting combination of cheeses, not from the garnishes.

Allow around 2oz (55g) of each cheese per person.

Offer diversity by choosing cheeses with different textures. Use the classifications on pages 10–23 to give you an idea of the range of textures available.

For variety of flavor, provide at least one goat's or sheep's milk cheese, rather than relying only on cow's milk cheeses.

Pre-cut a couple of wedges to show guests how it's done. You could remove the rind from blue or hard cheeses to keep anyone from cutting across the wedge instead of into smaller wedges.

THE WINE

The union of cheese and wine has moved writers to fill endless columns with riveting descriptions of distinguished or disreputable marriages, but there really is no right or wrong. Some combinations simply make the senses buzz while others definitely do not.

Fresh, **Aged Fresh**, and **Soft White** cheeses prefer dry, crisp fruity wines and ciders that won't dominate.
Semi-soft cheeses, especially washed rind, need a feisty, aromatic white or *eau de vie* to pair with their sweetness.
Hard cheeses pair well with red wines. The harder and darker the cheese, the heavier, richer, and redder the wine.
Blue cheeses work superbly with sweet pudding wines or aromatic whites. The sweetness cuts through the sharpness of the cheese.
Flavor-added cheeses work with different types of wines; it really depends on what flavor has been added.

HARD
Berkswell p173

SOFT WHITE
Camembert de Normandie p44

BLUE
Valdeón p166

FRESH
Innes Button p184

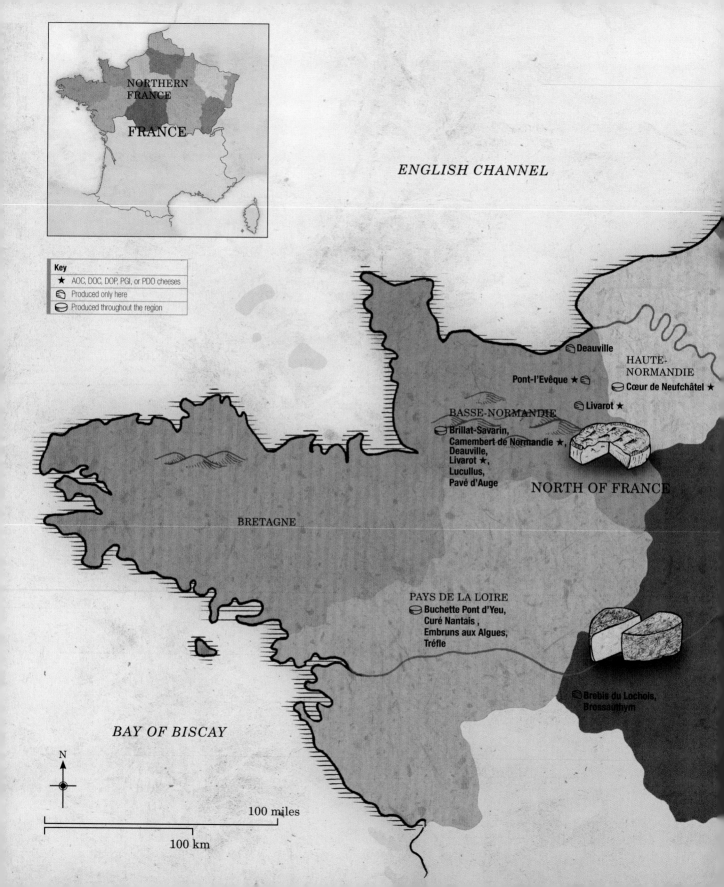

NORTHERN
FRANCE

FRANCE

ENGLISH CHANNEL

Key
★ AOC, DOC, DOP, PGI, or PDO cheeses
▱ Produced only here
◎ Produced throughout the region

▱ Deauville

HAUTE-
NORMANDIE

Pont-l'Evêque ★ ▱

◎ Cœur de Neufchâtel ★

▱ Livarot ★

BASSE-NORMANDIE
◎ Brillat-Savarin,
Camembert de Normandie ★,
Deauville,
Livarot ★,
Lucullus,
Pavé d'Auge

NORTH OF FRANCE

BRETAGNE

PAYS DE LA LOIRE
◎ Buchette Pont d'Yeu,
Curé Nantais,
Embruns aux Algues,
Tréfle

▱ Brebis du Lochois,
Brossauthym

BAY OF BISCAY

N

100 miles

100 km

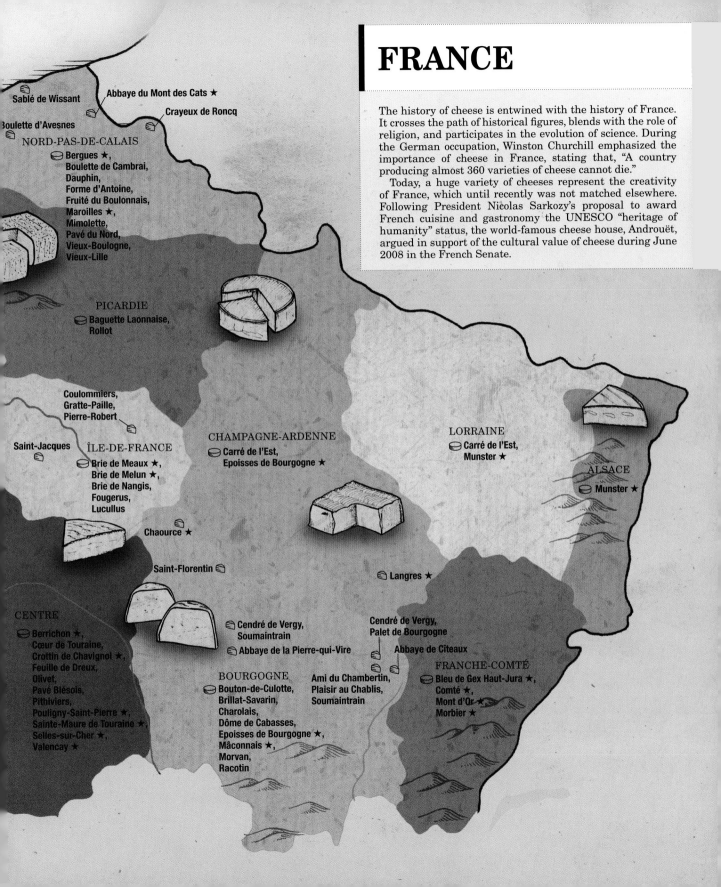

FRANCE

The history of cheese is entwined with the history of France. It crosses the path of historical figures, blends with the role of religion, and participates in the evolution of science. During the German occupation, Winston Churchill emphasized the importance of cheese in France, stating that, "A country producing almost 360 varieties of cheese cannot die."

Today, a huge variety of cheeses represent the creativity of France, which until recently was not matched elsewhere. Following President Nicolas Sarkozy's proposal to award French cuisine and gastronomy the UNESCO "heritage of humanity" status, the world-famous cheese house, Androuët, argued in support of the cultural value of cheese during June 2008 in the French Senate.

Sablé de Wissant

Abbaye du Mont des Cats ★

Crayeux de Roncq

Boulette d'Avesnes

NORD-PAS-DE-CALAIS

Bergues ★,
Boulette de Cambrai,
Dauphin,
Forme d'Antoine,
Fruité du Boulonnais,
Maroilles ★,
Mimolette,
Pavé du Nord,
Vieux-Boulogne,
Vieux-Lille

PICARDIE

Baguette Laonnaise,
Rollot

Coulommiers,
Gratte-Paille,
Pierre-Robert

Saint-Jacques

ÎLE-DE-FRANCE

Brie de Meaux ★,
Brie de Melun ★,
Brie de Nangis,
Fougerus,
Lucullus

CHAMPAGNE-ARDENNE

Carré de l'Est,
Epoisses de Bourgogne ★

Chaource ★

Saint-Florentin

LORRAINE

Carré de l'Est,
Munster ★

ALSACE

Munster ★

Langres ★

Cendré de Vergy,
Soumaintrain

Abbaye de la Pierre-qui-Vire

Cendré de Vergy,
Palet de Bourgogne

Abbaye de Cîteaux

CENTRE

Berrichon ★,
Cœur de Touraine,
Crottin de Chavignol ★,
Feuille de Dreux,
Olivet,
Pavé Blésois,
Pithiviers,
Pouligny-Saint-Pierre ★,
Sainte-Maure de Touraine ★,
Selles-sur-Cher ★,
Valencay ★

BOURGOGNE

Bouton-de-Culotte,
Brillat-Savarin,
Charolais,
Dôme de Cabasses,
Epoisses de Bourgogne ★,
Mâconnais ★,
Morvan,
Racotin

Ami du Chambertin,
Plaisir au Chablis,
Soumaintrain

FRANCHE-COMTÉ

Bleu de Gex Haut-Jura ★,
Comté ★,
Mont d'Or ★,
Morbier ★

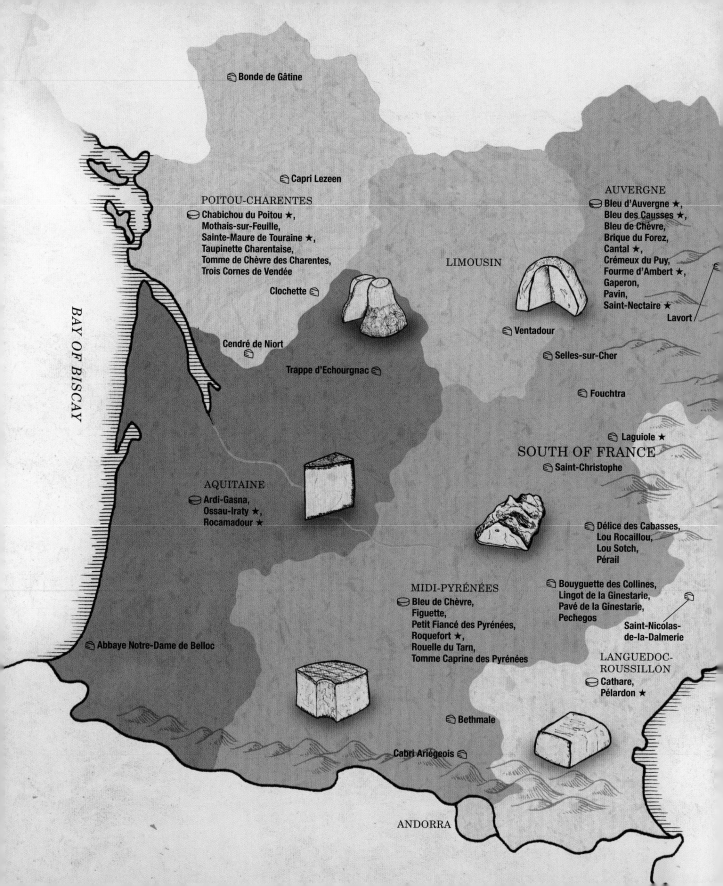

🧀 Bonde de Gâtine

🧀 Capri Lezeen

POITOU-CHARENTES
🧀 Chabichou du Poitou ★,
Mothais-sur-Feuille,
Sainte-Maure de Touraine ★,
Taupinette Charentaise,
Tomme de Chèvre des Charentes,
Trois Cornes de Vendée

Clochette 🧀

LIMOUSIN

AUVERGNE
🧀 Bleu d'Auvergne ★,
Bleu des Causses ★,
Bleu de Chèvre,
Brique du Forez,
Cantal ★,
Crémeux du Puy,
Fourme d'Ambert ★,
Gaperon,
Pavin,
Saint-Nectaire ★
Lavort

🧀 Ventadour

🧀 Selles-sur-Cher

🧀 Fouchtra

🧀 Laguiole ★

SOUTH OF FRANCE
🧀 Saint-Christophe

🧀 Cendré de Niort

Trappe d'Echourgnac 🧀

BAY OF BISCAY

AQUITAINE
🧀 Ardi-Gasna,
Ossau-Iraty ★,
Rocamadour ★

🧀 Délice des Cabasses,
Lou Rocaillou,
Lou Sotch,
Pérail

🧀 Bouyguette des Collines,
Lingot de la Ginestarie,
Pavé de la Ginestarie,
Pechegos

MIDI-PYRÉNÉES
🧀 Bleu de Chèvre,
Figuette,
Petit Fiancé des Pyrénées,
Roquefort ★,
Rouelle du Tarn,
Tomme Caprine des Pyrénées

Saint-Nicolas-
de-la-Dalmerie 🧀

**LANGUEDOC-
ROUSSILLON**
🧀 Cathare,
Pélardon ★

🧀 Abbaye Notre-Dame de Belloc

🧀 Bethmale

Cabri Ariégeois 🧀

ANDORRA

FRANCE

SOUTH OF FRANCE

Key
★   AOC, DOC, DOP, PGI, or PDO cheeses
⬭   Produced only here
⬬   Produced throughout the region

RHÔNE-ALPES

⬭ **Abondance ★**,
Arômes au Gêne de Marc,
Banon ★,
Banon aux Baies Roses ★,
Banon à la Sarriette,
Beaufort ★,
Bleu de Chèvre,
Bleu de Termignon,
Bleu du Vercors-Sassenage ★,
Comté ★,
Fourme de Montbrison ★,
Persillé de Tignes,
Picodon ★,
Raclette de Savoie,
Reblochon de Savoie ★,
Rigotte de Condrieu ★,
Saint-Marcellin,
Saint-Nectaire ★,
Sarments d'Amour,
Tarentais,
Tome des Bauges ★,
Tomme aux Herbes,
Tomme de Savoie,
Tommette Brebis de Alpes,
Tommette de Chèvre des Bauges

⬭ **Tomme de Chartreux**

⬭ **Emmental de Savoie**

⬭ **Abbaye de Tamié,**
Signal

⬭ **Saint-Félicien**

PROVENCE-ALPES-CÔTE D'AZUR

⬭ **Rove Cendré,**
Roves des Garrigues,
Saint-Domnin,
Tétoun de Santa Agata,
Tomme à l'Ancienne,
Truffe de Valensole

MONACO

GOLFE DU LION

N

MEDITERRANEAN SEA

100 miles

100 km

CORSE

LIGURIAN SEA

TYRRHENIAN SEA

U Bel Fiuritu

CORSE

⬬ **A Casinca,**
A Filetta,
Brocciu
Fleur du
Maquis ★,
Fium'Orbu,
Pot Corse,
Tomme de
Brebis Corse,
U Pecurinu,
Venaco

MEDITERRANEAN SEA

Abbaye de Cîteaux

The Abbey of St. Nicolas de Citeaux was founded 900 years ago, but it was only in 1925 that the resident Trappist monks began to make this delicious and exclusive cheese. It is rarely found outside the region because only 60 tons of it are made each year from the milk of 70 Montbéliarde cows.

TASTING NOTES This sweet, smooth, and creamy cheese with a grayish-yellow rind is worth seeking out. It is relatively mild compared with other washed rind, Trappist-style cheeses.

HOW TO ENJOY It is delicious served with fruity and light red wines, such as a Beaujolais or a Bourgogne.

FRANCE Dijon, Bourgogne
Age 2 months
Weight and Shape 1lb 10oz (750g), round
Size D. 7in (18cm), 1½in (H. 4cm)
Milk Cow
Classification Semi-soft
Producer Abbey of St Nicolas de Cîteaux

Abbaye du Mont des Cats

Produced since 1890 by monks at the Abbey of Saint-Marie-du-Mont in northern France, Mont des Cats is a semi-soft, washed cheese made from the milk of cows from neighboring farms.

TASTING NOTES The thin, leathery, orange rind covers a pale yellow, supple, elastic interior. The cheese melts in the mouth with a subtle, yet pronounced, milky flavor and the rustic aroma of hay.

HOW TO ENJOY It is delicious washed down with beer or a light, fruity wine, such as a Loire red or a dry white cadet.

FRANCE Godewaersvelde, Nord Pas-de-Calais
Age 2 months
Weight and Shape 4lb 6oz (2kg), round
Size D. 10in (25cm), 1½in (H. 3.5cm)
Milk Cow
Classification Semi-soft
Producer Abbaye du Mont des Cats

Abbaye Notre-Dame de Belloc

This rich, fermier cheese, made from the milk of a local red-nosed breed of ewes, is one of the last few "Abbaye" or Trappist cheeses produced by monks at an abbey in the traditional way.

TASTING NOTES Its long aging period gives it a very rich taste, with a pronounced caramel-like, fruity flavor. Beneath its crusty, grayish-brown rind, the paste is firm yet supple and softer than most other ewe's milk Basque cheeses, with a surprisingly mild scent.

HOW TO ENJOY Avoid strong red wines that might mask the flavor; try sweet whites, such as Pacherenc du Vic-Bilh.

FRANCE Urt, Aquitaine
Age Best around 6 months
Weight and Shape 12lb (5.5kg), round
Size D. 10in (25cm), H. 3½in (8.5cm)
Milk Ewe
Classification Hard
Producer Abbaye de Belloc

Abbaye de la Pierre-qui-Vire

This Benedictine abbey in the Yonne region was founded in 1850 by a priest named Dom Muard. Since 1920, it has also become known for its delicious, semi-soft, washed cheese. It is similar to Epoisses, and is made from the milk of the monks' herd of 40 cows.

TASTING NOTES The brick-red rind covers a soft, smooth, and supple cheese that has a distinct country taste and a strong aroma.

HOW TO ENJOY As part of a cheeseboard or mix into mashed potatoes. Serve with any lively, full-bodied red Burgundy, such as Beaune.

FRANCE Saint-Léger-Vauban, Bourgogne
Age 6–10 weeks
Weight and Shape 7oz (200g), round
Size D. 4in (10cm), H. 1in (2.5cm)
Milk Cow
Classification Semi-soft
Producer Abbaye de la Pierre-qui-Vire

Abbaye de Tamié

At the Abbaye of Tamié, in the Savoie mountains, the incumbent monks produce a cheese that is similar to the well-known Reblochon but not as strong. The finished product is sold wrapped in blue paper decorated with the white cross of Malta.

TASTING NOTES This semi-soft, washed cheese has an orange-coloured, thin leathery crust, supple, springy texture; and a mild, sweet, milky taste.

HOW TO ENJOY This elegant, subtly flavored cheese stands proudly on a cheeseboard, served with a light and fruity red, white or rosé Savoie wine, such as an Apremont or Mondeuse.

FRANCE Savoie, Rhône-Alpes
Age 1–2 months
Weight and Shape 1lb 10oz (750g), round
Size D. 7in (18cm), H. 2in (4.5cm)
Milk Cow
Classification Semi-soft
Producer Abbaye de Tamié

Abondance AOC

AOC-protected since 1990, this hard cheese is produced by various cheesemakers using milk from three breeds of native cows, which are renowned for their excellent milk: Montbéliardes, Tarines, and Abondance. To sustain the quality and flavor of the milk, the cattle are not fed silage or any other fermented fodder.

TASTING NOTES This strong-smelling cheese has an immediate subtle taste that can be light or full flavored, depending on the season and producer.

HOW TO ENJOY Pair this smooth and supple cheese with a local white wine, preferably a dry one, or a Beaujolais.

FRANCE Rhône-Alpes
Age Best around 2–3 months
Weight and Shape 11–33lb (5kg–15kg), wheel
Size D. 14–18in (40–46cm), H. 3–4in (7.5–10cm)
Milk Cow
Classification Hard
Producer Various

A Casinca

Robust, almost wild, Corsican goats roam freely over vast landscapes, infusing their milk with various natural aromas. The hand-moulded delight A Casinca is one of the best washed-rind cheeses that they produce.

TASTING NOTES Although it has a pronounced taste and a rather strong smell, A Casinca is by no means unrefined. Aging and the gentle climate improve it, creating a unique nutty flavor.

HOW TO ENJOY For an exotic taste, serve A Casinca with a white wine, such as Condrieux, which is made from grapes grown in sunny climates.

FRANCE Corse	
Age 1½–4 months	
Weight and Shape 14oz (400g), round	
Size D. 6in (15cm), H. 1in (3cm)	
Milk Goat	
Classification Semi-soft	
Producer Various	

A Filetta

The name reflects the roots of this artisanal cheese; *a filetta* means "fern" in the Corsican language. As an added reminder of its provenance, this semi-soft cheese is most often produced decorated with a fern leaf on top.

TASTING NOTES This truly original taste, tinged with fern and the smell of a cellar, which can be a bit strong for some palates, is definitely worth a try. The grazing is quasi-wilderness, so this cheese has more personality and more natural flavor than many others.

HOW TO ENJOY Perfect served with a fig jam, to offset its trademark sharpness, and with a Corsican red or white wine.

FRANCE Corse	
Age About 6 weeks	
Weight and Shape 12oz (350g), round	
Size D. 4in (10cm), H. 1in (3cm)	
Milk Ewe	
Classification Semi-soft	
Producer Various	

Ami du Chambertin

Raymond Gaugry created this artisan cheese in 1950 as an accompaniment to the famous wine, Gevry Chambertin, that is made close by. Although the cheese is made in a modern creamery, much of the work is done by hand.

TASTING NOTES The rind is washed with local Marc de Bourgogne brandy, giving it an orange color and a powerful taste. The paste has a mouth-watering, creamy texture.

HOW TO ENJOY Ami du Chambertin is best appreciated with a glass of Gevrey-Chambertin or a Chassagne Montrachet—delicious wines that have a long finish and are very flavorsome.

FRANCE Brochon, Bourgogne	
Age 2 months	
Weight and Shape 9oz (250g), round	
Size D. 3½in (8.5cm), H. 2in (4.5cm)	
Milk Cow	
Classification Semi-soft	
Producer Gaugry dairy	

Ardi-Gasna

Ardi-Gasna means "sheep's cheese" in the Basque language, so it's no surprise that this hard cheese comes from the milk of ewes grazing on alpine pastures high in the Pyrénées. It can be eaten all year round, but the best cheeses are made using milk from lush spring or summer grazing.

TASTING NOTES It grows sharper with age, but even the youngest cheeses have a sophisticated, nutty taste and a pleasant aroma.

HOW TO ENJOY A fruity red wine is the perfect match for a young cheese. Pair sharper ones with full-bodied reds. Serve with jam, honey, or walnuts.

FRANCE Aquitaine	
Age 2–24 months, best at 5 months	
Weight and Shape 10lb (5kg), round	
Size D. 13in (32.5cm), H. 3in (7.5cm)	
Milk Ewe	
Classification Hard	
Producer Various	

Arômes au Gêne de Marc

This fermier cheese is produced using an ancient method of curing and preserving. A ripe cheese is placed in a barrel of marc—the damp skins, pips, and stalks of pressed grapes—that slowly permeate the cheese.

TASTING NOTES It has a strong and bittersweet flavor that is distinctly yeasty. As the cheese ages, its texture evolves from creamy to hard.

HOW TO ENJOY This cheese is an ideal partner to a light Beaujolais-village or a sweet dessert wine such as Muscat de Beaumes de Venise.

FRANCE Rhône-Alpes	
Age 1 month	
Weight and Shape 3–5½oz (85–150g), disk	
Size D. 2½–3in (6–7cm), H. ¾–1in (2–3cm)	
Milk Cow	
Classification Aged fresh	
Producer Various	

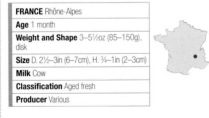

Baguette Laonnaise

A distinctive creamery or industrially produced cheese, Baguette Laonnaise is usually brick shaped but can also be found resembling a baguette. This feature, and the fact that it is produced in the city of Laon, gives the cheese its name.

TASTING NOTES It has a moist, red, washed rind and a highly pronounced flavor that is similar to those of the Maroilles (see p68).

HOW TO ENJOY You can eat this semi-soft cheese alongside all very full-bodied red wines of substance and character, and you could even wash it down with a glass of beer.

FRANCE Picardie	
Age 2–3 months	
Weight and Shape 1lb (450g), brick	
Size 6in (15cm), H. 2in (4.5cm)	
Milk Cow	
Classification Semi-soft	
Producer Various	

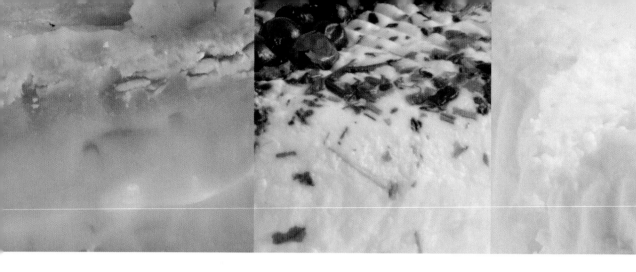

Banon AOC

A speciality of the mountains of
Lure in Provence, this cheese is sold
rustically wrapped in layers of chestnut
leaves and bound with raffia. The
Banon has benefited from AOC status
since 2003.

TASTING NOTES When young, the flavor
is mild and lactic, becoming slightly
nutty with age. As the leaves dry, molds
develop, the pâte softens and the flavor
becomes more nutty with a distinct
goaty tang.

HOW TO ENJOY This cheese is a real
pleasure to share with friends. Serve
with all fruity and lively red, white,
and rosé Provençal wines.

FRANCE Rhône-Alpes		
Age 2 weeks–2 months		
Weight and Shape 3½–4½oz (100–125g), round		
Size D. 3½in (8.5cm), H. 1in (2.5cm)		
Milk Goat		
Classification Aged fresh		
Producer Various		

Banon aux Baies Roses

Provence has a history making goat's
cheese that can be traced back to the
Roman times; some even claim that the
"Banon" cheese was enjoyed by the 1st
century Roman emperor, Antoninus
Pius. This fresh variation is decorated
with pink peppercorns (*baies roses*), the
dried berries from the Baies rose plant.

TASTING NOTES The mild, nutty flavor
of this cheese is counterpointed by the
sweet, distinct anise character of the
pink peppercorns.

HOW TO ENJOY This a beautiful-looking
addition to the cheeseboard can be
served with a fresh rose to decorate.

FRANCE Rhône-Alpes		
Age 2–8 weeks		
Weight and Shape 3½–4½oz (100–125g), round		
Size D. 3½in (8.5cm), H. 1in (2.5cm)		
Milk Goat		
Classification Fresh		
Producer Various		

Banon à la Sarriette

The Provençal climate provides perfect
growing conditions for some of the most
wonderful aromatic flowers and plants,
such as lavender and thyme, that
subtly flavor the milk of the grazing
goats. In this version of the region's
Banon, the herb savory creates yet
another layer of flavor.

TASTING NOTES The herb has a strong
sharp flavor; its pungency adds
a new dimension to this creamy,
slightly nutty cheese.

HOW TO ENJOY Serve with an aromatic
wine, such as a Gewürztraminer.

FRANCE Rhône-Alpes		
Age 2–8 weeks		
Weight and Shape 3.5–4.5oz, round		
Size D. 3½in (8cm), H. 1in (2cm)		
Milk Goat		
Classification Fresh		
Producer Various		

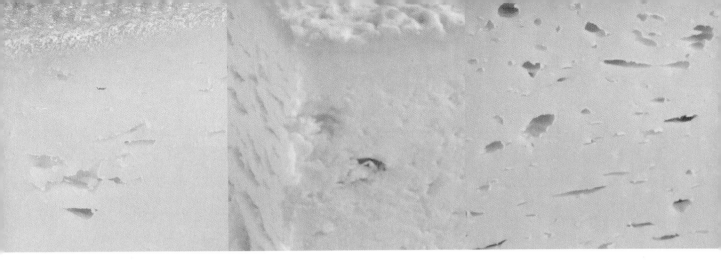

Bergues

This *fermier* cheese is named after the town in which it originated, and is still produced at Bergues in Flandres, around 8 miles from the Belgian border. It is a very popular cheese throughout northern France.

TASTING NOTES During the curing stage, this semi-soft cheese is repeatedly washed with brine and beer. This gives it a sharp, distinctive flavor against its supple and elastic texture.

HOW TO ENJOY It can be grated, broiled, or baked with vegetable dishes, soups, and pasta, and it is best enjoyed when washed down with a chilled beer.

FRANCE Nord-Pas-de-Calais	
Age at least 2 months	
Weight and Shape 4lb 6oz (2kg), round	
Size D. 8in (20cm), H. 2in (4.5cm)	
Milk Cow	
Classification Semi-soft	
Producer Various	

Berrichon

Since the 16th century, the Sancerre region has been successfully breeding goats, which has led to the production of a range of superb goat's cheeses like Berrichon (also known as Sancerrois), a big brother to Crottin de Chavignol.

TASTING NOTES As it ages the rind becomes more wrinkled and dusted with gray and blue molds. The texture also changes from firm and grainy to dense and compact, with a pronounced tang and a light goaty aroma.

HOW TO ENJOY It is excellent paired with local dry white wines, such as Sauvignon or fruity Pinot.

FRANCE Centre	
Age 3–5 weeks	
Weight and Shape 3½oz (100g), round	
Size D. 2½in (6cm), H. 2½in (6cm)	
Milk Goat	
Classification Aged fresh	
Producer Various	

Bethmale

Produced in the Pyrenees, Bethmale is one of the region's best-known cow's milk cheeses and is named after the village where it is made. It has a royal seal of approval, too, as it is said to have been favored by King Louis VI in the 12th century.

TASTING NOTES The flavor of Bethmale differs depending on how it is produced. Industrial varieties are very mild, while *fermier* varieties have a more pronounced taste.

HOW TO ENJOY Pair this cheese with all fruity and robust wines of Fitou, Corbières, Roussillon, Madiran.

FRANCE Midi-Pyrénées	
Age 3–4 months	
Weight and Shape 11lb–15lb (5kg–7kg), round	
Size D. 12–16in (30–40cm), H. 2–3in (4.5–7.5cm)	
Milk Cow	
Classification Hard	
Producer Various	

Bleu d'Auvergne AOC

Named after the province in which it originated, Bleu d'Auvergne has been AOC protected since 1975. It is similar to Roquefort, but this cheese is made using cow's rather than ewe's milk.

TASTING NOTES This blue cheese has a very sharp, engaging flavor and is best when made with milk from herds that have grazed the lush summer and fall mountain pastures.

HOW TO ENJOY This is a delicious addition to salad dressings or hot pasta dishes, or served with chicory, nuts, and raw mushrooms alongside a robust red or sweet white wine.

FRANCE Cantal, Auvergne	
Age 2–3 months	
Weight and Shape 5½lb (2.5kg), drum	
Size D. 8in (20cm), H. 4in (10cm)	
Milk Cow	
Classification Blue	
Producer Various	

Bleu des Causses AOC

Like Roquefort, this cheese is ripened in natural caves called *fleurines* in the limestone plateaus of the Causses. Bleu des Causses is made with cow's milk and is aged longer than most blues. It has been AOC protected since 1979.

TASTING NOTES The flavor differs depending on the season in which it is produced. Ivory-yellow summer cheeses are milder than the stronger-tasting, white winter cheeses.

HOW TO ENJOY It is excellent in salads and on cheeseboards, and goes well with all lively, well-balanced red wines that have an aromatic note, such as Cornas, Lirac, and Jurançon.

FRANCE Midi-Pyrénées	
Age 3–6 months	
Weight and Shape 5lb 3oz–5lb 13oz (2.3kg–2.6kg), drum	
Size D. 7–8in (18–20cm), H. 3–4in (7.5–10cm)	
Milk Cow	
Classification Blue	
Producer Various	

Bleu de Chèvre

As a blue goat's cheese, Bleu de Chèvre is a rare thing. Most French blues are made with cow's milk and a few, such as Roquefort, are made using ewe's milk. This cheese is produced on only a handful of small farms, mainly in the mountains, so it is little-known outside the region.

TASTING NOTES Bleu de Chèvre is dense with erratic patches of blue. It melts in the mouth with a subtle but herbaceous tang from the goat's milk, but is milder than cow's and ewe's milk blues.

HOW TO ENJOY Eat with fresh figs and a glass of sweet Muscat de Beaume de Venise.

FRANCE Auvergne, Rhône-Alpes, Midi-Pyrénées	
Age 2 months	
Weight and Shape 8lb (3.6kg), round	
Size D. 7½in (19cm), H. 4in (10cm)	
Milk Goat	
Classification Blue	
Producer Various	

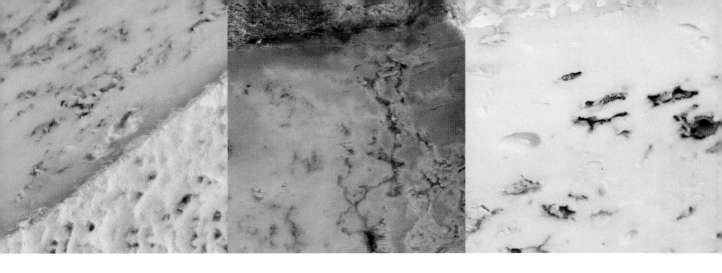

Bleu de Gex Haut-Jura AOC

Granted AOC status in 1977, this unusually dense, almost hard, blue cheese is produced in small, traditional dairies using milk from cows grazing the pastures of the Jura mountains.

TASTING NOTES The yeasts and molds in the mountain grasses and flowers pass through the milk into the cheese, giving the soft interior a speckled blue appearance and a slightly bitter, savory flavor. Eat it after wiping off the white powdery mold covering it.

HOW TO ENJOY Serve as the locals do with boiled potatoes and a fruity, regional red wine—a Beaujolais or Burgundy.

FRANCE Franche-Comté	
Age Around 2–3 months	
Weight and Shape 11lb–13lb 3oz (5–6kg). wheel	
Size D. 12in (30cm), H. 3–4in (7.5–10cm)	
Milk Cow	
Classification Blue	
Producer Various	

Bleu de Termignon

This blue cheese is produced to very precise specifications. Just four producers make it in summer using the milk of cows that graze 4300ft up the mountain pastures of the French Alps. The spare, irregular bluing is not the result of piercing, but of wild molds entering through cracks in the rind.

TASTING NOTES Beneath the rough, crusty, brown-gold rind is a dense, yet crumbly interior with a strong, almost spicy, tang and earthy, refined flavor.

HOW TO ENJOY Team this tasty blue cheese with a glass of Chignin Bergerson or a mellow wine, such as a Tokay.

FRANCE Rhône-Alpes	
Age 4–5 months	
Weight and Shape 15½lb (7kg), drum	
Size D. 11.8in (29cm), H. 6in (15cm)	
Milk Cow	
Classification Blue	
Producer Various	

Bleu du Vercors-Sassenage AOC

AOC protected since 1998, this cheese is named after the town of Sassenage where, in the 14th century, subjects were ordered to pay their taxes in cheese. Unlike most traditional blues, it is lightly pressed and thinner, which gives it a more supple texture.

TASTING NOTES The rind is thin, leathery, and brown; the paste pale yellow, dense yet soft, marked with irregular thick streaks and blue patches. Delicate for a blue, it has a slightly bitter aftertaste.

HOW TO ENJOY Eat alongside a glass of robust, lively, Beaujolais-Villages and Côtes-du-Rhône-Villages.

FRANCE Rhône-Alpes	
Age 2–3 months	
Weight and Shape 11lb–13lb 4oz (5–6kg), wheel	
Size D. 12in (15cm), H. 3in (7.5cm)	
Milk Cow	
Classification Blue	
Producer Various	

Beaufort AOC

Of all the great cheeses of the world, Beaufort encapsulates everything that is magical, traditional, and truly awesome about cheese, and demonstrates how, in a harsh and rugged terrain, humans have worked alongside Mother Nature and adapted to the rhythm and demands of the seasons.

In the 14th and 15th centuries, the local church and landowners of the Savoie-Beaufortain in the French Alps, instigated a widespread program to remove much of the woodlands to create mountain pastures. These pastures—as colorful and spectacular as a Monet painting—are unploughed and unfenced, and contain the thousands of different species of wild herbs, meadow flowers, and grasses that provide the native Abondance, and Tarine cows with fresh grazing in summer, and aromatic hay in winter. The resulting milk is sweet, nutty, aromatic, and complex.

It takes the milk of about 35 cows to make one Beaufort cheese. Because of this, herdsmen have, since ancient times, combined their milk, forming cooperatives, and shared the tasks of herding, milking, cheesemaking, and maturing.

Cheese produced in the lush summer pastures is known as Beaufort *d'Alpage*; those produced from a single herd that graze above 4,921ft (1,500m) are called Chalet *d'Alpage*, and are some of the largest artisan cheeses in the world. Winter cheeses, known as Beaufort *d'Hiver*, are paler as they are made when the cows enjoy a more concentrated diet of hay cut from the mountain pasture.

Beaufort is another cheese that is protected by the AOC label, and can only be made in an area covering approximately 1,112 acres in the Rhône-Alpes' Beaufortain, Tarentaise, and Maurienne valleys, as well as a section of the Val d'Arly.

TASTING NOTES Young Beaufort is firm but not hard. It melts in the mouth, and has a rich, sweet, complex flavor. The Chalet *d'Alpage* is aged longer and has more honeyed, aromatic notes and a long, savory tang that hints of meadow flowers.

HOW TO ENJOY This is not a cheese to melt over bread or put in a sandwich (although both would be heaven), and certainly not to be bought in miserable thin slices! It should be eaten in generous mouthfuls accompanied by a bottle of the best Pinot Noir you can afford. Fresh walnuts, grown throughout the Savoy, also make a great partner. Beaufort's rich sweetness is also excellent with Champagne, as well as Chardonnay and Riesling, but avoid dry whites that take away its flavor.

The milk *only comes from the Tarentaise and Abondance cows, whose diet is strictly controlled.*

FRANCE Rhône-Alpes	
Age 5–18 months	
Weight and Shape 44lb–154lb 3oz (20–70kg), round	
Size D. 14–27½in (35–75cm) H. 4½–6in (11–16cm)	
Milk Cow	
Classification Hard	
Producer Various	

A CLOSER LOOK

Beaufort has been protected by the AOC label since 1968, resulting in strict control of each stage of production. This includes the milk used, which is never pasteurized, the distinct concave shape, and every aspect of its maturation.

A few tiny holes are formed during the fermentation of the curd.

The cloth rind is rubbed with brine enriched with scrapings from old cheeses and whey, creating a grainy, russet crust that protects the cheese from drying out.

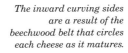

The inward curving sides are a result of the beechwood belt that circles each cheese as it matures.

COAGULATION This process only takes 20–30 minutes. The curds are then cut and the temperature raised to both scald the milk and to squeeze out moisture from the curd. The curd is piled into cloth and carefully removed from the cauldron.

Exterior

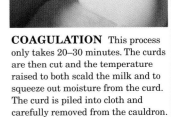

PRESSING The curd is encircled with a *cercle*, a belt made of beech, and pressed for 20 hours. It is turned regularly during this time.

During its long maturation, small horizontal cracks appear near the edge, because the rind dries faster than the interior.

Interior

Bonde de Gâtine

Produced in the marshy Gâtine area of Poitou, the Bonde de Gâtine is a high-quality *fermier* goat's cheese that requires two liters of milk to make just one 14oz cheese. It has a thin wrinkled rind, which is dusted with blue, gray, and white molds.

TASTING NOTES The paste has a pronounced acidity and saltiness that melts in the mouth, leaving behind it a rich aftertaste.

HOW TO ENJOY Team it with a dry and fruity wine, such as a Sancerre Blanc, which complements the creamy, acidic, and fruity flavors.

FRANCE Gâtine, Poitou-Charentes	
Age 6–10 weeks	
Weight and Shape 14oz (400g), drum	
Size D. 2in (4.5cm), H. 3in (7cm)	
Milk Goat	
Classification Aged fresh	
Producer Patrick Cantet	

Boulette d'Avesnes

In the past, this *fermier* cheese was made exclusively from buttermilk; nowadays, it is made with the fresh curds of Maroilles and mashed with parsley, tarragon, cloves, and pepper. It is shaped by hand, dyed with peppery annatto, and dusted with paprika.

TASTING NOTES The paprika from the rind gives it a hot peppery bite, while the semi-soft, ivory-colored paste adds a spicy, herbaceous, and sharp flavor.

HOW TO ENJOY Pair with all strong, very full-bodied red wines, such as Cahors. A shot of gin will also bring out its unusual combination of flavors.

FRANCE Flandre-Hainaut, Nord-Pas-de-Calais	
Age 3 months	
Weight and Shape 7oz (200g), cone	
Size D. 3in (7.5cm), H. 4in (10cm)	
Milk Cow	
Classification Fresh	
Producer Pont du Loup, Fauquet, and Leduc	

Boulette de Cambrai

Made by hand in Cambrai, near the Belgium border where it has long been popular, this cow's milk cheese is a delicious combination of fromage frais, tarragon, parsley, chives, and seasoning. Unlike Boulette d'Avesnes, Boulette de Cambrai is always consumed fresh.

TASTING NOTES This fresh rindless cheese is mildly aromatic and has a deliciously herby flavor, but it will become bitter if allowed to age for too long.

HOW TO ENJOY Spread on crusty bread and pair with a light and fruity red wine, such as Beaujolais.

FRANCE Nord-Pas-de-Calais	
Age 1–5 days	
Weight and Shape 10oz (280g), cone	
Size D. 3in (7.5cm), H. 4in (10cm)	
Milk Cow	
Classification Fresh	
Producer Various	

Bouton-de-Culotte

Bouton-de-Culotte, or trouser buttons, are small Mâconnais that are stored during the fall for winter use. By winter, the rind becomes dark brown and hard and this goat's cheese can be grated into the local *fromage fort*.

TASTING NOTES It has a very distinct goaty taste that hints of ground nuts, feels dry in the mouth, and has a sharp, tongue-tingling finish.

HOW TO ENJOY Enjoy this cheese with all the powerful full-bodied vintages of Mâconnais and Côte Chalonnaise.

FRANCE Bourgogne	
Age 2 months	
Weight and Shape 2oz (60g), tiny drum	
Size D. 2in (5cm) base, 1½in (4cm) top, H. 1.5in (3.5cm)	
Milk Goat	
Classification Aged fresh	
Producer Various	

Bouyguette des Collines

The pale ivory, soft, wrinkled rind of this hand-formed goat's cheese is decorated with a sprig of rosemary, making it a very attractive addition to a cheeseboard. Its thin rind means the paste breaks down very quickly and becomes soft and creamy.

TASTING NOTES Bouyguette des Collines has a slight taste of thyme and rosemary. Initially the cheese is smooth, then, after 20 days of maturing, its flavor becomes more pronounced.

HOW TO ENJOY It is best paired with a dry white wine, such as Sancerre, Riesling or Chinon, but is also good with a rosé.

FRANCE Tarn, Midi-Pyrénées	
Age 2–3 weeks	
Weight and Shape 5½oz (150g), oval	
Size L. 8in (20cm), H. 1½in (4cm)	
Milk Goat	
Classification Aged fresh	
Producer Segalafrom	

Brebis du Lochois

This modern, French ewe's milk cheese, comes from central France (a region traditionally associated with goats), where the flock grazes on very good pastures. Cheeses that are dusted with ash are called Cendré Lochois.

TASTING NOTES Lochois has a tender and generous paste, as well as a smooth buttery flavor and herby aromas. The beech ashes give it a somewhat smoky and woody character.

HOW TO ENJOY It tastes delicious served with figs and jam, and goes well when paired with white wines from Touraine, such as Sancerre or Montlouis.

FRANCE Touraine, Centre	
Age 2 weeks	
Weight and Shape 4oz (110g), round	
Size D. 3in (7.5cm), H. 1in (2.5cm)	
Milk Ewe	
Classification Aged fresh	
Producer Brebis du Lochois	

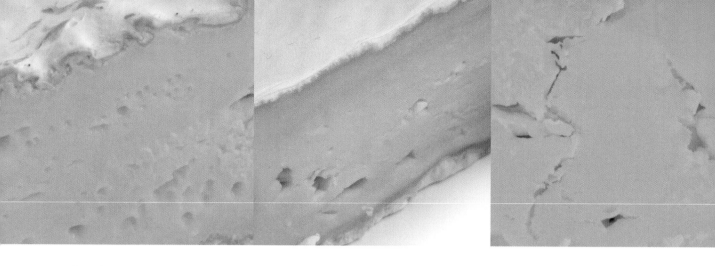

Brie de Melun AOC

Unlike other Bries, the coagulation of the curd in this cow's milk cheese is very slow, since it relies mainly on lactic fermentation rather than rennet. This produces a very thick curd, and eventually, a thick, crusty white rind with red, yellow, and brown pigments and molds.

TASTING NOTE It can be sold fresh, when it is sour yet sweet, or when fully mature, when it has a very fruity flavor and a strong scent of fermentation.

HOW TO ENJOY It can be enjoyed with all red wines of Burgundy, Bordeaux, and Côtes-Du-Rhône that are lively, full-bodied, and have bouquet.

FRANCE	Ile-de-France
Age	Best around 2 months
Weight and Shape	3lb 5oz (1.5kg), wheel
Size	D. 9½in (24cm), H. 1½in (3.5cm)
Milk	Cow
Classification	Soft white
Producer	Various

Brie de Nangis

Originally made in Nangis, south east of Paris, this Brie almost disappeared when superseded by Brie de Melun. However, it has since been revived by a single producer in Tournan-en-Brie and remains true to the original. It is at its best when made from milk from cows grazed on spring and summer grass.

TASTING NOTE Like Brie de Melun, this Brie has a white mold rind and a soft, creamy paste. Unlike Brie de Melun, it has a very fruity, rather than more savory or meaty flavor.

HOW TO ENJOY Pair this Brie with a glass of lively, full-bodied Bourgogne, Bordeaux or Côtes-du-Rhône.

FRANCE	Ile-de-France
Age	4–5 weeks
Weight and Shape	2¼lb (1kg), round
Size	D. 9in (23cm), H. 2in (5cm)
Milk	Cow
Classification	Soft white
Producer	Rouzaire

Brillat-Savarin

Although named after a renowned 18th-century gourmand and food writer, Brillat-Savarin was in fact created in the 1930s by Henri Androuët, a famous cheesemaker and *affineur*. This triple-cream cheese, with a fat content of 75 percent for every 3.5oz, is not for the dieter

TASTING NOTE When young, it has no rind and a texture like thick crème fraîche; if eaten once it has developed its thin white coat, the paste will have softened to become luscious, creamy, and soft.

HOW TO ENJOY It goes well with all light fruity wines, in particular Champagnes with some character.

FRANCE	Basse-Normandie, Bourgogne
Age	2–4 weeks
Weight and Shape	1lb 2oz (500g), round
Size	D. 5in (12cm), H. 1½in (3.5cm)
Milk	Cow
Classification	Soft white
Producer	Lincet

FRANCE

42

Brique du Forez

This traditional cheese from the Auvergne region takes its name from its brick-like shape. It is characterised by a thin white rind that develops a blue-gray hue. It used to be made using a mixture of cow's and goat's milk, but now it is made solely with cow's milk.

TASTING NOTES The white mantle smells mushroomy and sharp, while the interior is creamy and almost runny, with a nutty flavor and a long finish in the mouth.

HOW TO ENJOY Team this creamy cheese with light and fruity white, rosé and red wines of Auvergne, Roanne, and Beaujolais.

FRANCE Auvergne (Livradois)		
Age 2–3 months		
Weight and Shape 12–14oz (350–400g), brick		
Size L. 5–5½in (12–13cm), W. 1½–2.5in (3½–5½cm), H. 1in (2.5cm)		
Milk Cow		
Classification Soft white		
Producer Various		

Brocciu AOC

This famous Corsican fresh cheese is made by unusual production processes: whey is added, rather than discarded, during the process, giving it a unique taste in addition to some precious nutrients. It is then drained in small rush baskets (*canestres*).

TASTING NOTE Fresh Brocciu is mild tasting and creamy; however, ripened Brocciu (also referred to as Brocciu Pasu) is strong and a little spicy.

HOW TO ENJOY Brocciu can be used in many recipes, including salads, omelets and cheesecakes. It is delicious served with just salt, sugar, rosemary, or honey, and a light wine.

FRANCE Corse		
Age 2–3 days		
Weight and Shape 1½–3lbs (675g–1.3kg), basket		
Size Various		
Milk Ewe		
Classification Fresh		
Producer Various		

Brossauthym

This is a unique cheese, because it is thought to be the only ewe's cheese produced in the Loire region. Flavored with thyme, it has a natural rind and oval shape, and it makes a decorative addition to any cheeseboard.

TASTING NOTE This fresh cheese is tasty, thyme-flavored and has a mellow, melt-in-the-mouth finish.

HOW TO ENJOY Serve with aromatic red wines, such as a well-structured Ajaccio or a full-bodied Patrimonio.

FRANCE Touraine, Centre		
Age 1 month		
Weight and Shape 8oz (225g), oval		
Size L. 4⅓in (11cm), H. 2in (4.5cm)		
Milk Ewe		
Classification Aged fresh		
Producer M. Froideveaux		

Buchette Pont d'Yeu

This log-shaped goat's cheese takes its name from the island of Yeu in the Vendée region of France. It has a natural rind that is sprinkled with wood ash.

TASTING NOTES The flavor of the thick paste varies depending on the level of maturation of the cheese. When it is young (at about three weeks), it is nutty, but as it ages, it develops a peppery taste.

HOW TO ENJOY Serve on a cheeseboard alongside crusty bread, berries, and jam. The Buchette is best enjoyed with a fruity white wine, such as Lillet.

FRANCE Pays de la Loire	
Age 3–8 weeks	
Weight and Shape 7oz (200g), log	
Size L. 4in (10cm), H. 2in (5cm)	
Milk Goat	
Classification Aged fresh	
Producer Various	

Cabri Ariégeois

The passionate farmers in Ariège have created this modern French cheese, which has become one of the best goat's cheeses on the market. Based on the famous Mont d'Or cheese, Cabri Ariégeois is bound up in a strip of spruce bark.

TASTING NOTES Very smooth and creamy, this washed cheese has a pronounced, sharp flavor and a hint of pine that comes from the bark.

HOW TO ENJOY This cheese is best appreciated alongside a full-bodied and structured red wine with a strong berry flavor, such as a Côte de Roussillon.

FRANCE Ariège, Midi-Pyrénées	
Age From 4–6 weeks	
Weight and Shape 11lb 2oz (500g), round	
Size D. 10in (25cm), H. 2½in (6cm)	
Milk Goat	
Classification Semi-soft	
Producer Fromagerie Fermier Cabrioulet	

Camembert de Normandie AOC

This, one of the most famous French cheeses, is said to have been created in 1791 by Marie Harel, a farmer's wife in Camembert. The most important invention, though, was its wooden box, which enabled it to be shipped around the world. The AOC granted in 1983 states it must be made with raw milk.

TASTING NOTES Its flavor is fruity, with a slight aroma of mushrooms and mold. Locals prefer Camembert when the heart is white and not yet creamy.

HOW TO ENJOY Serve with fruity, elegant red wines of Burgundy and Côtes-du-Rhône, or a traditional Normandy cider.

FRANCE Basse-Normandie	
Age Best around 1 month	
Weight and Shape 9oz (250g), round	
Size D. 4½in (11cm), H. 1½in (3.5cm)	
Milk Cow	
Classification Soft white	
Producer Various	

Cantal AOC

AOC protected since 1956, Cantal is the forefather of all cheeses from the Auvergne region. It is made using the cheddaring process typical of many English traditional hard cheeses, and is unique in being the only French cheese produced this way.

TASTING NOTES The flavor differs depending on the age of the cheese: a well-ripened Cantal is strong in taste, while a young cheese has a mild, nutty and milky flavor.

HOW TO ENJOY Pair Cantal with a light fruity wine, such as a Côtes d'Auvergne, Côtes Roannaises, or Beaujolais.

FRANCE Auvergne	
Age Best around 3–6 months	
Weight and Shape 77–99lb, cylinder	
Size D. 14–18in (35–46cm), H. 14–16in (35–39cm)	
Milk Cow	
Classification Hard	
Producer Various	

Capri Lezeen

These farmhouse goat's cheeses are produced by the GAEC du Capri Lezéen in the marshy part of Poitou. They have quite a sticky yellow rind, with traces of light blue mold, and are sold wrapped in a signature chestnut leaf, packaged up in a wooden box.

TASTING NOTES The creamy, runny paste and soft rind has a slightly nutty taste and only a subtle goaty flavor.

HOW TO ENJOY Pair Capri Lezeen with a dry white wine, such as a Sancerre or Viognier. It tastes delicious served alongside fresh figs or berries.

FRANCE Lezay, Poitou-Charentes	
Age 2–3 weeks	
Weight and Shape 6oz (175g), round	
Size D. 4in (10cm), H. ½in (1.5cm)	
Milk Goat	
Classification Aged fresh	
Producer GAEC du Capri Lezéen Patrick Cantet	

Carré de l'Est

As its name suggests (it means "square of the east"), this co-operative or industrial washed-rind cheese is square in shape and is most famous in the eastern regions of France (Lorraine, the Ardennes, and Champagne).

TASTING NOTES Soft and grainy when young, this cheese becomes almost liquid when mature. It has a salty flavor and the orange, sticky rind that gives it a smokey bacon tang. Those covered with white mold are milder.

HOW TO ENJOY Spread this semi-soft cheese on bread for a delicious snack and team with light fruity wines, such as Châteauneuf-du-Pâpe or Gigondas.

FRANCE Champagne, Ardennes and Lorraine	
Age About 3 weeks	
Weight and Shape 4½–9oz (125–250g), square	
Size D. 4in (10cm), H. 1½in (3.5cm)	
Milk Cow	
Classification Semi-soft	
Producer Various	

Brie de Meaux AOC

Made just 31 miles (50km) east of Paris in the region of Ile-de-France, Brie de Meaux can trace its history back to Emperor Charlemagne who, in 774CE, extolled the virtues of Brie in his Chronicles.

FRANCE

At the Congress of Vienna, *1814, Brie de Meaux was declared the "King of Cheeses."*

The worldwide reputation of Brie de Meaux was established in 1814, when it was declared *Le Roi des Fromages,* "The King of Cheeses" at a culinary tournament during the Congress of Vienna. The close proximity of Ile-de-France to the markets of Paris and the charming wooden box in which it is sold have also contributed to its rise to fame.

Brie de Meaux is one of only 40 French cheeses protected by the AOC label, which guarantees the quality of a cheese as well as where and how it is made (see p8). To qualify, Brie must be made in specific areas with calf rennet and 6.6 gallons (25 litres) of unpasteurized milk. The curd must be ladled by hand into the molds and each cheese must be dry salted then ripened slowly at a specific temperature and humidity.

Brie de Meaux and Camembert de Normandie (see p44) are often considered similar, but in fact they each have their own distinct character influenced by size, microflora, unique climate, and grazing.

TASTING NOTES Brie de Meaux is probably the strongest of all the soft white cheeses. The aroma should be of mold, damp leaves, and mushrooms, becoming more intense with age. At its peak, it has a glossy pale straw to butter-yellow colored soft interior that oozes irresistibly toward you, and a characteristic rich taste like wild, smoky mushroom soup made with beef consommé. If it smells strongly of ammonia, then it will deliver a vicious bite. However, one man's meat is another man's poison.

If you prefer Brie that is runny rather than with a chalky band of immature curd through the center, buy it near its "best by" date. Don't be alarmed by any white mold that grows down the cut surface, this just tells you the cheese is alive and well, and merely trying to protect its soft interior from drying out. It's best kept in its original paper or wax paper. Plastic wrap prevents the cheese from breathing and the ammonia, released during ripening, will be trapped and, within a day or so, the cheese will start to sweat.

HOW TO ENJOY It would almost be a crime to do anything with Brie de Meaux except allow it to reach room temperature and enjoy it with a red Côte-du-Rhône, Bordeaux, or Burgundy or, as befits the Cheese of Kings, a glass of vintage Champagne.

FRANCE Ile de France	
Age 6–8 weeks	
Weight and Shape 6½lb (3kg), wheel	
Size D. 10in (25cm), H. 3¼in (8cm)	
Milk Cow	
Classification Soft white	
Producer Various	

A CLOSER LOOK

From Paris to Peru, Brie de Meaux is enjoyed the world over. Surprisingly, there are only a handful of producers, and most cheeses are then matured and aged by special *affineurs*, each creating their own unique style.

THE LADLE To achieve the smooth, voluptuous custardlike interior and to prevent the fat and protein from being lost in the whey, cheesemakers must handle the fragile, floppy curd by hand, using a perforated ladle known as a *pelle à brie*, first used in the 12th century.

RIND The cheese is softest under the rind where the mold is working to ripen the curd.

SALTING The cheeses are dry salted by hand. This helps to seal the cheese as well as draw out the moisture.

RIPENING The cheeses spend a minimum of four weeks in a special cellar where they are turned regularly. First, a sprinkling of red or brown streaks or spots known as *ferment du rouge* start to appear, then the more virulent white molds, *penicillium candidum* and *penicillium camemberti* gradually cover the rind in a fine coat of white velvet.

The fat content is around 26 percent, significantly less than hard cheeses such as Cheddar (see pp180–181).

Whole cheese, slice removed.

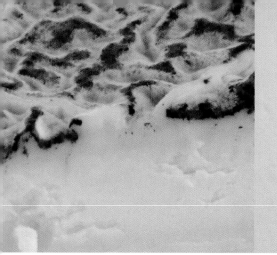

Cathare

This goat's cheese is distinctive because of the pattern outlined in the charcoal powder sprinkled on its rind. The Occitan cross that it bears has been the emblem of the Languedoc region since the Cathar heresies of the 12th and 13th centuries; it also refers to the Occitain language still spoken in parts of southern France and northern Spain.

TASTING NOTES This recently created cheese has a smooth, fine texture and a subtle goat's milk taste that is enriched by the aging process.

HOW TO ENJOY This is delicious teamed with a full-bodied and fruity wine, such as a Gaillac.

FRANCE Languedoc-Rousillon	
Age 2 weeks	
Weight and Shape 7oz (200g), flat disc	
Size D. 6in (15cm), H. ½in (1.5cm)	
Milk Goat	
Classification Aged fresh	
Producer La ferme de Cabriole	

Cendré de Niort

Cendré traditionally refers to the method of maturing cheese in a box of wood ash to form the rind, rather than simply sprinkling the coat with ash. Most of these cheeses originate in wine-growing regions; they were made when milk was abundant, preserved in wood ash until harvest time, and then served to the hungry grape pickers.

TASTING NOTES This *fermier* cheese has a real countryside aroma and a fairly milky flavor. The chestnut leaf it is wrapped in imparts a vegetal hint.

HOW TO ENJOY Open a fruity and light red wine with Cendré de Niort, such as a Chinon or an Alsace Pinot Noir.

FRANCE La Fragnée, Poitou-Charentes	
Age 6 weeks	
Weight and Shape 4½oz (125g), round	
Size D. 4in (8cm), H. 1in (2.5cm)	
Milk Goat	
Classification Aged fresh	
Producer Patrick Cantet	

Cendré de Vergy

Cendré de Vergy is another example of a cheese made by the method of burying a young cheese in wood ash for a month. A number of cheeses can be used for this process, including an Epoisses de Bourgogne. Aisy Cendré is a similar cheese, but it is made by another producer.

TASTING NOTES This artisan cheese has a mix of sweet and strong flavors, with a slightly smoked taste and very creamy texture—eat with a spoon!

HOW TO ENJOY Pair with a Meursault or Chambole Musigny—delicious wines that have a long finish and are very flavorsome.

FRANCE Bourgogne (Epoisses and Gevrey Chambertin)	
Age 2 weeks	
Weight and Shape 8½oz (100g), round	
Size D. 4in (10cm), H. 1½in (3.5cm)	
Milk Cow	
Classification Semi-soft	
Producer Berthault and Gaugry dairies	

Chabichou du Poitou AOC

This natural-rinded cheese comes from the Loire, home to the majority of French goat's cheeses. It has been protected by the AOC label since 1990, and its production can be *fermier*, cooperative, or industrial.

TASTING NOTES The thin, white rind, with its yellow and blue mold, conceals a cheese with a distinct aroma and a pronounced to sharp flavor, compared to other goat's cheeses.

HOW TO ENJOY Delicious with the lively, fruity red wines of the Neuville-de-Poitou, Dissay, and Saint-martin-la-rivière regions.

FRANCE Poitou-Charentes	
Age 3 weeks	
Weight and Shape 3½oz (100g), cylinder	
Size D. 2½in (6cm), H. 2½in (5cm)	
Milk Goat	
Classification Aged fresh	
Producer Various	

Chaource AOC

Said to have been created by the monks of Pontigny, the name of this soft white-rinded cheese comes from the town that is the center of that region. It was originally sold fresh or demi-sec, but now it is preferred as a more mature cheese. AOC protected since 1970.

TASTING NOTES Its white, crusty, and downy rind becomes pigmented with brown as it ages. It has a creamy texture and a milky, fruity flavor with a faint aroma of mushrooms, becoming sharper and salty as it matures.

HOW TO ENJOY Team it with fruity white wines of Saint-Bris-le-Vineux, Chablis, and Irancy, or fruity reds and rosés.

FRANCE Saligny, Bourgogne	
Age 2 weeks–2 months	
Weight and Shape 1lb 5oz (600g), small cylinder	
Size D. 5in (12cm), H. 2½in (6cm)	
Milk Cow	
Classification Soft white	
Producer Lincet	

Charolais

This *fermier* cheese made from goat's milk hails from the Bourgogne region. A distinctive-looking cheese, Charolais is shaped like a small barrel and often displays a characteristic bluish rind.

TASTING NOTES Charolais has a firm and compact paste and a natural rind. Faintly sour, it holds a distinct flavor of milk and almonds.

HOW TO ENJOY Serve with chestnuts and walnuts or a loaf of sourdough bread. Fruity wines, such as Fleurie, are the most appropriate for drinking alongside this cheese.

FRANCE Bourgogne	
Age 2–6 weeks	
Weight and Shape 4oz (120g), barrel	
Size D. 2in (4.5cm), H. 3in (7.5cm)	
Milk Goat	
Classification Aged fresh	
Producer Various	

PERSILLE DE TIGNES The gradual
development of fine gray, brown, and
white molds are like an intricately woven
spider web, and are actively encouraged by
the cheesemaker because they contribute
to the breakdown of the curd. (See p76).

Chevrotin des Aravis AOC

One of the few washed-rind goat cheeses, Chevrotin des Aravis is named after the type of milk used and the Vallée des Aravis where it is made. It is similar in appearance and texture to Reblochon; a moist, yellowish-orange rind is covered with a fine white mold. It was granted an AOC in 2002 as the 40th member.

TASTING NOTES This cheese has a mild, slightly goaty flavor. The fine-textured paste melts slightly at the edges.

HOW TO ENJOY It is best paired with a sharp-tasting red wine, such as a Mondeuse or Chignin-Bergeron.

FRANCE Rhône-Alpes	
Age 2 months	
Weight and Shape 1lb 5oz (600g), round	
Size D. 3½in (9cm), H. 2in (4cm)	
Milk Goat	
Classification Semi-soft	
Producer Various	

Chevrotin des Bauges AOC

This *fermier* cheese is produced in the mountain region of Savoie, known for its magnificent scenery and colorful, diverse natural pastures. This area is home to many of France's best-loved cheeses, including Reblochon, which Chevrotin resembles except that it is made with goat's milk.

TASTING NOTES A thick, rustic rind covers a smooth, supple, melting paste with small irregular eyes. The creamy, sweet flavor has a hint of goat.

HOW TO ENJOY Pair this cheese with a fruity, dry white Savoie wine, such as the Roussette.

FRANCE Rhône-Alpes	
Age 21 days	
Weight and Shape 10½oz (300g), round	
Size D. 3½–4½in (9–11.5cm), H. 1½in (4cm)	
Milk Goat	
Classification Semi-soft	
Producer Various	

Ch'ti Roux

The deep tangerine-orange color of this cheese is the result of roucous or annatto being added to the milk, and the rind being washed with a mix of dark beer and annatto. Ch'ti Roux is one of many cheeses made by the family of Bernard-Wierre Effroy in the Nord-Pas-de-Calais, from its own cows.

TASTING NOTES This firm-textured cheese has quite a powerful, spicy, and salty flavor with a long, slightly peppery finish.

HOW TO ENJOY A dark beer or a wine from Bourgogne, such as Côte de Baune or Beaujolais, will complement this flavorsome cheese.

FRANCE Nord-Pas-de-Calais	
Age 4 months	
Weight and Shape 14oz (400g), brick	
Size L. 4½in (11cm), W. 1in (2.5cm), H. 2in (4.5cm)	
Milk Cow	
Classification Semi-soft	
Producer Saint Godeleine Farm (M. Bernard)	

Clochette

This name of this goat's cheese reflects its dramatic-looking shape—*clochette* translates as "little bell". It is produced in the Poitou-Charentes region, which is also home to another well-known goat's cheese, Chabichou. Clochette has a dry and crusty rind of natural mold, but a firm and tender paste.

TASTING NOTES The pleasant aroma of dried hay and goats derives from its mold and from the cellar in which it was ripened. It has a smooth texture and a warm, powerful flavor.

HOW TO ENJOY Eat it warm with olives or nuts and serve alongside full-bodied Burgundy wines.

FRANCE Roullet-Saint-Estéphe, Poitou-Charentes	
Age 2–3 weeks	
Weight and Shape 8oz (225g), bell	
Size D. 3in (7.5cm), H. 4in (10cm)	
Milk Goat	
Classification Aged fresh	
Producer GAEC Jouseaume	

Cœur de Neufchâtel AOC

Neufchâtel is a cow's milk cheese that is produced in Haute-Normandie, and has benefited from the AOC label since 1969. As its name suggests, this version is heart-shaped, but it can also be found as a small cylinder or brick, when it is simply called Neufchâtel.

TASTING NOTES The white rind is dry, velvety, and crumbly with a mushroomy aroma. The paste is firm but slightly grainy, with a subtle milk taste and salty tang.

HOW TO ENJOY Its flavor works well with good crusty breads; locals like to melt it on warm bread and eat it for breakfast.

FRANCE Haute-Normandie	
Age 8–10 weeks	
Weight and Shape 7oz (200g), heart	
Size L. 4in (10cm), H. 1in (2.5cm)	
Milk Cow	
Classification Soft white	
Producer Various	

Cœur de Touraine

The Loire is famous not only for its great chateaux, but also for its goat's cheeses. This heart-shaped cheese (reflecting its name—the "heart" of Touraine) with its ash-covered rind is very popular.

TASTING NOTES Like all traditional Loire goat's cheese, the inside is a bit sticky on the palate and the rind is edible—including the mold, which is very savory. The overall taste is mild; a little salty yet mouth-watering.

HOW TO ENJOY Cœur de Touraine is a real delight with nut bread or raisin bread and a white wine, such as a Mont Louis.

FRANCE Centre	
Age 3 weeks at least	
Weight and Shape 5½oz (150g), heart	
Size W. 3½in (9cm), H. 1½in (4cm)	
Milk Goat	
Classification Aged fresh	
Producer Various	

Coulommiers

A more petite member of the Brie family, Coulommiers is produced in the Ile-de-France region, near Paris. A *fermier* or industrially-produced cheese, it has a downy white rind that is dotted with reddish ferments and a supple texture.

TASTING NOTES Coulommiers has a rather pronounced tang and leaves a long aftertaste. The pale yellow paste is smooth and melts in the mouth.

HOW TO ENJOY Delicious eaten as part of a cheeseboard at the end of the meal, or for lunch. It is best served with lively and fruity red wines, such as a Côtes-de-Beaune.

FRANCE Seine-et-Marne, Ile-de-France	
Age 4–8weeks	
Weight and Shape 1lb 2oz (500g), round	
Size D. 5in (12cm), H 1in (2.5cm)	
Milk Cow	
Classification Soft white	
Producer Nugier, Dongé dairies	

Crayeux de Roncq

The farmer and cheesemaker Marie-Therese Couvreur teamed up with cheese *affineur* Philippe Olivier to create this cheese, which is named *crayeux* for its chalky center. Washed regularly with salt water and beer, its distinct aroma belies a mild and creamy taste under an orange-colored crust. Produced in very small volume, it is rarely seen outside the region.

TASTING NOTES It has a subtle, nutty flavor between sweet and acid, which leaves a pleasing, unusual aftertaste.

HOW TO ENJOY The best match for this cheese is a structured red wine, such as a Médoc or Graves.

FRANCE Roncq, Nord-Pas de Calais	
Age 2 months	
Weight and Shape 15oz (425g), square	
Size L. 4in (10cm), W. 4in (10cm), H. 2in (4.5cm)	
Milk Cow	
Classification Semi-soft	
Producer Marie-Therese Couvreur	

Crémeux du Puy

This soft cheese is injected with blue mould and is produced in the Auvergne region, which is renowned for its excellent cheeses. It has a thick blue rind, which is overlaid by a delicate layer of white mold.

TASTING NOTES It has a creamy, delicate taste, with a hint of mushrooms and flavors of the cave in which it was left to mature.

HOW TO ENJOY Extremely flavorsome, with a texture not unlike Reblochon, Crémeux du Puy makes a popular addition to any cheeseboard. Serve this delicious cheese with some fresh, crusty bread and a glass of Côtes-du-Rhône.

FRANCE Haute-Loire, Auvergne	
Age 6–8 weeks	
Weight and Shape 1¾oz (50g), disc	
Size D. 3in (8cm), H. 2in (5cm)	
Milk Cow	
Classification Blue	
Producer Various	

Crottin de Chavignol AOC

It has an unfortunate name because *crottin* literally means horse dung, but this is actually a reference to the shape and color of this cheese when at full maturity. However, most are sold much younger when the rind is pale brown-white. AOC protected since 1976.

TASTING NOTES Known for its piquant taste, it can be eaten at various stages. When young, it is tender in texture, becoming harder, dry, crumbly, and sharp as it ages.

HOW TO ENJOY Best paired with the most vigorous full-bodied wines to enjoy the flavor of both wine and cheese.

FRANCE Centre	
Age Best around 2 months	
Weight and Shape 2oz (60g), small drum	
Size D. 2in (5cm), H. ¾in (2cm)	
Milk Goat	
Classification Aged fresh	
Producer Various	

Curé Nantais

This cheese is believed to have been introduced to the Pays de la Loire region by a Vendéen monk who was enduring the food shortage of the French Revolution. Now it is produced by a dairy that respects the traditional methods of making it. It is also known as Fromage du Pays Nantais dit du Curé.

TASTING NOTES A strong-tasting cheese with a soft and slightly elastic golden paste, featuring a few small holes.

HOW TO ENJOY It tastes delicious served with crusty bread and onion relish. Accompany it with a fruity Muscadet, such as a Melon Blanc.

FRANCE Pays de la Loire	
Age 1 month	
Weight and Shape 14oz (400g), round	
Size D. 4in (10cm), H. 2in (5cm)	
Milk Cow	
Classification Semi-soft	
Producer Curé Nantais dairy	

Dauphin

It is said that when Louis XIV was travelling through the Hainaut (in modern Belgium) with the Dauphin, his son and heir, he liked this cheese so much that he asked local cheesemakers to name the cheese in his son's honor. This distinctive cheese's washed, reddish rind encases a semi-soft paste.

TASTING NOTES A member of the Maroilles family, this is a strong, spicy, and aromatic cheese flavored with tarragon, parsley, pepper, and cloves.

HOW TO ENJOY This full-flavored cheese makes an interesting addition to any cheeseboard and is best paired with a robust wine, such as Côtes-du-Rhône.

FRANCE Nord-Pas-de-Calais	
Age 2–3 months	
Weight and Shape 14oz (400g), dolphin	
Size L. 5in (12.5cm), H. 1½in (3.5cm)	
Milk Cow	
Classification Flavor-added	
Producer Various	

FRANCE

Deauville

This modern French cheese combines attributes from two of Normandie's most famous washed-rind cheeses: Pont l'Evêque and Livarot. In spite of that, Deauville also has its own unique character and style.

TASTING NOTES The rich and flowery qualities of the cows' grazing pastures comes through in the flavor of this slightly milky semi-soft cheese, which has a sticky and supple texture.

HOW TO ENJOY Some apple marmalade and a glass of fresh cider make the perfect accompaniments to this tasty cheese.

FRANCE Normandie	
Age 7 weeks	
Weight and Shape 8oz (225g), round	
Size D. 5in (12cm)	
Milk Cow	
Classification Semi-soft	
Producer Fromagerie Thebault	

Délice des Cabasses

The term *délice,* meaning "delight", will give you a clue to the qualities of this very fresh, soft ewe's milk cheese made in the Pyrénées. It is a legitimate name for such an enticing cheese.

TASTING NOTES With a pleasing yet unobtrusively mild taste, Délice des Cabasses is fresh, delicate, and has a subtle sweetness. It is best enjoyed in the spring or summer months.

HOW TO ENJOY This cheese can find a place in any meal—from fruity to salty—and is delicious served with a fresh and simple-tasting light wine.

FRANCE Aveyron, Midi-Pyrénées	
Age 2 weeks	
Weight and Shape 3oz (85g), round	
Size D. 2½in (6cm), H. 1in (3.5cm)	
Milk Ewe	
Classification Fresh	
Producer M. Dombres	

Dôme de Vézelay

This is a raw-milk *fermier* cheese that is produced in very small volume and therefore rarely found outside the Yonne region. It is distinctive in its unusual shape, which is, as indicated by its name, that of a dome.

TASTING NOTES Vézelay has a natural rind and a fine, mellow paste. It has a subtle flavor that is later echoed by a spicier aftertaste.

HOW TO ENJOY This cheese combines well with sweet flavors such as honey or fig jam and with fruity and aromatic white wines such as a Chablis, a Mâcon blanc or a Meursault.

FRANCE Bourgogne (Yonne)	
Age 10 days at least	
Weight and Shape 4oz (120g), dome	
Size D. 3in (7.5cm), H. 2in (4.5cm)	
Milk Goat	
Classification Fresh	
Producer Various	

Comté AOC

This ancient French cheese, also known as Gruyere de Comté, has been made in small village-based cooperative dairies, or *fruitière*, for over eight centuries. This system has created a sense of solidarity and pride, and has preserved the traditions and the small-scale production techniques that have helped ensure Comté continues to be one of France's most popular cheeses.

It takes about 120 gallons (530 liters) of milk to make just one 80lb (35kg) Comté wheel, the daily yield of 30 cows. On average, each *fruitière* has 19 members or local dairy farms, located within an eight-mile radius.

The method, and the area in which Comté is made, has not changed for centuries, and is now defined by Appellation d'Origine Contrôlée (AOC) regulations as the rugged mountains and wide plateaux of the Massif du Jura, a region which spans the Jura, the Doubs (both of which are in the Franche-Comté), and the Ain (in the Rhône-Alpes).

It is the richness and diversity of its mountain pastures and markedly different seasons that give Comté its unique flavor along with the two native breeds of cow that must be used: the native Montbéliarde cow, known for its sweet milk, makes up around 95 percent of the herds, the rest are French Simmental cows.

During spring, the meadows, a blaze of colorful flowers, echo with the clanging bells as the cows return from winter in the valleys. During the winter, the cows are fed on a diet of hay cut from the summer pastures.

TASTING NOTES Each *fruitière* has its own distinct profile that reflects the soil, climate, and flora where the cows graze—from melted butter, milk chocolate, hazelnuts, and fudge to aromas of toast, plum jam, leather, pepper, and dark chocolate, others can be more reminiscent of butterscotch and hazelnuts and even sweet oranges.

HOW TO ENJOY The French enjoy Comté at virtually any time of day. As it melts well, it can be found in numerous French dishes from quiches, soups, and gratins to fondue, sauces, and salads. Its creamy texture and fruity tang marries well with fish and white meat and the local Jura wines or Chardonnay, Chenin Blanc, or Viognier.

The milk of the Montbéliarde cow is known for its sweetness.

FRANCE Franche-Comté, and Rhône-Alpes	
Age 4–18 months	
Weight and Shape 77–88lb (35–40kg), wheel	
Size D. 24–28in (60–70cm), H. 4in (10cm)	
Milk Cow	
Classification Hard	
Producer Various	

A CLOSER LOOK

Local *affineurs* take the young cheeses from the *frutière* and, with a love of their craft and centuries of knowledge, coax the very best from each cheese.

RIND Comté is recognized by its thin, beige rind.

THE AFFINAGE The *affineur* must decide on the time and conditions that suit the potential of each wheel. Regular turning, brushing, and rubbing with salty brine is vital to the process.

GRADING When the affinage is complete, each batch is graded out of 20 based on its taste, texture, and appearance. Cheeses with a grading of at least 15 get a green Comté Extra label; those between 12 and 14 are awarded a brown label reading Comté; but those with a rating below 12 do not qualify for the AOC Comté label.

The texture is firm, dry, slightly grainy, and more dense than Cheddar.

Interior

Exterior

The green "extra" label indicates a score by the grader of at least 15 out of 20.

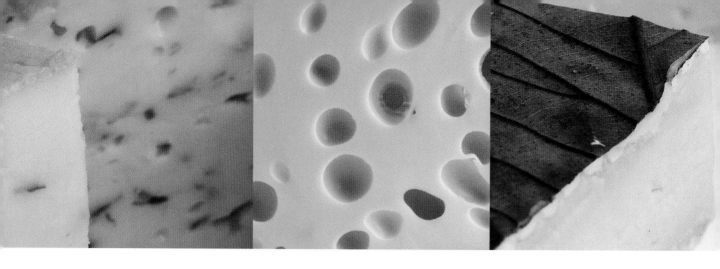

Embruns aux Algues

This cheese will certainly impress dinner guests. Embruns aux Algues is made in the same way as Curé Nantais, but it is rounder in shape and the curd is mixed with seaweed. This encourages the rind to develop a coral, pink-orange color and sticky texture.

TASTING NOTES A taste sensation, the special seaweed gives this cheese a salty and powerful flavor and a distinctive aroma of the sea.

HOW TO ENJOY It is delicious eaten with fresh bread and onion relish. Team it with a fruity Muscadet, such as a Melon Blanc.

FRANCE Pays de la Loire	
Age 1 month	
Weight and Shape 7oz (200g), round	
Size D. 4in (8.5cm), H. 1½in (3.5cm)	
Milk Cow	
Classification Flavor-added	
Producer Curé Nantais dairy	

Emmental de Savoie

Production of this now-popular hard cheese began in France in the 19th century, thanks to the imagination of German-Swiss cheesemakers. It is a distinctive-looking cheese, with a firm, ivory to pale paste punctuated with holes of about ½–1in (1.5–3cm).

TASTING NOTES Emmental has a smooth texture and a mild, pleasant flavor—it is fruity but also has a sweet and slightly nutty taste.

HOW TO ENJOY This popular choice for any cheeseboard can also be grated into recipes or simply served in chunks as a canapé. It goes well with all light and fruity wines.

FRANCE Savoie, Rhône-Alpes	
Age 6 months	
Weight and Shape 176lb–220lb (80–99kg), wheel	
Size Various, D. 34in (87cm), H. 10in (25cm) (pictured)	
Milk Cow	
Classification Hard	
Producer Various	

Feuille de Dreux

This very distinctive, ancient artisan cheese was historically eaten by workers in the fields as a snack and is still enjoyed by local farmers today. The decorative addition of a chestnut leaf on the top also has a practical purpose—it stops the cheeses sticking to each other when stacked.

TASTING NOTES This soft white cheese has a fruity, mushroomy flavor, and the faint smell of the chestnut leaf mingles with a pleasant, moldy aroma.

HOW TO ENJOY Excellent on a formal cheeseboard or as a simple snack with crackers or bread. Serve with a fruity, lively red wine, such as a Chinon.

FRANCE Center	
Age Around 2 months	
Weight and Shape 1lb 2oz (500g), round	
Size D. 7in (18cm), H. 1in (2.5cm)	
Milk Cow	
Classification Soft white	
Producer Various	

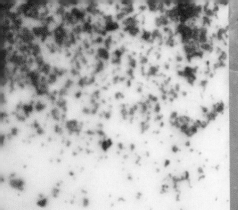
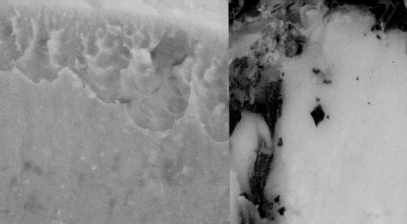

Figuette

This small and charming fig-shaped goat's cheese from the Pyrénées is sometimes covered with dried grasses, ash, or, as shown here, paprika in order to make it even more decorative and appealing to the tastebuds.

TASTING NOTES Figuette is sweet and has a lactic flavour. The delicious aromas come from the various coatings that it is given.

HOW TO ENJOY Eat it with a little honey to enhance its sweetness and tone down its goaty flavor. Bergerac wines are light and therefore most appropriate with this cheese.

FRANCE Midi-Pyrénées	
Age Fresh	
Weight and Shape 6oz (175g), fig	
Size D. 3in (8cm), H. 2in (4.5cm)	
Milk Goat	
Classification Fresh	
Producer Various	

Fium'Orbu

The sticky-rinded artisanal cheese Fium'Orbu is named after a small river in a little-known unspoilt part of Corse. As with other cheeses made on this mountainous Mediterranean island, its complex flavors and unique qualities can be partially attributed to the warm climate, the robust local breeds and the wild, diverse grazing.

TASTING NOTES Soft, tender, and buttery, the complex herbaceous flavors originate from the ewe's fragrant grazing. Washing endows this semi-soft cheese with a lingering meaty tang.

HOW TO ENJOY Corsicans eat it with fig jam accompanied by a fruity red wine.

FRANCE Corse	
Age 8–12 weeks	
Weight and Shape 16oz (450g), round	
Size L. 31/2in (8.5cm), W. 3in (8cm), H. 1in (3cm)	
Milk Ewe	
Classification Semi-soft	
Producer Various	

Fleur du Maquis

Covered with herbs and chilies, this unusual artisan cheese is called the "flower of the maquis"—the maquis being the Corsican landscape. Not only does it look better than other cheeses, it also smells pretty good. It is also known as Brindamour.

TASTING NOTES The combination of herbs and spicy chilies does not overwhelm the flavor, thanks to the proportions being cleverly thought out; the cheese itself is quite tender, and the overall taste is rather honeyed.

HOW TO ENJOY This is a full-flavored cheese, so serve it alone, at the end of a meal, with a local red like Cap Corse.

FRANCE Corse	
Age 3 months	
Weight and Shape 1lb 10oz (750g), round	
Size D. 5in (12cm), H. 2in (4.5cm)	
Milk Ewe	
Classification Aged fresh	
Producer Various	

Forme d'Antoine

This recently created, semi-soft cow's milk cheese is produced in the Nord Pas-de-Calais region. It is formed into an unusual but attractive dome shape, and encased in an orange crusty rind which is formed over six weeks through the process of regular washings.

TASTING NOTES It has quite a strong flavor balanced with a milky and spicy taste. The semi-soft paste has a milky aroma.

HOW TO ENJOY Pair this cheese with a full-bodied wine, such as a Côte de Beaune or Beaujolais, or with a sweet wine, such as Gewürztraminer.

FRANCE Nord-Pas-de-Calais	
Age 4 months	
Weight and Shape 14oz (400g), dome	
Size D. 5in (12cm), H. 2in (4.5cm)	
Milk Cow	
Classification Semi-soft	
Producer M. Bernard	

Fouchtra

The rind is similar to that of Cantal and St. Nectaire, and is dusted with a colorful mix of white, red, and sulphur-yellow molds. It has a subtle, mild taste and its flavor reflects the flora found in the volcanic mountains where it is produced. It is also made using cow's milk.

TASTING NOTES This cheese has a surprisingly soft and silky texture. The distinctive and memorable flavor has a lingering almondy aftertaste.

HOW TO ENJOY A full-bodied, structured red wine, such as Saint Joseph or Vacqueyras, is the best match for this flavorsome cheese.

FRANCE Auvergne	
Age 3 months	
Weight and Shape 13lb 4oz (6kg), wheel	
Size D. 6in (16cm), H. 3in (7cm)	
Milk Goat or cow	
Classification Semi-soft	
Producer Various	

Fougerus

An artisan cheese that was originally made for family consumption, Fougerus has been commercially produced since the beginning of the 20th century. In size it is slightly bigger than its Brie relative, Coulommier.

TASTING NOTES The fern leaves used to decorate the cheese give it a "forest" aroma, and the rind has a moldy, mushroomy scent. Soft in texture, it melts in the mouth with a rather pronounced tang.

HOW TO ENJOY This decorative cheese brightens up a cheese board. Try pairing it with a lively fruity red wine, such as a Côte de Beaune.

FRANCE Ile-de-France	
Age at its best 3–4 weeks	
Weight and Shape 1lb 2oz (500g), round	
Size D. 6in (15cm), H. 1½in (4cm)	
Milk Cow	
Classification Soft white	
Producer Various	

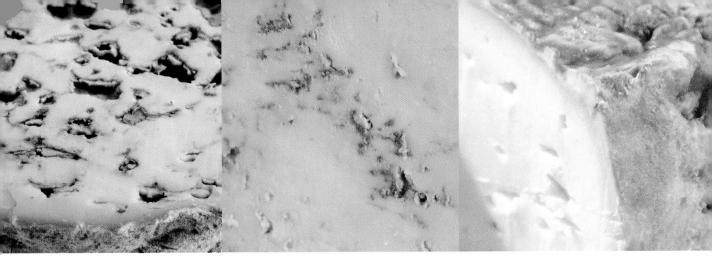

Fourme d'Ambert AOC

One of the oldest cheeses in France, this blue cheese dates from the Roman period. The AOC was granted in 1972 and since then methods of production have been streamlined to bring it into line with its AOC partner, Fourme de Montbrison.

TASTING NOTES It has quite a pronounced flavor, with some bitterness. The texture is creamy, bold, and rich, while the aroma gives a hint of the cellar in which it is aged.

HOW TO ENJOY Serve with wines such as Coteaux d'Auvergne, Côtes Roannaises, and a full-bodied Beaujolais, or try it with a sweet Sauternes or Banyuls.

FRANCE Auvergne	
Age 3 months	
Weight and Shape 3lb 5oz (1.5kg), cylinder	
Size D. 5in (12cm), L. 7in (17cm)	
Milk Cow	
Classification Blue	
Producer Various	

Fourme de Montbrison AOC

Fourme d'Ambert and Fourme de Montbrison are made in their two different namesake towns, but because they are very similar, they share an AOC. *Fourme* comes from the Latin *forma,* meaning form or shape.

TASTING NOTES Montbrison tends to be less creamy, slightly stronger and more complex than Fourme d'Ambert, with a long, spicy finish. The pale yellow interior is streaked with uneven blotches and broken lines of blue.

HOW TO ENJOY Team it with local wines like Coteaux d'Auvergne or Côtes Roannaises or a sweet wine.

FRANCE Rhône-Alpes	
Age 3 months	
Weight and Shape 3lb 5oz (1.5kg), cylinder	
Size D. 5in (12cm), H. 8in (21cm)	
Milk Cow	
Classification Blue	
Producer Various	

Fruité du Boulonnais

Recently created and already warmly received, Fruité du Boulonnais is characterized by an unusual and excellent paste and an orange crusty rind that is formed during eight weeks of regular washing.

TASTING NOTES You can eat this cheese at various stages and its flavor will be anything from smooth to strong, depending on its age. It has a gentle and pleasant milky aroma.

HOW TO ENJOY Pair with a French "real ale" from the growing number of small breweries springing up in Nord-Pas-de-Calais, such as a beer from the Castelain Brewery.

FRANCE Nord-Pas-de-Calais	
Age 4 months	
Weight and Shape 12oz (350g), cylinder	
Size D. 6in (15cm), H. 5cm (2in)	
Milk Cow	
Classification Semi-soft	
Producer M. Bernard	

Gaperon

In the past, the number of these cheeses hanging in the kitchen was an indication of a farmer's wealth and therefore his daughter's dowry. This speciality of Auvergne was originally made by mixing buttermilk with fresh milk; buttermilk is no longer used, but it is still ripened by airing.

TASTING NOTES Beneath the dry, hard rind is an elastic paste containing garlic and pepper, which gives it a pronounced flavor. Since it is hung and cured by the fire, it has a smoky tang.

HOW TO ENJOY It is a delicious cheese for snacking. Partner with robust, full-bodied wines, such as Côtes-du-Rhône.

FRANCE Auvergne	
Age 1–2 months	
Weight and Shape 12½oz–1lb 2oz (350g–500g), flattened ball	
Size D. 3½in (9cm), H. 2½–3in (6cm–7.5cm)	
Milk Cow	
Classification Semi-soft	
Producer Various	

Gour Noir

This delicious artisan cheese, made from goat's milk and sprinkled with wood ash, is the product of farmers of the Auvergne who are passionate about cheesemaking and their products. These same cheesemakers also make Gour Blanc, a variety without ash.

TASTING NOTES Beneath the soft, wrinkly rind, the taste changes according to its age: it can be very sweet or spicy, but it is always full of subtle flavors and has a delicate hint of goat's milk.

HOW TO ENJOY Serve Gour Noir with a slice of simple country bread. It is complemented well by a light Loire wine, such as a Chateaumeillant.

FRANCE Auvergne	
Age 2–6 weeks	
Weight and Shape 7oz (200g), oval	
Size L. 4in (10cm), H. 1in (3.5cm)	
Milk Goat	
Classification Aged fresh	
Producer La Fromagerie Corbreche	

Gratte-Paille

This white-rinded cheese, created in the 1970s, is a real treat for those who are not put off by a high fat content. Made with triple cream (70 percent cream for every 3½oz/100g of cheese), the rind bears the imprint of the straw mats on which it is ripened.

TASTING NOTES The triple cream gives Gratte-Paille a rich, very milky taste, while the almost buttery paste has an oily texture and sometimes a mushroomy flavor.

HOW TO ENJOY Combine it with other foods; grate on vegetable and chicken dishes and use in sauces. It is delicious served with strawberries!

FRANCE Seine-et-Marne, Île-de-France	
Age About 4 weeks	
Weight and Shape 10½oz (300g), brick	
Size H. 3½in (7.5cm), W. 2½in (6cm)	
Milk Cow	
Classification Soft white	
Producer Rouzaire dairy	

Laguiole AOC

Also known as Fourme de Laguiole, this is a very old cheese that dates back centuries, first produced by monks in their monastery in the Aubrac mountains. Laguiole has benefited from the AOC label since 1961.

TASTING NOTES Laguiole has a firm, smooth texture; a strong smell with a penetrating bouquet; and a spicy tang but a mild, milky flavor. As the cheese ages, it becomes more delicious.

HOW TO ENJOY It is excellent for snacks or served on a cheeseboard at the end of a meal. You can serve it with all fruity wines of Marcillac, du Fel, Costières du Gard.

FRANCE Laguiole, Midi-Pyrénées	
Age 4–6 months	
Weight and Shape 66–88lb (30–40kg), cylinder	
Size D. 16in (40cm), H. 14–16in (35cm–40cm)	
Milk Cow	
Classification Hard	
Producer Jeune Montagne cooperative	

Langres AOC

With its orange-coloured rind, Langres resembles Epoisses de Bourgogne, while its name comes from the plateau of Langres in Champagne, where it was traditionally sold. The annatto used in the wash gives the rind its color. AOC protected since 1991.

TASTING NOTES This strong-smelling cheese has a penetrating bouquet, and it tastes a little spicy when young. The texture changes with age, starting out grainy and becoming very creamy, sticky, and melt-in-the-mouth.

HOW TO ENJOY Pair it with any of the full-bodied red wines of the Bourgogne region to match its strong flavor.

FRANCE Langres, Champagne Ardenne	
Age 2–3 months	
Weight and Shape 10oz (300g), cylinder with sunken top	
Size D. 4in (10cm), H. 2in (5cm)	
Milk Cow	
Classification Semi-soft	
Producer Schertenleib Dairy and Reumillet	

Lavort

Shaped like a crater as a tribute to the Auvergne volcanoes, this ewe's cheese was created in the late 20th century. The five bands of rush leaves were originally positioned around it to prevent the cheese from collapsing as it matured.

TASTING NOTES Its creamy and delicate paste has numerous holes and differs in texture depending on the level of maturity. The finish has a subtle taste of hazelnuts.

HOW TO ENJOY It is excellent in a crunchy salad, so much so that it is featured in several local salad-based specialities.

FRANCE Puy Guillaume, Auvergne	
Age 3–6 months	
Weight and Shape 12oz–1lb 2oz (350–500g), drum	
Size Various, D. 6in (15cm), H. 4½in (11cm) (pictured)	
Milk Ewe	
Classification Hard	
Producer Fromagerie de Terre-Dieu	

Epoisses de Bourgogne AOC

According to legend, Epoisses was created in the 16th century by the local monks. It was based on the first washed-rind cheese created at Maroilles Abbey in Thierache, Northern France around 960CE.

The monks were forbidden meat on fast days, and with over a hundred of these—not to mention compulsory fish on Friday—cheese was an essential part of their diet. The washed-rind cheeses with their strong, pungent meaty taste must have seemed like a gift from above. When the monastery closed, the monks left behind the recipe which was then passed from mother to daughter. However, it was all but lost until Robert and Simone Berthaut decided to revive the old recipe in 1956. Other producers have since joined the revival, and, in 1991, Epoisses was awarded an AOC Protected Designation Origin.

To qualify for AOC status it must be made in the departments of the Cote d'Or, the Yvonne and the Haute Marne, and a small area West of the famous town of Dijon. Despite being made by only 4 producers, it is found in cheese shops as far afield as the United States, China, and Australia.

TASTING NOTES Epoisses *Frais*, at 30 days, is firm, moist, slightly grainy with a softening around the thin, pale orange rind and is mild and lactic with a subtle savory, yeasty tang. At 40 days, Epoisses *Affinee* has a sticky, wrinkled, terracotta rind and pungent spicy aroma and a smooth velvety texture. When the outer edges are near to collapsing, the inside is not far behind and the aroma, described by some as reminiscent of smelly socks, is matched by the wickedly strong, strangely meaty taste.

HOW TO ENJOY No cheeseboard is complete without a washed-rind cheese, and Epoisses is among the greatest. Smear it on nut and raisin bread or, if you love strong cheese, bake and serve it with crusty bread or dollop some on sliced potatoes and bake. Cooking brings out its sweeter side, but its intense flavor and aroma means it should be used sparingly. The smooth velvety texture and strong aromatic flavor demands a fine red Burgundian Pinot Noir or a rich buttery Chardonnay, but a spicy aromatic Riesling or Marc de Bourgogne are also equally good companions.

The milk for Epoisses come from Brune, French Simmental, and Montbeliarde cows.

FRANCE Bourgogne and Champagne Ardenne	
Age 4–6 weeks	
Weight and Shape 9oz (250g), round	
Size D. 6in (16.5cm), H. 1in (3cm)	
Milk Cow	
Classification	
Producer Various	

A CLOSER LOOK

The unique appearance of Epoisses is caused by regularly hand washing the cheeses in brandy and brine, which also made it one of the most pungent of the washed-rind cheeses.

APPLYING BRANDY

The monks of Epoisses, taking advantage of their proximity to the great vineyards of Burgundy, decided to wash the cheese in a strong local brandy or *marc* which imparts a distinct alcoholic whiff and creates an intense, sticky, orange rind.

SMEAR-RIPENING Every day for 4–6 weeks, the young cheeses are washed in a mix of brine and a special bacteria called *brevibacterium linens*, a process often referred to as smear-ripening.

PACKAGING The cheeses are packed in small round wooden boxes with wood from the Jura mountains. Traditionally, they were lined with chestnut leaves, but these are now banned due to health regulations. Now, attractive brown paper leaves are used instead. The perforated micro film stretched over the box in which it is sold prevents the buyer from feeling if the cheese is ripe. Instead you judge its maturity by the intensity of its color.

YELLOWING Smear-ripening causes the rind to gradually change from pale yellow-orange to an increasingly sticky, glistening tangerine orange with a fine dusting of white flora or yeast.

The washed rind is orange to terracotta in color, and pungent in flavor.

The interior is moist and creamy-colored.

Round, portion removed

Lingot de la Ginestarie

This small, fresh ewe's milk cheese is produced in the Pyrénées by M. Teosky, a passionate farmer who is originally from Poland and who grazes both ewes and goats on his pastures.

TASTING NOTES A farmhouse cheese, Lingot de la Ginestarie is soft, becoming almost runny with age, and tastes sweet with a fresh and pleasant countryside aroma.

HOW TO ENJOY Its brick shape makes it distinctive-looking on a cheeseboard, and its fresh, delicate taste is best paired with a light red wine such as a Chinon.

FRANCE Tarn, Midi-Pyrénées	
Age 2 weeks	
Weight and Shape 5oz (140g), brick	
Size L. 4in (10cm), W. 2in (5cm), H. 2in (5cm)	
Milk Ewe	
Classification Aged fresh	
Producer M. Teosky	

Livarot AOC

One of the most ancient cheeses of Normandie, Livarot was probably invented by local monks. Its nickname, "the Colonel," comes from the five stripes of sedge grass that encircle the cheese's washed rind and resemble the stripes used on military uniforms to denote an officer's rank.

TASTING NOTES A good Livarot should have a firm, orange-brown, slightly sticky rind and a strong spicy flavor.

HOW TO ENJOY Team a perfectly ripe cheese with any well-knit red wine, but it is equally good with a cider, such as one from Normandy, or a sweet late-harvest Alsace wine.

FRANCE Basse-Normandie	
Age 3 months	
Weight and Shape 1lb 2oz (500g), drum	
Size D. 5in (12cm), H. 2in (5cm)	
Milk Cow	
Classification Semi-soft	
Producer Fromagerie E Graindorge; Fromagerie Thebault	

Lou Rocaillou

Lou Rocaillou means "the craggy cheese" in local dialect, referring to the causse Méjean, a large limestone plateau where the ewes whose milk creates this cheese enjoy grazing.

TASTING NOTES Rocaillou has a white molded rind and a smooth, supple, and fine paste that almost melts in the mouth. Whether it is eaten young or kept until it is more mature, it is always a very sweet cheese.

HOW TO ENJOY It makes a delicious snack whether eaten on its own or spread on fresh bread. As part of a cheeseboard, it offers an interesting alternative to sharper cheeses.

FRANCE Aveyron, Midi-Pyrénées	
Age 2 weeks	
Weight and Shape 3oz (85g), round	
Size D. 2in (5cm), H. 1½in (3.5cm)	
Milk Ewe	
Classification Aged fresh	
Producer M. Dombres	

Lou Sotch

Lou Sotch is a small, oval ewe's milk cheese from the Grands Causses Nature Park in the Aveyron area. With its thin wrinkly rind dusted with white mold, it looks a little like Rocamadour, a small goat's milk cheese, but this cheese is more flavorful.

TASTING NOTES A smooth paste, tender rind, and nutty powerful taste makes Lou Sotch a delightful alternative for all lovers of goat cheese.

HOW TO ENJOY Eat with savory chutneys and serve with a chilled dry white wine as an aperitif.

FRANCE Aveyron, Midi-Pyrénées	
Age 12–20 weeks	
Weight and Shape 1oz (2.5cm), oval	
Size L. 6in (15cm), H. ½in (1.5cm)	
Milk Ewe	
Classification Aged fresh	
Producer M. Dombres	

Lucullus

This soft white cheese is produced in Normandy and named after a famous Roman general and gourmet. It is made by adding generous quantities of cream to the milk before it is coagulated. Its high cream content means it is more stable than other soft white cheeses, so keeps for longer in the refrigerator.

TASTING NOTES It develops a soft white rind with a mushroomy aroma. It has a wickedly rich, luxurious feel in the mouth and a nutty flavor. Forget the fat content—just enjoy the taste!

HOW TO ENJOY Eat on crackers or crusty bread and team with a light fruity wine with bouquet, such as red Bouzy.

FRANCE Ile-de-France and Basse Normandie	
Age 3–4 weeks	
Weight and Shape 8oz (225g), drum	
Size D. 3in (7.5cm), H. 2in (5cm)	
Milk Cow	
Classification Soft white	
Producer Various	

Mâconnais AOC

The Mâconnais is made from pure goat's milk or from a combination of goat's and cow's milk, which is available all year round. It is produced in the Bourgogne region and was given the AOC label in 2005.

TASTING NOTES It has a unique taste: a faint goaty and slightly nutty flavor, and a delicate aroma of spring herbs. Eaten fresh, it is white and creamy; left to mature, it becomes harder and slightly salty.

HOW TO ENJOY It is best served with the dry and fruity whites of the Mâconnais region, such as Beaujolais and Mâcon.

FRANCE Bourgogne	
Age 1–2 weeks	
Weight and Shape 2oz (60g), truncated cone	
Size D. 2in (5cm) at base, 1.5in (3½cm) at top, H. 1½in (3.5cm)	
Milk Goat and cow	
Classification Aged fresh	
Producer Various	

Maroilles AOC

The most famous cheese in the north of France, Maroilles was invented by monks in 962 CE. Regular turning and washing eliminates the natural white mold and promotes the development of the bacteria that gives the rind its distinctive orange-red color.

TASTING NOTES Maroilles' paste is golden-yellow, soft, and oily, and it has a strong flavor and aroma with a sweet, lingering aftertaste.

HOW TO ENJOY A local favourite involves using Maroilles in a sauce for chicken dishes. Eat it alongside all very strong, vigorous red wines, such as Châteauneuf-du-Pâpe.

FRANCE Nord-Pas-de-Calais	
Age 4 months	
Weight and Shape 1¾lb (800g) square	
Size L. 5in (13cm), W. 5in (13cm) H. 1½in (4cm)	
Milk Cow	
Classification Semi-soft	
Producer Various	

Mimolette

This hard cheese originated in the Netherlands, but since the 17th century it has also been made in northern France. It is produced using the same methods as Edam, but is colored with annatto and aged for a minimum of six months.

TASTING NOTES As it ripens, the paste of this colorful cheese changes from bright orange to orange-brown, and the texture becomes brittle. The flavor is mild but becomes stronger with age.

HOW TO ENJOY Eat as an appetizer. Serve with all light and fruity wines, such as Côte de Beaune, but it is commonly served with beers, port or Madeira.

FRANCE Nord-Pas-De-Calais	
Age 3–24 months	
Weight and Shape 5½lb–6lb (2.5kg–2.7kg), ball	
Size D. 6in (16cm), H. 5in (13cm)	
Milk Cow	
Classification Hard	
Producer Various	

Mont d'Or AOC

The Mont d'Or mountains lie on the French–Swiss border, and it is there that this cheese is made between the end of August and the middle of March. It has been produced in both countries for centuries; however, it is the French who have been granted an AOC label (in 1981).

TASTING NOTES This creamy cheese has a delicate taste with a hint of the spruce band that binds it and helps it to keep its shape while maturing.

HOW TO ENJOY Scoop it out with a spoon at the end of the meal or melt it in the oven and eat it like fondue.

FRANCE Franche-Comté	
Age 1 month	
Weight and Shape 4oz (115g), round	
Size D. 3in (7.5cm), H. ½in (1cm)	
Milk Cow	
Classification Semi-soft	
Producer Various	

Morbier AOC

This washed-rind cheese is made by the cheesemakers of Comté in the Jura mountains. It is characterized by a horizontal dark line in the center of the cheese. Traditionally, the producers sprinkled soot from wood fires over the morning curd, then covered it with curd from the evening milking. Today, wood ash is used to recreate the look.

TASTING NOTES It has a soft and delicate paste, a rather pronounced flavor, and a mild, milky aroma. The more it ages, the sweeter and stronger the taste.

HOW TO ENJOY Serve with a local Arbois wine or light and fruity wines like Beaujolais or Jura.

FRANCE Franche-Comté	
Age 2–3 months	
Weight and Shape 11lb–19lb 13oz (5–9kg), wheel	
Size D. 14–16in (36–41cm), H. 3–4in (7.5–10cm)	
Milk Cow	
Classification Semi-soft	
Producer Various	

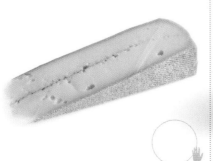

Morvan

This is a soft cheese that is typically eaten during spring and summer. It is a fermier cheese that is produced in Bourgogne and named after the Regional Nature Park of Morvan, a beautiful nature preserve of woods, forests, and mountains.

TASTING NOTES This cheese is best eaten fresh. It is slightly nutty and has a faint goaty flavor.

HOW TO ENJOY Eat it with fresh seasonal berries. Team with a light white wine such as Mâconnais, Beaujolais, or Mâcon.

FRANCE Bourgogne	
Age 3 weeks	
Weight and Shape 3½oz (115g), drum	
Size D. 3in (7cm), H. 1½in (4cm)	
Milk Goat	
Classification Aged fresh	
Producer Various	

Mothais-sur-Feuille

Goats were introduced to the Poitou province by the Moors during the 15th century and now play a significant role in the local economy. This farmhouse cheese undergoes an unusual production method for a goat cheese; it is placed on a chestnut leaf and ripened at a high humidity, rather than in dry conditions, so it retains more moisture.

TASTING NOTES With a soft, sticky white rind and creamy texture, the Mothais-sur-Feuille has a light, moldy aroma and a long-lasting, delicate aftertaste.

HOW TO ENJOY Partner this melt-in-the-mouth cheese with a full-bodied red wine from Poitou.

Region Poitou-Charentes	
Age 2 weeks	
Weight and Shape 8–9oz (225–250g), round	
Size D. 4in (10cm), H. 1in (2.5cm)	
Milk Goat	
Classification Aged fresh	
Producer Various	

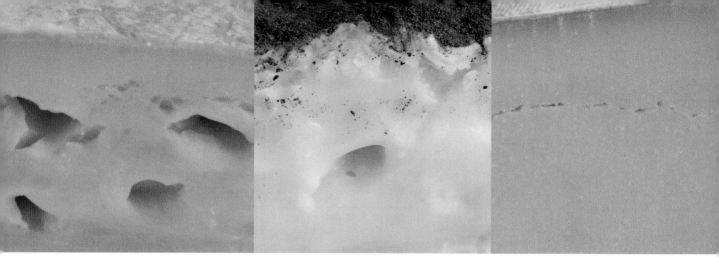

Munster AOC

Munster is an ancient, washed-rind cheese of monastic origin that dates back to the Middle Ages. It is also known as "Géromé" when made in the Lorraine region. Its AOC status was established in 1969.

TASTING NOTES When properly matured, it has a strong penetrating smell and the flavor of rich milk. There is also a version available that comes flavored with cumin.

HOW TO ENJOY Eat this like a local: serve it with cumin on boiled potatoes. Pair a young cheese with Gewürztraminer, and an older one with very full-bodied reds like Côte-Rôtie or Haut-Médoc.

FRANCE Alsace and Lorraine	
Age 2–3 months	
Weight and Shape 10oz– 3lb 3oz (280g–1.5kg), round	
Size D. 5–7in (13–19cm), H. 1–3in (2.5–8cm)	
Milk Cow	
Classification Semi-soft	
Producer Various	

Olivet

Named after the town on the Loire River in which it was first made, Olivet is produced in a variety of forms. Cendré (shown here), matured in ashes, has a rather gritty, ash-gray rind; au Foin has a white rind covered with a few strands of dry grass; and Poivre is covered in crushed pepper.

TASTING NOTES Olivet has a subtle taste of salt and mushrooms, tinged with a slight scent of mold.

HOW TO ENJOY Serve with rosé wines from the region, such as a Pinot Meunier from Orléanais or any fruity red, such as a Borgueil.

FRANCE Centre	
Age 1 month	
Weight and Shape 10½oz (300g), round	
Size D. 5in (12cm), H. 1in (2.5cm)	
Milk Cow	
Classification Soft white	
Producer Various	

Ossau-Iraty AOC

The name of this hard cheese refers to the valley of Ossau, in Béarn, and the forests of Iraty, in the Basque Country, and encompasses a number of wonderful cheeses made using the milk of the Manech ewes that graze in this breathtakingly beautiful region.

TASTING NOTES Ossau-Iraty has a sharp and somewhat nutty taste, and the rind is pretty firm, especially after a long maturation. If you have a strong palate, try the Espelette pepper variety.

HOW TO ENJOY Eat in traditional fashion with *itxassou*, a local black cherry jam, which counterbalances its sharpness. It is also featured in numerous local dishes.

FRANCE Aquitane	
Age 3 months minimum	
Weight and Shape 4½lb–15lb 7oz (2–7kg), round	
Size D. 7–11in (18–28cm), H. 3–4½in (7–15cm)	
Milk Ewe	
Classification Hard	
Producer Various	

Palet de Bourgogne

This is a 20th-century creation of the well-known Burgundian cheesemaker, Raymond Gaugry. This cheese is based on Epoisse and is washed every two days with brine and Marc de Bourgogne so that it becomes wet and reddish in color.

TASTING NOTES The paste of this strongly scented cheese is fine and creamy, and has a powerful and penetrating flavor that is not unlike the Epoisses and the Ami du Chambertin, but not as strong.

HOW TO ENJOY This full-flavored cheese is best eaten alongside a light red wine, such as a Savigny-les-Beaune.

FRANCE Gevrey-Chambertin, Bourgogne	
Age 4 weeks	
Weight and Shape 4½oz (125g), round	
Size D. 3½in (9cm), H. 1in (3.5cm)	
Milk Cow	
Classification Semi-soft	
Producer Fromagerie Gaugry	

Pavé d'Auge

An old variation of Pont-L'Evêque, this semi-soft cheese is nowadays a generic name for several square, washed-rind cheeses produced in the Auge area. These include Pavé de Moyaux (the name of an area), Pavé du Plessis (the name of a dairy), and Trouville (named after a small seaside town). *Pavé* is the French for the rough paving stones found in most old local towns.

TASTING NOTES Pavé d'Auge has a spicy flavor and strong tang that can be a little bitter.

HOW TO ENJOY Pair this with a strong, full-bodied red wine with some bouquet: Bourgueil, Fleurie, or Pomerol.

FRANCE Basse-Normandie	
Age 2 months	
Weight and Shape 1lb 10oz (750g), square	
Size L. 4½in (11cm), W. 4½in (11cm H. 2in (5cm)	
Milk Cow	
Classification Semi-soft	
Producer Various	

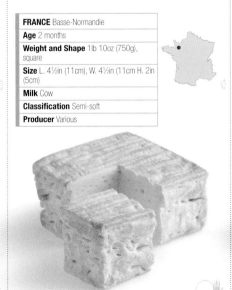

Pavé Blésois

This artisan cheese is produced in both a square and a rectangle shape, and its dry surface is covered in an elegant and interesting silvery blue mold. It is made in the Blesois region of France, near the River Loire.

TASTING NOTES It has an aroma of goat's milk. The paste is clean and smooth, with a hazelnut note and a tongue-tingling aftertaste.

HOW TO ENJOY An excellent country cheese, Pavé Blesois makes a great addition to a simple salad and is best served with a dry and simple light white wine, such as a Chinon.

FRANCE Centre	
Age 6 weeks	
Weight and Shape 9oz (250g) square, 10oz (300g) rectangle	
Size Square: L. 3in (8cm), W. 3in (8cm), H. 1½in (4cm); Rectangle: L. 5in (12cm), W. 3in (7cm), H. 1½in (3.5cm)	
Milk Goat	
Classification Aged fresh	
Producer Various	

Pavé de la Ginestarie

A unique cheese, Pavé de la Ginestarie is produced from the milk of goats that live in the Pyrenées mountains, but exactly how it is made is a well-kept secret. What is known is that there are traces of straw in the rind and that its bacteria form part of the ripening process.

TASTING NOTES An organic, white-rinded cheese, it has a pale paste with a hint of straw in the flavor. It has a subtle taste but a long-lasting finish.

HOW TO ENJOY For a delicious combination, pair this delicate cheese with fresh blackberries or currants to give it a real sweetness.

FRANCE Tarn, Midi-Pyrénées	
Age 3 weeks	
Weight and Shape 1oz (30g), square	
Size D. 3½in (9cm), H. ¾in (2cm)	
Milk Goat	
Classification Aged fresh	
Producer M. Teosky	

Pavé du Nord

This cheese is also known as Pavé de Roubaix, named after the textile city of Roubaix located in the north of France. Historically, the cheese could always be found on the weavers' tables. Its attractive, carrot-orange interior, like Mimolette, is derived from the use of annatto in its production.

TASTING NOTES It has a rock-hard, orange to brown rind and a very hard, compact texture with a few small holes, and an intense, mouth-tingling, tangy finish.

HOW TO ENJOY Shave or thinly slice as an appetizer with a beer, or use to add character and flavor to cheese sauces.

FRANCE Nord-Pas-de-Calais	
Age 6–24 months	
Weight and Shape 8lb 13oz (4kg), brick	
Size L. 11in (27cm), W. 5in (13cm), H. 3in (8cm)	
Milk Cow	
Classification Hard	
Producer Various	

Pavin

Produced in the mountains of Forez using a similar method to that for Saint-Nectaire, this semi-soft cheese is named after a lake in the Auvergne. Pavin is washed with a mix of brine and annatto to create a sticky orange rind that is dusted with a fine white mold.

TASTING NOTES The paste is light yellow in color and is tinged with the scent of mushrooms, and it has the flavor of hazelnuts.

HOW TO ENJOY Serve it with a full-bodied wine from the Bourgogne, such as a Pommard or Mercurey.

FRANCE Auvergne	
Age About 8 weeks	
Weight and Shape 1lb (450g), round	
Size D. 5in (13cm), H. 2in (4cm)	
Milk Cow	
Classification Semi-soft	
Producer Various	

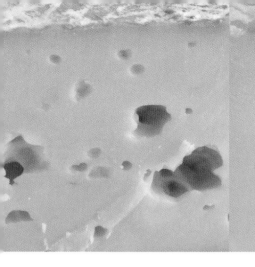

Pechegos

This cheese derives its name from a plateau in the Tarn region. It is here that the goats whose raw milk is used in the production of Pechegos graze. The finished washed cheese has a distinctive-looking copper-colored rind and is bound with spruce bark.

TASTING NOTES Pechegos has a very creamy texture, similar to the famous Mont d'Or on which the recipe is based. It is a real taste sensation, with many different mushroomy and truffle flavors.

HOW TO ENJOY Serve it alongside potatoes or eggs, with a full-bodied white, such as Jurancon, or a red, such as Madiran.

FRANCE Tarn, Midi-Pyrénées		
Age 8 weeks		
Weight and Shape 10oz (300g), round		
Size D. 4in (10cm), H. 1½in (4cm)		
Milk Goat		
Classification Semi-soft		
Producer Le Pic Cooperative		

Pélardon AOC

Pélardon is a generic name for small goat cheeses produced in the Cévennes region of France, near the Alps. These include Pélardon des Cévennes (shown here), Pélardon d'Anduze, and Pélardon d'Altier.

TASTING NOTES Pélardon cheeses have a creamy and dense texture; a full, rich milky and nutty flavor; and a lingering aftertaste. The rind is barely formed, thin, soft, and wrinkled, and as it matures it develops a natural mold.

HOW TO ENJOY Lightly broil or bake and accompany with a red Costières de Nîmes or a full-bodied Côtes du Rhône, such as Gigondas or Vacqueyras.

FRANCE Languedoc-Roussillon		
Age 2–3 weeks		
Weight and Shape 3–4½oz (85–125g), disc		
Size D. 2½–3in (6–7.5cm), H. 1in (2.5cm)		
Milk Goat		
Classification Aged fresh		
Producer Various		

Pérail

Although it has existed for centuries, this small cheese used to be made only as a way to prevent wastage, using up small quantities of milk when there was not enough left to make Roquefort. Nowadays it is considered to be a renowned speciality.

TASTING NOTES Pérail has a less pronounced flavor than most ewe's milk cheeses, probably because of its rather short aging period. With its smooth paste and tender rind, it has a soft yet distinguishable nutty taste.

HOW TO ENJOY Serve with rose hip jam. It pairs well with all lively wines from the south of France.

FRANCE Aveyron, Midi-Pyrénées		
Age Best around 2 weeks		
Weight and Shape 3–5oz (85–140g), disc		
Size D. 3–4in (8–10cm), H. 1in (2cm),		
Milk Ewe		
Classification Aged fresh		
Producer M. Dombres		

Reblochon de Savoie AOC

Although Reblochon has been made in the summer Alpine pastures since the 13th century, it was unheard of until after the French revolution. The reason for secrecy was the introduction of a tax. In the 14th century, farmers who grazed their cattle in the magnificent Haute-Savoie pastures overlooking Lake Annecy were forced to pay a tax based on the milk yield of their cattle.

To avoid payment of the tax, the farmer would only partially milk his cows in the presence of the tax man, then, once he departed, the cows were remilked. This additional "tax-free" milk was then made into Reblochon—from the old Savoie word *reblocher*, to "remilk" or "pinch the cow's udder again," and was kept for family consumption only.

After the French revolution, the tax was removed and the farmers were free to sell their cheese. Reblochon has been protected by the AOC regulations since 1976, which states that the milk can only come from the indigenous Abondance, Tarine, and Montbéliarde cows that graze the alpine pastures in summer and dine on hay cut from those rich summer pastures in winter. The feeding of silage or concentrates is banned because it can taint the sweetness of the milk, and the stipulation that it can only be made from unpasteurized milk ensures production is always near the source of the raw material.

Reblochon must be made and matured in the Haute-Savoie and north-eastern parts of the Savoie by individual farmers, *fermier*, cooperatives, *fruitiere*, or commercial dairies, *industriel*, who receive their milk from local farms.

TASTING NOTES When young, the cheese has the sweetness of stolen fruit. As it matures it is no longer sweet but tastes of freshly pickled, crunchy walnuts and a hint of the mountain flowers. Its supple, creamy texture flows over and caresses the palate like warm, English custard. The *fermier* cheese has a more intense, complex flavor and a farmyard aroma, but do not be deterred.

The interior captures the aroma of the wild flowers and herbs of the Haute-Savoie pastures.

HOW TO ENJOY Traditionally served with crusty *pain de campagne* (a sourdough bread), a few slices of sweet *jambon de pays* (air-dried ham), and pickled gherkins. However, it melts like a river of cheese and is amazing grilled on bread, vegetables, as a topping for soups or baked with potatoes and cream, or on ratatouille.

Apremont, a crisp local white wine, light beer, or sweet cider make perfect companions; or try a soft red with low tannin, such as Merlot.

The Haute-Savoie pastures *and Lake Annecy.*

FRANCE Rhône–Alpes	
Age 4–12 weeks	
Weight and Shape 9–1¼lb (240–550g), round	
Size D. 3½–5in (9–12cm), H. 1in (3cm)	
Milk Cow	
Classification Semi soft	
Producer Various	

A CLOSER LOOK

Reblochon is a piece of history and a reflection of the unique geology of the region, the indigenous breed of cows, and the people who make it.

THE CASEIN LABEL A round green casein stamp on the rind means it's a *fermier*, "farmhouse", cheese, made in an Alpine chalet or farms in the Thones area. A red stamp means it has been made in a factory, or by the milk of more than one herd within a wider defined area.

Round of Reblochon

The supple interior oozes beneath the rind.

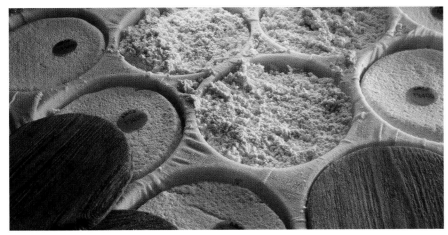

PRESSING A large piece of white cloth is stretched over a tray of cheese molds. The curd is then ladled into each mold and a small wooden disc placed over the top to lightly press the curd.

FORMING THE RIND In cool cellars, often carved into the hillside under the mountain chalets, the rind grows a mix of gray and white molds, which are discouraged by regular brushing and washes in brine. The rind should be dry not damp, smooth not cracked or split, and feel supple.

The rind ranges from pinkish-yellow when young to a pale terracotta-red, usually covered with whitish flora.

PACKAGING Reblochon is wrapped with a little wooden disc on the base and sometimes on top so you need to rely on your cheese merchant to tell you if it is ripe.

The wrinkles and irregularities in the rind are formed when the cloth is trapped in the curd during pressing.

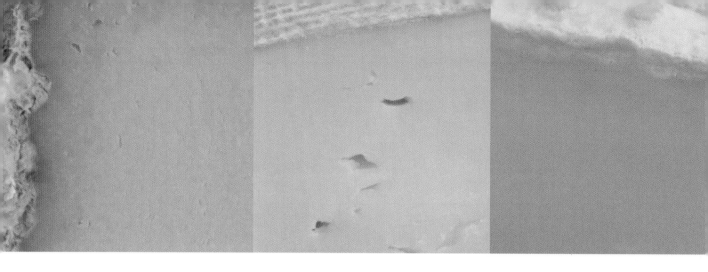

Persillé de Tignes

Although *persillé* translates as "parsley," it in fact refers to the fine blue-green mold that appears naturally inside the cheese rather than as a result of piercing to encourage the blue. The mustard-colored pigment on the rind is thought to be linked to the fact that the goats whose milk is used graze on sulphurous soil.

TASTING NOTES It is lactic and herbaceous with richer flavors in summer and fall. As it ripens, it becomes dry, spicy, and intense, and it breaks easily.

HOW TO ENJOY Persillé can be enjoyed with all fruity and light red wines, such as a Crépy or Saumure.

FRANCE Rhône-Alpes		
Age 2–6 months		
Weight and Shape 2lb (900g), cylinder		
Size D. 4½in (11cm), H. 3½in (9cm)		
Milk Goat		
Classification Hard		
Producer Various		

Petit Fiancé des Pyrénées

First created in 1989, this unpasteurized goat's cheese is made from the milk of an alpine breed of goats. After the whey is drained from the curds, the cheese is circled with a band of ash wood and washed repeatedly for six weeks as it matures.

TASTING NOTES The washing process gives the cheese a moist texture, and the ash binding infuses it with a woody aroma. The finished cheese has a supple melting interior.

HOW TO ENJOY Petit Fiancé des Pyrénées is best paired with a fruity white wine, such as a Condrieux.

FRANCE Midi-Pyrénées		
Age 6 weeks		
Weight and Shape 10oz (300g), round		
Size D. 5in (12cm), H. 1in (3.5cm)		
Milk Goat		
Classification Semi-soft		
Producer Fromagerie Fermier Cabrioulet		

Picodon AOC

This cheese is made from the milk of the goats that graze on the mountain grass and shrubs of the Ardèche and Drome regions. These pastures are filled with strong aromas and flavors, which in turn produce milk of the highest quality. Picodon has been AOC protected since 1983.

TASTING NOTES The goats' diet gives Picodon its spicy flavor; however, the paste is so dry that the flavor is best obtained by sucking the cheese.

HOW TO ENJOY Picodon tastes delicious when added to salads or paired with lively, full-bodied red and white wines from the Côtes-du-Rhône.

FRANCE Rhône-Alpes		
Age 1 month		
Weight and Shape 4oz (115g), round		
Size D. 3in (7.5cm), H. 1in (2.5cm)		
Milk Goat		
Classification Aged fresh		
Producer Various		

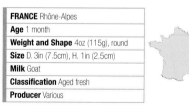

Pierre-Robert

Pierre-Robert originally owes its name to Robert Rouzaire, the producer, and his friend Pierre. This soft white cheese is now made by Rouzaire's son. It is not a cheese for anyone watching their calorie intake; this triple-cream cheese has extra cream added to the milk to give it a fat content of 75 percent for every 3½/100g and a luxurious, rich taste.

TASTING NOTES This very creamy, buttery and slightly sour cream tang melts in the mouth when young. Over time, it becomes richer and tangy.

HOW TO ENJOY It is delicious with pears, or with a full-bodied Bourgogne, such as Pommard or Mercurey.

FRANCE Seine-et-Marne, Ile-de-France	
Age 1 month	
Weight and shape 1lb (450g), round	
Size D. 5in (12cm), H. 2in (5cm)	
Milk Cow	
Classification Soft white	
Producer Fromagerie Rouzaire	

Pithiviers

Produced in Bondaroy, near Orléans, Pithiviers used to be made in summer when milk was plentiful and then stored in hay until the fall. Now it is produced all year round, but it is still covered in fine strands of dried grasses, herbs and meadow flowers.

TASTING NOTES The white rind is sprinkled with hay, and the paste is soft with a slight fragrance of mold and mushrooms, exuding a tangy flavor.

HOW TO ENJOY Team Pithiviers with the pale red Pinots of Orléanais and the fruity, lively light red wines of Orléans and Touraine (Chinon and Bourgeuil).

FRANCE Centre	
Age 4–5 weeks	
Weight and Shape 10½oz (300g), round	
Size D. 5in (12cm), H. 1in (2.5cm)	
Milk Cow	
Classification Soft white	
Producer Various	

Plaisir au Chablis

Named "the pleasure of Chablis" after the wine used in its production, this semi-soft cheese is from the same family as the Epoisses de Bourgogne. It is also known as Affidélis, and is a sticky, creamy cheese that is usually sold in a wooden box.

TASTING NOTES Being washed once a week with Chablis, a crisp white wine, gives it a fruity, alcoholic taste. Like all washed-rind cheeses, Plaisir has a strong taste.

HOW TO ENJOY As the name suggests, this is best served with a crisp white wine, especially a Chablis.

FRANCE Brochon, Bourgogne	
Age 6 weeks	
Weight and Shape 6½oz (180g), round	
Size D. 3in (8cm), H. 1in (3.5cm)	
Milk Cow	
Classification Semi-soft	
Producer Fromagerie Gaugry; Fromagerie Berthault	

Pont-l'Evêque AOC

Originally called Angelot, this washed-rind cheese is probably one of the oldest French cheeses. It is even mentioned by Guillaume de Lorris in his 13th century allegorical poem "Roman de la Rose." Pont-L'Evêque was granted an AOC in 1976.

TASTING NOTES The creamy, yellow, smooth paste develops small holes as it ripens, and has a lingering, sweet taste. Older cheeses have a stronger flavor.

HOW TO ENJOY Try eating this cheese alongside a glass of stout, or with a glass of full-bodied red wine, from Bordeaux, Burgundy, or Côtes du Rhône.

FRANCE Pont-l'Evêque, Basse Normandie	
Age 5–6 weeks	
Weight and Shape 12oz (350g), square	
Size L. 4in (10cm), W. 4in (10cm) H. 1in (2.5cm)	
Milk Cow	
Classification Semi-soft	
Producer Fromagerie E Graindorge, Fromagerie Thebault	

Pot Corse

Pot Corse is a *fromage fort*, a recipe developed by the French as a means of using leftover cheese. The remnants of ewe's milk cheeses are gathered together and combined with a little white wine, garlic, spices, and perhaps some herbs, then spread on bread like butter. This Corsican variation is presented in a small pot.

TASTING NOTES The strong, powerful and buttery flavor has vegetal overtones.

HOW TO ENJOY Do as the Corsicans do and match it with spicy food and a full-bodied red wine. Its pretty presentation is a bonus.

FRANCE Corse	
Age 20 weeks	
Weight and Shape 10oz (300g), jar	
Size No size	
Milk Ewe	
Classification Fresh	
Producer Various	

Pouligny-Saint-Pierre AOC

This goat cheese, AOC protected since 1972, is nicknamed "the Pyramid" or "the Eiffel Tower" because of its shape. It has a dry, vaguely knobby, pale cream to reddish rind which is dusted with a blue-gray mold.

TASTING NOTES With a moist, soft, and crumbly paste, the flavor changes from sour to salty to sweet. It has an aroma of the straw and of the milk of the Alpine goats used to produce it.

HOW TO ENJOY It is superb for a cheeseboard or broiled. Team it with a fruity Chenin or Sauvignon wine from the Touraine and Berry regions.

FRANCE Centre	
Age 3–5 weeks	
Weight and Shape 7oz (200g), pyramid	
Size D. 3in (7.5cm), H. 3½in (8cm)	
Milk Goat	
Classification Aged fresh	
Producer Various	

Raclette de Savoie

The name is derived from the French verb *racler*, meaning to scrape, as this cheese was traditionally placed in front of an open fire and, as it melted, scraped on to hot potatoes or bread. Some are made with added flavors, such as Raclette fumée, which is smoked over beechwood; au vin blanc, rubbed with a white wine; and *la moutarde*, made with mustard seeds.

TASTING NOTES The supple, elastic texture melts superbly and has a sweet taste that is stronger when melted.

HOW TO ENJOY Slice and grill or broil with potatoes, and serve with cooked meats and fruity red or white Savoy wines.

FRANCE Rhône-Alpes	
Age Minimum 2 months	
Weight and Shape 8¾lb–15lb 7oz (4.5–7kg), wheel	
Size D. 11–14in (28–36cm), H. 2in–3in (5.5–7.5cm)	
Milk Cow	
Classification Semi-soft	
Producer Various	

Racotin

During the production process, the curd of this goat cheese is drained, and it is the natural flora in the milk that brings a yellow tinge to the blue-white crinkled rind of the finished product. Similar to Charolais, but smaller, it is aged by Bernard Sivignon, a renowned affineur based in Bourgogne.

TASTING NOTES Racotin has a dense, firm, slightly grainy texture and a goaty flavor with a peppery, buttery tang.

HOW TO ENJOY Fresh raspberries and nutty bread are good accompaniments to this goat cheese, along with a crisp white wine.

FRANCE Bourgogne	
Age 3–4 weeks	
Weight and Shape 3½oz (100g), cylinder	
Size D. 2in (5cm), H. 2⅓in (6cm)	
Milk Goat	
Classification Aged fresh	
Producer Various	

Rigotte de Condrieu AOC

This farmhouse cheese is quite rare because it is made with goat's milk, unlike most rigottes, which are made with cow's milk. It is a very old cheese, and has been AOC protected since 2008.

TASTING NOTES Rigotte de Condrieu tastes milky but does not have a very pronounced flavor. It has a natural rind, a robust paste, and a honey and acacia aroma.

HOW TO ENJOY It goes perfectly with the light and fruity wines of Côtes du Lyonnais, Beaujolais, and Côtes du Rhône.

FRANCE Rhône-Alpes	
Age 2 weeks	
Weight and Shape 2oz (60g), round	
Size D. 1½in (4cm), H. 1in (3cm)	
Milk Goat	
Classification Aged fresh	
Producer Various	

Rocamadour AOC

This goat cheese was once known as Cabécou de Rocamadour, but since it gained its AOC status in 1996, it has been renamed simply Rocamadour, after the best-known market in the region. This change in name sets it apart from other Cabécou cheeses that are not made in the Rocamadour area, and so cannot carry the AOC label.

TASTING NOTES With a tender and creamy paste, Rocamadour tastes mild and slightly milky, but has a delicious sweet and nutty aftertaste.

HOW TO ENJOY Serve with figs and pair and a fruity, robust red wine, preferably of the Cahor region.

FRANCE Aquitaine	
Age 1–3 weeks	
Weight and Shape 1oz (30g), disc	
Size D. 2in (4.5cm), H. ½in (1.5cm)	
Milk Goat	
Classification Aged fresh	
Producer Various	

Rollot

This semi-soft washed-rind cheese used to be exclusively round, but in recent years, a factory version has been produced, called Cœur de Rollot, which has been molded into a heart shape.

TASTING NOTES This powerful cheese is similar in taste to a Maroilles (see p68) and has a spicy tang. The paste has a soft, sticky texture.

HOW TO ENJOY The heart-shaped version looks decorative on an after-dinner cheeseboard. You can serve it with all lively and fruity wines, such as Saint-Emilion, Côte Rôtie, and Savigny-les-Beaune.

FRANCE Picardie	
Age 6–8 weeks	
Weight and Shape 7–10oz (200–300g), round or heart	
Size D. 3in (7.5cm), H. 1½in (4cm)	
Milk Cow	
Classification Semi-soft	
Producer Various	

Rouelle du Tarn

This creamy goat cheese was created by a farmer from the Tarn region in 1984. Its unusual and distinctive shape is achieved by ladling the curd into a mold with a hole in the middle. It is then sprinkled with ash to create a white-gray rind. The combination of these techniques makes it an aesthetically-pleasing addition to any cheeseboard.

TASTING NOTES Rouelle du Tarn has a milky, deliciously creamy flavor and a hazelnut note.

HOW TO ENJOY Ideal with all fruity and light red wines, particularly a Saumur or Chinon.

FRANCE Midi-Pyrénées	
Age 1 month	
Weight and Shape 9oz (250g), round	
Size D. 4in (10cm), H. ½in (1cm)	
Milk Goat	
Classification Aged fresh	
Producer Various	

Rove Cendré

Generously sprinkled with ash, the Rove Cendré comes from a farm that has around 200 Rove goats with their distinct long horns and red coats. It is made only from March to December, although the hardy goats remain outdoors, grazing on the wild fragrant pastures, berries, and small bushes.

TASTING NOTES The texture is smooth and creamy, and the flavor is aromatic and herbaceous.

HOW TO ENJOY Rove Cendré 's ash coating and fresh lemony tang make it an attractive apéritif. Serve with fresh figs and berries, and a glass of Provençal rosé.

FRANCE Provence-Alpes-Côte D'Azur	
Age 2 weeks	
Weight and Shape 2½oz (75g), oval	
Size D. 2in (5cm), H. 1in (3cm)	
Milk Goat	
Classification Aged fresh	
Producer Various	

Roves des Garrigues

This fresh cheese is named after the Rove breed of goat that is native to the Mediterranean and now very rare. Rove goats produce very little milk each day (about 2 liters compared with an average of 5 liters in other breeds), but what it does produce is extremely dense and flavorsome.

TASTING NOTES The paste is pure white with a soft melt-in-the-mouth sensation and a fresh lemony tang that is overlaid with a hint of thyme and wild herbs.

HOW TO ENJOY Excellent served with a quince paste and washed down with a glass of red Côtes du Ventoux.

FRANCE Provence-Alpes-Côte D'Azur	
Age 1–2 weeks	
Weight and Shape 2½oz (75g), round	
Size D. 2in (5cm), H. 1½in (4cm)	
Milk Goat	
Classification Fresh	
Producer Various	

Sablé de Wissant

A recent creation made in Wissant, on France's northern coast, this semi-soft cheese is rolled in bread crumbs to give it a rough, sandy (or *sablé*) rind that absorbs the pale local beer in which it is washed.

TASTING NOTES Supple with small holes, this cheese feels rich and creamy in the mouth. It has the aroma and taste of beer—yeasty and slightly sweet with a pungent farm-yardy finish.

HOW TO ENJOY Great on a cheeseboard because of its unusual appearance, but like all washed-rind cheeses, it should be use sparingly in cooking. Serve with a light ale or a glass of Champagne.

FRANCE Wissant, Nord-Pas-de-Calais	
Age 7 weeks	
Weight and Shape 13oz (350g), square	
Size D. 5in (12cm), H. 2in (5cm)	
Milk Cow	
Classification Semi-soft	
Producer Bernard Brothers	

Roquefort AOC

Folklore has it that Roquefort was created some 2000 years ago when a love struck shepherd, distracted by his young love from tending his sheep, left his lunch, a piece of bread and cheese, in the cave where he had been sheltering. A few days later he remembered the cheese and found it had developed a greenish mold through the center.

Since then, shepherds have been maturing their cheese in the deep limestone caves of Cambalou. No chemicals, unwanted molds, or stainless steel shelves are used to disturb the delicate balance that has for centuries produced one of the world's finest cheeses. The natural caves are about 984ft (300m) wide, and go down four to five levels.

The often harsh climate with its hot, dry summers and cold winters, and the rugged, rocky geography has for centuries been home to a local breed of hardy indigenous sheep. Lactation lasts from December to July, and each sheep, grazing on the tussock grasses and wild herbs, produces around 3½–5 pints (2–3 liters) of rich, flavorsome milk.

It takes milk from 6–8 ewes to make one 6lb 6oz (3kg) cheese.

Roquefort has been protected since 1411 when Charles VI signed a charter granting the people of Roquefort-sur-Soulzon the rights to make it, and in 1926 it was the first cheese to be granted Appellation d'Origine Contrôlée (AOC) status. Only those unfamiliar with the process would compare other ewe's milk cheese with Roquefort.

TASTING NOTES When fully aged, the mold will have fanned out to the edges of the buttery mass in streaks and pockets and the flavor is spicy, strong, and mouth-watering. Sadly, some Roquefort is consumed too young when there is barely a hint of blue and the texture is crumbly rather than cohesive and the bite has no backbone.

HOW TO ENJOY Roquefort is sublime when eaten in chunks with sourdough bread, and spectacular in sauces, or when crumbled on top of salads or pasta. Traditionally it is paired with Port or Sauternes, but it is fantastic with just about any dessert wine as they cut though the salty tang and highlight the sweetness of the milk.

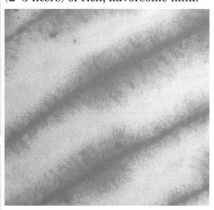

Pencillium roqueforti, *the fungus responsible for Roquefort's blue-gray mold.*

France Midi-Pyrénées	
Age 3 months	
Weight and Shape 5½–6¼lb (2.5–2.9kg), drum	
Size D. 8in (20cm), H. 3–4in (8.5–10.5cm)	
Milk Ewe	
Classification Hard	
Producer Various	

A CLOSER LOOK

There are only seven producers of Roquefort in the world, each using the same basic process and yet each achieves their own distinct and individual character. The biggest is the Roquefort Société.

Pockets of mold.

THE CAVES The numerous cracks and fissures of the limestone caves allow the cool air and indigenous molds to circulate. To encourage the growth of the blue *penicillium roqueforti* molds, large loaves of locally grown rye bread are placed in the caves and over three months grow a fine furry gray coat which, when dried and powdered, is sprinkled over the newly formed cheeses.

Once pierced, the spore-laden air quickly penetrates the nooks and crannies of the loosely packed curd, developing pockets of delicious blue-green mold.

FOIL WRAPPING The cheeses are wrapped in foil four weeks after their arrival in the caves to prevent any further mold growth on the rind.

The rind is very open and porous.

Drum, quarter removed

Saint-Christophe

Although this goat cheese is made in the same way as Saint-Maure de Touraine, it is made outside the area designated by the AOC regulations, so the cheesemaker must use another name. It is available plain or with ash, as seen here.

TASTING NOTES Matured in a very moist environment, it develops a soft, sticky, wrinkled rind and creamy texture. It is distinctly goaty, with a nutty taste and a light, moldy aroma.

HOW TO ENJOY It is excellent with any of the crisp white wines of the Loire or a light red wine of the Chinon.

FRANCE Saint-Christophe-Vallon, Midi-Pyrénées	
Age 2–3 weeks	
Weight and Shape 10oz (280g), log	
Size L. 5½in (14cm), W: 2in (5.5cm), H: 1½in (4.5cm)	
Milk Goat	
Classification Aged fresh	
Producer Pavé Jacquin	

Saint-Domnin

This is an Alpine goat cheese that has a character all its own. It is made in the Alpes-de-Haute-Provence, near ancient Sisteron, and is decorated with sprigs of the lavender that thrives on the region's rocky plateaus. It is also known as Carré Saint-Domnin.

TASTING NOTES The smooth texture melts in the mouth and is imbued with the scent of lavender and the subtle flavors associated with this sun-drenched land.

HOW TO ENJOY It makes the perfect ending to a hearty lunch; serve with a Provençal rosé or a sweet Muscat de Beaumes-de-Venise.

FRANCE Provence-Alpes-Côte-D'Azur	
Age 2 weeks	
Weight and shape 5½oz (150g), square	
Size L. 4in (10cm), W. 4in (10cm), H. 1in (3cm)	
Milk Goat	
Classification Aged fresh	
Producer Various	

Saint-Félicien

A natural-rinded cheese, Saint-Félicien was originally produced using goat's milk but now it is made with cow's milk. Made in the Rhône-Alpes area, it is similar to, but slightly larger than Saint-Marcellin.

TASTING NOTES The rind is very soft, wrinkly, and creamy; the interior varies from firm to almost runny and very creamy, with a delicate nutty flavor.

HOW TO ENJOY Accompany it with a sharp, strong-tasting red wine such as Saint Amour or a white Vin de Paille from Jura.

FRANCE Saint Félicien, Rhône-Alpes	
Age 2 weeks	
Weight and Shape 7oz (200g), round	
Size D. 5in (12cm), H. ½in (1cm)	
Milk Cow	
Classification Aged fresh	
Producer Étoile du Vercors Dairy	

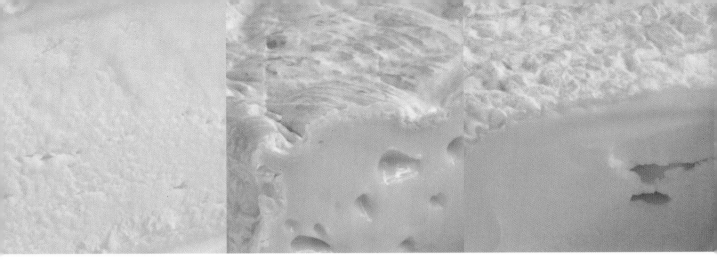

Saint-Florentin

Saint-Florentin, a town near the famous wine area of Chablis, is also located in the heart of one of France's great dairy regions. The traditional-style cheeses, with their reddish-brown crusts, are now quite rare, having been replaced by paler, factory-made cheeses that are sold when very young.

TASTING NOTES The smooth, shiny rind has a strong penetrating aroma, while the supple interior has a fresh, slightly salty flavor and can be quite spicy.

HOW TO ENJOY It makes a delicious addition to a fresh salad, and is best served with a robust Burgundy.

FRANCE Bourgogne	
Age 2 months	
Weight and Shape 1lb (450g), round	
Size D. 5in (12cm), H. 1in (2.5cm)	
Milk Cow	
Classification Semi-soft	
Producer Fromagerie Lincet	

Saint-Jacques

The farm on which this soft white cheese is made lies on the edge of the famous forest of Rambouillet, near Paris. Originally a cereal farm with a small herd of cows, the dairy side has gradually taken over, and they now produce hand made cheese six days a week using milk from their own herd.

TASTING NOTES The thin, very soft rind encases a creamy interior that varies in texture from firm to almost runny. Its flavor hints delicately of mushrooms.

HOW TO ENJOY Complement it with a soft and gentle claret, such as Pomerol, so as not to overpower it.

FRANCE Ile-de-France	
Age 4–5 weeks	
Weight and Shape 12½oz (350g), round	
Size D. 5in (13cm), H. 1in (3cm)	
Milk Cow	
Classification Soft white	
Producer Ferme de la Tremblaye	

Saint-Marcellin

This pale and creamy cheese has been made in homes and small farms in the Dauphine region for centuries. It is traditionally produced from goat's milk, but today, all but a handful are made from cow's milk.

TASTING NOTES The taste, texture and appearance vary according to how the cheese is ripened, but the best have an orange-tinged rind and are soft inside. Saint-Marcellin can be firm to creamy, almost liquid, with a light, subtle lemony freshness and a nutty aroma.

HOW TO ENJOY It is superb when baked; serve with a light and fruity Beaujolais or fruity Côtes du Rhône.

FRANCE Rhône-Alpes	
Age 2–6 weeks	
Weight and Shape 3oz (85g), round	
Size D. 3in (7.5cm), H. 1in (2.5cm)	
Milk Cow or goat	
Classification Aged fresh	
Producer Various	

LANGRES The cheese has been rubbed
frequently with a mix of the natural dye
annatto and brine, giving it a gorgeous
tangerine-orange sticky rind that attracts
white *Penicillium candidum* mold once the
washing stops. (See p63.)

Saint-Nectaire AOC

One of the great cheeses of France, Saint-Nectaire is made with milk from Salers cows that graze the rich and perfumed volcanic pastures of the uplands of the Auvergne region. The traditional methods of production have been AOC protected since 1955.

TASTING NOTES At maturity, the thick rind gives off a subtle, slightly pungent aroma of straw and mushrooms, while the paste should have a pronounced taste of nut, milk, and lush pastures.

HOW TO ENJOY Eat on its own with crusty bread and any light fruity wines, especially Côteaux d'Auvergne and Côtes Roannaises.

FRANCE Auvergne	
Age 8–10 weeks	
Weight and Shape 3lb 5oz (1.5kg), wheel	
Size D. 8in (20cm), H. 1½in (4cm)	
Milk Cow	
Classification Semi-soft	
Producer Various	

Saint-Nicolas-de-la-Dalmerie

At the monastery of St. Nicholas, founded in 1965, the monks live off the land and keep goats. Using raw milk from the herd, they create an aromatic cheese, redolent with the flavor of thyme. As the rind develops, it turns from gentle orange to chestnut in color. The interior is stark white.

TASTING NOTES Tangy, fruity, deep flavors typical of only the best goat cheese characterize this fine example, which is firm to the touch but melts in the mouth.

HOW TO ENJOY Accompanied by a glass of fruity dry white wine.

FRANCE Languedoc, Languedoc-Roussillon	
Age 3 weeks	
Weight and Shape 3½oz (100g), bar	
Size W. 1½in (4cm), L. 3½in (8.5cm), H. 1in (3cm)	
Milk Goat	
Classification Aged fresh	
Producer Le Monastère Orthodoxe Saint-Nicolas	

Sarments d'Amour

For centuries, the vineyards around Lyon have been home to herds of goats, which produce the milk for these charming cheeses. These vineyards are the inspiration behind the "branch of love" that decorates this modern French cheese; the protruding vine stem lends it an attractive air.

TASTING NOTES Sarments d'Amour has a dense white paste that feels luscious in the mouth and a subtle, but distinct, goat flavor.

HOW TO ENJOY Its charming appearance and small size make it perfect for an appetizer; serve it with a crisp rosé or even a sparkling wine.

FRANCE Rhône-Alpes	
Age 1 week	
Weight and Shape 1oz (30g), cone	
Size Various	
Milk Goat	
Classification Aged fresh	
Producer Various	

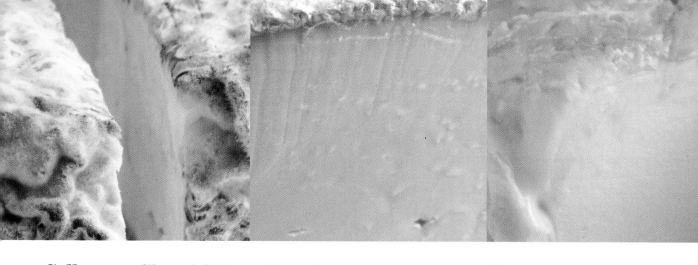

Selles-sur-Cher AOC

This popular goat cheese has been AOC protected since 1975 to maintain its traditional artisan methods of production. About 1.3 liters of milk are needed to make a single Selles-Sur-Cher; it is then coated with ash on which a bluish-gray mold develops.

TASTING NOTES It has a firm texture but melts in the mouth. The taste is a combination of sour, salty, and sweet. The locals eat the rind because they believe it gives the truest taste.

HOW TO ENJOY Team Selles-Sur-Cher with all dry whites and rosés of Blésois, and light and fruity reds of Touraine, such as Chinon and Bourgueil.

FRANCE Centre	
Age 10–21 days	
Weight and Shape 4½–5oz (125–140g), round	
Size Various, D. 3in (7.5cm), H. 1in (2.5cm) (pictured)	
Milk Goat	
Classification Aged fresh	
Producer Various	

Signal

This seasonal cheese is made only from March to November from the milk of goats that graze near Lac d'Aiguebellette in Savoie. This is France's third-largest lake, and it is set against a stunning backdrop of meadows, forests and the mountains of Epine, which were crossed in 218BCE by Hannibal, his army, and 37 elephants.

TASTING NOTES The very dense and rich paste is quite similar to that of Charolais, while the flavor has a hint of mountain flowers.

HOW TO ENJOY Eat this flavorsome cheese with ripe, fresh fruit, such as pears and mountain berries.

FRANCE Savoie, Rhône-Alpes	
Age 3 weeks	
Weight and Shape 5½oz (150g), round	
Size Various	
Milk Goat	
Classification Aged fresh	
Producer La Chèvrerie du Signal	

Soumaintrain

This brine-washed cheese is a member of the Epoisses family, but Soumaintrain is larger and tends to be eaten when much younger when it has a very thin orangey rind. The summer cheese is creamy and fresh, but it can be left to mature until winter, when it has a slightly harder rind.

TASTING NOTES The rind is barely formed, moist, and orange in color, while the paste is soft but grainy, becoming smoother with age. It has a spicy tang and a penetrating aroma.

HOW TO ENJOY Team this young cheese with full-bodied Burgundies, such as Nuits and Beaune.

FRANCE Epoisses, Bourgogne; Brochon, Bourgogne	
Age 6 weeks	
Weight and Shape 12oz (350g), round	
Size D. 5in (12cm), H. 1in (2.5cm)	
Milk Cow	
Classification Semi-soft	
Producer Fromagerie Berthault; Fromagerie Gaugry	

Tarentais

This authentic *fermier*, or farmhouse, cheese originates in the Tarentaise Valley in the mountains that border Italy. It is washed with a regional white wine. The best cheeses are those aged by *affineur* Denis Provent, in Chambery.

TASTING NOTES Tarentais has buttery and flowery flavors and a long finish. Although it is usually eaten fresh, it can be allowed to mature to take on a more piquant flavor.

HOW TO ENJOY It is superb broiled or served on its own with bread or quince paste, and it goes well with a salad or roast vegetables.

FRANCE Rhône-Alpes	
Age 15 days–3 months	
Weight and Shape 8½oz (240g), cylinder	
Size D. 6in (15cm), H. 3½in (8.5cm)	
Milk Goat	
Classification Aged fresh	
Producer Various	

Taupinette Charentaise

This cheese is at its best in spring. The curd of Taupinette is ladled into dome-shaped molds to mature. The crinkled, gray-white rind of the finished product closely resembles sphere-shaped coral.

TASTING NOTES Taupinette has a mild, sometimes nutty flavor that becomes more robust stronger as it ages and the mold spreads. It has a smooth texture when young.

HOW TO ENJOY Serve this attractive cheese with a red wine such as Pinot Noir or Saint Joseph.

FRANCE Poitou-Charentes	
Age 3 weeks	
Weight and Shape 9oz (250g), sphere	
Size D. 3in (7.5cm), H. 2in (5cm)	
Milk Goat	
Classification Aged fresh	
Producer Various	

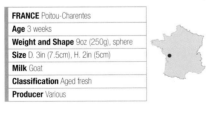

Tétoun de Santa Agata

The name of this goat cheese translates to "Santa Agata's nipple" because of the peppercorn on its peak. The cheese sits on a bed of sweet, herbaceous Provençal olive oil and finely chopped herbs, giving it an original taste and appearance.

TASTING NOTES The contrast of smooth, white creamy paste with olive oil and fresh herbs gives this delicately flavored cheese a wonderfully aromatic quality.

HOW TO ENJOY For full effect, serve it alone, spread on bread, or lightly melted. Excellent with a light rosé de Provence wine.

FRANCE Provence-Alpes-Côte D'Azur	
Age 1–2 weeks	
Weight and Shape 4½oz (125g), cone	
Size D. 2⅜in (6cm) base, H. 2⅜in (6cm)	
Milk Goat	
Classification Fresh	
Producer Various	

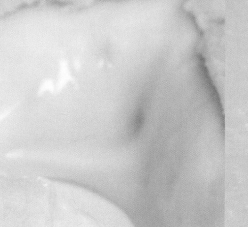

Tome des Bauges AOC

The milk for this semi-soft cheese comes from the cows grazing on the Alpine pastures of the Natural Park of Bauges. The meadows of wild flowers provide a rich diet for the cows, which is reflected in the sweet, complex flavors of this cheese.

TASTING NOTES One of the tastiest of the Tomme de Savoie cheeses, since it is made with full milk and lightly pressed to give it a supple texture with tiny holes. The rind becomes thick, wrinkled, and gray with age.

HOW TO ENJOY Combine it with hazelnuts and prunes, or add to omelets, soups or a salad with fennel and endive.

FRANCE Rhône-Alpes	
Age Around 5 weeks	
Weight and Shape 2½oz (75g), round	
Size D. 7in (18cm), H. 1½in (4cm)	
Milk Cow	
Classification Semi-soft	
Producer Various	

Tomme à l'Ancienne

Invented by a couple living near the town of Banon, Tomme à l'Ancienne is made with pure goat's milk and is ladled by hand into disc-shaped molds to create delicate soft texture.

TASTING NOTES This cheese is marinated in a strong local brandy—the *eau de vie* (the water of life)—along with some pepper, cloves, thyme, and bay leaves. This combination gives it a wonderful complexity of flavors.

HOW TO ENJOY It is delicious served with fresh figs and nuts and either a glass of *eau de vie* or a local rosé wine.

FRANCE Provence-Alpes-Côte D'Azur	
Age 2 weeks–2 months	
Weight and Shape 3½oz (100g), disc	
Size D. 3in (8cm), H. 1in (3cm)	
Milk Goat	
Classification Semi-soft	
Producer Various	

Tomme de Brebis Corse

This typical Corsican hard cheese has a rustic, brown wrinkled crust and is made with ewe's milk. It is similar to the Basque cheese Ossau-Iraty.

TASTING NOTES This cheese contains a wonderful mix of delicate Corsican aromas, including pepper, the native aromatic scrub or 'maquis'.

HOW TO ENJOY Fig jam makes a very tasty accompaniment. Serve with a good Corsican wine, a Chinon, a Menetou Salon, or a Faugères.

Region Corse	
Age 3 months	
Weight and Shape 5½lb (2.5kg), cylinder	
Size D. 7½in (19cm) , H. 3½in (9cm)	
Milk type Ewe	
Classification Hard	
Producer Various	

Tomme Caprine des Pyrénées

This *fermier* goat cheese is produced in the Pyrénées, a region better known for its excellent ewe's milk cheese. This hard cheese is at its best when made during the spring and summer months, which is when the mountainside pastures are at their most verdant.

TASTING NOTES The taste is rich and buttery, and it has a melt-in-the-mouth texture. The pleasant aroma is flowery and exotic.

HOW TO ENJOY Team this rustic goat cheese with a sweet Jurançon wine.

FRANCE Midi-Pyrénées	
Age 6–8 weeks	
Weight and Shape 6lb (2.7kg), wheel	
Size D. 7in (18cm), H. 3in (7.5cm)	
Milk Goat	
Classification Hard	
Producer Various	

Tomme de Chartreux

Chartreux is a member of the Tomme de Savoie family, which is a generic name for Savoie cheeses that differ from producer to producer. This cheese, with its flavoring of mountain herbs, has characteristics reminiscent of the Swiss Raclette (see p241), but with a bite. This similarity is not surprising because the family makers of this cheese originate from Switzerland.

TASTING NOTES It varies from mild and milky to nutty with a rich savory tang and a pleasant farmyard aroma.

HOW TO ENJOY Try with fresh fruit and a light, fruity Savoie wine or richer regional wines, such as Mondeuse.

FRANCE Alex, Rhône-Alpes	
Age 8–16 weeks	
Weight and Shape 5lb 3oz (2.4kg), round	
Size D. 3½in (9cm), H. 3in (8cm)	
Milk Cow	
Classification Semi-soft	
Producer Schmidhauser Dairy	

Tomme de Chèvre des Charentes

It is produced by just one farmer on the small Island of Ré, near La Rochelle. This goat cheese is washed twice a week with a mix of brine and local white wine to develop the complexity of aromas and flavors for which it is renowned.

TASTING NOTES The flavor is rich, with a sea breeze tang that is derived from the Atlantic Ocean surrounding the island. The rind is hard and compact.

HOW TO ENJOY Serve lightly grilled on crusty bread with apples, walnuts, or with a mellow white wine, such as a Muscat.

FRANCE Poitou-Charentes	
Age Minimum 3 months	
Weight and Shape 8lb (3.6kg), wheel	
Size D. 12in (30cm), H. 2½in (6cm)	
Milk Goat	
Classification Semi-soft	
Producer Various	

Sainte-Maure de Touraine AOC

Goats were introduced to the Loire in the 8th century by the Saracens who also left behind a lasting legacy of cheesemaking. Today, the *chèvre*, "goat cheeses," of the Loire are perceived by cheese lovers around the world as the benchmark against which all aged fresh goat cheeses are measured.

They include six AOC cheeses—Chabichou du Poitou (p49), Crottin de Chavignol (p54), Pouligny-Saint-Pierre (p78), Selle-sur-Cher (p88), Valençay (p97), and Sainte-Maure. They are made in every conceivable shape from tiny buttons, bells, and pears to bricks, rounds, cylinders, logs, and pyramids. They are all undeniable classics, but Sainte-Maure de Touraine, until modern times referred to simply as *le long chèvre*, is one of the most popular. The rind is dusted with ash and covered with tufted blue molds, patches of gray, and mottled with pinks and yellow. The high rainfall, warm summers, lush pastures, woodlands, wide rivers, and rolling hills of the Loire provide the perfect environment for the goats to produce a high yield of excellent, aromatic milk. The best are made between Easter and All Saints Day at the beginning of November.

TASTING NOTES The wood ash provides a stark contrast against the pure white, slightly grainy interior. As the molds develop, it becomes more dense and the lemony fresh, slightly nutty flavor intensifies to a more aromatic, herbaceous taste typical of Loire goat's cheeses. It should not, however, develop the musky goat taste that many people find distasteful until the surface becomes deeply wrinkled and covered with dark gray and reddish molds.

HOW TO ENJOY Its unusual shape makes it an attractive addition to a cheeseboard, like all the Loire *chèvre*. It is also an integral part of Chèvre Salad, France's ubiquitous salad, with thick rings grilled on slices of crusty bread bringing out its rich, aromatic, nutty side. Sadly, chefs across the world have assumed that any goat cheese can be used, but in fact *chèvre* refers solely to the Loire-style goat cheeses. The crisp whites, light Rosés, or fruity red wines of the Loire make the best drink companions.

A CLOSER LOOK

Like most aged fresh cheeses, Sainte-Maure is best when allowed to age gracefully in the hands of an *affineur*, who will sell them at varying stages of ripeness depending on the tastes of the clientèle.

As the cheese matures, the wrinkles will become deeper and more pronounced.

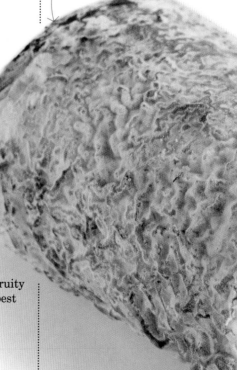

Alpine and Saanen goats are the breeds whose milk is used to make Sainte-Maure.

FRANCE Centre and Poitou Charentes		
Age 10–28 days		
Weight and Shape 9oz (250g), cylinder		
Size D. 1½in (4cm), L. 7in (18cm)		
Milk Goat		
Classification Aged Fresh		
Producer Various		

SHAPING The soft, wet, fragile curds achieved by coagulation are ladled into log-shaped molds to drain and take shape.

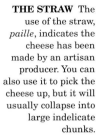

THE STRAW The use of the straw, *paille*, indicates the cheese has been made by an artisan producer. You can also use it to pick the cheese up, but it will usually collapse into large indelicate chunks.

The surface is encased with a dusty blue-gray mold.

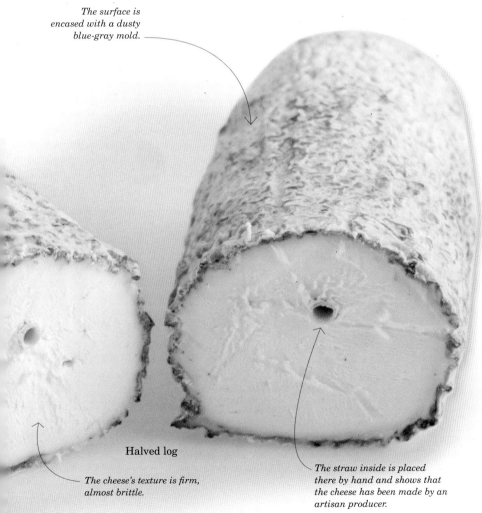

Halved log

The cheese's texture is firm, almost brittle.

The straw inside is placed there by hand and shows that the cheese has been made by an artisan producer.

THE ASH The logs are sprinkled with a mix of salt and wood ash. Initially, only the ash covers the bright, white, moist young curd. It must be at least 10 days old when sold, to comply with the AOC rules.

AGING Gradually, the cheese starts to lose moisture, a soft thin wrinkly rind develops, and the surface attracts a variety of micro flora. First, the familiar white velvet of *penicillium candidum*, then, within 12 days, a delicate blue powder pufflike mold appears that will take over from the white mold.

Tomme aux Herbes

Tomme aux Herbes is a variety of the famous French tomme cheeses. It has a thin layer of herbs pressed into the rind.

TASTING NOTES It is supple yet dense and more buttery than most tommes, it absorbs the essence of the aromatic herbs that coat the rind, dominated by thyme and rosemary.

HOW TO ENJOY Nothing beats a tomme purchased locally and consumed along with warm crusty bread and a local red, such as Cornas.

FRANCE Rhône-Alpes		
Age 3 months		
Weight and Shape 4lb (1.8kg), round		
Size D. 8in (20cm), H. 2½in (6cm)		
Milk Cow		
Classification Semi-soft		
Producer Various		

Tomme de Savoie

Tomme de Savoie, the generic name for the cheeses or "tommes" of Savoie, vary from producer to producer, village to village, and season to season. Some may be flavored with herbs, or spices such as cumin, or aged under a thick layer of *marc*, the residue left after wine pressing.

TASTING NOTES The flavor ranges from mild and milky to nutty with a savory tang. It has a herbaceous or farmyard aroma. A label showing four red hearts is a guarantee of quality.

HOW TO ENJOY Excellent baked or broiled. Try with light, fruity Savoie wines or a lively Mondeuse or les Abymes.

FRANCE Rhône-Alpes		
Age 1–2 months		
Weight and Shape 3–6lb (1.35–2.7kg), round		
Size D. 7–12in (18–30cm), H. 2–3in (5–8cm)		
Milk Cow		
Classification Semi-soft		
Producer Various		

Tommette Brebis des Alpes

The high altitudes of this region produce glorious pastureland, that influences the wonderful flavors of cheeses produced here. This particular example is made in small quantities and is distinguished by its brown rind. The "Brebis" of its name signifies the use of ewe's milk.

TASTING NOTES This cheese has a mix of delicate aromas and herbaceous flavors, evocative of Alpine meadows.

HOW TO ENJOY Gooseberry jam makes a tasty accompaniment. Serve with a fruity and bodied red wine, such as Chinon or Menetou Salon.

FRANCE Rhône-Alpes		
Age 2–4 months		
Weight and Shape 3lb (1.35kg), round		
Size D. 5in (11.5cm), H. 1½in (4cm)		
Milk Ewe		
Classification Semi-soft		
Producer Various		

Tommette de Chèvre des Bauges

This rarely produced, authentic goat cheese originates in the Bauges mountains in Savoie. *Tommette* refers to a small tommes—a French term that simply means a small cheese that is usually made on small farm in mountain regions. It has a hard, dry, gray-brown crust.

TASTING NOTES The slightly moist, soft and sticky paste fills the mouth with mountain flavors. It has subtle and structured aromas.

HOW TO ENJOY Team this goat cheese with a fruity, full bodied white wine of Condrieux.

FRANCE Rhône-Alpes		
Age 2 months		
Weight and Shape 1½lb (675g), round		
Size D. 4½in (11cm), H. 3in (7.5cm)		
Milk Goat		
Classification Semi-soft		
Producer Various		

Trappe d'Echourgnac

Since 1868, the nuns at the Abbaye d'Echourgnac have been using milk from neighboring farms to make and ripen this artisan cheese. Produced only in small quantities, it is well worth seeking out.

TASTING NOTES Washing with walnut liquor gives the rind an attractive dark brown color, and the supple paste has a smokier taste and a simple, balanced flavor.

HOW TO ENJOY It becomes runny and slightly stringy when cooked, but is especially good for stuffing into homemade ravioli. Serve with cider or a red or rosé from Cahors.

FRANCE Dordogne, Aquitaine		
Age 2 months		
Weight and Shape 10½oz (300g), round		
Size D. 4in (10cm), H. 2in (5cm)		
Milk Cow		
Classification Semi-soft		
Producer Abbaye d'Echourgnac		

Trèfle

Association des Fromagers Caprins Perche et Loir is a group group of seven artisan cheesemakers and goat farmers who got together in 2002 to create a new cheese using the milk of their goat herds. The cheese is shaped like a four-leafed clover; *trèfle* means clover in French, hence its name.

TASTING NOTES Beneath its soft, thin coat of blue-gray mold, the paste is tender and the taste peppery and long-lasting.

HOW TO ENJOY Serve it with sweet ripe figs and fresh berries alongside a Sauvignon Blanc.

FRANCE Pays de la Loire		
Age 2 weeks		
Weight and Shape 4.6oz, 4-leaf clover		
Size D. 3½in (9cm), H. 1in (3.5cm)		
Milk Goat		
Classification Aged fresh		
Producer Various		

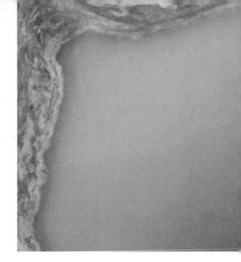

Trois Cornes de Vendée

After a halt of several years, production of this fresh goat cheese, with its distinctive triangular shape, was resumed in the 1980s near the seaside city of Marans. The curious name comes from the shape of the famous goat's horn belonging to Monsieur Seguin, a character in the tales of the French writer Alphonse Daudet.

TASTING NOTES The paste is bold and rich with a bittersweet flavor. It is best eaten fresh, but can be cured for one or two weeks.

HOW TO ENJOY Try with dry white Loire wines such as Sancerre or Chinon.

FRANCE Poitou-Charentes	
Age 1 month	
Weight and Shape 8oz (225g), triangular	
Size H. 3½in (9cm), W. 1in (2.5cm)	
Milk Goat	
Classification Aged fresh	
Producer Various	

Truffe de Valensole

The area around the village of Valensole, in the Haute-Provence region, is renowned for its truffles. This hand-shaped cheese reflects its origins by being covered with a fine layer of black charcoal to resemble these highly scented and much-prized mushrooms.

TASTING NOTES Soft and almost mousse-like with a delicate lemony freshness and a hint of herbs on the finish.

HOW TO ENJOY For pure luxury, try it stirred into pasta with a fine shaving of fresh truffles. Serve with a light white wine, such as Coteaux Varois, or with a light fruity red, such as Beaujolais.

FRANCE Provence-Alpes-Côte D'Azur	
Age Around 2 weeks	
Weight and Shape 3½oz (100g), ball	
Size Various	
Milk Goat	
Classification Aged fresh	
Producer Various	

U Bel Fiuritu

This washed-rind cheese has a thick, slightly sticky, orange rind that is dusted with white and gray mold and exudes a pungent farm-yardy aroma. It is one of the few Corsican ewe's milk cheeses made with pasteurized milk.

TASTING NOTES Supple, smooth, and creamy with small holes scattered through the pale yellow paste. Its sweet aromatic flavor reflects the Corsican landscape and the wild herbs and grasses on which the sheep graze.

HOW TO ENJOY U Bel Fiuritu can be enjoyed with full-bodied, structured red wines, such as a Muscat du cap Corse or a 12-year-old Frontignan.

FRANCE Venaco, Corse	
Age 4–10 weeks	
Weight and Shape 14oz (400g), round	
Size D. 4½in (11cm), H. 1½in (4cm)	
Milk Ewe	
Classification Semi-soft	
Producer Pierucci Dairy	

U Pecurinu

U Pecurinu is a dense washed-rind cheese from Corsica, an island renowned for its unique and flavorful cheeses, thanks to its warm climate, robust local breeds, and wild and diverse grazing.

TASTING NOTES This semi-soft cheese is tender and buttery and has a complex herbaceous flavor with vegetal overtones. The repeated washing leaves a lingering meaty tang and pungent farmyard aroma.

HOW TO ENJOY Corsicans often eat this cheese with fig jam; a fruity red wine makes the perfect accompaniment.

FRANCE Corse	
Age 2–16 weeks	
Weight and Shape 14oz (400g), round	
Size D. 4½in (11cm), H. 1½in (4cm)	
Milk Ewe	
Classification Semi-soft	
Producer Various	

Valençay AOC

It is said that this cheese was once made in the shape of a pyramid, but on seeing it, Napoleon became angry because it reminded him of his Egyptian defeat and he angrily chopped off the top with his sword, creating a truncated shape. Valençay has been AOC protected since 1998.

TASTING NOTES This natural-rinded cheese is covered in salted charcoal ashes. It has a soft, moist paste and a mild and slightly nutty flavor.

HOW TO ENJOY Valençay is delicious paired with all fruity and lively white wines of the Berry and Touraine regions of France, especially Sancerre.

FRANCE Centre region	
Age 5 weeks	
Weight and Shape 7–9oz (200–250g), truncated pyramid	
Size D. 2½–3in (6–7cm) base, 1–1½in (3.5–4cm) top, 2½–3in (H. 6–7cm)	
Milk Goat	
Classification Aged fresh	
Producer Various	

Venaco

Named after a small picturesque village in central Corsica where it was once made, this is one of the best known Corsican cheeses. It is a washed-rind fermier cheese and is best when produced between spring and fall, the milk benefiting from the sheep grazing lush pastures.

TASTING NOTES Beneath its thin and sticky orange rind, the paste is dense yet soft and sticky with a full-bodied and very spicy taste.

HOW TO ENJOY Spread sparingly on bread with herbs, garlic, or olive oil for an excellent snack. Sharp and tasty, it is best with big reds like Gigondas.

FRANCE Corse	
Age 3–4 months	
Weight and Shape 1lb 2oz–1lb 10oz (500–750g), round	
Size D. 4in (10cm), H. 1½in (4cm)	
Milk Ewe	
Classification Semi-soft	
Producer Various	

SELLES-SUR-CHER Over the fine ash coating, a fine, velvetlike white *Penicillium candidum* mold is overlaid by splotches of blue-gray *Penicillium glaucum*. As the cheese dries out, the original skin shrinks and wrinkles. (See p88).

Ventadour

Ventadour originates from Corrèze—part of the Limousin—which lays claim to 3,106 miles (5,000km) of river, including the Corrèze itself. The unadulterated countryside of this rural idyll allows farmers such as Xavier Cornet to indulge a passion for cheesemaking; he established his well-respected dairy in 1977.

TASTING NOTES The taste of this goat cheese changes according to its age: it can be very sweet or spicy but is always full of subtle flavors, with a delicate hint of goat.

HOW TO ENJOY Eat with a white Loire wine, such as Sancerre.

FRANCE Corrèze, Limousin	
Age 3–6 weeks	
Weight and Shape 5oz (140g), round	
Size D. 3in (8cm), H. 2½in (6cm)	
Milk Goat	
Classification Aged fresh	
Producer Xavier Cornet	

Vieux-Boulogne

Considered to be one of the most odorous cheeses in the world, Vieux-Boulogne is washed with beer several times during the production process. Despite its strong aroma, the taste is not aggressive or overpowering.

TASTING NOTES The rind is orange and the paste rubbery with small holes. Surprisingly enough, Vieux-Boulogne is not sharp; instead, it has a rich and mellow flavor.

HOW TO ENJOY It is too strong for most dishes and is best enjoyed with crusty bread and a variety of drinks—from a good-quality beer to Champagne or full-bodied red wines.

FRANCE Nord-Pas-de-Calais	
Age 7–9 weeks	
Weight and Shape 1lb 5oz (600g), square	
Size L. 4in (10.5cm), W. 4in (10.5cm), H. 1½in (4cm)	
Milk Cow	
Classification Semi-soft	
Producer Various	

Vieux-Lille

Once eaten down in the pits by miners, the nickname of this cheese is "Puant de Lille," or "the smelly cheese of Lille," because of its strong farm-yard aroma. It is similar to Maroilles (see p68), but is soaked, rather than washed, in brine and aged for longer.

TASTING NOTES It has a very powerful, sometimes piquant, salty taste with a thin, barely formed, slightly sticky pale orange-colored rind and supple, dense, and slightly dry texture.

HOW TO ENJOY Serve it with juniper berries and a variety of drinks, such as beer, black coffee, or even light wines—the taste is not as pungent as the scent.

FRANCE Nord-Pas-de-Calais	
Age 3–4 months	
Weight and Shape 1½lb (675g), square	
Size L. 5in (12cm), W. 5in (12cm), H. 2in (5cm)	
Milk Cow	
Classification Semi-soft	
Producer Various	

More Cheeses of France

The following cheeses are rare—either because they are only available seasonally or because they are produced in very remote areas. As a result, it has proved impossible to photograph them, but as they are important and interesting examples of French cheese, we are including them.

So, read, savor, and seek out.

Abbaye de Troisvaux

This is one of several cheeses that are produced at the Abbaye de Troisvaux. This semi-soft, washed-rind cheese is based on Trappist-style cheeses like Trappe de Beval. Another of these cheeses is Losange de Saint-Paul, which is also a washed-rind cheese but it is molded into a lozenger shape.

TASTING NOTES The elastic rind is a yellow-orange color from being washed with beer during maturation. The paste is smooth and creamy, without any bitterness, and has a mild aroma.

HOW TO ENJOY Team this cheese with a light and fruity red wine, such as a Beaujolais or a Bourgogne.

FRANCE Nord-Pas-de-Calais	
Age 5–6 weeks	
Weight and Shape 17oz (480g), round	
Size D. 10in (25cm), H. 1½in (4cm)	
Milk Cow	
Classification Semi-soft	
Producer Abbaye de Troisvaux	

Bastelicaccia

Originating in the south of Corse, Bastelicaccia is a ewe's-milk cheese with a thin and fragile rind. It is made using a little rennet; this addition makes the curdling last longer and creates a creamy, smooth paste.

TASTING NOTES Old-school Bastelicaccia, made during the winter months, is fine, fragile, and very creamy. The fresher and younger it is, the more character it has. Most producers, however, age Bastelicaccia longer, resulting in a more robust flavor.

HOW TO ENJOY As this is a rare cheese, it is an impressive addition to any cheeseboard. Serve it with light red wine, such as a Chinon.

FRANCE Corse	
Age 2–8 weeks	
Weight and Shape 14oz (400g), drum	
Size D. 5in (13cm), H. 1½in (4cm)	
Milk Ewe	
Classification Semi-soft	
Producer Various	

Boulette de Papleux

A variation on Boulette d'Avesnes (see p40), Boulette de Papleux is made from young, imperfect Maroilles cheeses rather than from fresh curd. It is then mashed with pepper, cloves, tarragon, and parsley.

TASTING NOTES Its deep red, beer-washed rind is covered with paprika, while the paste is ivory white and flecked with herbs. It is a very strong, hot, spicy cheese in both flavor and aroma.

HOW TO ENJOY A hearty winter cheese, because it is strong. It goes well with beer, very full-bodied wines, such as Cahors or Brouilly, or a shot of gin.

FRANCE Nord-Pas-de-Calais	
Age 2–3 months	
Weight and Shape 7oz (200g)	
Size D. 3in (7.5cm) , H. 4in (10cm)	
Milk Cow	
Classification Flavor-added	
Producer Various	

Crabotin

This is an unfairly little-known goat's milk cheese. The name is derived from the Occitan language; *crabot* simply means *caprine*, which translates as relating to goats. The cheese is washed with brine during maturation, producing a distinctive looking orange-colored rind.

TASTING NOTES This delicious cheese has a soft paste, a mild and quite creamy, fruity flavor, and a very goaty aroma.

HOW TO ENJOY Crabotin is excellent eaten with fresh crusty bread and fruit preserves. It is very well paired with Madiran wine.

FRANCE Aquitaine, Midi-Pyrénées	
Age 6 weeks	
Weight and Shape 1lb 2oz (500g), round	
Size D. 6in (15cm), H. 1in (2.5cm)	
Milk Goat	
Classification Semi-soft	
Producer Various	

Crémet du Cap Blanc-Nez

A beautiful and rare heavy-cream, white-rinded farmhouse cheese that takes its name from the white clay cliffs of the Cap Blanc-Nez, between Boulogne-sur-Mer and Calais.

TASTING NOTES The high cream content gives it a very rich taste that leaves a long finish in the mouth. The salty flavor is reminiscent of the breezes coming off the sea.

HOW TO ENJOY This is delicious eaten with bread and honey. Team it with a Champagne or a fruity white wine, such as Mont Louis from the Loire valley.

FRANCE Wiere Effroy, Nord-Pas-de-Calais	
Age 3 weeks	
Weight and Shape 1lb (450g), dome	
Size Various	
Milk Cow	
Classification Soft white	
Producer Saint Godeleine Farm (M. Bernard)	

Fort de Béthune

Cheeses of the Nord-Pas-de-Calais are known for their strong flavors—and one of strongest of them all is Fort de Béthune. This cow's-milk cheese was once a favorite of the mining community, who would team it with local beer. It is made by soaking the pungent local Maroilles cheese in brine for three months.

TASTING NOTES The fermentation process used for this cheese gives it a very creamy, silky texture, but with an almost eye-wateringly strong flavor.

HOW TO ENJOY Eat this spread on bread alongside a glass of a full-bodied red wine, such as a Faugères from Languedoc, or an *eau de vie*.

FRANCE Nord-Pas-de-Calais	
Age 3 months	
Weight and Shape Various	
Size Various	
Milk type Cow	
Classification Various	
Producer Various	

Mascare

This goat's-milk cheese originates in the 'provençales' Alps, in Banon. It has a thin, natural rind that is wrapped in a decorative chestnut leaf. It is a seasonal cheese and is only made by one producer, so it is rarely found outside its local area.

TASTING NOTES Beneath its soft, creamy rind, Mascare has a mild lactic to nutty flavor and a soft, almost runny paste around the edge as it ripens.

HOW TO ENJOY At its best when served simply with fresh crusty bread from the local market along with a fruity, lively red, white, or rosé wine, preferably from the Mont Ventoux or Durance area.

FRANCE Provence-Alpes-Côte D'Azur	
Age 3 weeks	
Weight and Shape 3½oz (100g), square	
Size D. 3in (7.5cm), H. 1in (2.5cm)	
Milk Goat	
Classification Aged fresh	
Producer Fromagerie de Banon – M. Greggo	

Mont Ventoux

This goat cheese is unique for its very unusual shape. It is molded into a cone shape to represent Mount Ventoux, the famous mountain that dominates the skyline in the Luberon area. The top half of the cheese is white, representing the limestone part of the mountain, and the lower half is black (with ash), representing the forest.

TASTING NOTES This is a tender and smooth cheese with real farmland flavors and aromas.

HOW TO ENJOY Add this distinctive cheese to your cheeseboard and serve alongside a local full-bodied red wine of Vaucluse, such as a Gigondas or Mont Ventoux.

FRANCE Provence-Alpes-Côte D'Azur	
Age 10 days	
Weight and Shape 1oz (30g), cone	
Size Various	
Milk Goat	
Classification Aged fresh	
Producer Various	

Nîmois

An interesting addition to a cheeseboard, this newly developed goat cheese is washed with the local red wine of Costières de Nîmes as part of the production process, giving the rind a distinctive dark red color.

TASTING NOTES Nîmois has a pronounced and powerful flavor. Because of this, it should be eaten on its own, without any accompaniments.

HOW TO ENJOY Best enjoyed on its own with a red wine of Costières de Nîmes or Pic St. Loup.

FRANCE Languedoc-Roussillon	
Age 3 weeks	
Weight and Shape 1¾oz (50g), round	
Size D. 2in (5cm), H. 2in (5cm)	
Milk Goat	
Classification Aged fresh	
Producer Various	

Persillé des Aravis

The name comes from the irregular dark green veining that looks like parsley, or *persille* in French. This goat's-milk cheese is produced in the Aravis Valley in the Haute-Savoie. Two similar cheeses are made in nearby valleys: Persillé des Grand-Bornand and Persillé des Thônes.

TASTING NOTES It has a very savory and sharp, spicy flavor with a strong aftertaste. It has a texture similar to aged Cheddar and is best when made in summer and fall.

HOW TO ENJOY Good with all full-bodied red wines, such as Mondeuse, Beaujolais-Village, and Chinon.

FRANCE Rhône-Alpes	
Age 2 months	
Weight and Shape 2¼lb (1kg), cylinder	
Size D. 4in (10cm), H. 6in (15cm)	
Milk Goat	
Classification Hard	
Producer Various	

Tomme de Bargkass

Tomme de Bargkass comes from the Vosges mountains in Lorraine; *Barg* means mountain and *kass* means cheese in the local dialect. It is here that farmers also produce Munster cheese (see p70).

TASTING NOTES The paste is soft, elastic and has a few holes. It gives off a light, soft aroma and has a flavor of hazelnut with a slightly acidic aftertaste.

HOW TO ENJOY Locals often eat this cheese with black sourdough bread. Team it with a Bourgogne, such as Pommard, or a Rhône wine, such as Châteauneuf-du-pape.

FRANCE Vosges, Lorraine	
Age 6 months	
Weight and Shape 3lb (1.4kg), round	
Size D. 12in (30cm), H. 2½in (6cm)	
Milk Cow	
Classification Hard	
Producer M. Minoux	

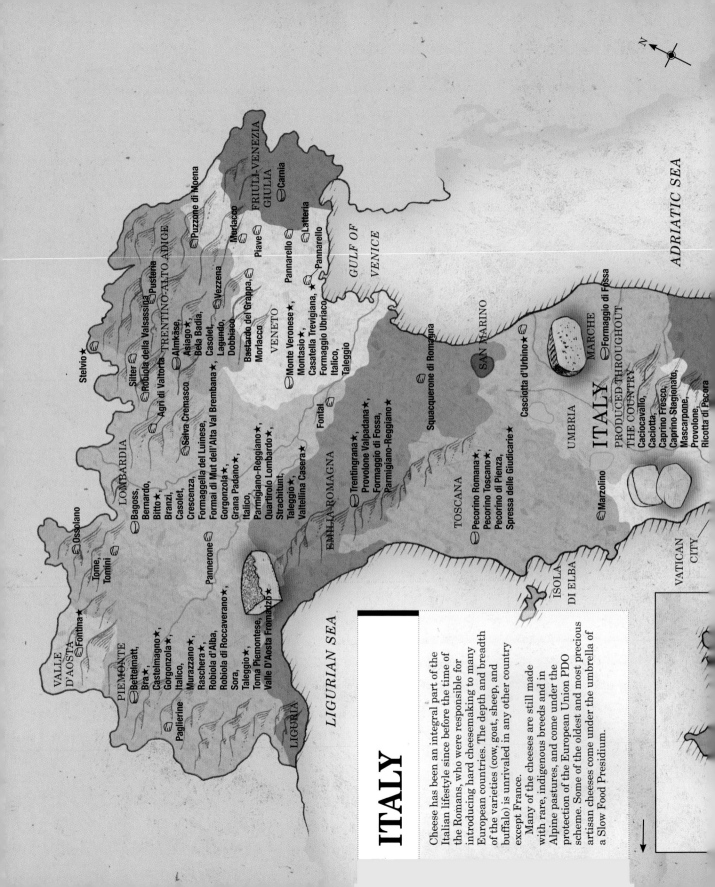

ITALY

Cheese has been an integral part of the Italian lifestyle since before the time of the Romans, who were responsible for introducing hard cheesemaking to many European countries. The depth and breadth of the varieties (cow, goat, sheep, and buffalo) is unrivaled in any other country except France.

Many of the cheeses are still made with rare, indigenous breeds and in Alpine pastures, and come under the protection of the European Union PDO scheme. Some of the oldest and most precious artisan cheeses come under the umbrella of a Slow Food Presidium.

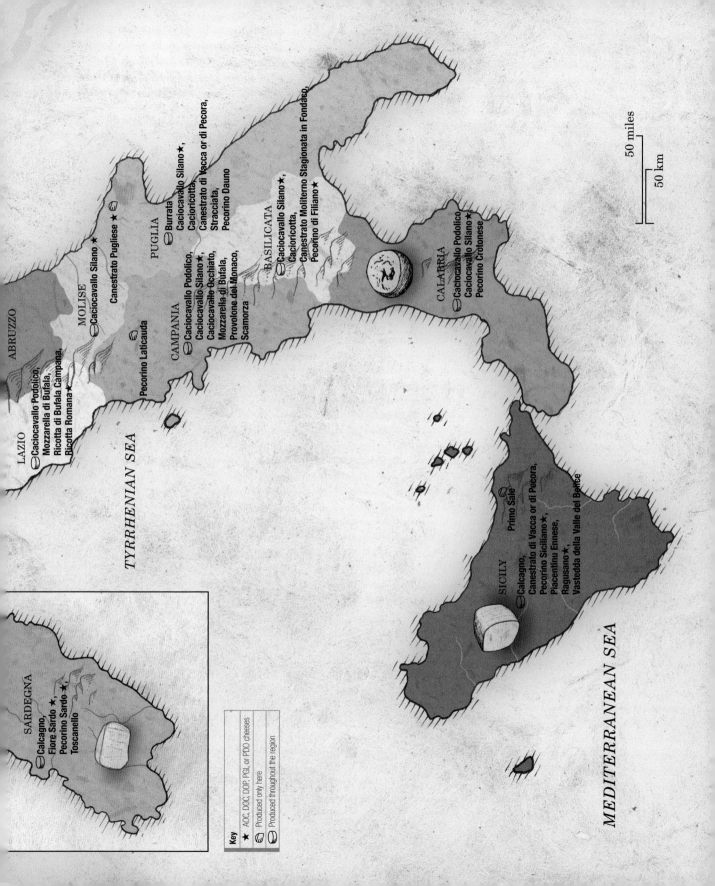

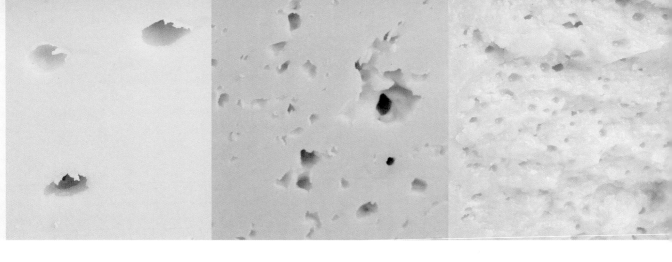

104

Almkäse

Deriving its name from the German *Alm,* meaning "Alpine pasture," this part full-cream, part-skim raw milk cheese is one of the oldest in Bolzano. The cheeses are turned, scraped, and brushed every day for three months until they are an ivory-white to deep straw-yellow and dotted with small holes or "eyes."

TASTING NOTES Firm with sweet rather than sharp high notes, it has a floral aroma reminiscent of Alpine meadows.

HOW TO ENJOY It grates and melts well. Wrap in thin slices of sautéed eggplant and serve with olive bread and a white Schiava Grigia.

ITALY Trentino-Alto Adige		
Age 6–8 months		
Weight and Shape 15lb 7oz–31lb (7–14kg), flat wheel		
Size D. 14–15½in (35–40cm), H. 3–4in (8–10cm)		
Milk Cow		
Classification Hard		
Producer Various		

Asiago PDO

Made only within officially recognized production areas, this cheese takes its name from the homonym plateau. It is available as two types: Asiago Pressato is made in low-lying pastures and is semi-soft with irregular-shaped holes; Asiago d'Allevo is hard and made using milk from mountain pastures.

TASTING NOTES Springy and moist in texture, Asiago Pressato is aromatic, fairly salty, and slightly piquant. Asiago d'Allevo is drier, crumbly to the bite, and has a savory, spiced flavor.

HOW TO ENJOY Perfect with a Cabernet Sauvignon, from Friuli's Colli Orientali, or Torcolato Maculan.

ITALY Trentino-Alto Adige		
Age 20–40 days		
Weight and Shape 24¼–33lb (11–15kg), wheel		
Size D. 12–16in (30–40cm), H. 4½–6in (11–15cm)		
Milk Cow		
Classification Semi-soft		
Producer Various		

Bagòss

Bagòss is the local nickname for the residents of Bagolino. Made from raw milk from cattle grazing on mountain pastures, this hard cheese must be matured for at least 12 months, but on average is at least 24–36 months old. During aging, the cheeses are brushed with raw linseed oil, which gives the rind an ocher brown color.

TASTING NOTES Has strong aromas of saffron, then of floral pastures and hay. Early fresh green notes combine with a slight almond taste and a tangy finish.

HOW TO ENJOY Use as a table cheese, or grate over pasta. Try with a robust red wine like Amarone.

ITALY Lombardia		
Age Over 12 months		
Weight and Shape 30–48½lb (14–22kg), flat wheel		
Size D. 16–20in (40–50cm), H. 5–5⅛in (12–14cm)		
Milk Cow		
Classification Hard		
Producer Various		

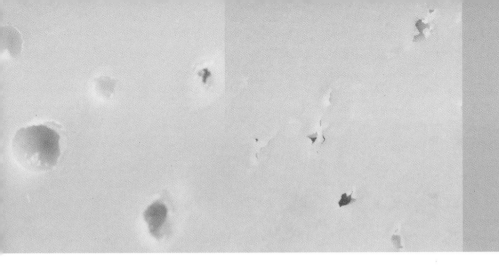

Bastardo del Grappa

Made in mountain dairy huts around Grappa during the summer months, this cheese gained the name "Bastardo" from being made using a mix of sheep's, goat's, and cow's milk, depending on availability. Now purely a raw cow's milk cheese, it has a dark mustard-yellow rind with burnt brown blotches.

TASTING NOTES The light, straw-colored paste darkens with age and has small eyes throughout. It has a floral aroma and a full flavor with notes of wild herbs, which intensifies as it matures.

HOW TO ENJOY Eat with semolina or potato gnocchi, along with a Cabernet Franc or a sparkling Chardonnay.

ITALY Veneto	
Age 6 months	
Weight and Shape 5½–11lb (2.5–5kg), wheel	
Size D. 10–12in (25–30cm), H. ¾–3in (2–8cm)	
Milk Cow or goat	
Classification Semi-soft or hard	
Producer Various	

Bettelmatt

Legend has it that the flavor of this red-rinded cheese comes from a herb known as *mottolina*, found only in the high pastures of Val d'Ossola, but it could be just the quality of grazing that creates this unique taste. Bettelmatt is made in summer from the raw milk of Brawn Mountain cattle, using similar methods to those for making Gruyère.

TASTING NOTES Sometimes dotted with irregular medium eyes, it has a strong, buttery, herby aroma and tastes sweet yet salty with an earthy finish.

HOW TO ENJOY Used traditionally as a table cheese; it is good with polenta and for filling for *agnolotti* pasta.

ITALY Piedmonte	
Age 2–6 months	
Weight and Shape 17lb 10oz–22lb (8–10kg), flat wheel	
Size D. 18–21½in (45–55cm), H. 3in (8cm)	
Milk Cow	
Classification Semi-soft and hard	
Producer Various	

Bitto PDO

Named after the fast-flowing River Bitto, this cheese is made in the summer months in mountain dairies or *calecc*—unroofed stone refuges that are covered with canvas when in use. This is where the maturation process begins, but it is then completed in the valley cheese stores and can last for ten years.

TASTING NOTES When young, this cheese has a mild fragrant flavor that develops into unmistakably nutty notes and caramel hints after at least six months maturation.

HOW TO ENJOY Use in local dishes such as *pizzoccheri*, a flat pasta, and *sciatt*, small buckwheat fritters.

ITALY Lombardia	
Age 70 days–1 year	
Weight and Shape 17lb 10oz (8–25kg), flat wheel with concave size	
Size D. 20in (50cm), H. 3½–5in (9–12cm)	
Milk Cow and goat	
Classification Hard	
Producer Various	

CANESTRATO MOLITERNO
The curd is pressed by hand into rush
baskets, then removed and rubbed with
olive oil and sometimes vinegar to create
this waxy, smooth rind with a dusting of
brown and white molds. (See p112).

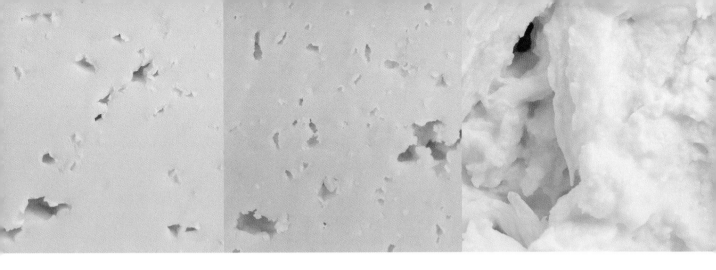

Bra PDO

Named after the town of Bra, famous for the cheese festival held by the Slow Food organization, Generic Bra is made from cow's milk from lowland dairies and can contain small amounts of ewe's or goat's milk. Bra Tenero is a semi-soft cheese aged for 45–60 days; Bra Duro is ripened for at least 180 days.

TASTING NOTES Bra Tenero is soft, mild, and aromatic, while Bra Duro has a delicious tang that can almost sting the tongue with its intensity.

HOW TO ENJOY Eat Bra Tenero as a main dish, or use Bra Duro grated over pasta. Serve with red Bricco dell'Uccellone or white Gavi dei Gavi.

ITALY Piemonte		
Age 1–2 months (tenero); 6–9 months (duro)		
Weight and Shape 11–19lb 13oz (5–9 kg), flat wheel		
Size D. 12–16in (30–40cm), H. 3–3½in (7–9cm)		
Milk Cow		
Classification Semi-soft		
Producer Various		

Branzi

Originating in the village of the same name, Branzi cheese uses the milk of Brawn Mountain cattle. In the past it was made only in Alpine huts in the summer, but now it is produced all year. A variety of *formai de mut,* it has a pale yellow paste laced with holes and encased in a yellow-brown crust.

TASTING NOTES When young, the sweet and milky flavor has a slight aroma of grass. When aged, it can be grated and tastes stronger, tangy, and nutty.

HOW TO ENJOY Used in *polenta taragna* (polenta with cheese and butter), and with gnocchi made from chestnut flour. Serve with Valcalepio Rosso.

ITALY Lombardia		
Age 1–7 months		
Weight and Shape 11–33lb (5–15kg), flat wheel		
Size D. 16–18in (40–45cm), H. 3½in (9cm)		
Milk Cow		
Classification Hard		
Producer Various		

Burrata

A *pasta filata* cheese very similar to mozzarella, differing only in the stretching technique employed to produce it and the fact that Burrata contains a filling made with the cream from the whey. *Burrata* means "buttered" in Italian, and this cheese certainly lives up to its name.

TASTING NOTES Eat it fresh at room temperature. It has a full buttery aroma and tastes mild and sweet with the consistency of very soft mozzarella.

HOW TO ENJOY Toss with avocado, tomatoes, and olive oil, or eat with a salty cured ham. Serve with Primitivo di Manduria or Moscato di Trani.

ITALY Puglia		
Age 24–48 hours		
Weight and Shape 9oz–1lb 2oz (250–500g), sphere		
Size D. 3–5in (7–12cm)		
Milk Cow		
Classification Fresh		
Producer Various		

Caciocavallo

This semi-soft cheese is an archetype of the Italian cheese-making technology *pasta filata,* or "stretched-curd." Mainly made in southern Italy, there are many regional variations; it is produced using ewe's, goat's, cow's, or buffalo milk, and it can also be smoked.

TASTING NOTES During the first 30 days of maturation it is sweet, milky, and buttery; after 90 days it becomes pungent with oily and gamey flavors.

HOW TO ENJOY Serve with rustic bread and a sparkling white wine.

ITALY All over		
Age From a few days until one year		
Weight and Shape 2¼–22lb (1–10kg), sphere		
Size Various. D. 4½–8in (11–20cm), H. 9in (23cm) (pictured)		
Milk Cow		
Classification Semi-soft or hard		
Producer Various		

Caciocavallo Occhiato

This classic *pasta filata* cheese has plenty of round eyes, as the *occhio* in the name suggests. It is produced using milk of cattle that naturally graze on the mountain pastures in Campania.

TASTING NOTES Typically generous with propionic aroma, it is elastic when young, and friable when aged. More sweet than tangy, citrusy, and floral hints are also present.

HOW TO ENJOY Eat on its own, in a salad, or with vegetables. Pair it with Aglianico Sorrentino wine or, for those who like sweet tastes, try a Lacryma Christi del Vesuvio.

ITALY Campania		
Age 3–6 months		
Weight and Shape 17lb 10oz–26½lb (8–12kg), oval or sphere		
Size Various. D. 12in (30cm), H. 13in (33cm) (pictured)		
Milk Cow		
Classification Semi-soft or hard		
Producer Various		

Caciocavallo Podolico

Semi-hard when young, this full-fat cheese hardens after four months of aging. It is a typical Caciocavallo cheese, made using the milk of Podolian cattle that graze on Appenine mountain pastures.

TASTING NOTES Extremely aromatic with vegetal cues of mountain herbs and flowers. Basically sweet, it has a very high solubility with persistent nutty and spicy hints.

HOW TO ENJOY When the cheese is well aged, simply serve dressed with olive oil. It is great alongside Aglianico del Volture di Paternoster or Moscato di Saracena.

ITALY Lazio, Campania, and Calabria		
Age 1 month–1 year		
Weight and Shape 4½–6½lb (2–3kg), oval or sphere		
Size Various. D. 6in (15cm) (pictured)		
Milk Cow		
Classification Hard		
Producer Various		

Caciocavallo Silano PDO

Originating in the Middle Ages, this semi-soft cow's milk cheese was already well known during the 14th century and continues to be popular now. It appears light-straw colored when young and brown when aged.

TASTING NOTES A typical stirred paste with small and sparse eyes. Its taste is aromatic and sharply sweet with milky and buttery cues when young, becoming pungent as it matures.

HOW TO ENJOY Traditionally used as a main dish or in stuffed pasta. It's happily balanced with Greco Bianco di Melissa or Rosato di Scavigna.

ITALY Basilicata, Calabria, Campania, Molise, and Puglia	
Age 1 month–1 year	
Weight and Shape 2¼–5½lb (1–2.5kg), various shapes (oval pictured)	
Size Various. D. 7½in (19cm), H. 3½in (9cm) (pictured)	
Milk Cow	
Classification Semi-soft	
Producer Various	

Caciotta

One of the most popular Italian cheeses, Caciotta is made throughout the country, using every type of milk—often mixed. Sold as a fresh cheese or semi-soft, it could also be ripened to become hard.

TASTING NOTES Usually mild and sweet with a milky and creamy aroma when made using cow's milk; is intense, buttery, and mushroomy when made using sheep's or goat's milk, or a mix.

HOW TO ENJOY Eat as a snack. Unites nicely with Italian Spumante Classico, or pair with a young red wine like Rosso di Franciacorta, or, when available, Vino Novello.

ITALY All over	
Age From a few days to 2–3 months	
Weight and Shape 2¼lb (1kg), cylinder	
Size D. 8in (20cm), H. 2in (5cm)	
Milk All	
Classification Various	
Producer Various	

Calcagno

This traditional sheep's cheese is made by simply adding black peppercorns to fresh curd, draining the cheeses in hand-woven rush baskets and, once salted, aging them for at least three months. The baskets leave behind a pattern on the brownish-yellow rind.

TASTING NOTES Calcagno becomes grainy with age, and as it matures the taste becomes saltier, pungent, and spicy, and the sheep flavor more distinct.

HOW TO ENJOY Serve a younger cheese with roasted peppers and use an older cheese for grating over pasta or vegetable dishes. Team with Torgiano Rosso, or a late-harvested white wine.

ITALY Sardegna and Sicilia	
Age 3–10 months	
Weight and Shape 22lb–33lb (10–15kg), cylinder	
Size D. 10–15½in (26–40cm), H. 6in (16cm)	
Milk Ewe	
Classification Flavor-added	
Producer Various	

Gorgonzola PDO

Everything about Gorgonzola is sexy—its rustic yet elegant appearance, its voluptuous, melt-in-the-mouth texture, its musky aroma, and its sweet, spicy tang. Even its name is seductive. It is thought to be the first blue cheese, and its origin is steeped in folklore and legend.

The most charming version is the story of a careless youth who, distracted by his young love, left a bundle of moist curd hanging overnight on a hook in a damp cellar. The following day, hoping to disguise his mistake, he added the curd to the morning batch. Weeks later, he found the cheese has a greenish mold through the center. Curious, he sampled it and found it so good he repeated the procedure and the rest, as they say, is history.

Gorgonzola's first name was Stracchino di Gorgonzola, derived from the Italian word *stracca* meaning "tired", as it was made in the autumn when the exhausted cows returned from the mountain pastures to the watery meadows of Lombardia where Gorgonzola was the main trading town for centuries.

Today, Gorgonzola is made under strict regulations by around 40 small family dairies and large factories. A few artisan cheesemakers still use unpasteurized milk and follow the traditional "two day curd" method, allowing the curd to become naturally inoculated by mold, then mixing it with the curd from the morning milking. Since the mid 1900s, however, most Gorgonzola has been made in factories using pasteurized milk and the "one day curd" method with the blue mold added to the milk, producing more even blueing than the traditional cheese, though not as strong a flavor.

Gorgonzola is made in large drums and, when ripe, the sides bulge like a riverbank ready to collapse. Around the edges, it can be slightly grayish—but it should never brown, as this indicates excessive drying and poor handling.

TASTING NOTES The uneven and erratically spread streaks and patches of blue mold impart a sharp, spicy flavor to the rich, creamy cheese. It tastes creamier and sweeter than Stilton, but is similar in strength, whereas Roquefort is stronger, sharper, and slightly more salty.

HOW TO ENJOY Dollop it onto thick wedges of walnut loaf or stir it into steaming pasta with a little cream or mascarpone and toasted pinenuts. Toss into salads with sun-dried tomatoes, kidney beans, and a honey dressing, or add to sauces and dips. It is exquisite drizzled with a little honey, and with most sweet wines including Marsala, a robust red, and even a rosé.

The molds, *each bears the number of the individual producer, which is imprinted on the cheese.*

ITALY Lombardia and Piedmont
Age 3–6 months
Weight and Shape 13lb 4oz–28½lb (6–13kg) , drum
Size D. 10–12in (25–30cm), H. 6–8in (15–20cm)
Milk Cow
Classification Blue
Producer Various

A CLOSER LOOK

In 1970, a Consortium was created to ensure Gorgonzola was only made with milk from designated areas, by approved producers. Only those that meet the tough standards are stamped with the Consortium "G".

WOODEN BELT Once firm, the cheese is removed from the mold, rubbed and rolled in salt or in brine baths to save labor costs, then encased in a wide belt made of thin, slatted, wood, and left to mature.

MATURING Traditionally ripened in *casere*, "natural caves", ideal conditions for natural mold formation, now they are ripened in purpose-built store rooms to ensure they attain the consistency and high quality demanded by today's market.

PIERCING AND GRADING At four weeks, each cheese is pierced with thick needles, encouraging the spread of the blue-green mold. This is carried out in a place called purgatory, where the cheese is kept at around 425°F (220°C) and up to 95 percent humidity. A grader takes a sample of cheese to check for the even distribution of the blue mold.

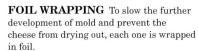

FOIL WRAPPING To slow the further development of mold and prevent the cheese from drying out, each one is wrapped in foil.

The ivory white interior is paler than other blue vein cheeses and almost translucent

Once exposed to air, the blue mold grows along the tunnels made by the piercing rods.

Drum, quarter

The sticky white rind is overlaid with a medley of orange, brown, red, gray, and blue molds.

Canestrato Moliterno

Clotted using kid goat's rennet, this hard cheese is molded and drained in rush baskets, then ripened in stores called *fondachi*, located a minimum of ½ mile (700m) above sea level.

TASTING NOTES *Primitivo* is less than six months old and is sweet and salty; *stagionato,* aged for six to 12 months, is pungent and salty. *Extra*, aged over 12 months, is very hard, brittle, pungent, and salty.

HOW TO ENJOY Delicious with slices of apple when young, while more mature cheeses are ideal for grating. Perfect with a glass of Aglianico del Volture Riserva.

ITALY Basilicata	
Age 2–18 months	
Weight and Shape 4½–6lb (2–3kg), cylinder	
Size D. 8–10in (20–25cm), H. 4–6in (10–15cm)	
Milk Ewe or goat	
Classification Hard	
Producer Various	

Canestrato Pugliese PDO

Like all Canestrato cheeses, this ewe's milk cheese derives its name from the reed baskets used to drain it. The rind is rubbed with olive oil and wine vinegar as the cheese matures to give a golden color.

TASTING NOTES The firm and straw-colored paste has small eyes. Its milky taste has sweet notes, becoming salty and pungent with a hint of roast lamb.

HOW TO ENJOY Fabulous grated on pasta, in regional artichoke dishes, or over stuffed lamb and veal cutlets. Pair with a red like Nero d'Avola or a sweet Primitivo di Manduria Dolce Naturale.

ITALY Corate, Puglia	
Age 2–12 months	
Weight and Shape 15½lb (7kg), cylinder	
Size D. 10in (25cm), H. 4in (10cm)	
Milk Ewe	
Classification Hard	
Producer Caseificio Pugliese	

Caprino Fresco

The name of this cheese concisely describes it: *capra* means goat and *fresco* means fresh. Caprino Fresco is produced by the ancient method of allowing the curd to coagulate over 24 hours using only a small quantity of rennet. At least ten varieties of this cheese are produced all over Italy.

TASTING NOTES This crumbly cheese is fragrant with a delicate, lemony fresh acidity, and it has a nutty, slightly goaty aroma.

HOW TO ENJOY Typically it is served with bread or crackers, but it can be used for stuffing pasta or bresaola. Pair it with a glass of Franciacorta Millesimato.

ITALY All over	
Age 2–5 days	
Weight and Shape 1¾–5½oz (50–150g), small logs	
Size D. 1–2in (3–5cm), L. 4–6in (10–15cm)	
Milk Goat	
Classification Fresh	
Producer Various	

Caprino Stagionato

Caprino Stagionato is made throughout Italy, particularly in areas where the grazing is poor because, unlike cows and ewes, goats are browsers and are happy to feed on rough, rocky pastures.

TASTING NOTES It has a fine dusting of white mold overlaid with grey and blue. The paste is ivory and tastes better as it matures, when it develops a nutty and more distinctive goaty aroma and taste.

HOW TO ENJOY Caprino Stagionato is perfect as a table cheese and delicious grated over pasta dishes. Team it with a glass of Merlot di Torre Rosazza.

ITALY All over	
Age 1–6 months	
Weight and Shape 4½–6lb (2–3kg), cylinder	
Size D. 8–10in (20–25cm), H. 4–6in (10–15cm)	
Milk Goat	
Classification Hard	
Producer Various	

Carnia

This hard cheese is made from the milk of the Bruna Alpina cattle that graze the Alps. The best ones are made with raw milk and aged for over a year, but to ensure a regular income, most producers sell it at around six months.

TASTING NOTES Sweet when young and becoming more aromatic as it matures. However, as the pastures change, so does the aroma and flavor of the cheese; at times herbaceous or fruity.

HOW TO ENJOY Carnia is typically used in *frico*, a local omelet-type dish, and is best served with a local wine like Refosco Isonzo del Friuli or Verduzzo Friulano Passito.

ITALY Friuli-Venezia Giulia	
Age 6–12 months or more	
Weight and Shape 17lb 10oz (8kg), wheel	
Size D. 12in (30cm), H. 2½in (6cm)	
Milk Cow	
Classification Hard	
Producer Various	

Casatella Trevigiana

The inclusion of *casa*, meaning home, in this fresh cheese's name hints at its original use. It was produced in homes for the family's consumption rather than for sale. Now, though, it is made commercially throughout the area in small cooperatives.

TASTING NOTES A soft, tender, shiny creamy cheese with milky and buttery notes and a melt-in-the-mouth texture. Small irregular eyes can be present.

HOW TO ENJOY Traditionally used to stuff Bresaola rosettes as part of a warm winter Italian dish. Casatella goes well with Prosecco Millesimato Bisol, a sparkling wine.

ITALY Veneto	
Age 5–10 days	
Weight and Shape 14oz–5lb (400g–2.2kg), wheel	
Size D. 3–9in (8–22cm), H. 1½–2½in (4–6cm)	
Milk Cow	
Classification Fresh	
Producer Various	

RICOTTA AFFUMICATA A week after pressing, the cheeses are smoked over green conifer wood fires. The outside turns a warm nut brown, and the inside absorbs the smoky aromas of the fire, but not the color. (*See p135.*)

Casciotta d'Urbino PDO

This historic cheese dates back to 1545, when it was mentioned in the writings of the Montefeltro Duke; it is also said to have been a favorite of Michelangelo. A semi-soft cheese, Casciotta is made from a combination of ewe's milk and some cow's milk.

TASTING NOTES A white or slightly yellow cheese with an elastic texture and an aroma and taste that is sweet with vegetal notes.

HOW TO ENJOY Traditionally a table cheese, it complements Verdicchio dei Castelli di Jesi Casal Serra or Malvasia delle Lipari.

ITALY Montemaggiore al Matauro, Marche	
Age 20–30 days	
Weight and Shape 1¾–2¾lb (800g–1.2kg), small cylinder	
Size D. 5–6in (12–16cm), H. 2–3in (5–7cm)	
Milk Ewe and cow	
Classification Semi-soft	
Producer Fattorie Marchigiane Cons. Co-op	

Casolet

Produced in the Adamello mountains, Casolet, meaning "small cheese." The rind is stamped with the *rosa camuna*, an ancient drawing of a rose found in the rock carvings of Capo di Ponte.

TASTING NOTES The thin orange rind is dusted with white and gray molds. The straw-yellow paste is velvety and supple with an aroma of fermented fruits, while the sweet herbaceous flavors change with the pastures.

HOW TO ENJOY Eat with dried fig conserve along with Vendemmia Tardiva Cavit or Franciacorta Millesimato Bellavista.

ITALY Lombardia and Trentino-Alto Adige	
Age 2–12 months	
Weight and Shape 3–4¾lb (1.3–2kg), triangle	
Size D. 8–10in (20–25cm), H. 2–3in (5–8cm)	
Milk Cow	
Classification Semi-soft	
Producer Various	

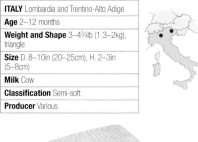

Castelmagno PDO

An ancient cheese, made from the milk of Piedmontese cows, Castelmagno was traditionally encouraged to develop some internal blueing through cracks in the rind and the fine curd. Nowadays, most is sold before the natural bluing has developed.

TASTING NOTES The crust is wrinkled, the interior is white-yellow and very friable or crumbly in the center, and it is delicate when young, becoming strong and very savory when ripe.

HOW TO ENJOY Traditionally eaten on its own and married with Barolo or used in fondues or *veloutees* (creamy cheese sauces). It is also delicious with honey.

ITALY Piemonte	
Age 2–6 months	
Weight and Shape 4½–15½lb (2–7kg), drum	
Size D. 6–10in (15–25cm), H. 5–8in (12–20cm)	
Milk Cow	
Classification Hard	
Producer Various	

Crescenza

This fresh cheese gets it name from the Latin *carsenza*, meaning "flat bread," because when it is kept in a warm place, the cheese ferments, swelling up like rising bread and bursting through its thin rind.

TASTING NOTES Crescenza is a fresh and delicate cheese with a balanced sweet taste and pleasant, lemony, milky, and creamy aroma. The paste is moist and sticky.

HOW TO ENJOY In Italy, Crescenza is sometimes used for preparing a delicate sauce with chestnuts or in puff-pastry dishes. It goes well with Pinot Nero or Valcalepio Rosso.

ITALY Lombardia	
Age 5–10 days	
Weight and Shape 4lb–4½lb (1.8–2kg), rectangle	
Size L. 6–8in (15–20cm), H. 1½–2in (4–5cm)	
Milk Cow	
Classification Fresh	
Producer Various	

Dobbiaco

Unlike most Italian cheeses, this is a rectangular or large brick-shaped cheese, so it lends itself to cutting. It is made from cow's milk in the mountain town of Dobbiaco in the attractive region of Val Pusteria.

TASTING NOTES The rind is reddish or brownish-red and slightly sticky. The paste is supple and straw-yellow with a few irregular small eyes. Fresh and lemony, it becomes sweet at the end with a buttery, vegetal, and nutty aroma.

HOW TO ENJOY Great on a cheeseboard with black rye bread and a generous aromatic wine or served with polenta.

ITALY Trentino-Alto Adige	
Age 3–5 months	
Weight and Shape 11lb (5kg), long brick	
Size L. 15½in (40cm), W. 4in (10cm), H. 4in (10cm)	
Milk Cow	
Classification Semi-soft	
Producer Latteria di Dobbiaco	

Fiore Sardo PDO

Fiore Sardo possibly dates back to the Bronze Age, and some cheeses are still made by shepherds in mountain huts over open fires, then stored in the rafters to imbue them with their smoky overtones.

TASTING NOTES The brown rind, rubbed with olive oil, has a distinctive aroma and appearance. The texture is hard and crumbly with the distinct sweet taste of ewe's milk and a long-lasting, smoky, salty, pungent finish.

HOW TO ENJOY Serve as an hors d'oeuvres with fresh fava beans, or when aged, it can be grated over numerous pasta or vegetable dishes.

ITALY Sardegna	
Age 3–6 months	
Weight and Shape 3⅓–8lb 13oz (1.5–4kg), drum	
Size D. 6–10in (15–25cm), H. 4–6in (10–15cm)	
Milk Ewe	
Classification Hard	
Producer Various	

Fontal

Fontal is a combination of two great cheeses: the famous mountain cheese Fontina, and Emmental. It is produced industrially in much of Northern Italy all year round, rather than only in summer, like Fontina.

TASTING NOTES The rind is reddish-brown while the paste is dense, straw-yellow, smooth, and slightly elastic. It is a very aromatic cheese, with milky and buttery notes and a hint of almonds.

HOW TO ENJOY Fontal melts superbly, so it is ideal in fondues or melted over vegetables, especially wild mushrooms. Pair it with Pignolo di Filiputti and Terre d'Agata di Salaparuta.

ITALY Gottolengo, Lombardia	
Age 45–60 days	
Weight and Shape 17lb 10oz–22lb (8–10kg), wheel	
Size D. 12–15½in (30–40cm), H. 3–4in (7–10cm)	
Milk Cow	
Classification Semi-soft	
Producer Various	

Fontina PDO

An exceptional cheese, Fontina is made twice a day from the milk of the Valdostana cows that graze at the foot of Mount Blanc. Dating back to the Middle Ages, this semi-soft cheese is thought to take its name from a local family, "Fontin."

TASTING NOTES The washed rind is reddish and sticky while the supple paste has small holes and a mild, nutty flavor that hints of the herbaceous pastures on which the cows graze.

HOW TO ENJOY Famously used in a *fonduta*, a dish in which the cheese is whipped with eggs and cream. It goes well with full-flavored red wines.

ITALY Saint-Cristophe, Valle D'Aosta	
Age 3 months	
Weight and Shape 17lb 10oz–26½lb (8–12kg), flat wheel	
Size D. 12–15½in (30–40cm), H. 3–4in (7–10cm)	
Milk Cow	
Classification Semi-soft	
Producer Various	

Formaggella del Luinese

This cheese is produced from goats that graze on Alpine pastures but, unlike most goat cheeses, it is made using fresh milk that is held in vats for around 30 hours at 39°F (4°C) before being coagulated. The curd is then cut very small to give it a soft, compact texture.

TASTING NOTES The rind is wrinkled and white; the paste moist and a little friable. It has a great goaty aroma, a mixture of herbs and goat's fleece, and tastes mainly sweet.

HOW TO ENJOY A superior cheese, it is excellent with Cabernet Sauvignon di Walch or Moscato Strevi Passito.

ITALY Lombardia	
Age 20–30 days	
Weight and Shape 1¾–2lb (700–900g), flat cylinder	
Size D. 5–6in (13–15cm), H. 3–5in (8–12cm)	
Milk Goat	
Classification Aged fresh	
Producer Various	

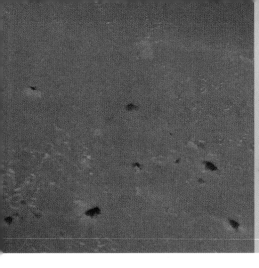
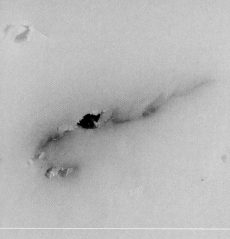
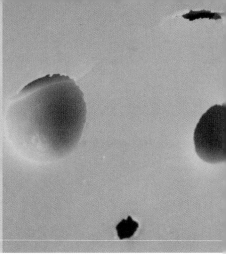

Formaggio di Fossa

Fossa, or "hole," refers to the technique by which cheeses are stored in holes carved into the walls of caves in Sagliano, which are then sealed with chalk paste to ensure a constant temperature as the cheeses ripen.

TASTING NOTES Covered in green, yellowish, and white mold, the taste is very variable, but typically it has a pungent smell and a sharp bitterish taste. It is an unforgettable cheese!

HOW TO ENJOY Grate over regional pasta, such as passatelli or tortelloni, and minestrone. Impressive when served with Cagnina di Romagna, or even better with Albana Passito.

ITALY Emilia Romagna and Marche	
Age 3–4 months	
Weight and Shape Various, Various	
Size Various	
Milk Ewe, cow, or both	
Classification Semi-soft	
Producer Various	

Formaggio Ubriaco

Ubriaco, or "drunken," refers to the technique of placing young cheeses in barrels of crushed grape skins and seeds left over from wine-making. Over two to three days, they are sprinkled with wine then left to mature and harden for a week or more.

TASTING NOTES The creamy richness of the cheese marries well with the distinct flavor and aroma of the wine, which varies according to the preferences of the cheesemaker.

HOW TO ENJOY Superb when served with a baked potato or when partnered with polenta and mushrooms. Try with an aromatic wine.

ITALY Veneto	
Age 2–12 months	
Weight and Shape 5½–11lb (2.5–5kg), drum	
Size D. 8–10in (20–25cm), H. 2–3in (5–8cm)	
Milk Cow	
Classification Flavor-added	
Producer Latteria di Soligo, La Casara di Roncolato Romano	

Formai de Mut dell'Alta Val Brembana PDO

Mut, or "mountain cheese" refers to the Alpine grazing of the cows that make this cheese. This hard cheese is produced in summer in 40 *casere*, or "mountain dairies," and in winter 2,500 wheels are made in the valley.

TASTING NOTES Beneath the thin, straw-tinged, ivory rind the paste is compact and springy with widely scattered holes. The delicate taste has an aroma of forage fragrances.

HOW TO ENJOY Use in polenta or pasta dishes. Try with Dolcetto d'Ovada.

ITALY Lombardia	
Age 7 weeks–6 months	
Weight and Shape 17lb 10oz (8kg), wheel	
Size D. 12in (30cm), H. 3in (8cm)	
Milk Cow	
Classification Hard	
Producer Various	

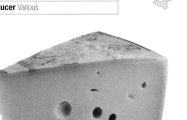

Grana Padano PDO

Created in the 12th century by the Cistercian monk of Chiaravalle Abbey, this hard cheese is now made in numerous dairies in the Padana Valley and is the biggest of all PDO cheeses.

TASTING NOTES The reddish-yellow or yellow rind is very thick while the paste is hard, white, or straw-yellow and brittle. It has a sweet fruity taste, and a fragrant, buttery aroma with hints of dried fruits.

HOW TO ENJOY It is classically used on homemade pasta and ravioli, and in hundreds of other recipes. Goes well with bold whites, reds and sparkling wines.

ITALY Lombardia		
Age 1–2 years		
Weight and Shape 53–88lb (24–40kg), drum		
Size D. 14–17½in (35–45cm), H. 1–10in (18–25cm)		
Milk Cow		
Classification Hard		
Producer Various		

Italico

Invented by Egidio Galbani in 1906 along with Bel Paese, Italico is now produced in numerous dairies in northern Italy alongside other well-known cheeses such as Bella Italia, Bella Milano, or Cacio Reale.

TASTING NOTES With a smooth, straw-yellow rind, Italico has a mild delicate paste, sometimes with small irregular eyes. Sweet, with milky and buttery notes, it melts in the mouth, having a pleasant elasticity when chewed.

HOW TO ENJOY A perfect table cheese, pair it with raw onions or celery. Serve with a sparkling white wine such as Talento Millesimato di Carpenè Malvolti.

ITALY Lombardia, Piemont, and Veneto		
Age 60 days,		
Weight and Shape 2¼–4½lb (1–2kg), small cylinder		
Size D. 6–8in (15–20cm), H. 3–5in (8–12cm)		
Milk Cow		
Classification Semi-soft		
Producer Galbani, Milano		

Latteria

This cheese was created in Latteria Turnaria, where the shareholders are the cheesemakers who all have use of the facilities and take turns to make their own individual-style cheeses.

TASTING NOTES The aroma has hints of milk and cream when the cheese is young, and flowers and hay when aged. It has a sweet and salty taste and an elastic texture until two to three months, from when it becomes compact and floury.

HOW TO ENJOY Enjoy Latteria with bread, olive oil, and a glass of red wine: perhaps the smoky I Balzini di Filiputti, or a full-bodied Amarone di Valpolicella.

ITALY Lombardia, Veneto and Friuli		
Age 1–12 months		
Weight and Shape 13–17lb 10oz (6–8kg), wheel		
Size D. 10–14in (25–35cm), H. 2–3in (5–8cm)		
Milk Cow		
Classification Semi-soft, or hard		
Producer Various		

Mozzarella di Bufala PDO

Mozzarella is made around the world and varies from lush, juicy pure white balls to yellow, rubbery blocks of cow's milk only suitable for family pizzas. But none can match Mozzarella di Bufala, made with milk from the handsome water buffalo of Campania.

The buffalo was introduced to Italy in the 7th century as a working beast to plough the marshes south of Naples, but as the Roman Empire disintegrated, the drainage systems and rivers silted up. The buffalo and the land were eventually abandoned as malaria became rife. It was not until the 12th century that records show cheese was made from its milk.

In the 18th century, the marshes were once again drained, malaria all but eradicated, the once wild buffalo now domesticated, and production of Mozzarella became widespread throughout Campania in southern Italy. The recipe was introduced from the Eastern Mediterranean and Middle East where you can find other stretched curd or *pasta filata* cheeses in Israel and Cyprus.

Rich in calcium, high in protein, and with a high vitamin and mineral salt content, it is highly nutritious and easily digested, plus, at 21 percent fat (270kcal per 100gm), Mozzarella is surprisingly low in fat. Protected under Italian and European law, it is strictly monitored to ensure the quality and provenance of the product. In fact, authentic Mozzarella di Bufala can only be made in seven provinces in Central-South Italy: Caserta and Salerno, and part of Benevento, Naples, Frosinone, Latina, and Rome.

ITALY Campania and Lazio		
Age From 1 day		
Weight and Shape Various		
Size Various		
Milk Water buffalo		
Classification Fresh		
Producer Various		

The water buffalo *of Campania.*

TASTING NOTES When cut, it has a grainy texture composed of many layers, like cooked chicken. Pearls of milky whey should seep out. It is very sweet and mild, like aged but not sour milk, with an earthy, mossy aroma and a taste reminiscent of new leather. Springy at first, it becomes softer, but never crinkled, slippery, or salty, and is bitter and sour only when overripe.

HOW TO ENJOY Its role is to give texture rather than taste to a dish and to trap, absorb, and intensify the juices and ingredients between its luscious layers of curd, producing some of the most memorable culinary combinations. Perfect on pizza; salads of olive oil, balsamic vinegar, sun-ripened tomatoes, and basil; Melanzane alla Parmigiana made with layers of eggplant and Mozzarella in a tomato sauce; or in a *carrozza* (carriage), sandwiched between two slices of bread, battered, and fried. When using fresh Mozzarella to top a pizza or fill a calzone, it is best to slice it and allow it to drain for several hours in a colander so that the crust doesn't become soggy.

A CLOSER LOOK

The extraordinarily versatile and irresistibly stretchy texture of Mozzarella di Bufala make it loved the world over. However, with its short shelf life and premium price, it is not readily available outside of Europe, so cow's milk alternatives are more widely available. If authentically made, their texture may be similar, but they lack the earthy, mossy, and new-leather notes of buffalo's milk.

THE CURD the freshly-made curd is allowed to ferment for a few hours before being cut into blocks then put through a mill that sheds it into small pieces. The rubbery pieces are covered with boiling water.

Whole ball

THE TEXTURE To achieve the desired texture, the rubbery curd and boiling water is stirred until the lumps turn into a smooth, plastic looking mass.

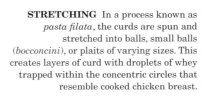

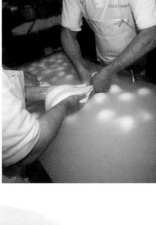

STRETCHING In a process known as *pasta filata*, the curds are spun and stretched into balls, small balls (*bocconcini*), or plaits of varying sizes. This creates layers of curd with droplets of whey trapped within the concentric circles that resemble cooked chicken breast.

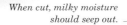

Ball, torn

When cut, milky moisture should seep out.

It must not be soft or mushy when cut, but fibrous and elastic, so that, if poked, it springs back to its original shape.

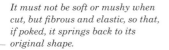

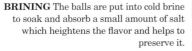

BRINING The balls are put into cold brine to soak and absorb a small amount of salt which heightens the flavor and helps to preserve it.

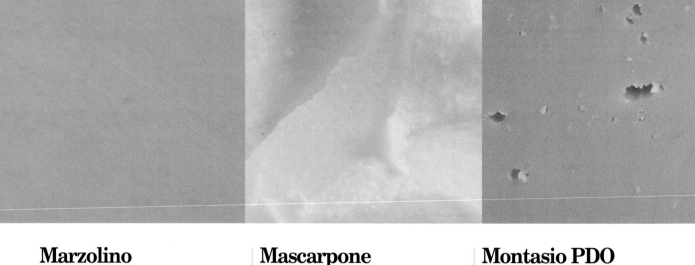

Marzolino

Marzolino means "little March," as traditionally this ewe's cheese was only produced at the beginning of lactation in March. When 14-year-old Catherine De' Medici became Queen Consort of King Henry II, in 1533, this cheese was supplied to the Court of France in order to alleviate her homesickness.

TASTING NOTES It has a straw-yellow or white paste with irregular eyes, and is full of sweet flavors and floral and vegetal hints.

HOW TO ENJOY *Bomboloni* ("doughnuts") are made with Marzolino, bread, oil, and pepper. Good with Ansonica dell'Argentario or Sagrantino Passito.

ITALY Roccalbegna Grosseto, Toscana
Age 15–90 days, best at 30 days
Weight and Shape 1lb 2oz–3lb 3oz (500g–1.5kg), oval
Size D. 6–8½in (15–22cm), H. 3½–5in (9–13cm)
Milk Ewe
Classification Semi-soft
Producer Caseificio "Il Fiorino," Roccalbegna Grosseto

Mascarpone

This fresh cheese is made by heating cream and allowing the natural acidity to gradually separate or curdle it, before draining off the whey. It dates back to the 12th century and was known to be a favorite of Napoleon.

TASTING NOTES Milky colored and velvety smooth, like rich heavy cream, it has a marked sweet and lemony taste and a full, persistent, and buttery aroma.

HOW TO ENJOY Essential for making tiramisù and Charlottes, and fantastic served with apple slices with sugar and lemon. For a wonderful combination, pair it with a classic dessert wine.

ITALY All over
Age Ready after 1 day
Weight and Shape 3½–7oz (100–200g), pots
Size No size
Milk Cow
Classification Fresh
Producer Various

Montasio PDO

Created by an unknown monk from the Moggio Abbey during the 13th century, the production of this hard cheese has been protected by the Montasio consortium since 1987 and is now also covered by the PDO scheme.

TASTING NOTES The taste depends on the age: fresh, semi-aged, or very old. It can be milky and buttery when young, and savory and aromatic when aged. Small eyes can be present.

HOW TO ENJOY Try Montasio with large ravioli and asparagus. Pair it with a glass of Sassò di Felluga, with its intense spiciness, or the sweet Picolit del Collio.

ITALY Veneto
Age 2–12 months
Weight and Shape 13lb 4oz–17lb 10lb (6–8kg), wheel
Size D. 12–14in (30–35cm), H. 3in (8cm)
Milk Cow
Classification Hard
Producer Consorzio per la Tutela del Formaggio Montasio

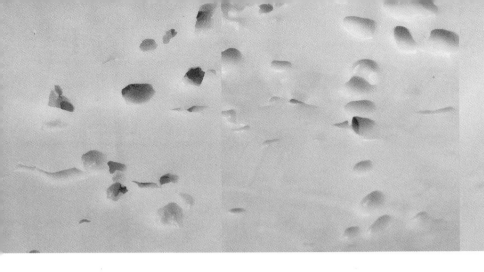

Monte Veronese PDO

This was created in 1273 when Bishop Bartholomeus della Scala authorized the Cimbri shepherds to live in the Lessinia Alps. Even today, pastures and grazing cows are the basic elements of this traditional product.

TASTING NOTES With a brown-yellow rind (sometimes treated with oil), it is compact and elastic with a sweet herbaceous taste when young, which becomes crumbly and floral in middle age, and spicy and fruity when old.

HOW TO ENJOY Great with fruit and nuts. Team with a full-bodied red, such as Recioto di Soave; when very old, pair it with a sweet Torcolato Maculan.

ITALY Veneto	
Age 2, 4 or 8 months	
Weight and Shape 13lb 4oz–19lb 3oz (6–9kg), wheel	
Size D. 10–14in (25–35cm), H. 3–4½in (7–11cm)	
Milk Cow	
Classification Hard	
Producer Various	

Morlacco

Named after the Morlocca nomadic people, who arrived in Italy as shepherds from the Balkans and the river Grappa, this prized cheese was originally made with skim milk, as the cream was sold for butter. Today it is made with semi-skim milk.

TASTING NOTES The thin rind bears the imprint of the basket mold, while the ivory paste is soft, yet crumbly, with delicate floral and fruity notes.

HOW TO ENJOY Simply serve it with pepper and olive oil, or cook with gnocchi. It is delightfully matched with Merlot dei Colli Trevigiani: a ruby red, full-bodied, tannic, and balanced wine.

ITALY Cesiomaggiore, Veneto	
Age 3–5 months, better at 3	
Weight and Shape 9lb–17lb 10oz (4–8kg), round	
Size D. 8–12in (20–30cm), H. 3–5in (7–12cm)	
Milk Cow	
Classification Semi-soft	
Producer Caseificio Montegrappa, Formaggio di Spelonca	

Murazzano PDO

One of the Robiolas family of cheeses, Murazzano was documented by Pliny the Elder during the Roman Empire. Today it is still an authentic farmhouse cheese, and is produced by many small dairies.

TASTING NOTES The rind is white-yellow, the texture smooth, fine, and elastic, and the flavor is a careful balance of sweet and acid with a creamy aroma and vegetal hints.

HOW TO ENJOY It is used in the famous Murazzano's timbale, and for preparing Bruss (a cream with spices and Grappa, or other spirits). It matches perfectly with Langhe Freisa di Cozzo, or the rich, red Verduno Pelavegra.

ITALY Piemonte	
Age 4–10 days	
Weight and Shape 10–14oz (300–400g), round	
Size D. 4–6in (10–15cm), H. 1–1½in (3–4cm)	
Milk Ewe, or ewe and cow	
Classification Semi-soft	
Producer Various	

Ossolano

This traditional cheese is made in summer in mountain huts from the milk of the Bruna Alpina cattle that graze the Ossola Alps. The secret of the cheese's flavor lies in the mottolina herbs, which only grow in that region.

TASTING NOTES The rind is brown and the paste creamy or straw-yellow, sometimes with small eyes. With a sweet taste, it has an intense, herby aroma and is slightly bitter.

HOW TO ENJOY An impressive way to serve this cheese is melted over turkey breasts. It pairs well with a red Sizzano di Zanetta, where the bouquet has a hint of violets, and Ghemme.

ITALY Corate, Piemonte		
Age 2–6 months		
Weight and Shape 11–15lb 7oz (5–7kg), wheel		
Size D. 12–16in (30–40cm), H. 2½–3in (6–8cm)		
Milk Cow		
Classification Semi-soft		
Producer Latteria Sociale Antigoriana		

Paglierine

Also called Braculina or Paglietta, this cheese takes its name from the *paglia* ("straw") on which it was traditionally placed to allow excess whey to drain off. Created in 1891 by Signor Quaglia, in San Francesco al Campo, near Turin.

TASTING NOTES The white, bloomy rind covers a soft, delicate, creamy paste that melts in the mouth and has a fresh, mushroomy aroma and taste.

HOW TO ENJOY Fill Paglierine with nuts, raisins, white pepper, and chiles, Italian-style, or serve with sesame and ham on crusty bread. Pair with a balanced red such as Dolcetto d'Asti, or an intense white Roero.

ITALY Rifreddo, Piemonte		
Age 15–20 days		
Weight and Shape 10oz–1lb 2oz (300–500g), small cylinder		
Size D. 4–6in (10–15cm), H. 1½–2in (3–4cm)		
Milk Cow		
Classification Soft white		
Producer Caseificio Oreglia		

Pannarello

One of only a handful of Italian cheeses that are made by adding extra cream to the milk before it is curdled. This technique is reflected in its name: *panna*, which means "cream."

TASTING NOTES Very delicate in the mouth and very creamy, Pannarello has a scalded milk aroma and taste, and when eaten it feels almost elastic, but pleasantly so.

HOW TO ENJOY Pannarello is perfect for fondues or paired with mixed-berry jams. Try serving it with the sparkling and fruity white Prosecco Cartizze Bisol, or the fresh and grassy white Roero Arneis.

ITALY Giavera del Montello, Veneto		
Age 1–2 days		
Weight and Shape 11–19lb 2oz (5–9kg), cylinder		
Size D. 10–12in (25–30cm), H. 6–8cm		
Milk Cow		
Classification Fresh		
Producer Latteria Montello, Latteria Modolo Dino		

Pannerone

Unlike most cheeses, Pannerone is made without salt, so the flavor is instead derived from the action of the natural bacteria. The Slow Food Organization hopes to expand production of this cow's milk cheese.

TASTING NOTES Soft, with myriad small holes and a persistent alcoholic aroma, it is at first quite mild, but the finish has a distinct almondy taste and bitter tang, which has led to its near demise.

HOW TO ENJOY A must-have cheese on an Italian Christmas Eve, stirred into steamed vegetables. Serve with aromatic Pelago Umani Ronchi, or the intense Refosco dal Peduncolo Rosso.

ITALY Pandino, Lombardia	
Age 15–20 days	
Weight and Shape 22–29lb (10–13kg), cylinder	
Size D. 11–12in (28–30cm), H. 8in (20cm)	
Milk Cow	
Classification Semi-soft	
Producer Caseificio Uberti 1896, Pandino Carena, Caselle Lurani	

Pecorino Crotonese

The art of making Pecorino Crotonese is described in a book written in 1759. This hard cheese takes its name from the city of Crotone and is made from the milk of ewe and goats that graze the mountain pastures. The brownish-yellow rind bears the imprint of the rush basket used to drain it.

TASTING NOTES The straw yellow paste is firm, friable, and sometimes has small eyes. The taste is pungent and sweet, with vegetal aromas.

HOW TO ENJOY Delicious grated on macaroni or mixed in with ground beef and eggplant. Team it with full-bodied Cirò or fruity Bivongi Bianco.

ITALY Calabria	
Age 2–12 months	
Weight and Shape 3lb 3oz–5½lb (1.5–2.5kg), cylinder	
Size D. 6–8in (15–20cm), H. 5in–6in (12–15cm)	
Milk Ewe and goat	
Classification Hard	
Producer Various	

Pecorino Dauno

Also called Canestrato Foggiano, this ewe's milk cheese is shaped using reed basket molds and coagulated with lamb's and kid goat's rennet. The curd is cut to the size of rice to create a hard, dense cheese.

TASTING NOTES Under a yellowish-brown rind, the paste is a yellowish straw color. It tastes sweet, with plenty of aromatic hints of honey and toasted seeds.

HOW TO ENJOY A typical local dish is Pecorino Dauno and *penne sparie*, (pasta with asparagus, tomatoes, eggs, black pepper, and olive oil). It goes well with Malvasia Nera di Lecce or Aleatico di Puglia Liquoroso.

ITALY Puglia	
Age 6 months	
Weight and Shape 6½–11lb (3–5kg), cylinder	
Size D. 10–12in (25–30cm), H. 6–8in (15–20cm)	
Milk Ewe	
Classification Hard	
Producer Various	

PRIMO SALE Many ancient Italian cheeses were drained in woven or plaited rush baskets, creating intricate and attractive patterns on the cheese, which also identified the producer. (See p129.)

Pecorino di Pienza

Sadly, this ancient cheese, also called *Pecorino delle crete senesi* (*creta* is a sort of clay) is now mostly made with pasteurized ewe's milk. The rind varies in color since it is rubbed during maturation with a mixture of oil and tomato or clay.

TASTING NOTES It is very sweet and has an elastic texture that becomes firm and crunchy with age. The flavor is fruity and floral, and when well matured, has hints of toasted hazelnuts.

HOW TO ENJOY Often used for filling stuffed peppers and artichokes, or grated over grilled lamb. It goes perfectly with Chianti dei Colli Senesi.

ITALY Toscana	
Age 1–4 months	
Weight and Shape 2¼lb–4½lb (1–2kg), round	
Size D. 6–8in (15–20cm), H. 2½–3in (6–8cm)	
Milk Ewe	
Classification Hard	
Producer Various	

Pecorino Romano PDO

In 100BCE, Pecorino Romano was described by Marcus Terentius Varro as essential for the rations of the Roman legions, as it provided fat, protein, and salt and could survive the rigors of soldiers on the move. Lamb's rennet is still used for coagulation.

TASTING NOTES The firm, compact paste is crumbly and crunchy and has the sweetness typical of ewe's milk, with a salty tang and hints of lanolin.

HOW TO ENJOY Grate over pasta and risottos, and serve with Carasau bread (dry bread), and a glass of Monteso di Chianti Rùfina or Vernaccia Sarda.

ITALY Toscana	
Age 5–12 months	
Weight and Shape 8–14in (20–35kg), cylinder	
Size D. 10–14in (25–35cm), H. 10–15½in (25–40cm)	
Milk Ewe	
Classification Hard	
Producer Various	

Pecorino Sardo PDO

Pecorino Sardo Dolce is made from calf's rennet, while Maturo is made using lamb's rennet. Both are made from the milk of sheep that are free grazing, rather than housed in barns.

TASTING NOTES Dolce is a young, elastic, white cheese with buttery and floral notes. Maturo is more intense, and full of pleasant pungent and salty flavors. Meat broth notes can also be present.

HOW TO ENJOY Excellent with french onion soup and lamb dishes. It is also a basic ingredient in the local dish *culingiones*, a sort of ravioli with ricotta and herbs. Pair with Dolcetto di Dogliani and Nuragus di Cagliari.

ITALY Sardegna	
Age Dolce 1–2 months, Maturo 8 months	
Weight and Shape 2¼–2¾lb (1–2.3kg), drum	
Size D. 6–8in (15–20cm), H. 3–5in (8–13cm)	
Milk Ewe	
Classification Hard	
Producer Various	

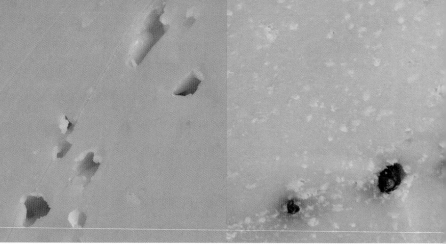

Pecorino Siciliano PDO

This cheese is documented as far back as 900BCE, when Odysseus meets the Cyclops Polyphemus in Homer's *Odyssey*. As in ancient times, this cheese is still hand-made using lamb's rennet. The brown-yellow rind is imprinted with a rush basket design.

TASTING NOTES Yellow and sometimes studded with whole black peppercorns, it is firm and friable with a pungent, salty, full, and long-lasting flavor.

HOW TO ENJOY Serve young cheeses with vegetables; aged ones with bread and olives or grated over pasta. Team with Anthìlia Donnafugata or sweet Zibibbo.

ITALY Sicilia	
Age 4–12 months	
Weight and Shape 9–26½lb (4 12kg), wheel	
Size D. 5½–15in (14–38cm), H. 4–7in (10–18cm)	
Milk Ewe	
Classification Hard	
Producer Various	

Pecorino Toscano PDO

A historic cheese, during the Roman Empire it was referred to by Pliny the Elder as *Caseus Lunensis*, and in 1832 Ignazio Malenotti, in his book *Manuale del Pecoraio*, wrote about its use of vegetable rennet from *Cynara cardunculus* flowers.

TASTING NOTES The oil-rubbed rind is yellow or brownish-yellow. The paste is yellow or white with a sweet taste and milky aroma. Aged, it becomes crumbly and savory with dry, fruity notes.

HOW TO ENJOY Eat with a lettuce or chicory salad, along with Morellino di Scansano or Moscadello di Montalcino.

ITALY Toscana	
Age 1–6 months	
Weight and Shape 2¼–7lb 11oz (1–3.5kg), drum	
Size D. 6–8in (15–22cm), H. 3–5in (7–12cm)	
Milk Ewe	
Classification Hard	
Producer Various	

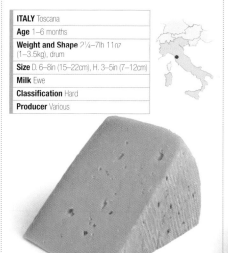

Piacentinu Ennese

First recorded in the days of the Roman Empire, this cheese is also known as Maiorchino. It is flavored with saffron and black pepper and is shaped in traditional reed baskets. The makers are currently applying for PDO status.

TASTING NOTES The outside and inside are marked yellow-orange from the addition of saffron. It tastes lightly sweet, but is also pungent and astringent with saffron and black pepper notes.

HOW TO ENJOY Fantastic for melting, it is also often used for Bucatini pasta with artichoke hearts. Match it with Etna Rosso or Cerasuolo di Vittoria.

ITALY Sicilia	
Age 2–4 months	
Weight and Shape 9lb 9oz (4.5kg), cylinder	
Size D. 8½in (21cm), H. 5½in (15cm)	
Milk Ewe	
Classification Flavor-added	
Producer Various	

ITALY

Piave

Made throughout the area around the Piave river, this hard cheese is produced in *Latteria*—small cooperatives where cheesemakers share facilities—but each makes their own individual cheeses. They are currently applying for PDO status.

TASTING NOTES The rind is straw-yellow becoming brown–yellow with age. The texture ranges from elastic to firm, compact, and friable. It has a rich, intense fruity sweetness, becoming more aromatic when aged.

HOW TO ENJOY Delicious for snacking, cheeseboards, or grating. Serve with full-bodied fruity reds like Pinot Noir.

ITALY Belluno, Veneto	
Age Fresco 1–2 months, Mezzano 2–6 months, Vecchio over 6 months	
Weight and Shape 13lb 4oz–15lb 7lb (6–7kg), wheel	
Size D. 12–13½in (30–34cm), H. 3in (8cm)	
Milk Cow	
Classification Hard	
Producer Lattebusche, Busche-Cesiomaggiore, Belluno	

Primo Sale

In Sicily this ewe's-milk cheese is also called *Picurino* ("lamb"), and it is believed to be the cheese mentioned in Homer's *Odysseus* as the one made by Cyclops in his cave.

TASTING NOTES It has a sharp acidity, but with sweet notes. The texture is crunchy, with irregular eyes that exude whey. The pungent aroma is full of herby hints.

HOW TO ENJOY Serve it on the table sliced into thin layers and dressed with olive oil, salt, black pepper, and chopped fresh mint. It is often used in fish dishes, too. It goes well with local wines, or pair it with a Pinot Grigio.

ITALY Mirto, Messina, Sicilia	
Age 7–10 days	
Weight and Shape Various, Various	
Size Various	
Milk Ewe	
Classification Fresh	
Producer Coop. Rochdale, Mirto, Messina Grifolatte, Colfiorito di Foligno, Perugia	

Provolone

A *pasta filata* cheese, like Caciocavallo, Provolone was traditionally the cheese of the poor, because just a little piece gave a lot of flavor. Originally from southern Italy, it was brought to the North at the end of the 19th century by the Margiotta and Auricchio families.

TASTING NOTES It can be mild, sweet, and milky when clotted with calf rennet, but has a stronger flavor when the milk is coagulated with kid rennet.

HOW TO ENJOY The Dolce variety can be grilled when young; use Piccante or aged in risotto. Pair with Gotturnio di Poggiarello, or Collio Rosso di Russiz.

ITALY All over	
Age 1–12 months	
Weight and Shape 4½–22lb (2–10kg),: various	
Size Various	
Milk Cow	
Classification Semi-soft	
Producer Various	

Parmigiano-Reggiano PDO

To taste a piece of Parmigiano-Reggiano, also known as Parmesan, is to taste a piece of Italian geological, culinary, and cultural history. This cheese is influenced by the soil, the grazing, the climate, and the Consortium who rigidly control its production according to a recipe barely changed since the 12th century.

The official stamp *of the Consorzio.*

In 1955, the Consorzio del Formaggio Parmigiano-Reggiano protected the name "Parmigiano-Reggiano," and lately "Parmesan," and specified it could only be made in the provinces of Modena, Parma, Reggio Emilia, and Bologna in the region of Emilia-Romagna and Mantova in Lombardia. It is also stipulated that the cows whose milk is used to produce it could be fed no silage, only fresh grass, hay, or alfalfa. As a result, the cheeses change subtly with the seasons.

Parmigiano-Reggiano is made with skim milk, which reduces the fat content; however, it is also very hard when mature, with significantly lower moisture content than Cheddar. In Italy it is sold in large rough, grainy chunks chiselled to order from the magnificent shiny drum.

ITALY Emilia-Romagna and Lombardia
Age 18–36 months
Weight and Shape 83lb (38kg), convex drum
Size D. 20in (50cm), H. 18in (45cm)
Milk Cow
Classification Hard
Producer Various

TASTING NOTES Parmigiano-Reggiano should never taste sour or dull, but fresh, fruity, and sweet like fresh pineapple; strong and rich but not overpoweringly salty; and certainly not vicious or bitter, nor should it ever smell acrid. Spring cheeses are a soft yellow with a delicate flavor and herbal scent attributed to the wildflowers on which the cows graze. Newly formed wheels of summer-made cheese exude butterfat, so they are drier and more pungent while those made in fall are noted for their higher casein content. The diet of hay in winter produces a paler cheese but is richer tasting. Brittle and crumbly, not plastic or supple, and pale yellow, a chunk will last for weeks and a little goes a very long way.

HOW TO ENJOY Superb simply eaten in chunks and probably the most versatile cheese in the world for cooking, as it dissolves when heated leaving behind a sweet, fruity, tangy flavor in virtually any savory dish you choose to make, from bread to sauces, soups, salads, and pasta.

Parmigiano-Reggiano will keep for weeks in the refrigerator but the rough surface may grow some mold, which can be scraped off. Or, if you have bought a large chunk, or use it infrequently (an unthinkable possibility), keep it in, and grate it straight from the freezer. It will quickly defrost on a hot dish. The full-bodied flavor lends itself to crisp white wines, robust reds, and even dessert wines.

A CLOSER LOOK

Parmigiano-Reggiano is made on 500 farms producing around 3.5 million cheeses per year. A staggering 160 gallons of milk are required to make one 85lb (38kg) drum, and each must reach the Consorzio's strict regulations.

DRAINING Large, copper cauldrons are used to make the cheese. After the curd is broken up, an enormous mass forms at the bottom of the cauldron, requiring two people to raise it using a very strong piece of cloth, knotted and slung around a length of wood. This huge mass is then cut into two quantities, which are left to hang for 24 hours to drain off excess whey.

BRANDING Cheeses that pass the rigorous tests are branded with "Parmigiano-Reggiano" to indicate they can be aged for another two years or more; the addition of *"Mezzano"* means they are suitable for immediate consumption. Later, some will be branded with "Extra" to indicate they have passed an additional test, or "Export" if they are of first-class quality. Those that do not meet the requirements have their brand polished off and are sold as *Grana*, which simply means "hard cheese" in Italian.

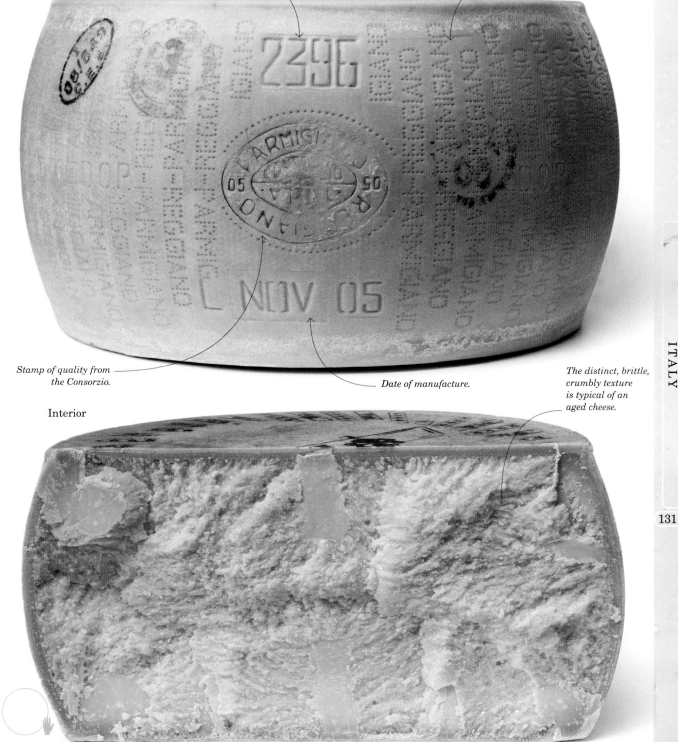

Exterior

The unique number identifies the dairy.

The stamp circles the width of the cheese, ensuring that every portion has the cheese name on it, confirming authenticity.

2396

NOV 05

Stamp of quality from the Consorzio.

Date of manufacture.

The distinct, brittle, crumbly texture is typical of an aged cheese.

Interior

Provolone del Monaco (PDO transitory list)

Legend has it that this cheese was created by a visiting monk, while the milk is linked to a race of dairy cattle, named Agerolese, that was bred by the House of Bourbon in the 18th century. It is aged in natural caves, or *tufa*, that are formed near mineral springs.

TASTING NOTES The aromatic herbs of the Lattari mountain pastures, such as thyme, oregano, and marjoram, give the milk, and cheese, a delicious flavor.

HOW TO ENJOY Simply serve it with olive oil and fresh aromatic herbs, such as wild fennel, parsley, and basil. Pair with a robust red or a sweet Marsala.

ITALY Campania	
Age 1–2 months, or 2 years in caves	
Weight and Shape 3lb 3oz–6lb 6oz (1.5–3kg), pear or sausage-shaped	
Size Various	
Milk Cow	
Classification Hard	
Producer Various	

Provolone Valpadana PDO

This *pasta filata* cheese is produced in two varieties: it is Dolce when made using calf liquid rennet, and Piccante when produced using the paste rennet from young goats.

TASTING NOTES Dolce is elastic, smooth, and velvety, and has a sweet, lightly salty, milky, and buttery flavor. Piccante is dense and compact, grainy, pungent, and salty with nutmeg hints.

HOW TO ENJOY Try it with nuts and pears. Use the Dolce variety in mild dishes; Piccante in stronger flavored ones. Serve with Freisa d'Asti, or Lambrusco Secco di Sorbara (sparkling red wine).

ITALY Emilia-Romagna	
Age 1–12 months	
Weight and Shape 2¼–220lb (1–100kg), flask, salamino, pancetta, pear, melon, mandarino	
Size Various	
Milk Cow	
Classification Semi-soft	
Producer Various	

Puzzone di Moena

Puzzone means "stinking," in reference to the very strong odor of this cheese. It is a singularly hard cheese and the rind is washed weekly with salty tepid water. Locally, it's called *Spretz Tzaorì*, meaning "savory cheese."

TASTING NOTES This strong-smelling cheese has an orange sticky rind and an elastic, white interior that melts in the mouth. The flavor is a balance of sweet, sour, and bitter tastes with a hint of citrus fruit on the finish.

HOW TO ENJOY Locals eat it with boiled potatoes, olive oil, salt, vinegar, and chopped chives. Good with Teroldego Rotaliano Rosso, or Pinot Noir.

ITALY Fassa Valley, Trentino-Alto Adige	
Age 5–10 months	
Weight and Shape 19lb 13oz (9kg), wheel	
Size D. 14–17½in (35–45cm), H. 4–10in (10–25cm)	
Milk Cow	
Classification Semi-soft	
Producer Caseificio Sociale Predazzo e Moena, Predazzo, Trento	

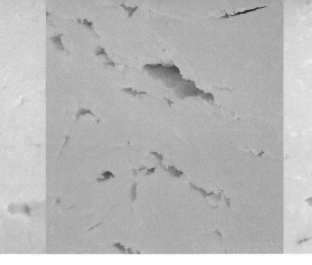

Quartirolo Lombardo PDO

Traditionally this cheese was made using milk from cattle that had grazed the sweet, aromatic hay harvested at the beginning of fall—the fourth (*quartirola*) and final cut before winter. Today it is produced all year round.

TASTING NOTES Ivory-white outside and inside, with a friable, grainy texture. Both sour and a little sweet, it is very refreshing, having an aroma of yogurt and a suggestion of wild herbs.

HOW TO ENJOY Used in the specialty dish of Quartirolo pie, or serve with celery and parsley. Try with Valbissera di san Colombano, or Malvasia delle Lipari.

ITALY Lombardia	
Age 5–10 days	
Weight and Shape 3lb 3oz–7lb 11oz (1.5–3.5kg), flat square	
Size L. 7–8½in (18–22cm), W. 1½in–3in (4–8cm), H. 1½in–3in (4–8cm)	
Milk Cow	
Classification Semi-soft	
Producer Various	

Ragusano PDO

Ragusano is a *pasta filata* cheese and the symbol of the Sicilian dairy industry. The unusual dumbbell shape was created to make it easy to transport by mule from the mountains to the villages, and gave it the name *Quattrofacce* ("four faces"). This is not a compliment, as a person with four faces is considered unreliable!

TASTING NOTES The yellow paste has small eyes and a taste that is sweet-sour-salty, pungent, and astringent, with vegetal and animal hints.

HOW TO ENJOY Marinate in olive oil and garlic, then dress with white vinegar and oregano. Match with Grecanico.

ITALY Sicilia	
Age 3–12 months	
Weight and Shape 22–35lb (10–16kg), dumbbell	
Size L. 17–21⅓in (43–55cm), W. 6–7in (15–18cm), H. 6–7in (15–18cm)	
Milk Cow	
Classification Hard	
Producer Various	

Raschera PDO

A classic mountain cheese that is quoted in the *Summa lacticiniorun* by Pantaleone da Confienza in 1477, where he describes how strips of lamb's stomach are soaked in water to remove the natural rennet.

TASTING NOTES It has a thin, leathery, brown rind dusted with white and an elastic, pale white, velvety interior with a few irregular eyes or holes. Mild and sweet-sour taste with marked vegetal notes like grass, hay, and cauliflower.

HOW TO ENJOY Very good for fondues and a great vol-au-vent filling. It tastes delicious alongside a glass of Nebiolo d'Alba, or Sciachetrà.

ITALY Piemonte	
Age 1–3 months	
Weight and Shape 11lb–17lb 10oz (5–8kg), square with rounded edges	
Size D. 12–16in (30–40cm), H. 2½–3½in (6–9cm)	
Milk Cow	
Classification Hard	
Producer Various	

ROSA CAMUNA The famous Rosa Camuna imprint is derived from an ancient drawing of a rose found in rock carvings in Capo di Ponte, Lombardy. This version is found on the cheese Rosa Camuna, a petal-shaped version of Casolet (see p115).

Ricotta Affumicata

Ricotta is typically made from whey left over from making large, hard cheeses. Once drained, the tiny white lumps of curd are lightly pressed and dry-salted, then smoked over green conifer-wood fires for about a week; when they are ready to eat. Cheese aged for a month can be grated.

TASTING NOTES The relatively high moisture content turns the outside a warm nut-brown. The texture is soft, very fine, and crumbly with a light, fresh, delicate taste and hints of pine.

HOW TO ENJOY At its best with blueberry jam, acacia honey, and rye bread. Pair it with crisp, light white wines.

ITALY Friuli-Venezia Giulia and Veneto	
Age 15–30 days	
Weight and Shape 7oz–1lb 2oz (200–500g), money bag	
Size Various	
Milk Cow	
Classification Flavor-added	
Producer Various	

Ricotta di Pecora

Ricotta means "cooked twice." First, the milk is heated for cheesemaking; then the whey is heated to make the solids left in the whey float to the surface, where they are skimmed off into rush baskets or plastic molds.

TASTING NOTES The fragile, tiny white lumps are milky with an acidic touch, and it has aromatic lemony notes due to the addition of a little sour milk before the whey is heated.

HOW TO ENJOY Use in the national dish *Tortelloni di ricotta ed erbette* and in the dessert *Cannoli siciliani*. Pair with a fresh, dry white Gavi di Gavi or a sparkling Spumante Classico Italiano.

ITALY All over	
Age 1–2 days	
Weight and Shape 1lb 2oz–6½lb (0.5–3kg), basket	
Size Various	
Milk Ewe	
Classification Fresh	
Producer Various	

Robiola d'Alba

It is believed that this fresh cheese took its name from Robbio Lomellina, an area where it has been made for centuries, or possibly from *rubeola* ("red"), the color of the bacteria that is used to develop on the rind.

TASTING NOTES Rubiola d'Alba is smooth, mild, and delicate, with a taste that is more sweet than sour. It has a creamy and buttery aroma, with vegetal and floral hints.

HOW TO ENJOY A traditional Italian dish is an omelet made with Robiola d'Alba. The cheese is best served with a dry red wine such as Alabarda Barbera d'Alba, or Dolcetto d'Alba.

ITALY Piemonte	
Age 6–7 days	
Weight and Shape 10oz–1lb 2oz (300–500g), round	
Size D. 4–5in (10–12cm), H. 1½–2in (3–4cm)	
Milk Cow, ewe, or goat	
Classification Fresh	
Producer Various	

Robiola di Roccaverano PDO

Thought to have been introduced by the Celts, who settled in Liguria around 1000CE, and named after the village of Roccaverano, this is Italy's only historic goat's milk cheese. The Roccaverano goat is now rare, replaced by high-yielding breeds.

TASTING NOTES The rind is white to pale brown with a fine gray mold, while the paste is creamy and smooth, having a balance of sweet-sour-salt with a hint of lanolin from the ewe's milk.

HOW TO ENJOY Eat as it is, or dress with olive oil and aromatic herbs. Match it with generous reds, such as Barbaresco.

ITALY Piemonte	
Age 7–10 days	
Weight and Shape 9 14oz (250–400g), round	
Size D. 4–5½in (10–14cm), H. 1½–2in (4–5cm)	
Milk Goat mixed with cow, and/or ewe	
Classification Semi-soft	
Producer Various	

Robiola della Valsassina

Like other Robiola cheese, the name comes from the Latin *ruber*, meaning "red", because of the reddish bacteria that can develop on the rind. In the past it was made with goat's milk, but now it is produced using cow's milk.

TASTING NOTES The rind is brown-red and dusted with gray-blue molds, while the paste is white or yellow with a supple, velvety texture. It is a little grainy and tastes quite sweet, with delicate mushroom and milky notes.

HOW TO ENJOY Use to fill potatoes or in an omelet with spicy local sausage. Pair it with Inferno, or Sassella Negra.

ITALY Cremeno, Lombardia	
Age 20–30 days	
Weight and Shape 14oz–1lb 2oz (400–500g); square	
Size L. 4in (10cm), W. 4in (10cm), H. 1½in (4cm)	
Milk Cow	
Classification Semi-soft	
Producer Invernizzi Daniele, Cremeno, Lecco	

Salva Cremasco (PDO transitory list)

The name Salva comes from *salvare*, "to save," and refers to the fact that the cheese was made in May from excess milk when the yield from the cows was too great, creating another vital source of income.

TASTING NOTES It has a gray, green, or reddish washed rind but is as white inside. The texture is friable and grainy, and the taste equally sweet and sour. It has a milky-yogurt aroma with citrus fruit notes.

HOW TO ENJOY Eat in risotto with porcini. Team it with Cabernet Sauvignon La Stoppa or a sweet Malvasia di Candia.

ITALY Trescore Cremasco, Lombardia	
Age 2 months, better after 1 year	
Weight and Shape 6½–9lb 9oz (3–4kg), square	
Size L. 6½–7½in (17–19cm) W. 6½–7½in (17–19cm) H. 3½–6in (9–15cm)	
Milk Cow	
Classification Semi-soft	
Producer Caseificio San Carlo, Coccaglio, Brescia Az. Agr. Eredi Carioni, Trescore Cremasco, Cremona	

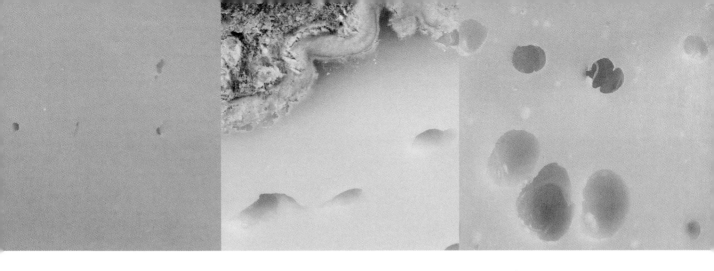

Scamorza

Also called *Mozzarella Passita* (withered mozzarella), Scamorza is a *pasta filata* that is made all year round in southern Italy. It is shaped by hand into two balls, one slightly smaller than the other. Scamorza Affumicata is a version smoked over wood or straw.

TASTING NOTES It is white to straw yellow outside, and the paste has an elastic texture, sweet taste, and milky aroma. Scamorza Affumicata is brown on the outside, brown-yellow inside, and the smoky aroma enhances the sweet taste.

HOW TO ENJOY Eat fresh or melted. Team with Pomino Rosso Frescobaldi, or Spumante Classico Italiano.

ITALY Campania	
Age 2–10 days	
Weight and Shape 7oz–1lb (200–500g), balls or large pears	
Size H. 3–5in (8–12cm)	
Milk Cow	
Classification Semi-soft (pasta Filata)	
Producer Various	

Sora

Known as the "witch's cheese," as it is said to have been first made by a "witch cheesemaker," However, the name means "shoe" in local dialect, as its flattened shape, bearing the imprint of the cloth in which it is pressed, resembles the sole of a shoe.

TASTING NOTES Soft, dense, and smooth with some eyes, it has a subtle yet complex taste of the milk used to make it, with floral, fruity, or citrus notes. It is especially good in summer.

HOW TO ENJOY Delicious rolled up in slices of ham or used in fondues and sauces. Pair with any dry, white, local Cortese wine.

ITALY Piemonte	
Age 1–3 months	
Weight and Shape 4–4½in (1.8–2kg), flat round	
Size L. 6–8in (15–20cm), W. 6–8in (15–20cm), H. 1½–2in (4–5cm)	
Milk Ewe, cow, or goat	
Classification Semi-soft	
Producer Various	

Spressa delle Giudicarie PDO

This ancient, mountain cheese was traditionally made with milk that was skimmed several times, as the farmers could sell butter for a higher price than cheese. Today it is made with partially skimmed milk.

TASTING NOTES It has a straw-yellow or brown rind and a crunchy texture when low in fat, being yellower, sweeter, and more buttery when higher in fat. The strong aroma comes from the pastures on which the cows graze.

HOW TO ENJOY Enjoy this on its own, or with barley soup. Team it with fruity red wines.

ITALY Trentino-Alto Adige	
Age 4–12 months	
Weight and Shape 17lb 10oz–22lb (8–10kg), wheel	
Size D. 12–14in (30–35cm), H. 4–4½in (10–11cm)	
Milk Cow	
Classification Hard	
Producer Various	

Taleggio PDO

Mention of Taleggio dates back to the 10th and 11th centuries, where there is evidence of it being traded. However, the name has only been used since the 20th century and refers to the Val Taleggio in the province of Bergano—an area also famous for its great cheeses such as Grana Padano (see p119) and Gorgonzola (see pp110–111)—where it is made.

The dramatic landscape *of the Alpine valley of Val Taleggio in Italy's northern Bergamo province in Lombardia.*

Taleggio was created to preserve the local milk, and the natural caves of Valsassina, in Lecco, Lombardia, provide the perfect ripening room Their deep crevices or fissures providing natural air-conditioning and soft breezes to spread the molds that grow in the rind. With increasing awareness and popularity, Taleggio is now made from both pasteurized and raw milk in many small dairies as well as larger factories where the recipe has been adapted to modern technology while still remaining true to the traditional methods essential to retain its unique character.

The best, however, are undoubtedly those made with raw milk from the summer alpine pastures and matured in the caves.

ITALY Lombardia, Piedmont, and Veneto	
Age 25–40 days	
Weight and Shape 3½–4½lb (1.7–2kg), square	
Size D. 16in (40cm) and 28in (70cm), H. 4in (10cm)	
Milk Cow	
Classification Hard	
Producer Various	

The surface of every cheese is imprinted with the distinctive four-leafed brand of the Consorzio Tutela Taleggio. The imprint is visible even if the cheese is sold in portions. It's a guarantee of quality and origin, and even the paper that wraps the cheese when it is sold must be of a certain type and carry the Taleggio brand.

TASTING NOTES The molds and yeasts of the rind speed up the breakdown of the curd, ripening it from the outside toward the center. It exudes a gentle but insistent herbaceous fragrance of fermenting fruit, hay, and mountain flowers like eating rich cream of broccoli soup. It's not necessary to remove the crust before eating or cooking with it, but it is a little gritty, so it is best to gently scrape it.

Sadly, Taleggio is often sold and eaten underripe, or before it comes to room temperature, when it is dull, rubbery, and grainy and the true character has either been killed off with excessive refrigeration or remains hidden.

HOW TO ENJOY An excellent table cheese, it can be eaten as is or used in various recipes because it melts so readily. Typically served at the end of the meal with apples, pears, or figs, or in pastas, risottos, soups, omelets, and salads as well as some types of pizza and crêpes. Best with a local wine from Franciacorta, like Terre di Franciacorta DOC, a sturdy red from Cabernet, Barbera, and Nebbiolo grapes, or the outstanding bottle-fermented sparkling wines that qualify as Franciacorta DOCG, most notable is Ca' del Bosco.

A CLOSER LOOK

Taleggio are aged by the producer or an *affineur* in the local caves or specially controlled rooms where the temperature, humidity, and native microflora play a vital role.

The enzymes produced from the microflora on the crust break down the curd by working from the outside, a process known as "mold-ripening."

The interior is soft, almost liquid, under the rind.

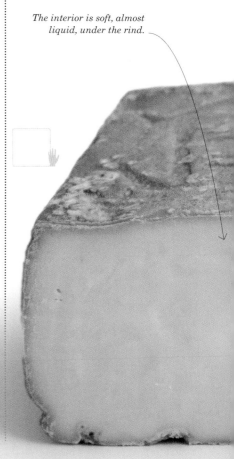

DRAINING The cheese is drained on special tables called *spersori*, and then placed in molds with rounded edges. The consortium brand along with the maker's number pressed into the soft cheese.

SALTING Each cheese is rubbed in dry salt or soaked in brine for 8–12 hours. The cheeses are put in wooden boxes each holding eight cheeses.

THE IMPRINT The four-leaf brand from the Consorzio becomes more distinct as the cheese ages and the brand is outlined by the fine gray and white molds that dust the rind.

The orangy-pink color of the rind becomes more pronounced with age.

Half square

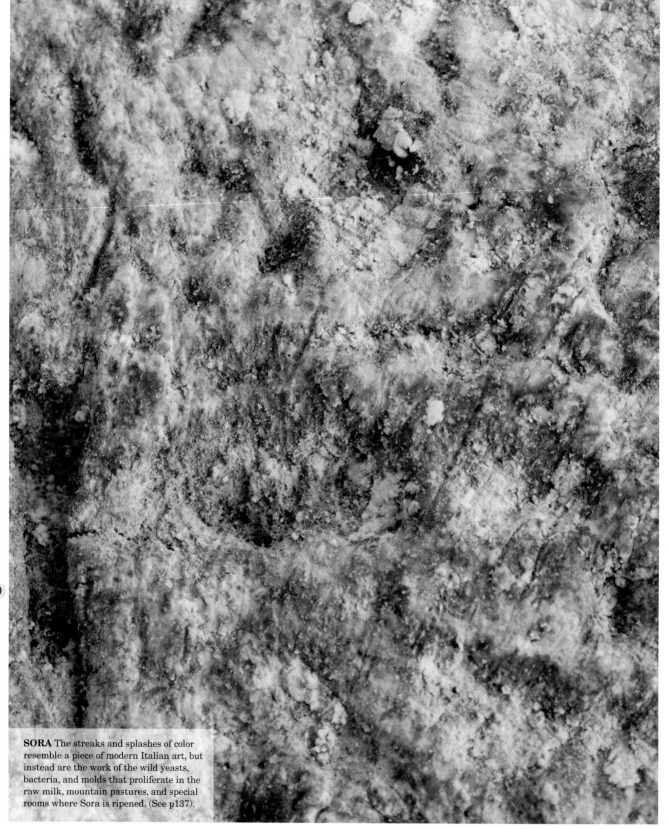

SORA The streaks and splashes of color resemble a piece of modern Italian art, but instead are the work of the wild yeasts, bacteria, and molds that proliferate in the raw milk, mountain pastures, and special rooms where Sora is ripened. (See p137).

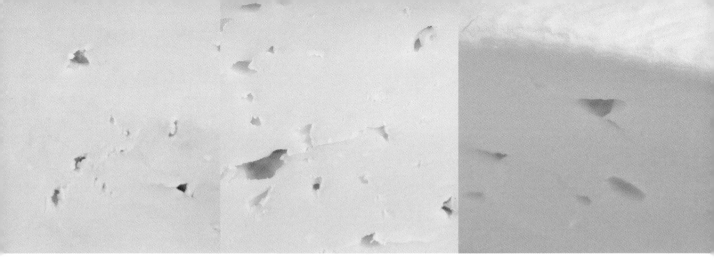

Strachìtunt

Made using the milk from Bruna Alpina cows since the late 1800s, Strachìtunt has recently been revived by a group of producers who formed a small consortium. They now produce around 50 cheeses a week.

TASTING NOTES Unlike most Italian blues, it has a dense, compact texture, very fine, erratic blueing and a dry, wrinkled crusty rind. The taste is sweet with a hint of spiced mushrooms.

HOW TO ENJOY For an authentic flavor, try this with gnocchi and polenta. Match it with an austere red, such as the velvety Valtellina Superiore, or a sweet, late-harvest white wine.

ITALY Lombardia	
Age 3–5 months	
Weight and Shape 9–11lb (4–5kg), wheel	
Size D. 9½–11in (24–28cm), H. 6–7in (15–18cm)	
Milk Cow	
Classification Blue	
Producer Arrigoni Valtaleggio	

Toma Piemontese PDO

Made since the Roman Empire, Toma could be the Italian version of the French cheese Tomme, which is made in the nearby Savoy region. It is a gourmet, versatile cheese.

TASTING NOTES Toma Piemontese has a hundred tastes, depending on its weight, ripening time, and art of the cheesemaking! It is sweet and melts easily, with vegetal and woody notes.

HOW TO ENJOY Use grated in Bruss or Pastasciutta, or melted in many recipes. Team it with a dry Magnus Langhe Chardonnay, or a light and dry sparkling red Barbera del Monferrato.

ITALY Piemonte	
Age 1–4 months	
Weight and Shape 4½oz–17lb 10oz (2–8kg), wheel	
Size D. 6–14in (15–35cm), H. 2½–5in (6–12cm)	
Milk Cow	
Classification Semi-soft	
Producer Various	

Tome and Tomini

There are 20–30 different Tome and Tomini (small cheeses each with their own unique character). One of the best-known is Tomino di Melle, made with whole milk and invented in 1889 by a cheesemaker and her nephew.

TASTING NOTES This supple, springy cheese is mild with a sweet acidity. It has a creamy taste and sometimes vegetal, nutty, or woody hints.

HOW TO ENJOY Typically used to make Bagnet: a tomato sauce with parsley, garlic, and minced anchovies. It is a perfect match for lively reds such as Rocca Giovino Dolcetto d'Alba, or the striking Diano d'Alba Superiore.

ITALY Arona, Piemonte	
Age 1–3 days, sometimes 10 days	
Weight and Shape 1¾–1lb 2oz (50–500g), mainly small cylinder	
Size D. 2½–3in (6–7cm)	
Milk Cow, or mixed	
Classification Soft white	
Producer Luigi Guffanti, 1876, Arona, Novara	

More Cheeses of Italy

The following cheeses are rare —either because they are only available seasonally or because they are produced in very remote areas. As a result, it has proved impossible to photograph them, but as they are important and interesting examples of Italian cheese, we are including them.

So, read, savor, and seek out.

Trentingrana PDO

In 1926, a dairyman from Trentino married a dairywomen from Mirandola, home of Parmigiano Reggiano, who brought to the Non Valley the art of making *grana* cheese. They created Trentingrana; today the production and sales of this cheese are controlled by the Trentingrana Cheese Consortium.

TASTING NOTES Under a thick yellow rind is a hard, brittle interior with a sweet, fruity taste and hints of cooked butter and spiced meat broth.

HOW TO ENJOY Grate over salads and pasta or vegetables. Team it with a sparkling white Ferrari Riserva or a sweet Vin Santo di Nosiola.

ITALY	Emilia-Romagna
Age	1–2 years
Weight and Shape	77lb (35kg), drum
Size	D. 14–15in (35–38cm), H. 8–8½in (20–22cm)
Milk	Cow
Classification	Hard
Producer	Various

Vezzena

During the Austro–Hungarian Empire, Vezzena was the preferred cheese of the House of Habsburg, and Franz Joseph I of Austria wanted it on his table at all times. Today, as then, the milk used comes from cows grazing around 1mi (1500m) above sea level.

TASTING NOTES A brown or brown-yellow rind protects the straw-yellow, hard inside, with its small holes. Sweet and pleasant-tasting, it has a strong aroma, mainly of green and fermented grass with a hint of toasted seeds.

HOW TO ENJOY Serve aged Vezzena on its own or with fruit. Try it with a white Nosiola Spagnolli or Refrontolo Passito.

ITALY	Lavarone, Trentino-Alto Adige
Age	4–12 months
Weight and Shape	17lb 10oz–26½lb (8–12kg), round
Size	D. 12–16in (30–40cm), H. 3½–5in (9–12cm)
Milk	Cow
Classification	Hard
Producer	Caseificio degli Altipiani del Vezzena di Lavarone

Agrì di Valtorta

This cheese is rarely found outside the small valley where it has been made for centuries. Slightly soured whey is used to curdle the milk, then after coagulation the curds are put into small ricotta molds and left to stand before being salted by hand.

TASTING NOTES Soft in texture, it has a milky aroma that recalls the aromatic herbs and mountain grasses on which the cattle have fed. It is creamy with a slightly sour, savory taste.

HOW TO ENJOY Eat on its own with vegetables or spread on fresh bread. Good with aromatic Bianco Valcalepio.

ITALY	Valtoria, Lombardia
Age	From 3 days
Weight and shape	1¾–3½oz (50–100g), squat cone
Size	D. 1½–2in (3–4cm), H. 3–4in (8–10cm)
Milk	Cow, goat
Classification	Fresh
Producer	Latteria Sociale, Monaci Sebastiano

Bela Badia

This soft cheese, with a smooth, dry crust, is a recent addition to the ranks of Italian cheeses. It takes its name from the Badia valley in which it was created and is appreciated for its high lactic bacteria content.

TASTING NOTES The light, straw-colored paste of Bela Badia becomes intense with time and has a fresh, creamy, and sweet taste. As the cheese is chewed, its flavor is enhanced by generous milky and grass hints.

HOW TO ENJOY Eat this cheese grilled and accompany it with a glass of Riesling Renano or sparkling Brut Hausmannhof Riserva.

ITALY Trentino-Alto Adige	
Age 2 months	
Weight and Shape 4½lb (2kg); flat wheel	
Size D. 3in (7cm), H. 3–4in (8–10cm)	
Milk Cow	
Classification Fresh or semi-soft	
Producer Various	

Bernardo

A classic, fresh, summer cheese made only with milk from cows grazing on high Alpine pastures. It is virtually rindless and is a reddish-yellow in color, due to a little saffron powder being added to the curds during production. It can be matured, during which time it will develop a brownish-yellow rind and an intense aromatic flavor.

TASTING NOTES The added saffron gives a floral aroma and a sweet, slightly bitter taste to this delicate cheese.

HOW TO ENJOY Eaten fresh with crusty bread, it pairs well with a red or a white Valcalepio wine.

ITALY Lombardy	
Age 10–15 days	
Weight and Shape 1lb 2oz–2¼oz (500g–1kg); flat wheel	
Size D. 6in (15cm), H. 2in (5cm)	
Milk Cow and goat	
Classification Fresh	
Producer Various	

Cacioricotta

Affectionately known in southern Italy as the "hockey puck" for its flat and round shape, this cheese comes from a strong tradition of Italian farmhouse types. It is half ricotta and half a fresh cheese, made from a combination of ewe's and goat's milk.

TASTING NOTES It has a very mild aroma of sweet milk when fresh, and is citrusy, tangy, and pungent when aged.

HOW TO ENJOY Usually used fresh in Mediterranean salads, or grated over pasta when aged. Pair it with Messapia of Leone de Castris, or Marsala Vergine di Terre Arse.

ITALY Puglia and Basilicata	
Age From 2–3 weeks, until 2–3 months	
Weight and Shape 14oz–2lb ¼oz (400g–1kg); small cylindrical form, or truncated cone	
Size D. 5½–9½in (13–24cm), H. 1½–3in (4–7cm)	
Milk Goat and ewe	
Classification Fresh, hard when ripened	
Producer Various	

Canestrato di Vacca or di Pecora

Named after the rush basket (*canestro*) in which it is made, this cheese is coagulated or curdled with kid rennet. The curd is still manipulated by hand in the traditional way that dates back to the days of the Roman Empire.

TASTING NOTES Cow's milk Canestrato is sweet, becoming salty and nutty when mature, while the Pecora (ewe's milk) is more aromatic and has a nutty aroma at around six months.

HOW TO ENJOY Use in salads, grated over pasta, in béchamel sauce, or stuffed vegetables. It goes well with Greco di Tufo, or light and fruity red wines.

ITALY Puglia and Sicily	
Age 2–10 months	
Weight and Shape 3lb 3oz–17lb 10oz (1.5–8kg); cylinder	
Size D. 8–14in (20–35cm), H. 2½–4in (6–10cm)	
Milk Cow or ewe	
Classification Hard	
Producer Various	

Lagundo

This cheese ranges from semi-soft to firm in consistency, depending on the ripening time. Made from cow's milk, it develops a marked brown rind from being washed. Lagundo is the village in which it first originated, but is also known as *Bauernkäse*, which is German for farmer's cheese.

TASTING NOTES With irregular eyes thoughout the white or straw-colored paste, it is full flavored with a sweet, butter aroma and a tang in the taste.

HOW TO ENJOY Eat with rye bread or melt onto potatoes. Try with Pinot Bianco (Wiessburgunder) or Moscato Giallo (Goldenmuskateller).

ITALY Trentino-Alto Adige	
Age 2 months, better after 6 months	
Weight and Shape 17lb 10oz (8kg), brick	
Size Various	
Milk Cow	
Classification Semi-soft or hard	
Producer Small farmers	

Pecorino di Filiano PDO

An ancient cheese that is made in the Basilicata region using milk from the native ewes, *gentile di puglia*. The cheeses are ripened in local caves.

TASTING NOTES It has a golden-yellow or, when treated with oil and vinegar, brown-yellow rind imprinted with the pattern of the basket molds. The firm, crunchy paste is light yellow with very small eyes. Sweet and buttery when young, it becomes pungent, salty, and strongly aromatic when mature.

HOW TO ENJOY Used in the dish *Pecorino maritato*, or grated over boiled broad beans. Pair with local red wines.

ITALY Basilicata	
Age 6 months or more	
Weight and Shape 5½–11lb (2.5–5kg), drum	
Size D. 6–10in (15–25cm), H. 3–7in (8–18cm)	
Milk Ewe	
Classification Hard	
Producer Various	

Pecorino Laticauda

This hard cheese is named after the Laticauda breed of sheep that was introduced from Africa in the 18th century, then crossed with the local Pagliarola race.

TASTING NOTES The thin, waxy rind is yellow-orange over an ivory white, grainy, and friable paste. With a sweet and salty taste, it has an aroma of cut grass, wild flowers, and citrus fruit.

HOW TO ENJOY Serve fresh as a table cheese, or use to stuff and fill artichokes and in delicious local cheese pies. Try with Vino Bianco Avignonesi and Vino Nobile di Montepulciano.

ITALY Faicchio, Campania	
Age 3–6 months	
Weight and Shape 4½lb (2kg), drum	
Size D. 8in (20cm), H. 5in (12cm)	
Milk Ewe	
Classification Hard	
Producer Azienda Torre Vecchia, Faicchio, Benevento	

Pusteria

Its Italian name is Pusteria, but since it is produced in a bilingual area, it also has German names of Pustertaler, Bergkäse, or Hocpustertaler. It is produced in the Puster Valley, mainly from Pustertaler Sprinzen cattle. Until 1800 it was made only in summer.

TASTING NOTES Under the yellow-orange rind is a white paste with irregular eyes and an elastic texture. The taste is sweet, becoming bitter and pungent. It has mild vegetal and floral aromas.

HOW TO ENJOY It is used in Spätzle noodles, grilled with butter. Try serving with Muller Thurgau.

ITALY Bolzano, Trentino-Alto Adige	
Age 60–70 days	
Weight and Shape 20lb (9kg), wheel	
Size D. 14in (35cm), H. 3½in (9cm)	
Milk Cow	
Classification Semi-soft	
Producer Milkon Alto Adige, Bolzano	

Ricotta di Bufala Campana (PDO transitory list)

In some Italian regions, buffalo are used to produce milk instead of cows, because they adapted better to the humid climate and poor grazing. This cheese uses whey left over from making Mozzarella di Bufala Campana.

TASTING NOTES Refreshing with a sweet, slightly acidic flavor and a delicate grainy texture.

HOW TO ENJOY Use in many Italian recipes. Try it with white Falanghina Spumante, or red Palummo Passito.

ITALY Lazio	
Age 1–2 days	
Weight and Shape 1lb 2oz–5½lb (500g–2.5kg), basket mold	
Size Various	
Milk Buffalo	
Classification Fresh	
Producer Various	

Ricotta Romana PDO

In 2BCE, Cato the Elder made reference to this delicate ewe's-milk whey cheese, and the recipe was recorded by Columella in 1CE and Galen of Pergamum in 2CE. Today, it has been granted the European Union's Protected Designation of Origin.

TASTING NOTES This refreshing cheese has a smooth, fine, grainy texture, with a taste more sweet than sour and a citrus aroma. The flavor changes depending on the pastures on which the sheep graze.

HOW TO ENJOY Ricotta Romana is a major ingredient in the dessert "Fingers of Apostle." Pair with Frascati Superiore.

144

ITALY Lazio	
Age 1 day	
Weight and Shape 1lb 2oz–4½lb (500g–2kg), truncated cone	
Size Various	
Milk Ewe	
Classification Fresh	
Producer Various	

Silter

This Celtic-named cheese dates back to the 17th century. Silter comes in two types: those made in the high mountain pasture, and those made in the valley.

TASTING NOTES Under a brownish-yellow rind is a straw-yellow paste that has a friable, crumbly texture when aged. The mountain cheese has more vegetal and floral aromas, while the valley cheese has hints of hay and dry fruits.

HOW TO ENJOY It is a delicious ingredient in Cannelloni alla zucca (pasta rolls filled with pumpkin and Silter). Pair it with sparkling white Franciacorta Millesimato, or Sagrantino Passito.

ITALY High Camonica and Sebino Valley, Lombardia	
Age 4–12 months	
Weight and Shape 22–44lb (10–20kg), wheel	
Size D. 14–15½in (35–40cm), H. 4–6in (10–15cm)	
Milk Cow	
Classification Hard	
Producer Romelli Giacomo, Pedena-Breno	

Squacquarone di Romagna

In 1CE, Gaius Petronius Arbiter, the author of Satyricon, called this cheese Caseum mollem. In the local dialect the name means "without consistence," because it is mousselike and easily melts in the mouth.

TASTING NOTES A shining white cheese, it has a very soft, high-moisture texture, a creamy, buttery aroma, and a balance of sweet and sour with citrus hints.

HOW TO ENJOY Traditionally it is used to stuff pasta, along with beef marrow, but try it simply in a fresh salad. Pair it with a dry white Albana di Romagna, or a red such as Sangiovese Superiore.

ITALY Bologna, Emilia–Romagna	
Age 1–4 days	
Weight and Shape 2¼–6½lb (1–3kg)	
Size Various	
Milk Cow	
Classification Fresh	
Producer Caseificio Pascoli, Savignano sul Rubiconde	

Stelvio PDO

This washed-rind cheese takes its name from the highest Alps pass and has been traded in the Tirol since Medieval times. Since it is made in a bilingual area, Stelvio is also known as Stilfser.

TASTING NOTES It has a yellow-orange to orange-brown rind and straw-yellow paste with irregular holes, and a compact, supple, and springy texture. Its sweet–sour flavor is sometimes pleasantly bitter, with aromatic hints of hay and steamed vegetables.

HOW TO ENJOY Often melted on polenta or used in barley or lentil soups. Pair with Merlot Kretzer, or Lagrein Dunkel.

ITALY	Stelvio National Park, Lombardia
Age	2–4 months
Weight and Shape	17lb 10oz–22lb (8–10kg), cylinder
Size	D. 14½–15in (36–38cm), H. 3–4in (8–10cm)
Milk	Cow
Classification	Semi-soft
Producer	Milkon Alto Adige, Bolzano

Stracciata

This artisan cheese is produced by cutting or tearing the curd, which is then stretched into ribbons that are folded and shaped. The result is a sweet, fresh, fatty paste which is sold as it is or used to fill Burrata cheese.

TASTING NOTES A shining, white, creamy cheese, Stracciata is mild and sweet with fresh lactic notes. It easily melts in the mouth, leaving a taste like warm melted butter.

HOW TO ENJOY Serve this refreshing summer cheese as a main dish with fresh salad and tomatoes, and a glass of Locorotondo Spumante, or Aleatico di Puglia Liquoroso.

ITALY	Puglia
Age	1–2 days
Weight and Shape	7oz–1lb 2oz (200–500g), long cylinder or ball
Size	Various
Milk	Cow
Classification	Fresh
Producer	Various

Toscanello

Toscanello belongs to the Caciotta group of cheeses and is also known as Caciotta di Pecora. Toscanello means "Little Tuscany," which is where this ancient cheese originated, before its production migrated to Sardegna.

TASTING NOTES When young, Toscanello has a mild sweet and sour taste and supple texture with milky, vegetal notes. When aged, it has a marked sweet and salty taste, a friable texture and floral and fruity notes.

HOW TO ENJOY Sardinians serve it with Mallureddu, or use it in risotto. Pair with Sovana Rosso, or Sauvignon Castello della Sala.

ITALY	Sardegna
Age	1–6 months
Weight and Shape	3–5½in (1.5–2.5kg); round
Size	D. 7–8in (18–20cm), H. 3–4in (8–10cm)
Milk	Ewe
Classification	Semi-soft
Producer	Various

Valle D'Aosta Fromadzo PDO

Well known in the 15th century, this hard cheese is made using morning and evening milk, then left to stand before the cream is skimmed off. Some cheeses contain up to 10 percent goat's milk.

TASTING NOTES Often flavored with juniper, cumin, or wild fennel, it is supple with tiny holes and has a slightly sweet taste that becomes stronger and more aromatic when aged.

HOW TO ENJOY Grate onto toast or into soups, such as spinach or cabbages. Pair it with a dry red wine such as Enfer d'Arvier, or Vallée d'Aosta Donnas.

ITALY	Valle D'Aosta
Age	2–10 months
Weight and Shape	2¼–15½in (1–7kg), wheel
Size	D. 6–12in (15–30cm), H. 2–8in (5–20cm)
Milk	Cow
Classification	Hard
Producer	Various

Valtellina Casera PDO

This cheese is made in Valtellina, an isolated valley in the Alps, using milk from the Bruna Alpina cows known for their excellent, sweet-flavored milk.

TASTING NOTES The thin, yellow rind covers a dense but creamy interior, with small, irregular eyes. Its sweet-and-sour-flavor becomes salty when aged. The aromatic flavor has honey and floral notes, sometimes with a bitter finish.

HOW TO ENJOY It is the basic ingredient of Pizzoccheri, and is used to fill Sciatt, stuffed buckwheat pancakes. Best teamed with a red Sassella Negri.

ITALY	Lombardia
Age	2–4 months
Weight and Shape	15lb 7oz–26½lb (7–12kg), wheel
Size	D. 12–17½in (30–45cm), H. 3–4in (8–10cm)
Milk	Cow
Classification	Hard
Producer	Various

Vastedda della Valle del Belice (PDO transitory list)

Unlike other Italian *pasta filata* cheeses, this is made with ewe's milk, in particular from the local Belice breed. Vastedda is derived from *vasta*, the base of the cheese-shaping dish.

TASTING NOTES The fine white rind covers a shiny, straw-yellow, very moist, soft paste. The flavor is sour and sweet and becomes aromatic after a few days with hints of herbs and flowers.

HOW TO ENJOY Eat as an appetizer with a glass of Regaleali Tasca d'Almerita.

145

ITALY	Sicilia
Age	2–3 days
Weight and Shape	1lb 2oz–1lb 7oz (500–700g), cylinder
Size	D. 6–6½in (15–17cm), H. 1–1½in (3–4cm)
Milk	Ewe
Classification	Fresh
Producer	Various

BAY OF BISCAY

La Peral

ASTURIAS

Cebreiro

**Afuega'l Pitu ★,
Ahumado de Pría,
Cábrales ★,
Casín ★,
Gamonedo ★,
Taramundi**

CANTABRIA

**Cantabria ★,
Liébana,
Picón Bejes Tresviso ★**

Pasiego de
las Garmillas

PAÍS
VASCO

GALICIA

**Arúza-Ulloa ★,
San Simón da Costa,
Tetilla ★**

Valdeón ★

NAVARRA

**Idiazábal ★,
Roncal ★**

LA RIOJA

Camerano ★

**Castellano,
Ibérico,
Pata de Mulo,
Zamorano ★**

CASTILLA-LEÓN

N

VIANA DO
CASTELO

VILA
REAL

Cabra Transmontano ★

BRAGA

BRAGANÇA

Cabra Transmontano ★

Beato de Tábara

Cañarejal

Zamorano ★

ARAGÓN

Tronchón

PORTO

AVEIRO

VISEU

GUARDA

Serra da Estrela ★

PORTUGAL

Monte Enebro

SPAIN

COIMBRA

MADRID

LEIRIA

CASTELO
BRANCO

Castelo Branco ★

Los Montes de Toledo

CASTILLA-LA MANCHA

Ibérico

SANTARÉM

PORTALEGRE

Nisa ★

EXTREMADURA

**Ibores ★,
Tortas Extremeñas**

LISBOA

ÉVORA

Évora ★

SETÚBAL

Azeitão ★

Cabra Rufino

Azores

BEJA

Serpa ★

Murcia al Vino ★

MURCIA

Payoyo

ANDALUCÍA

FARO

GOLFO DE
CÁDIZ

ATLANTIC OCEAN

COSTA DEL SOL

Madeira

Islas Canarias

COSTA DE LA LUZ

MEDITERRANEAN SEA

GIBRALTAR

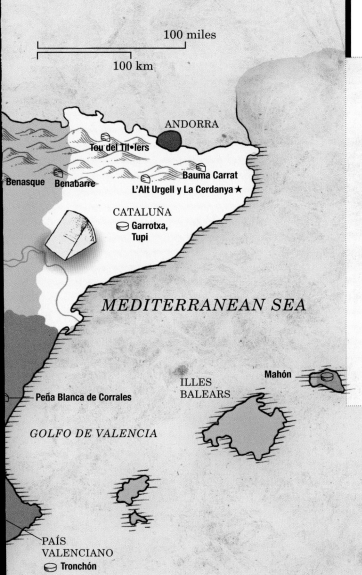

SPAIN AND PORTUGAL

SPAIN During the 9th century, when many rural folk and their livestock took refuge with the monasteries, monks became the principal producers of cheese. When livestock populations grew, the monasteries needed more pastures, which saw the beginning of transhumance, or the migration of shepherds. This movement of animals and shepherds helped spread the science of cheesemaking across the country. Many of the cheese shapes or patterns originated from whatever local materials were available: ceramic bowls of the Levante, sycamore leaves, carved wood, or even grass belts. During the last forty years, transhumance almost disappeared, but in the late 1900s, cheese experienced a well-deserved resurgence, although artisan cheesemaking was almost entirely replaced by large cooperatives.

PORTUGAL With the Atlantic Ocean to the west and high mountains to the east, Portugal received protection from the invasion of Goths, Vandals, and Moors. That protection and the harsh climate led to cheese playing a very minor role in Portuguese cuisine. Those that were made, however, were exceptional, and most used (and still do) the thistle or Cardoon to curdle the rich milk of the hardy sheep.

With the boom of the economy and the tourist industry since the 1960s, Portugal has seen a revival of artisan cheeses and cheesemaking, as well as the introduction of bigger manufacturing plants. They can now boast 10 cheeses that qualify for PDO and PGI status.

Key

★	AOC, DOC, DOP, PGI, or PDO cheeses
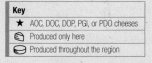	Produced only here
	Produced throughout the region

ISLAS CANARIAS

LANZAROTE

Palmero ★

TENERIFE

LA PALMA

Flor de Guía

Majorero ★

GOMERA

FUERTEVENTURA

Herreño

HIERRO

GRAN CANARIA

MOROCCO

ATLANTIC OCEAN

MADEIRA

PORTO SANTO

São Jorge ★

MADEIRA

DESERTA GRANDE

ATLANTIC OCEAN

BUGIO

AZORES

CORVO

FLORES

GRACIOSA

Ilha Graciosa

TERCEIRA

FAIAL

SÃO JORGE

ATLANTIC OCEAN

SÃO MIGUEL

SANTA MARIA

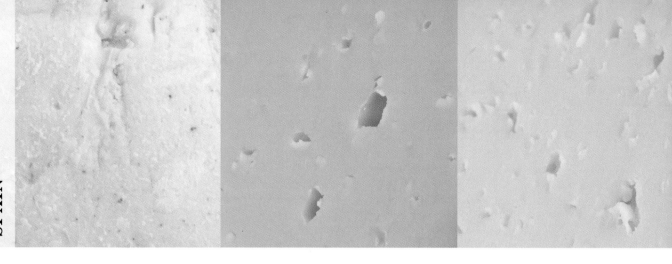

Afuega'l Pitu DOP

A small, wrinkled cheese with a sticky exterior shaped into a cone or like a pumpkin, Afuega'l Pitu is molded by hand in a cloth. The most striking version has its curd seasoned by hot pimentón (Spanish smoked paprika) and is matured for two months.

TASTING NOTES Afuega'l Pitu, meaning "stick in the throat", after its tart, creamy texture, is made from acidified white curd. The dusty red pimentón variety has a seriously fiery finish.

HOW TO ENJOY Fresh white Afuega'l Pitu has a thick, yogurty consistency and is excellent with jam or honey; the hot variety needs a dry sherry.

SPAIN Asturias		
Age Fresh 7 days; with pimentón 2 months		
Weight and Shape 7oz–1lb 5oz (200–600g), cone or pumpkin		
Size D. 3–5½in (8–14cm), H. 3–5in (8–12cm)		
Milk Cow		
Classification Flavor-added		
Producer Various		

148

Ahumado de Pría

A lightly smoked, creamy northern cheese with an orange rind, this was originally made in smoky shepherd's huts in high summer pastureland that is also famed for its sweet butter.

TASTING NOTES Matured for two months before being gently smoked over beech and oak, allowing the fragrance of added ewe cream to complement the heady aromas of cow's milk produced on mountain pastures.

HOW TO ENJOY Ideal with an apéritif, it is delicious with the fruity white wines of Galicia, or try it dipped in cinnamon, cumin, and breadcrumbs, then fried and served with muscatel grape jelly.

SPAIN Asturias		
Age 2–6 months		
Weight and Shape 1lb 5oz (600g), cylinder		
Size D. 5in (12cm), H. 4in (10cm)		
Milk Cow, with ewe cream		
Classification Flavor-added		
Producer Various		

L'Alt Urgell y La Cerdanya DOP

This tender and approachable cheese hails from the high Catalan Pyrenees, and is the initiative of a cooperative dairy that is famous for its Cadí butter. Washed in brine, the cheese develops a thin leathery orange-red rind and small holes in the pale interior.

TASTING NOTES The aroma is reminiscent of grassy meadows, the paste is springy, and the initial impression is mild and buttery, but with unexpected depth.

HOW TO ENJOY Melts well in gratins and sauces for vegetable and fish dishes, and pairs extremely well with a chilled dry cava or fruity or sweet white wines.

SPAIN La Seu d'Urgell, Cataluña		
Age 6–12 weeks		
Weight and Shape 4½–5½lb (2–2½kg), round		
Size D. 7½–8in (19½–20cm)		
Milk Cow		
Classification Semi-soft		
Producer La Cooperativa del Cadí		

Arzúa-Ulloa DOP

An elegant round cheese with a waxy clean yellow rind and soft almost squishy, smooth interior, it remains the most popular within Galicia. Various artisan producers near the river Ulla make it, hence its name.

TASTING NOTES Although the paste is unexpectedly mild, more like butter than cheese, it is deeply aromatic, and its sweet, milky flavors develop with quiet confidence on the palate.

HOW TO ENJOY Relish its gentle flavors simply on breadsticks, or spread the cheese like butter onto wholemeal, sourdough, or pumpernickel. Pairs well with a white Ribeiro wine.

SPAIN Galicia	
Age 15–30 days	
Weight and Shape 1lb 2oz–7lb 11oz (500g–3.5kg), round	
Size D. 4–10in (10–26cm), H. 2–5in (5–12cm)	
Milk Cow	
Classification Semi-soft	
Producer Various	

Bauma Carrat

Toni Chueca, with Rose Heras, left the city in 1980 to make cheese using milk from their own herds, but now focuses on making the cheeses and acquiring excellent milk from a single farmer.

TASTING NOTES Fragile and striking, the deep black ash rind protects the bright white smooth, moist interior. The paste is fresh yet luxuriously creamy, with a distinct but not strong goaty taste.

HOW TO ENJOY Ripe tomatoes alone are excellent partners to Carrat, and its perfect Catalan partner would be *escalivada*—grilled eggplants, green peppers, and Aragón olives—with a fruity white wine such as Alella.

SPAIN Borreda, Cataluña	
Age 15–21 days	
Weight and Shape 14oz (400g), square	
Size L. 4in (10cm), W. 4in (10cm), H. 1in (3cm)	
Milk Goat	
Classification Aged fresh	
Producer Formatge Bauma SL	

Beato de Tábara

Santiago Lucas Leon and his sons shepherd their own flock in the Sierra de la Culebra and make this artisan cheese, inspired by the illustrated manuscripts of the monastery at San Martín de Tábara, by hand.

TASTING NOTES Cool on the palate, its stone-gray rind and aroma of cellars take you to dark underground spaces, while the bright white paste brings you back to the meadows. An elegant and exceptional cheese.

HOW TO ENJOY To be true to the monastic purity of the cheese's inspiration, it is best appreciated on its own, or after dinner with a refreshing Riesling.

SPAIN San Martin de Tábara, Castilla-León	
Age 60–100 days	
Weight and Shape 1lb 2oz–2¼lb (500g–1kg), cylinder	
Size D. 4–6in (10–15cm), H. 2½–3in (6–7cm)	
Milk Goat	
Classification Hard	
Producer Santiago Leon Lucas	

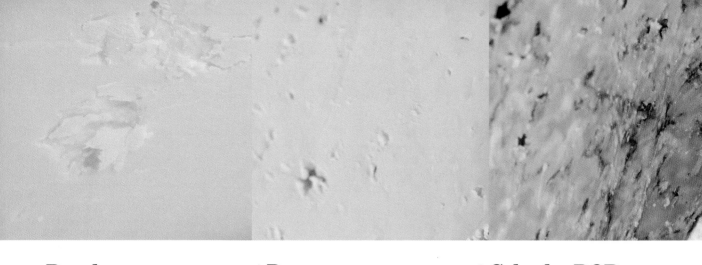

Benabarre

Blessed with an absolutely stunning setting, this dairy sits in the foothills of the Pyrenees facing the valleys of Aran, where its herds of Granadina goats pasture. The cheese is shaped like a pumpkin and possesses the size and weight of a small rock.

TASTING NOTES Matured in cellars ventilated by clean mountain air, the natural molds on the rind develop aromas of fresh mushroom. The paste is compact, revealing flavors of hazelnuts, acorns, and wild herbs.

HOW TO ENJOY Serve simply, accompanied by a good red Somontano wine and a bowl of dark Aragón olives.

SPAIN Benabarre, Aragón	
Age 14–60 days	
Weight and Shape 14oz–1lb 5oz (400–600g) or 5½–6½lb (2.5–3kg). square	
Size L. 4½–9in (11–23cm), W. 4½–9in (11–23cm), H. 2–3in (5–8cm)	
Milk Goat	
Classification Semi-soft	
Producer Quesos Benabarre	

Benasque

Produced in the stunning Benasque valley in the heart of the Pyrenees, also known as the "Valle Escondido", or hidden valley, on a family-run farm. The cattle graze on natural mountain pastures, supplemented with a diet of dry food, ensuring that milk quality remains consistent year-round.

TASTING NOTES Hand-molded and slowly matured in underground cellars, it is moist yet crumbly, with a hint of salt and a full-bodied strong, tangy finish.

HOW TO ENJOY A well-rounded cheese best served simply with fresh crusty white bread and a glass of the local Somontano wine.

SPAIN Huesca, Aragón	
Age 3–6 months	
Weight and Shape 2¼lb (1kg), round	
Size D. 5in (12cm), H. 2–3in (5–7cm)	
Milk Cow	
Classification Hard	
Producer Quesería el Benasques	

Cabrales DOP

A notorious strictly artisan blue cheese matured in the damp, mold-rich caves of the rugged, isolated Picos de Europa mountains, where mixed herds pasture. Its original maple-leaf covering has now been replaced by green foil.

TASTING NOTES The thin, soft gray rind envelops a creamy paste that is heavily streaked with blue veins and punctuated with irregular cavities. Although the cheese's aroma is a touch fetid, a keen creaminess comes through.

HOW TO ENJOY This very strong cheese is best sampled at the end of a meal with a dry Asturian cider, as even young Cabrales will overwhelm most pairings.

SPAIN Asturias	
Age 3 months minimum	
Weight and Shape 1lb 5oz–8lb 13oz (600g–4kg), drum	
Size D. 6–8½in (15–22cm), H. 3–4in (7–10cm)	
Milk Cow, ewe, and goat	
Classification Blue	
Producer Various	

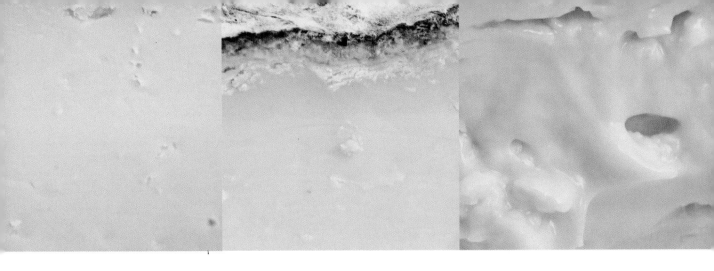

Cabra Rufino

For 40 years the Rufino family has been aging these five-day-old *tortas*. Each piece is methodically turned, washed, and checked daily. The best are made in the fall, when the goats enjoy the local acorns, making the cheese particularly creamy. Its full name is Queso de Cabra Rufino.

TASTING NOTES Seasonality and aging affect the cheese, which ranges from dense and compact with a crumbly yet moist paste and a strong, genuine spicy bite, to unctuous in the autumn.

HOW TO ENJOY Ideally, relaxing in the local Bar Rufino, with country-style bread and a strong wine or beer.

SPAIN Olivia de la Frontera, Extremadura	
Age 60–120 days	
Weight and Shape 1lb 5oz (600g), round	
Size Various	
Milk Goat	
Classification Semi-soft	
Producer Quesos Artesanos Rufino	

Camerano DOP

Also known as La Aulaga Camerano, this is the brainchild of Monica Figuerola. Shaped in traditional wicker molds and aged for up to two months, this is a resolutely artisan cheese made only in spring and summer.

TASTING NOTES The natural mold has a powerful aroma of mushrooms. The texture of the cheese itself is close, and dissolves on the palate into subtle flavors of goat and mountain herbs.

HOW TO ENJOY Eaten as a dessert with honey, grapes, or quince when young, or served simply with toasted pistachios, country bread, and a young Rioja wine.

SPAIN Munilla, La Rioja	
Age 7 days fresh; 60 days cured	
Weight and Shape 1lb 5oz (600g), drum	
Size D. 4½–6in (11.5–15cm), H. 2–4in (5.5–10cm)	
Milk Goat	
Classification Semi-soft	
Producer Quesería la Aulaga	

Cañarejal

This artisan torta, a contemporary northern version of the more famous Torta La Serena, was an initiative of the local sheep-farming Santos family. It is produced using milk from the Santos' flock of robust Awassi sheep, which graze the local grasslands.

TASTING NOTES Made with thistle rennet, this is the creamiest of all the Spanish tortas. Very aromatic, with soft, earthy flavors, it has a typical bitter finish.

HOW TO ENJOY Open the thin rind to expose the silky interior, and scoop out with a teaspoon or breadsticks. It is also delicious melted on a rare fillet steak served with caramelized onions.

SPAIN Pollos, Castilla-León	
Age 2–3 months	
Weight and Shape 9oz–1lb 2oz (250–500g), round	
Size D. 4–5in (10–12cm), H. 2–2½in (5–6cm)	
Milk Ewe	
Classification Semi-soft	
Producer Cañarejal SL	

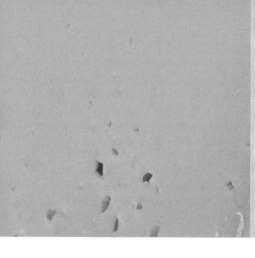

Cantabria DOP

Also known as Queso Nata de Cantabria, this was originally made in the Cóbreces Cistercian monastery, but is now produced by numerous small and medium-sized family dairies using milk from the abundant dairy cattle found pasturing in sheltered green valleys.

TASTING NOTES Its smooth waxy rind hides a pale interior, with a dense, springy texture and a mellow, sweet, and buttery flavor, sometimes with a tart finish.

HOW TO ENJOY Eat on crusty toast with chestnut honey, quince, or apple jelly. Also ideal picnic fare with a salad and a dry white or young red wine.

SPAIN La Cavada, Cantabria	
Age Minimum 15 days	
Weight and Shape 14oz–6lb (400g–2.8kg), round or brick	
Size D. 8in (20cm), H. 4in (10cm) (pictured)	
Milk Cow	
Classification Semi-soft	
Producer Various	

Casín DOP

Casina cattle feed on lush, mountain meadow to provide milk for one of the oldest cheeses in Asturias. The unique recipe involves repeated rolling of the curds during the first week, before they are kneaded into shape to producing Casín's peculiar grainy paste.

TASTING NOTES With a strong smell that suggests rancid butter, the taste is very fiery and oily on the palate. The dense, creamy-looking paste is oddly grainy.

HOW TO ENJOY Producers imprint their name on the cheese with a wooden stamp, making Casín a very attractive option to serve whole on a cheeseboard. Best enjoyed with beer or cider.

SPAIN Asturias	
Age 60 days	
Weight and Shape 9oz–2¼lb (250g–1kg), hemisphere	
Size D. 4–8in (10–20cm), H. 1½–3in (4–7cm)	
Milk Cow	
Classification Semi-soft	
Producer Various	

Castellano

Little known and understood mainly by its brand name, Castellano cheese can actually be of outstanding character when made well because the Castilla-León region produces the best, creamiest ewe's milk in Spain.

TASTING NOTES When aged for six months and made with raw milk, it gains piquancy and a smooth texture that reveals a distinct caramelized onion flavor of sheep and an intense finish.

HOW TO ENJOY An apéritif cheese ideal with bold red wines such as Somontano or Priorato, it is also excellent with unsalted nuts and dried fruit, quince jelly or paste, or fresh pears and apples.

SPAIN Castilla-León	
Age 2–6 months	
Weight and Shape 4½–6½lb (2–3kg), drum.	
Size D. 4½–7½in (11–19cm), H. 3–4in (8–10cm)	
Milk Ewe	
Classification Hard	
Producer Various	

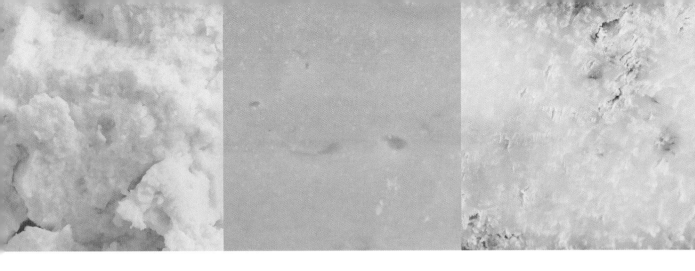

Cebreiro

Reminiscent of a chef's hat or stout mushroom in shape, Cebreiro is rarely found away from its mountain home in Galicia. The characteristic shape is achieved when the curd is put in a bag and a hoop slipped over the top to hold it in position; as the hoop is not tall enough, the curd spills over the top.

TASTING NOTES The fresh white paste is moist and close-textured but granular. It has a fresh, lightly acidic yogurt tang, with an aroma of warm butter.

HOW TO ENJOY Serve with honey and fruit jams and preserves, or use in gratins and béchamel sauce. Cebreiro happily pairs with chilled young Albariño wine.

SPAIN Lugo, Galicia	
Age 3–7 days	
Weight and Shape 10oz–4½lb (300g–2kg), chef's hat	
Size D. 3½–6in (9–15cm), H. 3in (7cm)	
Milk Cow	
Classification Fresh	
Producer Queixerias Castelo de Branas; Carmen Arrojo Valcarcel Xan Busto	

Flor de Guîa

An exceptional and very rare cheese, curiously only ever made by women, it is named Flor de Guîa (thistle flower) after the local thistle used to coagulate the milk. Shaped with a grass belt, the cheese develops gently rounded sides.

TASTING NOTES Creamiest of all Canarian cheeses, Flor de Guîa has an unctuous, rich texture that melts in the mouth, releasing its mildly acidic, aromatic flavor and the typical bitterness of thistle rennet on the finish.

HOW TO ENJOY Complements fruity white wines from Galicia, tropical fruit such as bananas, and fruit jams such as those made from berries. A rare treat.

SPAIN Gran Canaria, Islas Canarias	
Age 2–3 weeks	
Weight and Shape 4½–11lb (2–5kg), wheel	
Size D. 8½–12in (22–30cm), H. 1½–2⅜in (4–6cm)	
Milk Ewe and cow	
Classification Semi-soft	
Producer Various	

Gamonedo DOP

A blue mountain cheese overshadowed by its neighbor Cabrales (*see p150*), but with quite an individual character: harder pressed, elegant-looking rind, less blue veining, and lightly smoked before placing in the natural curing caves.

TASTING NOTES This cheese blues lightly in patches nearer to the hard dry rind and has a gentle spikiness, revealing hints of damp mushroom, salt, and a nutty aftertaste of hazelnuts.

HOW TO ENJOY Relish in the rustic flavor of a cheese made in shepherds' cabins on the mountain passes of the Picos de Europa. Gamonedo del Valle is a milder, more accomplished cheese.

SPAIN Cangas de Onis and Onis, Asturias	
Age 3–5 months	
Weight and Shape 1lb 2oz–15lb 7oz (500g–7kg), drum	
Size D. 4–12in (10–30cm), H. 2½–6in (6–15cm)	
Milk Cow, with some ewe or goat	
Classification Blue	
Producer Various	

SPAIN

153

Mahón DO

Granted Denomination of Origin status in 1985, Mahón comes from the Balearic Island of Menorca. The tiny island has a colorful history, with invasions by the Carthegians, Romans, Arabs, French, and lastly the British in the 18th century, who introduced the Friesian cow.

Port of Mahón, *Menorca, from which the cheese takes its name.*

Records show that Mahón was traded around the Mediterranean from about the 13th century. However, it owes its international reputation to the local merchants who, in the late 1800s, started taking the farmers' cheese in exchange for goods. Known as *recogedor-afinador*, gatherer-ripeners, they ripened the young cheeses in underground caves where the airflow, temperature, and humidity provided the cheese with a unique microclimate. This practice continues, with about 300 family-owned dairy farms selling their milk to the big cooperatives. Today, the best-known *afinador* is Nicolas Cardona.

TASTING NOTES At 20–60 days it is supple, buttery. and mild; semi-cured at 2–5 months, the flavor increases and the texture becomes firmer; cured, or *añejo*, at 5–10 months, it is hard and slightly granular, not unlike Parmigiano-Reggiano (see pp130–131), and has an aroma and taste of peaches with a sea-salt finish.

Green-labeled Mahón is made by hand from raw milk on small farms and finished by an *afinador,* whose skill is to bring out the best in each cheese. The harder, more piquant style with its red label and bright orange rind is made in cooperatives and has an unexpectedly sharp, mouth-puckering bite.

HOW TO ENJOY Traditionally served as an appetizer, drizzled with olive oil and topped with a sprig of fresh rosemary. Serve it alongside a glass of sherry, which brings out the personality of the cheese. However, like all hard cheeses, it is extremely versatile and is used in many recipes from the Spanish omelet to tapas and pastries. The more matured or cured Mahón pairs well with beer or even *sake* (Japanese rice wine).

SPAIN Menorca, Balearic Islands
Age 20 days–5 months
Weight and Shape 3lb 4oz (1.5kg), square "cushion"
Size D. 8in (20cm), H. 2in (5cm)
Milk Cow
Classification Hard
Producer Various

A CLOSER LOOK

Mahón is lovingly nurtured and matured by the skillful *afinadores* who buy the generic young cheeses and age them according to their own individual methods.

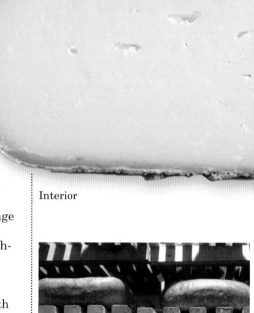

Interior

THE RACKS the cheeses are stored on wooden racks in underground caves where the *afinador* carefully controls the temperature, humidity, and flow of fresh air.

All aged Mahón is speckled with small, irregular holes, caused by the fermentation that happens as the cheese ripens.

CLOTH PRESSING The young artisanal cheese is wrapped in cloth (*fogasser*) and tied by its corners. This is pressed manually, forcing out excess whey and forming the cheese into its distinct "cushion" shape.

The upper surface of matured artisanal Mahón bears the pattern of the creases and folds of the *fogasser*.

The ocher-yellow color of the rind is created not by bacteria but by rubbing butter, paprika, and olive oil into the rind to enhance its appearance and prevent mold.

Exterior

Garrotxa

One of the new generation of Spanish artisan cheeses to come to prominence in recent years, this is notable for its subtle goaty flavor and dark gray velveteen rind, or *pell florida*. First produced in 1981 by a single maker, Garrotxa is now made by several other artisan cheesemakers in the region.

TASTING NOTES A fresh slice, unusually chalky for Spanish cheese, invokes memories of mountain herbs, walnuts, and mushrooms; the lingering finish has distinct creamy overtones of goat.

HOW TO ENJOY Ideal for tapas or at the end of a meal, served with almonds, walnuts, and a robust white Priorat.

SPAIN Cataluña	
Age 2–4 months	
Weight and Shape 2¼lb (1kg,) round	
Size D. 6in (15cm), 3in (H. 7cm)	
Milk Goat	
Classification Semi-soft	
Producer Various	

Herreño

Similar cheeses are produced all over these rugged islands under the various island names, but this has the most interesting texture and flavor. When smoked, there are beautiful burnished lines on the rind from the racking.

TASTING NOTES It is bright white and refreshingly acidic when young, while smoked Herreño is a satisfying balance of light smoke, usually fig or prickly pear branches, and delicate flavor.

HOW TO ENJOY When young, it pairs well with white and rosé wines; aged it is better with red wines. Excellent lightly melted and served with red or green *mojo* sauces or in the local cheesecake.

SPAIN El Hierro, Islas Canarias	
Age 10–60 days	
Weight and Shape 12oz–8lb 13oz (350g–4kg), cylinder	
Size D. 3½–10in (8.5–25.5cm), H. 2½–3⅓in (6–8.5cm)	
Milk Goat, cow, and ewe	
Classification Semi-soft	
Producer Sociedad Cooperativa Ganaderos de El Hierro; Valverde	

Ibérico

Imprinted with the marks of the woven-basket mold, Ibérico is a blend of cow's, goat's, and ewe's milk, typical of many traditional Spanish cheeses, and makes up more than 50 percent of the nation's consumption of cheese.

TASTING NOTES The rind is often colored to indicate age, and the blend of milks brings together the best of each one: creamy and mellow from the cow, sweet and nutty from the ewe, and herbaceous notes from the goat.

HOW TO ENJOY The flavor changes subtly with the seasons, but Ibérico is always delicious in a toasted sandwich or used for a gratin, whatever time of year.

SPAIN Castilla-La Mancha; Castilla León	
Age 1 month minimum	
Weight and Shape 2¼–7lb 11oz (1–3½kg), drum	
Size D. 3½–8½in (9–22cm), H. 3–5in (7–12cm)	
Milk Cow, goat, and ewe	
Classification Hard	
Producer Various	

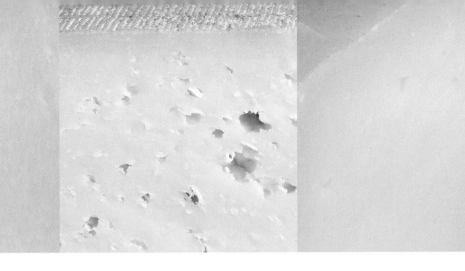

Ibores DOP

A rustic cheese whose roots lie in the migrating herds of native Verata and Retinta goats and the wild vegetation and oak forests of the area, it is found either plain or brushed with olive oil and pimentón (smoked paprika).

TASTING NOTES The firm white paste is rich with aromas of broom, lavender, and thyme, while the copper-colored pimentón rind imparts a warmth to the cheese's tangy finish.

HOW TO ENJOY Sprinkle a slice with pimentón, lightly toast, and serve with an apéritif or as a light supper with salad. Ideal with a crisp dry white wine and unsalted nuts.

SPAIN Caceres, Extremadura	
Age 2 months minimum	
Weight and Shape 1lb 7oz–2½lb (650g–1.2kg), drum	
Size D. 4½–6in (11–15cm), H. 2–3½in (5–9cm)	
Milk Goat	
Classification Semi-soft	
Producer Queserías de las Villuercas; Berrocales Trujillanos	

Idiazábal DOP

This ancient cheese comes from the Basque mountains, where shepherds spent summer in the high pastures, before returning in the fall with their cheeses. Stored in the rafters of the shepherds' huts over the summer, the cheese took on a wood-smoke flavor.

TASTING NOTES Hard and chewy, with tiny holes and a coppery rind, Idiázabal is smoked with beech wood, adding a light smokiness to the distinctive caramel sweetness of the ewe's milk. Artisan varieties are a rare treat.

HOW TO ENJOY Try a Basque recipe such as squid and Idiázabal risotto, or serve simply with Txacoli or a Basque cider.

SPAIN Navarra	
Age 3–6 months	
Weight and Shape 2¼–6½lb (1–3kg), drum	
Size D. 4–12in (10–30cm), H. 3–5in (8–12cm)	
Milk Ewe	
Classification Flavor-added	
Producer Various	

Liébana DOP

Small cheeses (*quesucos*) are made in each village in the foothills of the Picos de Europa. Mainly fresh or semi-soft, sometimes smoked, they are made with cow's or sometimes ewe's or goat's milk.

TASTING NOTES Lemony when fresh, but most are supple, buttery, and aromatic, with a hint of caramel when made with ewe's milk. The rinds are typically thin, rough, and straw-colored, or bright white if fresh. Smoking adds piquancy.

HOW TO ENJOY Serve on a cheeseboard alongside dried fruits and nuts, and a selection of young wines. Young cheeses are delicious with mountain honey.

SPAIN Cantabria	
Age 2 weeks minimum	
Weight and Shape 14oz–1lb 2oz (400g–500g), round	
Size D. 3–5in (8–12cm), H. 1–4in (3–10cm)	
Milk Cow and occasionally ewe and goat	
Classification Fresh or semi-soft	
Producer Various	

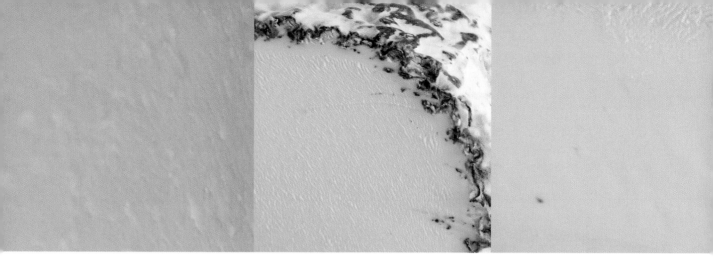

Majorero DOP

The scrubby desert landscape of Fuerteventura nourishes the Majorero goats that produce this exceptional cheese. The rind, rubbed with olive oil, bears the imprint pattern of a palm frond belt. Some are rubbed with either paprika or *gofio* (roasted corn flour).

TASTING NOTES Supple to firm, Majorero ranges from creamy fresh with a subtle goaty flavor, through to a more robust nutty, almondy sweetness.

HOW TO ENJOY Traditionally grated into vegetable soups or summer salads, and served with a minerally white island wine. Young Majorero makes a superb fondue flavored with orange zest.

SPAIN Fuerteventura, Islas Canarias	
Age 20 days minimum	
Weight and Shape 2¼lb–13lb 4oz (1–6kg), round	
Size D. 6–14in (15–35cm), H. 2½–3½in (6–9cm)	
Milk Goat	
Classification Hard	
Producer SAT Ganaderos de Fuerteventura	

Monte Enebro

When most would be retiring, Rafael Báez chose to create this *pata de mulo*, or mule's-hoof-shaped, goat's cheese, with its distinctive rind covered in gray and black molds. It was the first modern artisan cheese in Spain to gain international recognition.

TASTING NOTES Dense curds are gently compressed, and the flavor matures over time from a light citric creaminess to an assertive, pungent bite.

HOW TO ENJOY Savor with muscatel dessert wine, add to beetroot salad, or fry in tempura batter and serve with orange blossom honey, accompanied by a light, white La Mancha wine.

SPAIN Avila, Castilla-León	
Age 6–8 weeks	
Weight and Shape 3lb (1.4kg), mule's hoof	
Size L. 9in (23cm), W. 12cm (5in), H. 2½in (6½cm)	
Milk Goat	
Classification Natural rind	
Producer Queserias del Tietar	

Los Montes de Toledo

This is the innovation of a spirited individual, Anna Maria Rubio. The Toledo Mountains neighbor Ibores, where goats dominate, so local goat farmers joined the cooperative and provide milk for this soft, unique torta.

TASTING NOTES A clean aroma and silky texture with flavors that vary with the seasons from more acidic with a touch of salt to sweeter during the spring, it is a mild cheese.

HOW TO ENJOY Sublime on crusty white bread with fruits and nuts: pistachios, apples, and quince paste. Pair with fruity white wine or chilled dry fino.

SPAIN Navalmorales, Castilla-La Mancha	
Age 2–3 months	
Weight and Shape 2¼lb (1kg), round	
Size D. 6½in (17cm), H. 1½in (4cm)	
Milk Goat	
Classification Semi-soft	
Producer La Merendera Sociedad Cooperativa	

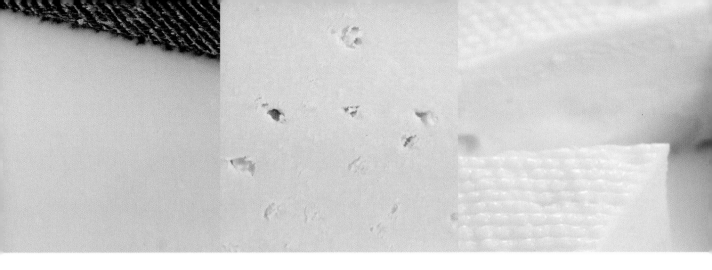

Murcia al Vino DOP

Spain's hot and arid region of Murcia has a growing cheese industry based on the exceptionally productive native goats, Murciano-Granadina, honed by genetic selection over generations. This cheese is washed with local Jumilla and Yecla red wines.

TASTING NOTES A washed-curd cheese with a slightly elastic texture and distinct, aromatic flavor, with hints of almonds from the rich milk and a slightly winey, fermenting fruit finish.

HOW TO ENJOY Try the cheese in salads, lightly fried, or grilled on toast and served with the young white or rosé wines from Jumilla and Yecla.

SPAIN Jumilla, Murcia	
Age 3 weeks minimum	
Weight and Shape 10oz–4½lb (300g–2 kg), drum	
Size D. 3–7in (7–18cm), H. 2½–3½in (6–9cm)	
Milk Goat	
Classification Semi-soft	
Producer Various	

Palmero DOP

Spain's largest cheese comes from the greenest of the Canary Islands, where the Palmero goat feeds on rich pasture, moving steadily up the slopes as the weather warms.

TASTING NOTES Diverse and lush grazing gives this lightly smoked cheese a rich flavor. Palmero is pleasantly crumbly, salty, earthy, and lightly acidic, with a toasted aroma.

HOW TO ENJOY As Palmero breaks up easily, it is commonly used in local cuisine grated into the mojo sauces or sliced alongside fish, vegetable, and potatoes. Also good on its own with the local mineral-rich Malvasia wines.

SPAIN La Palma, Islas Canarias	
Age 1–3 months	
Weight and Shape 15lb 7oz–33lb (7–15kg), wheel	
Size D. 5–23½in (12–60cm), H. 2½–6in (6–15cm)	
Milk Goat	
Classification Semi-soft	
Producer Various	

Pasiego de las Garmillas

A fragile primitive cheese made without a mold that was originally from the valley of Pas, it is now made to more contemporary standards and available at the weekly market in the town of Ampuero and beyond.

TASTING NOTES So fresh that the pale rind has barely formed, its interior is soft and fatty, with an aroma of fresh yogurt and mountain streams.

HOW TO ENJOY Its delicate, sweet flavors work well with crusty bread, salted anchovies, and piquillo peppers, accompanied by a very cold dry cider. Used for the local *quesada pasiega*.

SPAIN Ampuero, Cantabria	
Age 15–20 days	
Weight and Shape 1lb 2oz (500g), flat disk	
Size D. 5½in (14cm), H. ¾in (2cm)	
Milk Cow	
Classification Fresh	
Producers Queso Las Garmillas	

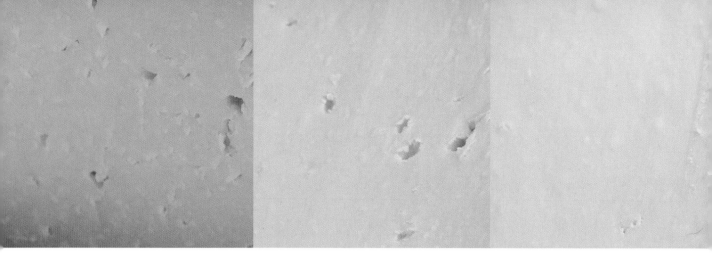

Pata de Mulo

Named "mule's hoof" because of its shape, this was traditionally molded by hand in cheesecloth, then rolled on a table until the typical shape was achieved. Thankfully, since the late 1990s, production of this disappearing cheese has been reinvigorated.

TASTING NOTES A rounded flavor, grainy texture, nutty nose, light oil on the palate, and persistent finish are typical of this very Castilian aged ewe's cheese, with its straw-colored wrinkled rind.

HOW TO ENJOY Attractive for slicing into salads or displayed on a cheeseboard, it pairs beautifully with young red or rosé wines of Ribera del Duero or Navarra.

SPAIN Castilla-León	
Age 2–6 months	
Weight and Shape 4½lb (2kg), flattened oval log	
Size L. 9in (23cm), W. 5in (13cm), H. 3in (8cm)	
Milk Ewe	
Classification Hard	
Producer Various	

Payoyo

Set up in 1997 by 14 farmers, this cooperative makes cheeses using milk from native Payoyo goats and rare-breed Grazalema sheep that roam the green pastures of the Sierra de Grazalema, 900m (2,750ft) above sea level.

TASTING NOTES The strictly artisan methods used mean that even the rennet derives from the Payoyo goat. The plain rind can be coated with lard or paprika, and it has a firm texture that reveals a soft, rounded nutty taste, with hints of toffee.

HOW TO ENJOY Ideal with an apéritif. Serve with almonds and a Manzanilla dry sherry or a cold refreshing beer.

SPAIN Sierra de Grazalema, Andalucia	
Age 6–12 weeks	
Weight and Shape 2¼–5½lb (1–2.5kg), cylinder	
Size D. 5–6½in (12–17cm), H. 3–4in (8–10cm)	
Milk Goat	
Classification Hard	
Producer Quesos Artesanales de Villaluenga SL	

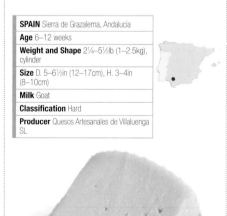

Peña Blanca de Corrales

Assertive ewe's milk cheese with a rind of red and ochre molds, this is an original recipe using lactic coagulation, and its makers very successfully capture the terroir of the Sierra de Espadas where it is made.

TASTING NOTES The aroma is reminiscent of a Cabrales, but the dense paste has the texture of fresh curds, with hints of leather, caramelized onions, and wool.

HOW TO ENJOY Its restrained piquancy works well with other Mediterranean flavors: fino or palo cortado sherry, black olives, extra virgin olive oil, and fresh crusty bread.

SPAIN Almedíjar, Valencia	
Age 90 days	
Weight and Shape 5lb (2.2kg), cylindrical	
Size D. 7½in (19cm), H. 3in (8cm)	
Milk Ewe	
Classification Hard	
Producer Quesería Los Corrales	

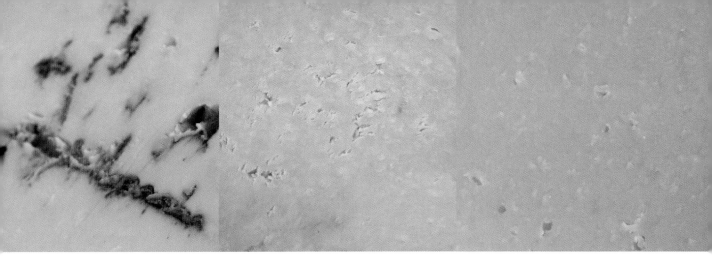

La Peral

This relatively modern foil-wrapped blue cheese from Asturias is made by the third generation of creator Antonio León's family. Production remains small scale and consistent, resulting in an accessibly priced, very pleasant cheese.

TASTING NOTES A sticky yellow rind with a pale yellow interior lightly inked with blue veins, it emits a gentle buttery smell. The shiny curd-like cheese has a creamy salty flavor that gradually develops into a clean, fresh mild blue.

HOW TO ENJOY Savor this cheese with blackberries and walnuts, accompanied by either an Asturian cider or a Pedro Ximenez sherry.

SPAIN Illas, Asturias	
Age 60–150 days	
Weight and Shape 4½lb (2kg), tall cylinder	
Size D. 7in (18cm), H. 3½in (9cm)	
Milk Cow with ewe's cream	
Classification Blue	
Producer Herederos de Antonio León	

Picón Bejes Tresviso DOP

From the villages of Bejes and Tresviso in the Picos de Europa, this ancient blue cheese has the hallmark sharp flavor characteristic of cheeses made in these high peaks. Abandoned mines and natural caves provide excellent damp space for curing.

TASTING NOTES The light gray rind with orange overtones conceals an interior veined with dense blue streaks. A pungent blue cheese with a distinctive balance of bite, butter, and salt.

HOW TO ENJOY Sprinkle with ground hazelnuts or serve with prunes; pair with muscatel or a sweet red Priorat.

SPAIN Cantabria	
Age 3–6 months	
Weight and Shape 1lb 2oz–6½lb (500g–3kg), drum	
Size D. 4–8in (10–21cm), H. 2½–5in (6–13cm)	
Milk Cow, goat, and ewe	
Classification Blue	
Producer Various	

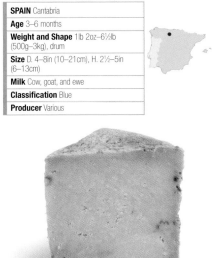

Roncal DOP

Records for this Pyrenean sheep's cheese date back to the 13th century, and detail control of the herds as they were moved between their summer and winter pastures, and routes up and down the Roncal valley. The cheese is pressed, then aged in cloth.

TASTING NOTES Dense with a smooth straw- to gray-colored rind that bears the imprint of the cloth. With age, there may be hints of dried fruit, a growing piquancy, and a lingering aftertaste.

HOW TO ENJOY Serve simply with crusty white bread and a good Navarran red wine or cider. Artichoke gratin with Roncal is a popular local dish.

SPAIN Roncal, Navarra	
Age 4 months minimum	
Weight and Shape 2¼–6½lb (1–3kg), drum	
Size D. 6–8in (15–20cm), H. 4–4½in (10–11cm)	
Milk Ewe	
Classification Hard	
Producer Various	

Manchego DOC

Manchego takes its name from the dry plateau of La Mancha, south of Madrid and not far from Toledo. Baptized by the Arabs, *Al Mansha* (land without water), La Mancha is a vast, dry flat region with few trees, scorched by temperatures of up to 122°F (50°C) and minimal rainfall. It is a magnificent part of Spain with a sense of timelessness and history, dotted with old ruins, scrawny sheep, and the windmills made famous by Don Quixote.

Modern irrigation has meant vast acres of vines, olive groves, sunflowers, and crops have replaced much of the indigenous shrubs, acorns, blackthorn, vetch, and wild grasses of the *dehesa* (uncultivated land). However, sufficient natural, uncultivated land still exists in the mountains, woodlands, around riverbanks, and on the plains, to provide summer grazing for the hardy sheep, whose thick, aromatic milk gives Manchego its character. In fall and winter, their diet is supplemented with sweet tendrils from vines and the stubble from crops and hay.

Most Manchego is made in factories, but milking is still largely done by hand. It is an awesome sight to see the shepherds as they work methodically through the herds, often upward of 700 at a time. Each sheep is lifted off its back legs so the milk from the swollen udder collects in the bucket, yielding but a few liters of milk each a day. Yet every drop is imbued with the essence of the wild thyme, aromatic herbs, and withered acorns that form their diet. The resulting thick, sweet, aromatic milk is what makes Manchego unique.

TASTING NOTES The depth and complexity of flavor depends on age, but all Manchego has an unmistakable richness reminiscent of Brazil nuts and caramel, with a distinct aroma of lanolin and roast lamb, and a slightly salty finish. The texture is dry yet creamy. It can be slightly oily on the surface and may feel a little greasy in the mouth, but that just makes it taste better. Each mouthful is a taste of Spanish culture, history, and gastronomy.

Cheeses that reach a great age have a peppery bite to the finish and, if cut into thin wedges and marinated in the strong aromatic local green olive oil, the flavor is intensified.

HOW TO ENJOY Like all hard cheeses, Manchego keeps well and is gorgeous eaten just as it is; however, like any hard cheese, it is extremely versatile and, when cooked, lends a nutty, sweetness to the dish.

Manchego will absorb tannin, so enjoy it with a robust or young rough red, crisp white, or perhaps the best combination is with sherry, either dry or sweet.

The vast, *dry plains of La Mancha.*

SPAIN Castilla La Mancha		
Age 6–18 months		
Weight and Shape 6½lb (3kg), drum		
Size D. 8in (20cm), H. 4in (10cm)		
Milk Ewe		
Classification Hard		
Producer Various		

A CLOSER LOOK

Most Manchego is now made with pasteurized milk in modern factories that comply with EU regulations. However, great care has been taken to ensure the finished cheese is as close to traditional handmade cheeses as possible.

PRESSING AND AGING Once the curd is in the molds, they are placed on a horizontal press to expel excess whey. Artisan cheeses are then aged in stone barns, sometimes dug into the sides of the limestone hills. Factory cheeses are aged in large, airy barns.

MARKING To qualify for the DOC label, the cheese must bear the distinct zigzag markings along the sides and the *flor,* "flower," design on the top and bottom. Originally, the zigzag marks were made by encircling the fresh curd with plaited esparto grass and placing it on hand-carved wooden boards to drain. Regrettably, the boards and grass have been replaced with plastic molds, imprinted with the zigzag pattern.

ESPAÑA
Denominación de Origen
MANCHEGO
74979
FO

The texture of the ivory-colored interior is firm and dry, yet rich and creamy.

Interior

The distinctive yellow to brownish-beige rind gathers a multitude of molds that must be washed and scrubbed and sometimes waxed before being sold.

Exterior

San Simón da Costa

Shaped as a large teardrop or spinning top with a small nipple on the top, it is thought to have its origins in Celtic culture. Its distinctive smooth copper-colored rind is the result of gentle smoking over birch wood.

TASTING NOTES The smoky taste blends elegantly with the buttery aroma and taste, while the overall flavour is mild with some salt, a pleasant balance of acidity, and sweetness in the aftertaste.

HOW TO ENJOY A good melting cheese, this works well in rice, pasta, and vegetable dishes, or added to salads. Delicious with a glass of a young red Valdeorras wine and some peanuts.

SPAIN Galicia	
Age 3 weeks	
Weight and Shape 1¾lb–3lb 3oz (800g–1.5kg), large cone	
Size D. 5–6in (12–15cm), H. 5–7in (13–18cm)	
Milk Cow	
Classification Flavor-added	
Producer Various	

Taramundi

The creation of a splinter cooperative who wanted to respond to the growth in popularity of local cheese and take advantage of the rich mountain milk, Taramundi is inspired by the sweeter, more elastic cheeses of Switzerland.

TASTING NOTES Made plain or with walnuts or hazelnuts, this cheese has an unusual but pleasant flavor—a mix of toast, butter, and sweetness—and a springy texture.

HOW TO ENJOY An excellent hors d'oeuvre alongside crudités, it also has the same superb melting qualities as raclette. Perfect when combined with young, fruity white wines or cider.

SPAIN Taramundi, Asturias	
Age 2–3 months	
Weight and Shape 1lb 2oz–2¼lb (500g–1kg), wheel	
Size D. 4–8in (10–20cm), H. 1½–2½in (4–6cm)	
Milk Cow and goat	
Classification Flavor-added	
Producer Various	

Tetilla DO

This popular cheese from northwestern Spain is well known beyond its borders due to its mellow taste and distinctive shape—the name Tetilla means "small breast". Original farmhouse production has been almost totally replaced by a strong dairy industry.

TASTING NOTES It is ready to eat after only seven days, when the deep bright yellow interior is sweet, clean, buttery, and unctuous; with maturity, Tetilla becomes firmer and more resilient, with a slight acidity on the finish.

HOW TO ENJOY Delicious when served at the end of a meal, with either quince paste or a sharp apple purée.

SPAIN Galicia	
Age 7 days minimum	
Weight and Shape 1lb 2oz–3lb 3oz (500g–1.5kg), flattened cone	
Size D. 3½–6in (9–15cm), H. 3½in–6in (9–15cm)	
Milk Cow	
Classification Semi-soft	
Producer Various	

Tortas Extremeñas

Once considered fit only for peasants, these lush cheeses have recently taken Europe by storm with their near-liquid interiors. There are three versions, including Torta de Barros (pictured), Torta del Casar, and Torta La Serena.

TASTING NOTES Thistle rennet gives these cheeses a distinctive earthy flavor and a gentle bitterness on the finish; the paste is very soft and rich, with aromas reminiscent of dry hay.

HOW TO ENJOY Heat in the oven until warmed right through, cut a hole in the top of the cheese, and scoop out the soft interior with a teaspoon or breadsticks.

SPAIN Extremadura	
Age From 8 weeks	
Weight and Shape 1lb 2oz–3lb (500g–1.3kg), round	
Size D. 4½–6in (11–16cm), H. 2–2½in (5–6cm)	
Milk Ewe	
Classification Semi-soft	
Producer Various	

Tou del Til·lers

This tender soft cheese with its white mold rind is a thoroughly modern cheese created at a dairy founded in 1995. It is situated in the heart of the Pyrenees, in Pallars Sobirà, where varied high pasture enriches the quality of the milk.

TASTING NOTES The rind reveals notes of ammonia and, although there are hints of fresh mushroom and rich cream, the pungent, gluey, and assertive flavor of this cheese is hard to deny.

HOW TO ENJOY Full of character, it is best enjoyed with a dense white country-style loaf and a strong red wine such as a Terra Alta or Somontano.

SPAIN Sort, Cataluña	
Age 6–12 weeks	
Weight and Shape 14oz–1lb 2oz (400–500g) and 2¼lb (1kg), round	
Size D. 5in and 8½in (13 and 22cm), H. 1 and 1½in (3 and 4cm)	
Milk Cow	
Classification Soft white	
Producer Tros de Sort	

Tronchón

A delightful volcano-shaped cheese, Tronchón is imprinted with original carved wooden molds made by the shepherds. The tradition of taking mixed herds of goat and sheep into the Sierra del Maestrazgo extends its spread throughout the provinces of Tarragona, Teruel, and Castellón.

TASTING NOTES Mountain pastures endow this soft, buttery cheese, available either fresh or cured, with hints of lavender and oregano.

HOW TO ENJOY Serve fresh ewe's milk Tronchón with crusty bread and green olives; the cured goat's milk variety is sharper and pairs well with young reds.

SPAIN Aragón and Pais Valenciano	
Age From 45 days	
Weight and Shape 1lb 2oz–4½lb (500g–2kg), round with a crater	
Size D. 4–6in (10–15cm), H. 3–4in (7–10cm)	
Milk Ewe or goat, or a blend	
Classification Hard	
Producer Various	

SPAIN

165

Tupí

This spread, which is a very ancient shepherd's recipe that is firmly back on the modern-day Catalan cheese menu, is made from the second fermentation of fresh and cured cheeses, blended with olive oil and brandy or liqueur.

TASTING NOTES Matured in small ceramic clay pots, this is a strangely compulsive cheese. It has the texture of porridge, a strong piquant flavor, and a slightly fetid aroma, but develops a surprisingly satisfying finish.

HOW TO ENJOY Its soft texture makes it perfect for canapés on dry bread, but it is not a cheese for the faint-hearted. It pairs well with cold beers and ciders.

SPAIN Cataluña	
Age A few weeks	
Weight and Shape 5½oz (160g) and 7oz (200g), pots	
Size No size	
Milk Cow	
Classification Fresh	
Producer Various	

Valdeón DO

The innovative Alonso brothers, Tomás and Javier, produce this on the León side of the Picos de Europa, where the climate of Valdéon is less humid than that of Picón. The resulting less-virulent mold produces a less intense flavor than similar blues. Valdeón is often marketed as Picos de Europa.

TASTING NOTES The rind is rough, sticky, speckled with molds, and wrapped in sycamore leaves. Distinctly spicy, but not strong, and flavored with a touch of salt, it leaves an elegant aftertaste.

HOW TO ENJOY Serve with hazelnuts, walnuts, and prunes, and with port or cider. It also makes an excellent sauce.

SPAIN León, Castilla-León	
Age 2–3 months	
Weight and Shape 5½lb (2.5kg), drum	
Size D. 7½in (19cm), H. 3½in (9cm)	
Milk Cow, occasionally with goat	
Classification Blue	
Producer Queserías Picos de Europa	

Zamorano DO

The dry pastures of northern Castilla contribute to Zamorano's complex character. Shepherding and moving herds between summer and winter pasture have a strong heritage here, and the dramatic landscape offers a great variety of vegetation and climate.

TASTING NOTES The quality and character of the ewe's milk allow the cheese to be matured for long periods. It develops an intense, slightly tart, nutty complexity with a distinct sheepy aroma.

HOW TO ENJOY Select a Gran Reserva, aged for 12 months, and serve alone at the end of a meal, or perhaps with quince paste, and the local wine Toro.

SPAIN Castilla-León	
Age 100 days minimum	
Weight and Shape 4½lb–8lb 13oz (2–4kg), drum	
Size D. 8–9½in (20–24cm), H. 3½–5½in (9–14cm)	
Milk Ewe	
Classification Hard	
Producer Various	

Azeitão DOP

This rustic-looking cheese wrapped in gauze hails from the lush foothills of the Arrabida mountains, where the flora and local soil conditions strongly influence the quality of the milk.

TASTING NOTES The curds are molded in cloth, the rind is brine-washed, and the paste is pale yellow. It has a sweet, slightly acidic and very delicate taste, with fatty spice on the finish.

HOW TO ENJOY Cut open the top, scoop out the runny paste, dollop into mini cooked pastry shells, and sprinkle with oregano to serve with an apéritif, or eat with nutty bread and wash down with Tempranillo or Albarinho wine.

PORTUGAL Setúbal	
Age 20–30 days	
Weight and Shape 3½–9oz (100–250g), soft round	
Size D. 2–4½in (5–11cm), H. ¾–2½in (2–6cm)	
Milk Ewe	
Classification Semi-soft	
Producer Various	

Cabra Transmontano DOP

This cheese, which comes from the area famous for port is made from the hardy and resilient Serrana goat. The herds are moved from high to low altitudes as the weather moves into winter, and spring time brings the opportunity for milking and, of course, cheesemaking.

TASTING NOTES Rich in butterfat and protein, the paste is firm with a slightly unctuous texture. The flavor is lemony and zesty, with earthy undertones.

HOW TO ENJOY It is excellent for grating or crumbling over a summer salad and can be served as a table cheese, paired with a tawny Port or fruity white wine.

PORTUGAL Bragança and Vila Real	
Age 60 days	
Weight and Shape 1lb 5oz–2lb (600–900g), round	
Size D. 5–7½in (12–19cm), H. 1–2½in (3–6cm)	
Milk Goat	
Classification Semi-soft	
Producer Various	

Castelo Branco DOP

This DOP, which is also called Beira Baxta, describes three cheeses made with thistle rennet. Castelo Branco, which is a white ewe's milk cheese, is the most common, but there is also a yellow version blended with goat's milk and a hotter, more mature recipe.

TASTING NOTES It is tangy with a slightly bitter finish, becoming more spicy as it is matured for up to 60 days. Young cheeses have a soft texture that gets firmer and chewier with age.

HOW TO ENJOY In all its variations, this cheese adds interest to a cheeseboard, alongside dried fruit and nuts. Serve with reds such as Pinot Noir.

PORTUGAL Castelo Branco	
Age 45–60 days	
Weight and Shape 1lb 10oz–2¼lb (750g–1kg), round	
Size D. 5–6in (12–16cm), H. 2½–3in (6–7cm)	
Milk Ewe	
Classification Semi-soft	
Producer Various	

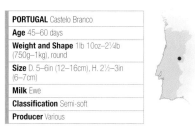

167

Évora DOP

The home of this hand-shaped washed-rind cheese is the famous walled town of Évora, where it was once traded as currency. Merino ewe's milk and cardoon thistle rennet combine to create one of the best cheeses of its kind.

TASTING NOTES This is a delicious, light-yellow cheese with a crumbly texture, light acidity, spicy fruity flavor, and salty finish. Spring pastures create a creamier, fruitier, and stronger version.

HOW TO ENJOY It is traditionally thinly sliced and accompanied by olives, cured meats, and sourdough bread dowsed in olive oil, it is also an excellent salad cheese. Pair it with Sangiovese wines.

PORTUGAL Évora	
Age 30–90 days	
Weight and Shape 4–10oz (120–300g), cylinder	
Size D. 3–4in (7–10cm), H. 1¼in (3–3.5cm)	
Milk Ewe	
Classification Semi-soft	
Producer Various	

Ilha Graciosa

The cheesemaking technique used to produce Ilha Graciosa has been handed down by settlers of the Azores' most northern island for many centuries. It is similar to São Jorge, but is matured for a shorter period.

TASTING NOTES The island's fertile volcanic soil and damp climate provide the lush pastures that characterize this firm straw-yellow cheese, with its strong, clean spicy taste and aroma.

HOW TO ENJOY Graciosa cheese is well suited to eating before or after meals with the local minerally white wines or sugarcane rum. Very mature versions are ideal for grating over gratin dishes.

PORTUGAL Ilha Graciosa, Azores	
Age 90 days	
Weight and Shape 22lb (10kg), cylinder	
Size D. 12in (30cm), H. 6in (15cm)	
Milk Cow	
Classification Hard	
Producer Various	

Nisa DOP

Merina Branca, the local breed of ewes, produce the rich milk for this traditional cheese, which farmers and locals have enjoyed for years. Local thistle rennet coagulates the milk, and the cheese may be preserved in terra-cotta pots of olive oil called *talhas*.

TASTING NOTES The texture of this yellow-white cheese with a well-formed crust is dense, with small eyes in the paste. Nisa has a slightly sweet taste and is very rich and creamy.

HOW TO ENJOY One of Portugal's most popular cheeses, it is perfect on a cheeseboard with fruits such as plums or apricots, and a crisp white wine.

PORTUGAL Portalegre	
Age 3–4 months	
Weight and Shape 7oz–3lb (200g–1.3kg), round	
Size D. 4–5in (10–13cm), H. 5–6in (12–16cm)	
Milk Ewe	
Classification Semi-soft	
Producer Various	

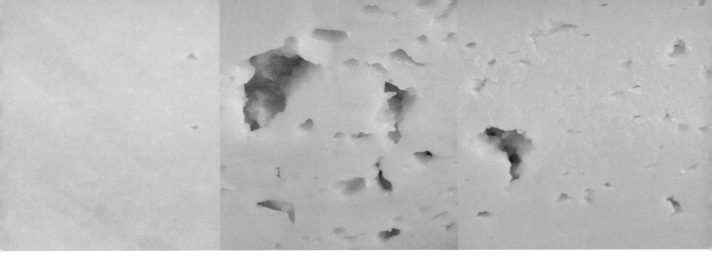

São Jorge DOP

Introduced by a group of Flemish sailors who made Madeira their home, it dates back to the 15th century and is based on a Gouda-type recipe. It is so named because the island was discovered on St. George's Day.

TASTING NOTES The abundant grass and salty pastures allow the cheese to gain a strong spicy flavor, a clean bouquet, and a hard but crumbly texture. It is akin to a cross between Cheddar and Gouda, with some small holes.

HOW TO ENJOY Ideal for fondues, São Jorge also makes a fine addition to a traditional cheeseboard with fresh fruit such as pears and muscatel grapes.

PORTUGAL São Jorge, Madeira
Age 4–6 months
Weight and Shape 22lb–24¼lb (10–11kg), cylinder
Size D. 12in (30cm), H. 5in (12.5cm)
Milk Cow
Classification Hard
Producers Various

Serpa DOP

Serpa is similar to Serra, but is made with the milk of the Laconne ewes, rather than the Bordeleira. The hot dry climate and sparse aromatic grazing gives the cheese a rich and fruity taste.

TASTING NOTES A full, creamy cheese, Serpa is soft, clean, and slightly salty on the palate, with a tangy finish. The cardoon or thistle rennet used to make it adds a lightly acidic aftertaste and a slight bitterness.

HOW TO ENJOY It is perfect paired with red wine as an apéritif. Scoop out the middle with breadsticks, then fill the shell with mild onions and potatoes, and bake. Complete enjoyment.

PORTUGAL Beja
Age 30 days
Weight and Shape 7oz–3lb 3oz (200g–1.5kg), round
Size D. 4–7in (10–18cm), H. 5–8in (12–20cm)
Milk Ewe
Classification Semi-soft
Producers Various

Serra da Estrela DOP

Made from milk of the Bordeleira da Serra da Estrela ewes, Serra has a long history dating back to the time of the Romans. The flocks are moved to different pastures within the northern mountains, and they feed on wild herbs, flowers, and grasses.

TASTING NOTES The supple and luscious yellow paste, coagulated with thistle rennet, possesses a mild acidity with the sweetness of toffee and a hint of strawberries and thyme.

HOW TO ENJOY Bring the cheese to room temperature, cut off the top like a lid, and eat with breadsticks or a spoon along with marmalade or quince paste.

PORTUGAL Guarda
Age 45 days
Weight and Shape 1lb 2oz–2¼lb (500g and 1kg), round
Size D. 4–7in (10–18cm), H. 5–8in (12–20cm)
Milk Ewe
Classification Semi-soft
Producer Various

GREAT BRITAIN AND IRELAND

SCOTLAND Harsh, unpredictable weather; long, dark, unforgiving winters, and brief summers meant that cheeses were originally made mainly by the old clan folk and crofters for their own consumption. Inspiration for cheeses came from various sources, including the Vikings and the Irish.

Today there are around 20 Scottish artisan cheesemakers producing both traditional and unique cheeses from cow's, goat's, and ewe's milk.

IRELAND Irish cheesemaking dates back centuries thanks to high rainfall levels, lush pastures, proximity to Europe, and the influence of itinerant monks. In recent decades, the industry has seen a major revival of farmhouse-based productions, beginning in 1976 when Veronica Steele created Milleens, Ireland's first modern farmhouse cheese.

Raw and pasteurized milk from goats, cows, and sheep is now used here for a wide variety of styles and flavors, including superb soft fresh cheeses, blues, hard Cheddar, and Dutch and Swiss styles. The Irish Farmhouse Cheese Association (CAIS) lists more than 40 farmhouse cheesemakers in the country.

ATLANTIC OCEAN

NORTH SEA

NORTHERN IRELAND

SCOTLAND

GREAT BRITAIN

Orkney

Iona Cromag

Blue Monday,
Caboc,
Crowdie,
Strathdon Blue
Cuillin Goats

Clava Brie

Bishop Kennedy

Dunlop

Lanark Blue

Cairnsmore Ewes

Kebbuck

Allerdale

Doddington

Northumberland

N

100 km

100 miles

IRISH SEA

IRELAND

REPUBLIC OF IRELAND

Corleggy
Bellingham Blue
Glebe Brethan
Grace
Mossfield Organic
Knockdrinna Gold, Lavistown
Cooleeney
Cashel Blue, Crozier Blue
Mount Callan
St Tola Log
Knockalara
Baylough Cheddar
St Gall
Ardrahan
Ardsallagh
Coolea
Durrus
Milleens
Beenoskee
Desmond, Gubbeen

ENGLAND

Ribblesdale Original Goat
Lancashire
Blacksticks Blue
Lincolnshire Poacher
Stichelton
Shropshire Blue, Stilton,
White Stilton ★
Red Leicester, Shropshire Blue, Stilton,
White Stilton
White Stilton ★
Whitehaven
Cheshire
Innes Button
Cheshire
Sage Derby
Fowlers Forest Blue
Berkswell
Snodsbury Goat
St Eadburgha, St Oswald
Hereford Hop, Stinking Bishop
Windrush
Daylesford Cheddar, Penyston
Double Gloucester,
Single Gloucester ★
Oxford Isis
Cerney Pyramid
Birdwood Blue Heaven
Finn, Perroche, Ragstone
Dragons Back
Suffolk Gold
Shipcord
Barkham Blue
Waterloo
Tunworth
New Forest Blue, Old Sarum
Old Winchester, Rosary Plain
Isle of Wight Blue
Duddleswell, Sussex Slipcote
Lord of the Hundreds
Fairlight
Wealden, Wealway
Flower Marie, Golden Cross

WALES

Ffteys
Gorau Glas
Caerphilly
Caerphilly
Saval, Teifi Farmhouse, Hafod
Cerwyn
Perl Las
Pont Gar
Pant-Ys-Gawn
Talley Mountain Goat's Cheese, Talley Mountain Mature Cheese
Campscott
Cheddar
Vulscombe
Curworthy
Keltic Gold
Cornish Blue
St Endellion
Yarg Cornish Cheese ★
Quickes Hard Goat
Norsworthy, Posbury
Beenleigh Blue
Sharpham, Sharpham Rustic, Ticklemore Goat

Inset:

Little Ryding
Tymsboro
Bath Soft Cheese, Wyfe of Bath
Wedmore
Pendragon
Black-eyed Susan
Dorset Blue Vinney
Ogleshield
Village Green
Farleigh Wallop, Little Wallop
Blissful Blue Buffalo
Exmoor Blue ★
Capricorn Goat
Woolsery English Goat
Cheddar
Caerphilly, Rachel, Cheddar
White Nancy

WALES Wales is primarily a pastoral country boasting beautiful and varied landscapes with high mountain ranges, luscious lowlands, and a mild variable climate. The grasses, wild herbs, and flowers give a unique character to the milk of the goats, cows, and sheep that graze there.

Simple cheese has been made in Wales for centuries and was an essential part of the local economy, but the best known is Caerphilly, initially made on lowland farms for the mining community.

The past 25 years brought an extraordinary revival of on-farm cheesemaking. Welsh cheese producers now make a variety of traditional and modern cheeses, from mild creamy goat's to robust blues.

ENGLAND A great wedge of the geology and history of England can be told through its iconic cheeses, such as Cheddar, Lancashire, and Red Leicester. However, in the last 25 years there has been an upsurge in small, English artisan cheeses, not only resulting in an increase in complex and flavorful cheeses, but also ensuring a future for some of the rare native breeds that give cheese the subtleties, nuances, and quality so essential for these handmade products. Cheese is a reflection of individual cheesemakers, their craft, and their passion. As a result, the cheeses of England are a reflection of the very landscape, its people, and the animals that graze it.

Allerdale

This was Carolyn Fairbairn's first cheese when she began her dairy career in the basement of the family home in 1979, using milk from her herd of goats. Nowadays, she works alongside her daughter Leonie, translating the flavors of Cumbria's lush green grazing into delicious cheese.

TASTING NOTES This sweet, moist cheese has a clean hint of almond and a texture similar to Cheshire (see p176), its maturation in cloth allows different layers of flavors to permeate.

HOW TO ENJOY Oven-baked or grilled; serve on a bed of baby spinach with a drizzle of oil and a full-bodied white.

ENGLAND Thursby, Cumbria	
Age 3–5 months	
Weight and Shape 5½lb (2.5kg), truckle	
Size D. 5½in (14cm), H. 5½in (14cm)	
Milk Goat	
Classification Hard	
Producer Thornby Moor Dairy	

Barkham Blue

The buttery consistency of Channel Island milk, which colors the interior deep yellow, characterizes this excellent cheese that looks as good as it tastes. Ammonite-shaped with an attractive rustic mold-covered rind, it has blue-green veining from the *Penicillium roqueforti* mold.

TASTING NOTES Rich and creamy, this blue melts in the mouth and, while it admirably avoids harshness, it achieves a satisfying and spicy depth. A blue for anyone who usually avoids blue.

HOW TO ENJOY Serve on its own, in a soup, or in a salad with Conference pears, mixed leaves, and dressing.

ENGLAND Barkham, Berkshire	
Age 6 8 weeks	
Weight and Shape 3lb (1.3kg), ammonite	
Size D. 7in (18cm), H. 3in (7.5cm)	
Milk Cow	
Classification Blue	
Producer Two Hoots Cheese	

Bath Soft Cheese

Graham Padfield, a third-generation farmer, began making cheese in 1993, but the recipe for Bath Soft dates back to the time of Admiral Lord Nelson, who, in 1801, was sent some by his father as a gift. Today's organic version of this cheese is packed in parchment bearing a distinctive red wax seal.

TASTING NOTES Reminiscent of a mellow Brie, this mild cheese begins with a fresh hint of spring onion and matures to a creamier, more mushroomy taste.

HOW TO ENJOY Remove from the refrigerator an hour beforehand, and enjoy as part of a cheeseboard with Bath Oliver Biscuits and wheat beer.

ENGLAND Bath, Somerset	
Age 4–6 weeks	
Weight and Shape 8oz (225g), square	
Size L. 4in (10cm), W. 4in (10cm), H. 1¼in (3cm)	
Milk Cow	
Classification Soft white	
Producer Bath Soft Cheese Company	

Beenleigh Blue

One of a very few British blue cheeses made from ewe's milk (and available from August to January), this is the creation of Robin Congdon, a skilled blue-cheese aficionado whose dairy skirts the banks of the river Dart.

TASTING NOTES Rich, sweet, and slightly crumbly, with a blue-green mold running through it, this cheese has hints of burnt caramel that show what an excellent ewe's milk cheese it really is. The rough exterior has a slight stickiness.

HOW TO ENJOY Use in a salad or serve on its own, complemented with a sweet Devon cider.

ENGLAND Sharpham Barton, Devon		
Age 5-plus months		
Weight and Shape 6½–7½lb (3–3.5kg), drum		
Size D. 8in (20cm), H. 4–5in (10–13cm)		
Milk Ewe		
Classification Blue		
Producer Ticklemore Cheese		

Berkswell

This consistent award winner at the British Cheese Awards was created by Stephen Fletcher and his mother, Sheila, on their 16th-century farm near the village of Berkswell. It is now made by their cheesemaker Linda Dutch, who uses milk from their flock of East Friesland sheep.

TASTING NOTES Originating from a traditional recipe, this characterful cheese provides a satisfying mouthful: firm texture, sweet, nutty, caramel hints, and a surprisingly tangy finale.

HOW TO ENJOY Its texture makes it ideal for dishes that call for grated cheese; when cooked, it forms a delicious crust.

ENGLAND Berkswell, West Midlands		
Age 4–6 months		
Weight and Shape 6½lb (3kg), flying saucer		
Size D. 8in (20cm), H. 3½in (9cm)		
Milk Ewe		
Classification Hard		
Producer Ram Hall Dairy Sheep		

Birdwood Blue Heaven

The young stock from Jonathan and Melissa Ravenhill's herd of Shorthorns graze on the unimproved limestone grassland of Minchinhampton Common. With an addition of *Penicillium roqueforti*, Melissa creates a semi-soft mold-ripened blue cheese.

TASTING NOTES The creamy, soft paste, streaked with patches of blue and encased in a natural molded crust, is pleasantly piquant.

HOW TO ENJOY Perfect for canapés or on a cheeseboard with crusty bread and a drizzle of extra virgin olive oil. Serve with a Cotswold Brewery wheat beer.

ENGLAND Minchinhampton, Gloucestershire		
Age 6–8 weeks		
Weight and Shape 14oz (400g) and 3lb 3oz (1.5kg), flat round		
Size D. 2in (5cm) and 8in (20cm), H. 2in (5cm) and 6in (15cm)		
Milk Cow		
Classification Blue		
Producer Birdwood Farmhouse Cheesemakers		

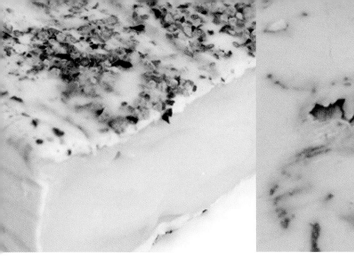

Black-eyed Susan

Taking its name from the flower of the daisy family, this is created using the dairy's young Brie-like Goldilocks cheese. Black peppercorns are crushed to exactly the right consistency—still retaining a certain bite—and the cheese is then rolled in them, before being allowed to ripen.

TASTING NOTES The glory lies in the contrast between the spicy outside and the runny "gold" within. Made with milk from Jersey cows, the ripened interior is reminiscent of thick Jersey cream.

HOW TO ENJOY Serve simply with crackers, and enjoy with your favorite Chardonnay or cider.

ENGLAND North Brewham, Somerset	
Age 4 weeks	
Weight and Shape 5½oz (150g), round	
Size D. 4in (10cm), H. 1in (2.5cm)	
Milk Cow	
Classification Soft white	
Producer Daisy and Co.	

Blacksticks Blue

Named after a group of chestnut trees that resemble a collection of black sticks in winter, the Blacksticks range was originally developed for the restaurant trade. By popular request, it has made it into stores. Blacksticks Blue is a contemporary soft blue-veined cheese, milder and creamier than other British blues such as Stilton.

TASTING NOTES Blacksticks Blue starts by delighting the nose, then strokes the tongue, and finally lingers delightfully on the palate with a mild spicy tang.

HOW TO ENJOY Pair with hot buttered Irish soda bread, or use in a rich blue sauce for grilled steak or pasta.

ENGLAND Inglewhite, Lancashire	
Age 9–12 weeks	
Weight and Shape 5½lb (2.5kg), drum	
Size D. 8¼in (21cm), H. 2½in (6cm)	
Milk Cow	
Classification Blue	
Producer Butlers Farmhouse Cheese	

Blissful Blue Buffalo

Once in the carpet business, cheesemaker Ian Arnett is now more interested in the tufted Hampshire sward that the buffalo graze upon to produce his fine blues. Not one to compromise, he can make a mighty strong blue.

TASTING NOTES Rich and creamy, this is one of a handful of British buffalo's milk blues. The cheese is tangy, moist, smooth and light, and you can taste the sweetness of the milk and the richness of the countryside.

HOW TO ENJOY It is best served on its own because it is so unusual, with a good bottle of red to wash it down.

ENGLAND Lydeard St Lawrence, Somerset	
Age 4–6 weeks	
Weight and Shape 2¼lb (1kg), drum	
Size D. 5in (13cm), H. 3½in (9cm)	
Milk Buffalo	
Classification Blue	
Producer Exmoor Blue Cheese Company	

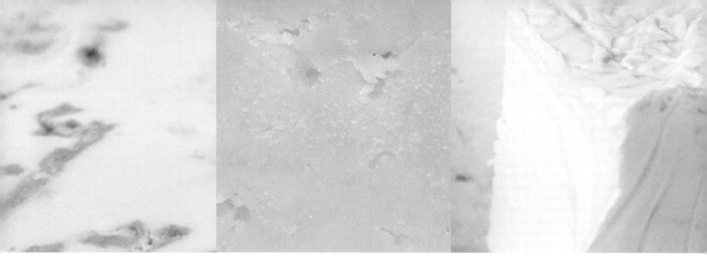

Buffalo Blue

From the only maker of buffalo blue cheese in Yorkshire, this is handmade from the milk of local water buffalo. One of Judy Bell's aims in using milk from sheep and buffalo was to help people with dairy allergies. She created something rather special in the process.

TASTING NOTES It looks light—soft and creamy—and it is light, although there is, of course, a reminder that it is a "blue" in its nutty, slightly salty taste.

HOW TO ENJOY Stir a healthy portion of cheese and a dollop of half and half into a potato soup before liquidizing, to produce a deliciously rich and creamy broth.

ENGLAND Newsham, North Yorkshire	
Age 8–10 weeks	
Weight and Shape 6½lb (3kg) drum	
Size D. 8in (20cm), H. 8in (20cm)	
Milk Buffalo	
Classification Blue	
Producer Shepherds Purse Cheeses	

Campscott

Middle Campscott Farm in Devon, with fields overlooking the Atlantic Ocean, specializes in organic sheep's and goat's cheese. The full-flavored Campscott is matured for at least two months, when it develops a firm texture and thin gray rind.

TASTING NOTES Unpasteurized milk allows the characteristics of the seasons to come through: drier with a nutty taste in summer; creamier and sweeter in winter.

HOW TO ENJOY The younger cheese is excellent on its own; the more mature varieties are delicious grated and grilled, or sprinkled over salads or pasta.

ENGLAND Lee, Devon	
Age 2–3 months	
Weight and Shape: 2¼lb (1kg) and 4½lb (2kg), cylinder	
Size D. 4¼in (10.5cm) and 5½in (14cm), H. 4in (10cm) and 6in (15cm)	
Milk Ewe	
Classification Hard	
Producer Middle Campscott Farm	

Capricorn Goat

Lubborn Creamery nestles in a green Somerset Valley and specializes in making continental styles of cheeses. Ripened for seven weeks, this cheese develops a thin delicate white mold rind.

TASTING NOTES Like the goats themselves, this cheese changes character with age. Eaten young, it has a slight nutty flavor; however, as it ripens, this develops into a salty-sweetness, and the paste is softer and creamier.

HOW TO ENJOY Crumble the young cheese into salads, or grill. Savor the mature cheese simply as it comes, with a glass of Sauvignon Blanc.

ENGLAND Cricket St Thomas, Somerset	
Age 7 weeks	
Weight and Shape 4¼oz (120g) cylinder	
Size D. 2½in (6cm), H. 1½in (4cm)	
Milk Goat	
Classification Soft white	
Producer Lubborn Creamery	

Cerney Pyramid

Handsome and fresh, this eye-catching cheese is made by hand from a recipe developed by Lady Angus of Cerney: a full-fat Valençay-type cheese from a unique starter culture. It is coated with oak ash and a sea salt mix from France, and shaped into a truncated pyramid.

TASTING NOTES Luxuriously smooth, with a creamy texture, it exudes a fresh, clean taste with floral notes. It is far milder than expected from a goat's cheese, but develops as it matures.

HOW TO ENJOY A striking addition to the cheeseboard, this black-and-white truncated pyramid is heavenly with crackers and a dry white wine.

ENGLAND South Cerney, Gloucestershire	
Age 1 month	
Weight and Shape 9oz (250g), pyramid	
Size D. 2½in (6cm), H. 1½in (4cm)	
Milk Goat	
Classification Fresh	
Producer Cerney Cheese	

Cheshire

A cheese woven into the fabric of English history, Cheshire was mentioned in the Domesday Book. Since the cattle were grazed on salt marshes, the salt content caused the cheese to ripen slowly and gave it a crumbly texture. Available white, most are coloured with annatto.

TASTING NOTES Dense, slightly dry with a very fine crumbly texture and a mild fresh acidity, Cheshire has a savory, salty tang that lingers in the mouth.

HOW TO ENJOY Grill it (as in traditional Welsh rarebit), bake it, crumble it in soups and salads, or marry it with a glass of real ale.

ENGLAND Today produced in Cheshire, Shropshire, and Wales	
Age 2–6 months	
Weight and Shape 48½lb (22kg), cylinder	
Size D. 12in (30cm), H. 10½in (26cm)	
Milk Cow	
Classification Hard	
Producer Various	

Cornish Blue

In 2001 Philip and Carol Stansfield, looking for a way to diversify their dairy farm, spotted the gap in the market for a young blue cheese that could compete with imported blue cheese. This mild blue was the result, and the Stansfields have since won many awards.

TASTING NOTES With a creamy texture like Gorgonzola and thick streaks of blue, it is surprisingly mild and sweet, becoming spicier and tangier as it ages.

HOW TO ENJOY Perfect for pepping up—but not overpowering—risotto, sauces, appetizers, and more; it goes beautifully with fruit and a glass of Champagne.

ENGLAND Liskeard, Cornwall	
Age 14 weeks	
Weight and Shape 13¼lb (6kg), round	
Size D. 11in (28cm), H. 7in (18cm)	
Milk Cow	
Classification Blue	
Producer Cornish Cheese Company	

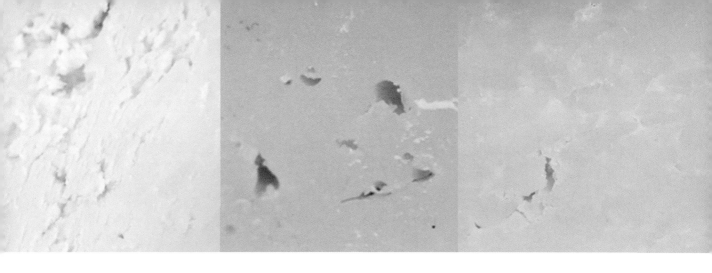

Cotherstone

Cotherstone and similar cheeses were once common in the wild and beautiful Pennines, but today—at Quarry Farm on the banks of the river Tees— Joan Cross is the only remaining producer of this cheese, thanks to a recipe handed down to her by her mother.

TASTING NOTES Cotherstone's interior is pale yellow, moist, crumbly, and fatty, and it develops a buttery richness of flavor that is edged with a fruity tang on the finish.

HOW TO ENJOY The signature tanginess goes well with a variety of wines, but in the Dales they favor a glass of dark stout as the requisite accompaniment.

ENGLAND Teesdale, County Durham
Age 1–3 months
Weight and Shape 11lb 2oz–6⅓lb (500g–3kg), millstone
Size D. 3–8½in (7.5–22cm), H. 3in (7.5cm)
Milk Cow
Classification Hard
Producer Cotherstone Cheese

Curworthy

With its own natural rind or, more strikingly, a black wax coating, the traditional Curworthy is based on a 17th-century cheese and uses milk from the farm's herd of Friesian cows. The cheese is one of six varieties produced by Rachel Stephens at Stockbeare Farm in Devon.

TASTING NOTES The texture is dense and chewy, with a lovely buttery feel when young, and it matures into a more tangy, peppery flavor.

HOW TO ENJOY It is ideal on a cheeseboard or served with an Alsace Gewürztraminer, which will complement Curwothy's young, buttery flavor.

ENGLAND Okehampton, Devon
Age 2–6 months
Weight and Shape 1–5lb (450g–2.2kg), drum
Size D. 3½–8in (9–20cm), H. 2½–4in (6–10cm)
Milk Cow
Classification Hard
Producer Curworthy Cheese

Daylesford Cheddar

Created in 2001 by Joe Schneider for Lady Bamford, using organic milk from the Daylesford estate in the Cotswolds, and made in a modern creamery next to the Daylesford Farmshop. Made like traditional Cheddar, this has won various awards, including Best English Cheese in 2002.

TASTING NOTES Hard yet chewy, this has a rich full-bodied tang that mellows out to a savory lingering finish that hints of green grass and toffee.

HOW TO ENJOY Versatile in cooking, but it also stands proud on any cheeseboard paired with a not-too-tannic red wine, such as a Pinot Noir or Merlot.

ENGLAND Daylesford, Gloucestershire
Age 9–18 months
Weight and Shape 20lb (9kg), truckle
Size D. 10in (25cm), H. 16in (40cm)
Milk Cow
Classification Hard
Producer Daylesford Organic Creamery

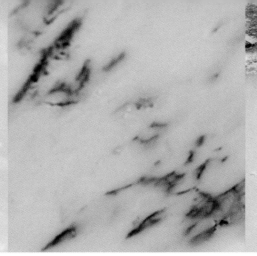

Doddington

Made at Doddington Dairy, situated at the bottom of the Cheviot Hills, this cheese is described by its makers Neill and Jackie Maxwell as lying somewhere between a Leicester and Cheddar. They have been making ice cream and cheeses since 1990 after learning their craft in the Netherlands and France.

TASTING NOTES An attractive brick-red rind and a hard, compact, slightly dry texture, with a rich, sweet caramel taste and a long-lasting nuttiness.

HOW TO ENJOY Serve with fruit and nuts, wrapped in warm bread, or grated over salads or pasta, along with a medium-bodied red wine such as a Merlot.

ENGLAND Wooler, Northumberland
Age 12–14 months
Weight and Shape 11lb and 22lb, drum
Size D. 9in (23cm) and 12½in (32cm), H. 4½in (11cm)
Milk Cow
Classification Hard
Producer Doddington Dairy

Dorset Blue Vinny

Once upon a time, every self-respecting Dorset farmhouse made this cheese—an excellent use for milk left over from the buttermaking. But with changing times, the recipe itself nearly died out, until Mike Davies revived it in the 1980s. He makes it with a combination of skim and full fat milk, so it is more moist than the original.

TASTING NOTES As it is unpasteurized and the butterfat content of the milk varies according to the time of year, this cheese is sometimes crumbly and sometimes creamy; nutty but not too strong.

HOW TO ENJOY Try with traditional Dorset knob biscuits and a sweet cider.

ENGLAND Stock Gaylard, Dorset
Age 12–14 weeks
Weight and Shape 13lb (6kg), round
Size D. 10in (25cm), H. 12in (30cm)
Milk Cow
Classification Blue
Producer Mike Davies, Woodbridge Farm

Double Gloucester

This iconic cheese can be traced back to the 15th century, when Severn Vale farmers made it from famed Cotswold sheep. Gradually, milk from Gloucester cows replaced it. Today, it is made throughout England, but not necessarily with Gloucester milk.

TASTING NOTES With a leathery rind, this hard cheese has a strong, savory, and mellow flavor. It is made with full-fat milk and colored deep orange with annatto seeds.

HOW TO ENJOY Eat plain, cook with it, or watch it being rolled down Coopers Hill in Gloucester in May, as per tradition.

ENGLAND All over
Age Around 4 months
Weight and Shape Various, wheel
Size Various
Milk Cow
Classification Hard
Producer Various

Duddleswell

You would expect a delicious cheese from a farm set in a region officially designated as an Area of Outstanding Natural Beauty. The Hardy family started High Weald Dairy in 1988, in the beautiful surroundings of Ashdown Forest; Duddleswell has echoes of traditional Dales cheeses, with all the nutritional benefits of ewe's milk.

TASTING NOTES Smooth and creamy with a sweet, nutty release, Duddleswell is a hard-pressed cheese with a thin and leathery natural rind.

HOW TO ENJOY Feature as part of a cheeseboard, or instead of pecorino; great with pasta or topping a salad.

ENGLAND Horsted Keynes, West Sussex	
Age 3–4 months	
Weight and Shape 7lb (3.2kg), truckle	
Size D. 9½in (24cm), H. 2¾–3¼in (7–8cm)	
Milk Ewe	
Classification Hard	
Producer High Weald Dairy	

Exmoor Blue PGI

Ian Arnett makes a range of traditional handmade hard and soft blue-veined cheeses with vegetarian rennet, using local cow, sheep, goat, and buffalo milk. Exmoor Blue is the only one with PGI status, which means that it is made according to strict guidelines, including using local unpasteurized Jersey milk.

TASTING NOTES Balance is the key to this semi-soft blue veined cheese, where the zing of the blue still allows other subtle, mildly salty flavors to reach the palate.

HOW TO ENJOY Partake with simple appreciation on the cheeseboard and, if you can find it, Somerset cider brandy.

ENGLAND Taunton, Somerset	
Age 4–5 weeks	
Weight and Shape 1lb 2oz (500g) and 2¾lb (1.25kg), flat round	
Size D. 4¾in (12cm) and 7in (18cm), H. 2½in (6cm)	
Milk Cow	
Classification Blue	
Producer Exmoor Blue Cheese Company	

Fairlight

The free-range, mainly British Saanen goats on this farm are raised along biodynamic principles, producing a salt-free fresh cheese in a traditional way. Made fresh every day, and hung in muslin, it offers a mild purity that is universally appealing.

TASTING NOTES Fresh and clean, with a soft, silky texture, it is also available rolled in organic cracked pepper (Peasmarsh); in garlic pepper, parsley, and salt crumb (Icklesham); and infused with fresh chives (Winchelsea).

HOW TO ENJOY Spread on bread or a cracker, use it in a salad or in cooking, or try it in a cheesecake recipe.

ENGLAND Hastings, East Sussex	
Age 6 days	
Weight and Shape 7oz (200g), log	
Size L. 3in (7.5cm), H. 1½in (4cm)	
Milk Goat	
Classification Fresh	
Producer Hollypark Organics	

Cheddar

The story of Cheddar can be traced back to the Romans who introduced hard cheeses to Britain. It was the feudal system, however, that led to the development of the large, buxom traditional British cheeses because it placed the majority of land in the hands of a few great landowners who could afford to make very large cheeses.

Yet, it was not until the 16th century that this hard cheese made in the Mendip Hills near the Cheddar Gorge in Somerset became known as Cheddar. The lush grazing, rolling hills and natural caves offered the ideal conditions for large herds and meant the cheesemakers tended to make huge 60–120lb (27–54kg) cheeses requiring 2–3 years to mature.

The rolling hills *of England's West Country.*

Since then it has been emulated throughout the world, especially Canada, Australia, and New Zealand where the majority is made in blocks rather than elegant clothbound cylinders. But only those made from cows that graze the green and verdant hills of England truly deserve the name Cheddar.

TASTING NOTES To taste an unpasteurized, clothbound cheddar made from the milk of cows whose diet is fresh grass, clover, buttercups, and daisies, is to taste a piece of England. The bite is firm but yielding like chocolate, the aroma earthy and slightly savory. The flavor differs from farm to farm, but there is always the rich sweetness of the milk, a classic acidity, sometimes nutty, often with an explosion of flavor in the mouth and a lingering cheese and onion tang.

HOW TO ENJOY For generations, Cheddar has been an integral part of the English diet, in sandwiches, as quick snacks, in lunches, or displayed in huge wedges on cheese platters, embellished with pickled walnuts, and crusty bread. It is also superb in sauces, melted over baked potatoes, or grated over numerous vegetable dishes and broiled. Best with a Merlot or Pinot Noir, but avoid Clarets, as they have too much tannin.

FARMHOUSE CHEDDAR

Although the texture and quality of block cheddar has improved enormously in recent years, it can never achieve the same hardness and depth of flavor as those made by hand with the raw milk of a single farm. The following produce prime examples of excellent farmhouse Cheddar.

Ashley Chase Dairy, Dorset
Cheddar Gorge Cheese Company, Somerset
Denhay Cheddar, Dorset
Green's of Glastonbury, Somerset
Keen's, Somerset
Montgomery's, Somerset
Quickes Traditional Cheeses, Devon
Westcombe Cheddar, Somerset

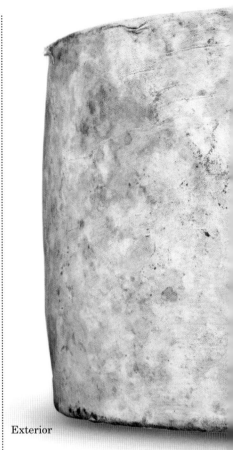

Exterior

The fine gray mold that grows over the cloth reduces the moisture loss so that the cheese can develop its characteristic hard, dense, creamy texture and earthy aroma.

A CLOSER LOOK

Cheddar can be sold as young as six months, when it has a softer texture and mild, almost buttery taste. At 12 months, the texture is firmer, almost chewy, and the taste is more intense. At 18 months, the texture is drier, sometimes with crunchy calcium crystals and the flavor more savory.

Wedge

ENGLAND Dorset, Devon, and Somerset	
Age 6–24 months	
Weight and Shape 56lb (26kg), cylinder or block	
Size D. 12½in (32cm), H. 10½in (26cm)	
Milk Cow	
Classification Hard	
Producer Various	

CHEDDARING To create the unique texture of Cheddar, the mass of curds is molded into brick-sized blocks and piled two bricks high. This process is repeated every 15–20 minutes until the bricks flatten out, the acidity rises, and more whey is forced out.

MILLING The flattened bricks are then milled or "minced" to finger-sized pieces and pitched by hand using giant forks to aerate and cool the curd before salting.

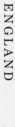

The interior is a soft sunshine butter-yellow color with an orange tinge as it ages.

Interior

Farleigh Wallop

Produced by Peter Humphries at White Lake Cheeses in Somerset, and created by Alex James (Blur bassist) and Juliet Harbutt (chairman British Cheese Awards), this lovely Camembert-style cheese is decorated with a sprig of thyme, pressed into the velvety crust.

TASTING NOTES Uncomplicated yet far from overly simple, this lovely-looking cheese liquefies with age, exuding hints of mushroom and thyme, with a gentle almondy nuttiness on the finish.

HOW TO ENJOY Enjoy it as is—a visual pleasure, too—or try it in a light-as-air soufflé or grilled over roasted beetroot with a dry New Zealand Riesling.

ENGLAND Glastonbury, Somerset	
Age 4–6 weeks	
Weight and Shape 4oz (125g), round	
Size D. 3¼in (8cm), H. 1¼in (3cm)	
Milk Goat	
Classification Soft white	
Producer White Lake Cheeses	

Finn

Charlie Westhead, Haydn Roberts, and their team produce cheeses in a dairy atop Dorstone Hill, with glorious views over the Wye Valley towards the Black Mountains. As with French double-cream cheeses, ten percent additional cream is added to the milk before the cheesemaking begins, giving it a creamy riches.

TASTING NOTES Inside its creamy-white rind lies a soft but firm cheese with a creamy acidity, a salty-sweet mingling, and a hint of mushrooms.

HOW TO ENJOY Bake with it, or savor the extra richness set off to perfection by the plainest of crackers.

ENGLAND Dorstone, Herefordshire	
Age 3 weeks	
Weight and Shape 10½oz (300g), round	
Size D. 4in (10cm), H. 2in (5cm)	
Milk Cow	
Classification Soft white	
Producer Neal's Yard Creamery	

Flower Marie

Kevin and Alison Blunt produce this unique ewe's milk cheese, with its soft rind and moist interior that is often compared to the feel of melting ice cream. They have been making cheese on the farm since 1989; this one lives up to its name—demure-looking, but with a suggestion of naughtiness, captured in a lemony freshness.

TASTING NOTES: The sweetness of the ewe's milk lends a caramel subtlety that is gentle and moist, while the rind has a mushroomy taste and aroma.

HOW TO ENJOY Serve it spread on a chunk of fresh, soft crusty bread, accompanied by a glass of fine port.

ENGLAND Whitesmith, East Sussex	
Age 4–5 weeks	
Weight and Shape 7oz (200g), square	
Size D. 2½in (6cm), H. 2in (5cm)	
Milk Ewe	
Classification Soft white	
Producer Golden Cross Cheese Company	

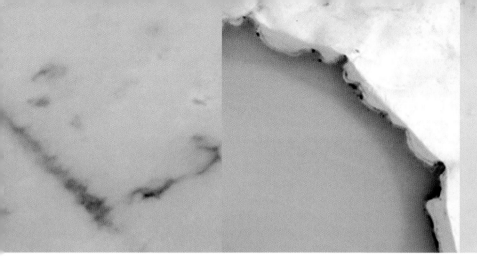

Fowlers Forest Blue

Fowlers can lay claim to the title of oldest cheesemaking family business in England, the keepers of cheesemaking secrets whispered down through the generations. They are also proud of the high-calcium water from the 1,000-ft (300-m) borehole, which adds to the cheese's flavor and texture.

TASTING NOTES This is a handcrafted traditional blue cheese, which matures in humidity-controlled cellars. Soft-rinded, firm, and creamy, it is lightly veined, salty, and mildly tangy.

HOW TO ENJOY Melt together with Warwickshire ale and Worcestershire sauce, and spread on toast.

ENGLAND Earlswood, West Midlands	
Age 3 months	
Weight and Shape 11lb (5kg), cylinder	
Size D. 8in (20cm), H. 6in (15cm)	
Milk Cow	
Classification Blue	
Producer Fowlers of Earlswood	

Golden Cross

Kevin and Alison Blunt's herd of 300 goats grazes outside all summer and enjoys a diet of hay all year round, which contributes to continuing success at the British Cheese Awards. From their milk comes a St Maure-style cheese, each log lightly dusted with charcoal and matured to a creamy, full flavor.

TASTING NOTES Sweeter in taste than you might expect, it is soft and delicate, and redolent of those grassy pastures that the goats so enjoy.

HOW TO ENJOY Complemented by celery on a cheeseboard, it is also an excellent cheese for all sorts of dishes, thanks to its gorgeous texture.

ENGLAND Whitesmith, East Sussex	
Age 3–4 weeks	
Weight and Shape 9oz (225g), log	
Size L. 5½in (14cm), H. 2in (5cm)	
Milk Goat	
Classification Soft white	
Producer Golden Cross Cheese Company	

Hereford Hop

The lightly roasted hops give this cheese its instantly recognizable appearance, but it is the skill of the almost-legendary Charles Martell that ensures the quality under the surface. He has also helped to preserve rare breed Gloucester cattle and to revive interest in perry, which is like cider, but made with local pears.

TASTING NOTES Mellow sweetness is thrown into relief by the aroma and taste of the cheese's coat of hops, like a hint of beer permeating through.

HOW TO ENJOY A delightful addition to the cheeseboard, particularly with a dollop of homemade apple chutney.

ENGLAND Dymock, Gloucestershire	
Age 10–12 weeks	
Weight and Shape 5lb (2.2kg), round	
Size D. 8½in (22cm), H. 2¾in (7cm)	
Milk Cow	
Classification Flavor-added	
Producer Charles Martell & Son	

Innes Button

This tiny unpasteurized goat's cheese, made by Stella Bennett, was the first cheese ever to win Supreme Champion twice at the British Cheese Awards. It is now a favorite of culinary gurus such as Anton Mosimann and Nigel Slater, and top London cheese shops.

TASTING NOTES **Perfection itself—soft, almost mousse-like, it melts in the mouth, releasing its lemony freshness with hints of walnuts and white wine on the finish. Available with ash, pink peppercorns, or chopped nuts.**

HOW TO ENJOY **Savor on its own, spread on soft, warm bread, or grill and serve with a Sauvignon Blanc or Viognier.**

ENGLAND Tamworth, Staffordshire	
Age 3–7 days	
Weight and Shape 1¾oz (50g), button	
Size D. 2in (5cm), H. 1in (2.5cm)	
Milk Goat	
Classification Fresh	
Producer Innes Cheese	

Isle of Wight Blue

Guernsey cows that munch on the riches of the Isle of Wight's fertile Arreton Valley help give this tangy yet mellow cheese its creamy texture. Richard Hodgson gave up a career as a film editor to make cheese, while his mother, Julie, joined him after selling the family's small hotel.

TASTING NOTES **A thick gray molded rind hides a mellow, nutty paste, which is smooth in texture with a slight spicy bite from the blue.**

HOW TO ENJOY **Simply enjoy it as it comes or as part of a cheeseboard, or layer it with slices of fresh pear for rather special party canapés.**

ENGLAND Sandown, Isle of Wight	
Age 3–5 weeks	
Weight and Shape 8oz (230g), drum	
Size D. 3½in (9cm), H. 1¾in (4.5cm)	
Milk Cow	
Classification Blue	
Producer Isle of Wight Cheese Company	

Keltic Gold

Full of pungency and character all at the same time, this cheese from Sue Proudfoot is rind-washed three times a week with local cider until it is ripe. The resulting sticky terra-cotta rind should not be ignored, but instead form part of the pleasure of the eating.

TASTING NOTES **Prepare to be deluged by layers of delicious notes, varying from bacon to yeast, with distinct nuttiness in between and farmyardy finish.**

HOW TO ENJOY **Make a vegetarian version of a Cornish pasty with apple, onion, and sage wrapped around Keltic Gold, or melt it with a little freshly grated nutmeg for an alpine-style fondue.**

ENGLAND Bude, Cornwall	
Age 4–6 weeks	
Weight and Shape 3lb 3oz (1.5kg), drum	
Size D. 8in (20cm), H. 3in (7.5cm)	
Milk Cow	
Classification Semi-soft	
Producer Whalesborough Farm Foods	

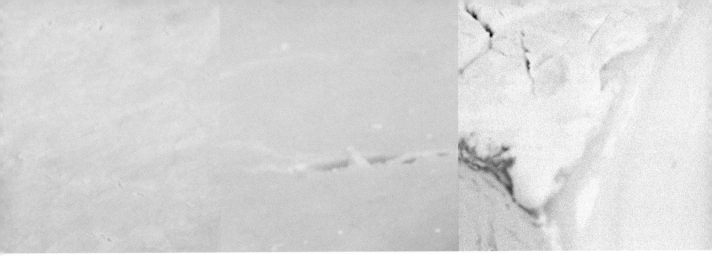

Lancashire

One of the great "territorial" cheeses of England, Lancashire comes in three main styles: creamy, tasty, and crumbly, the latter being a fast-ripening and high-acid recent creation. Its history goes back as far as the 13th century, when every farmer's wife made use of surplus milk.

TASTING NOTES Made by combining the curd from three consecutive days, it has a mottled appearance, soft, vaguely lumpy feel in the mouth, and buttery richness balanced by an oniony tang.

HOW TO ENJOY Its meltingly smooth, even consistency makes it ideal for anything from cheese on toast to tasty pies.

ENGLAND Around the Forest of Bowland, Lancashire
Age 4–12 weeks for "creamy"; 12-plus weeks for "tasty"
Weight and Shape 41½lb (19kg), cylinder
Size D. 12in (30cm), H. 10in (25cm)
Milk Cow
Classification Hard
Producer Various

Lincolnshire Poacher

Once a traditional folk song, it is now also a cheese invented by Simon Jones and made with his brother Tim. It was originally a brilliant solution to the abundant supplies of spring milk from their herd of Holsteins, and has become a much-loved modern British cheese. It was Supreme Champion at the British Cheese Awards in 1996.

TASTING NOTES This is similar to an excellent mature Cheddar-style cheese. Hard and chewy, lively and complex, it offers a full taste experience.

HOW TO ENJOY Eat it plain, grate it, melt it, or bake it with onions, bacon, and potatoes for a fine gratin.

ENGLAND Alford, Lincolnshire
Age 12–24 months
Weight and Shape 44lb (20kg), cylinder
Size D. 12in (30cm), H. 9in (23cm)
Milk Cow
Classification Hard
Producer FW Read & Sons Ltd

Little Ryding

Previously made by Mary Holbrook of Timsbury, it is now made by the Bartlett brothers, to whom she sold her recipe after deciding to concentrate on goat's cheese. In 2004, using milk from their own flock, James and David's first cheese went on sale, to great applause.

TASTING NOTES Handmade with a Camembert-like rind and creamy middle, this is like traditional British Sunday lunch on a plate, with flavors of burnt onions and roast lamb, and yet a caramel sweetness, too.

HOW TO ENJOY: Serve simply with thin crackers and a side order of homemade caramelized onion chutney.

ENGLAND North Wootton, Somerset
Age 3–8 weeks
Weight and Shape 7oz (200g), round
Size D. 4in (10cm), H. 1¼in (3cm)
Milk Ewe
Classification Soft white
Producer Wootton Organic Dairy

Little Wallop

It was a big move for Juliet Harbutt, founder of the British Cheese Awards, to establish her own cheese label; being who she is, she had to get it right. In partnership with columnist and musician Alex James, that's exactly what she has done.

TASTING NOTES Produced exclusively for them by White Lake Cheese, Little Wallop is washed in local cider brandy and wrapped in vine leaves. When young, it exudes a mild, creamy freshness, which later matures into a nutty, distinctly goaty complexity.

HOW TO ENJOY A beautiful-looking cheese to grace any cheeseboard.

ENGLAND Glastonbury, Somerset	
Age 3–6 weeks	
Weight and Shape 4oz (115g), round	
Size D. 3¼in (8cm), H. 1½in (4cm)	
Milk Goat	
Classification Natural rind	
Producer White Lake Cheese	

Lord of the Hundreds

Radiating out from the hamlet of Stonegate are the slopes of the Rother Valley, a landscape that leaves clues of its many qualities within the subtleties of this cheese. Cheesemaker Cliff Dyball gave up a career in London as an insurance broker for rewards of a different kind.

TASTING NOTES It has a rustic reddish brown rind, dusted with gray, and a compactly satisfying density within. Think pecorino; expect a dry, grainy texture, with mild nuttiness alongside a deep burnt caramel sweetness.

HOW TO ENJOY The maker recommends quince jelly as the perfect complement.

ENGLAND Stonegate, East Sussex	
Age 6–8 months	
Weight and Shape 5½–10½lb (2.5–4.8kg), round	
Size D. 7–9½in (18–24cm), H. 3–4½in (7.5–11cm)	
Milk Ewe	
Classification Hard	
Producer The Traditional Cheese Dairy	

New Forest Blue

Gwyn and Ness Williams use pure Ayrshire milk from a herd grazed on the Hampshire Downs; it is, they say, "the best milk we have ever tasted, and fantastic for cheesemaking". The recipes for their cheeses—including this excellent example—are designed to bring out the milk's charmingly idiosyncratic characteristics.

TASTING NOTES It has a light blue touch, with an attractive sharpness from that extra blue tang.

HOW TO ENJOY Pep up risotto, crumble over salads, or savor the full taste of "Ayrshire" by serving this cheese as simply as possible.

ENGLAND Redlynch, Wiltshire	
Age 6–8 weeks	
Weight and Shape 3lb 3oz (1.5kg), cylinder	
Size D. 6¾in (17cm), H. 4½in (11cm)	
Milk Cow	
Classification Blue	
Producer Loosehanger Cheeses	

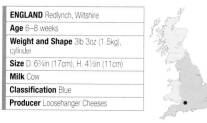

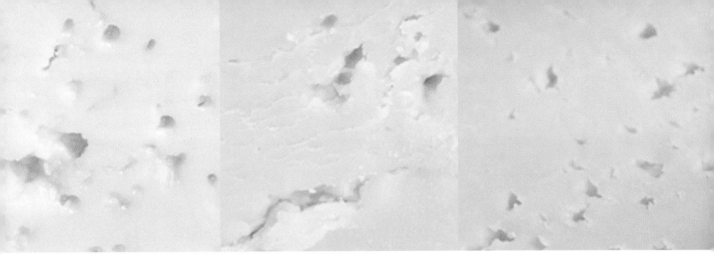

Norsworthy

Originally a naval engineer from Durham, Dave Johnson now has his own herd of 180 goats in Devon and makes a series of hard and soft cheeses. Based on a Dutch recipe, Norsworthy is made from unpasteurized milk using the Dutch washed-curd method.

TASTING NOTES Its pleasant and mild taste deepens and lingers. Matured for a month, it develops a fine crusty brown rind and a white paste within that becomes more crumbly as it ripens.

HOW TO ENJOY Delicious served with a chunk of fresh crusty country-style bread, accompanied by an English pale ale or a Merlot.

ENGLAND Norsworthy, Devon	
Age 1 month	
Weight and Shape 4½–5½lb (2.5kg), round	
Size D. 7in (18cm), H. 4½in (11cm)	
Milk Goat	
Classification Semi-soft	
Producer Norsworthy Dairy Goats	

Northumberland

It was a book about sheep and their cheeses that first set Mark Robertson along the artisan cheese road in 1984, and he received so much support and encouragement that he ended up diversifying into goats and cows. Over the years, he has taken inspiration from various sources.

TASTING NOTES A Gouda-style cheese, it is smooth, moist, mild, and creamy, with hints of green grass and red onions. Also available in flavored versions.

HOW TO ENJOY The perfect choice for making traditional Northumberland pan haggerty, with its layers of potato, onion, and grated cheese.

ENGLAND Blagdon, Northumberland	
Age 12 weeks	
Weight and Shape 5lb (2.3kg), round	
Size D. 9in (20cm), H. 7½in (3cm)	
Milk Cow	
Classification Hard	
Producer Northumberland Cheese Company	

Ogleshield

When Cheddar cheesemaker Jamie Montgomery had two Americans to stay, they all spent some enjoyable hours using his Jersey milk in various "experiments". Thus Jersey Shield was born. Bill Oglethorpe at Neal's Yard Dairy then began another round of experiments, using the washed-rind technique to arrive at this cheese.

TASTING NOTES Beneath the orange rind is a yellow heart with an aroma as robust as its flavor—onion soup and yeasty bread. A cheese to get to know.

HOW TO ENJOY Think of raclette; this is an excellent West Country alternative that melts like a dream.

ENGLAND North Cadbury, Somerset	
Age 4–5 months	
Weight and Shape 12¼lb (5kg) wheel	
Size D. 12½in (32cm), H. 3½in (9cm)	
Milk Cow	
Classification Semi-soft	
Producer JA & E Montgomery	

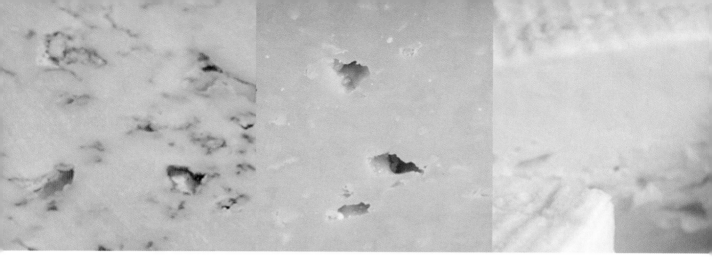

Old Sarum

With this dairy's cheeses, you know that the Ayrshire cow's milk will produce that characteristic smooth-as-velvet texture. Old Sarum comes in the form of a tall, elegant cylinder with a natural gray-brown rind, a moist interior, and blue-gray veins amid a yellow paste.

TASTING NOTES In the tradition of the Italian soft blue cheese Dolcelatte, this is a sweet-tasting blue that melts in the mouth like rich, spicy butter.

HOW TO ENJOY As an indulgent lunchtime treat, serve in a crusty baguette with crispy, preferably rare-breed bacon.

ENGLAND Redlynch, Wiltshire	
Age 6–8 weeks	
Weight and Shape 3lb 3oz (1.5kg), tall cylinder	
Size D. 6¾in (17cm), H. 4½in (11cm)	
Milk Cow	
Classification Blue	
Producer Loosehanger Cheeses	

Old Winchester

Mike and Judy Smales, who have been making their cheeses for eight years, came up with Old Winchester—still creamy, but with "subtle nuttiness"—to satisfy customers who were looking for a fuller flavored cheese. It is also known as Old Smales.

TASTING NOTES Old Winchester's hard, smooth crust protects the hard, almost brittle warm yellow interior, with its distinctive nuttiness and lasting salty-sweet finale.

HOW TO ENJOY Use as either a table cheese or a vegetarian alternative to hard Italian cheeses.

ENGLAND Landford, Wiltshire	
Age 16 months	
Weight and Shape 9lb (4kg), boulder	
Size D. 9in (23cm), H. 3in (7.5cm)	
Milk Cow	
Classification Hard	
Producer Lyburn Farmhouse Cheesemakers	

Oxford Isis

Created by Harley Pouget and his father, who is best known for his Oxford Blue, this cheese is lightly washed with five-year-old full-flavored locally produced mead (made from fermented honey) that continues to mature in the bottle.

TASTING NOTES The sticky orange rind has a pervasive aroma that is both spicy and pungent, while the interior is velvety, almost runny, with a sweet yeasty taste from the mead.

HOW TO ENJOY Serve on a cheeseboard with crusty bread and, if you can find it, a glass of mead.

ENGLAND Oxford, Oxfordshire	
Age 6–8 weeks	
Weight and Shape 8oz (225g), round	
Size D. 4in (10cm), H. 1in (2.5cm)	
Milk Cow	
Classification Semi-soft	
Producer Oxford Cheese Company	

Pendragon

Philip Rainbow, one of a handful of producers in Britain to use buffalo's milk, makes this firm Cheddar-style cheese. Pendragon takes its name from strong historical connections Somerset has with the Arthurian myths. It is also available lightly smoked.

TASTING NOTES The hard, waxy yellow paste has a mild sweetness and its understated character appeals to those who like a clean flavor. Being made with buffalo milk means that the cheese is admirably low in cholesterol.

HOW TO ENJOY Assemble a sophisticated cheeseboard, using Pendragon to give variety among cow's and goat's cheeses.

ENGLAND Ditcheat, Somerset	
Age 4–12 months	
Weight and Shape 4½lb (2kg) and 7½lb (3.5kg), round	
Size D. 7in (18cm) and 10in (25cm), H. 2¾in (7cm)	
Milk Buffalo	
Classification Hard	
Producer Somerset Cheese Company	

Penyston

The Friesians of Daylesford Organic enjoy the clean, unspoiled pastures of this timeless part of England; you can even taste the seasons in the cheese. Penyston might call to mind the popular Norman cheese Pont l'Evêque, but it has its own distinguishing features and is mild for a washed rind.

TASTING NOTES Described as delivering "waves of flavor", the cheese leads from a meaty aroma to a full-bodied orange stickiness as it ages.

HOW TO ENJOY Use in an upmarket cheese and tomato sandwich, preferably made with a loaf of organic country-style bread.

ENGLAND Daylesford, Gloucestershire	
Age 8 weeks	
Weight and Shape 10½oz (300g), square	
Size L. 4in (10cm), W. 4in (10cm), H. 1¼in (3cm)	
Milk Cow	
Classification Semi-soft	
Producer Daylesford Creamery	

Perroche

These elegant individual cylinders, available plain or rolled in fresh herbs, use milk from a farm near Ashleworth in Gloucestershire. Although now produced by Charlie Westhead, Haydn Roberts, and the team, the cheese's name derives from the creamery's previous managers, Perry James and Beatrice Garroche.

TASTING NOTES Gently does it with this process, resulting in a light, mousse-like texture with a subtle goaty taste and clean, almondy finish.

HOW TO ENJOY Delia Smith herself makes a point of recommending Perroche as a beautifully mild cheese that grills well.

ENGLAND Dorstone, Herefordshire	
Age 1 week	
Weight and Shape 5½oz (150g), cylinder	
Size D. 2½in (6cm) base, 2in (5cm) top, H. 2¾in (7cm)	
Milk Goat's milk	
Classification Fresh	
Producer Neal's Yard Creamery	

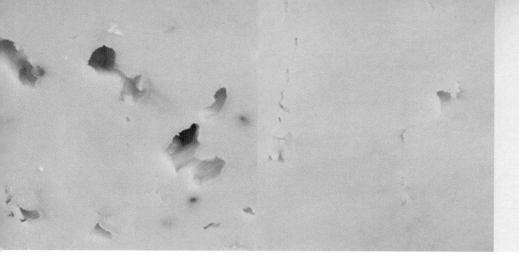

Posbury

Posbury is a Dutch-style cheese based on Dave Johnson's Norsworthy (see p189). Flavored with garlic, onion, horseradish, and paprika, this flavor-added cheese shows an excellent balance of tastes.

TASTING NOTES The orange rind conceals a white paste dotted with holes and orangey flecks. Posbury's flavor is mild and creamy, but the horseraddish gives it a warm kick on the palate.

HOW TO ENJOY This is excellent sandwich material, particularly nestled between slices of wholemeal bread.

ENGLAND Norsworthy, Devon	
Age 4-plus weeks	
Weight and Shape 4½–5½lb (2–2.5kg), round	
Size D. 7in (18cm), H. 4½in (11cm)	
Milk Goat	
Classification Flavor-added	
Producer Norsworthy Dairy Goats	

Quickes Hard Goat

The Quicke family has farmed the same land for more than 450 years. Aound 40 years ago, Sir John and his wife, Prue, built the dairy where their daughter Mary continues to produce cheese, including this recently created Cheddar-style goat cheese.

TASTING NOTES Firm, almost chewy, it has a subtle goaty taste and an aromatic, almondy tang with a fresh acidity. This is an excellent alternative for people with an allergy to cow's milk.

HOW TO ENJOY This cooks superbly. Try wilting spinach or similar greens in a little water, add with the cheese to a roux of rice flour and milk, then purée.

ENGLAND Newton St Cyres, Devon	
Age 6–10 months	
Weight and Shape 53lb (24kg), truckle	
Size D. 14in (35.5cm), H. 12in (30cm)	
Milk Goat	
Classification Hard	
Producer Quickes Traditional	

Rachel

Peter Humphries makes two washed-rind cheeses: Morn Dew, with cow's milk, and this one, made with goat's milk. It looks distinguished, with its fine orange leathery rind, dusted with white, gray, and even yellow with molds—it is the most popular cheese he produces.

TASTING NOTES Rachel is sweet, curvy, and slightly nutty, with a whole raft of taste experiences: rich and tangy, meaty and savory, but with a citric sharpness and a sweet nutty finish.

HOW TO ENJOY Savor on its own or in a salad, paired with a glass of Sancerre or a single-varietal cider.

ENGLAND Pylle, Somerset	
Age 3 months	
Weight and Shape 4½lb (2kg), round	
Size D. 7in (18cm), H. 2¾in (7cm)	
Milk Goat	
Classification Semi-soft	
Producer White Lake Cheeses	

Ragstone

Another great cheese from Charlie Westhead, Ragstone was originally made in his first creamery based near Sevenoaks in Kent, and it was the nearby Ragstone Ridge that lent its name to this cheese.

TASTING NOTES The wrinkly rind will call to mind a Brie, and it is certainly a lovely-looking product. Creamy yet light on the tongue, it has a hint of mushroomy notes and a lemony tang.

HOW TO ENJOY This cheese melts superbly. Alternatively, bake in the oven, drizzled with a little olive oil, until it is at melting point. Serve warm and oozy, on a bed of mixed leaves.

ENGLAND Dorstone, Herefordshire	
Age 3 weeks	
Weight and Shape 10½oz (300g), log	
Size L. 6in (15cm), H. 2in (5cm)	
Milk Goat	
Classification Soft white	
Producer Neal's Yard Creamery	

Red Leicester

Named after the city of Leicester, this traditional English cheese is made in a similar way to Cheddar, but colored with annatto. Prolific by the late eighteenth century, its quality was partly ascribed to the county's excellent grazing. Farmhouse production in the county had died out by the mid 1900s, until 2005 when the Leicestershire Handmade Cheese Company revived it.

TASTING NOTES The distinctive tangerine coloured interior is dense, waxy, and smooth, with a sweet, mellow nuttiness that strengthens as it matures.

HOW TO ENJOY Serve on toast, in tarts, or use it to add color to a cheeseboard.

ENGLAND Leicestershire	
Age 4–5 months	
Weight and Shape 22lb (10kg) and 44lb (20kg), wheel	
Size D. 14in (35.5cm) and 18in (46cm), H. 5in (13cm) and 7in (18cm)	
Milk Cow	
Classification Hard	
Producer Various	

Ribblesdale Original Goat

The late Iain Hill and his wife Christine created this fresh, delicate cheese, and niece Iona now carries on their work. It is made in the Yorkshire Dales' Ribble Valley, where the natural pastures and high rainfall provide excellent grazing for the goats.

TASTING NOTES With a firm yet supple texture like young Gouda, it is delicately goaty and has chicory and almond flavors.

HOW TO ENJOY Serve on its own, grate it, melt it, or, above all, bake it with figs. Works well with an oaky Chardonnay or Merlot.

ENGLAND Horton-in-Ribblesdale, North Yorkshire	
Age 8–12 weeks	
Weight and Shape 4½lb (2kg), boulder	
Size D. 8in (20cm), H. 2½in (6cm)	
Milk Goat	
Classification Hard	
Producer Ribblesdale Cheese Company	

Stilton PDO

In the early 18th Century, the town of Stilton was a major staging post on the London to York road, and the landlord of the Bell Inn in Stilton started serving a soft, blue-veined cheese made in the nearby Leicestershire town of Melton Mowbray.

Such was the popularity of the cheese that Cooper Thornhill, the enterprising landlord, was soon sending Stilton to London, upward of a thousand a week by the mid-1700s. The cheese was therefore named after the place from which it was made famous, rather than where it was made.

Initially made on small farms, the intricate and time-consuming nature of its production soon influenced Stilton-makers to join forces, and in 1875 the first Stilton was produced by hand in a small factory. In 1910, the Stilton Makers Association was registered as a trademark, ensuring the cheese could only be made in the counties of Nottinghamshire, Derbyshire, and Leicestershire, and This decision ultimately saved the cheese from mediocrity or even extinction—the fate of other fine British fine territorial cheeses.

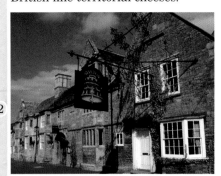

The Bell Inn, *which is in the town of Stilton, Peterborough, England.*

Today, Stilton is one of a handful of British cheeses granted Protected Designation Origin (PDO) status by the European Commission. There are just seven dairies licensed to make Stilton.

TASTING NOTES Each maker's cheese is slightly different, but all are sharp and aggressive when eaten too young and mellow out to a rich, spicy butter taste with hints of cocoa on the finish and sometimes a touch of walnuts or a slight sharp acidity.

HOW TO ENJOY Ideal for sauces, dressings, and soups, especially broccoli or celery soup, baked in a quiche or tart, paired with spinach or crumbled over a grilled steak, or into a salad with a sweet balsamic dressing.

The sweet richness of vintage Port can overpower Stilton. Instead, try a tawny Port or a crisp yet sweet wine like Montbazillac, but not Sauterne, which is too sweet. Alternatively, try an aromatic dry Riesling or light beer.

The tradition of pouring Port into Stilton came about to kill the creatures that gathered at the bottom of Stilton bells. Nowadays, with modern refrigeration, there is no need to spoil the Stilton or waste good Port.

A CLOSER LOOK

To create the smooth buttery texture characteristic of Stilton, the freshly drained curds are left to ripen overnight, significantly longer than most other cheeses.

Jagged blue lines radiate erratically from the center to the outside like shattered porcelain.

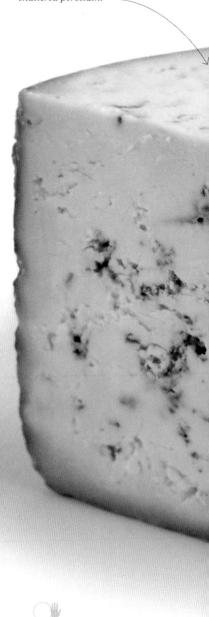

BRITAIN	Nottinghamshire, Derbyshire, and Leicestershire
Age	9–14 weeks
Weight and Shape	17lb (7.5 kg), tall cylinder
Size	D. 8in (20cm), H.12in (30cm)
Milk	Cow
Classification	Blue
Producer	Various

SALTING The curd is milled before being measured into special pans so the salt can be mixed through by hand.

THE MOLDS The curds are placed in tall, open-ended, stainless steel, cylindrical molds and placed on wooden slates where gravity and the weight of the curd gradually forces out whey through the holes in the sides of the hoops and through the bottom. Some 17 gallons (77 liters) of milk are required to make one 15lb (7.5kg) Stilton. Once the cheese can stand on its own, it is removed and the curds allowed to drain overnight.

PIERCING At about 6 weeks, each cheese is placed on a special stand and pierced with 18–20 long, narrow stainless steel needles to allow air to enter the body of the cheese.

GRADING Before being released to the retailers, each batch is graded. An "iron" is used to bore into the cheese and extract a plug. By visual inspection and by smell, the grader can determine whether the cheese is up to the mark.

Quarter cylinder

The interior should be straw yellow, not brown or dull.

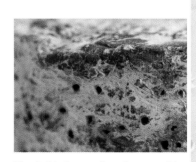

The rind is dry, rough, and crusty, with the pierced holes quite visible.

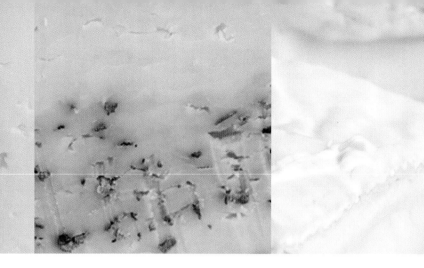

Rosary Plain

Chris and Claire Moody began making cheese in 1986, originally using milk from their own small herd of goats. As they became more successful, however, the pair made the pragmatic decision to buy in milk from a herd of pedigree Saanen goats. Their fresh cheese Rosary Plain is a consistent award-winner at the British Cheese Awards.

TASTING NOTES Moist, fresh, meltingly soft, and delightfully aromatic, it also comes in flavored garlic and herb, pepper-coated, and ash-coated versions.

HOW TO ENJOY Use as a table cheese, for melting or spreading, or add it at the last moment to a fluffy omelette.

ENGLAND Landford, Wiltshire	
Age 3 days	
Weight and Shape 3½oz (100g), round	
Size D. 2in (5cm), H. 1½in (4cm)	
Milk Goat	
Classification Fresh	
Producer Rosary Goats Cheese	

Sage Derby

Derby is one of England's oldest and most famous cheeses. The custom of adding finely chopped sage, thought to have health-giving properties, to the fresh curd began in the 17th century. Today, most are factory-made, but the West Midlands family producer, Fowlers of Earlswood, still makes Sage Derby traditionally.

TASTING NOTES Softer than Cheddar, this pale yellow cheese has a melted butter taste and a delightful, but subtle, herbal flavor from the sage.

HOW TO ENJOY With its ribbon of herbs, this makes a colorful and distinctive addition to the cheeseboard.

ENGLAND West Midlands	
Age 10–20 weeks	
Weight and Shape 3lb 3oz (1.5kg), round	
Size D. 8in (20cm), H. 4in (10cm)	
Milk Cow	
Classification Flavor-added	
Producer Various	

St. Eadburgha

The Staceys have farmed at the foot of the Cotswolds for more than 35 years, and named this Camembert-style cheese after the great-granddaughter of Alfred the Great, to whom a local church is dedicated. It is made from the milk of Montbeliarde and Friesian cows that graze in pear orchards and on lush, grassy pastures.

TASTING NOTES This is at its best when it is soft in the middle, when the flavor becomes more pungent and meaty.

HOW TO ENJOY Delicious warmed until the inside starts to run, or on the cheeseboard with cider, a light ale, or a full-bodied red wine.

ENGLAND Broadway, Worcestershire	
Age 4–12 weeks	
Weight and Shape 6oz–6½lb (175g–3kg), round	
Size D. 3½–13¾in (9–35cm), H. 1½in (4cm)	
Milk Cow	
Classification Soft white	
Producer Gorsehill Abbey Farm	

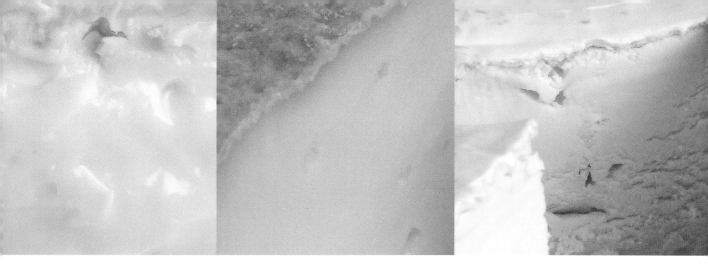

St. Endellion

Started by two farming families in 1996, the creamery—which overlooks the rugged Atlantic coast—has made a name for itself with its innovative approach to cheesemaking. This is a Brie-style cheese made with Cornish double cream.

TASTING NOTES Luxury is the keynote here. As the cheese ripens, the paste softens to a wonderful creamy consistency with a full-bodied flavor, fresh tanginess, and hint of mushroom.

HOW TO ENJOY Leave loosely wrapped for a couple of hours, before serving as part of a cheeseboard. It is especially good with a spicy white wine.

ENGLAND Trevarrian, Cornwall	
Age 6 weeks	
Weight and Shape 7oz (200g) and 2lb 3oz (1kg), round	
Size D. 8in (20cm) and 35½in (90cm), H. 1in (3cm) and 1½in (3.5cm)	
Milk Cow	
Classification Soft white	
Producer Cornish Country Larder	

St. Oswald

This cheese, another from Mike Stacey, is named after a former Bishop of Worcester. It is washed in brine and matured for at least one month, and the rind changes from yellow to a sticky orange-brown as it matures. St. Oswald is the latest addition to this dairy's repertoire.

TASTING NOTES The smooth, supple paste becomes almost runny and has a full, rich meaty flavor, with onion notes that become stronger as it ages.

HOW TO ENJOY Serve as it comes with a good full-bodied red wine and dried fruit. Or put a few dollops in among finely sliced potatoes, and bake.

ENGLAND Broadway, Worcestershire	
Age 1–3 months	
Weight and Shape 12oz (350g) and 5½lb (2.5kg), round	
Size D. 4½in (11cm) and 13¾in (35cm), H. 1¾in (4.5cm)	
Milk Cow	
Classification Semi-soft	
Producer Gorsehill Abbey Farm	

Sharpham

Reminiscent of a small Brie, Sharpham is produced by one of the first British creameries to make this style of cheese. The estate began making it by hand, to its own recipe, in 1980, using milk from the estate's herd of Jersey cows, which graze beside the river Dart near Totnes.

TASTING NOTES It has a wonderfully creamy texture (firm to begin with, but softens with ripening) and a unique depth of intense flavor, with some mushroom character.

HOW TO ENJOY Good on its own, but also a handsome-looking choice for gracing the cheeseboard. Matches well with a red wine from the Sharpham Estate.

ENGLAND Totnes, Devon	
Age 4–8 weeks	
Weight and Shape 9oz–2¼lb (250g–1kg), square and round	
Size D. 3¾in (9.5cm) and 7½in (19cm), H. 1½in (4cm) and 1¾in (4.5cm)	
Milk Cow	
Classification Soft white	
Producer Sharpham Partnership	

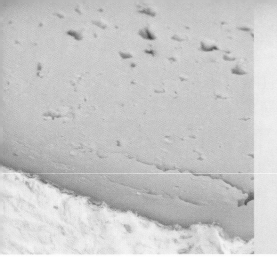
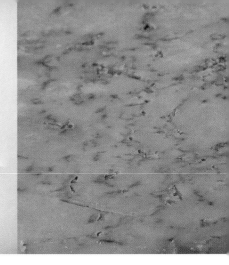

Sharpham Rustic

One of several cheeses produced on this estate, also famous for its outstanding wines, Rustic is made using sweet, rich milk from the Jersey herd. The curd is placed, unpressed, in a colander to give it its unusual shape and knobbly rind. Also available with chives and garlic.

TASTING NOTES Deep yellow with a natural mold-coated rind, this moist cheese has a wonderful creamy texture and a buttery sweet flavor balanced by a fresh, gentle acidity.

HOW TO ENJOY Serve on its own or crumbled over warm asparagus or into a roast beetroot and pea shoot salad, with a glass of cider or fruity red wine.

ENGLAND Totnes, Devon
Age 6–8 weeks
Weight and Shape 3¾lb (1.7kg), elliptical
Size D. 7in (18cm), H. 3½in (9cm)
Milk Cow
Classification Semi-soft
Producer Sharpham Partnership

Shipcord

Suffolk is not traditionally known as a cheesemaking region, so when the Richards family, long-standing dairy farmers, decided to start cheesemaking in 2006, local cheese lovers greeted them enthusiastically. Each cheese is named after a river meadow on the farm.

TASTING NOTES The curds and whey are scalded, reminiscent of French tommes, giving the cheese a close texture and a "long" creamy amd nutty flavor that develops a tangy acidity as it matures.

HOW TO ENJOY Its creamy texture makes it a perfect snacking cheese, along with crackers, celery, apple, or grapes, but Shipcord also melts and grills well.

ENGLAND Baylham, Suffolk
Age 6–12 months
Weight and Shape 9½–10½lb (4.3–4.8kg), wheel
Size D. 10in (25cm), H. 4in (10cm)
Milk Cow
Classification Hard
Producer Rodwell Farm Dairy

Shropshire Blue

Rather oddly named, as it was actually first created in Inverness, Scotland, in 1970, this cheese is based on the recipe for Stilton with the addition of annatto giving it its attractive mandarin orange color. It was eventually adopted by the Stilton makers who now make it.

TASTING NOTES Milder than Stilton, but equally creamy in texture, its streaks of blue stand out against the orange interior. There is a hint of caramel sweetness behind its spicy, blue tang.

HOW TO ENJOY Spectacular crumbled into salads or melted in soups, this cheese is equally at home on a cheeseboard, with an accompanying port or brown ale.

ENGLAND Leicestershire and Nottinghamshire
Age 10–13 weeks
Weight and Shape 17½lb (8kg), cylinder
Size D. 8in (20cm), H. 10in (25cm)
Milk Cow
Classification Blue
Producer Various

Single Gloucester PDO

One of the few English cheeses with Protected Designation of Origin (PDO), it was rescued from extinction by Charles Martell of Stinking Bishop fame. Traditionally, evening milk was skimmed to make butter, then mixed with full milk the next morning to make the cheese. Producers must have at least one Gloucester cow.

TASTING NOTES Firm but yielding, it has a mild, buttery flavor, with subtle hints of vanilla and nuts, and a gentle acidity.

HOW TO ENJOY Best enjoyed with apples or pears and pickled walnuts, served with perry, a traditional pear cider.

ENGLAND Gloucestershire	
Age 2–3 months	
Weight and Shape 5lb (2.25kg), wheel	
Size D. 8½in (22cm), H. 2¾in (7cm)	
Milk Cow	
Classification Hard	
Producer Various	

Snodsbury Goat

On their farm in Worcester, Colin and Alyson Anstey produce a range of hard cow's milk cheeses based on traditional cheeses that were once made in the county. In 2005, they decided to branch out, and created this clothbound goat's cheese based on Double Gloucester.

TASTING NOTES Dense with a smooth creaminess, it has a distinct almondy nuttiness rather than the more distinct goaty taste you find in softer goat's cheeses, with hints of chicory and wild herbs on the finish.

HOW TO ENJOY Serve on crackers with some home-made pickle, or grate over salads and soups.

ENGLAND Worcester, Worcestershire	
Age 4–6 months	
Weight and Shape 4lb (1.8kg), drum	
Size D. 8in (20cm), H. 4in (10cm)	
Milk Goat	
Classification Hard	
Producer Anstey's of Worcester	

Stichelton

Stichelton, the original name for the village of Stilton, provided leading cheesemaker Joe Schneider with his inspiration for this cheese. After his success with Daylesford Cheddar, he decided to set up his own dairy in 2006 and make a blue. Based on the Stilton recipe, it cannot be called Stilton because it is made with raw milk.

TASTING NOTES Creamy white with bold blue streaks, Stichelton is complex and delicious, and moves from a fruitiness to a spicy sweetness, all carried within a creamy texture.

HOW TO ENJOY Serve on the cheeseboard, with crackers and a glass of port.

ENGLAND Cuckney, Nottinghamshire	
Age 12–14 weeks	
Weight and Shape 15½lb (7kg), cylinder	
Size D. 8in (20cm), H. 8½in (22cm)	
Milk Cow	
Classification Blue	
Producer Stichelton Dairy	

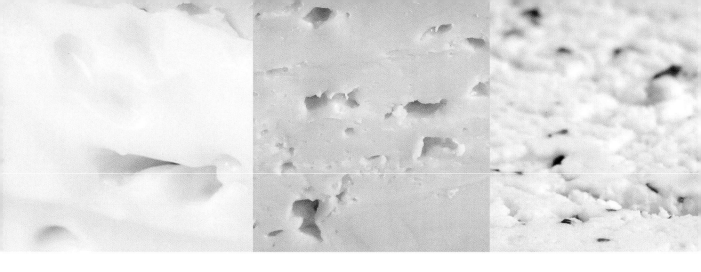

Stinking Bishop

Named after an old variety of pear used to make the perry (fermented pear juice) in which the cheese is washed, Stinking Bishop was created by Charles Martell in 1972. It has become one of the best-known and loved of English washed-rind cheeses, and even featured in one of Nick Park's Wallace and Gromit films.

TASTING NOTES Rich and meaty, with a hint of sweetness, it is milder than the smell suggests. The supple paste and sticky golden rind are encapsulated in a thin band of wood.

HOW TO ENJOY Ideal on the cheeseboard with pears and a robust red wine.

ENGLAND Dymock, Gloucestershire	
Age 5–8 weeks	
Weight and Shape 1lb 2oz (500g) and 3lb 3oz (1.5kg), round	
Size D. 5in (13cm) and 8¼in (21cm), H. 1¾in (4.5cm) and 2in (5cm)	
Milk Cow	
Classification Semi-soft	
Producer Charles Martell & Son	

Suffolk Gold

Creamy milk from this family-run dairy's small herd of pedigree Guernsey cows (graced with names such as Madge and Armilla) is used to make this cheese, which is lightly pressed and aged to develop a golden rind. Established in 2004, the dairy also produces a soft white, blue, and fresh cheeses.

TASTING NOTES The high butterfat content in the Guernsey milk comes through in the mild sweetness and deep yellow color, while the texture is firm with a few small holes.

HOW TO ENJOY Perfect with oatcakes and an apple, or melted under the broiler.

ENGLAND Coddenham, Suffolk	
Age 10–12 weeks	
Weight and Shape 6½lb (3kg), wheel	
Size D. 8in (20cm), H. 2in (5cm)	
Milk Cow	
Classification Semi-soft	
Producer Suffolk Farmhouse Cheeses	

Sussex Slipcote

The name derives from an old English word meaning a "little" (slip) piece of "cottage" (cote) cheese, and the organic milk used to make it comes from farms especially selected by this dairy on the edge of Ashdown Forest. Traditionally made with cow's milk, it is given a sweeter taste here with ewe's milk. It comes in different flavors, including garlic and herb, and peppercorn.

TASTING NOTES Very moist, almost mousse-like, it has a lemony fresh tang that finishes with sweet notes.

HOW TO ENJOY Best spread on bread or biscuits, but also a good addition to a baked potato or pasta.

ENGLAND Horsted Keynes, West Sussex	
Age 10 days	
Weight and Shape 3½oz (100g), button	
Size D. 2¼in (5.5cm), H. 1¾in (4.5cm)	
Milk Ewe	
Classification Fresh	
Producer High Weald Dairy	

Swaledale Goat

David and Mandy Reed set up their cheesemaking company in 1987, using an old recipe handed down through generations of Swaledale farmers—and possibly back to the eleventh century, when it was introduced by Cistercian monks from Normandy.

TASTING NOTES The firm white paste has a sweet taste with traces of the salty brine in which it is soaked, and a mild goat flavor. It develops a natural brown rind, or is waxed at three days old for a slightly softer texture.

HOW TO ENJOY Choose for subtle flavor in soufflés and tarts, or serve on a plain cracker with a light ale.

ENGLAND Gallowfields, North Yorkshire
Age 6–12 weeks
Weight and Shape 5½lb (2.5kg), round
Size D. 6½in (16cm), H. 3¼in (8cm)
Milk Goat
Classification Hard
Producer Swaledale Cheese Company

Ticklemore Goat

Originally conceived by Robin Congdon of Ticklemore Cheeses, this is now made by award-winning cheesemaker, Debbie Mumford, a former colleague, on the beautiful thousand-year-old Sharpham Estate farm, alongside the estate's cow's milk cheeses.

TASTING NOTES The stark white paste is fine, crumbly, and delicate, and dotted with small holes. The goat flavor comes through as herbaceous with a hint of marzipan.

HOW TO ENJOY This works well in soufflés and tarts, or on the cheeseboard with a fruity red wine, or perhaps a glass of Sharpham rosé.

ENGLAND Totnes, Devon
Age 2–3 months
Weight and Shape 3lb 3oz (1.5kg), basket
Size D. 7in (18cm), H. 3¼in (8cm)
Milk Goat
Classification Hard
Producer Sharpham Partnership

Tickton

Tom and Tricia Wallis started experimenting with goat's milk on their farm after discovering their granddaughter was lactose intolerant. Now they make a range of cheeses in small batches, including Tickton.

TASTING NOTES Fresh, milky, mushroomy and only mildly goaty with a smooth, slightly grainy texture that melts like marshmallows in the mouth. The sprinkling of pepper imparts a warm, spicy but not overpowering bite.

HOW TO ENJOY Perfect with a crisp white wine and as the rind is very thin it is excellent melted or baked on root vegetables, steak, or chicken.

ENGLAND Cottingham, East Yorkshire
Age 2–6 weeks
Weight and Shape 6oz (170g), log
Size L. 3½in (8.5cm), H. 2in (4.5cm)
Milk Goat
Classification Soft white
Producer Lowna Dairy

ENGLAND

199

Yarg Cornish Cheese

Yarg Cornish Cheese, one of the most attractive and unusual cheeses created since the revival of British artisan cheeses started in the early 1980s, was first made by Alan and Jenny Gray in Withiel on the edge of Bodmin Moor. Trying to think of a good local name, they eventually decided that Yarg, Gray spelled backward, sounded Cornish and was uniquely theirs.

In 1984, the Horrell family, who farmed nearby, started making the Yarg and later in partnership with Catherine and Ben Mead, who built a new dairy on their farm, Pengreep, in West Cornwall. The Horrells have since retired and all the cheese is now made at Pengreep Dairy.

The Meads returned to the family farm, leaving behind their London careers—Catherine to work on the cheese and Ben to work with the dairy herd. Since then, he has invested an enormous amount of time and resources to creating the best possible soil and diversity of pastures resulting in exceptional quality milk from their mixed herd of Ayrshire, Jersey, and Friesian cows. They are an amazing dedicated team and now make 200 tons of cheese a year in their highly sustainable bespoke dairy.

TASTING NOTES With age, the leaves start to break down the rind, making it very soft and creamy. As the cheese matures, the fine crumbly texture has a fresh, creamy taste while the edible nettles impart a delicate, slightly mushroomy aroma and a wonderful taste, not so different from spinach or asparagus. Wild Garlic Yarg is similar but softer with a very subtle taste of garlic.

HOW TO ENJOY Without doubt, Yarg adds style and character to any cheeseboard. It has a low melting point and quickly adds a touch of glamour to crostinis, baguettes, baked potatoes, and pasta. Not overpowering, it partners well with fish and is perfect for use in vegetable gratins. The Meads serve it with a local cider, Perry (fermented pear juice), or mild ale. It also goes well with almost any wine, especially fruity whites or even a dessert wine.

A CLOSER LOOK

Each cheese is a labor of love, made by hand in open vats by a team of dedicated cheesemakers. Every nettle that makes up the unique rind is individually picked, no stems or stalks, no holes or debris, and not a sun scorch mark in sight.

Nettles *are hand picked locally in May when they don't sting, and are frozen to use later in the year.*

ENGLAND Truro, Cornwall	
Age 6–12 weeks	
Weight and Shape 7lb (3.3kg), wheel	
Size D. 11in (28cm), H. 3½in (9cm)	
Milk Cow	
Classification Flavor-added	
Producers Lynher Dairies	

NETTLING The freshly formed, pale ivory cheese is taken to the nettling room where the nettles are applied by hand ensuring every leaf overlaps and no cheese is exposed.

MATURING The cheeses are matured and carefully monitored to ensure even distribution of the white mold, so each cheese emerges as a unique masterpiece and an example of human's ingenuity working alongside Mother Nature.

Mild, crumbly, and has a subtle flavor from the nettles.

THE RIND As the cheese ripens, a fine gray mist appears around the jagged edges of the green leaves making a very attractive eye-catching surface.

The combination of nettles and molds speed up the breakdown of the curd near the rind.

Interior

Tunworth

Good friends Stacey Hedges and Julie Cheyney use milk from a local herd of Holstein cows that graze on the Hampshire Downs to make this highly acclaimed Camembert-style cheese. Although they started their venture in their own kitchens, they have now progressed to a converted cowshed dairy on the family farm.

TASTING NOTES A wrinkled, mold-dusted rind conceals a sumptuous, creamy paste with a warm mushroom flavor.

HOW TO ENJOY For complete melt-in-the-mouth indulgence, warm in the oven until gooey soft, or transport it whole, in its wooden packaging, for a picnic.

ENGLAND Herriard, Hampshire	
Age 6–8 weeks	
Weight and Shape 9oz (250g), round	
Size D. 4½in (11cm), H. 1¼in (3cm)	
Milk Cow	
Classification Soft white	
Producer Hampshire Cheeses	

Tymsboro

Former archaeologist Mary Holbrook developed this cheese, using milk from her own herd, which grazes the Mendip Hills. Following tradition, the goats are milked only from spring through to the fall, their period of outdoor grazing. A coating of charcoal and salt gives this cheese an attractive gray-white rind.

TASTING NOTES This is creamy at the edge and drier, dense and more flavorful in the middle. Tymsboro has a subtle flavor of lemon and almonds, which strengthens and deepens as the cheese matures.

HOW TO ENJOY Eat as it comes, with fresh fruit, or melted over poached pears.

ENGLAND Timsbury, Somerset	
Age 3–8 weeks	
Weight and Shape 9oz (250g), truncated pyramid	
Size D. 3¼in (8cm) base; 1½in (4cm) top, H. 3in (7.5cm)	
Milk Goat	
Classification Aged Fresh	
Producer Sleight Farm	

Village Green

Green by name, green by nature, the brightly colored wax contains a brilliant white cheese made by Cornish Country Larder at its dairy farm in Somerset. With its sweet nuttiness, it's the perfect introduction for those unsure about goat's cheese.

TASTING NOTES Pure white, dense, and slightly crumbly, Village Green has a refreshing, lemony zing, with the subtle, aromatic character of the goat's milk coming through on the finish.

HOW TO ENJOY A very versatile choice for cooking, it is also a great alternative to Cheddar on the cheeseboard, with a slice of apple and a glass of port.

ENGLAND North Bradon, Somerset	
Age 3–18 months	
Weight and Shape 2¾lb (1.25kg), block	
Size D. 3½in (9cm), H. 2¾in (7cm)	
Milk Goat	
Classification Hard	
Producer Cornish Country Larder	

Vulscombe

Created in 1982 by Josephine and Graham Townsend, this was one of the first English goat's milk cheeses on the market. Made by lactic fermentation rather than with rennet, Vulscombe has a slightly thicker feel than other, similar cheeses.

TASTING NOTES Unlike most fresh cheeses, it feels thick rather than light in the mouth, but it has a citrussy freshness and a barely discernible herbaceous goaty tang.

HOW TO ENJOY With its decorative bay leaf, it looks good a cheeseboard. Easy to spread on crackers or bread, or try it in a twice-baked soufflé.

ENGLAND Cruwys Morchard, Devon	
Age Up to 5 weeks	
Weight and Shape 6oz (170g), round	
Size D. 3in (7.5cm), H. 1½in (4cm)	
Milk Goat	
Classification Fresh	
Producer Vulscombe Cheese	

Waterloo

The name is no coincidence, as this was originally made on the Duke of Wellington's estate from Guernsey milk. Nowadays, the Wigmores make it with locally sourced milk from behind their home, which hides a wonderful dairy, once a workshop and stables.

TASTING NOTES Bite through the soft, lightly molded rind into the pale, soft paste for a mild, creamy taste when young that matures to a rich, buttery flavor as the cheese ages.

HOW TO ENJOY This is delicious at room temperature with some cold green grapes, or warm it through and serve with a tangy red onion chutney.

ENGLAND Riseley, Berkshire	
Age 4–10 weeks	
Weight and Shape 1½lb (675g), round	
Size D. 6½in (16cm), H. 1¾in (4.5cm)	
Milk Cow	
Classification Soft white	
Producer Village Maid Cheese	

Wealden

Nut Knowle Farm was established in 1979. It now makes a wide variety of cheeses using vegetarian rennet and produced by their herd of pedigree British Toggenburg and British Saanen goats, which live on a natural diet of cereals and lush meadow hay.

TASTING NOTES Wealden comes in two forms: a soft, fresh cheese with a creamy, mild goat tang or aged for 3–4 weeks, when it has a pungent, earthy flavor and wrinkly, edible rind.

HOW TO ENJOY Cut the cheese in half, and dip in egg wash and breadcrumb, then deep-fry and serve with some seared young venison, chilli jam, and salad.

ENGLAND Gun Hill, East Sussex	
Age 1–4 weeks	
Weight and Shape 2¾oz (80g), round	
Size D. 2in (5cm), H. 2in (5cm)	
Milk Goat	
Classification Soft white	
Producer Nut Knowle Farm	

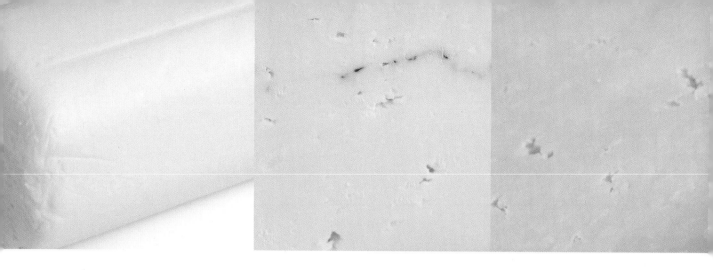

Wealdway

Another cheese from Nut Knowle Farm's goats, Wealdway is a small log that comes either plain or coated in herbs and seeds, or as a larger, mature version coated in charcoal. The curds are hand-ladled into molds and drained under their own weight.

TASTING NOTES The basic Wealdway is soft and fairly dry in texture, with a mild goat flavor, but because it is eaten young, the cheese also possesses a sharp piquancy.

HOW TO ENJOY To make the most of the log shape (very attractive for dinner parties), cut into medallions and serve grilled as an entrée.

ENGLAND Gun Hill, East Sussex	
Age 3 weeks	
Weight and Shape 5½oz (150g), log	
Size D. 2¼in (5.5cm), L. 5½in (14cm)	
Milk Goat	
Classification Fresh	
Producer Nut Knowle Farm	

Wedmore

Created by Chris Duckett, famous for his authentic Caerphilly, Wedmore is a Caerphilly matured with a thin layer of finely chopped chives. Originally made at the Duckett's farm in Wedmore village, it is now made by Jemima Cordle at Westcombe Dairy, with equal care and passion for quality.

TASTING NOTES Wedmore is ready to eat after just two weeks, when it is waxy on the surface, but crumbly and moist inside. The mild saltiness is balanced by the tang of chives.

HOW TO ENJOY Great either on its own or paired with a local cider, or sweeten with slices of crisp apple.

ENGLAND Westcombe, Somerset	
Age 2 weeks	
Weight and Shape 4⅓lb (2kg), wheel	
Size D. 6¾in (17cm), H. 3in (7.5cm)	
Milk Cow	
Classification Flavor-added	
Producer Duckett's Caerphilly	

Wensleydale

Introduced by French monks in the 11th century and immortalized by Wallace and Gromit in the 20th, it was originally made with ewe's milk, but replaced with cow's milk by the 17th century. Wensleydale Dairy Products is the only Yorkshire-based producer. They use both cow or ewe milk.

TASTING NOTES Pale white with a firm but dense slightly flaky texture, it has a subtle wild honey flavor balanced by the cheese's refreshing acidity.

HOW TO ENJOY With crackers, of course! In Yorkshire, they also like to pair that sweetness with a piece of apple pie.

ENGLAND Wensleydale, North Yorkshire	
Age 6–12 weeks	
Weight and Shape 11lb (5kg), cylinder	
Size D. 7in (18cm), H. 7in (18cm)	
Milk Cow	
Classification Hard	
Producer Wensleydale Dairy Products	

Whitehaven

Whitehaven is now owned by Ravens Oak Dairy, which was bought by Butlers Farmhouse Cheeses. It is still made by hand at the dairy, however, in small batches to ensure that it retains its smooth, soft texture and farmhouse character.

TASTING NOTES Smooth and soft with a white mold rind, Whitehaven has a subtle almond flavor when young, which develops into a deeper goaty tang as the cheese ripens.

HOW TO ENJOY Try baking it until creamy on the outside, but still cool on the inside; if you want the untainted hit of goat, leave to ripen until gooey.

ENGLAND Burland, Cheshire	
Age 6–8 weeks	
Weight and Shape 5½oz (150g), round	
Size D. 3in (7.5cm), H. 1½in (4cm)	
Milk Goat	
Classification Soft white	
Producer Ravens Oak Dairy	

White Nancy

Pete Humphries worked for Bath Soft Cheese Company before setting up in partnership with Roger Longman and handmaking cheeses using milk from Roger's 600-strong herd of goats. This is a cheese made by thermization, a process that involves heat, but not to the same extent as that involved in the process of pasteurization.

TASTING NOTES Moist and crumbly, White Nancy has a fresh, lemony taste, with hints of tarragon and almonds.

HOW TO ENJOY Try it cut into cubes and dropped like croutons into a hot soup, such as leek and potato, or crumble it into a salad.

ENGLAND Pylle, Somerset	
Age 2 months	
Weight and Shape 1lb 2oz (500g), round	
Size D. 4½in (11cm), H. 2¾in (7cm)	
Milk Goat	
Classification Soft white	
Producer White Lake Cheeses	

White Stilton PDO

White Stilton has a Protected Designation of Origin (PDO), meaning it can be made only in Derbyshire, Nottinghamshire, and Leicestershire; other requirements are that it is made from locally produced milk, which must be pasteurized. A popular base for many blended or flavor-added cheeses.

TASTING NOTES Much underrated, White Stilton has a fresh, creamy mild flavor allied with a fine, crumbly moist texture.

HOW TO ENJOY Savor as it comes, or crumbled into salad. White Stilton with apricot goes very well with a sweet dessert wine.

ENGLAND Derbyshire, Nottinghamshire, and Leicestershire	
Age 3–4 weeks	
Weight and Shape 17½lb (8kg), cylinder	
Size D. 8in (20cm), H. 10in (25cm)	
Milk Cow	
Classification Hard	
Producer Various	

ENGLAND

205

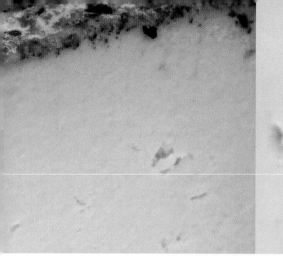

Windrush

Modelled on traditional French methods, Windrush is made by two Australians, Renee and Richard Loveridge, who moved to the Windrush Valley in 2003 and quickly established a dedicated local following. It is also available flavored with herbs, peppercorns, or garlic.

TASTING NOTES Windrush is only made in small batches. It has a luxurious creamy texture and a lemon fresh tang with hints of fruitiness and white wine.

HOW TO ENJOY Crumble it into tarts or eaten simply as it is with a cool Sauvignon Blanc.

ENGLAND Windrush, Oxfordshire	
Age 5 days	
Weight and Shape 4oz (115g), round	
Size D. 2½in (6cm), H. 1¼in (3cm)	
Milk Goat	
Classification Fresh	
Producer Windrush Valley Goat Dairy	

Woolsery English Goat

Woolsery English Goat is the result of Annette Lee's dedication to unique artisan cheesemaking as well as the lush green slopes of Dorset that allow the goats to graze on an abundance of grass and hay.

TASTING NOTES Moist and open-textured with a subtle but distinct goaty taste that hints of pine nuts and green grass. It has a sea-breeze salty finish.

HOW TO ENJOY Eat on the cheeseboard, together with some apple or pear. It is perfect for a cheese omelet or grated and used in cooking in place of Cheddar.

ENGLAND Up Sydling, Dorset	
Age 8–12 weeks	
Weight and Shape 5lb (2.2kg), cylinder	
Size D. 2½in (6cm), H.2½in (6cm)	
Milk Goat	
Classification Hard	
Producer Woolsery Cheese	

Wyfe of Bath

Named after Chaucer's pilgrim, this is made by Graham Padfield, a third-generation farmer and a family pioneer in the cheese world. He has established an excellent reputation in the region for cheesemaking skills.

TASTING NOTES The yellow paste, bounded by a natural brown rind, is smooth and springy with a mild flavor redolent of buttercups and meadows.

HOW TO ENJOY It seems a waste to cook with this excellent award-winning cheese, instead serve it on a cheeseboard with crusty bread and a fruity Beaujolais.

ENGLAND Bath, Somerset	
Age 4 months	
Weight and Shape 6½lb (3kg), basket	
Size D. 10in (25cm), H. 15in (38cm)	
Milk Cow	
Classification Semi-soft	
Producer Bath Soft Cheese	

Bishop Kennedy

Now made by Inverloch Cheese, Bishop Kennedy was created in 1992 by Howgate Creamery. It was modelled on Reblochon, but is dowsed in whisky and named after the bishop who founded St. Andrews University in Scotland.

TASTING NOTES With an orange-red rind and a velvety smooth paste, Bishop Kennedy has a spicy, yeasty tang and the powerful aroma of warm gym socks.

HOW TO ENJOY Irresistible on the cheeseboard, but also wonderful grated over mashed potatoes or melted on top of a rare juicy steak.

SCOTLAND Campbeltown, Argyll and Bute	
Age 3 months	
Weight and Shape 1.7kg (3lb 12oz), wheel	
Size D. 23cm (9in), H. 4cm (1½in)	
Milk Cow	
Classification Semi-soft	
Producer Inverloch Cheese	

Blue Monday

Named after the New Order song, Blue Monday was created by Alex James of British band Blur and cheese expert, Juliet Harbutt. It is the only cube shaped blue cheese in the world.

TASTING NOTES Soft and creamy with hints of gold leaf and the sea breeze on highland pastures. It has a kick of malt and chocolate, yet a surprisingly mild spicy blue.

HOW TO ENJOY The unique shape lends itself to the cheeseboard, but Blue Monday also makes a great soufflé or blue cheese mousse, and can be used in cheese caviar.

SCOTLAND Tain, Highland	
Age 3 months	
Weight and Shape 1½lb (675gm), cube	
Size D. 3½in (9cm), H. 3½in (9cm)	
Milk Cow	
Classification Blue	
Producer Highland Fine Cheese	

Cairnsmore Ewes

Made with milk from the farm's own flock of ewes, Cairnsmore Ewes is aromatic, with a rusty-red sandpaper rind that resembles the landscape of Mars. Clothbound and aged for a minimum of six months, it achieves a wonderful full flavor.

TASTING NOTES With hints of old-style caramel toffee, it is moist on the mouth and has hints of boot polish developing into a salty sweetness. Very satisfying.

HOW TO ENJOY Ideal for the cheeseboard, but also good with a crisp salad with pickled onions and warm crusty bread, or in a quiche with lots of chopped chives.

SCOTLAND Wigtownshire, Dumfries and Gallow	
Age 6–8 months	
Weight and Shape 3lb 3oz (1.5kg), truckles	
Size D. 7in (18cm), H. 9in (23cm)	
Milk Ewe	
Classification Hard	
Producer Galloway Farmhouse Cheeses	

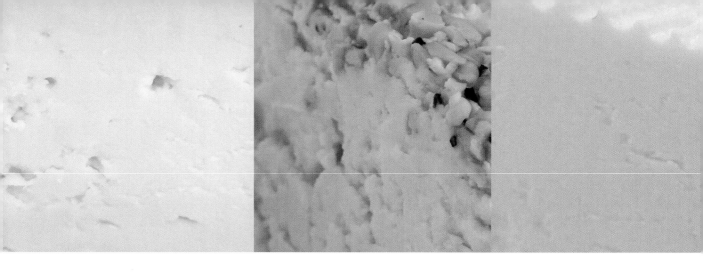

Clava Brie

At Connage Highland Dairy, the Clark family is making some truly wonderful cheeses using their own Jersey Cross, Holstein Friesian, and Norwegian Red cows. They graze on the lush pastures of clover and wild herbs at the banks of the Moray Firth.

TASTING NOTES Under the crusty white rind, the paste is soft and creamy with the subtle taste of sweet meadows and mushrooms. With age, the taste becomes more complex and slightly bitter.

HOW TO ENJOY Serve alongside a hard cheese on a cheeseboard, or melt it onto smoked ham and toasted bread smeared with English mustard.

SCOTLAND Ardersier, Inverness	
Age 3 weeks	
Weight and Shape 9oz (250g) and 2 ¼lb (1.5kg), round	
Size D. 4⅓in (11cm) and 10in (25cm), H. 1in (3cm)	
Milk Cow	
Classification Soft white	
Producer Connage Highland Dairy	

Crowdie

Believed to have been introduced by the Vikings, Crowdie was traditionally made by crofters—tenant farmers— with skimmed milk. In Gaelic, it is known as *Gruth*.

TASTING NOTES A fresh lemon acidity and the taste of crushed almonds on the top of the mouth. The crumbly and creamy finish hints of freshly baked yeasty bread.

HOW TO ENJOY A great alternative to heavy cream in the Scottish dessert, Cranachan, or spread on oatcakes with fine smoked salmon.

SCOTLAND Tain, Highland	
Age From 2 days	
Weight and Shape 4½oz (120g), log	
Size L. 3in (8cm), H. 1½in (4cm)	
Milk Cow	
Classification Fresh	
Producer Highland Fine Cheese Dairy	

Cuillin Goats

Named after the mountains on the Isle of Skye that rise majestically behind the West Highland Dairy, Cuillin Goat is the creation of Kathy Biss, an old-school cheesemaker, who has also written books and teaches the art of cheesemaking.

TASTING NOTES Fresh, soft, and slightly sharp on the tongue, it has a somewhat citrus nose, mild goaty taste, and the subtle smell of highland grazing.

HOW TO ENJOY Great in summer salads with olives and red onions, it also sits well on a cheeseboard, or simply crumbled over oatcakes with a dusting of black pepper and sea salt.

SCOTLAND Achmore, Higland	
Age 1–2 weeks	
Weight and Shape 7oz (210g), round	
Size D. 3½in (9cm), H. 1in (3.5cm)	
Milk Goat	
Classification Fresh	
Producer West Highland Dairy	

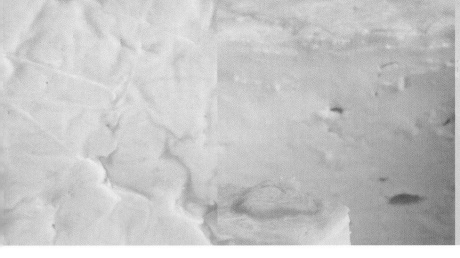
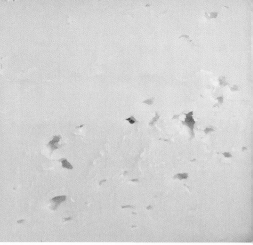

Dunlop

Revived in the mid-1980s by Anne Dorward, Dunlop is now made by a handful of cheesemakers across Scotland. The best are made with traditional Ayrshire milk.

TASTING NOTES Sweet and mild to taste, it has a pale primrose yellow rind and a buttery Cheddar paste. At six months, the texture is similar to soft fudge; at 12 months it is firm and fragrant.

HOW TO ENJOY An afternoon tea favorite, enjoy it with hot scones and Assam tea. Alternatively, add slices to oatcakes with mustard and a dram of whisky. Children love it on toast with warm milk.

SCOTLAND All over	
Age 6–12 months	
Weight and Shape 44lb (20kg), cylinder	
Size D. 12in (30cm), H. 12in (30cm)	
Milk Cow	
Classification Hard	
Producer Various	

Iona Cromag

Made by the Reade family on the Isle of Mull, Iona Cromag has a sticky pink-orange rind that is washed in whisky from the nearby Tobermory Distillery.

TASTING NOTES Supple and sticky, the buttery flavor is balanced with the whisky, achieving an enticing, hot, creamy finish, and a taste reminiscent of wild mushrooms baking under the autumn sun.

HOW TO ENJOY A real player on the cheeseboard, serve it with Muscat grapes or ripe Turkish figs and a dram of whisky.

SCOTLAND Tobermory, Isle of Mull	
Age 4–6 months	
Weight and Shape 1lb 2oz (500g) and 4½lb (2kg), drum	
Size D. 4½in (11cm) and 9in (23cm), H. 1½in (4cm)	
Milk Ewe	
Classification Semi-soft	
Producer Isle of Mull Cheese	

Kebbuck

Made by the wonderful people of Camphill Trust near Dumfries, this fine distinctive cheese is washed then literally hung out to dry in a cloth. After two months, the rind develops a brown, prehistoric appearance.

TASTING NOTES A sponge-like center with a crispy outer crust, Kebbuck has a subtle sweet to peppery taste with a mild finish of bees wax. You can almost taste the cows trampling the grass in the morning dew.

HOW TO ENJOY Great on a British cheeseboard, or simply on its own with Scrumpy cider. It can also be added to the topping of a buttery apple crumble.

SCOTLAND Dumfries, Dumfriesshire	
Age 2 months	
Weight and Shape 1¾lb (800g), teardrop	
Size D. 5in (12cm), H. 2½in (6cm)	
Milk Cow	
Classification Semi-soft	
Producer Loch Arthur Creamery	

Caboc

While the Romans played a significant role in improving cheesemaking in England, their influence did not cross the borders into Scotland. Instead, most cheese was made by crofters, most likely introduced by the Vikings.

Caboc is similar to Crowdie (see p208), a traditional Scottish cheese made from milk that has curdled naturally without rennet. While Crowdie is made with skimmed milk, Caboc is made with extra cream. It is said to have been created in the 15th century by Mariota de Ile, daughter of The Macdonald, Lord of the Isles. Forced to flee to Ireland to avoid abduction and marriage by the Campbells. When she returned home to the Isle of Skye, she brought with her the recipe for Caboc, turning the rich milk of the island into a richer and more fitting cheese for the Lord of the Isle and his clan.

Like so many great recipes, it survived by being passed on, generation to generation, although it had all but disappeared until its revival in 1962 by Susannah Stone, a distant descendant of the creator.

Using raw milk from their own farm, she set about recreating the recipe. Today it is made in exactly the same way at Highland Fine Cheese Company, owned and run by her son Ruaraidh. The milk comes from the most northerly herds on mainland Scotland in Caithness, a barren, treeless area that is fairly flat and exposed to the cold northerly winds. As a result, the cows are of sturdy stock, traditional friesian with some Ayrshire, and store more fat to protect them from the harsh elements; this gives the protein and solids rich milk, ideal for cheesemaking.

TASTING NOTES Made with cream enriched milk, it feels very rich, smooth, and buttery with a nutty taste but slightly sharp on the finish like sour cream, while the toasted pinhead oats give it a nutty yeasty flavor and a pleasant gentle crunchy feel.

HOW TO ENJOY Caboc is at home on any grand dining room cheese table, but is also versatile in the kitchen. Slice onto a blood orange or clementine salad with a handful of bitter salad leaves, or stir into fluffy mashed potatoes served with sliced roast ham and onion relish. A Stone family favorite is to grill some on haggis from the excellent local butcher served with a glass of Glenmorangie whisky made just down the road.

Sturdy *Highland cattle*

SCOTLAND Tain, Ross-shire	
Age 3+ months	
Weight and Shape 3¾oz (110g), logs	
Size D. 1½in (4cm), L. 3¼in (8cm)	
Milk Cow	
Classification Fresh	
Producers Highland Fine Cheeses	

A CLOSER LOOK

Like many artisan cheeses, Caboc's development was due to the raw materials available—an abundance of milk and Scottish oats.

MILK CHURNS The cream is skimmed from the milk, having been collected from two dairy farms in Caithness, and poured into a small round vat where starter cultures are added, then stirred and left to slowly ripen in milk churns for upward of 3 months.

MANUAL PRESSING The cream and milk sours and is poured into bags hung to drain.

SHAPING The soft curd is very malleable and is easily shaped into logs.

THE OATMEAL Rolling the small cheese in toasted pinhead oatmeal was an invention of Susannah's. She felt the flavor was enhanced with the addition of the meal and that it added a nice texture.

Log, sliced

The texture is more like cream cheese than cheese.

The crunchy oatmeal is the perfect counterbalance to the soft, creamy interior.

Lanark Blue

Humphrey Errington uses Roquefort mold, then ages the cheese for three months. During this time, it develops into a cheese with a complex flavor due to the wild heather and natural pastures on which the ewe's graze.

TASTING NOTES It is soft as putty in the center, has a crumbly outer crust, and is sharp as grapefruit with the meatiness of aged rib of highland beef. It can have elements of sweetness and be steely blue.

HOW TO ENJOY Great on a cheeseboard alongside stalks of celery and crisp crackers or grated over a substantial warm winter salad with hot roasted onions and winter squash.

SCOTLAND Carnwath, Lanarkshire	
Age 3 months	
Weight and Shape 4lb (1.8kg), drum	
Size D. 6in (16cm), H. 5in (12cm)	
Milk Ewe	
Classification Blue	
Producer H J Errington	

Orkney

Made by Hilda Seator on her farm on the isolated, windswept Orkney Island, it has the consistency, but not the taste of, Wensleydale. It is a lactic cheese, so no rennet is used.

TASTING NOTES Pale with a chewy bite and a lemony zest. There is a hint of butternut squash, and a yeasty breathe like an old brewing room, on the finish.

HOW TO ENJOY It can be enjoyed with a single malt whiskey when crumbled onto cornbread, or alongside traditional fruit cake with a cup of afternoon tea. A good breakfast cheese, it goes well with grilled ham, and warm, lightly-cooked eggs.

SCOTLAND Kirkwall, Orkney Islands	
Age 4 weeks	
Weight and Shape 7lb 7oz (3.5kg), pressed rounds	
Size D. 5in (12cm), H. 2in (5cm)	
Milk Cow	
Classification Hard	
Producer Grimbister Farm	

Strathdon Blue

Made in Tain on the east coast of Scotland by Rory Stone, makers of Caboc (see p210–211), one of Scotland's oldest cheeses, and Blue Monday (see p207), it develops smudges of silver-gray mold, and patches of sky blue on the sticky golden rind.

TASTING NOTES Well-spread blue veining and a slight peppery taste and spicy tang. It can sometimes finish with the essence of mousse-like milky chocolate.

HOW TO ENJOY Outstanding in twice-baked soufflés or with walnuts and dressed salad leaves, it sits well on raisin bread, and is great melted on steaks.

SCOTLAND Tain, Highland	
Age 3 months	
Weight and Shape 6lb (2.8kg), wheel	
Size D. 12in (30cm), H. 4in (10cm)	
Milk Cow	
Classification Blue	
Producer Highland Fine Cheese	

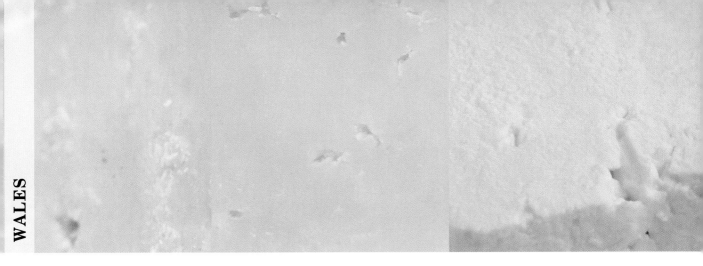

Cerwyn

Cerwyn is produced on Pant Mawr Farm, situated in the heart of the Preseli Mountains, and was established in 1983 when the Jennings family returned from setting up a dairy enterprise in Libya and North Yemen.

TASTING NOTES Hard but unpressed with a smooth, velvety texture and buttery color, its mature flavor has a slight raw onion tang, and nutty aftertaste.

HOW TO ENJOY It is perfect for the cheeseboard, served with a rich Bordeaux. It is also delicious with fresh fruit and preserves, and excellent in sauces for dishes such as macaroni and cheese, and for melting on toast.

WALES Clynderwen, Pembrokeshire	
Age 6 months	
Weight and Shape 3lb (1.4kg), wheel	
Size D. 7in (18cm), H. 2in (5cm)	
Milk Cow	
Classification Hard	
Producer Pant Mawr Farmhouse	

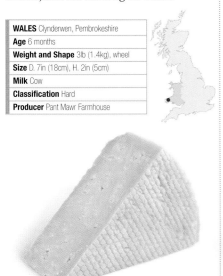

Dragons Back

Caws Mynydd Du means "Black Mountains Cheese" and was set up by the Meredith family to use the ewe's milk from their own farm that nestles at the foot of the Black Mountains. Dragons Back is based on a traditional Caerphilly recipe.

TASTING NOTES Attractive rustic rind, the rich ewe's milk provides the firm, yet creamy texture, and sweet flavor with a slight citrus aftertaste.

HOW TO ENJOY Ideal for cheeseboards with Soave, or late-harvest Riesling. It grates well, and melts perfectly. Grate it into a piping hot bowl of leek and potato soup.

WALES Brecon, Powys	
Age 8 weeks	
Weight and Shape 2lb (900g), truckle, or 6½lb (3kg), wheel	
Size D. 4½in (11cm), H. 4in (10cm); D. 8in (20cm), H. 4½in (11cm)	
Milk Ewe	
Classification Hard	
Producer Caws Mynydd Du	

Ffetys

Nigel Jefferies and his wife Rhian established a creamery in 2008 to manufacture soft cheeses from their herd of 50 goats. Their cheeses include Ffetys, a Feta-type cheese, and a variety of curd cheeses called Peli Pabo.

TASTING NOTES Soft and crumbly with a creamy consistency, it has a classic salty, lemony tang, a slight peppery quality, and just a hint of goat.

HOW TO ENJOY Excellent in salads; baked in savory tarts with red onions and thyme; in pasta and omelets; or stuffed into home baked bread with rosemary. Serve with a New Zealand Sauvignon Blanc or dry Riesling.

WALES Dulas, Isle of Anglesey	
Age 3 months	
Weight and Shape 7oz (200g), blocks	
Size L. 9in (23cm), W. 6in (15cm), H. 2in (5cm)	
Milk Goat	
Classification Fresh	
Producer Y Cwt Caws	

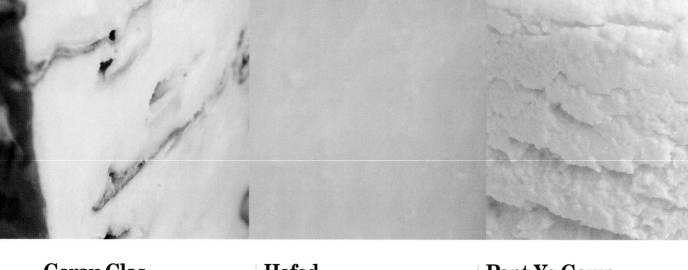

Gorau Glas

Margaret Davies started cheesemaking to add value to the milk from the family dairy herd, and has gone from strength to strength, with Gorau Glas, "Blue Moon," a small blue truckle with a gray-green mold the most successful.

TASTING NOTES Deliciously creamy with a subtle, yet distinctively spicy aftertaste when young, as it matures the flavor gives a strong blue sensation on the palette.

HOW TO ENJOY A versatile cheese, try it crumbled in a bitter leaf salad with sliced ripe pears and toasted walnuts, or served with fresh figs and Sauternes, or perhaps Tawny Port.

WALES Dwyran, Isle of Anglesey	
Age 8–10 weeks	
Weight and Shape 12oz (350g), small truckle	
Size D. 1in (3.5cm), H. 1in (3.5cm)	
Milk Cow	
Classification Blue	
Producer Quirt Farm	

Hafod

Sam Holden, son of the founder of the Soil Association, created Hafod in 2008 on the longest established organic farm in Wales, using a cheddar recipe and their own Ayrshire cow's milk.

TASTING NOTES The rich, creamy quality of the milk gives the cheese a full yet pure taste, and with age, it becomes hard and chewy with a lively, complex tang, and a green, grassy finish.

HOW TO ENJOY Ideal for the cheeseboard, and delicious with crusty bread and a glass of chilled beer. It has a good melting quality and is excellent in gratin dishes.

WALES Credigion, West Wales	
Age 12 months	
Weight and Shape 22lb (10kg), cylinder	
Size D. 10in (25cm), H. 10in (25cm)	
Milk Cow	
Classification Hard	
Producer Holden Dairy Farm	

Pant-Ys-Gawn

Made by Abergavenny Fine Foods, the first commercial producers of goat cheese in Wales, it has proved extremely successful in supermarkets across the country. Named after the family farm where it was first made, it is available with or without fresh herbs.

TASTING NOTES It is a fresh, pure white, clean, and mild-tasting cheese with a smooth, creamy texture. It is refreshing and crisp with a mild goaty finish.

HOW TO ENJOY Spread thickly on crusty bread; melt over bruschetta with vine tomatoes; or make a delicious savory cheesecake mixed with fresh herbs. Serve with Sancerre or rosé.

WALES Abergavenny, Monmouthshire	
Age 3 weeks	
Weight and Shape 3½oz (100g), drum	
Size D. 2½in (6cm), H. 1in (3cm)	
Milk Goat	
Classification Fresh	
Producer Abergavenny Fine Foods	

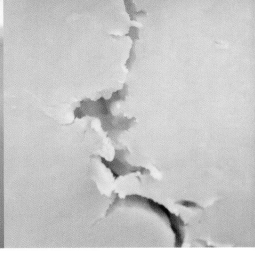

Perl Las

Thelma Adams, a cheesemaker from Wales, started making traditional Caerphilly, in 1987 with raw milk from her own herd. Perl Las, which translates from Welsh as "Blue Pearl," followed in 2001.

TASTING NOTES It has an earthy, moldy aroma, typical of a true blue, with a smooth, creamy texture, and a mellow yet strong taste with a spicy, vaguely herbaceous finish.

HOW TO ENJOY A good blue for the cheeseboard, melted on hot fillet steak, or used in a dressing for fresh, crisp salads. Best with a dry Riesling, Tawny Port, or beer.

WALES Boncath, Carmarthenshire		
Age 12–16 weeks		
Weight and Shape 1lb 5oz (600g) and 5½lb (2.5kg), wheel		
Size D. 4in (10cm) and 8in (20cm), H. 3in (8cm) and 4in (10cm)		
Milk Cow		
Classification Blue		
Producer Caws Cenarth		

Pont Gar

Carmarthenshire Cheese was founded in 2006 by Steve and Sian Elin Peace. Having worked in the dairy industry for 25 years, they decided to join forces to create their own range of soft cheeses using the excellent local milk.

TASTING NOTES A soft white Brie-style cheese, it has a mild, velvety texture with a hint of mushrooms, and a sweet buttery taste with a slight sharpness on the finish. It can also be smoked or made with herbs.

HOW TO ENJOY This cheeseboard classic is delicious with seasonal fruits and nuts. Serve with a New World Merlot or cider.

WALES Carmarthen, Carmarthenshire		
Age 5 weeks		
Weight and Shape 3lb (1.4kg), wheel		
Size D. 4½in (11cm), H. 1½in (4cm)		
Milk Cow		
Classification Soft white		
Producer Carmarthenshire Cheese Company		

Saval

John Savage at Teifi Farmhouse Cheeses has created a number of hard cheeses, including a traditional Caerphilly, and washed rind cheeses from raw milk. Some have been made in conjunction with Britain's first *affineur*, James Aldridge.

TASTING NOTES This is a dumpling-shaped cheese with a pink-orange rind, supple and elastic yellow interior, a distinct, pungent farmyard aroma, and a savory, meaty finish.

HOW TO ENJOY A must for cheese lovers, and beautifully accompanied by a dry Gewürztraminer. It also makes a pungent addition to a fondue.

WALES Llandysul, Powys		
Age 6–7 weeks		
Weight and Shape 4½lb (2kg), dumpling		
Size D. 10in (26cm), H. 2in (5cm)		
Milk Cow		
Classification Semi-soft		
Producer Teifi Farmhouse Cheese		

Caerphilly

The only traditional cheese associated with Wales, Caerphilly was a favorite of the Welsh miners and made on numerous small-scale farms in Glamorgan and Monmouth between the early 1800s and 1914.

Caerphilly Castle *in the historical town of Caerphilly.*

The years after the First World War were tough on the farming community and, with the advent of the railway, farmers were able to sell their milk, rather than preserve it as cheese, and subsequently cheese production dwindled. After the Ministry of Food stopped all production of Caerphilly until 1954, traditional Welsh Caerphilly did not reappear until the 1980s.

Fortunately, at the turn of the 20th century, some Somerset Cheddar makers, seeing the economic advantages, decided to turn their hands to Caerphilly, as it was ready to sell within a few weeks compared to twelve months for Cheddar. A few, like Ducketts, continued after the war but making less and less until the cheese revolution in the 1980s, coinciding with the campaign for traditional cheese by Patrick Rance.

Today there are a handful of farmhouse Caerphillys made in the Welsh valleys by Caws Cenarth, Trethowan's Dairy, and Nantybwla. Most is matured for a few months rather than a few days and more likely to be found in top London restaurants than a miner's lunch box.

TASTING NOTES Caerphilly has a delicious fresh taste and sometimes, when the grazing is at its best, its usual herbaceous sweetness is infused like a rustic béchamel sauce by the scent of crushed bracken moistened by autumnal rains.

With age it becomes softer, creamier, and more supple as it grows a bluish gray coat which sometimes sneaks onto the surface of the cheese and indicates it is still alive and well; you just need to scrape it off.

HOW TO ENJOY
Caerphilly's mild, lemony fresh flavor means it can be used in sweet or savory dishes, but it is especially delicious with Welsh Rabbit (also known as Rarebit). The cheese is very good melted on toast or with crusty bread, but it can be mixed with beer, egg, Worcestershire sauce, and mustard for an interesting combination. Serve with beer, local cider, or a white wine from one of the new Welsh vineyards.

A CLOSER LOOK

A simple cheese in appearance and taste, yet what liberates mediocrity into greatness is the quality of the raw materials, the method, and above all the passion the makers have for their art.

RIND The molds that grow on the rind of the Caerphilly give it a mottled appearance.

WALES All over	
Age 4 days to 4 months	
Weight and Shape 9½lb (4.5kg), wheel	
Size D. 10in (25cm), H. 3¼in (8cm)	
Milk Cow	
Classification Hard	
Producer Various	

CUTTING THE CURD The curd is cut using special knives, long enough to reach the bottom of the vat. As they are drawn slowly through the milk, they cut the curd in three ways, producing ½in (1cm) very soft and floppy cubes.

DRAINING THE WHEY The curd is stirred by hand in the whey until the desired acidity is reached, traditionally determined when an imprint of a hand remains on the pressed curd. The whey is then drained, the curd cut again and piled into molds lined with cheesecloth. All of this is done by hand. The molds are stacked three to four cheeses high under the press separated by metal trays and then the pressure is applied. They remain in the press for 20–30 minutes.

Cheeses that are allowed to mature for 3–4 months develop a magnificent thick gray coat and more complex flavor.

MATURING The following day, they are soaked in a brine bath, dried off, and put in a cold room where they remain for 4–7 days before being sold.

The interior is a yellow-white color like a magnolia, with fine, paler, almost white marbling throughout.

Talley Mountain Goat Cheese

What makes the cheeses, fudge, yogurt, and smoothies from Kid Me Not so good is that their goats graze the hills of the farm, so the milk is always fresh. Nearby cheesemakers, Carmarthenshire Cheese, make the cheese on their behalf.

TASTING NOTES A cake-shaped cheese with a thin white rind; dense, chalky texture; and a fresh lactic flavor with hints of tarragon and mushrooms. It becomes creamier with age.

HOW TO ENJOY Delicious broiled, crumbled, or with pasta. Like all goat cheese, its best companion is a Sauvignon Blanc.

WALES Llandeilo, Carmarthenshire	
Age 6 weeks	
Weight and Shape 11lb (5kg), cake	
Size D. 12in (30cm), H. 2in (5cm)	
Milk Goat	
Classification Soft white	
Producer Kid Me Not	

Talley Mountain Mature Cheese

Set on 50 acres of rolling green hills, Cothi Valley Goats is home to the 240 dairy goats and youngsters that provide the delicately aromatic milk for numerous cheeses that include a blue and Ranscombe, with its rustic, tuffty blue-gray mold.

TASTING NOTES It has a firm yet fine grainy texture, fresh acidity, and an almondy taste typical of hard goat's milk cheeses.

HOW TO ENJOY At its best on a cheeseboard, but also adds complexity to most sandwiches, tarts, and quiches. Best with crisp whites or soft reds.

WALES Llandeilo, Carmarthenshire	
Age 2 months	
Weight and Shape 11lb (5kg), round	
Size D. 12in (30cm), H. 2½in (6cm)	
Milk Goat	
Classification Hard	
Producer Cothi Valley Goats	

Teifi Farmhouse

After moving from the Netherlands, John Savage set up his dairy in the heart of Wales, and modeled his first cheese, Teifi Farmhouse, after Gouda—the cheese of his homeland.

TASTING NOTES The lush, wild pastures in the Teifi valley give the cheese an exceptional flavor—herbaceous, fruity, with a savory tang. Smooth and supple when young, it becomes dry, almost brittle, with age.

HOW TO ENJOY A classic for any cheeseboard, and can be used in cooking where a strong cheese is required. Perfect with Chardonnay.

WALES Llandysul, Carmarthenshire	
Age 6–12 months	
Weight and Shape 33lb (15kg), boulder	
Size D. 4in (10cm), H. 2½in (6cm)	
Milk Cow	
Classification Hard	
Producer Teifi Farmhouse	

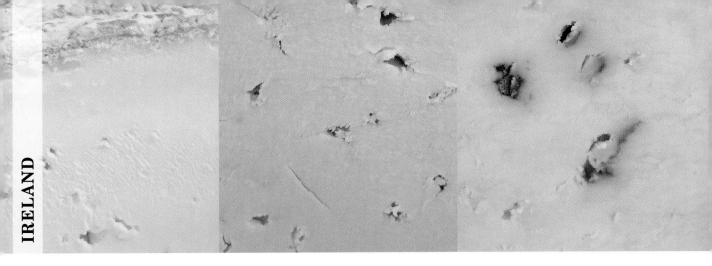

Ardrahan

Founded in county Cork by Eugene and Mary Burns in the 1980s to make use of the milk from their own herd, Ardrahan remains one of Ireland's best loved washed-rind cheeses.

TASTING NOTES Pale golden in the center with a sticky terracotta rind, it has a supple, dense, creamy interior with a sweet savory taste and meaty aftertaste that intensifies with age. A smoked version is also produced.

HOW TO ENJOY It melts superbly, so it can be melted over vegetables, or added to an omelet. It is also suitable for a cheeseboard, and can be enjoyed with a glass of beer.

IRELAND Kanturk, Cork	
Age Small: 4–6 weeks, big: 12–14 weeks	
Weight and Shape 2¼lb (1kg), wheel	
Size D. 7in (18cm), H. 3in (10cm)	
Milk Cow	
Classification Semi-soft	
Producer Ardrahan Farmhouse	

Ardsallagh

Jane and Gerard Murphy run the Ardsallagh farm and dairy. Their 400 goats provide the milk that enables them to produce a range of handmade hard and soft cheeses including an excellent Crottin, as well as yogurt and bottled milk.

TASTING NOTES When young it has a mild, nutty freshness; with age it becomes hard, and can be grated when it has an almondy mellowness. It finishes with an aromatic tang. Also delicious smoked.

HOW TO ENJOY On the cheeseboard, Ardsallagh pairs well with reds, such as Montepulciano d'Abruzzo, or cider. It's also good for use in quiches and tarts.

IRELAND Carrigtwohill, Cork	
Age 4 months minimum	
Weight and Shape 250g–11kg, rounds	
Size D. 3–14in (8–35cm), H. 1½–5in (4–12cm)	
Milk Goat	
Classification Hard	
Producer Ardsallagh Goats Products	

Bellingham Blue

One of Ireland's best blue cheeses, it is made from raw milk from Glyde Farm's closed herd of Friesians by dedicated cheesemaker Peter Thomas.

TASTING NOTES Moist with blue-green mold and a natural rind, it is mild and gentle when young, then develops a rich, mellow, peppery tang with age.

HOW TO ENJOY Extra mature cheeses work well with a glass of Barolo, or Sauternes. Superb melted over steak, or for stuffing chicken breasts and great for soufflés, pasta, and in salads with pears or pomegranate seeds and toasted nuts.

IRELAND Castlebellingham, Louth	
Age 6–14 months	
Weight and Shape 6½lb (3kg), wheel	
Size D. 8in (20cm), H. 3in (7.5cm)	
Milk Cow	
Classification Blue	
Producer Glyde Farm	

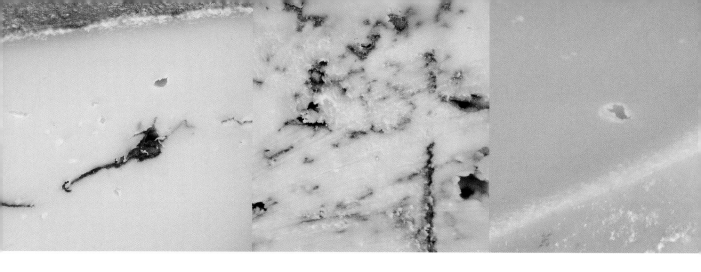

Beenoskee

German born Maja Binder produces some of Ireland's most unusual raw milk cheeses at Dingle Peninsula Dairy. The milk is naturally salty, since the cows graze close to the sea, and local seaweed is used for flavoring. Flavored and seaweed flecked cheeses are also produced.

TASTING NOTES The crusty rind of seaweed adds a natural, sea-salt flavor to the fudgey, divinely creamy flavor of the rind, and there's the warm, spicy aroma of the paste.

HOW TO ENJOY As a cheeseboard cheese, this needs nothing more than a glass of Alsace Riesling and some quince paste.

IRELAND Castlegregory, Kerry
Age 6–12 months
Weight and Shape 8lb 13oz–19lb 13oz (4–9kg), wheel
Size Various
Milk Cow
Classification Hard
Producer Dingle Peninsula Cheese Dairy

Cashel Blue

One of Ireland's best-loved blues, Cashel Blue is made by the Grubb family at Beechmount Farm, with milk from the farm's own pedigree British Friesian herd.

TASTING NOTES This soft, silky textured creamy blue with green-blue marbling has a medium flavor, with a gentle buzz from the mold veining.

HOW TO ENJOY For maximum flavor, serve this cheeseboard cheese at room temperature with a ripe pear and a sweet Semillon or St. Emilion wine. Great melted onto grilled steak, crumbled into salads, or into a smooth celery soup.

IRELAND Fethard, Tipperary
Age 9–35 weeks
Weight and Shape 3lb 3oz (1.5 kg), drum
Size D. 5in (13cm), H. 3½in (9cm)
Milk Cow
Classification Blue
Producer J & L Grubb

Coolea

This Gouda-style cheese has received many awards since it first came into production in 1980. It is now made by second-generation cheesemaker Dicky Willems and his wife, Sinead.

TASTING NOTES This smooth, hard, pale-gold cheese has a handful of small holes. It is fruity and mild when young, but intensifies to a rich, nutty caramel spiciness as it ages. Rich milk from hilly grazing adds a herbaceous character to the mix.

HOW TO ENJOY Coolea grates and melts well, and is good in omelets or salads. Enjoy it with a full-bodied red wine or warming Tawny Port.

IRELAND Fermoy, Cork
Age 2–24 months
Weight and Shape 10lb (4.5kg) and 20lb (9kg), boulder
Size D. 10in (25cm) and 14in (35cm), H. 4in (10cm)
Milk Cow
Classification Hard
Producer Coolea Farmhouse Cheese

Cooleeney

Cooleeney, Ireland's answer to Camembert, is handmade by a fourth-generation farming family in Tipperary, where lush grazing pastures provide rich, sweet milk.

TASTING NOTES Raw-milk Cooleeney is sensuously rich in texture, with aromas of mushrooms and herbs, a full buttery flavor, and good acidity.

HOW TO ENJOY It should be left out to soften before eating, and is best accompanied with a crusty baguette and grapes. The wine needs to be gentle—a light red Valpolicella would suit.

IRELAND Moyne, Tipperary	
Age 8–14 weeks	
Weight and Shape 7oz (200g) and 3lb 12oz (1.7kg), round	
Size D. 3in (8cm) and 9⅛in (24cm), H. 1in (2.5cm) and 2in (4.5cm)	
Milk Cow	
Classification Soft-white	
Producer Cooleeney Cheese	

Corleggy

Silke Cropp's Corleggy cheese from County Cavan was born out of a farmhouse cheese revolution that helped put Ireland on the culinary map. Goats and cows dine out on the nearby drumlin pastures that are rich with herbs.

TASTING NOTES Corleggy has notes of lush sweet grass and wild herbs. Its natural rind is brine-washed and flavorful.

HOW TO ENJOY This cheese is perfect with plums or figs. It also grates well and can be used in sauces or soufflés.

IRELAND Belturbet, Cavan	
Age 2–4 months	
Weight and Shape 14oz (400g) and 2¼lb (1kg), cylinder	
Size D. 4in (10cm) and 6in (16cm), H. 5in (12cm)	
Milk Goat	
Classification Hard	
Producer Corleggy Cheeses	

Crozier Blue

Ireland's first ewe's milk blue cheese, Crozier Blue, was developed in 1993. The sister to Cashel Blue, it is similar in taste to Roquefort (see pp82–83).

TASTING NOTES The Crozier flock of British Friesland ewes graze on limestone to give the soft, creamy, and subtly crumbly cheese a steely dry piquancy and peppery punch.

HOW TO ENJOY Crozier Blue can be served as a first course with ripe pears, walnuts, and delicate salad leaves, or after dinner, with a glass of late-bottled vintage Port or Tokaji. Use it on blue-cheese pizza, in a quiche, or added to risotto.

IRELAND Fethard, Tipperary	
Age 10–35 weeks	
Weight and Shape 3lb 3oz (1.5kg), drum	
Size D. 5in (13cm), H. 4in (10cm)	
Milk Ewe	
Classification Blue	
Producer J & L Grubb	

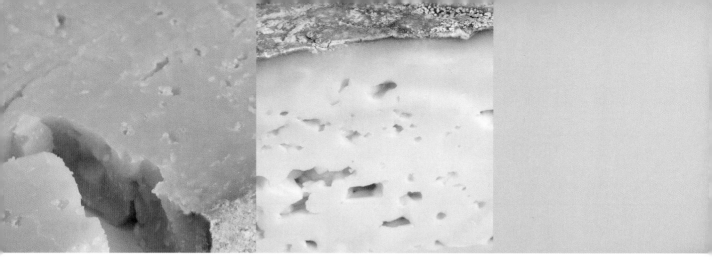

Desmond

Desmond, which was named after an iconic local peak, was originally farmhouse based, but now, production has transferred to Newmarket Creamery, where the cheesemakers oversee the proceedings. A sister cheese, Gabriel, is made with a slightly different temperature of milk.

TASTING NOTES A long-matured, Swiss style, thermophilic cheese, it has a hard texture packed with piquant peppery spice and a rich, lengthy aftertaste.

HOW TO ENJOY On the cheeseboard, it is best with an Alsatian white wine. Use in fondues and sauces or over pasta and leafy salads.

IRELAND Schull, Cork	
Age 10 months–3 years	
Weight and Shape 15lb 7oz (7kg), wheels	
Size D. 12in (31cm), H. 4in (10cm)	
Milk Cow	
Classification Hard	
Producer West Cork Natural Cheeses	

Durrus

One of the original "big four" west Cork cheeses. Thirty years later, Jeffa Gill still makes her washed-rind cheese in Dunmanus Bay, using time-honored methods and raw milk.

TASTING NOTES This orange-hued washed rind cheese is speckled with tiny holes. It is smooth, creamy, and sensuously textured, with sublime grassy flavors and warm fruity notes that become nuttier and richer with age.

HOW TO ENJOY Durrus is superb after dinner with Sancerre or Merlot. Durrus Melt, a type of fondue, is a classic modern Irish recipe.

IRELAND Durrus, Cork	
Age 3–8 weeks	
Weight and Shape 9oz–3lb (250g–1.4kg), round	
Size D. 4–6½in (10–17cm), H. 2in (5cm)	
Milk Cow	
Classification Semi-soft	
Producer Durrus Cheese	

Glebe Brethan

David and Mairead Tiernan first made this wonderful hard, creamy cheese in 2004. Its strengths have been attributed to the excellent milk from their herd of Montbeliarde cows.

TASTING NOTES When young, this smooth and golden yellow cheese with intermittent holes, is fruity and creamy. Aging adds spice, nuttiness, and a gentle aromatic buzz, finished with a zesty tang.

HOW TO ENJOY This versatile cheese can be enjoyed as it comes with just an Alsace Pinot Gris. It is also nice in tartlets with caramelized onions, or in a smooth fondue or sauce.

IRELAND Dunleer, Louth	
Age 6–24 months	
Weight and Shape 88lb 3oz–99lb 3oz (40–45kg), wheels	
Size D. 23½–26in (60–66cm), H. 4in (10cm)	
Milk Cow	
Classification Hard	
Producer Glebe Brethan Farmhouse	

Grace

Grace is one of a range of organic fresh cheeses packed in jars, covered with sunflower oil, and flavored with various herbs and spices.

TASTING NOTES It has a very fresh, soft, creamy taste with herbaceous grassy notes from the sunflower oil. The other cheeses in the range are flavored with olives, nettles, chives, or pepper.

HOW TO ENJOY Eat on crusty bread, crackers, or sandwiches with peppery salad leaves and tomatoes. It's good for baked potatoes, as an instant dip, or as a base for smoked salmon pâté, and it makes an excellent luxurious cheesecake.

IRELAND Ladestown, Westmeath	
Age A few days	
Weight and Shape 5½oz (150g), glass jar	
Size No size	
Milk Cow	
Classification Fresh	
Producer Moonshine Dairy Farm	

Gubbeen

Gubbeen is a farmhouse cheese made with milk from the farm's herd of Friesian and Kerry Cows. The orange sticky bacteria on the rind, which has been named Gubbeenensis, is now world famous.

TASTING NOTES Washed in brine, Gubbeen is smooth and creamy, with tiny holes. It has gentle herb and floral notes with a meaty finish.

HOW TO ENJOY Match Extra Mature Smoked Gubbeen with fruit cake. After dinner, it is superb with Chianti or Bordeaux. Gubbeen melts and omelets.

IRELAND Schull, Cork	
Age 12–16 weeks	
Weight and Shape 1lb 2oz–9lb 15oz (500g–4.5kg), round	
Size D. 5–12in (12cm–30cm), H. 2–4in (5–10cm)	
Milk Cow	
Classification Semi-soft	
Producer Gubbeen Cheese	

Knockdrinna Gold

Helen Finnegan only started making cheese in 2004, but she has already won awards for her goat's and ewe's milk cheeses, and more recently for her cow's milk cheese, Lavistown (see p224).

TASTING NOTES Knockdrinna Gold is creamy and nutty. It is rind washed with organic white wine, lending a rich golden color and citrusy notes. A soft creamy goat's cheese and semi-soft ewe's milk cheese are also produced.

HOW TO ENJOY On the cheeseboard or a mixed cheese platter, it is best served with a grassy Sauvignon Blanc. It is ideal baked in a goat's cheese tart.

IRELAND Stoneyford, Kilkenny	
Age 2 months	
Weight and Shape 6½lb (3 kg), round	
Size D. 9in (23cm), H. 3in (8cm)	
Milk Goat	
Classification Semi-soft	
Producer Knockdrinna Farmhouse Cheese	

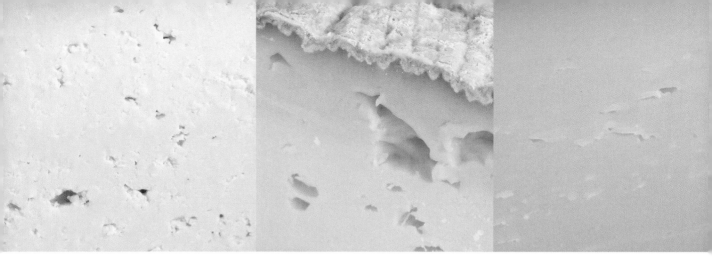

Lavistown

More than a quarter of a century ago, Lavistown was first made at Lavistown House by Olivia Goodwillie. It is now made by Helen Finnegan at Knockdrinna.

TASTING NOTES This low-fat Caerphilly style cheese has a thin, leathery, pale-cream rind dusted with white, gray, and pink molds. It is tangy and fresh when young, but becomes more crumbly with a hint of spice with age.

HOW TO ENJOY Pair it with wedges of dessert apple and a glass of ale. It adds something special to apple pie or can be placed underneath the mincemeat before baking your Christmas mince pies.

IRELAND Stoneyford, Kilkenny	
Age 3 weeks–70 days	
Weight and Shape 7lb 11oz (3.5kg), wheel	
Size D. 9in (23cm), H. 3½in (9cm)	
Milk Cow	
Classification Hard	
Producer Knockdrinna Farmhouse Cheese	

Milleens

Ireland's first farmhouse artisan cheese, Milleens, was created in 1976 by Veronica Steele. Veronica nicknamed the smallest Milleens a "*dote*"—an Irish term for something cherished.

TASTING NOTES It is a washed-rind cheese with an orange-pink hue and inviting soft texture that becomes unctuously runny. The flavor is mushroomy and herbaceous, with full woodland aromas.

HOW TO ENJOY Serve with good bread, preferably Irish soda, and a glass of Barolo or Claret. Milleens can be added at the last minute to risotto or melted into vegetable soups, such as broccoli or cauliflower.

IRELAND Eyeries, Cork	
Age 2–3 months	
Weight and Shape 9oz (250g) and 2¾lb (1.25kg), round	
Size 4in (10cm) and 9in (23cm), H. 1in (3cm) and 1½in (4cm)	
Milk Cow	
Classification Semi-soft	
Producer Milleens Cheese	

Mossfield Organic

This award-winning, organic farmhouse cheese is from Offaly, where the farm's Friesian and Rotbunt herd is kept on a variety of grazing, adding subtle nuances to the milk.

TASTING NOTES This Gouda-style cheese has a moist, supple consistency and elegant mellow notes, becoming full bodied and crumbly as it ages. It is also available with tomato and herbs, and garlic and basil.

HOW TO ENJOY Mossfield is great for the cheeseboard, with a glass of claret, or in tarts and quiches. The flavored alternatives add zest to baked potatoes.

IRELAND Clareen, Offaly	
Age 3–9 months	
Weight and Shape 11lb (5kg), wheels	
Size D. 11½in (29cm), H. 4in (10cm)	
Milk Cow	
Classification Semi-soft	
Producer Mossfield Organic Cheese	

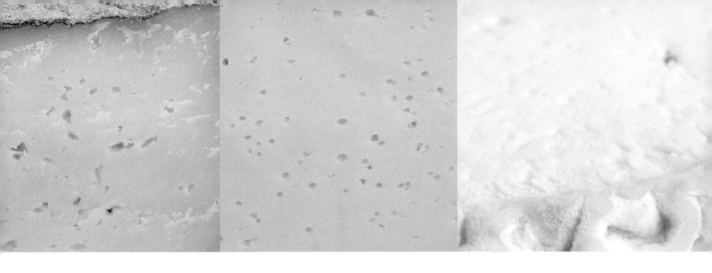

Mount Callan

Michael and Lucy Hayes created this cheese in 2000. This small, traditional, Cheddar-style cheese is bound in cheese cloth and then matured on wooden shelves in a stone curing room.

TASTING NOTES A few tell-tale cracks in the hard gray rind suggest a lovely moistness in the creamy, golden interior. It has well-developed, earthy flavors and, with age, develops a blast of heat on the finish.

HOW TO ENJOY It adds rich personality to a cheeseboard. Like Cheddar, it is great in sauces or grated. Superb with a full bodied red or port.

IRELAND Ennistimon, Clare
Age 9–18 months
Weight and Shape 9lb (4kg) and 33lb (15kg), cylinder
Size D. 6in (15cm) and 12in (30cm), H. 5in (13cm) and 15in (38cm)
Milk Cow
Classification Hard
Producer Mount Callan Farmhouse Cheese

St. Gall Extra Mature

In Fermoy, Cork, Frank, and Gudrun Shinnick have developed a superb range of farmhouse cheeses, including this hard cheese made with raw cow's milk.

TASTING NOTES It has a naturally hard rind, a rich gold color, and small holes punctuating the creamy consistency. Sweet milky flavors are rounded with toasty, almost cookie-ish, notes and a fresh, spicy acidity to finish.

HOW TO ENJOY This needs no adornment, just a glass of decent red wine. In cooking, it melts well for Welsh Rarebit, mixed with chopped spring onions or tomatoes.

IRELAND Fermoy, Cork
Age 3–6 months
Weight and Shape 11lb (5kg), round
Size D. 12in (30cm), H. 4in (10cm)
Milk Cow
Classification Hard
Producer Fermoy Natural Cheeses

St. Tola Log

St. Tola is made from organic goat's milk from the Burren region of Clare, where limestone and alpine plants provide a wild, rocky landscape. Siobhan Ni Ghairbhith also makes Crottin and a hard goat's milk cheese.

TASTING NOTES This classic *chèvre*-style log has a pale, wrinkly rind tinged with pink and a silky texture with a subtle nutty, goaty flavor and crisp finish.

HOW TO ENJOY Serve it melted or fresh with sourdough bread and grapes, or with slices of pear and a white Bordeaux. Crumble it into salads or serve on warm toasted brioche drizzled with honey, and enjoy with a Sauternes.

IRELAND Burren, Clare
Age 3–5 weeks
Weight and Shape 2¼lb (1kg), log
Size L. 8½in (21cm), D. 3in (8cm)
Milk Goat
Classification Aged Fresh
Producer Inagh Farmhouse Cheese

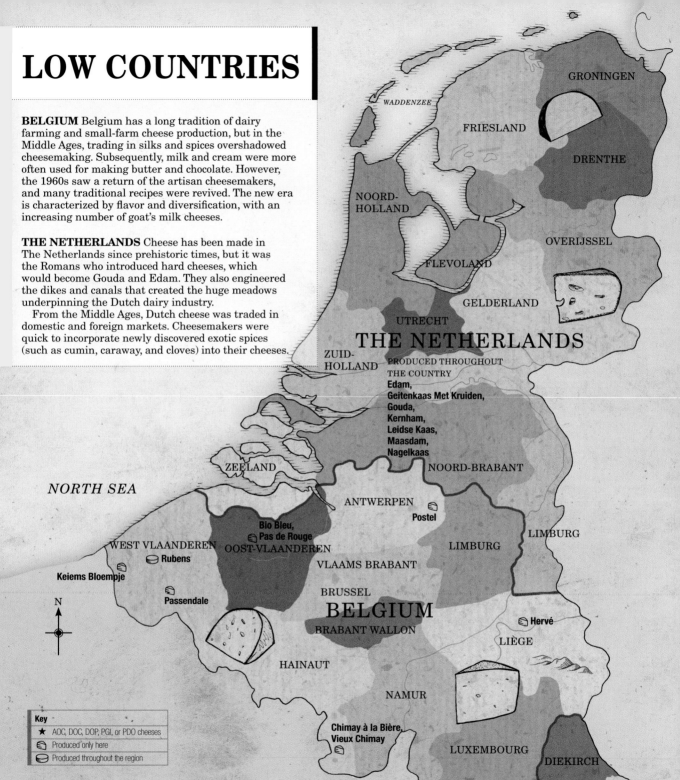

LOW COUNTRIES

BELGIUM Belgium has a long tradition of dairy farming and small-farm cheese production, but in the Middle Ages, trading in silks and spices overshadowed cheesemaking. Subsequently, milk and cream were more often used for making butter and chocolate. However, the 1960s saw a return of the artisan cheesemakers, and many traditional recipes were revived. The new era is characterized by flavor and diversification, with an increasing number of goat's milk cheeses.

THE NETHERLANDS Cheese has been made in The Netherlands since prehistoric times, but it was the Romans who introduced hard cheeses, which would become Gouda and Edam. They also engineered the dikes and canals that created the huge meadows underpinning the Dutch dairy industry.

From the Middle Ages, Dutch cheese was traded in domestic and foreign markets. Cheesemakers were quick to incorporate newly discovered exotic spices (such as cumin, caraway, and cloves) into their cheeses.

GRONINGEN

WADDENZEE

FRIESLAND

DRENTHE

NOORD-HOLLAND

OVERIJSSEL

FLEVOLAND

GELDERLAND

UTRECHT

THE NETHERLANDS

ZUID-HOLLAND

PRODUCED THROUGHOUT THE COUNTRY
**Edam,
Geitenkaas Met Kruiden,
Gouda,
Kernham,
Leidse Kaas,
Maasdam,
Nagelkaas**

NOORD-BRABANT

ZEELAND

NORTH SEA

ANTWERPEN
Postel

**Bio Bleu,
Pas de Rouge**

WEST VLAANDEREN
Rubens
OOST-VLAANDEREN

LIMBURG

LIMBURG

Keiems Bloempje

Passendale

VLAAMS BRABANT

BRUSSEL

BELGIUM

BRABANT WALLON

Hervé

LIÈGE

HAINAUT

NAMUR

**Chimay à la Bière,
Vieux Chimay**

LUXEMBOURG

DIEKIRCH

LUXEMBOURG

GREVEN-MACHER

LUXEMBOURG

N

Key
★ AOC, DOC, DOP, PGI, or PDO cheeses
Produced only here
Produced throughout the region

50 miles

50 km

Bio Bleu

Made by the Hinkelspel dairy cooperative (*hinkelspel* means "hopscotch" in English). Bio Bleu's slightly sticky rind is red-brown and covered in gray, blue, and some white molds.

TASTING NOTES The pale yellow, creamy interior has a mass of well-spread blue streaks. It has an intense steely blue tang, long-lasting and very peppery, with an acidic bite and spicy overtones.

HOW TO ENJOY Delicious with fall fruit such as sweet grapes and Doyenné pears, or in a salad with chicory and nuts. Pair with sweet white wines.

BELGIUM Oost-Vlaanderen	
Age 8–10 weeks	
Weight and Shape 1¾lb–1lb 2oz (800g–1kg), drum	
Size D. 4in (10cm), H. 4in (10cm)	
Milk Cow	
Classification Blue	
Producer Coöperatieve Het Hinkelspel	

Chimay à la Bière

In 1850, a group of Cistercian monks started building Scourmont Abbey and established a herd of Friesian cows to make butter and, later, Trappist cheeses such as this one, which is washed in Chimay Trappist beer. Today, the milk used comes from 250 producers in the region.

TASTING NOTES The firm leathery rind has a heady aroma of hops and the farmyard, while the creamy, supple interior is fruity, with a distinct taste of toasted hops continuing on the finish.

HOW TO ENJOY This is a superb melting cheese, or serve it simply, accompanied by a Belgian beer, ideally from Chimay.

BELGIUM Chimay, Hainaut	
Age 4 weeks	
Weight and Shape 4½lb (2kg), wheel	
Size H. 2½in (6cm), D. 7½in (19cm)	
Milk Cow	
Classification Semi-soft	
Producer Chimay Fromage	

Hervé

Probably the most famous of Belgium's cheeses, this is similar to Limburger (see p236) and named after the town where it is made. Washed repeatedly in brine over three months, the rind becomes sticky and covered in orange-brown mold. It is sometimes flavored with herbs or made with heavy cream.

TASTING NOTES Its pale yellow interior is springy and creamy. The flavor ranges from surprisingly sweet and mellow to strong, spicy, and anything but mellow.

HOW TO ENJOY Its pungency demands a strong companion, so enjoy with dark breads, and wash down with Belgian-style Trappist beers and ales.

BELGIUM Hervé, Liège	
Age 3 months minimum	
Weight and Shape 7oz (200g), brick	
Size L. 2½in (6cm), W. 2½in (6cm), H. 2in (5cm)	
Milk Cow	
Classification Semi-soft	
Producer Hervé Société	

Keiems Bloempje

"Keiems" refers to a part of the city of Diksmuide, a region of lush meadows formed by the intricate system of dykes and canals, or *polders*, while "Bloempje" is the Walloon for "flower" and refers to the *Penicillium candidum* bloom that coats the cheese. Some types are flavoured with herbs and garlic.

TASTING NOTES Made from raw organic milk, it has a thick, creamy texture, mushroom aroma, and fresh milky taste with a mushroom and green grass finish.

HOW TO ENJOY Try it grilled on bread or spread on crispbreads with a sweet homemade chutney; complement with Chardonnay or a light beer.

BELGIUM Diksmuide, West Vlaanderen	
Age 4–8 weeks	
Weight and Shape 12oz (350g) or 15½lb (7kg), round	
Size D. 4¼in (11cm), H. 1½in (4cm)	
Milk Cow	
Classification Soft white	
Producer Het Dischhof	

Pas de Rouge

The name Pas de Rouge refers to a hop in Belgium's version of the old school-playground game of hopscotch. A washed-rind Trappist-style cheese, it is made with organic raw cow's milk and has a red-orange leathery rind that develops a white mist of *Penicillium* mould as it matures.

TASTING NOTES Supple and buttery, with small, scattered holes, Pas de Rouge has a lightly farmyardy aroma and overtones of hazelnut, with a meaty taste as it comes of age.

HOW TO ENJOY Eat it like the locals: with brown bread, butter, and coffee or a typically Belgian Trappist beer.

BELGIUM Gent, Oost Vlaanderen	
Age 6–8 weeks	
Weight and Shape 5½lb (2.5kg), round	
Size D. 8¾in (22cm), H. 2¾in (7cm)	
Milk Cow	
Classification Semi-soft	
Producer Coöperatieve Het Hinkelspel	

Passendale

This popular Flemish cheese, based on an old monastic recipe, resembles a loaf of bread, with its distinctive caramel brown rind lightly dusted with white mold. It is named after the village made infamous by the World War I Battle of Passendale.

TASTING NOTES Firm, yet pliable with very small and irregular holes in it pale yellow creamy interior has a buttery taste becoming more mellow with age.

HOW TO ENJOY A stalwart of the continental breakfast buffet with cold hams and smoked meats and sausages. Serve with light beers or white wines.

BELGIUM Passendale, West Vlaanderen	
Age 3–6 months	
Weight and Shape 6½lb (3kg), round	
Size D. 6in (15cm), H. 3in (7cm)	
Milk Cow	
Classification Semi-soft	
Producer Kaasmakerij Passendale	

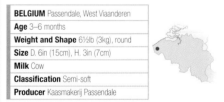

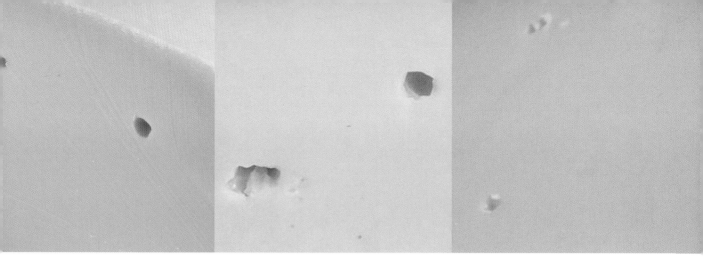

Postel

An orange-rinded cheese handmade by the monks at the Abbey of Postel using milk from their own herd of some 160 cows and others from near-by farms. Needless to say, this cheese is not made in high volumes, but is much loved by those in the know.

TASTING NOTES Hard and quite dry with a dark, earthy yellow color, Postel is a nutty-flavored cheese, with hints of spices such as cloves and nutmeg, becoming more intense with age.

HOW TO ENJOY Pair with a bottle of Postel beer, obviously. This is a good cheese for grating, as a snack, or as a topping baked potatoes.

BELGIUM Mol, Antwerpen	
Age 12–24 months	
Weight and Shape 4kg, loaf	
Size L. 10¾in (27cm), W. 5¼in (13cm), H. 4¼in (11cm)	
Milk Cow	
Classification Hard	
Producer Abbey of Postel	

Rubens

This distinctive washed-rind cheese is named in honor of the 17th-century Flemish Baroque painter Peter Paul Rubens. The recipe was revived in the 1960s and is now one of the most popular of all the Belgian cheeses.

TASTING NOTES Beneath the reddish-brown protective rind lies a firm yet supple paste with small holes. It has a rich, smooth flavor, with a subtle sweet-savory taste.

HOW TO ENJOY Like all semi-soft cheeses, Rubens melts and bakes well, and it is easy to slice for snacks or breakfast. Try it with slices of fresh apple, and serve with cider or a light red wine.

BELGIUM West Viaanderen	
Age 8–12 weeks	
Weight and Shape 6½lb (3kg), oval	
Size D. 12in (30cm), H. 4⅓in (9cm)	
Milk Cow	
Classification Semi-soft	
Producer Various	

Vieux Chimay

Like Chimay à la Bière (see p227), this is made at Scourmount Abbey. Annatto is added to the milk to give the finished cheese a warm tangerine color. With its flattened ball shape and thin golden brown crust, this makes it an attractive addition to a cheeseboard.

TASTING NOTES Although this cheese is described as hard, Vieux Chimay has a soft, chewy melt-in-the-mouth texture. The flavor is buttery with a hint of hazelnuts and a distinct but pleasant bitterness to the finish.

HOW TO ENJOY The makers recommend it melted into a lobster risotto, and paired with a glass of Chimay Tripel beer.

BELGIUM Chimay, Hainaut	
Age 6 months	
Weight and Shape 6½lb (3kg), flattened ball	
Size D. 6¾in (17cm), H. 4¼in (11cm)	
Milk Cow	
Classification Hard	
Producer Chimay Fromage	

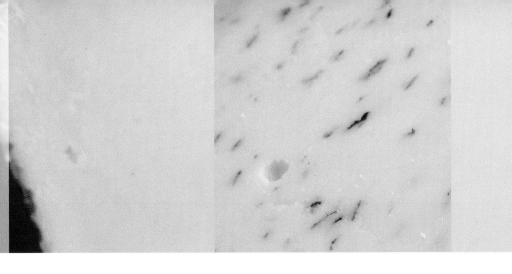

Edam

First mentioned in 1439, when Edam was shipped from the Port of Edam, just north of Amsterdam, and made with skimmed milk. Its distinctive red waxed coat is a familiar sight on deli counters the world over. The majority is exported, the Dutch preferring Gouda.

TASTING NOTES Beneath the thin rind it has a supple, smooth texture and sweet milky, buttery flavor, becoming more flavorsome and firmer with age.

HOW TO ENJOY A simple cheese, Edam is equally at home as a snack, in sandwiches, melted, grated, or served at breakfast with chocolate and eggs, as they do in the Netherlands.

THE NETHERLANDS All over	
Age 1–12 months	
Weight and Shape 2¼lb (1kg), ball	
Size D. 4in (10cm), H. 4in (10cm)	
Milk Cow	
Classification Semi-soft	
Producer Friesland Campina	

Geitenkaas Met Kruiden

Cheese lovers visiting Amsterdam should make time to visit one of the amazing cheese shops. Less well-known hard goat's cheeses such as this are definitely worth trying. The name means "Goat's Cheese with Nettles".

TASTING NOTES Supple like young Gouda, its stark white interior is scattered with flecks of chopped nettles; it has a subtle almond flavor from the goat's milk and a slight grassy, earthy finish.

HOW TO ENJOY Great as a snack or on a cheeseboard, paired with a cool beer.

THE NETHERLANDS All over	
Age 3–6 months	
Weight and Shape 17lb 10oz (8kg), boulder	
Size D. 8in (20cm), H. 4in (10cm)	
Milk Goat	
Classification Flavor-added	
Producer Various	

Kernhem

A modern Dutch cheese, this is named after the Kernhem Estate, a mystical place where, according to legend a white lady or ghost is regularly seen. Unlike most other Dutch cheeses, Kernhem is made with added cream and has a sticky orange rind from frequent washings in brine.

TASTING NOTES Kernhem's paste is soft and gooey, with a pronounced farmyard aroma, a nutty, creamy flavor, and a penetrating savory finish.

HOW TO ENJOY This is a cheese that cries out for tangy pickles, cold meats, and a glass of white wine.

THE NETHERLANDS All over	
Age 5–6 weeks	
Weight and Shape 5¼lb (2.5kg) flat round	
Size D. 8in (20cm), H. 2in (5cm)	
Milk Cow	
Classification Semi-soft	
Producer Friesland Campina	

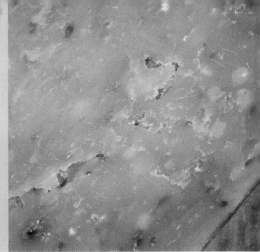

Leidse Kaas

Named after its town of origin, Leyden, Leidse Kaas's rind is imprinted with crossed keys, the city's emblem. Similar to Gouda, but made with semi-skimmed milk, it is scattered with cumin seeds. Spices such as cumin, cloves, and peppercorns were introduced in the 1600s by early Dutch explorers.

TASTING NOTES The dense, compact sunshine-yellow interior feels dry yet creamy and mellow, perfectly balanced by the aromatic cumin.

HOW TO ENJOY Excellent with all drinks ranging from beer to aromatic wines. It also adds a pleasant spice-filled note to salads, soups, and vegetable dishes.

THE NETHERLANDS All over	
Age 2–12 months	
Weight and Shape 22lb (10kg), boulder	
Size D. 12in (30cm), H. 4in (10cm)	
Milk Cow	
Classification Flavor-added	
Producer Various	

Maasdam

A Swiss-style cheese was originally created in the Netherlands as a less expensive alternative to Emmental, but its sweet, fruity taste, large holes, and bulging upper side proved very popular. Production continues to grow, with leading brand Leerdammer now sold across the world.

TASTING NOTES Very supple and elastic with large holes, its sweet, fermenting fruit flavor is a result of the special bacteria added to the milk.

HOW TO ENJOY A definite favorite for all the family as a snacking cheese or in sandwiches, salads, and, fondue. Pair with light fruity whites and rosé wines.

THE NETHERLANDS All over		
Age 4–12 weeks		
Weight and Shape 22lb (10kg), boulder		
Size D. 12–15½in (30–40cm), H. 6–8in (15–20cm)		
Milk Cow		
Classification Semi-soft		
Producer Bel Leerdammer; Friesland Campina		

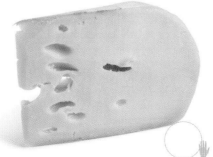

Nagelkaas

A traditional Gouda-style cheese originally from Friesland, made with cloves and cumin. As cloves resemble nails, they are called *kruidnagels*, or "spicy nails", and the cheese is known as "nail cheese". Its equivalent without cloves is known as Kanterkaas.

TASTING NOTES Despite being made from skimmed milk with only a 23 percent fat content, the cheese possesses a pronounced hot, spicy aromatic taste and firm, creamy texture, and becomes a deep yellow with age.

HOW TO ENJOY A little goes a long way, so use sparingly in salads and hot dishes, and complement with beer.

THE NETHERLANDS All over	
Age 4–12 months	
Weight and Shape 17lb 10oz (8kg), boulder	
Size D. 12in (30cm), H. 4in (10cm)	
Milk Cow	
Classification Flavor-added	
Producer Friesland Campina	

Gouda

The long-keeping properties of the Dutch cheeses, especially Gouda, and the geographical position of Holland on the west coast of Europe meant, historically, the cheeses could be shipped to France and further afield. By the 12th century, their popularity had spread across Europe and later became an essential item on the explorer's shopping list when they took to the seas.

Evidence of their importance can be seen in the existence of the weigh-houses and formal markets in virtually every town, such as the beautifully restored example in Gouda. Built in 1668, it was where the farmers brought their cheeses to be weighed and quality checked to estimate their tax. Today, you can find out your weight in cheese at the weekly markets in summer in Gouda, Alkmaar, and Edam.

What differentiates Gouda and Edam (see p230) from other cheeses is that some of the whey is replaced with hot water in the vat once the curd has been cut, a process known as washing the curd. This removes lactose from the curd, producing a sweeter, more mellow and slightly more elastic curd.

The fresco on the outside of the Gouda weigh-house.

The Netherlands	All over
Age	4 weeks–3 years
Weight and Shape	7oz–44lb (200g–20kg), round
Size	Various
Milk	Cow
Classification	Hard
Producer	Various

The best are the Boerenkaas, Farmhouse Gouda, made with raw milk by small farmers when the weather permits the cattle to stay outside and graze the fresh grasses of the polders, a remarkable landscape of dykes and windmills.

Over the centuries, other European countries have adopted the style of cheesemaking, notably Sweden and, in the last century, Dutch immigrants in America, Australia, and New Zealand have started making farmhouse versions that meticulously retain the old methods—although regulations prevent most from using raw milk.

TASTING NOTES At only a few months old, Gouda is supple with a sweet, fruity taste becoming firmer and fruitier, and by 18 months, the interior, with its small holes, has become deep yellow, hard, almost brittle and granular. Each bite reveals more of its complex character, from fruity to a hint of cocoa and groundnut, while the feel in the mouth is rich and smooth. Boerenkaas Gouda has a more outspoken taste that differs from farm to farm.

HOW TO ENJOY Young Gouda is ideal for sandwiches, snacks, and in salads, while the stronger taste of aged Gouda lends itself to the cheeseboard or cooked in hot dishes from gratins to tarts and pasta alongside a good Dutch beer or robust red like Pinot Noir or Barolo.

A CLOSER LOOK

The Netherlands produces 730,000 metric tons of cheese, of which 550,000 is exported. About 60 percent of Dutch cheese production is Gouda.

Young Gouda has a distinctive polished yellow rind.

Young Cheese

WASHING THE CURD In order to wash the curd, some of the whey is drained off and replaced by warm water, this is stirred in, and again some of the whey, now diluted, is drained off and replaced by more water. The water removes the lactose (milk sugars) from the curd. When the water is hot, it scalds the curd and so expels additional moisture. The result of this activity is to keep the acidity of the curd at a lower level than would normally be the case since the activity of the lactic bacteria is reduced.

ADDING FLAVOR The founding of the Dutch East Indies Company in the 17th century opened up the spice trade. The Dutch were quick to utilize these new and aromatic flavors in their cheeses—particularly cumin, caraway, peppercorns, and cloves.

VERTICAL PRESS The cheeses are removed from their molds and stacked in vertical presses, separated by boards, and lightly pressed for a few hours or even days.

Aged Gouda, aged for a minimum of 18 months has a black waxed rind.

With age, the exterior becomes hard, dry, and a deep sunshine yellow.

Mature cheese

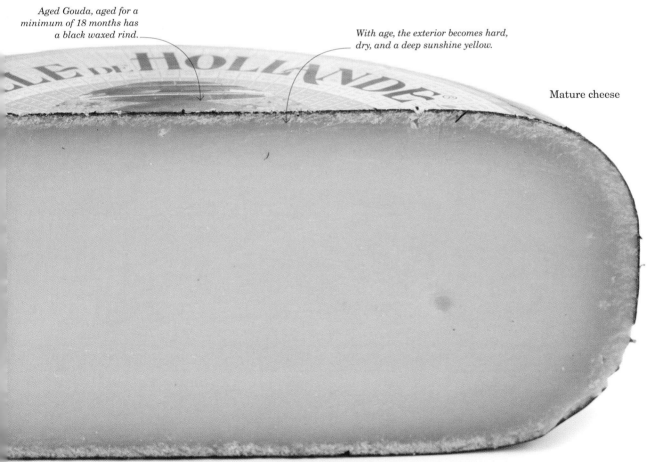

GERMANY, AUSTRIA, AND SWITZERLAND

N

GERMANY In the Alpine regions of Bayern (Bavaria), cheesemaking was influenced by the Swiss, and before them the Romans. Allgäu, the heart of German cheesemaking, draws its inspiration from the Swiss with its famous Allgäuer Emmental, which was introduced to the area in 1821. An abundant supply of high quality milk allows Bayern to produce 75 percent of Germany's cheeses, making it one of Germany's most important milk and cheese regions.

In the northern regions of Germany, traditional cheeses are often fresh or lactic-acidified milk products, as seen in The Netherlands and Denmark or with Trappist cheeses. Although many cheeses are produced in Bayern, some of Germany's more famous cheeses, such as Altenburger Ziegenkäse, are produced in the northern parts of Germany.

AUSTRIA Since the climate and pasture in Western Austria (Vorarlberg and Tirol) are similar to those in Switzerland, it is no wonder that the border-sharing cheesemakers have been swapping recipe for centuries. In the east, the influence came from the Balkans, which is why fresh-style cheeses are more prevalent.

SWITZERLAND The great cheeses of Switzerland, famous throughout the world, can trace their history back to before the coming of the Romans. The first reference to cheesemaking was made in 33 BCE, when the Rhaetians made "cheese" for the long, hard winter. Record show that by the Middle Ages, Swiss cheeses were being traded across much of Europe.

In modern times, despite much of the production moving to large factories, most Swiss cheeses are still made in small dairies or cooperatives. This is due to the primary objective of the Swiss agricultural policy—maintaining the landscape that characterizes Switzerland

SCHLESWIG-HOLSTEIN
Schichtkäse

MECKLENBURG-VORPOMMERN

GERMANY
PRODUCED THROUGHOUT THE COUNTRY
Tilsiterkäse

NIEDERSACHSEN
Harzer Käse

BRANDENBURG

NORDRHEIN-WESTFALEN

SACHSEN-ANHALT
Harzer Käse

Altenburger Ziegenkäse ★

SACHSEN

Harzer Käse

THÜRINGEN
Harzer Käse

HESSEN

RHEINLAND-PFALZ

SAARLAND

BAYERN
Allgäuer Bergkäse,
Allgäuer Emmental,
Limburger,
Weisslacker

BADEN-WÜRTTEMBERG

Tête de Moine ★,
Vacherin Mont d'Or ★

Tomme Vaudoise,
Vacherin Fribourgeois ★

Sbrinz ★

Appenzeller

Appenzeller

Bavaria Blu

Mondseer

St Severin

Gruyère ★

Sbrinz ★

Vorarlberger Bergkäse

AUSTRIA

Tomme Vaudoise

Hobelkäse

Sbrinz ★

Weinkäse,
Tiroler Graukäse

SWITZERLAND
PRODUCED THROUGHOUT THE COUNTRY
Mutschli,
Raclette

Sbrinz ★

Schabziger

Tiroler Graukäse,
Chorherrenkäse

Tiroler Graukäse,
Chorherrenkäse

LIECHTENSTEIN

Valle Maggia

Hobelkäse

100 miles

100 km

Key
★ AOC, DOC, DOP, PGI, or PDO cheeses
🗇 Produced only here
🗇 Produced throughout the region

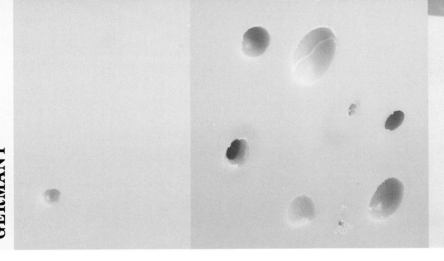

Allgäuer Bergkäse

Allgäu is known for its Swiss-style cheeses, introduced in 1841 by two Swiss cheesemakers. Bergkäse, or mountain cheese, is like a little Emmental (see pp242–243) with smaller holes and made in alpine huts during late spring and summer.

TASTING NOTES Dense with small holes, it has a sweet, buttery taste becoming more intense and slightly salty.

HOW TO ENJOY This is perfect for a Bavarian *Brotzeit*, an afternoon meal accompanied with sausage slices, bacon, and dark bread. Enjoy with a fine Bavarian beer.

GERMANY Bayern	
Age 3–6 months	
Weight and Shape 55lb 2oz (25kg), wheel	
Size D. 20in (50cm), H. 4in (10cm)	
Milk Cow	
Classification Hard	
Producer Various	

Allgäuer Emmental

Allgäu cheeses use milk from the brown Allgäu cattle that graze the spring meadows that are rich in alpine flowers. Allgäuer Emmental is based on the Swiss Emmental (see pp242–243), but is smaller and ripens more quickly.

TASTING NOTES Most is sold at around three months old when it is supple, golden yellow, and mild with a hint of hazelnut.

HOW TO ENJOY For breakfast, snacks, cheese-plates, and cooking. In Germany, thin slices are laid on or between white bread slices. Typically served with tea, coffee, or beer.

GERMANY Bayern	
Age 3–6 months	
Weight and Shape 176lb 6oz (80kg), wheel	
Size D. 35½in (90cm), H. 43½in (110cm)	
Milk Cow	
Classification Hard	
Producer Various	

Altenburger Ziegenkäse PDO

Sachsen and Thüringia in eastern Germany were home to this cheese. Very little of it was produced until German reunification, but it is now available all over the country.

TASTING NOTES Soft and creamy, but pure white in color, typical of goat cheese. It has a very pleasant, mild flavor and a goaty finish that is not too pronounced. The interior is punctuated with caraway seeds.

HOW TO ENJOY Perfect for cheeseboards, salads, or drizzled with sweet mustard to bring out the flavor. Enjoy it with a liqueur or a light white wine.

GERMANY Sachsen and Thüringia	
Age 4 weeks	
Weight and Shape 10oz–1lb 2oz (300–500g), round	
Size Various, D. 8in (20cm), H. 4in (10cm) (pictured)	
Milk Goat with some cow	
Classification Soft white	
Producer Altenburger Land	

Bavaria Blu

With a thick white coat and made with extra cream, Bavaria Blu is a fusion of Camembert and Gorgonzola. The blue mold is injected into the young cheese, a technique developed in Germany in the 1970s. Bavaria Blu is often referred to as the blue cheese for people who don't like blue cheese!

TASTING NOTES **Considerably milder than Gorgonzola or Camembert, it has a very rich, creamy taste and subtle spicy blue finish. The blue splodges through the interior make it very appealing.**

HOW TO ENJOY **Served on most German cheeseboards with a white Rhine wine such as Riesling and a nutty bread.**

GERMANY Allgäu, Bayern	
Age 4–6 weeks	
Weight and Shape 3lb 3oz (1.5kg), round	
Size D. 12in (30cm), H. 3in (7cm)	
Milk Cow	
Classification Blue	
Producer Käserei Champignon	

Harzer Käse

This has been made for centuries from "soured" skimmed milk on small farms throughout the country; in Germany, butter was always more important than cheese. Best known are Harzer, along with Olmützer Quargel (pictured), Handkäse, and Mainzer.

TASTING NOTES **Several of these "coins" are assembled into a roll, and are then separated for eating. When fresh, the paste is lemony sharp, but at about three weeks it becomes mellower.**

HOW TO ENJOY **Mixed with vinegar, salt, and onion, it is called "hand cheese with music". With dark German bread and cider, it is a satisfying afternoon meal.**

GERMANY The Harz mountain range (Niedersachsen, Sachsen-Anhalt, and Thüringen)	
Age 2–4 weeks	
Weight and Shape 3½oz (100g), log	
Size Various, D. 2in (5cm), H. ¾in (2cm) (pictured)	
Milk Cow	
Classification Fresh	
Producer Various	

Limburger

This washed-rind cheese was originally made in Belgium's Limbourg region. It became so popular that, since 1830, the majority of it has been made in Germany, mostly in the Allgäu from the excellent local milk.

TASTING NOTES **Its sticky orange-brown rind and intense farmyard smell comes from being washed in special bacteria. The taste is significantly milder, but still farmyard and meaty.**

HOW TO ENJOY **Served as "Brotzeit", afternoon tea with boiled potatoes and butter, or with vinaigrette and slices of onion, dark bread, and beer or cider.**

GERMANY Bayern	
Age 6–12 weeks	
Weight and Shape 5oz (150g), brick	
Size L. 5in (12cm), W. 1½in (4cm), H. 1in (3.5cm)	
Milk Cow	
Classification Semi-soft	
Producer Various	

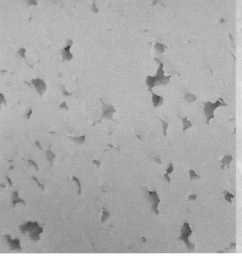

Schichtkäse

A very old recipe using skimmed milk, made in northern parts of Germany, it is a lactic cheese, which curdles without rennet. Similar to quark, but dryer, it is made of layers of curd—the top and bottom layers from skimmed milk; the middle layer from whole milk.

TASTING NOTES An acquired taste, it is vaguely aromatic and tart, with a texture similar to cottage cheese. The middle layer of the cheese looks more yellow because it is higher in fat.

HOW TO ENJOY Suitable for breakfast in place of quark or yogurt. Spread on a slice of dark bread as a snack. It also goes perfectly with tea or coffee.

GERMANY Schleswig-Holstein	
Age A few days	
Weight and Shape 3½oz–1lb 2oz (100–500g), packets or pots	
Size Various	
Milk Cow	
Classification Fresh	
Producer Various	

Tilsiterkäse

Named after the town of Tilsit, now Sowjetsk in Russia, it was apparently created by Dutch immigrants in the mid-nineteenth century, trying to recreate their famous Gouda. Brick-shaped, it can be waxed or made with added cream, herbs, pepper, or caraway seeds. Swiss Tilsit is round and firmer, with pea-sized holes.

TASTING NOTES Butter-yellow, springy, and sliceable, with many uneven slits, it ranges in flavor from mild and sweet-savory to strong and meaty.

HOW TO ENJOY Ideal for breakfast, sandwiches, and snacks along with a beer, Riesling, Sylvaner, or fruity red.

GERMANY All over	
Age 12–18 weeks	
Weight and Shape 8½lb (4kg), brick	
Size L. 12in (30cm), W. 6in (15cm), H. 6in (15cm (pictured))	
Milk Cow	
Classification Semi-soft	
Producers Various	

Weisslacker

Invented in 1874, Weisslacker means "white lacquer cheese", and it is so named because of its shiny, glass-like white rind, the result of being soaked in brine and is not unlike feta. This cheese is also known as Bayerische Bierkäse (Bavarian beer cheese), as it goes extremely well with this brew.

TASTING NOTES After two days in brine, it is crumbly and has a surprisingly strong smell and tang, with a salty bite.

HOW TO ENJOY Cut into chunks and serve with Bretzels (chewy pretzels), vinaigrette, and a lot of onions. This is a hearty meal best washed down with a lot of beer. Also used in Maultaschen.

GERMANY Bayern	
Age 3–6 weeks	
Weight and Shape 1lb 2oz–2¼lb (500g–1kg), brick	
Size L. 4–5in (10–12cm), W. 4–5in (10–12cm), H. 2½–4in (6–10cm)	
Milk Cow	
Classification Fresh	
Producer Various	

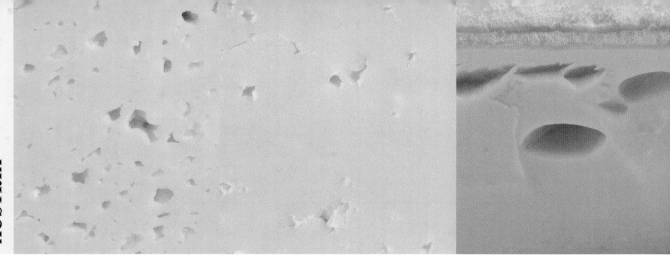

Chorherrenkäse

A special recipe that combines fresh milk and sometimes buttermilk makes for an innovative cheese also known as Prälatenkäse. Traditionally made in a Tyrolean dairy, Chorherrenkäse is dipped in white wax and is based on monastery or Trappist-style cheeses.

TASTING NOTES The combination of buttermilk and fresh milk gives a pleasant flavor and a smooth texture reminiscent of a warm summer day with a hint of meadow flowers.

HOW TO ENJOY A pleasant, undemanding cheese for the cheeseboard, or sliced for breakfast or as part of a buffet. Ideal with a local Grüner Veltliner wine.

AUSTRIA Tirol	
Age 4–6 weeks	
Weight and Shape 1¾lb (800g), loaf	
Size D. 10in (25cm), H. 7in (18cm)	
Milk Cow	
Classification Semi-soft	
Producer Bergland Voitsberg	

Mondseer

First made in Salzburg in 1830, this is named after the monastery of Mondsee. Also known as Schachtelkäse, its recipe is based on the Trappist-style washed-rind cheese brought to Austria by the Cistercian monks. It has a thin orange rind dusted with white mold.

TASTING NOTES The paste is a light yellow and has a sweet-sour flavor with a hint of flowery grass; as it ages, the flavor becomes more hearty and the texture supple and soft.

HOW TO ENJOY A fine cheese for many occasions: breakfast with tea, a light meal, or on a cheeseboard, accompanied by a Grüner Veltliner wine.

AUSTRIA Oberösterreich	
Age 6–8 weeks	
Weight and Shape 1lb 2oz–2¼lb (500g–1kg), round	
Size D. 5–10in (12–25cm), H. 2–3½in (5–9cm)	
Milk Cow	
Classification Semi-soft	
Producer Various	

St. Severin

In 1920, Friar Leonhard brought the recipe for this cheese to the monastery of Schlierbach in Upper Austria, and named the cheese after St. Severin, protector against famine. It is a little round soft cheese with a yellow to orange washed rind similar to Munster.

TASTING NOTES The smooth bright yellow paste has a hearty, full-bodied taste. The aroma, typical of Trappist cheeses, is farmyard and strong.

HOW TO ENJOY Great on a cheeseboard with crispy bread for an afternoon snack. Complement with a red Zinfandel, Merlot, or Pinot Noir, or a full-bodied white wine.

AUSTRIA Salzburg	
Age 3–6 weeks	
Weight and Shape 3½oz (100g), round	
Size D. 3½in (9cm), H. 2½in (6cm)	
Milk Cow	
Classification Semi-soft	
Producer Stift Schlierbach	

Tiroler Graukäse

Made with skimmed milk and soured naturally using a lactic starter, rather than rennet, this Tyrolean cheese is pressed, then milled and pressed again. The surface of the thin rind develops blue-gray to green-gray molds.

TASTING NOTES In the first few days, it is curdlike and crumbly, but left at room temperature for a few days it ripens and becomes smooth, softer, and almost runny. The taste is lemony fresh.

HOW TO ENJOY In Tirol, it is served with vinegar, pumpkin seed oil, and onion rings. The Styrian version is typically grated over flat cake on buttered bread. Try with salads and sautéed potatoes.

AUSTRIA Tirol and Steiermark		
Age 4 weeks		
Weight and Shape 4½lb (2kg), block		
Size L. 6in (15cm), W. 6in (15cm), H. 6in (15cm)		
Milk Cow		
Classification Hard		
Producer Various		

Vorarlberger Bergkäse

The Vorarlberg mountains overshadow Lake Constance. Their high pastures carpeted with wild flowers and grasses provide superb grazing for the cattle during the summer months, producing rich, flavorsome, milk to make this Bergkäse, or mountain, cheese.

TASTING NOTES The rind is thick and the paste supple, with cherry-sizes holes, and the grazing gives the cheese its buttery yellow color and subtle taste of wild honey with a savory, salty undercurrent with age.

HOW TO ENJOY Vorarlberger is equally at home as a snack, in a fondue, or grilled, complemented by a fruity Chardonnay.

AUSTRIA Vorarlberg		
Age 6–8 months		
Weight and Shape 110lb (50kg), wheel		
Size D. 20in (50cm), H. 5in (12cm)		
Milk Cow		
Classification Hard		
Producer Various		

Weinkäse

First made in Leibnitz, in a dairy near the Slovenian border when by chance the new cheese, temporarily stored in a nearby wine cellar, absorbed the wonderful aromas, and Weinkäse was born. Today it is made in nearby Enns valley and washed with red wine, creating an almost black rind dusted with white mold.

TASTING NOTES After six weeks, it has a fermenting fruit, slightly lemony tang and a hint of the Zweigelt wine, balanced by a smooth, tender texture.

HOW TO ENJOY Eye-catching cheeseboard addition with crusty bread. Pair with a red Zweigelt wine from Styrian country.

AUSTRIA Steiermark		
Age 6–8 weeks		
Weight and Shape 2¼lb (1kg), round		
Size D. 8in (20cm), H. 2in (5cm)		
Milk Cow		
Classification Semi-soft		
Producer Schärdinger Group		

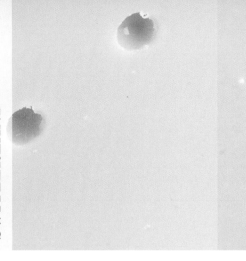
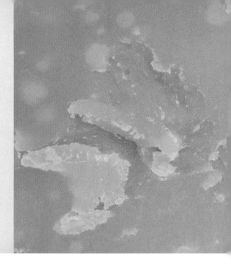

Appenzeller

Made in the hilly pre-alps of Switzerland for more than 700 years, this cheese has a brown-orange aromatic rind from washing with a secret blend of cider, white wine, herbs, and spices. Some are soaked for two months in brine creating a suppler interior and strong, rich flavor.

TASTING NOTES At six months, it has nutty notes and a distinct spicy finish, but develops a more intense flavor with age.

HOW TO ENJOY Popular for breakfast when young, or the cheeseboard when aged, with crusty bread, cider, beer, or a racy red wine such as Dole or Fitou.

SWITZERLAND Appenzell Ausserrhoden, Appenzell Innerrhoden, Sankt Gallen, and Thurgau	
Age 6–8 months	
Weight and Shape 13¼lb–17lb 10oz (6–8kg), wheel	
Size D. 14in (35cm), H. 5in (12cm) (pictured)	
Milk Cow	
Classification Semi-soft	
Producer Various	

Gruyère AOC

Switzerland's most popular cheese is named after the picturesque village of Gruyère, near Fribourg, and can trace its history back to 1072. The best are made in the mountains in summer when the cows graze the alpine pastures.

TASTING NOTES At 4 months, it is firm and dense with a nutty flavor. At 8 months, it has a wonderful complexity that is rich, strong, nutty, and earthy.

HOW TO ENJOY The essential ingredient for fondue. Grate over pasta, salads, or vegetables, or into sauces. Serve with walnuts, fruity bread, and a Dole or Burgundy red wine.

SWITZERLAND Fribourg	
Age From 12 months	
Weight and Shape 66–88lb (30–40kg), wheel	
Size D. 27½in (70cm), H. 6in (15cm) (pictured)	
Milk Cow	
Classification Hard	
Producer Various	

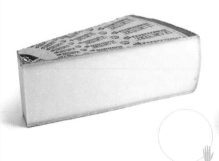

Hobelkäse

Made in the Bernese Oberland and Valais, where each summer the cows go to graze in the mountain pastures, and the farmers, each with a few cows, pool milk to make cheese. In fall, they return home and share out the cheeses at the annual "Chästeilet", a major event for the farmers and tourists.

TASTING NOTES Cut in paper-thin slices with a cheese-rake, Hobelkäse reveals the exquisite aroma of the flowery meadows captured in the milk.

HOW TO ENJOY Traditionally thinly sliced and rolled, and served with a prickling white wine from the Lake Geneva vineyards as an apéritif.

SWITZERLAND Bern and Valais	
Age 18 months	
Weight 17lb 10oz–22lb (8–10kg), wheel (pictured)	
Size D. 20in (50cm), H. 6in (15cm) (pictured)	
Milk Cow	
Classification Hard	
Producer Various	

Mutschli

Produced in most regions of the country from milk surplus in the village dairies, using cow's, goat's, or occasionally ewe's milk. Significantly smaller than most Swiss cheeses, it comes in various shapes and sizes.

TASTING NOTES Beneath the washed yellow to brown rind is a soft, mild paste, with few or no holes, and a light yellow color. Mutschli is a pleasant cheese and a children's favorite.

HOW TO ENJOY In Central Switzerland, Mutschli is typically fried in a pan and served with boiled potatoes, similar to raclette. Otherwise it is eaten mostly as part of breakfast or as a snack.

SWITZERLAND All over	
Age 5 weeks	
Weight and Shape 10oz (300g), round (pictured)	
Size D. 8in (20cm), H. 4in (10cm) (pictured)	
Milk Cow, goat, or ewe	
Classification Semi-soft	
Producer Various	

Raclette

The name originates from the French word *racler*, meaning "to scrape", and relates to the process of broiling the cheese, traditionally in front of an open fire, and scraping it onto bowls of piping hot potato. To meet demand, it is now made throughout Switzerland. Raw milk cheeses from the valleys are stamped with their origin – such as Bagnes, Orsières, and Goms.

TASTING NOTES A leathery washed brown rind encases a smooth, supple paste with a rich, fruity savory flavor.

HOW TO ENJOY Eaten grilled and topping potatoes, with pickled cucumbers and onions, and a local white or red wine.

SWITZERLAND All over	
Age 6 months	
Weight and Shape 13¼lb (6kg), wheel	
Size D. 18in (45cm), H. 4in (10cm)	
Milk Cow	
Classification Semi-soft	
Producer Various	

Sbrinz AOC

Sbrinz today is not very different from the one described by the Roman writer Pliny in 70 B.C. as "Caseus Helveticus", or "Swiss cheese". Although it is very hard, it is less crumbly than Parmigiano-Reggiano (see pp130–131) because it is made with full-fat milk.

TASTING NOTES Very hard and grainy, it has a distinct aroma from the flowery meadows, with spicy, slightly salty undercurrents.

HOW TO ENJOY Superb grated into pasta and soups, or serve accompanied by a fruity Swiss or Burgundy red or white wine, or Champagne, as an apéritif.

SWITZERLAND Luzern, Obwalden, and Unterwalden	
Age 18–48 months	
Weight 66–88lb (30–40kg), wheel	
Size D. 15½in (40cm), H. 12in (30cm) (pictured)	
Milk Cow	
Classification Hard	
Producer Various	

Emmentaler

One of the great classics of the cheese world, Emmental can trace its history back to 1293 but was first mentioned by name in 1542 when the recipe was given to the people of Langehthal in the Emme valley.

At the beginning of each summer, farmers would take their small herds to the summer pastures, known as *alpage*. Far from the nearest markets, they needed to make a cheese that required months to mature, so they pooled their milk, creating huge slow-ripening cheeses, which could ripen in the chalets until the cows returned to the valleys at the beginning of fall.

Little has changed since then except Emmental is now made all over Switzerland where there are high pastures, and takes place in mountain chalets or small owner-operated cooperatives. Hence, as you travel through the magnificent Alps, you can still see the timber-built chalets with their colorful flower boxes, wooden balconies and tiny windows, and the peaceful cows with their hand-painted bells grazing meadows abundant with wild flowers, grasses, and herbs. It is this that makes Swiss Emmental unique and unable to be emulated despite many copies the world over. Over winter, the cattle are housed in barns. Fed a diet of hay, the milk is more concentrated and intense but the color is a paler yellow and the cheeses often smaller.

TASTING NOTES When first cut, a perfume like a million meadow flowers is released. If you squeeze a small piece, you can feel its supple texture and, as it warms, you can taste the hushed tones of the alpine meadows, the sweetness of ripe, fermenting fruit, and herbaceous white wine that tingles on the palate. If you find one that has a tiny "tear" of moisture trapped in the holes, it will be as near to perfect as you will find.

HOW TO ENJOY Great for snacking, sandwiches, for breakfast, and on a cheeseboard, but comes into its own in a fondue where it is rich, creamy, and wonderfully stretchy while its sweet, nutty nature is underlined. Its stringy texture when cooked means, unlike most hard cheese, it does not break down in sauces but lends itself to being grated or melted, especially in a Croque Monsieur.

With its immense flavor and firm texture, Emmental can be served with big red or white wines or even a crisp, fruity white Swiss wine.

Cattle grazing *in the summer* alpage.

SWITZERLAND Central cantons		
Age 4–18 months		
Weight and Shape 165–220lb (75–100kg), wheel		
Size D. 31½–39in (80–100cm), H. 6–10½in (16–27cm)		
Milk Cow		
Classification Hard		
Producer Various		

A CLOSER LOOK

About 265 gallons (1,000 liters) of milk is needed for one cheese. As a result, like all the big mountain cheeses of Europe, they are made by cooperatives rather than individuals.

RIND The distinctive, repeating pattern on the rind guarantees authenticity to the consumer.

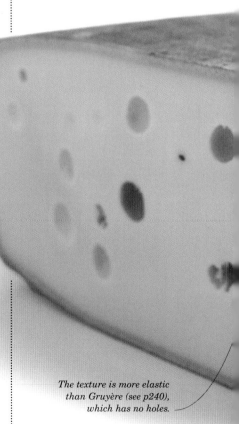
The texture is more elastic than Gruyère (see p240), which has no holes.

CUTTING THE CURD The milk is warmed in a large vat, traditionally a huge copper kettle, and three different starter cultures are stirred into the milk. The curd is cut with wires strung in a giant frame. In the traditional hemispherical vats, a "figure-eight" motion is required to cut the curd evenly into rice-sized pieces.

KNEADING AND PRESSING The curd is kneaded so it fills the hoop and is put into a press. It is then turned and the diameter of the hoop reduced. The process is repeated six or more times.

GRADING After 6–12 months, a grader using a special hammer like a piano tuner's will tap each cheese and, from the resonance or echo, can ascertain the size, distribution, and even shape of the holes and therefore its quality. The best are stamped in red with the alpine horn blower (common to all Swiss cheeses) and the words Switzerland and Emmental. The sides are branded with a unique identification number for traceability.

Quarter wheel

The propionic bacteria present during maturation gives off bubbles of carbon dioxide, and, unable to escape, these create the small holes characteristic of the cheese.

SWITZERLAND

243

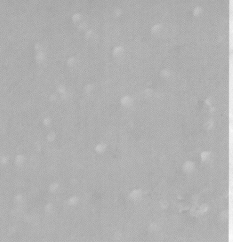

Schabziger

This unique and very distinctive lime-green zero-fat cheese has been made since the 11th century, when the local monks introduced fenugreek. Skimmed-milk curds are aged for a few weeks, then finely ground and mixed with ground fenugreek and wild clover.

TASTING NOTES Pressed into a small, truncated cone, it has a powerful, racy, almost eye-watering spicy tang as it melts in the mouth.

HOW TO ENJOY Mix 50:50 with butter, and spread over crusty white bread with onions or fresh chives. It spices up baked potatoes, fondues, and soups. Cider or Pinot Noir work well as partners.

SWITZERLAND Glarus	
Age 8 weeks	
Weight and Shape 3½oz (100g), truncated cone	
Size D. 2in (5cm), H. 4in (10cm)	
Milk Cow	
Classification Fresh	
Producer Geska	

Tête de Moine AOC

First made in the twelfth century by monks at Bellelay monastery, its production then shifted to farms owned by the monastery, when the cheese was given to the Church as a tithe. Originally named Bellelay after the monastery, it was renamed "head of the monks", in recognition of enthusiastic consumption.

TASTING NOTES Dense, smooth, and yellow as the result of meadow flowers, it has a buttery, slightly savory taste, revealed when pared into rosettes with the specially invented *girolle* machine.

HOW TO ENJOY Using the *girolle*, guests create rosettes, and enjoy with a Lake Geneva white and fresh walnuts.

SWITZERLAND Jura	
Age 8 months	
Weight and Shape 1lb 5oz–1¾lb (600–800g), cylinder	
Size D. 5in (12cm), H. 7in (18cm)	
Milk Cow	
Classification Hard	
Producer Various	

Tomme Vaudoise

Made in the French-speaking part of Switzerland, this has a thin, wrinkled rind dusted with white mold. The raw cow's milk cheese Tomme Fleurette develops reddish brown patches that break down the curd until it becomes almost liquid. Goat's milk cheeses are sold as Tomme de Chèvre.

TASTING NOTES Vaudoise is mild and creamy with a hint of mushrooms from the rind, while Fleurette has a more intense, rustic flavor as it softens.

HOW TO ENJOY Great with crispy bread, especially caraway or walnut, and a Vully or Chablis, or dip in breadcrumbs and lightly fry, and serve with salad.

SWITERLAND Vaud and Fribourg	
Age 4–6 weeks	
Weight and Shape 3½–5oz (100–150g), disc	
Size: D. 6in (16cm), 1in (3cm)	
Milk Cow or goat	
Classification Soft white	
Producer Various	

Vacherin Fribourgeois AOC

Vacherin Fribourgeois, not to be confused with Vacherin Mont d'Or, is a dense, deep yellow cheese. Produced in the canton of Fribourg, it first came to fame in 1448, when it was served to the daughter of the Scottish king and wife of the Duke Sigismund of Austria.

TASTING NOTES Supple and nutty, it has a long, tender aftertaste of alpine flowers and freshly cut hay. Its flavors intensify when the cheese is melted.

HOW TO ENJOY At its best in *fondue au vacherin*, made with three vacherins of different ages—like the best-ever cheese soup. Pair with Pinot Noir.

SWITZERLAND Fribourg	
Age 9 weeks–6 months	
Weight and Shape 13¼lb–17lb 10oz (6–8kg), wheel	
Size D. 18in (45cm), H. 4½in (11cm) (pictured)	
Milk Cow	
Classification Semi-soft	
Producer Various	

Vacherin Mont D'or AOC

This is produced from September until March, when the cows come down from the mountains to spend winter in the warm barns of individual farmers. In the summer, their milk is combined to make huge wheels of Gruyère.

TASTING NOTES Encircled with aromatic spruce bark, the almost liquid interior hints of farmyards, meadow flowers, and white wine, with a woody tang.

HOW TO ENJOY Spoon direct from the box, or make a little hole in the rind, pour in some white wine, and put the whole box in the oven at 425°F (220°C) for 30 minutes. Serve with a dry white.

SWITZERLAND Vaud	
Age 6–10 weeks	
Weight and Shape 14oz (400g) and 2¼lb (1kg), round	
Size D. 7in (18cm), H. 3in (8cm)	
Milk Cow	
Classification Semi-soft	
Producer Various	

Valle Maggia

Produced in villages in the valley of Maggia on the southern side of the Swiss alps, all the cheeses are round and covered with a thick gray mold. They are named after the particular valley in which they are produced: Verzasca, Piora, Bedretto, etc.

TASTING NOTES The ivory paste has tiny little holes and a smooth, buttery taste. There is also sometimes a subtle fragrance of the smoke that drifts into the storeroom from the farmer's fire.

HOW TO ENJOY Perfect sustenance for walking and hiking, enjoyed with dried pork or venison sausage, particularly with the local Merlot wine.

SWITZERLAND Ticino	
Age 6 months	
Weight and Shape 13¼lb–17lb 10oz (6–8kg), round	
Size D. 15½in (40cm), H. 5in (12cm) (pictured)	
Milk Cow; sometimes mixed with goat or ewe	
Classification Semi-soft	
Producer Various	

SCANDINAVIA

Scandinavia encompasses Denmark, Norway, Sweden, and Finland, and is known for its long, dark winter days and all-day summer sunlight. As a result of being isolated for much of the year and having short grazing times, farmers found it essential to preserve their most precious source of protein, often in the form of whey cheese. In Lapland, the far-north region of Scandinavia, the milk of the hardy reindeer is still used to make cheese, and the exceptionally rich milk produces cheese with an earthy, gamey flavor.

Key
- ★ AOC, DOC, DOP, PGI, or PDO cheeses
- Produced only here
- Produced throughout the region

FINLAND
PRODUCED THROUGHOUT THE COUNTRY
Juustoleipä, Oltermanni, Turunmaa

SWEDEN
PRODUCED THROUGHOUT THE COUNTRY
Ädelost, Grevéost, Herrgårdsost, Hushållsost, Mesost, Prästost, Västerbottenost

Ridder

NORWAY
PRODUCED THROUGHOUT THE COUNTRY
Jarlsberg, Nökkelost

Gammelost

Gjetost

DENMARK
PRODUCED THROUGHOUT THE COUNTRY
Bla Castello, Danablu, Danbo, Havarti

Esrom ★

Samsø

DENMARK Denmark, the most southern of the Scandinavian countries, has a milder maritime climate and flat meadows that are home to comfort-loving cows. Denmark has a thriving dairy industry, with cheeses exported around the world.

NORWAY With the exception of a long, narrow strip of grazing land bordering the sea, Norway is made up of forests, rugged mountains, and the Tundra in the north, which is why goats, rather than cows, prevailed.

SWEDEN Sweden's well-established dairy industry dates back to the 9th century when Benedictine monks, who were sent to convert the war-mongering Vikings to more peaceful way of life, introduced cheesemaking.

FINLAND Finland, which has one-third of its landmas in the Arctic Circle, has a thriving dairy industry that features many European-style cheeses, as well as its ow unique reindeer cheese (Juustoleipä) that is toasted in front of the fire.

N

100 miles

100 km

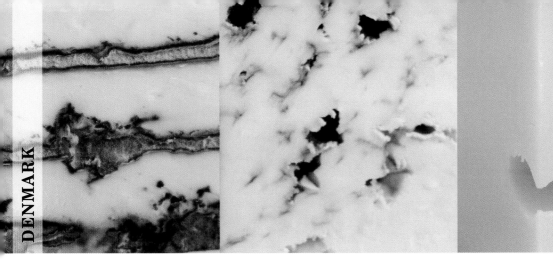

Bla Castello

Developed in the 1960s to meet demand for mild creamy blue cheese, Bla Castello, also known as Blue Castello, has a unique rind that can develop a combination of red and blue-green molds.

TASTING NOTES This rich and buttery cheese has a Brie-like texture, mild spicy accents of blue veins, an aroma that hints of mushrooms, and a flavor that develops steadily but never becomes too strong.

HOW TO ENJOY Ideal for younger palates, and eats well on bread and, of course, Danish crisp-bread. Matches well with Danish beer.

DENMARK All over	
Age 8–10 weeks	
Weight and Shape 5½oz (150g), half moon, and 2¼lb (1.6kg), round	
Size D. 4½in (11.5cm) and 8in (20cm), H. 2in (5.5cm) and 2½in (6cm)	
Milk Cow	
Classification Blue	
Producer Tholstrup	

Danablu

Invented in the early 20th century as an alternative to the imported French blues, and is now available worldwide. Danablu, also known as Danish Blue, is one of the most popular cheeses in Denmark.

TASTING NOTES This mature blue has deep purple-blue streaks, a smooth yet crumbly, moist texture, and a full flavor that is fresh with a sharp, salty, almost metallic blue bite and creamy finish.

HOW TO ENJOY A cheeseboard stalwart, pairs well with grapes, apples, or tomatoes, or try it with olives and pickles. It needs a slightly sweet wine or hoppy ale to offset its salty tang.

DENMARK All over	
Age 2–3 months	
Weight and Shape 6½lb (3kg), drum or block	
Size D. 8in (20cm), H. 4in (10cm)	
Milk Cow	
Classification Blue	
Producer Rosenborg	

Danbo

This milder version of Samsø (see p248) is one of Denmark's most popular cheeses, and is made with semi-skim milk. The smooth, barely formed yellow rind is often covered in red or orange wax. It is also known as King Christian or Christian IX in the United States.

TASTING NOTES It is pale, with a pleasant aroma. The pliable interior is spattered with small holes, and the taste is slightly sweet and nutty.

HOW TO ENJOY This breakfast cheese is also great for sandwiches and for general snacking. It partners well with dark breads such as Pumpernickel, and beers, apple juice, and ciders.

DENMARK All over	
Age 6–12 months	
Weight and Shape Various	
Size Various	
Milk Cow	
Classification Semi-soft	
Producer Various	

Esrom PGI

First made by Cistercian monks in the 12th century, this was reintroduced by the Danish Cheese Institute in 1951. Formerly named "Danish Port Salut," it was renamed "Esrom" after the ancient abbey in which it was first made. Esrom was granted PGI status in 1996.

TASTING NOTES Pale lemon with small holes, Esrom is sweet and buttery; it becomes more pungent with age, while still retaining its sweetness. Some styles are made with garlic or pepper.

HOW TO ENJOY It is ideal in a traditional Danish open sandwich, or eaten with cold cuts of hams and charcuterie.

DENMARK Hovedstaden	
Age 21–28 days	
Weight and Shape 7oz–4½lb (200g–2kg), brick	
Size Various, L. 8½in (22cm), W. 5in (12cm), H. 2½in (6cm) (pictured)	
Milk Cow	
Classification Semi-soft	
Producer Various	

Havarti

Probably Denmark's most famous cheese, Havarti was invented in the mid-1800s by Hanne Neilsen, who was the wife of a farmer from New Zealand. She traveled through Europe to learn cheesemaking and invented this cheese—a masterpiece with its added cream. It was originally named "Havarthi," after her farm.

TASTING NOTES Sweet, mellow, and very creamy, it has a buttery aroma that becomes sharper and saltier with hints of hazelnut. Some contain caraway seeds.

HOW TO ENJOY A great snacking cheese, it is ideal for Danish open sandwiches, slicing and broiling, or adding to salads.

DENMARK All over	
Age 4–12 weeks	
Weight and Shape 10lb (4.5kg), blocks or drums	
Size Various, L. 4½in (11cm), W. 2½in (6cm), H. 2in (5cm) (pictured)	
Milk Cow	
Classification Semi-soft	
Producer Various	

Samsø

This semi-soft cheese was created in the early 19th century when the king of Denmark invited Swiss cheesemakers to share their skills with Danish farmers. A pale elastic-textured cheese with irregular-shaped holes based on Emmental was the result. It is named after the Danish island of Samsø, a traditional Viking meeting place.

TASTING NOTES Mild, and buttery when young, as it ages, Samsø develops a sweet-sour pungency, and distinct hazelnut flavors.

HOW TO ENJOY Perfect for a fondue, melted on top of grilled potatoes, or sliced on a chunk of rye bread.

DENMARK Samsø, Mitjylland	
Age 8–12 weeks.	
Weight and Shape Various	
Size Various	
Milk Cow	
Classification Semi-soft	
Producer Various	

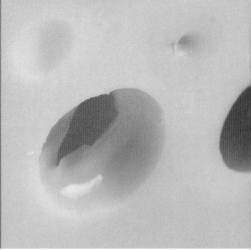

Gammelost

Gammelost means "old cheese," a name given because it grows a green-brown mold traditionally achieved by wrapping the cheese in straw soaked in gin and juniper berries. It is made with very low-fat skim milk, mainly in Sogn og Fjordane, and Hardanger.

TASTING NOTES Sharp and aromatic with a brittle, granular texture and a pungent tang reminiscent of aged Camembert or Danish Blue. Its brownish yellow interior is flecked with erratic, uneven streaks of blue.

HOW TO ENJOY An after-dinner favorite, robust enough to be enjoyed with strong digestives such as schnapps or grappa.

NORWAY Vestlandet	
Age 4–5 weeks	
Weight and Shape 6½lb (3kg), drum	
Size D. 4in (10cm), H. 8in (20cm)	
Milk Goat	
Classification Hard	
Producer Various	

Gjetost

Made in the Gudbrandsdalen Valley using milk, cream, and whey, Gjetost has the color of French mustard and the texture of fudge. It was once made using only goat's milk—*gjet* means "goat" in Norwegian. To differentiate the styles today, that made with pure cow's milk is called *mysost*, while *ekta gjetost* is made with pure goat's milk.

TASTING NOTES This is not to everyone's taste, but Norwegians love its sweet caramel and peanut butter flavors as well as its unique aromatic, goaty taste.

HOW TO ENJOY Gjetost is traditionally eaten thinly shaved on flatbread, or with spiced fruit cake at Christmas.

NORWAY Østlandet	
Age From a few days	
Weight and Shape 9oz–1lb 2oz (250–500g), block	
Size Various, L. 6in (15cm), W. 2½in (6cm), H. 1½in (4cm) (pictured)	
Milk Goat or cow	
Classification Fresh	
Producer Various	

Jarlsberg

First produced in the 1860s in Jarlsberg and Vestfold county, it was revived in the mid-1900s. Made from the rich milk produced from cows grazing in high summer pastures, it has large round holes and a lemony-yellow color.

TASTING NOTES It was inspired by Swiss Emmental, but Jarlsberg is softer, more supple, sweeter, and less nutty, with a fermenting fruit tang to the finish.

HOW TO ENJOY Try sliced in salads or as a party snack. This versatile cheese is also great in sandwiches with smoked ham, melted on toast, or served with crudités.

NORWAY All over	
Age 1–15 months	
Weight and Shape 22lb (10kg), wheel or block	
Size: Various	
Milk Cow	
Classification Semi-soft	
Producer Tine	

Nökkelost

Made with partially skimmed milk and generously scattered with finely chopped cumin seeds and cloves, this semi-soft cheese is based on Dutch Leidsekaas. Made in Norway since the 17th century, it is named after the crossed keys (*nökkel*) that are the emblem of the Dutch city of Leiden, and only two small dairies are still producing it.

TASTING NOTES Springy yet firm, it has a creamy feel and a warm spicy flavor that hints of Christmas.

HOW TO ENJOY Nökkelost adds a warm spiciness to tarts and baked vegetables, or serve simply with fresh apples and pears, pumpernickel, and beer.

NORWAY All over	
Age 12 weeks	
Weight and Shape Various	
Size Various	
Milk Cow	
Classification Semi-soft	
Producer Tine	

Ridder

Ridder is a semi-soft cheese that is washed in brine mixed with annatto, which gives it a sticky, orange rind. Named after the Norwegian word for "knight," it was invented in 1969 by the Swedish cheesemaker Sven Fenelius, and it is now available worldwide.

TASTING NOTES Sweet, buttery yet sharp, and slightly nutty, with a dense, pliable, pale yellow interior. As it ages, Ridder becomes more pungent.

HOW TO ENJOY An excellent dessert cheese when young, especially when it is served with fresh summer berries. It tastes more mellow when it is grilled or baked.

NORWAY Vestlandet (Western Norway)	
Age 12–15 weeks	
Weight and Shape 7lb (3.25kg); wheel	
Size D. 6in (15cm), H. 2–3in (5–7cm)	
Milk Cow	
Classification Semi-soft	
Producer Tine	

Ädelost

Ädelost, or "noble cheese," is Sweden's only original blue and was created as an alternative to the imported French blues. It is characterized by blue-gray pockets and short broken veins that are scattered through its pale, creamy interior. The thin, pale rind is dusted with gray, white, and blue molds.

TASTING NOTES Ädelost's high-moisture texture emphasizes the sharp, spicy, blue bite and salty tang of the cheese.

HOW TO ENJOY Crumble over salads or mix with extra virgin olive oil and balsamic vinegar to make a piquant salad dressing. Serve with a hoppy beer or local schnapps.

SWEDEN All over	
Age 8–12 weeks	
Weight and Shape 5½lb (2.5kg), drum	
Size D. 7in (18cm), H. 4in (10cm)	
Milk Cow	
Classification Blue	
Producer Various	

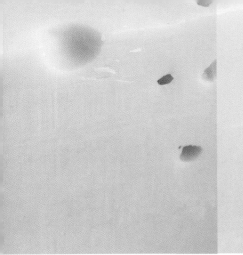

Grevéost

Commercially produced and based on Emmental (see pp242–23), Grevéost has a pale yellow, dense interior with holes of irregular size and shape. Produced in large wheels, and a "lite" variety, this cheese plays a daily role in Swedish cooking because its mild, sweet flavor appeals to young and old alike.

TASTING NOTES Sweet and nutty, it is firm to the bite, with a dense and pliable texture, but it lacks Emmental's depth.

HOW TO ENJOY Spread brioche with butter and fill with thin slices of the cheese and smoked ham. Also works well as a snack, melted, or grated into béchamel-type sauces.

SWEDEN All over	
Age 40 weeks	
Weight and Shape 33lb (15kg), wheel	
Size D. 14in (35cm), H. 4–5½in (10–14cm)	
Milk Cow	
Classification Semi-soft	
Producer Various	

Herrgårdsost

Created in the early 20th century as a local alternative to Gruyère (see p240), Herrgårdsost gets its name from the Swedish for "manor house." Although based on Gruyère, it is softer and more supple, with smaller round holes.

TASTING NOTES The pale yellow interior has a thin rind that is most often waxed. Nutty and with a similar taste to mild Cheddar, its zingy tang intensifies with age.

HOW TO ENJOY Like Gruyère, this is an excellent eating and cooking cheese. Try it with pickled gherkins, to accentuate its tangy character, and match with a fruity white wine.

SWEDEN All over	
Age 4–24 months	
Weight and Shape 33lb–39lb 11oz (12–18kg), round	
Size Various, D. 15½in (40cm), H. 5in (12cm) (pictured)	
Milk Cow	
Classification Semi-soft	
Producer Various	

Hushållsost

Hushållsost means "household cheese" in Swedish, and as such and with more than 700 years of history behind it, it is one of the country's best-known and most well-used cheeses. Unlike many Swedish cheeses, it is made unashamedly with full-fat milk.

TASTING NOTES Mild and creamy, with a straw-colored interior, Hushållsost has a lemon-fresh finish, an open texture with small irregular holes, and a barely formed rind.

HOW TO ENJOY Popular as part of the traditional breakfast buffet, it is also great for sandwiches, pizzas, tarts, and even melted on top of casseroles.

SWEDEN All over	
Age 4–12 weeks	
Weight and Shape 6½lb (3kg), drum	
Size D. 8–10in (20–25cm), H. 2–3in (5–8cm)	
Milk Cow	
Classification Semi-soft	
Producer Various	

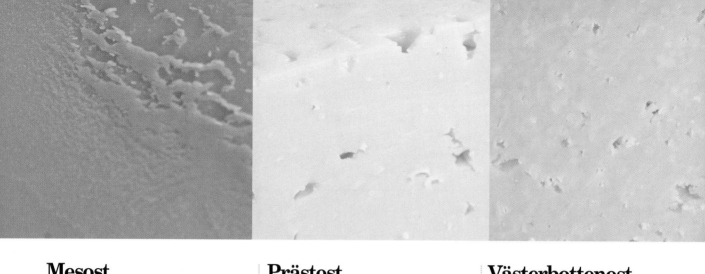

Mesost

This whey cheese came about from the need of the Scandinavian producers to use every element of their milk. The whey is cooked so that the proteins and fats separate and the remaining liquid evaporates, leaving behind a sticky brown caramelized mass of sugars. Sometimes cream or milk is added to increase the yield.

TASTING NOTES An acquired taste to those not brought up with it, the cheese is sweet with a creamy, caramel fudge flavor and bitter aftertaste.

HOW TO ENJOY It is usually served for breakfast with toast or bread, or as a snack.

SWEDEN All over	
Age From a few days	
Weight and Shape 2lb 4oz–17lb 6oz (1kg–8kg), blocks	
Size Various	
Milk Cow, goat, or ewe	
Classification Fresh	
Producer Various	

Prästost

Prästost or "priest cheese," dates from the 16th century when farmers paid a tithe to the local church in the form of goods, including milk. Once paid, the farmer's wife converted the balance of the milk into cheese and sold it at the local market to recoup some costs. Today it is factory-made.

TASTING NOTES Supple with rice-sized holes and a squishy texture, it is robust, sweet-sour, and leaves a sharp, fruity tingle on the palate.

HOW TO ENJOY Try it sprinkled on hearty soups, on chili con carne, or as an extra dimension to a cheeseboard with a fruity red.

SWEDEN All over	
Age Up to 12 months	
Weight and Shape 26lb 5oz–33lb (12kg–15kg), wheels	
Size Various, D. 4in (10cm), H. 1–3in (5–7cm) (pictured)	
Milk Cow	
Classification Semi-soft	
Producer Various	

Västerbottenost

Swedish cuisine is all about converting the bounty of the brief summer harvest into food that will last through the long, harsh winter. As a result, hard cheeses were made in homes and small dairies across Sweden. Västerbottenost, a mass-produced cheese invented in the mid-19th century, is modeled on these traditional cheeses.

TASTING NOTES It is hard and granular like aged Cheddar, with small irregular holes and a fruity tang that becomes more savory with age.

HOW TO ENJOY A great after-dinner cheese, best served with beer, Schnapps, or red wine.

SWEDEN All over	
Age Up to 12 months	
Weight and Shape 44lb (20kg), wheel	
Size D. 20in (50cm), H. 8in (20cm)	
Milk Cow	
Classification: Hard	
Producer Various	

SCANDINAVIA

252

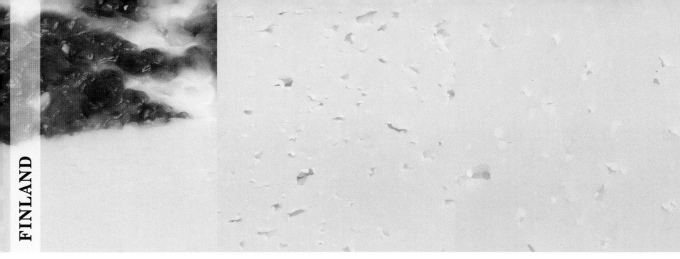

Juustoleipä

A unique cheese, Juustoleipä, or "cheese bread" was once made in homes using cow or reindeer milk. The curd was pressed into flat wooden platters then "toasted" in front of an open fire, hence the name. Today it is commercially made with cow's milk.

TASTING NOTES Beneath the lightly-toasted rind, the whitish-yellow interior is floppy and squeaky on the palate, with hints of coconut, pineapple, sweet milk, and eggs.

HOW TO ENJOY Rarely found outside Finland, where it is grilled and served with fruit jam for breakfast, or dropped into a cup of coffee, but not consumed.

FINLAND Finland and Lapland	
Age From a few days	
Weight and Shape 28oz (800g), flattened round	
Size D. 5½in (14cm), H. ½in (1.5cm)	
Milk Cow or reindeer	
Classification Fresh	
Producer Various	

Oltermanni

An Havarti-style cheese made by Valio, a large dairy owned by Finnish dairy farmers, who produce the cleanest milk in the EU due to their crystal clear water and freedom from industrial pollution. Outside Finland it is sometimes sold as Baby Muenster or Finlandia Cheese.

TASTING NOTES Similar to Turunmaa, it has a barely formed rind and small, irregular holes.

HOW TO ENJOY Like many Scandinavian cheeses, it is served at breakfast, sliced on rye bread, or melted over toast.

FINLAND All over	
Age 1–3 months	
Weight and Shape 2lb 4oz (1.1kg), cylinder	
Size D. 4½in (11cm), H. 4in (10cm)	
Milk Cow	
Classification Semi-soft	
Producer Valio	

Turunmaa

This cheese was originally made as a breakfast cheese in the grand manor houses of Turku, Finland's ancient capital in the 16th century. An Havarti-style cheese, it has a firm yet open texture, and a richness that comes from the excellent grazing in the area.

TASTING NOTES Chewy and creamy with tiny eyes and a rich, deep buttery taste. It has a savory tang liked grilled Cheddar on the finish, like a rather delicious but slightly rubbery omelet.

HOW TO ENJOY Like most Scandinavian cheeses it is served at breakfast or with slices of smoked ham and cold meats.

FINLAND All over	
Age 8–12 weeks	
Weight and Shape 13–22lb (6–10kg), drum	
Size D. 4–6in (10–15cm); H. 2–3in (5–7cm)	
Milk Cow	
Classification Semi-soft	
Producer Valio	

253

POLAND

CZECH
REPUBLIC

SLOVAKIA
PRODUCED
THROUGHOUT
THE COUNTRY
**Bryndza ★,
Oštiepok ★**

HUNGARY
PRODUCED
THROUGHOUT
THE COUNTRY
Kashkaval

ROMANIA

SLOVENIA

CROATIA

BOSNIA&
HERZEGOVINA

SERBIA

BULGARIA

MONTENEGRO

ADRIATIC SEA

MACEDONIA

Kaseri ★

ALBANIA

Galotiri ★

AEGEAN SEA

Kaseri ★

Kaseri ★

GREECE
PRODUCED
THROUGHOUT
THE COUNTRY
**Anthotyros ★,
Feta ★,
Kefalotyri ★
Manouri,
Myzithra**

Galotiri ★

IONIAN SEA

N

200 miles

200 km

EASTERN EUROPE AND THE NEAR EAST

GREECE In Greek mythology, Apollo's son presented a gift of "everlasting value" to the Greeks: the secret of making cheese, which was the food of the gods. Records of Greek cheesemaking can be traced back as far as the 10th century BCE, and today, Greeks eat more cheese per head than the French or Italians.

The variety of mountain and maritime natural pastures plus the sun-kissed climate provide ideal conditions for the tenacious native goats and hardy sheep that provide the milk for some of the world's oldest and greatest cheeses.

EASTERN EUROPE Since 552 CE, Eastern Europe's borders changed frequently and numerous forces occupied the region, which led to a melting pot of culinary influences, from Roman to Russian and Turkish to Central Asian. As a result, unique local cheeses are sold alongside Swiss and Danish Havarti-style cheeses made in Lithuania and Slovenia; a version of Mozzarella, called Lubelski, made in Poland; and numerous Feta-like cheeses.

When post-war communism led to mass production, small producers all but died out, but since the Iron Curtain dropped, artisan cheesemakers have re-emerged. The Eastern European dairy industry is now thriving, with many small traditional creameries producing a variety of European and local cheeses.

ISRAEL AND THE NEAR EAST Although archaeological sites dating from 7000 BCE show signs that the domestication of the then-evolving sheep and goat population could have led to the development of the first cheeses for this region, the harsh climate prevented the creation of the sophisticated cheeses that were seen in Europe.

In the 1980s, interest in cheese beyond just fresh and salted or dried styles started a new wave of artisan and industrial cheeses. European-trained cheesemakers were able to upgrade the quality and awareness of traditional cheeses and produce European-style cheeses.

BLACK SEA

TURKEY
PRODUCED
THROUGHOUT
THE COUNTRY
Beyaz Peynir

Tulum

SYRIA

Tulum

LEBANON
PRODUCED
THROUGHOUT
THE COUNTRY
Akkawi

CYPRUS
PRODUCED
THROUGHOUT
THE COUNTRY
**Anari,
Halloumi**

Graviera ★

Turkeez

Inbar

KRÍTI

ISRAEL

Ketem

PRODUCED
THROUGHOUT
THE COUNTRY
**Labane,
Zfatit**

Graviera ★

MEDITERRANEAN SEA

Key	
★	AOC, DOC, DOP, PGI, or PDO cheeses
🧀	Produced only here
🧀	Produced throughout the region

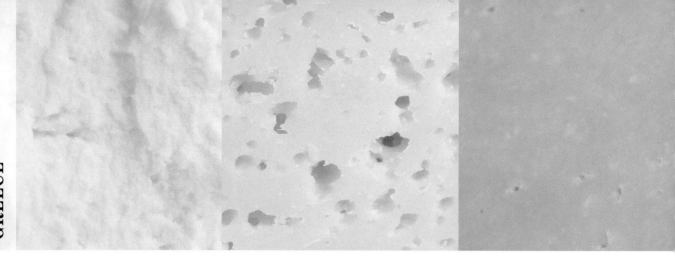

Anthotyros DOC

This has been made for centuries using the whey of ewe and goat's milk, or a mix of both, with the addition of small quantities of milk and cream. It is widely available throughout Greece as a soft or a hard cheese.

TASTING NOTES When fresh it is creamy and lemony with a unique floral taste; when aged it develops gray molds and is dry with a stronger, salty tang and a hint of smoke on the finish.

HOW TO ENJOY Traditionally used in savory or sweet pastries, and when aged it is grated over hot savory dishes. It is especially tasty when paired with fresh figs.

GREECE All over		
Age A couple of days up to 12 months		
Weight and Shape 12oz (350g), ball or truncated cone		
Size Various		
Milk Ewe and goat		
Classification Fresh and aged fresh		
Producer Various		

Graviera DOC

This is one of the most popular Greek cheeses. It is based on Gruyère but can be made with cow, goat, or ewe's milk, depending on the season. Graviera from Krìti (Crete) is made using ewe's milk and some goat, while Graviera Naxos is made with cow's milk with a little ewe or goat.

TASTING NOTES The Cretan Graviera is sweet and fruity like Emmental, with a delicate fragrance and burnt caramel finish. The Naxos version is richer, creamier and more nutty.

HOW TO ENJOY A classic all-around table cheese which can also be baked in cheese pastries.

GREECE Naxos and Kriti		
Age 3–5 months		
Weight and Shape 4½–17½lb (2–8kg), drum		
Size Various		
Milk Ewe, goat, or cow		
Classification Hard		
Producer Various		

Kaseri DOC

One of the oldest cheeses in the world, Kaseri is produced using a mix of goat's and ewe's milk (minimum 80 per cent ewe's). It is an aged *pasta filata* or stretched curd cheese, similar to Italian Provolone, which gives it a stringy texture when cooked.

TASTING NOTES Firm but supple with no rind, it becomes elastic when cooked. Quite salty, yet slightly sweet and pungent with a dry feel in the mouth.

HOW TO ENJOY A table cheese that is great for melting. Try on top of pita bread and smothered in fresh vine-tomato pulp and olives for your own Greek-style pizza.

GREECE Thessalia, Mitilini island, and Xanthi		
Age 12 weeks		
Weight and Shape 2–20lb (1–9kg), wheel		
Size Various		
Milk Ewe and goat		
Classification Semi-soft		
Producer Various		

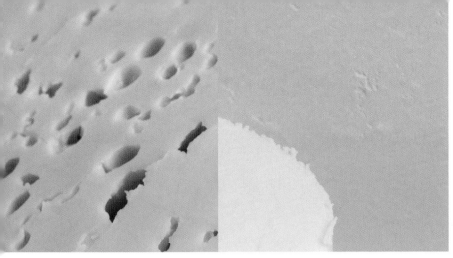

Galotiri DOC

Galotiri is one of the oldest Greek cheeses. It is predominantly made with ewe's milk, typically for household consumption rather than on a commercial scale. The fresh curds from successive days are placed in barrels and sealed with fat or hung from the rafters in sacks to drain until needed. If mold grows, it is scraped off to enable the whey to escape and the cheese to breathe.

TASTING NOTES Soft and spreadable with a refreshing, slightly sour and brackish taste, which is much appreciated by the Greeks.

HOW TO ENJOY Used in various traditional dishes, especially in spreads with herbs or spices.

GREECE	Epirus and Thessalia
Age	Few days to a few months
Weight and Shape	Various, small pots
Size	No size
Milk	Ewe, or ewe and goat
Classification	Fresh
Producer	Various

Myzithra

Made for thousands of years from whey of Feta and Kefalotyri, Myzithra is considered the ancestor of all Greek whey cheeses. It comes in two types: fresh Myzithra is unsalted or slightly salty and similar to cottage cheese, while aged is dry, salty, and firm.

TASTING NOTES Mild and refreshing when fresh, it has a nuttier and more salty taste when aged and a dusty, gray moldy rind.

HOW TO ENJOY Fresh Myzithra makes deliciously light sweet or savory dishes, while the dried version is ideal for grating over savory dishes such as pasta and pastries.

GREECE	All over
Age	From a couple of days
Weight and Shape	2.5–4.5lb (1–2kg) (fresh); 1–3lb (500g–1.5kg) (dried), pear
Size	Various
Milk	Ewe and goat
Classification	Aged fresh
Producer	Various

Kefalotyri DOC

Made throughout Greece since the Byzantine era, Kefalotyri is referred to as a "male or first cheese," a term used to describe cheeses made with full milk—as opposed to "female or second" cheeses, which are made with whey.

TASTING NOTES Firm but dry with numerous irregular holes, it has a fresh taste and distinct tang of ewe's milk. It also has a herbaceous tang as it finishes, which is reminiscent of olive oil.

HOW TO ENJOY Traditionally used in the classic Greek dish *saganaki*, where thick slices are fried, sometimes covered in egg and bread crumbs, and served with a squeeze of lemon.

GREECE	All over
Age	3–4 months
Weight and Shape	13–17½lb (6–8kg), drum
Size	Various
Milk	Ewe, and ewe and goat
Classification	Hard
Producer	Various

Manouri

A very old and popular Greek "white" or fresh cheese that is made from the drained whey from Feta production, with the addition of larger quantities of milk than used in Anthotyros.

TASTING NOTES Similar to Feta cheese but smoother, creamier, and less salty, Manouri is drained in cloth sacks and generally sold in logs.

HOW TO ENJOY Its low salt content means it is used in savory and sweet dishes, particularly pastries such as *spanakopita*, a baked spinach and cheese filo pastry pie, or sweet pastries, or simply served drizzled with honey.

GREECE	All over
Age	From a few days
Weight and Shape	1lb (500g), log
Size	L. 9½in (25cm) H. 3in (7cm)
Milk	Ewe or goat
Classification	Fresh
Producer	Various

Feta PDO

According to Greek mythology, the gods sent Apollo's son to teach the Greeks the art of cheesemaking; however, the first, but no less magical, record of cheesemaking was Homer's *Odyssey*. Written in the 8th century, Homer describes seeing Cyclops the giant making ewe's milk cheese in his cave, a simple recipe that would later become Feta.

Feta, granted protection in 2002 under the EU protected name scheme PDO (see p8), can now only be made in the mountainous regions of Macedonia, Thrace, Epirus, Thessaly, Sterea Ellada, Peloponnesus, and Mytilini from ewe's or goat's milk because it is in these areas that the herds still graze freely. As you watch the agile goats and endlessly patient sheep grazing the steep rugged hills and rock strewn pastures, it is easy to see why the comfort-loving cow never made Greece it home! There are no pesticides, insect repellents, or other pollutants used, and you can still catch the sound and a glimpse of the herds passing through small villages on the way to new pastures.

The hardy goats *graze the rugged landscape of Greece's mountainous regions.*

GREECE All over	
Age 2 months minimum	
Weight and Shape Various	
Size Various	
Milk Goat or ewe	
Classification Fresh	
Producer Various	

To those of us used to seeing sheep grazing ankle-deep in grass and clover, it is hard to imagine they can eke out sufficient food to survive, let alone produce milk for cheese from their diet of wild herbs, flowers, and tenacious grasses. But it is precisely why they produce some of the thickest, most aromatic milk in the world. The scent of the thyme, marjoram, and pine are captured and concentrated in the tiny fat globules in the milk.

TASTING NOTES Firm and compact yet easily crumbled, it has no rind and a myriad of small holes. Very white if made with pure goat's milk, it has a very fresh taste that hints of wild herbs, white wine, and a slightly goaty tang. Ewe's milk Feta feels a bit richer and creamier and is more ivory white. The taste is reminiscent of roast lamb, lamb fat, and lanolin. Both have a salt tang on the finish and a depth of flavor from the grazing.

HOW TO ENJOY Feta is eaten at every meal in Greece, notably in Spanokopita, the delicious cheese and spinach pies found all over Greece. Feta is also used in salads, usually with olives, tomatoes, raw onion, and olive oil, or mixed with any combination of raw or cooked vegetables. It does not dissolve completely when baked or melted, giving a lightness to many Greek dishes.

If you find Feta to be too salty, simply soak a chunk in cold water or milk for 10–15 minutes. This removes excess salt but does not mask its flavor.

A CLOSER LOOK

Feta is produced in homes, small family-run dairies, and large industrial units, but all respect the traditional recipe protected by the PDO status. It is an important component of the Greek diet, connected with the history and traditions of the country.

Feta is usually cut into small blocks and vacuum packed along with a little brine. Originally, shepherds who lived far from the sea where salt was bought would store their cheeses in olive oil.

CUTTING THE CURD Once the starter culture and rennet have done their job, the soft floppy curd is cut into ½–¾in (1–2cm) cubes using what looks like a giant wooden comb or square harp.

DRAINING The curds and whey are poured onto large draining tables with low sides, or traditionally it would have been put in a basket woven from reeds, and left to drain. During this time, the curd is turned 2–3 times over the next few hours and salted to speed up the expulsion of the whey.

The color changes depending on the ratio of the different milks used. Goat's milk is more white, whereas ewe's milk is more ivory.

Block of cheese

It crumbles easily, making it perfect for salads.

Kashkaval

Kashaval has been made since before the Roman Empire and the creation of mozzarella, and similar cheeses are produced across Eastern Europe and Central Asia. A *pasta filata* cheese—the curds have been heated and stretched prior to salting, then aged—its color ranges from pale yellow to yellow-brown, with a natural thin rind.

TASTING NOTES Flexible and crumbly, with a salty, sharp, almost bitter taste. There is also a hint of caramelized onions in the aftertaste.

HOW TO ENJOY Traditionally a table cheese, it can be fried, baked in pastry dishes, or grated over vegetables.

HUNGARY All over		
Age 8 weeks		
Weight and shape 15lb 7oz–19lb 13oz (7–9kg), irregular round		
Size D. 2–4½in (5–11.5cm), H. 1in (3cm)		
Milk Ewe, or ewe and cow		
Classification Hard		
Producer Various		

Bryndza PGI

Originally from the Carpathain Mountain region, Bryndza is a Feta-style cheese, probably introduced by the Greeks. Similar cheeses are made throughout Eastern Europe using cow, goat, or ewe's milk.

TASTING NOTES Similar to Feta, but softer, spreadable, and not as salty. It has a lemony acidity and ranges from soft, to firm and crumbly, depending on its age and the type of milk used.

HOW TO ENJOY Spread on warm grainy bread or crumble over baby salad leaves and tomatoes. Served as part of the traditional dish *bryndzové halušky* (potato dumplings with Bryndza).

SLOVAKIA All over		
Age 4 weeks or more		
Weight and shape 3½–10oz (100–300g), block		
Size L. 3–5in (7.5–12cm), 2–4in (W. 5–10cm), H. 1in (2.5cm)		
Milk Ewe, goat, or cow		
Classification Fresh		
Producer Various		

Oštiepok PGI

A traditional ewe's milk cheese, this is very similar to the Polish Oszcypek cheese. The curds are pressed into beautiful, hand-crafted wooden molds giving each a unique identity, then stored in the eaves of the house where it absorbs smoke from the fire below.

TASTING NOTES Smoky, slightly salty with a caramel taste from the milk and the rind ranges from a pale straw colored to deep orange-brown, depending on the age and smoking.

HOW TO ENJOY A table cheese, it combines well with cured meats and sausages.

SLOVAKIA All over		
Age 1–4 weeks		
Weight and Shape 5½oz–4½lb (150g–2kg), various shapes		
Size Various		
Milk Ewe		
Classification Hard		
Producer Various		

Beyaz Peynir

Known as "white cheese," this Feta-like cheese is made and consumed in large quantities all over Turkey. The recipe varies slightly from place to place, and it can be made from ewe, goat or cow's milk.

TASTING NOTES The taste varies from season to season depending on the mix of milks used. It can be salty to very salty, hard to soft, but the creamier version produced in Marmara is much sought after.

HOW TO ENJOY It plays a major role in Turkish cuisine from breakfast to salads, snacks, or as a filling in vegetable and pastry dishes.

TURKEY All over	
Age Minimum of 3 months	
Weight and shape 9oz–2¼lb (250g–1kg), various	
Size Various	
Milk Ewe, goat, or cow	
Classification Fresh	
Producer Various	

Tulum

One of the world's oldest cheeses, Tulum is made by packing specially cured goat's skins with fresh curd over a period of weeks. The skins are stitched up and left to age for three months, before being slit open for the cheese to be served from the skins.

TASTING NOTES Surprisingly mild with aromatic or sweet flavors depending on the milk and the seasons. Erzincan, the most common variety, can be quite strong and somewhat bitter.

HOW TO ENJOY A relatively expensive artisan cheese, it is best served simply drizzled with olive oil alongside fruit, figs, olives, or fresh vegetables.

TURKEY Eastern Anatolia and Aegean regions	
Age From 3 months	
Weight and shape 1lb 2oz–1lb 5oz (500–600g); pots or blocks	
Size Various, L. 4in (10cm), W. 4in (10cm), H. 4in (10cm) (pictured)	
Milk Ewe, goat, or a mixture	
Classification Fresh	
Producer Various	

Anari

Anari is made using whey from Halloumi, plus some goat or ewe's milk to improve the texture and taste. Traditionally, if it is not consumed fresh, it is salted and dried in the warm, dry air—which today happens by gentle heating.

TASTING NOTES Chalky white, it is soft, moist, and creamy with a very delicate, milky taste. Dried Anari is very hard and salty.

HOW TO ENJOY Fresh Anari is served with fruit or carob-based syrups, or used to make *bourekia*—sweet and savory pastries. Dried Anari is grated over salads, pasta or sauces.

CYPRUS All over	
Age From a few days to a few months	
Weight and shape Various	
Size Various, L. 4in (10cm), W. 4in (10cm), H. 4in (10cm) (pictured)	
Milk Goat and ewe	
Classification Fresh	
Producer Various	

261

Halloumi

Born out of a need to preserve milk and provide protein during the winter months when the sheep and goats stopped producing milk, Halloumi was, and still is, a vital part of the Cypriot diet.

What gives Halloumi its unique place in culinary history is not only its ability to keep its shape and not melt when cooked, but the source of its milk, the amazing Mouflon breed of sheep, which were introduced in the Neolithic period and over thousands of years adapted to their environment and became an integral part of the community. Sadly, they are now considered an endangered species although in other parts of the world they are bred for hunting and sport.

Handsome looking, they have a red-brown rough coat and striking thick spiral horns that arch back over the head.

Some Halloumi is still made traditionally in rural areas, but following huge international demand, most is now produced in factories. Although they adhere to the traditional recipe using goat's and ewe's milk, most mix it with some cow's milk since it is not seasonal

The Mouflon sheep, *introduced during the Neolithic period.*

CYPRUS	All over	
Weight and Shape	12oz (250g), blocks	
Size	L. 5in (12cm), H. 2½in (6cm)	
Milk	Goat, ewe, or cow	
Classification	Fresh	
Producer	Various	

and is less expensive; however, this does impact the taste.

Cyprus has applied for PDO status, which is expected to be confirmed in a few years.

TASTING NOTES Salty and tangy with a bouncy texture but, when cooked, the milk sugars or lactose in the cheese caramelize on the outside, giving it a sweet onion taste, while the texture is supple, springy, and squeaky.

The flavor varies according to the seasons and type of milk used. The best are made with raw goat's and ewe's milk during the spring and summer months when the free-ranging animals graze on a myriad of wild flowers, herbs, grasses, and bushes that cover the rocky island.

HOW TO ENJOY The main ingredient in a Cypriot breakfast, appetizer, or lunch, Halloumi is usually served alongside fresh fruit, such as melon and figs, or with vegetables. It is the only cheese that does not melt when heated, thanks to its unique texture, and is excellent cut into thick slices and barbecued or fried as an appetizer.

It is essential not to use oil when frying Halloumi, as this seals the cheese and stops the milk sugars from escaping, resulting in the cheese losing its sweet caramel flavor.

A CLOSER LOOK

Halloumi is not unlike the Italian *pasta filata* cheeses which are stretched. Halloumi is in fact kneaded, but it produces a similar texture.

HEATING Traditionally, raw goat's or ewe's milk, or a combination of both, was heated in a cauldron. Today, some cow's milk is usually mixed in and pasteurized in stainless steel vats.

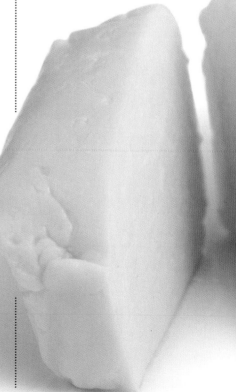

The early-formed rind is shiny from the brine in which it was stored.

CUTTING THE CURDS
The curds are cut with knives or wires on a frame and stirred in the hot whey to harden the curd and expel more whey.

The firm, dense texture is easy to slice for frying or grilling.

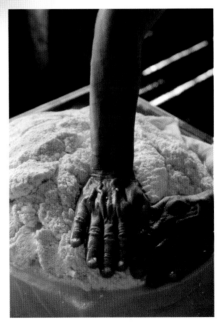

KNEADING The still slightly rubbery curds are cut into plastic molds and pressed by hand to remove the excess whey and create the texture.

Block of cheese, sliced

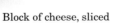

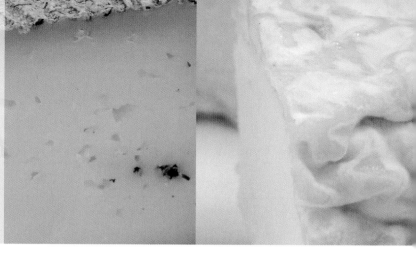

Akkawi

Very similar to Feta, Akkawi is sometimes soaked in water to remove the salt so it can be used in sweet dishes. Its name originates from Acre, the port town. It is still made in many homes, but increasingly it is made commercially in Europe for the Arab market.

TASTING NOTES Very white and firm with some small holes and a fresh, salty taste. It feels slightly fatty when made with cow's milk.

HOW TO ENJOY It is very versatile and is a staple ingredient of many Lebanese and Middle Eastern dishes, from salads to pastries, or simply as a snack.

LEBANON All over
Age 1–3 months
Weight and Shape Various, blocks
Size L. 4½–6in (11–15cm), W. 4–6in (10–15cm), H. 1½in (4cm)
Milk Ewe or cow
Classification Fresh
Producer Various

Inbar

After a visit to a Swiss dairy, Michal Melamed became fascinated with cheese making. She and her husband then moved to the Galilee where they built their dairy in Kibbutz Reshafim to make ewe and goat cheese. Inbar is a tribute to Alpine-style cheeses.

TASTING NOTES Firm yet supple with a hard, dry rind and delicate, yet aromatic, slightly nutty taste. Also made flavored with black pepper, thyme, red wine, mustard seeds, and even chiles.

HOW TO ENJOY Good on a cheeseboard, or slice thinly for sandwiches. Grate and melt in vegetable dishes.

ISRAEL Kibbutz Reshafim, Emek Hama'ayanot
Age From 2 months
Weight and Shape 4½lb (2kg), round
Size D. 10in (25cm), H. 3–4in (7–8cm)
Milk Ewe
Classification Flavor-added
Producer Shirat Roim Dairy

Ketem

Daniel and Anat Kornmehl, as part of a new generation of Israeli cheesemakers, have created a range of European-style goat cheeses in the Negev desert. Ketem ("spot" in English) is based on the much-loved French cheese, Pelardon (see p73).

TASTING NOTES Beneath its wrinkled white rind, it is firm yet creamy and melts in your mouth. When young it is distinctly goaty but mild; once mature it is strong, aromatic, sharp, and very stormy in character.

HOW TO ENJOY Best served as part of a cheeseboard, but it is also good grilled or baked.

ISRAEL Tlalim, Ramat HaNegev
Age 2–3 weeks
Weight and Shape 5½oz (160g), square
Size L. 4in (10cm), W. 4in (10cm), H. 1in (3cm)
Milk Goat
Classification Aged fresh
Producer Kornmehl Family Dairy

Labane

Found throughout the Middle East, Labane is made by draining thick, full-fat yogurt overnight in cloth and is made in many households for use as one of the basic ingredients of Eastern Mediterranean cuisine. Without doubt, the best are made with ewe's milk, but is increasingly made with cow's milk.

TASTING NOTES Deliciously rich and velvety smooth with a mildly lemony fresh tang. Those made with ewe's milk have a lovely sweetness.

HOW TO ENJOY Traditionally eaten at breakfast or served with olive oil, fresh local herbs, pine nuts, and pita bread.

ISRAEL All over	
Age A few hours	
Weight and Shape 9oz (250g) and 1lb 2oz (500g), pots	
Size No size	
Milk Cow, ewe, goat, or a mixture	
Classification Fresh	
Producer Various	

Turkeez

The Barkanit family dairy was one of the first in Israel—established in 1978. The family learned their skills in Europe and this attractive cheese, made from the milk of their own sheep and goats that graze the pastures of Harod Valley, is one of their best.

TASTING NOTES Velvety with a fresh acidity and a hint of salt, while the walnuts provide a crunchy, nutty balance. With age, it has a taste reminiscent of Roquefort (see pp82–83).

HOW TO ENJOY Good on cheeseboards, or break it into chunks and use in fruit salads, with smoked meats or grilled over pears. Excellent with sweet wines.

ISRAEL Kfar Yechezke'el, Gilboa	
Age From a few days	
Weight and Shape 5½oz and 1lb 2oz (150g and 500g), truncated cone	
Size D. 4in and 8in (10cm and 20cm), H. 3in and 6in (7cm and 15cm)	
Milk Goat	
Classification Fresh	
Producer Barkanit Dairy	

Zfatit

A popular Israeli cheese, Zfatit was first made in Safed (Hebrew, *Zfat*) in the 19th century by the Hame'iry family. It is now made in small baskets by various producers in Israel and around the world.

TASTING NOTES Bearing the imprint of the baskets, it is a little spongy but high in moisture with a silky texture. The combination of milky sweetness and salt makes it irresistible. Often flavored with herbs and spices.

HOW TO ENJOY Best on a sunny morning with a dash of olive oil, fresh tomatoes, basil, grated pepper, and accompanied by warm sourdough bread.

ISRAEL All over	
Age From a few days	
Weight and Shape 9oz (250g), round	
Size D. 8in (20cm), H. 2in (5cm)	
Milk Cow	
Classification Fresh	
Producer Various	

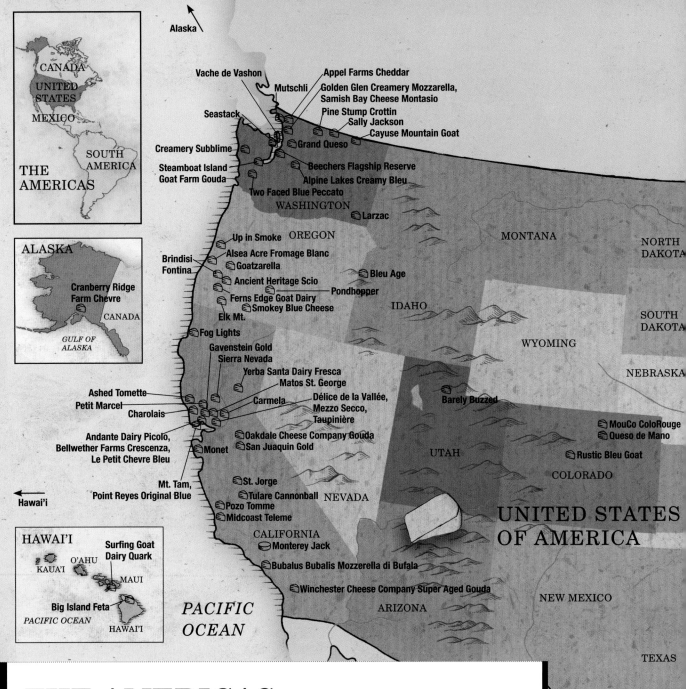

THE AMERICAS

USA Cheesemaking in North America began when the early settlers in the 17th century brought with them the skills of dairy farming and preserving milk in the form of butter and cheese. As more European settlers arrived, the range of cheeses made increased with Spanish-, Dutch-, Swiss-, French-, English-, and Italian-style cheeses all gaining popularity. It wasn't until the mid-1800s that commercial production of cheese began, particularly in Wisconsin, "The Dairyland State," with its vast, lush pastures and ideal climate for milk production. Nowadays, there are hundreds of factories and large producers creating copies of the European classics alongside hundreds of artisan cheesemakers across the States, making cheeses as unique and original as the makers and the landscape.

Map labels

THE AMERICAS

CANADA
UNITED STATES
MEXICO
SOUTH AMERICA

ALASKA
Cranberry Ridge Farm Chevre
CANADA
GULF OF ALASKA

HAWAI'I
Surfing Goat Dairy Quark
KAUA'I
O'AHU
MAUI
Big Island Feta
HAWAI'I
PACIFIC OCEAN

Alaska
Hawai'i

Vache de Vashon
Mutschli
Appel Farms Cheddar
Golden Glen Creamery Mozzarella, Samish Bay Cheese Montasio
Pine Stump Crottin
Sally Jackson
Cayuse Mountain Goat
Seastack
Grand Queso
Creamery Subblime
Steamboat Island Goat Farm Gouda
Beechers Flagship Reserve
Alpine Lakes Creamy Bleu
Two Faced Blue Peccato
WASHINGTON
Larzac
OREGON
Up in Smoke
Alsea Acre Fromage Blanc
Brindisi
Fontina
Goatzarella
Bleu Age
Ancient Heritage Scio
Pondhopper
Ferns Edge Goat Dairy
Smokey Blue Cheese
Elk Mt.
Fog Lights
Gavenstein Gold
Sierra Nevada
Yerba Santa Dairy Fresca
Matos St. George
Ashed Tomette
Petit Marcel
Charolais
Carmela
Délice de la Vallée, Mezzo Secco, Taupinière
Barely Buzzed
MouCo ColoRouge
Queso de Mano
Andante Dairy Picolo,
Bellwether Farms Crescenza,
Le Petit Chevre Bleu
Monet
Oakdale Cheese Company Gouda
San Juaquin Gold
Rustic Bleu Goat
Mt. Tam,
Point Reyes Original Blue
St. Jorge
Tulare Cannonball
Pozo Tomme
Midcoast Teleme
Monterey Jack
Bubalus Bubalis Mozzerella di Bufala
Winchester Cheese Company Super Aged Gouda

MONTANA
NORTH DAKOTA
IDAHO
SOUTH DAKOTA
WYOMING
NEBRASKA
UTAH
COLORADO
UNITED STATES OF AMERICA
CALIFORNIA
NEVADA
ARIZONA
NEW MEXICO
TEXAS
PACIFIC OCEAN

VERMONT

Hartwell

MAINE

Vaquero Blue

Baley Hazel Blue,
Constant Bliss,
Winnamere

VERMONT

NEW
HAMPSHIRE

Cabot Clothbound Cheddar

Coupole

Bouree,
Menuet

Blythdale Farm Camembert

Soft Wheel,
Twigg Square Cheese

Tarentaise

Vermont Ayr

Ascutney Mountain Cheese

NEW YORK

Dorset

Vermont Shepherd

MASSACHUSETTS

MINNESOTA

MAINE

City of Ships

Rosemary's Waltz,
R&R Cheddar

VERMONT

Widmers Cellars Aged Brick Cheese

Hubbardston Blue

WISCONSIN

NEW HAMPSHIRE

Kunik

MASSACHUSETTS

Mona

Ewe's Blue

Great Hill Blue

Bad Axe,
O'Cooch

Cave Aged Marisa

MICHIGAN

NEW YORK

RHODE ISLAND

Pleasant Ridge Reserve

Les Frères

Triple Cream Wheel,
Aged Green Peppercorn Chevre

Brigid's Abbey,
Hooligan

Bleu Mont Dairy Cheddar

Ouray,
Eden

Gruyère Surchoix

CONNECTICUT

Bridgewater Round

IOWA

PENNSLYVANIA

5 Spoke Creamery Browning Gold

Maytag Blue

OHIO

Telford Reserve

NEW JERSEY

Frisian Farms Mature Gouda

ILLINOIS

INDIANA

Mountain Top Bleu

DELAWARE

Fleur de la Terre

WEST
VIRGINIA

Everona Piedmont

MARYLAND

KANSAS

MISSOURI

Old Kentucky Tome,
Wabash Cannonball

VIRGINIA

KENTUCKY

Appalachian,
Grayson

Awe Brie

NORTH CAROLINA

TENNESSEE

OKLAHOMA

ARKANSAS

Clemson Blue

Belle Chèvre

SOUTH
CAROLINA

ALABAMA

GEORGIA

ATLANTIC OCEAN

Blanca Bianca,
Hoja Santa

LOUISIANA

Pecan Chèvre,
Thomasville Tomme

MISSISSIPPI

Fleur-de-Lis

GULF OF MEXICO

Claire de Lune

N

FLORIDA

200 miles

200 km

Key

★ AOC, DOC, DOP, PGI, or PDO cheeses

Produced only here

Produced throughout the region

CANADA Canada's cheese history dates back to 1635, when French colonists first produced cheese. Throughout the centuries, immigrants from Europe, the Middle East, and even India brought with them their favorite recipes, adding diversity and complexity to the variety of cheeses.

Until the 1990s, most cheeses were made on small farms for local consumption or in huge factories that produced blocks of strong cheddar. The renaissance of artisan cheesemakers, who used cow's, goat's, and ewe's milk, led Canadians to discover and voice their pride in their country's exceptional cheeses. Nearly 200 cheese companies exist today, which reflects increasing consumption.

Key
- ★ AOC, DOC, DOP, PGI, or PDO cheeses
- Produced only here
- Produced throughout the region

ARCTIC OCEAN

BEAUFORT SEA

BAFFIN BAY

LABRADOR SEA

YUKON TERRITORY

NORTHWEST TERRITORIES

NUNAVUT

NEWFOUNDLAND

GULF OF ALASKA

QUEEN CHARLOTTE ISLANDS

CANADA
PRODUCED THROUGHOUT THE COUNTRY
Cheddar Curds

HUDSON BAY

QUÉBEC

NEWFOUNDLAND AND LABRADOR

ALBERTA

Avonlea Clothbound Cheddar

Sieur de Duplessis

Le Paillasson de l'isle d'Orléans

BRITISH COLUMBIA

Bouquetin de Portneuf, La Sauvagine

Baby Blue

Old Grizzly

SASKAT-CHEWAN

MANITOBA

ONTARIO

Le Délice des Appalaches

Harvest Moon

Le Cendré des Prés

Allegretto

VANCOUVER ISLAND

Le Sabot de Blanchette

PRINCE EDWARD ISLAND

La Barre du Jour, Le Cru des Erables

Dragon's Breath Blue

NOVA SCOTIA

Seven-Year-Old Orange Cheddar

NEW BRUNSWICK

Bleu Bénédictin

Le Cabanon

Piaceré

Prestige

Oka Classique

Vicky's Spring Splendour

Comfort Cream

PACIFIC OCEAN

500 miles

500 km

N

ATLANTIC OCEA

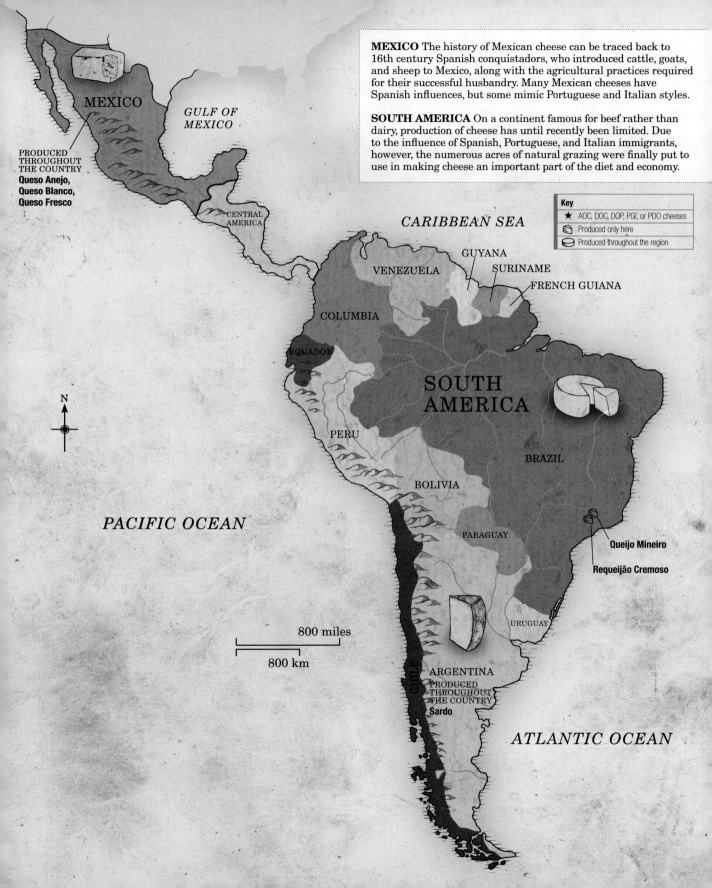

MEXICO The history of Mexican cheese can be traced back to 16th century Spanish conquistadors, who introduced cattle, goats, and sheep to Mexico, along with the agricultural practices required for their successful husbandry. Many Mexican cheeses have Spanish influences, but some mimic Portuguese and Italian styles.

SOUTH AMERICA On a continent famous for beef rather than dairy, production of cheese has until recently been limited. Due to the influence of Spanish, Portuguese, and Italian immigrants, however, the numerous acres of natural grazing were finally put to use in making cheese an important part of the diet and economy.

Key
★ AOC, DOC, DOP, PGI, or PDO cheeses
⬗ Produced only here
⬖ Produced throughout the region

MEXICO

GULF OF MEXICO

PRODUCED THROUGHOUT THE COUNTRY
Queso Anejo,
Queso Blanco,
Queso Fresco

CENTRAL AMERICA

CARIBBEAN SEA

VENEZUELA
GUYANA
SURINAME
FRENCH GUIANA

COLUMBIA

EQUADOR

SOUTH AMERICA

PERU

BRAZIL

N

BOLIVIA

PACIFIC OCEAN

PARAGUAY

Queijo Mineiro

Requeijão Cremoso

URUGUAY

800 miles

800 km

CHILE

ARGENTINA
PRODUCED THROUGHOUT THE COUNTRY
Sardo

ATLANTIC OCEAN

Aged Green Peppercorn Chevre

Coach Farm has acquired a reputation for outstanding quality over the last few years and has won numerous international awards. They make regular appearances at many of New York City's great farmer's markets.

TASTING NOTES Firm and crumbly, it has a lemony sourness that is perfectly accented, but not overpowered, by the mild green peppercorn flavor. The finish is delicate and clean.

HOW TO ENJOY Delicate yet complex, it is ideal with a summer salad of fresh greens and ripe tomatoes.

USA Pine Plains, New York	
Age 30 days	
Weight and Shape 3lb (1.35kg), brick	
Size L. 12in (30cm), H. 4in (10cm)	
Milk Goat	
Classification Soft white	
Producers Coach Farm	

270

Alsea Acre Fromage Blanc

The mild Oregon climate provides the Alsea Acre family farm with the ideal environment to create European-style cheeses all year round.

TASTING NOTES The pure goat's milk flavors arrive with a zesty fresh taste, alongside hints of citrus and pinenut. The finish is a complex and creamy taste on the palate.

HOW TO ENJOY Sprinkle over fresh salad greens with green grapes, roasted almonds, and toasted crostini. Enjoy with a chilled glass of Roussanne.

USA Alsea, Oregon	
Age From a few days	
Weight and Shape 8oz (225g), tubs	
Size No size	
Milk Goat	
Classification Fresh	
Producers Alsea Acre	

Andante Dairy Picolo

The cheesemakers at California's Andante Dairy are inspired by the various musical tempos of the cheesemaking process. This luxurious triple-cream cheese combines Jersey milk and crème fraîche.

TASTING NOTES Made with fresh farm cow's milk, Picolo has a pleasantly tart and sweet taste inspired by spring. When properly aged, it melts in the mouth.

HOW TO ENJOY Drizzle wedges of Picolo with citrus honey and accompany with a sweet baguette and a glass of sparkling Prosecco.

USA Petaluma, California	
Age 2–4 weeks	
Weight and Shape 4½oz (125g), round	
Size D. 2in (5cm), H. 1½in (4cm)	
Milk Cow	
Classification Soft white	
Producers Andante Dairy	

Appalachian

Meadow Creek Dairy, located in the mountainous southwest of Virginia, draws inspiration from various traditional European cheeses. Appalachian loosely resembles a French Tomme (see pp90–94).

TASTING NOTES The flavor is very delicate and raw with strong vegetal notes and a spicy finish. The texture is dense and chewy with a musty strong aroma.

HOW TO ENJOY Appalachian melts well, making it the perfect cooking cheese. However, the flavor is robust enough to serve the cheese on its own.

USA Galax, Virginia	
Age 60 days	
Weight and Shape 10lb (4.5kg) wheel	
Size D. 9in (23cm), H. 2in (5cm)	
Milk Cow	
Classification Semi-soft	
Producers Meadow Creek Dairy	

Appel Farms Cheddar

This cheese is handmade at Appel Farms in Washington State using the Cheddaring technique of authentic English cheddar (see p180–181). The milk comes from a herd of 300 cows fed on grass and corn silage grown on the farm. An alternative variety is flavored with black peppers

TASTING NOTES Aged a minimum of 3 months, the nutty and buttercup flavors become sharper on the palate as it matures.

HOW TO ENJOY An outstanding addition to homemade macaroni and cheese. Accompany with a fine Pilsner.

USA Ferndale, Washington	
Age 3–6 months	
Weight and Shape 5lb (2.25kg), wheel	
Size D. 10in (25cm), H. 2½in (6cm)	
Milk Cow	
Classification Hard	
Producers Appel Farms	

Ascutney Mountain Cheese

The Cobb Hill cheesemakers are part of a community of 23 households making agricultural products. They produce two raw milk cheeses from a small herd of Jersey cows. The farm uses no chemical fertilizers, additives, or feeds.

TASTING NOTES Loosely based on alpine cheeses, Ascutney Mountain is not quite as dense but still has a firm texture. The mild initial flavor develops toward a pineapple-like sweet and sour finish.

HOW TO ENJOY The sweet taste favors a good hoppy beer, like an IPA, and some savory chutney.

USA Hartland, Vermont	
Age 6–10 months	
Weight and Shape 10lb (4.5kg), wheel	
Size D. 15in (38cm), H. 5in (12cm)	
Milk Cow	
Classification Hard	
Producers Cobb Hill Cheese	

Ashed Tomette

Since 1976, Ana and Gilbert Cox have been making award-winning cheese from their herd of Alpine, La Mancha, and Nubian dairy goats on their farm just north of the town of Willits in Mendocino County.

TASTING NOTES The striking ash-covered disc has a firm yet flaky texture, with a cream-white center that has a subtle goaty taste and nutty overtones.

HOW TO ENJOY Match with a hearty Cabernet, and serve with a seasonal fresh fruit platter and warm crunchy sweet baguettes.

USA Willits, California	
Age 2–4 weeks	
Weight and Shape 2oz (60g), disc	
Size Various	
Milk Goat	
Classification Fresh	
Producer Shamrock Artisan Goat Cheese	

272

Awe Brie

From a farm located in the rolling hills of Kentucky and influenced by Western European cheesemakers, Awe Brie is the first Brie made within the United States to be produced using raw milk. In fact, all of the farm's cheeses are made using raw milk, piped fresh from the milking barn for processing.

TASTING NOTES The cheese is ripened to 60 days. Its snow-white exterior conceals a golden interior that has a silky texture and robust flavor.

HOW TO ENJOY In honor of Kentucky, a bourbon and fresh pear slices are the perfect marriage to serve alongside a cheeseboard of Awe Brie.

USA Austin, Kentucky	
Age 60 days	
Weight and Shape 2lb (900g), wheel	
Size Various	
Milk Cow	
Classification Soft white	
Producer Kenny's Farmhouse Cheese	

Barely Buzzed

Hand-rubbed with a blend of South American and Indonesian coffee beans finely ground with French lavender buds, and mixed with oil to suspend the dry ingredients in the rub, Barely Buzzed is aged in caves on Utah blue spruce. Its unusual name comes courtesy of a contest held by Beehive Cheese Company in 2007.

TASTING NOTES A smooth Cheddar-style cheese with a nutty flavor, the rub and sweet Jersey milk impart hints of butterscotch, caramel, and coffee.

HOW TO ENJOY This is ideal paired with a stout and crusty whole wheat bread.

USA Uintah, Utah	
Age 3–4 months	
Weight and Shape 9–11lb (4.1–5kg), wheel	
Size D. 10in (25cm), H. 3in (7.5cm)	
Milk Cow	
Classification Flavor-added	
Producer Beehive Cheese Company	

Bayley Hazen Blue

The Kehlers have been producing cheese from a pure Ayrshire herd only since 2002, but the complexity and sophistication of their products speaks to the incredible amount of research and training they have undergone as they strive for perfection.

TASTING NOTES A medium-strong and relatively dry blue cheese, Bayley Hazen Blue delivers a complex flavor. The blue is upfront and slightly peppery, while the cheese's finish is long and creamy.

HOW TO ENJOY Complemented well by Port or sweet wines, it is best served as part of a cheeseboard.

USA Greensboro, Vermont	
Age 4–6 months	
Weight and Shape 4lb (1.8kg), drum	
Size D. 6in (15cm), H. 9in (23cm)	
Milk Cow	
Classification Blue	
Producer Jasper Hill Farm	

Belle Chèvre

Located in Elkmont, Alabama, Fromagerie Belle Chèvre is among relatively few cheesemakers in the southern United States. Nonetheless, the creamery has gathered more than 50 awards over the years for its fresh goat's milk cheeses.

TASTING NOTES This traditional French-style chèvre is very rich and smooth, with a tangy flavor and distinct herbaceous finish.

HOW TO ENJOY Marries well with almost any preserve and perfect for any recipe that calls for fresh chèvre. Alternatively, serve plain with almonds, walnuts, and a crisp white wine.

USA Elkmont, Alabama	
Age Fresh	
Weight and Shape 8oz (225g), log	
Size D. 1in (2.5cm), L. 2in (5cm)	
Milk Goat	
Classification Fresh	
Producer Fromagerie Belle Chèvre	

Bellwether Farms Crescenza

This cheese is modeled on the famous Italian cheese Crescenza (see p116), right down to its traditional square shape, but with a twist of California coastal sea breeze flavor.

TASTING NOTES Handmade and sent to market at 1 week of age, it is milky white and high in moisture. The rich Jersey milk gives it a creamy flavor balanced by a pleasant tartness and yeasty finish.

HOW TO ENJOY Dollop a spoonful of homemade apricot compote over the top, serve with crunchy fresh baguette, and pair with a crisp Pinot Blanc.

USA Petaluma, California	
Age 1 week	
Weight and Shape 3lb 3oz (1.5kg), square	
Size D. 12in (30cm), H. ½in (1cm)	
Milk Cow	
Classification Fresh	
Producer Bellwether Farms	

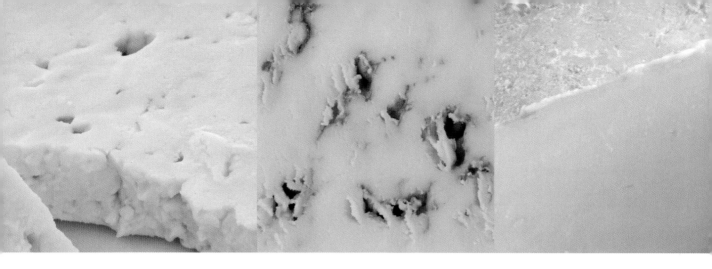

Big Island Feta

Dick Threlfall, a retired farrier who shod horses for more than 35 years, focuses on the feta, the herd, and the machinery, while Heather, having worked in the veterinary field, milks the goats and makes the soft cheese.

TASTING NOTES The pleasant slight tang has a hint of unusual flavors because the goats graze on pastures as well as tropical vegetation ranging from bamboo shoots to macadamia tree leaves.

HOW TO ENJOY Create a Hawaiian salad with toasted whole macadamia nuts, fresh-picked spinach, sweet island pineapple, and serve with a chilled Kona Brewing Big Wave golden ale.

USA Honokaa, Hawaii		
Age 3–12 weeks		
Weight and Shape 1lb (450g), block		
Size Various		
Milk Goat		
Classification Fresh		
Producer Hawaiian Island Goat Dairy		

Big Woods Blue

Despite losing much of their herd in a devastating fire on the farm in 2005, the Reads have been slowly rebuilding with the help of the local community and Slow Food groups, and continue to produce this magnificent raw milk cheese for blue lovers.

TASTING NOTES Creamy and mild, it is very approachable for blue-shy tasters, yet still complex and surprising for veterans. The robust and only slightly salty cheese melts in the mouth like milk chocolate.

HOW TO ENJOY The complexity of this cheese deserves to be matched with a great vintage port.

USA Nerstrand, Minnesota		
Age 4–6 months		
Weight and Shape 7lb (3.2kg), round		
Size D. 6in (15cm), H. 5in (12cm)		
Milk Ewe		
Classification Blue		
Producer Shepherd's Way Farms		

Blanca Bianca

Paula Lambert has spent more than 20 years working with cheese, drawing particular inspiration from her travels in Italy. The Mozzarella Company was founded to produce fresh mozzarella, but production now includes many of Paula's own creations, including this cheese washed with white wine.

TASTING NOTES Rich and full-flavored, the chewy paste fills the mouth and nose with sweet floral tastes. While not a particularly powerful washed-rind cheese when young, it develops a strong but pleasing punch as it matures.

HOW TO ENJOY Try with dark walnut raisin bread and a light beer.

USA Dallas, Texas		
Age 2 months		
Weight and Shape 1½lb (675g), flat wheel		
Size D. 7in (18cm), H. 2in (5cm)		
Milk Cow		
Classification Semi-soft		
Producer Mozzarella Company		

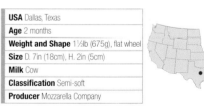

Bleu Mont Cheddar

Willie Lehner is a second-generation cheesemaker who trained in England and Switzerland. He buys milk from local certified organic producers and makes cheese off-site at other producers' cheesemaking facilities. All his cheeses are then transferred to a custom-built cave on his property to ripen.

TASTING NOTES With a very pleasant and tasty element of freshly turned earth, this handmade clothbound Cheddar has a medium-strong flavor with good grassy notes and a nice lingering finish.

HOW TO ENJOY Savor on its own with some chutney and dried figs or dates.

USA Blue Mounds, Wisconsin	
Age 12–18 months	
Weight and Shape 8lb (3.6kg), drum	
Size D. 6in (15cm), H. 4in (10cm)	
Milk Cow	
Classification Hard	
Producer Bleu Mont Dairy	

Blythedale Farm Camembert

Becky and Tom Loftus at Blythedale Farm in Corinth, Vermont, have been producing Camembert and Brie-style cheeses since 1994. They have stuck with the tried-and-true recipe, using milk from their herd of Jersey cows to produce these well-regarded cheeses.

TASTING NOTES While possessing the typical rich creamy flavor you would expect in a Camembert-style cheese, it has a softer and wetter rind, as well as a tarter initial flavor.

HOW TO ENJOY Use to make a great ham and Camembert sandwich on a baguette, or serve with crackers and Champagne.

USA Corinth, Vermont	
Age 4 weeks	
Weight and Shape 8oz (225g), round	
Size D. 5in (12cm), H. 1in (2.5cm)	
Milk Cow	
Classification Soft white	
Producer Blythedale Farm	

Bourrée

Dancing Cow Farm began producing cheese in 2006. Unlike many artisanal cheesemakers, after the cheese is made, Steve and Karen Getz hand the job of ripening over to the experts in the cellars at Jasper Hill, so that they can focus on maintaining high milk quality standards.

TASTING NOTES Although it is a washed-rind cheese, its aroma is relatively mild and floral. The texture is smooth, rich, and somewhat sticky on the palate, with a peanut-like flavor that grows more intense as it finishes.

HOW TO ENJOY Bourrée is best served with a strong ale and some chutney.

USA Bridport, Vermont	
Age 3 months	
Weight and Shape 1lb (450g), round	
Size D. 4in (10cm), H. 2in (5cm)	
Milk Cow	
Classification Semi-soft	
Producer Dancing Cow Farmstead Cheese	

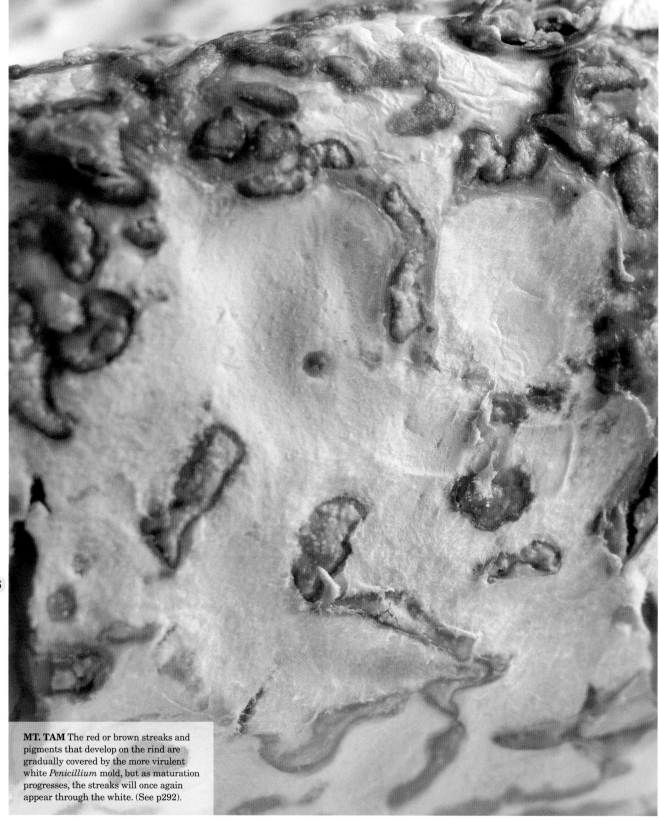

MT. TAM The red or brown streaks and pigments that develop on the rind are gradually covered by the more virulent white *Penicillium* mold, but as maturation progresses, the streaks will once again appear through the white. (See p292).

Bridgewater Round

Zingerman's has firmly built its ever-growing reputation on selling excellent, flavorsome, traditionally made foods, including a huge range of cheeses, and educating and inspiring their staff and customers alike. So it was almost inevitable that it would turn its hand to cheesemaking.

TASTING NOTES Made with added cream and spiked with freshly ground black pepper. Bridgewater Round has a rich, silky feel and taste, with a hint of mushrooms on the finish.

HOW TO ENJOY A star of the cheeseboard, it is complemented by nuts, dried fruit, and a crisp, fruity Chinon.

USA Ann Arbor, Michigan	
Age 4–8 weeks	
Weight and Shape 8oz (225g), round	
Size Various	
Milk Cow	
Classification Soft white	
Producer Zingerman's	

Brigid's Abbey

Brigid's Abbey is the most popular cheese out of about 12 varieties made at Cato Corner, a small family-run farm priding itself on the high quality of its Jersey milk. In true farmhouse style, this washed-rind cheese varies in texture with the seasons.

TASTING NOTES The cheese is at its most creamy during the winter months. The flavor is rich and earthy, with hints of straw. In the summer, it becomes quite firm and more vegetal-tasting.

HOW TO ENJOY This monastery-style cheese naturally pairs well with beer. Great with crudités, it is also delicious melted in grilled cheese sandwiches.

USA Colchester, Connecticut	
Age 3–4 months	
Weight and Shape 8lb (3.6kg), round	
Size D. 12in (30cm), H. 5in (12cm)	
Milk Cow	
Classification Semi-soft	
Producer Cato Corner Farm	

Bubulus Bubalis Mozzarella di Bufala

Making cheeses in the traditional style, Bubalus Bubalis is the only producer of water buffalo mozzarella, as well as ricotta cheese and scamorza (smoked mozzarella), in California.

TASTING NOTES A fresh, snow-white buffalo milk, hand-formed into a round and filled with creamy and delicate flavors with a silky finish.

HOW TO ENJOY Layer fresh mozzarella in slices with fresh basil leaves, roasted red peppers, golden tomatoes, crushed olives, and roasted eggplant slices, and drizzle with olive oil. Accompany with a glass of Friulano.

USA Gardena, California	
Age 1–7 days	
Weight and Shape 8oz (225g), ball	
Size Various	
Milk Water buffalo	
Classification Fresh	
Producer Bubalus Bubalis	

Cabot Clothbound

Cabot Creamery can trace its origins back to 1919, when a cooperative of 94 local farmers was formed in Vermont. This raw milk cheese, a handmade traditional bandaged Cheddar, is cave-aged in the cellars at Jasper Hill Farm.

TASTING NOTES Initially sweet and buttery on the palate, its finish is much more savory and heavy; rather than a classic Cheddar acidity, it has a fuller, rounder sour bite.

HOW TO ENJOY Serve simply with some hearty bread, homemade chutney, and a beer. Big red wines work well, too. Its flavor and texture also make Cabot Clothbound perfect for sandwiches.

USA Montpelier, Vermont	
Age 12 months or more	
Weight and Shape 12lb (5.4kg), cylinder	
Size D. 18in (46cm), H. 4in (10cm)	
Milk Cow	
Classification Hard	
Producer Cabot Creamery Cooperative	

Cave Aged Marisa

Sid Cooke is the master cheesemaker at the helm of this large Wisconsin creamery, which produces dozens of varieties of cheese, yet crafts each one with great care and attention. The majority is made with cow's milk, but this one uses ewe's milk.

TASTING NOTES A dense medium-firm natural rind cheese, it has an intense floral aroma and a very sweet initial flavor. As the flavor develops, it becomes more savory. There is a hint of lanoline to the finish.

HOW TO ENJOY It is great served with black fruit preserves or quince paste, and good hearty dark bread.

USA La Valle, Wisconsin	
Age 6 months	
Weight and Shape 6lb (2.7kg), round	
Size D. 12in (30cm), H. 4in (10cm)	
Milk Ewe	
Classification Hard	
Producer Carr Valley Cheese Company	

Charolais

This farmstead cheese made with alpine goat's milk has a distinct rind that provides an attractive contrast to its pure white interior. Cheeses are made in small 190-liter (50-gallon) batches using 1- to 2-day-old milk.

TASTING NOTES This is at its peak at about 60 days, when the flavors arrive to melt in your mouth with subtle and delicate hints of the Bodega coast.

HOW TO ENJOY Champagne complements a cheeseboard of Charolais, especially when served with fresh Gravenstein apples, honey-toasted walnuts, and a crusty sweet baguette.

USA Bodega, California	
Age 60 days minimum	
Weight and Shape 4–7oz (115–200g), cylinder	
Size D. 2in (5cm), H. 4in (10cm)	
Milk Goat	
Classification Aged fresh	
Producer Bodega Artisan Cheese	

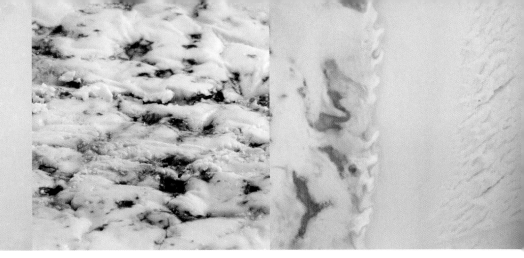

City of Ships

This small producer keeps her business local, buying milk from nearby farms and supplying cheese to local outlets, but the high-quality milk and expert ripening make this worth seeking out.

TASTING NOTES Highly complex flavors cover the full range of senses. Initially sweet, it yields to herbal and sea salty flavors, building to a strong lingering butterscotch finish that coats the tongue. The texture is tight and chewy, with a faint crunch.

HOW TO ENJOY To savor the best of its myriad flavors, serve it on its own or with other medium-strength cheeses and mild crackers with gentle textures.

USA Phippsburg, Maine	
Age 8 months	
Weight and Shape 6lb (2.7kg), rounded wheel	
Size D. 11in (28cm), H. 4in (10cm)	
Milk Cow	
Classification Hard	
Producer Hahn's End	

Clemson Blue

Produced at Clemson University, Clemson Blue dates back to 1941, when the cheese was aged in an abandoned railroad tunnel under Stumphouse Mountain. Since the late 1950s, the entire making and ripening process has taken place on campus.

TASTING NOTES The texture is medium-grained and slightly clumpy, but on the palate it quickly opens up into an exceptionally smooth creaminess. Its medium blue flavor is well balanced against a buttermilk sweetness.

HOW TO ENJOY Its moderate intensity allows it to be paired with both sweet wines and fruitier reds such as Merlot.

USA Clemson, South Carolina	
Age 6 months	
Weight and Shape 2lb (900g), flat disc	
Size D. 10in (25cm), H. 1in (2.5cm)	
Milk Cow	
Classification Blue	
Producer Clemson University	

Constant Bliss

The name comes from American Revolutionary history and seems improbably fitting because the cheese is aged just to the US legal minimum of 60 days and offers a rare glimpse into the world of soft raw milk cheeses, typically unavailable in the United States.

TASTING NOTES The thin dry rind has a stony aroma and slight bitterness enveloped by the paste's salty, buttery, almost popcorn-like flavor. With age, it becomes soft and rich, but not runny.

HOW TO ENJOY Feature on a cheeseboard with other premium cheeses. Even better, serve with Champagne and caviar.

USA Greensboro, Vermont	
Age 60 days	
Weight and Shape 8oz (225g), round	
Size D. 2in (5cm), H. 3in (7.5cm)	
Milk Cow	
Classification Soft white	
Producer Jasper Hill Farm	

Coupole

Allison Hooper's cheesemaking journey began in the 1970s, working in France. By 1985 she had formed Vermont Butter and Cheese Company with Bob Reese, where they make a variety of award-winning dairy products. Coupole, sprinkled with ash, exhibits all the best qualities of a French-style goat cheese.

TASTING NOTES Soft and smooth, but not runny, it has just enough punch to remind you of the goat's milk from which it is made, but is mild enough to charm first-time goat cheese tasters.

HOW TO ENJOY Perfect on a cheeseboard, or try it in a salad that includes nuts, pears, and a spicy salad green.

USA	Bare, Vermont
Age	45 days
Weight and Shape	8oz (225g), dome
Size	D. 2in (5cm), H. 2in (5cm)
Milk	Goat
Classification	Aged fresh
Producer	Vermont Butter and Cheese

Cranberry Ridge Farm Chèvre

Unique to Alaska, Cranberry Ridge Farm is one of only three cheesemakers located in Wasilla, where it produces French-style chèvre from a herd of Alpine, La Mancha, Nubian, and Saanen goats.

TASTING NOTES Aged for just 1 week, this fresh cheese has a subtle goat's milk flavor, light and clean to taste, with a delicate lemony essence.

HOW TO ENJOY Serve as a simple but delicious dessert with fresh golden raspberries and garnished with mint leaves, accompanied by Champagne.

USA	Wasilla, Alaska
Age	1 week
Weight and Shape	8oz (225g), tubs
Size	No size
Milk	Goat
Classification	Fresh
Producers	Rhonda & Matt Shaul

Délice de la Vallée

Délice de la Vallée is named in honor of both California's Sonoma Valley and the delicacy and flavor of the cheese.

TASTING NOTES A blend of fresh cow's and goat's milk, the cheese has a sweet essence and creamy delicate sensation on the palate.

HOW TO ENJOY Drizzle with a Meyer lemon and olive oil dressing, sprinkle with fresh basil, and serve with rustic breads and a bottle of chilled Friulano.

USA	Sonoma, California
Age	1–7 days
Weight and Shape	8oz (225g) and 2lb (900g),
Size	Various
Milk	Cow and goat
Classification	Fresh
Producer	Sheana Davis

Dorset

Located in Vermont's Champlain Valley, the dairy has roots dating back to the mid-19th century. It is now being revitalized by cheesemaker Peter Dixon and others, who produce several cheeses from their organic herds of Jersey cows and Oberhasilis goats.

TASTING NOTES Dorset is a lightly washed Taleggio-style cheese. Not particularly pungent, the soft but chewy cheese displays the butteriness of the Jersey milk well, with a round, sweet flavor.

HOW TO ENJOY Dorset benefits from being left to come to room temperature, as the flavor really opens up. Lovely with Malbec and dried fruit.

USA West Pawlet, Vermont	
Age 60 days	
Weight and Shape 2lb (900g), round	
Size D. 8in (20cm), H. 1in (2.5cm)	
Milk Cow	
Classification Semi-soft	
Producer Bardwell Farm	

Eden

Located just an hour north of New York City, Sprout Creek Farm makes a wide variety of cheeses from its mixed herd, using traditional methods and sustainable farming practices. The milk is produced seasonally. In harmony with its cheesemaking ventures, the farm also offers educational workshops to increase understanding of good farming practices.

TASTING NOTES Lightly washed in brine, it has an apple tartness to its flavor, with a long and full savory finish. The texture is supple and chewy.

HOW TO ENJOY This cheese is perfect to serve with cider.

USA Poughkeepsie, New York	
Age 3 months	
Weight and Shape 8lb (3.6kg), flat wheel	
Size D. 14in (35cm), H. 2in (5cm)	
Milk Cow	
Classification Semi-soft	
Producer Sprout Creek Farm	

Everona Piedmont

The Piedmont region of Virginia is in the foothills of the ancient Blue Ridge Mountains, and Dr. Pat Elliot has operated a full-time sheep farm here since 1992, alongside her farm-based family medical practice. Everona also produces the ewe's milk cheese Stony Man, as well as a range of flavored, or "infused," versions of Piedmont, and a wine-washed cheese, Pride of Bacchus.

TASTING NOTES Made with raw ewe's milk, it is filled with nutty, fruity, and even floral tones, with a creamy finish.

HOW TO ENJOY This pairs wonderfully with a crisp Sauvignon Blanc, served simply with fresh pear slices.

USA Rapidan, Virginia	
Age: 3–6 months	
Weight and Shape 1½lb (675g) and 6lb (2.7kg), wheel	
Size D. 8in (20cm), H. 3in (7.5cm)	
Milk Ewe	
Classification Hard	
Producer Everona Dairy	

Ewe's Blue

Located in New York State's Hudson Valley, Old Chatham has grown since 1993 to become one of the largest sheep dairies in the United States. Its range of sophisticated and well-executed cheese and yogurt products are widely available throughout the United States.

TASTING NOTES Similar in style to Roquefort, it is moist and creamy with pockets of blue-green mold and fruity, buttery notes; it has a more mineral-like character and less saltiness than its French counterpart.

HOW TO ENJOY Try it crumbled on top of salad greens, or enjoy it simply, with French bread and a glass of Sauterne.

USA Old Chatham, New York	
Age 6–8 months	
Weight and Shape 4lb (1.8kg), wheel	
Size D. 9in (23cm), H. 2in (5cm)	
Milk Ewe	
Classification Blue	
Producer Old Chatham Sheepherding Company	

Fleur-de-Lis

Bittersweet Plantation Dairy produces several artisan cheeses that reflect Lousiana's rich Creole and Cajun cultural and culinary heritage. This triple-cream Guernsey milk cheese is named in honor of the French *fleur-de-lis* symbol, as it was the French who founded the colony of Louisiana, and continue to live there in spirit.

TASTING NOTES Aged for four weeks, this white bloomy rind cheese, with its smooth, buttery center, makes for a perfect taste of France from Louisiana.

HOW TO ENJOY Complement Fleur-de-Lis with a delicate Riesling and a bowl of Louisiana pecans.

USA Gonzales, Louisiana	
Age 4 weeks	
Weight and Shape 8oz (225g), cylinder	
Size D. 3in (7.5cm), H. 2in (5cm)	
Milk Cow	
Classification Soft white	
Producer Bittersweet Plantation Dairy	

Fleur de la Terre

Located outside Indianapolis, Traders Point was established by Jane and Fritz Kunz out of a desire to protect not just traditional farming, but also the land itself from the pressures of suburban development. The organic farm produces cheese year-round from a herd of Brown Swiss cows.

TASTING NOTES It has an uncomplicated but interesting profile; despite its age, the cheese has a raw brightness of flavor and a tart finish, with a smooth but slightly chewy paste.

HOW TO ENJOY The fresh flavor is the highlight here, and should be paired with fresh fruits and a pear cider.

USA Zionsville, Indiana	
Age 4–6 months	
Weight and Shape 12lb (5.4kg), boulder	
Size D. 8in (20cm) , H. 5in (12cm)	
Milk Cow	
Classification Hard	
Producer Traders Point Creamery	

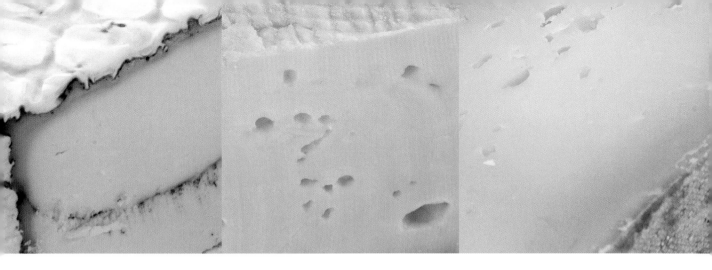

Fog Lights

This beautiful ash- and mold-covered cheese is named after the lights viewed through the Humboldt fog that often line the region of California's northern coast where Cypress Grove is found.

TASTING NOTES Each disc, which is covered with a bloomy rind, is aged for four weeks, producing an elegant finish of rich and creamy goat flavor.

HOW TO ENJOY Slice over a bed of fresh seasonal salad greens, drizzled with olive oil and white balsamic vinegar; complement with a Carignane wine. Or serve with slices of fresh apple, or even as a dessert with baked pears.

USA Arcata, California	
Age 4 weeks	
Weight and Shape 8oz (225g), disc	
Size D. 4in (10cm), H. 1½in (4cm)	
Milk Goat	
Classification Soft white	
Producer Cypress Grove Chèvre	

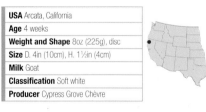

Les Frères

Located in Waterloo, Wisconsin, this farm with a herd of 950 Holstein cows is operated by the four Crave brothers and their families. It produces cheeses that reflect the family's French and Irish heritage such as Les Frères and its little brother, Petit Frère, but also includes mozzarella and mascarpone.

TASTING NOTES A washed-rind cheese, Les Frères has a very gentle and somewhat claylike aroma. Its rind is leathery and chewy, while the soft, very rich paste has a complex salty-sweet flavor.

HOW TO ENJOY Terrific on a cheeseboard with dark beers and dried fruit, or try it melted over potatoes and grilled onions.

USA Waterloo, Wisconsin	
Age 3 weeks	
Weight and Shape 1½lb (675g), round	
Size D. 7in (18cm), H. 1in (2.5cm)	
Milk Cow	
Classification Semi-soft	
Producer Crave Brothers Farmstead Cheese	

Frisian Farms Mature Gouda

Making farmstead Gouda in the Dutch tradition is part of Frisian Farms' commitment to its Dutch ancestry. It is located just outside Pella, Iowa, a predominantly Dutch community that has preserved its Dutch culture, including traditional windmills, an historical village, and an annual tulip festival. The Gouda is available in young, mature, and smoked versions.

TASTING NOTES Each golden wheel is filled with nutty flavors and fruity essences, with a sweet cream finish.

HOW TO ENJOY Savor with a Riesling, fresh grapes, and wheat crackers.

USA Oskaloosa, Iowa	
Age 6–8 weeks minimum	
Weight and Shape 20lb (9.1kg), wheel	
Size D. 14in (35cm), H. 6in (15cm)	
Milk Cow	
Classification Hard	
Producer Frisian Farms	

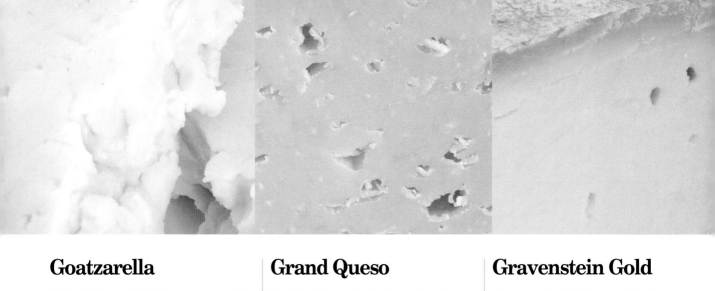

Goatzarella

Fifty Alpine and Nubian goats provide the organic milk for this supple, elastic mozzarella-style cheese. The goats are also the family pets and all know their names. Goatzarella is one of several goat's milk cheeses made by Fraga Farm, including a chèvre and a feta.

TASTING NOTES Made with vegetarian rennet, it is rich in cream with a grassy meadow flavor, and finishes with a silky texture on the palate.

HOW TO ENJOY For cooking rather than for the cheeseboard, it grates and melts superbly. Try it on fresh herbed foccacia with tomatoes and olive oil, paired with an Oregon Pinot Noir.

USA Sweet Home, Oregon	
Age 2–6 wccks	
Weight and Shape 8oz (225g), square	
Size D. 9in (23cm), H. 3in (7.5cm)	
Milk Goat	
Classification Fresh	
Producer Fraga Farm Goat Cheese	

Grand Queso

The Roths' stated mission when they began producing cheese in the United States was not to import cheese, but rather to utilize the traditions and technology. Although Grand Queso is reminiscent of Spanish Manchego, it has its own unique flavor profile.

TASTING NOTES It has a full, rounded taste and aroma that is sweet and very buttery, while the texture is gummy and slightly oily, but not heavy.

HOW TO ENJOY Grand Queso is a terrific option in Spanish and Mexican recipes calling for a hard full-flavored cheese. Or serve it grated over bruschetta topped with sun-dried tomatoes.

USA Monroe, Wisconsin	
Age 6 months	
Weight and Shape 5lb (2.25kg), wheel	
Size D. 6in (15cm), H. 5in (12cm)	
Milk Cow	
Classification Hard	
Producer Roth Käse USA	

Gravenstein Gold

Gravenstein Gold is named in honor of the Sebastopol Gravenstein, the home-grown variety of apple in which the cheese is washed and which is such a vital part of the rich history and economy of Sebastopol.

TASTING NOTES As the cheese is aged, the apple cider wash creates a balanced, complex array of flavors, including hints of apples and cream.

HOW TO ENJOY Ideal as an appetizer, Gravenstein Gold is particularly enjoyable with hard apple cider, fresh apple slices, and pumpkin seed bread.

USA Sebastopol, California	
Age 2–3 months	
Weight and Shape 3lb (1.35kg), wheel	
Size Various	
Milk Goat	
Classification Semi-soft	
Producer Redwood Hill Farm	

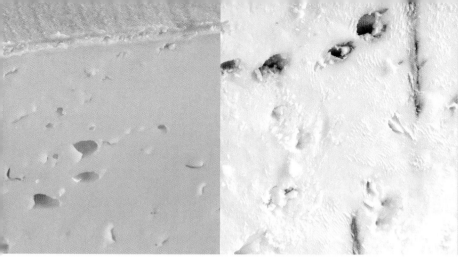

Grayson

Meadow Creek Dairy is located in the Blue Ridge Mountains of southwest Virginia, at an altitude of 2800ft (850m). According to the cheesemakers, it is the great air and water quality, along with ecologically responsible farming, that result in exceptionally high milk quality.

TASTING NOTES This intensely strong-smelling washed cheese possesses an appropriately strong vegetal flavor. Its firm texture holds up well on the palate, and it finishes surprisingly cleanly.

HOW TO ENJOY Grayson's intense flavor demands strong-flavors to match, such as crackers with black pepper, or rye bread with onion confit.

USA Galax, Virginia	
Age 4 months	
Weight and Shape 8lb (3.6kg), square	
Size D. 7in (18cm), H. 2in (5cm)	
Milk Cow	
Classification Semi-soft	
Producers Meadow Creek Dairy	

Great Hill Blue

This old dairy farm located south of Boston has been in the family for more than a generation. The dairy purchases Jersey and Holstein milk from several surrounding farms, but it is neither pasteurized nor homogenized. The resulting cheese has won numerous awards since its launch in 1996.

TASTING NOTES It has a surprisingly tight texture that opens on the palate like cool butter. Tangy with a good blue punch, it is just salty enough to complement the natural sweetness.

HOW TO ENJOY Delightful on its own or in a salad with apples and bacon; pair with aromatic Riesling or Viognier.

USA Marion, Massachusetts	
Age 6 months	
Weight and Shape 8lb (3.6kg), drum	
Size D. 9in (23cm), H. 4in (10cm)	
Milk Cow	
Classification Blue	
Producer Great Hill Dairy	

Gruyère Surchoix

The Roth family came to the United States from Switzerland in 1990 to capitalize on the great milk produced in Wisconsin. The family had been in the cheese business for generations, and the result is an American Gruyère that is of similar quality to the Swiss original, but with distinctive character.

TASTING NOTES The pale white cheese has an aroma of dried apples with a hint of mustiness. The flavor continues in that direction, but the lengthy finish turns to a meaty saltiness.

HOW TO ENJOY The perfect choice for fondue. Alternatively, serve with a selection of dry salamis and Riesling.

USA Monroe, Wisconsin	
Age 9–19 months	
Weight and Shape 16lb (7.3kg), wheel	
Size D. 14in (35cm), H. 5in (12cm)	
Milk Cow	
Classification Hard	
Producer Roth Käse USA	

Monterey Jack

Also known as Monterey Sonoma Jack or, colloquially, "Jack," Monterey Jack was given its official title by the Food and Drug Administration in 1955 to encompass all the varieties then on the market. A debate has raged as to whom actually created Monterey Jack, and the characters behind the story are as smooth, colorful, and sharp as a Dry Jack itself.

In the mid-1800s, Dona Juana Cota de Boronda made and sold a cheese called Queso del Pais door-to-door to help feed her family of 15 children. Meanwhile, Domingo Pedrazzi of Carmel Valley is known to have created a similar cheese that required the application of pressure from a device called a "housejack." He named it Pedrazzi's Jack Cheese.

It was the shrewd and less-than-popular local businessman David Jacks, however, that laid claim to Monterey Jack cheese, and it is said that he stole the idea of Queso del Pais and started major production using milk from his 14 dairy ranches in the 1890s. Jacks marketed the cheese as Jacks' Cheese.

What is not in doubt is that David Jack was the first person to manufacture the cheese on a large scale, however, according to research by Wendy Moss in 1966, it was the Franciscan monks in the 1700s who brought the recipe for a soft, creamy cheese known as Queso Blanco Pais from Spain, via Mexico.

Today, Monterey Jack is one of the best-loved American cheeses and can be found in most supermarkets. It accounts for about 10 percent of all cheese production in California.

TASTING NOTES Young Jack is very mild with a lactic taste. It is sometimes flavored with spices, pimientos, or jalapeño peppers. The Farmstead version is almost runny, has an earthy, mushroomy aroma, and a sweet creamy taste that hints of hazelnuts, with a citrus tang.

Mezzo Secco is a firmer fresh Jack. It first appeared in the 1930s as an alternative to Parmesan. Aged for 7–12 months or longer, it has a deep yellow-gold interior with a grainy, brittle texture and a deep full-bodied tang that is sweet and nutty. The best example is the Dry Jack made by Ig Vella of Vella Cheeses—a legend in his own life.

HOW TO ENJOY The supple texture of Young Jack is perfect for grilling, snacking, or in numerous Mexican-style dishes. Young Jack is perfect with a cool beer or cider. Dry Jack is great for sauces, omelets, soufflés, or grated on pasta, tacos, and enchiladas. Dry Jack needs the depth of one of California's great reds.

Drums of Dry Jack *mature on wooden racks of a cellar. Dry Jack is usually aged for 7–12 months.*

USA California	
Age 1 week–12 months	
Weight and Shape 5½lb (2.5kg) drum	
Size Various	
Milk Cow	
Classification Semi soft (Monterey Jack); Hard (Dry Jack)	
Producer Various	

A CLOSER LOOK

There are numerous Jacks on the market, and flavored ones are gaining in popularity. Young, Mezzo Secco. or Dry—the process remains largely the same—the difference is in the maturing

MEASURING THE CURDS Once the whey has been drained, the curds are carefully measured and placed in square pieces of cheesecloth, then knotted, ready for shaping.

SHAPING It takes great skill to shape the 10lb (5kg) mass of curds into a uniform ball without squeezing out too much whey.

MATURING The cheeses are aged for about five weeks until their edges firm up. At this stage, the cheese is soft and supple and ready for consumption as Young Jack. More mature varieties are hand-coated with a special mixture of vegetable oil, cocoa, and pepper, which ensures the cheese dries out slowly over the next seven or so months.

Young Jack is a pale ivory color, and very mild, smooth, and rubbery with small irregular holes.

The long soaking in brine creates a thin, barely formed rind, which may be waxed.

A whole Young Monterey Jack.

A Young Jack, halved

Hartwell

Marisa Mauro and Princess MacLean founded Ploughgate Creamery in 2008, after training with many great cheesemakers in Vermont. They have climbed the learning curve quickly, having successfully produced several excellent soft cow's, ewe's, and blended milk cheeses.

TASTING NOTES This traditional Brie-style cheese has an exceptionally well-developed rind, perfectly balanced in texture and flavor with the paste, which is sweet and full, but not heavy.

HOW TO ENJOY Hartwell is sturdy enough to be served warm, drizzled with honey and sprinkled with walnuts.

USA Craftsbury Common, Vermont	
Age 30 days	
Weight and Shape 8oz (225g), round	
Size D. 5in (12cm), H. 1½in (4cm)	
Milk Cow	
Classification Soft white	
Producer Ploughgate Creamery	

Hoja Santa

Paula Lambert has been making mozzarella at her creamery near Dallas for more than 20 years and has developed an exciting range of Italian-inspired cheeses. This is a fresh cheese similar to a French Banon, but wrapped in the Mexican hoja santa leaf.

TASTING NOTES A fresh goat's milk cheese, it has a very fine curd that feels light and clean in the mouth. What makes it unique from other fresh chèvre is the natural woody sassafras flavor that comes off the leaf .

HOW TO ENJOY Delicious on toast, but, to really bring out the flavor of the hoja santa, try this with some Chardonnay.

USA Dallas, Texas	
Age 4 weeks	
Weight and Shape 8oz (225g), drum	
Size D. 2in (5cm), H. 1½in (4cm)	
Milk Goat	
Classification Fresh	
Producer Mozzarella Company	

Hooligan

Hooligan, a washed-rind basket-molded cheese, is made by Mark Gillman, school teacher turned cheesemaker, who is a regular at New York's Union Square farmers' market. Cato Corner keeps its own herd of about 40 hormone- and antibiotic-free Jersey cows.

TASTING NOTES Cato Corner's best-known and most pungent cheese, the aroma is intense and slightly yeasty, the texture firm but moist, with a slight grittiness from the rind, and it melts on the palate, with a creamy sweet finish.

HOW TO ENJOY Excellent melted on toast with a little tomato or on its own with a good-quality Belgian ale.

USA Colchester, Connecticut	
Age 60 days	
Weight and Shape 1lb (450g), wheel	
Size D. 6in (15cm), H. 3in (7.5cm)	
Milk Cow	
Classification Semi-soft	
Producer Cato Corner Farm	

Hubbardston Blue

Now operated by the Kilmoyers, Westfield Farm has been producing high-quality goat's milk cheeses in all shapes, sizes, and types since 1971. Hubbardston is a surface-ripened blue cheese; the bright blue mold grows on the outside rather than internally, but as it ages the blue is overlaid with a distinctive gunmetal gray rind.

TASTING NOTES Very soft and creamy, sometimes runny, it is not particularly pungent, with mushroom-like flavors and a mild blue finish.

HOW TO ENJOY A very approachable blue, it works well with whole grain crackers, fresh figs, and a sweet white wine.

USA Hubbardston, Massachusetts	
Age 30–40 days	
Weight and Shape 8oz (225g), round	
Size D. 3in (7.5cm), H. 1in (2.5cm)	
Milk Goat	
Classification Blue	
Producer Westfield Farm	

Kunik

Nettle Meadow is currently home to more than 100 goats, in addition to a multitude of other farm animals that have been rescued or retired over the years. This cheese is an unusual triple-cream blend of goat's milk and cream from the farm's Jersey cows.

TASTING NOTES A remarkably sweet, honeylike cheese that has a mouthfeel ranging from custard when fresh to butter if the cheese has dried a bit.

HOW TO ENJOY Kunik is perfectly suited to very dark breads such as rye, where the sweetness of the cheese will really shine and cry out for an accompanying glass of Champagne.

USA Warrensburg, New York	
Age 2–4 weeks	
Weight and Shape 10oz (300g), round	
Size D. 4in (10cm), H. 2in (5cm)	
Milk Goat with cow's milk cream	
Classification Soft white	
Producer Nettle Meadow Goat Farm	

Larzac

Along the Touchet River in southwest Washington State's Walla Walla Valley lies the home of the first farmstead ewe's milk dairy using recipes based on cheeses from southern France. Larzac has an attractive thin layer of fine wood ash through the center.

TASTING NOTES Each batch is handmade to achieve a delicate soft texture, then cellared for a month to complete the aging that highlights the fresh sweet goat milk flavors in each cheese.

HOW TO ENJOY Larzac is perfect sliced over fresh butterleaf greens, roasted golden beets, and olive oil, and paired with a crisp Pilsner beer.

USA Dayton, Washington	
Age 4–6 weeks	
Weight and Shape 225g (8oz), truncated cylinder	
Size D. 4in (10cm), base, 2in (5cm), top, H. 3in (7.5cm)	
Milk Goat	
Classification Aged fresh	

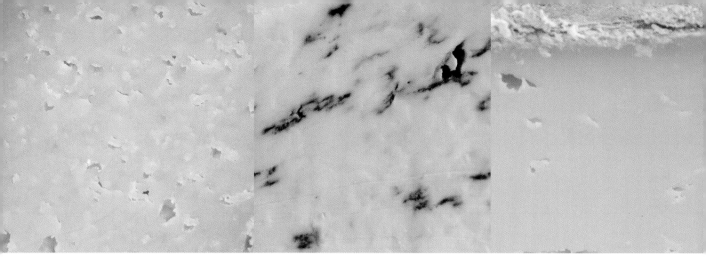

Matos St. George

This is made to honor the island of São Jorge in the Azores, from where Mary and George Matos originally come. The Matos family now makes its Portuguese-style farmstead cheese in Santa Rosa, California.

TASTING NOTES A perfect balance of creamy dense and rich flavors, with a firm Cheddar-like texture that offers hints of earthy meadow, enhanced over time with crunchy crystals that round out the full flavor of the Jersey cream.

HOW TO ENJOY A marvelous choice for macaroni and cheese with sun-dried tomatoes and olive oil, complemented by a glass of Barbera.

USA Santa Rosa, California	
Age 3–6 months	
Weight and Shape 9–16lb (4.1–7.3kg), wheel	
Size Various	
Milk Cow	
Classification Hard	
Producer Matos St. George	

Maytag Blue

Certainly one of the most famous and oldest original American cheeses yet, despite high demand, it is still produced by hand as it was when it was first made in 1941. Although the cheese is cave-aged, it always remains bleach white in appearance.

TASTING NOTES A blur similar to Roquefort but made with cow's milk, Maytag has an enigmatic flavor. Initially creamy and steely blue, it yields to a lemon-tartlike sweet-sourness on the finish.

HOW TO ENJOY In addition to service on the cheeseboard, this sturdy cheese is perfect for salads, melted on fillet steak, or even baked into fruit-based desserts.

USA Newton, Iowa	
Age 4 months	
Weight and Shape 4lb (1.8kg), drum	
Size: D. 7in (18cm), H. 4in (10cm)	
Milk Cow	
Classification Blue	
Producer Maytag Dairy Farms	

Menuet

Steve and Karen Getz began producing cheese in 2006, using organic milk from a herd of about 20 Jersey and Guernsey cows. Their raw milk cheeses are all handmade using fresh milk piped directly from the milking parlor into their cheese vats.

TASTING NOTES Menuet captures the essence of a traditional tome. While the nose is musty, the flavor is salty and meaty, with an interesting vegetable brothlike finish.

HOW TO ENJOY This cheese's unusually soothing appeal should be reflected in any accompaniment. Try it with crackers and tea.

USA Bridport, Vermont	
Age 4 weeks to 3 months	
Weight and Shape 2lb (900g), drum	
Size D. 8in (20cm), H. 3in (7.5cm)	
Milk Cow	
Classification Semi-soft	
Producer Dancing Cow Farm	

Mezzo Secco

Mezzo Secco is not as hard or dry as Monterey Jack, but firmer than a young, soft Jack. It was first created in the 1920s, in the days before the advent of refrigeration, when perishable foods were stored in "ice boxes," and cheese had to fend for itself.

TASTING NOTES Mezzo Secco's supple, dense golden interior has a rich and nutty full flavor, enhanced by a black pepper and vegetable oil coating.

HOW TO ENJOY This is always a great choice for picnics, or slice and serve it over grilled lamb burgers with a glass of Californian Pinot Noir.

USA Sonoma, California	
Age 4–6 months	
Weight and Shape 9–11lb (4.1–5kg), wheel	
Size D. 11in (28cm), H. 4in (10cm)	
Milk Cow	
Classification Hard	
Producer Vella Cheese Company	

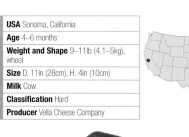

Mona

The cooperative began operating in 1997 to help small sheep dairy farms better negotiate the sometimes highly complex regulations involved with getting their milk to cheese plants. Now encompassing 15 dairies, it produces a few products under its own label.

TASTING NOTES It has a very fine slightly grainy texture in the mouth and a very sweet, salty, and full flavor, but its strongest feature is the length, often lasting minutes on the side of the tongue and inside the cheeks.

HOW TO ENJOY Mona is well suited to grating over pasta. An American Pinot Noir makes a good wine match.

USA River Falls, Wisconsin	
Age 6 months	
Weight and Shape 12lb (5.4kg), wheel	
Size D. 14in (35.5cm), 5in (12cm)	
Milk Ewe and cow	
Classification Hard	
Producer Wisconsin Sheep Dairy Cooperative	

Monet

Decorated with fresh marigold, borage, and viola flowers, the French chèvre-style Monet produced by Dee Harley is a true artist's palate reflecting the beautiful gardens that surround this coastal California dairy.

TASTING NOTES This fresh and clean chèvre's soft, smooth texture is the result of the gentle handling of the fresh goat's milk, and has hints of spring grass flavor year-round.

HOW TO ENJOY With its floral decoration, it makes a stunning centerpiece for a cheeseboard, or serve with a garden-fresh salad and a crisp Pinot Grigio.

USA Pescadero, California	
Age 1–3 weeks	
Weight and Shape 8oz (225g), ball	
Size D. 3in (7.5cm), H. 1in (2.5cm)	
Milk Goat	
Classification Fresh	
Producer Harley Farms Goat Dairy	

MouCo ColoRouge

This particular cheesemaker enjoys the changing of the seasons. The flavors within the cheese change as it ages and evolves. ColoRouge is rubbed with a brine solution to create the red-orange rind with its distinctive haze of white mold.

TASTING NOTES Hand-ladled to create a soft and creamy texture beneath the smear rind, it has mild buttery overtones that develop into complex and spicy notes.

HOW TO ENJOY Spread ColoRouge over crispy crackers, and serve with a rich tawny port and halved fresh red and green grapes.

USA Fort Collins, Colorado
Age 3–8 weeks
Weight and Shape 8oz (225g), round
Size D. 3in (7.5cm), H. 1in (2.5cm)
Milk Cow
Classification Semi-soft
Producer MouCo Cheese Company

Mt. Tam

Named after Mt. Tamalpais, a small mountain located on the Marin County coast of Northern California, just north of San Francisco Bay, Cowgirl Creamery's signature triple-cream cheese is made with organic cow's milk from the Straus Family Dairy.

TASTING NOTES Under the thick, white bloomy rind, Mt. Tam is creamy and dense in texture, with a rich flavor and a pleasant fruity finish.

HOW TO ENJOY Mt. Tam goes extremely well with a golden Pilsner or a Fumé Blanc, dried apricots, and fresh-baked crunchy Pugliese bread.

USA Point Reyes, California
Age 3–4 weeks
Weight and Shape 2oz (60g), round
Size D. 3in (7.5cm), H. 2in (5cm)
Milk Cow
Classification Soft white
Producer Cowgirl Creamery

Mountain Top Bleu

Firefly Farms originally kept its own herd of goats, but ultimately decided to buy milk from a local Amish cooperative in Pennsylvania, so that it could focus exclusively on cheese production. It make several varieties, but this small blue is particularly unusual.

TASTING NOTES The relatively uncommon pyramid shape hints at Mountain Top Bleu's unique flavor. While subtle, the blue is well balanced against grassy, bright, and enjoyably goaty flavors. Its texture is soft and velvety.

HOW TO ENJOY The cheesemaker suggests serving this with poached figs. A white Port would go well on the side.

USA Bittinger, Maryland
Age 5 weeks
Weight and Shape 8oz (225g), pyramid
Size D. 4in (10cm) , H. 3in (7.5cm)
Milk Goat
Classification Blue
Producer FireFly Farms

Oakdale Cheese Company Gouda

Dutch-born Walter and Lenneke Bulk re-create the cheeses of their homeland, Gouda and Edam, in central California, nestled between almond orchards and strawberry fields. It is available plain or flavored, including peppercorns, garlic, mustard, or jalapeño peppers.

TASTING NOTES Aged to perfection for about 10 weeks, the cheese has flavors that share elements of butterscotch and toasted almonds.

HOW TO ENJOY Create a golden grilled sandwich on French bread with a slice of country ham; serve with Sangiovese and fresh or dried fruit.

USA Oakdale, California	
Age 2–4 months	
Weight and Shape 9–11lb (4.1–5kg), boulder	
Size D. 9in (23cm), H. 7.5in (3cm)	
Milk Cow	
Classification Hard	
Producer Oakdale Cheese Company	

O'Cooch

Hidden Springs, located in a part of Wisconsin known as the Driftless Area, operates in close cooperation with its surrounding Amish neighbors, utilizing traditional sustainable methods. The high-quality milk is sourced from a herd of East Friesian and Lacaune sheep that thrive in this terrain.

TASTING NOTES This very firm-textured cheese is crumbly and slightly grainy on the palate, with a fat, sweet, and very nutty flavor. It has a delightful aroma of sheep on open pasture.

HOW TO ENJOY O'Cooch is delicious with honey and almonds, or on its own with a good red Burgundy.

USA Westby, Wisconsin	
Age 4 months	
Weight and Shape 2lb (900g), wheel	
Size D. 5in (12cm), H. 2⅜in (6cm)	
Milk Ewe	
Classification Hard	
Producer Hidden Springs Creamery	

Old Kentucky Tome

A great cheese from Capriole, founded by Judy and Larry Schadd, it is based on the mountain tommes of Europe, but has a thinner rind dusted with a fine powdery white mold. The quality of the cheeses exhibit the great care with which the Schadds keep their herd of more than 400 goats.

TASTING NOTES Its pure white, smooth texture feels light on the palate, and it has a slightly goaty nose, with a hint of toasted walnut on the finish.

HOW TO ENJOY Robust enough to stand up to many flavors, but Judy suggests a yellow tomato and ginger preserve. Pair with a Pinot Noir or other soft red.

USA Greenville, Indiana	
Age 4–8 months	
Weight and Shape 4lb (1.8kg), drum	
Size D. 10in (25cm), H. 4in (10cm)	
Milk Goat	
Classification Soft white	
Producer Capriole Farmstead Goat Cheeses	

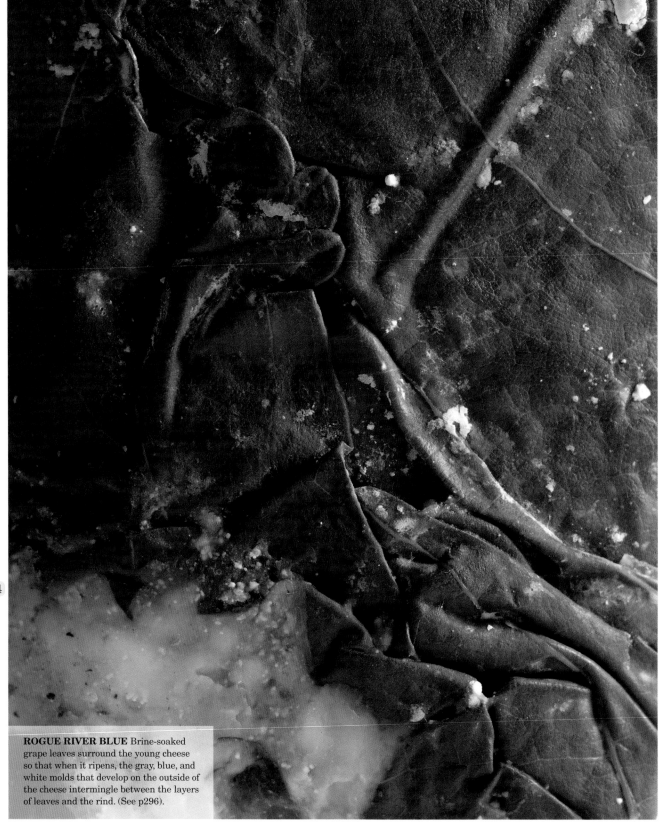

ROGUE RIVER BLUE Brine-soaked grape leaves surround the young cheese so that when it ripens, the gray, blue, and white molds that develop on the outside of the cheese intermingle between the layers of leaves and the rind. (See p296).

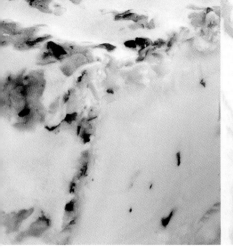
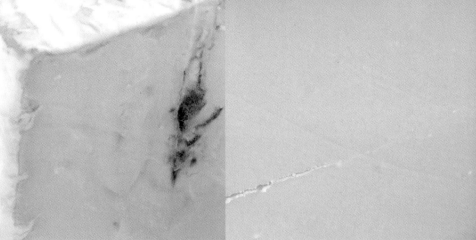

Pecan Chèvre

Sweet Grass Dairy in southern Georgia produces a variety of cow's and goat's milk cheeses on its farm. Some cheeses are traditional in style, but this one, with the addition of world-famous Georgia pecans, is unique.

TASTING NOTES Coated in ground pecans, which give it a delicious crunchy nut taste and texture, the cheese itself is creamy and fairly strong, with a tart bite to the rind.

HOW TO ENJOY This is a cheese that is at its best when served younger, rather than older. The cheesemaker suggests serving with fragrant fresh peaches when they are in season.

USA Thomasville, Georgia	
Age 3 weeks	
Weight and Shape 6oz (175g), pyramid	
Size D. 3in (7.5cm), H. 2in (5cm)	
Milk Goat	
Classification Aged fresh	
Producer Sweet Grass Dairy	

Le Petit Chèvre Bleu

One of the oldest continuously producing cheese companies in the Unites States, Marin French, located within California's Sonoma County, shows a strong French influence in each of its cheeses.

TASTING NOTES Aged for 30 days, this triple-cream Brie-style cheese strikes a good balance between rich flavors and delicate fine blue veining. It has a creamy texture, with a subtle, mild, white pepper spicy taste.

HOW TO ENJOY Spread on buttered toast in the morning, and savor with apricot preserves and fresh pear juice, or pair with a full-bodied Cabernet Sauvignon.

USA Petaluma, California	
Age 30 days or more	
Weight and Shape 4oz (115g), round	
Size D. 2½in (5.5cm), H. 4in (1¾cm)	
Milk Goat	
Classification Soft white	
Producer Marin French Cheese Company	

Pleasant Ridge Reserve

To demonstrate the superior quality of their milk, the Gingrich and Patenaude families worked together to develop this handmade Alpine-style cheese. It is produced only during peak pasture season from spring to fall, and the cows are moved into fresh pasture daily to graze naturally.

TASTING NOTES Daily washing imparts a strong aroma. The flavor ranges from very fruity and sweet when young, to savory and slightly sour as it matures.

HOW TO ENJOY A great melting cheese, it can be used like Gruyère in fondue or to make an excellent French onion soup.

USA Dodgeville, Wisconsin	
Age 8–12 months	
Weight and Shape 12lb (5.4kg), wheel	
Size D. 12in (30cm), H. 3in (7.5cm)	
Milk Cow	
Classification Hard	
Producer Uplands Cheese Company	

Pondhopper

Tumalo Farms combines the traditional methods of Dutch and Italian cheesemaking to produce its unique goat's milk cheeses in the Cascade Mountain Range.

TASTING NOTES The pale yellow-white interior has a few tiny eyes and smooth, creamy supple feel, with a hoppy taste balanced with a nutty tang from the goat's milk.

HOW TO ENJOY Pondhopper is a natural partner for a nutty ale accompanied by yeasty bread, especially one with dried cherries and walnuts.

USA Bend, Oregon	
Age 2–12 weeks	
Weight and Shape 9lb (4.1kg), wheel	
Size D. 10in (25cm), H. 3in (7.5cm)	
Milk Goat	
Classification Hard	
Producer Tumalo Farms	

Queso de Mano

Cheesemaker Jim Schott built his cheese business from the ground up, starting in 1989. Despite encountering many hurdles along the way, the farm now produces several pasteurized and raw award-winning cheeses. Queso de Mano was its first raw milk cheese.

TASTING NOTES Queso de Mano is very firm and slightly grainy on the palate. It is not a salty cheese, but medium dry, with a robust toasty hazelnut flavor and spicy finish.

HOW TO ENJOY Pairings for this cheese include toasted almonds or cherries. The suggested pairing with Beaujolais works very, very well.

USA Longmont, Colorado	
Age 4–6 months	
Weight and Shape 6lb (2.7kg), drum	
Size D. 6in (15cm), H. 4in (10cm)	
Milk Goat	
Classification Hard	
Producer Haystack Mountain Goat Dairy	

Rogue River Blue

Rogue Creamery, founded in the 1930s by one of America's great cheesemakers Thomas Vella, continues to enjoy great success. Under the management of David Gremmels, in 2008 Rogue River became the first American raw-milk cheeses to be certified for export.

TASTING NOTES Wrapped in grape leaves and soaked in pear brandy, it has great intensity and depth of flavor. Firm, yet moist and smooth in the mouth, it is less salty than many blues, and is creamy and sweet with a spicy finish.

HOW TO ENJOY Pair with dessert wines and pears or use in desserts such as poached pears or calvados soufflé.

Region Central Point Oregon	
Age 6–8 months	
Weight and Shape 5lb (2.25kg), drum	
Size D. 6in (15cm), H. 4in (10cm)	
Milk Cow	
Classification Blue	
Producer Rogue Creamery	

Rosemary's Waltz

Silvery Moon Creamery was founded in 2003 by Jennifer Betencourt who, after studying cheesemaking at Cornell, formed a partnership with Smiling Hill Farm. Although located in a relatively commercial area of Maine, the farm still works the same pristine pastures that have remained in the hands of the same family since the 1700s.

TASTING NOTES Very fresh and clean with a crumbly texture, it picks up the flavors of the rosemary and juniper on the rind without being overpowered.

HOW TO ENJOY Its mildness makes it a good base for numerous recipes. Try it shaved over baked sweet potato slices.

USA	Westbrook, Maine
Age	1 month
Weight and Shape	3lb (1.35kg), wheel
Size	D. 7in (18cm), H. 3in (7.5cm)
Milk	Cow
Classification	Fresh
Producer	Silvery Moon Creamery

R&R Cheddar

Founded in the 1700s, Smiling Hill Farm is ancient by American standards. It keeps a herd of Holsteins grazing on pastures free of chemical fertilizer and pesticides. Silvery Moon Creamery partnered with Smiling Hill in 2003, adding artisan cheese production to its existing diary business.

TASTING NOTES Mild but full of interesting subtlety, it has a chewy texture and tight grain; the flavor is sweet and full. Rather than salty or savory on the finish, it has an earthy minerality.

HOW TO ENJOY The texture and age make it ideal for melting in sandwiches, or enjoy on its own with a strong lager.

USA	Westbrook, Maine
Age	6 months minimum
Weight and Shape	17lb (7.7kg), drum
Size	D. 14in (35cm), H. 4in (10cm)
Milk	Cow
Classification	Hard
Producer	Silvery Moon Creamery

St. Jorge

The Fagundes family makes cheeses based on those from the Azores, a group of small islands west of Portugal, where Isabel Fagundes made cheese in the late 1800s. St. Jorge, the family's first, was released in 2000 and, like all their cheese, is made only with morning milk from their farm.

TASTING NOTES With a texture between Cheddar and Gouda, this raw milk cheese is long in flavor and slow to mature. After the initial sharp bite, it mellows to a creamy, sweet-fruity tang.

HOW TO ENJOY An excellent cheese for grating, it also makes a tasty snack with a glass of Cabernet Sauvignon.

USA	Hanford, California
Age	Up to 3 years
Weight and Shape	6–8lb (2.7–3.6kg), wheel
Size	D. 10in (25cm), H. 4in (10cm)
Milk	Cow
Classification	Hard
Producer	Fagundes Old World Cheese

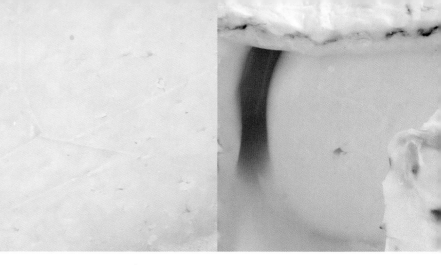

Sally Jackson

This semi-soft cheese is produced by one of the only American cheesemakers that hand-makes cheese over a wood-fired stove. This traditional method gives the cheese its unique flavor and texture.

TASTING NOTES Wrapped in chestnut leaves and aged for 2–4 months, the golden-cream color that the paste gains from the Guernsey milk welcomes you to enjoy its floral essence with hints of cream on the palate.

HOW TO ENJOY Each cheese deserves a toast with Champagne or a fruity ale to make a fine finish to a meal with friends.

USA Oroville, Washington
Age 2–4 months
Weight and Shape 2lb (900g), wheel
Size Various
Milk Cow
Classification Semi-soft
Producer Sally Jackson Cheeses

San Juaquin Gold

Named after the San Juaquin Valley in California, this American original is inspired by Swiss-mountain cheeses. It is produced with the milk of Holstein Farmstead cows, in keeping with the cheesemaker's concept of creating cheese in the European tradition.

TASTING NOTES It is aged for 16 to 24 months to create a full-flavored cheese with a buttery golden color and a crumbly texture. As it ages, the complex flavors of nuts and grass arise to the palate.

HOW TO ENJOY Grate it into a creamy pasta dish and serve with a full-bodied San Juaquin Syrah.

USA Modesto, California
Age 16–24 months
Weight and Shape 30lb (13.6kg), wheel
Size Various
Milk Cow
Classification Hard
Producer Farmstead Cheese

Seastack

The rock formations covering the coastal lines of the Pacific Northwest are the inspiration for the cheeses produced at the Mt. Townsend Creamery in Washington.

TASTING NOTES The coating of vegetable ash and sea salt prior to ripening is the key to the balance of flavors in this soft white cheese. It is a one-of-a-kind cheese, with a silky texture and earthy flavors that become piquant as it ages.

HOW TO ENJOY A perfect picnic and hiking cheese served with a fresh, crusty baguette, Viognier, and dried fruit. Equally, it makes a delicious finale to a fine meal with friends.

USA Port Townsend, Washington
Age 4–6 weeks
Weight and Shape 8oz (225g), round
Size Various
Milk Cow
Classification Soft white
Producer Mt. Townsend Creamery

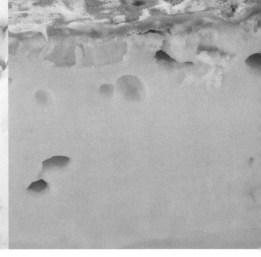

Sierra Nevada

Named after the Sierra Nevada Mountains, California, the cheesemakers of the same name also produce a range of natural and organic cheeses, including a Cheddar and various flavored Jack cheeses. However, their best cheeses are these authentic, old-style cream ones.

TASTING NOTES Sierra Nevada has a full-cream flavor and texture with hints of sweet grass, warm butter, and a sea-salty tang on the finish.

HOW TO ENJOY Spread on a bagel or fold into an omelet with smoked salmon and chives, alongside a glass of California Sauvignon Blanc.

USA Willows, California	
Age 1–3 weeks	
Weight and shape 7oz (200g), container	
Size No size	
Milk Cow	
Classification Fresh	
Producer Sierra Nevada	

Smokey Blue Cheese

Rogue Creamery age their cheeses in Roquefort-style caves, and after their success with Oregon Blue, the first blue made on the West Coast, its producers decided to be the first to smoke a blue. Hence Smokey Blue was born.

TASTING NOTES This cheese is smoked over a bed of local hazelnut shells, giving the robust, spicy blue a hint of hazelnuts with a touch of creamy caramel and smoke on the finish.

HOW TO ENJOY The marriage of this smoked blue with a bottle of Chocolate Stout and slices of stoneground-wheat baguette is a great way to enjoy a sunny afternoon.

USA Central Point, Oregon	
Age 3 months	
Weight and shape 5lb (2¼kg), wheel	
Size Various	
Milk Cow	
Classification Blue	
Producer Rogue Creamery	

Soft Wheel

Michael Lee started out as a cheese retailer, but since 2005 he has been producing his own cheese from a small herd of 25 goats. Respectful of seasonality, as and when needed, this cheesemaker often supplements his supply of milk with cow's milk from neighboring farms.

TASTING NOTES Soft Wheel is a pungent, washed-rind cheese. The rind is thick but soft and sticky, while the inside is rich and goaty with hints of chestnuts.

HOW TO ENJOY Spread on warm crusty bread and serve with dried fruit and nuts alongside an Alsace-style aromatic white wine or wheat beer.

USA West Cornwall, Vermont	
Age 80 days	
Weight and Shape 1½lb (700g), wheel	
Size D. 5in (12cm), H. 2in (5cm)	
Milk Goat and cow	
Classification Semi-soft	
Producer Twig Farm	

Surfing Goat Dairy Quark

The farm is located on the sunny Hawaiian slopes of Maui's Haleakala Crater, providing the herd of goats with native vegetation to forage on, as well as pasture, and adding distinctive regional flavors to the milk.

TASTING NOTES Smooth on the palate, with a sweet creamy taste and pleasant tangy goat milk finish.

HOW TO ENJOY Serve the Quark with fresh mango slices and macadamia nuts over salad greens. For a true tropical experience, complement with a Kona Brewing Co. Fire Rock Pale Ale.

USA Kula, Maui, Hawaii
Age A few days
Weight and Shape 8oz (225g), jar
Size No size
Milk Goat
Classification Fresh
Producer Surfing Goat Dairy

Tarentaise

Trained in the Haute-Savoie, the Putnams offer an excellent American interpretation of Alpine cheeses using their organically farmed Jersey cow's milk and traditional alpine cheesemaking equipment and techniques.

TASTING NOTES The deep golden color seems almost to translate right into the flavor, with its warm, toasty caramel notes and a touch of acidity on the finish. It has a strong cherrylike aroma when freshly cut. The texture is initially medium dry, but relaxes in the mouth.

HOW TO ENJOY Pairing with Vin de Savoie and some fresh apples is a good place to start. It makes terrific fondue, too.

USA North Pomfret, Vermont
Age 8 months
Weight and Shape 18lb (8.2kg), wheel
Size D. 20in (50cm), H. 4in (10cm)
Milk Cow
Classification Hard
Producer Thistle Hill Farm

Taupinière

Made in the historic town of Sonoma, this is based on the traditional taupinière cheese from the French region of Poitou-Charentes—the name reflects the shape of the cheese, which means "molehill" in French.

TASTING NOTES Slightly aged with a dense texture and pleasant cream flavor, the cheese is dusted in blue-gray charcoal powder to create a consistency of soft paste.

HOW TO ENJOY Heat in the oven ever so slightly, and serve with a fresh crusty bread and rich full-bodied red wine such as Zinfandel.

USA Sonoma, California
Age 2–6 weeks
Weight and Shape 6oz (175g), molehill
Size D. 3in (7.5cm), H. 2in (5cm)
Milk Goat
Classification Soft white
Producer Laura Chenel's Chèvre

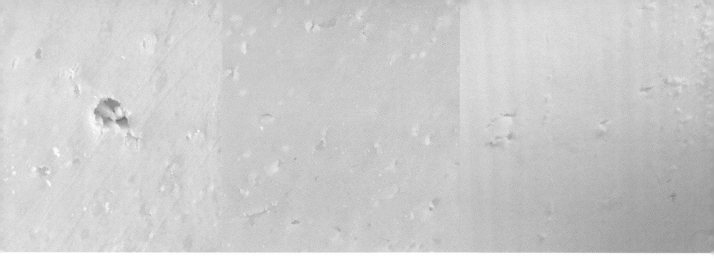

Telford Reserve

At Hendricks Farm, located just outside Philadelphia, they believe in traditional sustainable farming, including the use of a team of draft horses to work the farm. They produce roughly ten cheeses, alongside many other traditional farm products that feed almost exclusively into the local community.

TASTING NOTES Deliciously complex, with a tart bite often found in traditional Cheddar and a long butterscotch finish typical of premium aged Gouda. It has a firm but not crumbly texture.

HOW TO ENJOY Beer, preferably good lager, is the best match. Great with sourdough bread, country ham, and hot mustard.

USA Philadelphia, Pennsylvania	
Age 10 months	
Weight and Shape 8lb (, 3.6kg) wheel	
Size D. 16in (40cm), H. 5in (12cm)	
Milk Cow	
Classification Hard	
Producer Hendricks Farm and Dairy	

Thomasville Tomme

Sweet Grass Dairy is located on beautiful wooded terrain in southern Georgia. The Littles keep a small herd of goats and Jersey cows, from which they produce several different styles of cheese. This one is modeled after traditional tommes of the Pyrénées.

TASTING NOTES Although relatively mild in flavor, this cheese has an appealing simplicity that is best compared to farm-fresh milk: clean, rich, slightly sweet, and perfectly balanced. The texture is chewy and semi-soft.

HOW TO ENJOY Ideal for macaroni and cheese, its mellow flavor lends richness to recipes without being overpowering.

USA Thomasville, Georgia	
Age 3–6 months	
Weight and Shape 9lb (4.1kg), wheel	
Size D. 12in (30cm), H. 5in (12cm)	
Milk Cow	
Classification Semi-soft	
Producer Sweet Grass Dairy	

Triple Cream Wheel

Coach Farm produces exceptional milk from its large herd of Alpine goats and makes a wide range of products. Given the relatively small yield, every drop of cream goes into producing this 75 per cent fat triple-cream goat cheese.

TASTING NOTES Dense, rich, sweet, and buttery, with a subtle tart finish and barely a hint of the goat's milk, it does not exhibit a tendency to become runny or soupy, as is sometimes the case with triple-cream cheeses.

HOW TO ENJOY Too delicate to cook, try it with Champagne. To indulge, smear on pita wedges and top with caviar.

USA Pine Plains, New York	
Age 20–30 days	
Weight and Shape 4½lb (2kg), wheel	
Size D. 7in (18cm), H. 3in (7.5cm)	
Milk Goat	
Classification Soft white	
Producer Coach Farm	

BLUE CHEESE The holes where the stainless steel rods have penetrated the rind are clearly visible. These create fine tunnels that allow air to reach the interior, encouraging the blue mold added to the milk to turn blue.

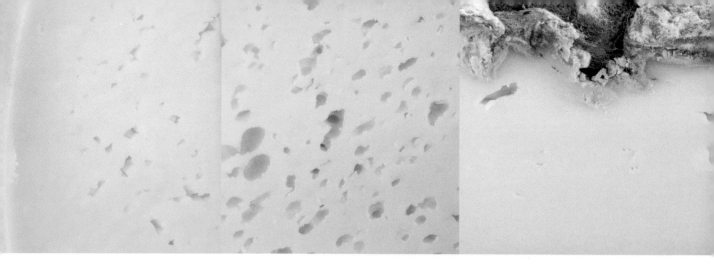

Tulare Cannonball

Made using Jersey cow's milk and the 500-year old traditional Dutch recipe for Edam, this is named in honor of Tulare County, where the dairy is located and which counts milk as its most valuable agricultural product.

TASTING NOTES It has the classic creamy texture associated with Edam, with a spicy aroma and slightly salty finish. The cheese is matured for a minimum of 5 months, when its flavor reaches its peak of perfection.

HOW TO ENJOY For an afternoon picnic, serve with a selection of fresh melon slices sprinkled with pine nuts, and pair with a fruity Beaujolais.

USA Visalia, California	
Age 5–6 months	
Weight and Shape 3–5lb (1.35–2.25kg), ball	
Size D. 5in (12cm), H. 6in (15cm)	
Milk Cow	
Classification Semi-soft	
Producer Bravo Farms	

Tumalo Tomme

Tumalo Tomme is named after Tumalo in Oregon's Cascade Mountains; the "tomme" comes from the style of artisan cheeses produced mainly in the French Alps that bear this name. It is made with raw milk from a mixed herd of Alpine, La Mancha, and Saanen goats.

TASTING NOTES The pine essence from the aging planks is reflected in the pastoral flavors that complement the earthy components of this washed-rind cheese. The finish has floral overtones.

HOW TO ENJOY Pear cider enhances the flavors of Tumalo Tomme, especially when served with pear compote and crusty walnut bread.

USA Redmond, Oregon	
Age 6 months	
Weight and Shape 3–5lb (1.35–2.25kg), wheel	
Size D. 6½in (17cm), H. 3in (7.5cm)	
Milk Goat	
Classification Semi-soft	
Producer Juniper Grove Farm	

Twig Farm Square Cheese

Not able to rely fully on the availability of goat's milk, Twig Farm sometimes follows the traditional practice of supplementing its supply with cow's milk. But for certain cheeses, including this one, it uses only milk from its own herd. Tying it in muslin or cheesecloth forms its irregular square shape.

TASTING NOTES Hazelnuts are the leading flavor, which rolls into a surprisingly mellow, sweet finish. The rind carries a certain pungency, but this does not penetrate the firm, dense paste.

HOW TO ENJOY Perfect with a honey derived from nut or herbal blossoms.

USA West Cornwall, Vermont	
Age 2–3 months	
Weight and Shape 2lb (900g), flat square	
Size L. 10cm (4in), W. 10cm (4in), H. 5cm (2in)	
Milk Goat	
Classification Hard	
Producer Twig Farm	

USA

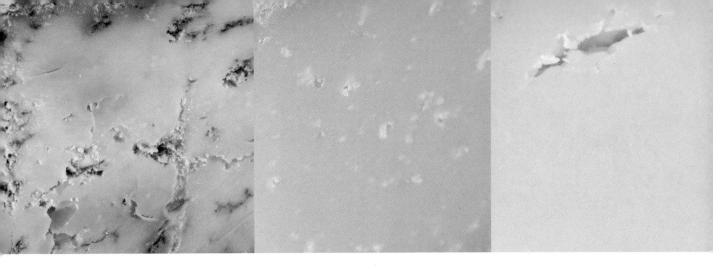

Vaquero Blue

This organic farm produces a wide range of handmade ewe's milk or mixed ewe's and cow's milk cheeses. Many, including this one, are cave-aged on the property. Their strictly seasonal production means that many of Willow Hill's cheeses come and go quickly, but patience is rewarded with exceptional quality and dynamic flavors.

TASTING NOTES Its appearance speaks volumes about the cave ripening, but this medium-strong, slightly musty blue is buttery and smooth on the palate.

HOW TO ENJOY Ideal for crumbling into salads or grilling on your favorite steak, paired with a Merlot or dry Riesling.

USA	Milton, Vermont
Age	6 months
Weight and Shape	4lb (1.8kg), cylinder
Size	D. 5in (12cm), H. 6in (15cm)
Milk	Ewe and cow
Classification	Blue
Producer	Willow Hill Farm

Vermont Ayr

This cheesemaker is keeper of a herd of increasingly uncommon Ayrshire cows on a farm in Vermont's Champlain Valley. The cheeses are made in small batches and lightly brined before being transferred to the cellar for ripening.

TASTING NOTES The grazing of timothy-grass, clover, brome, and alfalfa comes right through into the cheese. The texture is tight and nutty, but opens up to become creamy in the mouth. The flavor builds in intensity and lingers pleasantly before dissipating.

HOW TO ENJOY Serve Vermont Ayr with other medium to mild cheeses as part of a cheeseboard. Nice with Syrah wine.

USA	Champlain Valley, Vermont
Age	3 months
Weight and Shape	2–3lb (900g–1.35kg), round
Size	D. 5in (12cm), H. 3in (7.5cm)
Milk	Cow
Classification	Hard
Producer	Crawford Family Farm

Vermont Shepherd

Aside from producing this excellent cave-aged sheep's milk cheese, Patch Farm has served as a training ground for many aspiring cheesemakers. To highlight the importance of *terroir*, each wheel of cheese is delivered with a certificate detailing the herd's activity on the day of production.

TASTING NOTES Deliciously sweet and concentrated, its texture is very dense and relaxes nicely in the mouth. True to Pyrenean style, it has a long sweet-savory finish, with a hint of woolliness.

HOW TO ENJOY The classic pairing is with a black cherry conserve, but it works equally well with quince paste.

USA	Putney, Vermont
Age	6 months
Weight and Shape	3lb (1.35kg), convex drum
Size	D. 6in (15cm), H. 3½in (9cm)
Milk	Ewe
Classification	Hard
Producer	Vermont Shepherd Cheese

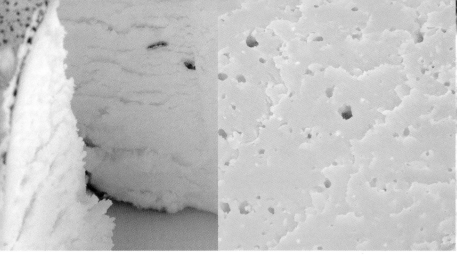

Wabash Cannonball

Capriole, founded by Judy Schadd, has an ever-evolving range of French-style goat cheeses distinctively its own. The Wabash Cannonball has been a success for years and was an American Cheese Society award winner in 1995.

TASTING NOTES Firm and slightly dry, with a thin white rind dusted with ash, this surface-ripened cheese has a goaty and slightly acidic flavor; the rind lends a pleasant muskiness. The finish is rich and buttermilky.

HOW TO ENJOY Ideal with dried fruit and sparkling wine. Bread and crackers distract from the flavor, so it is best to enjoy this one on its own.

USA Greenville, Indiana	
Age 3–10 weeks	
Weight and Shape 4oz (115g), flattened ball	
Size D. 1½in (4cm)	
Milk Goat	
Classification Aged fresh	
Producer Capriole Farmstead Goat Cheese	

Winchester Super Aged Gouda

Jules Wesselink was born and raised in the Netherlands, where he learned the traditional Dutch methods for making cheese. He has re-created these to produce this super aged "boere kaas," or farmhouse, Gouda.

TASTING NOTES Its smooth, thick rind protects the dense interior with its myriad holes and tiny calcium crystals that crunch in the mouth. By 15 months, the sweet, buttery flavor becomes sharp and assertive, with a nuance of toffee.

HOW TO ENJOY Superb on a cheeseboard with almonds, fresh crusty bread, and apples, accompanied by a cool lager.

USA Winchester, California	
Age 15 months	
Weight and Shape 11–12lb (5–5.4kg), wheel	
Size D. 12in (30cm), H. 6in (15cm)	
Milk Cow	
Classification Hard	
Producer Winchester Cheese Company	

Winnemere

Available only from midwinter through spring, this is always worth waiting for, and its slight variability from year to year always stirs excitement for the cheese to become available. Like Jasper Hill's other cheeses, the beer-washed Winnamere reflects European training.

TASTING NOTES It has a sweet sort of pungency, but also hints of wet stone. The full sweet flavor has an almost baconlike smokiness to it, while the paste's texture is so perfectly velvety that you hardly notice the soft rind.

HOW TO ENJOY Delicious with sweet beers or cider, this cheese presents very well on lightly toasted rounds of baguette.

USA Greensboro, Vermont	
Age 2 months	
Weight and Shape 1¼lb (550g), round	
Size D. 6in (15cm), H. 2in (5cm)	
Milk Cow	
Classification Semi-soft	
Producer Jasper Hill Farm	

More Cheeses of the USA

The following cheeses are rare, largely because they are only available seasonally or because they are produced in very remote areas. Although it has proved impossible to photograph them, they are important and interesting examples of cheeses of the USA, so we are including them.

So, read, savor, and seek out.

5 Spoke Creamery Browning Gold

The name 5 Spoke Creamery was inspired by the ambling bicycle journeys around the world of two friends, which they likened to the journey of discovery when making cheese. All the cheeses are handmade in the farmstead tradition, produced on site from the raw milk of a closed herd of grass-fed cows.

TASTING NOTES This hard cheese is aged for 24 months until it is full of rich buttery flavors and has a firm Cheddar-like texture.

HOW TO ENJOY Truly a fine pairing with toasted almonds, a fresh-baked sweet baguette, and a Golden Ale.

USA	Port Chester, New York
Age	24 months
Weight and Shape	9–11lb (4–4.9kg), cylinder
Size	D. 6in (16cm), H. 7½in (19cm)
Milk	Cow
Classification	Hard
Producer	5 Spoke Creamery

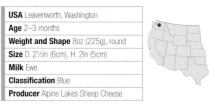

Alpine Lakes Creamy Bleu

The milk for this blue cheese comes from a herd of mixed East Friesland and Locaune sheep, which is then infused with traditional roqueforti mold to create a pristine, true blue flavor and rustic appearance.

TASTING NOTES Alpine Lakes Creamy Bleu is ripened and brought to market when 60 days old. By then it is rich, smooth, and creamy to taste with an ivory center streaked with blue. It intensifies in flavor with age.

HOW TO ENJOY Serve on a cheeseboard with fresh plums, cherries, and a crusty Walnut Levaine loaf alongside an aromatic, crisp White Port.

USA	Leavenworth, Washington
Age	2–3 months
Weight and Shape	8oz (225g), round
Size	D. 2½in (6cm), H. 2in (5cm)
Milk	Ewe
Classification	Blue
Producer	Alpine Lakes Sheep Cheese

Ancient Heritage Scio

The cheesemakers at Ancient Heritage Dairy were impressed by the flavor and texture of traditional, European ewe's milk cheese, so they decided to recreate one at home in Oregon. Ancient Heritage Scio was produced in honor of old-world cheesemakers.

TASTING NOTES The distinct flavors of this two-month aged, raw, ewe's milk cheese stand out as a sweet, moist, and dense taste on the palate with a hint of roasted nuts in the finish.

HOW TO ENJOY Ancient Heritage Scio is pleasantly delicious when paired with almonds, fresh-baked wheat breads, and a nutty Brown Ale.

USA	Scio, Oregon
Age	60 days
Weight and Shape	5lb (2.25kg), wheel
Size	D. 9in (23cm), H. 3in (7.5cm)
Milk	Ewe
Classification	Semi-soft
Producer	Ancient Heritage Dairy

Bad Axe

Hidden Springs Farm is a sustainable sheep dairy in the rolling hills of western Wisconsin, combining an old-fashioned, all-natural farmstead with just enough modern equipment and science to keep the quality at its peak. Bad Axe is named after the river that flows through the Westby Valley.

TASTING NOTES A delectably creamy and sweet semi-soft cheese. The flavor of the ewe's-milk cream stays pleasantly on the palate.

HOW TO ENJOY Pairs perfectly with a fresh baguette stuffed with arugula and tomatoes and served up for an afternoon picnic.

USA	Westby, Wisconsin
Age	8–12 weeks
Weight and Shape	6lb (2.7kg), wheel
Size	D. 15cm (6in), H. 7.5cm (3in)
Milk	Ewe
Classification	Semi-soft
Producer	Hidden Springs Creamery

Beechers Flagship Reserve

These beautifully cloth-bound wheels, aged as Reserve Cheddar, are inspired by traditional English Cheddar. They are produced using similar methods; they are pressed then bandaged or wrapped to protect the rind during ageing. The milk used is a blend of Holstein and Jersey.

TASTING NOTES At 13 months, the developed cheddar taste arrives on the palate with a creamy and clean flavor and a firm, slightly crumbly texture that finishes with a fruity essence.

HOW TO ENJOY Sliced and served with a country-style pâté, crusty sourdough baguette, and a nutty Brown Ale.

USA	Seattle, Washington
Age	12–16 months
Weight and Shape	16lb (7.2kg), truckle
Size	D. 8in (20cm), H. 9in (23cm)
Milk	Cow
Classification	Hard
Producer	Beechers Handmade Cheese

Bleu Age

Rollingstone Chevre, established in 1988, was the first farmstead goat cheese producer in Idaho. From the first goat, purchased to provide milk for the family, their herd has expanded to over 300, from which they now make a range of wonderful cheeses, including this unusual external blue mold one.

TASTING NOTES Beneath the thick, midnight-blue *Penicillum roqueforti* coat is a thin, almost liquid, sweet layer, then a firmer nutty interior. It has a distinct, but not strong, goaty taste and a spicy blue tang.

HOW TO ENJOY Serve with walnuts, slices of fresh pears, and a dry Riesling.

USA Parma, Idaho	
Age 30 days	
Weight and shape 6oz (175g), round or pyramid	
Size D. 3in (7.5cm), H. 2in (5cm)	
Milk Goat	
Classification Blue	
Producer Rollingstone Chevre	

Brindisi Fontina

Brindisi is the maiden name of cheesemaker Rod Volbeda's mother, and Fontina is one of Italy's great cheeses, made in the Alps since the 12th century. This American version is made using 100 percent Jersey cow's milk.

TASTING NOTES The Jersey milk gives the cheese a warm golden glow, a rich smooth feel on the palate, and a strong aroma and flavor. It has a nutty bite and a subtle, sweet cream finish.

HOW TO ENJOY Makes an excellent Brandy Fondue, with dark grain bread, roasted potatoes and apples, and a glass of apple brandy.

USA Salem, Oregon	
Age 3–9 months	
Weight and Shape 8–10lb (3.6–4.5kg), wheel	
Size Various	
Milk Cow	
Classification Semi-soft	
Producer Willamette Valley Cheese Company	

Carmela

The name of the producers of this cheese, Goat's Leap, reflects the energy and personality of the La Mancha goats that graze on the farm, and the fine life they lead amongst the hills of California's Napa Valley.

TASTING NOTES An elegant and sophisticated raw goat cheese, it is hand salted and dusted with paprika. Carmela is sweet to the taste and has a clean, goat's-cream finish. It is at its best when it is 12 months old.

HOW TO ENJOY The Carmela is an elegant addition to a Sunday brunch, served alongside honeycombs, fresh cherries, and Lambic Cherry Beer.

USA St. Helena, California	
Age 12 months	
Weight and Shape 5lb (2.2kg), wheel	
Size D. 8in (20cm), H. 4in (10cm)	
Milk Goat	
Classification Hard	
Producer Goat's Leap Cheese	

Cayuse Mountain Goat

Clare Paris makes raw goat's and ewe's milk cheeses including Shepherd's Gem, a hard ewe's milk cheese; Rosa Rugosa, a semi-soft ewe's and goat's milk cheese; and Cayuse, which is named after a mountain summit in Okanogan County.

TASTING NOTES It has a dense, creamy texture and a complex, yet subtle, character that has all the nutty and herbaceous attributes of a hard goat cheese without the feral goaty taste associated with French-style *chèvre*.

HOW TO ENJOY It is best on a cheese plate with *charcuterie*, herbed olives, and a flavourful Zinfandel.

USA Tonasket, Washington	
Age 6 months	
Weight and Shape 2–3lb (900g–1.35kg), wheel	
Size Various	
Milk Ewe and goat	
Classification Semi-soft	
Producer Lakhaven Farmstead Cheeses	

Claire de Lune

This semi-soft cheese forms part of the Pure Luck Texas legacy of organic farmstead goat cheese. The vision was established by Sara Bolton in 1979, but it continues today through her three daughters. They now have 100 Nubian and alpine goats that graze on the same five acres, now certified organic, that were purchased by Sara.

TASTING NOTES Ripened for 2–6 months, the supple interior is filled with sweet, creamy, goaty flavors that are accentuated by tang notes on the finish.

HOW TO ENJOY Pleasant when served with a glass of Cabernet Franc, currants, and a fresh walnut baguette.

USA Dripping Springs, Texas	
Age 2–6 months	
Weight and Shape 2½lb (1.1kg), round	
Size D. 6in (15cm), H. 3in (7.5cm)	
Milk Goat	
Classification Semi-soft	
Producer Pure Luck Texas	

Creamery Subblime

This cheese owes its name not just to its flavor, but to "Subby," a La Mancha doe in the farm's herd that once broke her neck and resembled a submarine while healing! All Estrella Family Creamery cheeses are made with raw milk and the animals graze on organically maintained pastures.

TASTING NOTES Aged for two months to semi-soft perfection, it has a delicate hint of goat and a tang of coastal salt air on the finish.

HOW TO ENJOY Best with a baguette, apple slices, a drizzle of wild honey, and a Washington State Chardonnay to highlight the elegant flavors.

USA Montesano, Washington	
Age 60 days	
Weight and Shape 8oz (225g), round	
Size Various	
Milk Goat	
Classification Semi-soft	
Producer Estrella Family Creamery	

Elk Mountain

The production of this semi-soft cheese is based on the method used to make European mountain-style cheeses such as the Tomme of the Pyrénées. This American version is named after Elk Mountain, near the Rogue River in Oregon, where it is made.

TASTING NOTES Best eaten when it has aged six months. This cheese is washed in a local Wild Mountain Oregon beer, and the paste has a very buttery flavor and firm texture.

HOW TO ENJOY A true pairing of this Oregon cheese would be with savory fig preserves while enjoying an Elk Mountain Ale.

USA Rogue River, Oregon	
Age 6 months	
Weight and Shape 8lb (3.6kg), wheel,	
Size D. 9in (23cm), H. 4½in (11cm)	
Milk Goat	
Classification Semi-soft	
Producer Phoila Farm	

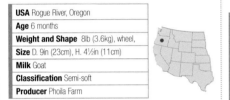

Ferns Edge Goat Dairy

Fern's Edge Dairy is nestled in the foothills of Mount Zion in the Cascade Hills of Oregon. The fresh, artisan cheese of the same name is handcrafted using the milk of the organic farm's goats, and seasoned with some of their home-grown herbs.

TASTING NOTES A fresh-flavored Chèvre, it is made by hand to create a delicate and soft texture, which is followed by a sweet cream finish.

HOW TO ENJOY Serve with fresh pears, some blanched almonds, and a sweet baguette, and wash it down with a crisp glass of Viognier.

USA Lowell, Oregon	
Age 1–3 weeks	
Weight and Shape 4oz (115g), log	
Size Various	
Milk Goat	
Classification Fresh	
Producer Ferns Edge Goat Dairy	

Golden Glen Creamery Mozzarella

Golden Glen Creamery is the only farmstead producer on the Washington coast that hand-makes and stretches fresh mozzarella.

TASTING NOTES Moist and creamy to start, it is rich in flavor and has a delicate texture that reflects the gentle process by which the cheese was made.

HOW TO ENJOY Toss in a salad with arugula, serve as a snack with a dribble of fresh pesto, or add to a fresh tomato and garlic pasta dish. Add a bottle of rich Washington Syrah to create a fine meal.

USA Bow, Washington	
Age 2–10 days	
Weight and Shape 8oz (225g), ball	
Size Various	
Milk Cow	
Classification Fresh	
Producer Golden Glen Creamery	

Midcoast Teleme

The Original Teleme was created by Giovanni Peluso, however, the tradition continues to this day thanks to the work of third-generation cheesemaker Frankin Peluso. It is still made using rice flour that has been coated Teleme within the state of California.

TASTING NOTES This fresh, butcher's-block shaped cheese is aged for one week in order to yield a velvety smooth, moist texture and a fresh clean flavor.

HOW TO ENJOY Italian Salami, Teleme, and a sourdough baguette make a classic San Francisco North Beach sandwich. Enjoy it with a glass of old vine Zinfandel.

USA San Louis Obispo, California	
Age 1 week	
Weight and Shape 6½lb (3kg), block	
Size L. 8in (20cm), W. 8in (20cm), H. 3in (7.5cm)	
Milk Cow	
Classification Fresh	
Producer Franklin's Cheeses	

Ouray

Sprout Creek Farm, who produce this semi-soft cheese, is owned by the non-profit organization, Society of the Sacred Heart. This society provides thousands of children with the chance to work with animals and to learn how a farm works.

TASTING NOTES Ouray has a thin, leathery rind dusted with gray molds. The dense, creamy paste is filled with earthy and buttery flavors and a sweet floral essence.

HOW TO ENJOY A fine cheese that is perfect paired with fresh currants, walnut bread, and a good apple cider.

USA Poughkeepsie, New York	
Age 2–4 months	
Weight and Shape 6½lb (3kg), drum	
Size Various	
Milk Cow	
Classification Semi-soft	
Producer Sprout Creek Farm	

Petit Marcel

Pugs Leap Farm is committed to sustainable practices and the principles of the Slow Food Movement, essentially that "buying locally brings health, economic, environmental, and social benefits to the community."

TASTING NOTES The soft, fresh, velvety flavors and overtly pleasant tang of this soft white cheese present a rich and delicate goat's milk flavor, coupled with a balance of saltiness from the start to the finish.

HOW TO ENJOY Petit Marcel is complemented by a handmade pâté, fresh baked breads, and a crisp, light Riesling.

USA Healdsburg, California	
Age 2 weeks	
Weight and Shape 2–3½oz (60–100g), round	
Size D. 2½in (6cm), H. 1½in (4cm)	
Milk Goat	
Classification Soft white	
Producer Pugs Leap Farm	

Pine Stump Crottin

This Crottin is made in the traditional French way, where the curd is gently ladled into molds and allowed to drain off without pressing. Over time it creates a snow-white, round drum with a thin white rind.

TASTING NOTES When young, this goat cheese is delicate and soft. As it ages, the cheese becomes dense and strengthens in flavor, maintaining its original earthy tones.

HOW TO ENJOY Warmed Crottin, sprinkled with cracked black pepper and olive oil over frisée greens is a meal that offers real pleasure when served with a fruity Marsanne.

USA Omak, Washington	
Age Over 60 days	
Weight and shape 4–8oz (115–225g), drum	
Size D. 3½–4in (9–10cm), H. 3in (7.5cm)	
Milk Goat	
Classification Aged fresh	
Producer Pine Stump Farms	

Pleasant Valley Dairy Mutschli

This original Washington creation is an artisan cheese that is produced from the milk of this family farmstead's cows. Mutschli was first made to be an American version of Swiss cheese, with the same smooth texture but no holes.

TASTING NOTES The raw milk offers a mild though sweet milk flavor that finishes with a hint of toasted walnuts.

HOW TO ENJOY Use it to create a rich warm dish of potatoes au gratin with fresh parsley, red onions, and toasted walnuts. Complement and accentuate its flavors with a nutty brown ale.

USA Ferndale, Washington	
Age 8 – 12 weeks	
Weight and Shape 2–6lb (900g–2.7kg), rounds	
Size Various	
Milk Cow	
Classification Hard	
Producers Pleasant Valley Dairy	

Point Reyes Original Blue

Since its debut in 2000, this Original Blue cheese, made in Point Reyes, California, has become a mainstay on cheeseboards and the recipient of numerous cheesemaking awards.

TASTING NOTES This blue cheese has a pleasant tang, with salty ocean flavors developing as the blue-gray veins mature throughout the creamy, smooth white wheel. The taste becomes more robust with age.

HOW TO ENJOY Crumble over a warm dish of green beans sprinkled with pancetta and savor the taste while enjoying a glass of California Cabernet.

USA Point Reyes, California	
Age 6–8 months	
Weight and Shape 6lb (2.7kg), wheel	
Size Various	
Milk Cow	
Classification Blue	
Producer Point Reyes Cheese	

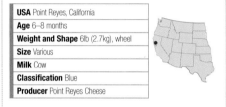

Pozo Tomme

Jim and Christine Macquire started making cheese in earnest when they moved to their small ranch near San Luis Obisbo in 1999. There they established their mixed herd of sheep and goats and soon after they created Pozo Tomme, their flagship cheese.

TASTING NOTES This semi-soft cheese develops a thin natural rind and old world flavors that range from earthy undertones to a distinct nuttiness. With age it becomes firm, and rich in butterscotch flavors.

HOW TO ENJOY Serve on its own or, when aged, grate over grilled vegetables or risotto, accompanied by a Pinot Grigio.

USA Santa Margarita, California	
Age 2–4 months	
Weight and Shape 5–6lb (2.25–2.7kg), wheel	
Size Various	
Milk Ewe	
Classification Semi-soft	
Producer Rinconada Dairy	

Rustic Bleu Goat

The cheesemakers Jumpin Good Goats relocated to Colorado in 2009, from where they continue to produce their award-winning farmstead products as well as other new, regionally inspired cheeses.

TASTING NOTES The unusual, washed-rind, goat's milk blue cheese is aged for four to six weeks and finishes with a hearty, earthy, and robust blue flavor.

HOW TO ENJOY Eat as a salad course, crumbled into a bed of candied walnuts and seasonal salad mix, or with fresh pears topped with a Champagne Vinaigrette.

USA Buena Vista, Colorado	
Age 4–6 weeks	
Weight and Shape 6lb (2.7kg), wheel	
Size Various	
Milk Goat	
Classification Blue	
Producer Jumpin Good Goats	

Samish Bay Cheese Montasio

Although this American cheese is based on the northeastern Italian cheese of the same name, it has a flavor and style of its own that is influenced by the grazing and coastal breeze of Samish Bay. The milk used comes from their own organic herd of Jersey, Dutch Belted, and Shorthorn cows.

TASTING NOTES Firm to the touch, it has a rich creamy taste that becomes more flavorful and complex with age.

HOW TO ENJOY Grate over warm ravioli or fresh cooked spinach pasta, and serve with a glass of Sangiovese.

USA Bow, Washington	
Age 6–9 months	
Weight and Shape 8lb 13oz (4kg), wheel	
Size D. 10in (25cm), H. 3½in (9cm)	
Milk Cow	
Classification Hard	
Producer Samish Bay Cheese	

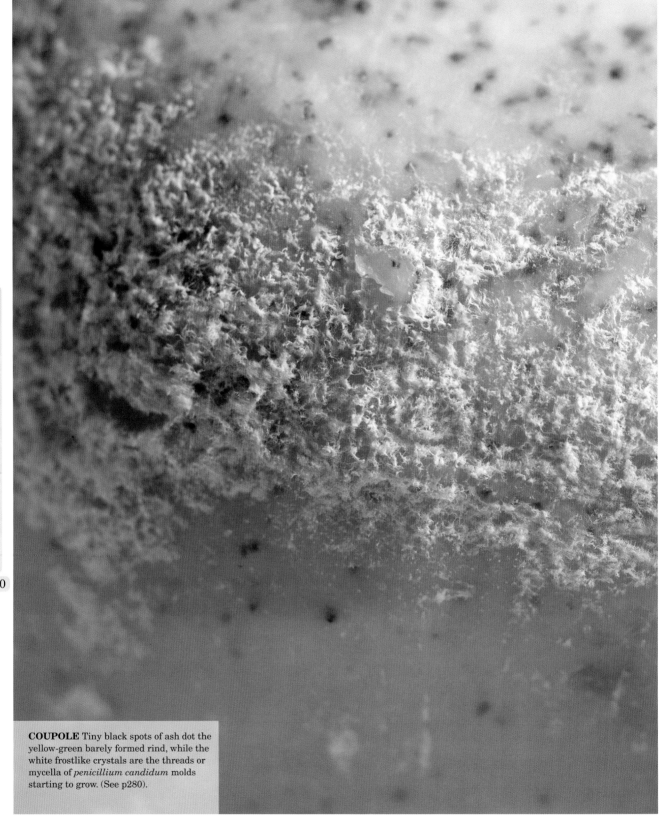

COUPOLE Tiny black spots of ash dot the yellow-green barely formed rind, while the white frostlike crystals are the threads or mycella of *penicillium candidum* molds starting to grow. (See p280).

Steamboat Island Goat Farm Gouda

Jason Drew, a supporter of the Slow Food movement, established Steamboat Island Goat Farm in 2006. His intention was to create handmade goat cheeses that could be produced with integrity and which would support his community and family farm.

TASTING NOTES Farm Gouda is a Cheddar-style cheese with a full flavor of goat's milk, along with balanced meadow and floral undertones and a nutty background.

HOW TO ENJOY Serve with sourdough rolls or as a great alternative to cow's milk Cheddar. Excellent with a Pilsner beer.

USA	Steamboat Island, Washington
Age	2–6 months
Weight and shape	2–10lb (900g–4.5kg), round
Size	Various
Milk	Goat
Classification	Hard
Producer	Steamboat Island Goat Farm

Two Faced Blue Peccato

The name refers to the fact that it is made using a combination of two milks: raw ewe and cow's. It is one of several blues made in the century-old barn on the banks of the Chehalis River.

TASTING NOTES A vein of musical blues runs through each wheel, inspired by the notes of the cheesemaking. The taste is a blend of earthy and floral flavors, encompassed in a soft, natural, and blue-gray rind.

HOW TO ENJOY Eat with fresh figs, honey, and toasted walnut bread for a late afternoon cheeseboard, alongside a Washington State Pinot Noir.

USA	Doty, Washington
Age	3 months
Weight and Shape	10lb (4.5kg) wheel
Size	Various
Milk	Ewe and cow
Classification	Blue
Producer	Willapa Hills Farmstead Cheese

Up in Smoke

The underlining character of the various cheeses produced by River's Edge Chevre is attributed to the abundance of grazing in the meadows alongside the Siletz River and the surrounding woodlands. Up in Smoke is, as the name suggests, smoked, then wrapped in smoked maple leaves that have been sprinkled with bourbon.

TASTING NOTES The combination of smoke, maple leaves, and hints of bourbon provide an unusual but elegant contrast to the lemony fresh tang and creamy texture of the cheese.

HOW TO ENJOY Serve with crusty bread or maple-toasted walnuts and smoked ale.

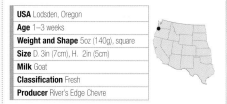

USA	Lodsden, Oregon
Age	1–3 weeks
Weight and Shape	5oz (140g), square
Size	D. 3in (7cm), H. 2in (5cm)
Milk	Goat
Classification	Fresh
Producer	River's Edge Chevre

Vache de Vashon

Influenced by the alpine regions of France, Italy, and Switzerland, Sea Breeze has created their own unique cellar-aged regional and original raw milk cheeses.

TASTING NOTES The essence of apples and pears tease the palette, with a sweet and delicate rich, buttery texture on the finish.

HOW TO ENJOY You can appreciate Vache de Vashon with a dry cider or Sauvignon Blanc along with sweet pound cake for dessert.

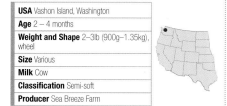

USA	Vashon Island, Washington
Age	2 – 4 months
Weight and Shape	2–3lb (900g–1.35kg), wheel
Size	Various
Milk	Cow
Classification	Semi-soft
Producer	Sea Breeze Farm

Widmers Cellars Aged Brick Cheese

Joe Widmer, a third generation cheesemaker in the town of Theresa, Wisconsin makes a large range of cheeses including this aged brick, a Wisconsin original first made in 1877 that is washed or smeared to create the orange sticky rind.

TASTING NOTES Supple and smooth, the flavor changes from mild and sweet with a subtle nuttiness to pungent and tangy when aged. Also available as a spread.

HOW TO ENJOY Slices for sandwiches, especially with pumpernickel bread, mustard, and onions. Good with ale.

USA	Theresa, Wisconsin
Age	8 –12 weeks
Weight and Shape	5lb (2.25kg), brick
Size	Various
Milk	Cow
Classification	Semi-soft
Producer	Widmers Cellars

Yerba Santa Dairy Fresca

The family originally came from Peru where they made cheese, but moved to the United States and in 1986 bought a farm where they strive to create a model of sustainable agriculture and excellent goats' milk cheeses.

TASTING NOTES Freshly made and delivered to market daily, the creamy taste and brine flavors come through the crumbly texture of this Feta-style cheese.

HOW TO ENJOY Serve a chef's sandwich of Fresca, olives, and roasted red peppers while enjoying with a robust California Zinfandel.

USA	Lakeport, California
Age	1–2 weeks
Weight and Shape	4oz (115g) and 8oz (225g), containers
Size	Various
Milk	Goat
Classification	Fresh
Producer	Yerba Santa Dairy

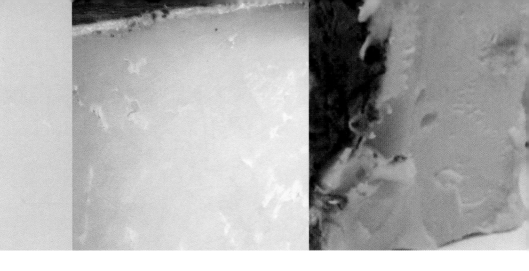

Allegretto

This washed-rind cheese is produced in Québec's far north Abitibi region, an unusual location for dairy sheep production. Its producers believe that the pasture's shorter growing season and the Nordic microclimate give the milk a richer, sweeter taste.

TASTING NOTES The large wheel has an off-white paste with a few pinholes. Its nutty aroma and sweet, full flavor make it very morish.

HOW TO ENJOY Melt on a special raclette grill, or under an ordinary broiler, and scrape onto a crusty baguette, or try it with steamed asparagus. Serve with an amber ale, dry Riesling, or Zinfandel.

CANADA La Sarre, Québec	
Age 60–75 days	
Weight and Shape 7½lb (3.5kg), wheel	
Size D. 12in (30cm), H. 4in (10cm)	
Milk Ewe	
Classification Semi-soft	
Producer Fromagerie La Vache à Maillotte	

Avonlea Clothbound Cheddar

This Prince Edward Island Dairy, well known for its delicious ice cream and funky cow-inspired T-shirts, has moved into cheesemaking using traditional clothbound Cheddar techniques.

TASTING NOTES The gray-green rind bears the impressions of the cloth. The aroma is of fruit and nuts, and has the taste of lingering herbs. The cheese's off-white interior is dense yet crumbly because of its long aging.

HOW TO ENJOY Melt on open-faced roast beef sandwiches, grate into cider and maple syrup soup, or mix into mashed potatoes. Enjoy with ale or Merlot.

CANADA Charlottetown, Prince Edward Island	
Age 12–18 months	
Weight and Shape 17½lb (8kg), tall cylinder	
Size D. 9½in (24cm), H. 8in (20cm)	
Milk Cow	
Classification Hard	
Producer Cows Inc.	

Baby Blue

Using raw and pasteurized milk, the Grace sisters produce a range of blue, hard, soft white, and fresh cheeses from their farm on Salt Spring Island, including this Brie-style blue.

TASTING NOTES The delicate subtle blue flavor has a sweet milk aroma, a buttery texture, and a slight cultured cream finish. Its richness and yellow interior are derived from the unique qualities of the Jersey milk.

HOW TO ENJOY Savor with a glass of Pilsner, Sauvignon Blanc, or Icewine. Melt over poached pears with toasted walnuts for a succulent dessert.

CANADA Salt Spring Island, British Columbia	
Age 30–45 days	
Weight and Shape 5½oz (160g), round	
Size D. 2in (5cm), H. 2in (5cm)	
Milk Cow	
Classification Blue	
Producer Moonstruck Organic Cheese	

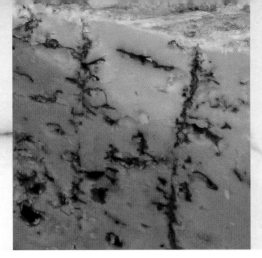

La Barre du Jour

Québec cheesemakers are creating new versions of European classics. This is a goat's milk version of the Swiss Raclette (see p241) and has a thin layer of red Espelette chilli sprinkled through the center like a spicy Morbier (see p69).

TASTING NOTES The thin line of red offsets beautifully the ivory white-colored interior, and the flavors are delicate and mild—until your taste buds detect the heat and spiciness of the chilli.

HOW TO ENJOY This delicious melting cheese can be used in a spicy version of raclette with steamed vegetables, grilled sausage, or shrimp. A dark beer or a Merlot would be a good match.

CANADA Mont-Laurier, Québec	
Age 45–60 days	
Weight and Shape 4lb (1.7kg), wheel	
Size D. 8in (20cm), H. 1½in (4cm)	
Milk Goat	
Classification Flavor-added	
Producer Fromagerie Le P'tit Train du Nord	

Bleu Bénédictin

Produced at Abbaye Saint-Benoît-du-Lac, a Benedictine monastery set among woodlands on the edge of a lake, this blue won Grand Champion at the 2000 Canadian Cheese Grand Prix.

TASTING NOTES Blue Bénédictin has pronounced streaks and patches of blue-green veins throughout the off-white paste, an aroma of mold and salt, and a lingering spicy, salty tang.

HOW TO ENJOY Serve melted over a juicy steak with a red wine jus. Many Canadian sommeliers match this champion with another Canadian icon, Icewine. The wine's sweetness perfectly balances the saltiness of the cheese.

CANADA Saint-Benoît-du-Lac, Québec	
Age 3–5 months	
Weight and Shape 4lb (1.8kg), wheel	
Size D. 8in (20cm), H. 4in (10cm)	
Milk Cow's milk	
Classification Blue	
Producer Abbaye Saint-Benoît-du-Lac	

Bouquetin de Portneuf

An artisanal farmstead-produced cheese based on the famed Crottin de Chavignol, this aged fresh goat's cheese is eaten from 10 days old up to 2 months. The change in its flavor profile is quite amazing.

TASTING NOTES Creamy when young with a rich, lingering flavor and a slight herbal, barnyard aroma; the older cheese is more dense in consistency, with light brown and gray molds on the rind and a piquant aftertaste.

HOW TO ENJOY Melt the young cheese into scrambled eggs with chives, or try with chanterelles, leeks, and puréed garlic. Chardonnay or Pilsner matches well.

CANADA Saint-Raymond de Portneuf, Québec	
Age 10–60 days	
Weight and Shape 3½oz (95g), cylinder	
Size D. 2in (5cm), H. 2in (5cm)	
Milk Goat	
Classification Aged fresh	
Producer Ferme Tourilli	

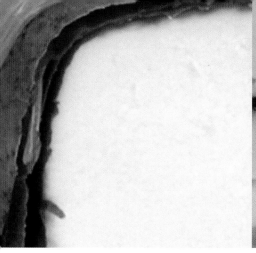
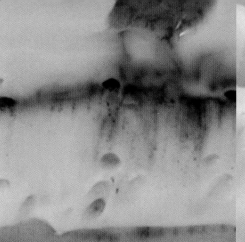
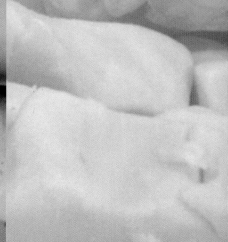

Le Cabanon

This artisanal farmstead cheese is made by Fromagerie La Moutonnière, one of the pioneers in ewe's milk cheese in Québec. It is wrapped in both maple and grape leaves that have first been soaked in alcohol, such as eau de vie.

TASTING NOTES Upon unwrapping the small cheese from its leafy cover, you discover an ivory-white rindless cheese. A slight herbal aroma introduces you to a lingering grassy flavor, and the soft paste melts delicately on the palate.

HOW TO ENJOY Serve with a crisp Viognier white wine, whole roasted garlic cloves, and a sliced baguette, or crumble into salads with a light vinaigrette.

CANADA Sainte-Hélène-de-Chester, Québec	
Age 30 days	
Weight and Shape 4½oz (130g), round	
Size D. 4in (10cm), H. 1½in (4cm)	
Milk Ewe	
Classification Aged fresh	
Producer Fromagerie La Moutonnière	

Le Cendré des Prés

This Camembert-style cheese was first made by Fromagerie Domaine Féodal in 2001. It is produced using local, organic Ayrshire cow's milk and has a decorative layer of maple ash running through its center.

TASTING NOTES The soft, creamy off-white paste has a sweet aroma and mushroom flavor; the ash adds a great visual component when the cheese is cut. The rind is soft and slightly spongy.

HOW TO ENJOY The cheesemaker suggests stuffing the cheese into a phyllo-wrapped seared pork tenderloin. Bake until the dough is golden. Riesling, Beaujolais, or Pilsner is best savored with this dish.

CANADA Berthierville, Québec	
Age 45–55 days	
Weight and Shape 3lb 3oz (1.5kg), wheel	
Size D. 8in (20cm), H. 1½in (4cm)	
Milk Cow	
Classification Soft white	
Producer Fromagerie Domaine Féodale	

Cheddar Curds

Eastern Canadian Cheddar makers discovered that the fresh unpressed curds were a delicious "squeaky" and salty snack popular with their regular patrons. Goat's and ewe's milk versions are now appearing in shops.

TASTING NOTES The white or orange-colored curds must be "squeaky" to be good. Some are flavored with garlic powder, barbecue or souvlaki spices, herbs, or maple seasoning.

HOW TO ENJOY As a snack, still warm from the vat, or in the Québec dish *poutine*—French fries with white Cheddar curds, topped with a brown velouté sauce. Enjoy with an ale.

CANADA All over	
Age Best within 48 hours of being made	
Weight and Shape 9oz (250g) bags, finger-shaped	
Size No size	
Milk Cow	
Classification Fresh	
Producers Various	

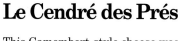

Comfort Cream

Niagara Peninsula's Upper Canada Cheese Company, the first in the recent wave of new artisanal cheesemakers in Ontario, produces this Camembert-style cheese. It is made using milk from a single herd of local Guernsey cows.

TASTING NOTES The warm yellow paste has a subtle mushroom aroma, and the rich Guernsey milk gives the supple interior a delicate, buttery flavor.

HOW TO ENJOY Bake in buttery phyllo dough with local wine jelly. Remove the rind, and melt the paste with other cheese to produce a variation of a Normandy seafood fondue. Serve with a Niagara Peninsula Chardonnay.

CANADA Jordan Station, Ontario	
Age 30–45 days	
Weight and Shape 10oz (300g), wheel	
Size D. 5in (12cm), H. 1½in (4cm)	
Milk Cow	
Classification Soft white	
Producer Upper Canada Cheese Company	

Le Cru des Erables

Influenced by the aromas of its surroundings, this washed-rind cheese is made in an old maple syrup shanty—where the sap is boiled and reduced to a thick, sweet syrup—then washed in a local maple sap liqueur.

TASTING NOTES Beneath the pale pink-orange rind, the light yellow paste has a smooth, satiny texture, while the full, persistent flavor has beefy undertones and a slight barn aroma.

HOW TO ENJOY Melt over mushrooms sautéed with garlic, or serve on a grilled slice of baguette as a great winter snack. Matches well with amber ale or Baco Noir red wine.

CANADA Mont-Laurier, Québec	
Age 45–60 days	
Weight and Shape 2¼lb (1kg), wheel	
Size D. 8in (20cm), H. 1in (3cm)	
Milk Cow	
Classification Semi-soft	
Producer Les Fromages de l'Erablière	

Le Délice des Appalaches

Named after the nearby Appalaches mountain range, the cheese is washed with ice cider, a unique frozen apple-based Québec drink. Apples are left to freeze outdoors, before being pressed to produce this regional speciality.

TASTING NOTES A pale orange rind, off-white paste, supple and velvety texture, scents of apples and nuts, and a mild flavor with a slight lactic aftertaste.

HOW TO ENJOY Serve with an apple-based beverage such as hard cider, Calvados, or ice cider. It melts very well, making it ideal for fondue or used in béchamel sauces to accompany pork dishes.

CANADA Plessisville, Québec	
Age 45–60 days	
Weight and Shape 7oz (200g), square	
Size L. 5in (12cm), W. 8in (20cm), H. 2in (5cm)	
Milk Cow	
Classification Semi-soft	
Producer Fromagerie Éco-Délices	

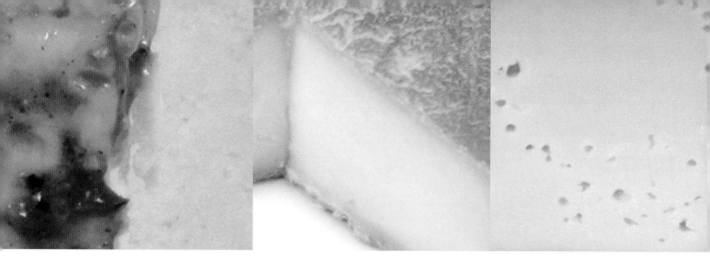

Dragon's Breath Blue

This small black bell of blue cheese covered in a thick black wax coating is made by Maja and Willem van den Hoek, who recommend that you slice off the top and inhale, and, if there is any mold under the wax, mix it in.

TASTING NOTES Under the black wax, the white paste has a few holes, a spicy blue aroma, with a subtle creamy saltiness and lingering flavors, but no bitterness or harshness—despite what its name might imply.

HOW TO ENJOY Stuff it into ravioli with leeks or stir it into freshly cooked pasta, or as a topping for dried apricots. Match to Icewine, beer, or dry Riesling.

CANADA Upper Economy, Nova Scotia	
Age 30–45 days	
Weight and Shape 7oz (200g), cylinder	
Size D. 2½in (6cm), H. 3in (7.5cm)	
Milk Cow	
Classification Blue	
Producer That Dutchman's Farm	

Harvest Moon

Gitta Sutherland makes this washed-rind cheese only at the full moon. Poplar Grove is in British Columbia's Okanagan Valley, renowned for its bountiful harvest of apples, nuts, and grapes.

TASTING NOTES The pale yellow paste has a buttery aroma, supple, silky texture, and delicate cream flavor. The pale orange rind, characteristic of washed cheeses, gives it a slight salty aroma.

HOW TO ENJOY Serve on a cheese platter with frozen grapes and candied or spicy walnuts. It goes well with a wheat beer or Okanagan Chardonnay.

CANADA Penticton, British Columbia	
Age 30–40 days	
Weight and Shape 7oz (190g), wheel	
Size D. 4in (10cm), H. 1in (2.5cm)	
Milk Cow	
Classification Semi-soft	
Producer Poplar Grove Cheese Company	

OKA Classique

One of Canada's best-known cheeses, this was originally produced at the Trappist monastery in Oka, Québec, using methods taught to the monks by a visiting brother from the Abbaye Port-du-Salut in France. Agropur, the province's largest dairy cooperative, now produces it commercially.

TASTING NOTES Washed in brine, this has a tangerine coloured sticky rind with a light yellow pinholed paste, and a nutty, salty aroma. With age, it becomes more meaty, piquant, and farmyardy.

HOW TO ENJOY Great on a cheeseboard, in tarts, or melted on potatoes. A Belgian-style beer is a good accompaniment.

CANADA Oka, Québec	
Age 45–75 days	
Weight and Shape 5lb (2.5kg), wheel	
Size D. 10in (25cm), H. 2in (5cm)	
Milk Cow	
Classification Semi-soft	
Producer Agropur Cooperative	

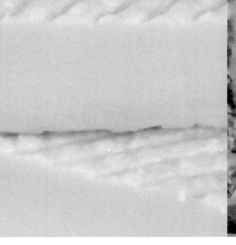

Old Grizzly

This aged traditional Gouda-style cheese is made by an award-winning Dutch artisanal cheesemaker, within sight of Alberta's Rocky Mountains. All of Sylvan Star's cheese are made with milk from its own herd.

TASTING NOTES Over the two-year maturing period, the milk proteins caramelize to a light brown color. When you break a piece off the large boulder-shaped wheel, a sweet cultured-cream aroma is evident and the cheese has a sweet-savory tang.

HOW TO ENJOY Grate over potatoes, soups, pasta, and casseroles, or use in sauces. Match with a big red or a strong beer.

CANADA Red Deer, Alberta	
Age 2 years	
Weight and Shape 22lb (10kg), wheel	
Size D. 14in (36cm), H. 4in (10cm)	
Milk Cow	
Classification Hard	
Producer Sylvan Star Cheese	

Le Paillasson de l'isle d'Orléans

This simple fresh cheese introduced in 1635 by the first French colonists on the Ile d'Orléans near Québec City, it had all but died out until being revived in 2003 by Jocelyn Labbe.

TASTING NOTES The lemon-fresh taste with the sweetness of fresh milk and a hint of saltiness. This cheese has a firm but moist texture perfect for grilling.

HOW TO ENJOY Serve fresh with fruit, or pan-fried with maple-caramelized apples, smoked salmon, and mesclun. Try with sautéed onions and shiitake mushrooms. A light white wine works well with this salty cheese.

CANADA Ile d'Orléans, Québec	
Age 3–10 days	
Weight and Shape 4oz (115g), disc	
Size D. 3in (7cm), H. ½in (1cm)	
Milk Cow	
Classification Fresh	
Producer Les Fromages de l'isle d'Orléans	

Piacere

Similar to a Corsican Fleur du Maquis (see p59), this cheese is coated with rosemary, summer savory, juniper berries, chili, and a touch of gray-green mold, and is made with ewe's milk produced by local Mennonite farmers.

TASTING NOTES Piacere's white interior has a delicate, slightly sweet flavor that balances well with the lingering flavors provided by the herb- and spice-coated rind. With age, the paste becomes very soft and creamy.

HOW TO ENJOY Superb on a cheeseboard, but Piacere also melts well when baked or broiled. A fruity white or a Merlot would be a good complement.

CANADA Millbank, Ontario	
Age 30–45 days	
Weight and Shape 1lb 10oz (750g), wheel	
Size D. 8in (20cm), H. 1in (2.5cm)	
Milk Ewe	
Classification Flavor-added	
Producer Monforte Dairy	

Prestige

Fromages Chaput make an interesting range of raw cow's and goat's milk cheeses based on French artisan recipes. Prestige is a large aged fresh cheese that is made to appeal to those who like a distinctly goaty cheese.

TASTING NOTES The smooth, dense white interior is covered in black olivewood ash overlaid by white and gray molds, adding complexity to the cheese's fresh, aromatic, and slightly peppery taste.

HOW TO ENJOY Perfect for a cheeseboard melted on crusty bread and served with thinly sliced cucumber or leafy green salad. Both Sauvignon Blanc and dry Riesling make good partners.

CANADA Châteauguay, Québec	
Age 45–60 days	
Weight and Shape 4lb (1.8kg), wheel	
Size D. 7in (17.5cm), H. 5in (12.5cm)	
Milk Goat	
Classification Aged fresh	
Producer Fromages Chaput	

Le Sabot de Blanchette

The Guitels have been making raw and pasteurized cheese from their own herd of cows and goats since 1995, using recipes from their homelands, France and Switzerland. Included among these is Le Sabot, based on the cheeses of the Loire.

TASTING NOTES The soft, satiny texture with a delicate sweetness counteracts the lactic goaty aromas. As it ages, blue molds appear on the thin wrinkly rind.

HOW TO ENJOY An attractive cheeseboard choice that also bakes superbly, especially in quiches and tarts. Serve with crisp whites, rosé, or light beer.

CANADA Saint-Roch-de-l'Achigan, Québec	
Age 30–45 days	
Weight and Shape 5½oz (150g), pyramid	
Size D. 1½in (4cm), H. 3in (7cm)	
Milk Goat	
Classification Aged fresh	
Producer Fromagerie La Suisse Normande	

La Sauvagine

Made by La Fromagerie Alexis de Portneuf, a large-scale producer of numerous cheeses, La Sauvagine is a double cream cheese washed in brine. It won Grand Champion at the 2006 Canadian Cheese Grand Prix.

TASTING NOTES The added cream makes it almost runny, rich, and buttery, with a hint of mushrooms. The washed orange rind with its dusting of white has a rustic, farmyardy taste.

HOW TO ENJOY This is superb on its own, but its supple texture means it also melts well, especially when broiled. The creamy richness goes well with ale or a juicy red from Cahors.

CANADA Saint-Raymond-de-Portneuf, Québec	
Age 30–45 days	
Weight and Shape 2¼lb (1kg), wheel	
Size D. 8in (20cm), H. 1in (3cm)	
Milk Cow	
Classification Semi-soft	
Producer La Fromagerie Alexis de Portneuf	

Seven-Year-Old Orange Cheddar

A farmer-owned cooperative, Pine River was established in 1885 on the banks of the river of the same name near Lake Huron. Today, Cheddar is its main business and is colored with annatto, to give it a bright mandarin-orange color, then aged for seven years.

TASTING NOTES The long, slow aging process causes calcium crystals to form, providing a flavor burst and sharp tang. The texture is hard, dry and crumbly.

HOW TO ENJOY This extremely versatile hard cheese is regularly found served with apple pie, an Ontario favorite. Enjoy with strong ale, stout, or porter.

CANADA Pine River, Ontario
Age 7 years
Weight and Shape 5½lb (2.5 kg), block
Size L. 12in (30cm), W. 10in (25cm), H. 18in (45cm)
Milk Cow
Classification Hard
Producer Pine River Cheese and Butter Co-op

Sieur de Duplessis

Pressed and washed in brine, then aged for a period of up to nine months, Sieur de Duplessis is Atlantic Canada's only unpasteurized ewe's milk cheese.

TASTING NOTES The mottled golden brown rind surrounds a firm, dense pale yellow interior that has the sweet, nutty taste of ewe's milk, with floral notes from the pastures. As the cheese ages, the flavor becomes more intense, with a rich meaty finish.

HOW TO ENJOY Although this is almost too good to cook, it has all the versatility of a hard cheese and lends its sweetness to any dish. Match with a full-bodied white, fruity red, or Indian Pale Ale.

CANADA Sainte-Marie-de-Kent, New Brunswick
Age 3–9 months
Weight and Shape 4½lb (2kg), wheel
Size D. 8in (20cm), H. 4in (10cm)
Milk Ewe
Classification Hard
Producer La Bergerie aux 4 Vents

Vicky's Spring Splendour

All of Fifth Town's cheeses are made with local goat's or ewe's milk, and aged in subterranean caves for extra flavor. Vicky's Spring Splendour is covered in a colorful mix of herbs and named after the local organic grower.

TASTING NOTES The herbs grow into the white rind, imparting their distinctive flavor to the cheese's soft, slightly chalky interior. The finish has a crisp acidity with vegetal notes.

HOW TO USE Elegant on a cheeseboard, it also adds another dimension crumbled into salads or baked in fresh figs. Serve with a Zinfandel or India Pale Ale.

CANADA Waupoos, Ontario
Age 30 days
Weight and Shape 4½oz (120g), log
Size L. 4in (10cm) H. 2in (5cm),
Milk Goat
Classification Soft white
Producer Fifth Town Artisan Cheese

Queso Anejo

Meaning "aged cheese," Queso Anejo is simply an aged version of Queso Fresco, or "fresh cheese" and was originally made purely with goat's milk, though nowadays it is more likely to be made with goat's and cow's milk, due to demand.

TASTING NOTES It becomes firm, chewy, yet crumbly with age and has mild herbacious notes that are heightened when cooked, A salty bite, and definitely hot when rolled in paprika.

HOW TO ENJOY Grated or shredded onto various dishes including Chili con carne, enchiladas, and tacos. It is also great crumbled over salads.

MEXICO All over	
Age 2–8 months	
Weight and Shape 6½lb–11lb (5–10kg) rounds or blocks	
Size L. 3½in (9cm) W. 3½in (9cm), H. ¾in (2.5cm)	
Milk Goat or Cow and Goat	
Classification Hard	
Producer Various	

Queso Blanco

Simply meaning "white cheese," this skimmed cow's milk cheese is prevalent throughout Mexico and Latin America. Resembling a cross between salty cottage cheese and Mozzarella, it is made by coagulating the milk with lemon juice and scalding the curds before pressing and kneading them.

TASTING NOTES Lemon fresh and with a buttery mild flavor, it is firm and elastic to the bite.

HOW TO ENJOY Used as a topping for spicy dishes such as enchiladas and empanadas, or crumbled over soups or salads. In Peru it is melted with spices to make a cold sauce for boiled potatoes.

MEXICO All over	
Age From a few days	
Weight and Shape Various	
Size Various	
Milk Cow	
Classification Fresh	
Producer Various	

Queso Fresco

Introduced by the Spanish it means simply "fresh cheese" and is consumed within a few days as it has high moisture content. Made by curdling cow's and goat's milk then lightly pressing the cheese, it is made in homes and large factories.

TASTING NOTES It is very white, creamy, spongy, slightly grainy, and mild with a fresh lemony acidity and slight saltiness somewhere between ricotta and Feta.

HOW TO ENJOY Crumbled over enchiladas or used as a filling in many Mexican dishes, it softens and becomes creamy when heated, but it will not melt.

MEXICO All over	
Age From 1 to 5 days	
Weight and Shape Various	
Size L. 3½in (9cm) W. 3½in (9cm) H. ¾in (2.5cm)	
Milk Cow or Goat	
Classification Fresh	
Producer Various	

Queijo Mineiro

A household staple in the hilly Minas Gerais region of Brazil that produces more coffee and milk than any other state in Brazil. Made by thousands of small producers, the cheese arrived in the region with the Portuguese explorers of the 1500s.

TASTING NOTES Soft and moist with a very mild salty tang and hint of lemon on the palate, it becomes yellow with a white center with age, and develops a deeper tang and slight bitterness.

HOW TO ENJOY Usually eaten at breakfast with French bread, it can be used as a filling in the traditional *Pão de queijo*, bread balls stuffed with cheese.

BRAZIL Minas Gerais	
Age From 4 to 10 days (to a few months when aged)	
Weight and Shape Various	
Size D. 3½in (9cm), H. 2in (5cm)	
Milk Cow	
Classification Semi-soft	
Producer Various	

Requeijão Cremoso

This very popular and now mass-produced cheese can be traced back to an Italian immigrant named Mario Silvestrini who developed the cheese back in 1911. The cheese is made using a secret recipe and is now synonymous with the large manufacturer Catupiry.

TASTING NOTES Soft white, tangy, and creamy, this cheese is easily spreadable, with the consistency of cream cheese but without the sweet taste.

HOW TO ENJOY A great snacking cheese, it can be eaten on bread or crackers, as a stuffing in savory pastries, or even on pizzas. It can also be used as a dessert.

BRAZIL Minas Gerais	
Age From 4 to 10 days (to a few months when aged)	
Weight and Shape Various	
Size D. 5in (12cm), H. 1½in (4cm)	
Milk Cow	
Classification Fresh	
Producer Laticínios Catupiry® Ltda	

Sardo

It takes its name and basic recipe from the famous Italian sheep's milk cheese Pecorino Sardo, which it emulates, and although its hard, grainy texture is similar, it is made with cow's milk and the thin rind is waxed with red or black wax.

TASTING NOTES Hard but less grainy than Italian Pecorino, it has a richness in the mouth and sharp, salty taste with a lingering raw onion bite on the finish.

HOW TO ENJOY Excellent grating cheese, it is sprinkled onto to various local dishes as well as pasta and salads, or thinly sliced as a snack.

ARGENTINA All over	
Age 9–18 months	
Weight and Shape 6½lb–11lb (3–5kg) drum	
Size D. 6in (16cm), H. 4½in (11cm)	
Milk Cow	
Classification Hard	
Producer Various	

JAPAN

Due to the introduction of yogurt drinks, an increase in the number of Western restaurants during the 1964 Tokyo Olympics and the Osaka Expo in 1970, and more Japanese natives traveling abroad in the 1980s, milk products, which were once considered inedible by the Japanese, became a part of the once rice-dominated Japanese diet.

Initially, most cheeses were processed, but after the year 2000, subsidies and technical support from the government led to an increase of cheesemakers, which is why Japan's northernmost island, Hokkaido, now boasts more than 30 cheesemakers. Most cheeses are like Camembert, Emmental, and Edam in style, but some retailers, such as Fromagerie Fermier, are experimenting with small, unique cheeses.

N

Key
★ AOC, DOC, DOP, PGI, or PDO cheeses
Produced only here
Produced throughout the region

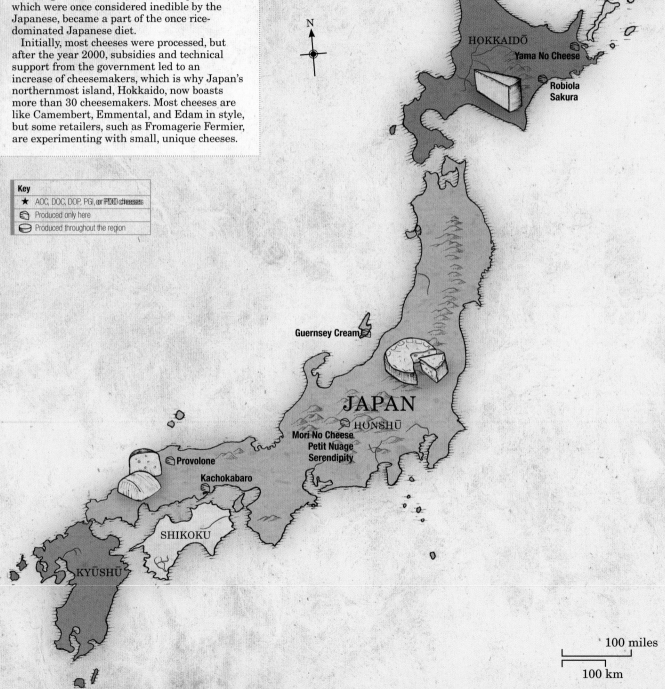

HOKKAIDŌ

Yama No Cheese

Robiola Sakura

Guernsey Cream

JAPAN

HONSHŪ

Mori No Cheese
Petit Nuage
Serendipity

Provolone

Kachokabaro

SHIKOKU

KYŪSHŪ

100 miles

100 km

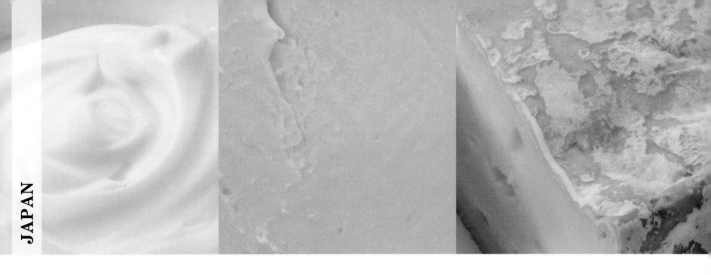

Guernsey Cream

Made on Sado Island, once a place of exile for political prisoners and even a deposed monarch, it is now a pleasant getaway and home to a herd of Guernsey cows. Originally from the small island off the southern coast of England, the breed thrives in the lush pastures on the island.

TASTING NOTES The thick, sweet milk with its yellow tinge is characteristic of Guernsey cows and gives this creamy cheese a smooth and moist feel.

HOW TO ENJOY With pickled plums, called *Kishu no Umeboshi*, and toasted bagels, which bring out the milk's character.

JAPAN Sado, Niigata
Age 2–10 days
Weight and Shape 3½oz (100g), pots
Size D. 3in (7cm), H 2⅜in (6cm)
Milk Cow
Classification Fresh
Producer J.A. Sado Milk Kobo

Kachokabaro

Say the name aloud and you realize it is Caciocavallo, the Italian cheese made in the shape of a small gourd. Made by one of Japan's most renowned cheesemakers, Yoshida Farm, who also make a Camembert, ricotta, fresh mozzarella, and *rakoret* (raclette).

TASTING NOTES It has a hard edible rind, firm, straw-colored fibrous texture, and is slightly sour with a rich lingering milky flavor when young. With age the taste becomes dense with *umami*.

HOW TO ENJOY Cut into chunks and put on a brochette, then melt or grate and use in various recipes.

JAPAN Kaga-gun Kibi Chuo, Okayama
Age 2–3 months
Weight and Shape 1lb 2oz–1lb 14oz (500g–850g), teardrop or pear
Size D. 4⅜in (11cm), L. 5⅞in (15cm)
Milk Cow
Classification Semi-soft
Producer Yoshida Farm

Mori No Cheese

A Japanese original, this washed-rind cheese has a sticky, mandarin-orange rind dusted with blue-gray molds. Made from the milk of a single herd of brown Swiss cows that graze the high mountain pastures giving the cheese a darker color and richer taste. *Mori* is the Japanese word for "forest," so the name literally means, "cheese of the forest."

TASTING NOTES Supple with lots of small eyes, both aroma and taste are reminiscent of fallen leaves in the forest with a wonderful strong robust flavor.

HOW TO ENJOY Excellent with medium- to full-bodied red wine or rice wine.

JAPAN Matsumoto, Nagano
Age 3–8 weeks
Weight and Shape 9–10½oz (250–300g), round
Size Various, D. 4⅛in (10.5cm), H. 1⅜in (3.5cm) (pictured)
Milk Cow
Classification Semi-soft
Producer Shimizu Farm

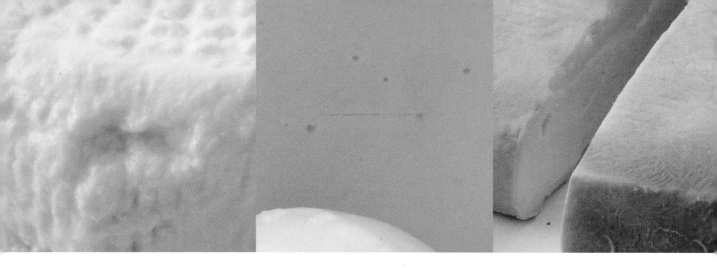

Petit Nuage

Based on the Corsican cheese Brocciu, Petit Nuage is made from the whey of Brown Swiss cows. Its name, "small cloud" in French, refers to its small size and white appearance. After draining, the fresh cheese is turned out of its molds bearing the imprint of the basket weave.

TASTING NOTES Made by heating the fresh whey, this cheese is very white and very mild with the sweetness of milk. The light, delicate almost mousse-like fine curd feels like eating a cloud.

HOW TO ENJOY Delicious as a dessert with jam or honey or in savory dishes, such as pasta or quiche.

JAPAN Matsumoto, Nagano
Age 2–10 days
Weight and Shape 7oz (200g), flat round
Size D. 3½in (9cm), H. 1in (2.5cm)
Milk Cow
Classification Fresh
Producer Shimizu Farm

Provolone

The expense of importing cheese from Europe to Japan has lead to the development of many great Japanese alternatives such as this one, which is based on the famous Italian stretched curd cheese of the same name (see p129).

TASTING NOTES It has a sweet melted butter taste, a fine slightly smoked rind that is covered with wax, and a subtle smoky aroma. Best eaten cooked, as the taste will be more intense.

HOW TO ENJOY Try baking it over rice cakes, especially those made with local rice, *Nitamai*, or on local beef, *Oku-Izumo*, and serve with soy sauce. Also works well baked with honey.

JAPAN Unnan, Shimane
Age 1–3 months
Weight and Shape 13oz (380g), drum
Size D. 3in (8cm), H 2in (4.5cm)
Milk Cow
Classification Semi-soft
Producer Kisuki Nyugyo

Robiola

Based on the popular Italian cheese of the same name (see p136), Robiola means "to become red" in Italian, and refers to the reddish hue that develops on the rind as a result of washing with "Grappa," or grape-based spirit. Shiranuka Farm is situated near the coast on the East Side of Hokkaido.

TASTING NOTES The rich, sweet milk is converted into a strong pungent, meaty cheese with the classic supple texture of washed rind cheeses.

HOW TO ENJOY Delicious melted on oysters, with potatoes, full-bodied red wine, or with locally made grape jam.

JAPAN Shiranuka Gun, Hokkaido
Age 4–8 weeks
Weight and Shape 2¼lb–3lb 3oz (1–1.5kg)
Size D. 8½in (22cm), H. 1in (2.5cm)
Milk Cow
Classification Semi-soft
Producer Shiranuka Farm

Sakura

The cherry blossom, known as *Sakura* in Japan, that for just a week every year paints the country a candy floss pink, inspired the cheesemaker to create Japan's first original cheese. Produced on the cooperative, Kyodo Gakusha Shintoku Farm.

TASTING NOTES Mild, lemony with a melt-in-the-mouth feel. When ripe, it becomes creamy beneath the soft rind and the aroma deepens.

HOW TO ENJOY An elegant addition to a cheeseboard and can be served with green tea or red wine, such as Pinot Noir. Also great with grilled Kobe beef.

JAPAN Shiranuka Gun, Hokkaido	
Age 2–4 weeks	
Weight and Shape 3oz (90g), round	
Size D. 2¾ in (6.5cm), H. 1in (3cm)	
Milk Cow	
Classification Soft White	
Producer Kyodo Gakusha Shintoku Farm	

Serendipity

Produced from spring to fall from goats that graze on the Japanese Alps in the village of Hakuba. Once formed, they are removed from their small round molds, and preserved in pots in rice oil and locally grown herbs.

TASTING NOTES It has a mild taste that balances well with the herbs and subtle rice oil, which is very light and draws out the delicate flavor of the cheese.

HOW TO ENJOY Best enjoyed with a little of the oil on fresh bread or spread on rice crackers with a glass of rosé. Also very versatile in cooking and salads.

JAPAN Matsumoto, Nagano	
Age From 10 days to a few months	
Weight and Shape 5½oz (160g), jars	
Size D. 2in (5.2cm), H 1in (2.5cm)	
Milk Goat	
Classification Fresh	
Producer Kaze No Tani Farm Hakuba	

Yama No Cheese

Yama literally means "cheese of the mountain," and is loosely based on the cheeses made in the French alps. Made on the eastern most part of Hokkaido, the North Island of Japan.

TASTING NOTES Long affinage gives it a firm, compact texture and a complex, nutty, rich lingering flavor and aroma. Its deep yellow color is the result of the lush, green summer pastures.

HOW TO ENJOY Delicious on a cheese plate served with coffee, roasted green tea, salad, or with Hakushaku potatoes.

JAPAN Shibetsu Gun, Hokkaido	
Age 6–18 months	
Weight and Shape 22½–24¾lb (10–11kg), wheel	
Size D. 14in (36cm), H 4in (10cm)	
Milk Cow	
Classification Hard	
Producer Mitomo Farm	

NORTHERN TERRITORY

QUEENSLAND

AUSTRALIA

SOUTH AUSTRALIA

NEW SOUTH WALES

GREAT AUSTRALIAN BIGHT

N

200 miles

200 km

🧀 Woodside Edith
🧀 Washington Washrind

Holy Goat La Luna,
Holy Goat Pandora

Richard Thomas Fromage Blanc,
Yarra Valley Dairy Persian Fetta

VICTORIA

Shaw River
Buffalo Mozzarella

Meredith Blue

Ironstone Extra

Gunnamatta Gold

Gippsland Blue,
Jenson's Red Washed Rind
Strzelecki Blue

Roaring Forties,
Stormy

BASS STRAIT

Healey's Pyengana

Heidi Farm Gruyère,
Heidi Farm Raclette

TASMANIA

Bruny Island C2,
Bruny Island Lewis

INDIAN OCEAN

NORTHERN
TERRITORY

CORAL SEA

AUSTRALIA

WESTERN
AUSTRALIA

SOUTH
AUSTRALIA

QUEENSLAND

PACIFIC OCEAN

NEW SOUTH
WALES

VICTORIA

TASMAN SEA

TASMANIA

NEW ZEALAND

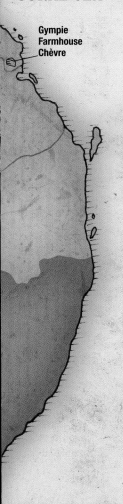

CORAL SEA

Gympie
Farmhouse
Chèvre

TASMAN SEA

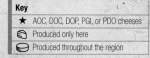

AUSTRALIA AND NEW ZEALAND

AUSTRALIA Although Australian dairy farming began when the first fleet landed in Sydney Cove in 1788, it was not until the end of the gold rush, almost a century later, that cooperatives made Cheddar and butter for export.

Milk production mostly takes place in cooler, southeastern coastal regions. Although low-cost industrial production, quarantine, and protective trade policies once created barriers to the production of artisanal cheeses, demand has resulted in adaptations of European recipes to Australian conditions during the past two decades. However, many local and international raw-milk benchmarks are still banned from sale.

NEW ZEALAND European migrants to New Zealand in the early 1800s had to bring cattle and cheesemaking skills with them. Small-scale family production of Cheddar and Cheshire gave way to farmer-owned cooperatives, and the first dairy factory opened in Edendale in 1882. With refrigerated shipping, Cheddar became a major export by the 1840s; by the 1920s, cheese and butter were being exported to England.

When Dutch cheesemakers migrated to New Zealand in the 1980s with their traditional recipes, the revival of small-scale artisan cheesemaking began. With a growing awareness of the wider cheese world, a growing band of passionate, hands-on cheesemakers began producing alternatives to the great cheeses of Europe and creating unique New Zealand artisan cheeses.

NEW ZEALAND

Mahoe Vintage Edam,
Mahoe Vintage Gouda

Crescent Dairy
Farmhouse

Canaan Labane

Mt Eliza Red Leicester

Mercer Maasdam,
Meyer Vintage Gouda

NORTH ISLAND

Waimata
Camembert

Meadowcroft Farm Goat's Curd

Mt Hector Kapiti

Te Mata Irongate,
Te Mata Pakipaki,
Te Mata Port Ahuriri

Neudorf
Richmond Red

Zany Zeus
Halloumi

SOUTH
ISLAND

Karikaas Vintage Leyden

Barry's Bay Cheddar

Whitestone Windsor Blue

Evansdale Farmhouse Brie

200 miles

200 km

Blue River Curio Bay Pecorino,
Blue River Tussock Creek Sheep Feta

Bruny Island C2

Nick Haddow is passionate about cheese and studied extensively in Europe before settling on Bruny Island, south of Hobart, with his partner Leonie in 2005. C2 was his first cheese, named after the vat in which it was created.

TASTING NOTES Best when at least 9 months old, when it develops a deliciously rich complex nutty flavor with a hint of caramel and mouth-tingling tang.

HOW TO ENJOY Ideal cheese for sauces or melting, or as it is on a cheeseboard. Match with a dry Tasmanian Riesling.

AUSTRALIA Bruny Island, Tasmania	
Age 9–12 months	
Weight and Shape 13lb (7kg), drum	
Size D. 8in (20cm), H. 7in (18cm)	
Milk Cow	
Classification Hard	
Producer Bruny Island Cheese Company	

Bruny Island Lewis

This is another quirky cheese from Nick Haddow based on a mountain recipe he studied in Savoie, France. With no milk produced on the island, the cheese is made from the milk from a single herd of Saanen goats near Cygnet on the mainland. It is named after a beloved family goat that once guarded the vegetable patch next to the dairy.

TASTING NOTES Ripened under an elegant thick natural slate-colored rind, the pure white dense interior is subtly nutty with fresh herbal overtones.

HOW TO ENJOY Enjoy simply with crusty sourdough bread and a glass of chilled Tasmanian sparkling wine.

AUSTRALIA Bruny Island, Tasmania	
Age 4–6 months	
Weight and Shape 3lb 3oz (1.5kg), drum	
Size D. 5in (12cm), H. 3in (7cm)	
Milk Goat	
Classification Hard	
Producer Bruny Island Cheese Company	

Gippsland Blue

Created in 1981 at Hillcrest farm in Gippsland, this natural gray rind cheese was the first artisan Australian blue. Based on Gorgonzola, its milk comes from the farm's Holstein Friesian cows and is matured on wooden shelves in special underground cellars built deep beneath the farm dairy.

TASTING NOTES This rich and creamy blue is at its best when it develops a soft and sticky texture punctuated with steely blue veins.

HOW TO ENJOY A very seasonal cheese—recommended from late fall to early summer—to be enjoyed with an Australian late-harvest sweet wine.

AUSTRALIA Neerim South, Victoria	
Age 2–3 months	
Weight and Shape 12lb (5.5kg), wheel	
Size D. 6in (15cm), H. 9½in (24cm)	
Milk Cow	
Classification Blue	
Producer Tarago River Cheese	

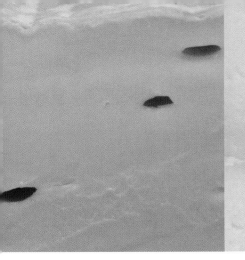

Gunnamatta Gold

Created by Trevor and Jan Brandon at the tiny Red Hill cheesery on Victoria's Mornington Peninsula, this cheese is handmade using organic milk from a farm at Fish Creek in Gippsland. Open to the public, the cheesery is only an hour from Melbourne and takes its name from one of the peninsula's best surf breaks.

TASTING NOTES Beneath the slightly sticky terra-cotta rind lies a soft and creamy cheese with a delicious rich finish and a hint of smoke.

HOW TO ENJOY Like all intense washed-rind cheeses, it needs a spicy, aromatic wine, such as a Mornington Peninsula Pinot Noir, and crusty bread.

AUSTRALIA Mornington Peninsula, Victoria	
Age 4–5 weeks	
Weight and Shape 9oz (250g), round	
Size D. 4in (10cm), H.1in (3cm)	
Milk Cow	
Classification Semi-soft	
Producer Red Hill Cheese	

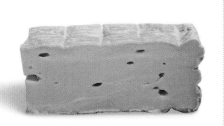

Gympie Farmhouse Chèvre

Camille Mortaud learned his craft in the Poitou-Charentes region of France, renowned for its aged fresh cheeses, and follows the traditions at Conondale in the hinterland behind the Sunshine Coast in southeast Queensland using milk sourced from nearby Kingaroy.

TASTING NOTES The rind turns a gray dusty blue the longer the cheese is aged and can be quite strong; the interior has a delightful savory flavor with a delicious lingering goaty finish.

HOW TO ENJOY Ideal with crusty bread and a crisp dry white wine, or melted and served with wild rocket salad.

AUSTRALIA Gympie, Queensland	
Age 3–4 weeks	
Weight and Shape 4oz (110g), cylinder	
Size D. 2in (5cm), L. 2⅓in (6cm)	
Milk Goat	
Classification Aged Fresh	
Producer Gympie Farm Cheese	

Healey's Pyengana

Dating back to 1901, this venerable cheese from the lush George River Valley is the oldest surviving traditional clothbound Australian cheese. Originally made by a cooperative, the "washed curd" Colby recipe was adopted by the Healey family and is now handmade from the milk of its herd of Holstein Friesian cows.

TASTING NOTES Made in various sizes, but the most sought after are the large wheels matured for at least a year until the moist, open texture develops herbal hints of pasture and honey.

HOW TO ENJOY Ideal with crusty bread and a Tasmanian cider or Pinot Noir.

AUSTRALIA Pyengana, Tasmania	
Age 9–18 months	
Weight and Shape 40½lb (18.5kg), wheel	
Size D. 12in (30cm), H. 8in (20cm)	
Milk Cow	
Classification Hard	
Producer Pyengana Cheese Factory	

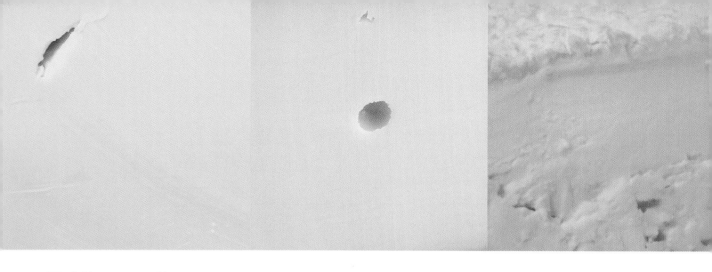
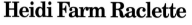

Heidi Farm Gruyère

Weighing in at 66lb (30kg), this is Australia's largest handmade artisan cheese, and has won many accolades since it was launched by Swiss migrant and cheesemaker Frank Marchand. Heidi Farm is now owned by National Foods, but the cheese is still handmade.

TASTING NOTES Sold at various ages, but at its best when aged for at least a year, when its smooth concentrated texture develops an intensely rich, slightly nutty flavor with a hint of honey.

HOW TO ENJOY A wonderful melting cheese, this is particularly good as a base for macaroni cheese. Great with a full-bodied red wine.

AUSTRALIA Exton, Tasmania	
Age 9–12 months	
Weight and Shape 66lb (30kg), wheel	
Size D. 18in (46cm), H. 4in (10cm)	
Milk Cow	
Classification Hard	
Producer Heidi Farm	

Heidi Farm Raclette

Very successfully adapted in the 1980s by farmer and master cheesemaker Frank Marchand from the traditional Swiss raclette, this uses Friesian milk from several local farms and has since won many national awards.

TASTING NOTES Beneath the cheese's sticky, slightly "smelly" terra-cotta rind lies a creamy pliable interior with a melange of grassy farm flavors and a hint of sweetness.

HOW TO ENJOY A delicious table cheese, or enjoy cut in half and grilled in the traditional manner in front of a hot grill. Serve with Pink Eye or similar potatoes and a dry Riesling.

AUSTRALIA Exton, Tasmania	
Age 2–4 months	
Weight and Shape 8lb 13oz (4kg), wheel	
Size D. 12in (30cm), H. 3in (7cm)	
Milk Cow	
Classification Semi-soft	
Producer Heidi Farm	

Holy Goat La Luna

Holy Goat was established at Sutton Grange Organic Farm in 2001, when Carla Meurs and Anne-Marie Monda returned from studying artisan goat's cheese in Europe. All cheese is handmade in their small dairy using organic milk from a herd of 60 very pampered goats.

TASTING NOTES Beneath the rind of this unusual ring of goat cheese covered with a creeping wrinkled gray mold lies a pure white curd with deliciously complex lingering nutty flavors.

HOW TO ENJOY Perfect with crusty bread and a glass of Sauvignon Blanc, La Luna also bakes and melts well.

AUSTRALIA Sutton Grange, Victoria	
Age 4–6 weeks	
Weight and Shape 3lb (1.4kg), disc	
Size D. 9in (23cm), H. 1½in (4cm)	
Milk Goat	
Classification Aged fresh	
Producer Holy Goat Organic Cheeses	

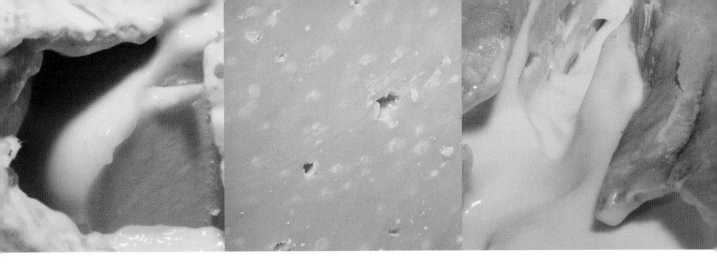

Holy Goat Pandora

The name says it all! This small drum is ripened under a cocktail of molds. It was created by Carla Meurs and Anne-Marie Monda to be enjoyed at one sitting, and customers claim it pairs with everything and never fails to please.

TASTING NOTES At its best when the chalky center has an irresistible soft creamy texture that rarely fails to satisfy with its luxurious feel and refreshingly mild goat flavor.

HOW TO ENJOY Cut off the lid, dig out the center in large dollops like clotted cream, and enjoy with a glass of Sauvignon Blanc or rosé.

AUSTRALIA Sutton Grange, Victoria	
Age 2–3 weeks	
Weight and Shape 7oz (200g), cylinder	
Size D. 2in (5cm), H. 2in (5cm)	
Milk Goat	
Classification Aged fresh	
Producer Holy Goat Organic Cheeses	

Ironstone Extra

After studying overseas, Steven Brown returned home to the family farm near Neerim South in Gippsland to set up a small dairy. Ironstone is based on a traditional Dutch Boerenkaas recipe. All cheese is made between spring and fall from the farm's small herd of Holstein Friesians, to ensure the rich pastures are reflected in the cheese.

TASTING NOTES Matured for up to two years, Ironstone Extra develops a sensational rich, buttery caramel flavor reminiscent of shortbread.

HOW TO ENJOY A wonderful addition to any cheeseboard, or serve in chunks with an apéritif.

AUSTRALIA Drouin West, Victoria	
Age 18–24 months	
Weight and Shape 11lb (5kg), boulder	
Size D. 9in (23cm), H. 4½in (11cm)	
Milk Cow	
Classification Hard	
Producer Piano Hill	

Jensen's Red Washed Rind

This bulging soft cheese from Tarago River near Neerim South in Gippsland, Victoria, is named after one of the dairy founders—cheesemaker Laurie Jensen. Made on the farm using Friesian Holstein milk, it is matured on wooden shelves and hand-washed until it develops a bright orange rind.

TASTING NOTES Beneath the "pongy" rind with its hint of yeast and eucalyptus lies a rich fudgy texture with a mild and creamy flavor.

HOW TO ENJOY Ideal for a cheeseboard. Serve with or without the rind, with crusty bread and sparkling white wine.

AUSTRALIA Neerin South, Victoria	
Age 4–5 weeks	
Weight and Shape 3lb (1.3kg), round	
Size D. 8in (20cm), H. 1in (3cm)	
Milk Cow	
Classification Semi-soft	
Producer Tarago River Cheese	

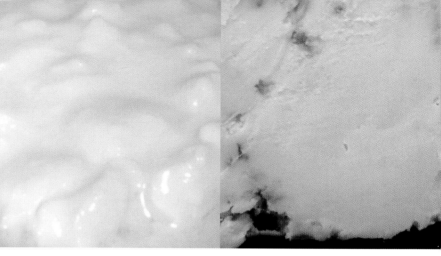

Meredith Blue

Handmade on the Cameron family dairy near Meredith using milk from the largest flock of dairy ewes in Australia, this, the first Australian sheep's milk blue, was created in 1990. It is still matured in old shipping containers next to the dairy, which has an enviable reputation for its goat's and ewe's milk cheeses and yogurt.

TASTING NOTES Ewe's milk is highly seasonal, but is at its best in early spring, when the soft ivory interior texture of the cheese develops dark pockets of salty blue molds.

HOW TO ENJOY Serve with toasted walnut bread or drizzled with local honey.

AUSTRALIA Meredith, Victoria
Age 8–12 months
Weight and Shape 2¼lb (1kg), drum
Size D. 5½in (14cm), H. 3in (7cm)
Milk Ewe
Classification Blue
Producer Meredith Dairy

Richard Thomas Fromage Blanc

This soft, tender hand-ladled cow's milk curd from Richard Thomas is fresh cheese at its simple best. Using milk from the Yarra Valley, it is beautifully presented in self-draining containers that ensure that the whey does not sour the cheese.

TASTING NOTES Its delicate silky exceptionally moist texture has the unmistakable sweet lactic perfume of a dairy, with a refreshingly mild lemony acidity.

HOW TO ENJOY At its best served cold as it comes, or with homemade preserves or fresh berries for a breakfast treat.

AUSTRALIA Yarra Valley, Victoria
Age 1–2 days
Weight and Shape 3½oz (100g), pot
Size D. 3in (7cm), H. 3in (8cm)
Milk Cow
Classification Fresh
Producer Richard Thomas

Roaring Forties

This full-flavored blue cheese is aptly named for the strong westerly winds that buffet King Island, which lies in Bass Strait and is famous for the many shipwrecks along its isolated coast. Straw mattresses washed up from the wrecks are said to be responsible for the island's grasses and ultimately the quality of the milk.

TASTING NOTES The combination of rich creamy milk, blue *"roqueforti"* molds, and a coating of dark blue wax ensures this dependable cheese is always very moist in texture with a sweet salty tang.

HOW TO ENJOY Serve with dark rye bread, and match with a sweet fortified wine.

AUSTRALIA Loorana, King Island, Tasmania
Age 10–12 weeks
Weight and Shape 3lb (1.3kg), drum
Size D. 7½in (19cm), H. 1½in (4cm)
Milk Cow
Classification Blue
Producer King Island Dairy

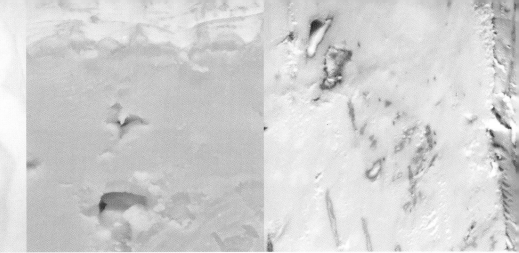

Shaw River Buffalo Mozzarella

Roger Haldene imported the first dairy buffalo into Australia in 1996 against all odds and red tape. The herd grazes on the lush coastal pastures beside the Shaw River, and son-in-law Andrew Royal is the cheesemaker.

TASTING NOTES Unlike in Europe, the herd is pasture-based year-round, with the richest, sweetest milk produced during the warmer months, especially late summer and early fall.

HOW TO ENJOY The slightly firm texture makes it ideal for pizza. Also delicious with vine-ripened tomatoes, fresh basil, and extra virgin olive oil.

AUSTRALIA Yambuk, Victoria	
Age Within a few days of production	
Weight and Shape 1oz (50g), ball	
Size D. 3½in (9cm), H. 2½in (6.5cm)	
Milk Buffalo	
Classification Fresh	
Producer Shaw River Buffalo Cheese	

Stormy

Another great Australian washed rind cheese, this is named after Stormy Bay on the windswept coast of King Island, Tasmania, renowned for its rich and creamy cheeses. Stormy was originally created by cheesemaker Frank Beurain, using techniques borrowed from the traditional washed-rind cheeses of Northern Europe.

TASTING NOTES The soft, buttery paste beneath the "whiffy" tangerine-colored rind has a very mild creamy flavor and slightly salty sea-breeze finish.

HOW TO ENJOY Great on a cheeseboard, melted on pizza with cracked pepper, or served with baked potatoes and beer.

AUSTRALIA Loorana, King Island, Tasmania	
Age 4–5 weeks	
Weight and Shape 5½oz (150g), brick	
Size L. 4in (10cm), W. 1½in (4cm), H. 1in (3cm)	
Milk Cow	
Classification Semi-soft	
Producer King Island Dairy	

Strzelecki Blue

"Count" Pawel Strzelecki was the first person to discover gold in Australia in 1835, and it seems appropriate that his name is now attached to this striking blue. It uses milk from a nearby single farm and is matured in underground cellars beneath the dairy.

TASTING NOTES A seasonal cheese at its optimum with spring or fall milk, it is quick to mature and best when its soft creamy interior is threaded with steely blue veins and the slightly sweet flavor has a distinct savory tang.

HOW TO ENJOY Perfect for a cheeseboard accompanied by a glass of dessert wine or a Gippsland Pinot.

AUSTRALIA Neerim South, Victoria	
Age 2–3 months	
Weight and Shape 4⅖lb (2kg), drum	
Size D. 8in (20cm), H. 7½in (19cm)	
Milk Goat	
Classification Blue	
Producer Tarago River Cheese	

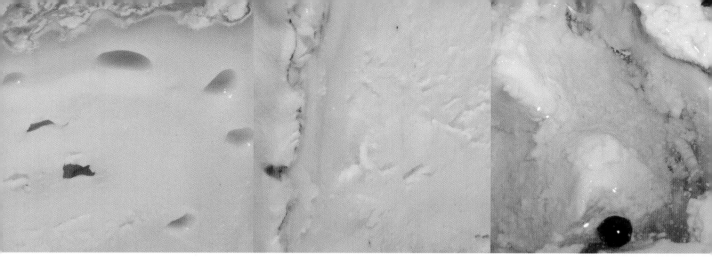

Washington Washrind

Victoria McClurg established Barossa Valley Cheese Company in Angaston's main street in 2003, after extensive winemaking travels in Europe. The dairy makes a range of washed-rind cheeses using cow's and goat's milk. The strongest is Washington.

TASTING NOTES A small orange disc with a very distinct and indiscreet aroma. Beneath the sticky rind lies a smooth silky paste with a mild creamy flavor.

HOW TO ENJOY Perfect on a cheeseboard, the yeasty flavors in the rind match well with the local Coopers ale and wood-fired sourdough bread. Use sparingly when cooking.

AUSTRALIA Angaston, South Australia	
Age 4–5 weeks	
Weight and Shape 8oz (220g), round	
Size D. 4in (10cm), H. 1in (3cm)	
Milk Cow	
Classification Semi-soft, washed	
Producer Barossa Valley Cheese Company	

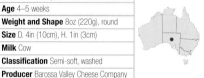

Woodside Edith

Kris Lloyd makes several dozen original cow's and goat's milk cheeses; Edith is one of the oldest and takes its name from the Frenchwoman who provided the original recipe. Its secret is milk quality, handling, and slow overnight fermentation, before being smothered in black vine ash and ripened.

TASTING NOTES Deliciously nutty when young, it ages gracefully, as the chalky center gradually breaks down to a smooth clotted texture.

HOW TO ENJOY Ideal on a cheeseboard matched with crusty bread and Sauvignon Blanc—but avoid eating the peppery hot rind when fully mature.

AUSTRALIA Woodside, South Australia	
Age 3–4 weeks	
Weight and Shape 7oz (200g), drum	
Size D. 2½in (6cm), H. 1½in (4cm)	
Milk Goat	
Classification Natural rind	
Producer Woodside Cheese Wrights	

Yarra Valley Dairy Persian Fetta

There are dozens of marinated feta-style cheeses in Australia, but the first was created by Richard Thomas in 1994, inspired by a Persian recipe and using milk collected from Yarra Valley Dairy's herd of Holstein Friesian cows.

TASTING NOTES Creamy chunks of curd are marinated in a powerful garlicky blend of oils infused with crushed garlic, fresh thyme, and spices.

HOW TO ENJOY A surprisingly versatile cheese that can be enjoyed straight from the jar on toast or crackers, drizzled over steamed vegetables, or as an instant dressing for a salad.

AUSTRALIA Yarra Valley, Victoria	
Age 1–2 months	
Weight and Shape 9oz (250g), tin	
Size D. 3in (7.5cm), H. 3in (8cm)	
Milk Cow	
Classification: Fresh	
Producer Yarra Valley Dairy	

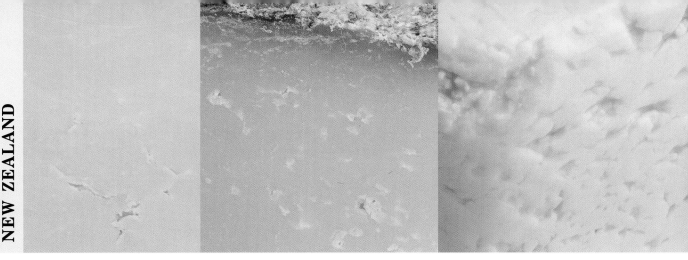

Barry's Bay Cheddar

Since 1989 the Walkers have kept alive the tradition started by early English settlers of making clothbound Cheddar on Banks Peninsular. When Don retired in 2008, Mike and Catherine Carey stepped enthusiastically into his shoes.

TASTING NOTES The only clothbound rinded Cheddar in New Zealand, its hefty rounds are waxed and matured for anything up to five years. At their best, these rounds are hard and granular, with a sweet but sharp mustard flavor.

HOW TO ENJOY Best with good bread and chutney, or an apple, and a bottle of handmade Canterbury beer.

NEW ZEALAND Barry's Bay, Canterbury	
Age 2–5 years	
Weight and Shape 3lb 3oz (1.5kg) and 9½lb (4.5kg) truckles, 79lb (36kg), round	
Size truckle: D. 4½in (11cm) and 6½in (17cm), H. 5½in (14cm) and 6½in (17cm); round: D. 15½in (40cm), H. 14in (35cm)	
Milk Cow	
Classification Hard	
Producer Barry's Bay Traditional Cheeses	

Blue River Curio Bay Pecorino

Blue River sources milk from 3,000 crossbred East Friesians sheep on its own farms throughout Southland. This impressive cheese is the result of the unique grazing and head cheesemaker Wayne Robertson's talent.

TASTING NOTES Hard and granular, almost crumbly, and straw-colored. Sweet and slightly gamey with an edge of salt, it is best at a year old when the paste remains moist and rich.

HOW TO ENJOY Eat in chunks with crusty bread and quince paste. Grate onto pasta, risotto, or polenta, or shave onto salads. Fruity red wines are a good match.

NEW ZEALAND Invercargill, Southland	
Age 10–14 months	
Weight and Shape 4½lb (2kg), round	
Size D. 5in (13cm), H. 4in (10cm)	
Milk Ewe	
Classification Hard	
Producers Blue River Dairy Products	

Blue River Tussock Creek Sheep Feta

Blue River took over the production of this traditional feta-style cheese from another Southland cheesemaker, Chobani. Using the same methods, it continues to make the best in New Zealand and export to the Middle East.

TASTING NOTES Pure white, definitely sheepy, and fatty, but balanced by the saltiness of the brine in which the blocks are stored until sold. This feta has a crumbly but moist texture.

HOW TO ENJOY Perfect for the classic Greek salad, drizzled with a fruity extra virgin olive oil. Match with a citrussy wheat beer or a glass of rosé.

NEW ZEALAND Invercargill, Southland	
Age 10–24 months	
Weight and Shape 4½lb (2kg), block	
Size L. 8in (21cm), W. 4½in (11cm), H. 3in (8cm)	
Milk Ewe	
Classification Fresh	
Producer Blue River Dairy Products	

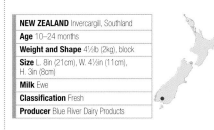

Canaan Labane

Simcha and Ilan Tur-Shalom arrived from Israel in 2003, determined to create the best Mediterranean-style cheeses. The result is a range of irresistible kosher cheeses bursting with character, especially the Labane, a yogurt-based cheese.

TASTING NOTES Light, almost fluffy, it melts in the mouth and tastes wickedly rich, yet is low in fat. Lemony fresh like yogurt, it has a subtle, delicate but never bland flavor.

HOW TO ENJOY Combine with olive oil and za'atar to make a superb traditional dip to serve with pita bread and olives, and a crisp white or rosé wine.

NEW ZEALAND Auckland, Auckland	
Age A few days	
Weight and Shape 7oz (200g), pot	
Size D. 4in (10cm), H. 2in (5cm)	
Milk Cow	
Classification Fresh	
Producer Canaan Cheese	

Crescent Dairy Farmhouse

Crescent Dairy Goats is the smallest cheesemaker in New Zealand with 17 goats, producing just one 4½lb (2kg) cheese a day, yet this hard cheese is a consistent winner year after year at the New Zealand Cheese Awards.

TASTING NOTES Varying one day to the next, sometimes with coconut milk discernible, sometimes cinnamon and thyme, but all develop a fresh, earthy goaty flavor. Best when still moist and slightly soft.

HOW TO ENJOY Too precious as a mere sandwich filling, it should be savored with a good Sauvignon Blanc.

NEW ZEALAND Auckland, Auckland	
Age 6–12 months	
Weight and Shape 3lb 3oz (1.5kg), round	
Size D. 4in (10cm), H. 2in (5cm)	
Milk Goat	
Classification Hard	
Producer Crescent Dairy Goats	

Evansdale Farmhouse Brie

Set up in 1979 by schoolteacher Colin Dennison, to utilize excess milk from the family's house cow, and managed by son Paul, Evansdale remains small, hands-on, and quirky. Its Farmhouse Brie has become a New Zealand icon.

TASTING NOTES Smaller and twice as thick as traditional brie, the Evansdale has a fluffy white *candidum* rind, a smooth and buttery center, and a taste that is both sweet and yogurty sharp.

HOW TO ENJOY: Excellent with buttery Chardonnay or spritzy Champagne. Try with fresh fruit platter of apricots, nectarines, and peaches.

NEW ZEALAND Waikouaiti, Otago	
Age 5–10 weeks	
Weight and Shape 3lb (1.3kg), round	
Size D. 6in (16cm), H. 3in (7cm)	
Milk Cow	
Classification Soft white	
Producer Evansdale Cheese	

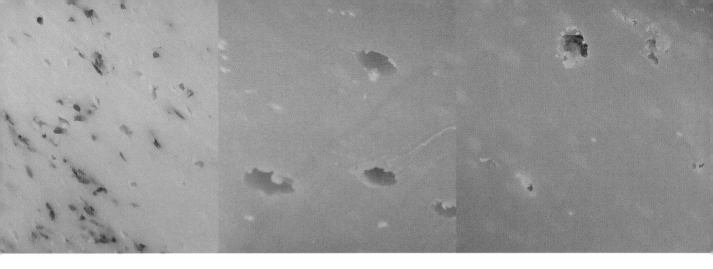

Karikaas Vintage Leyden

Set up by Rients and Karen Rypma in 1984, two of the Dutch cheesemakers who helped to resurrect traditional cheesemaking in New Zealand, the Karikaas Dairy is now owned by a very hands-on Diane Hawkins.

TESTING NOTES Flavored with cumin and a pale sunshine yellow, this Leyden is firm yet supple, sweet, spicy, and with a hint of curry. At two years old, it is drier, sharper, and caramel-sweet.

HOW TO ENJOY Great melted over potatoes, matched with strong, spicy cured meats. The cumin complements mulled red wine or dark ales and stout.

NEW ZEALAND Loburn, Canterbury	
Age 6–36 months	
Weight and Shape 22lb (10kg), boulder	
Size D. 12½in (32cm), H. 5in (12cm)	
Milk Cow	
Classification Flavor-added	
Producer Karikaas Dairy	

Mahoe Vintage Edam

New Zealand's most northern commercial cheesemakers are situated in lush Oromahoe in the Bay of Islands. The Rosevears have been making cheese from their own milk since 1986. Traditionally, this lower fat cheese is mild and rubbery, but when aged is more akin to Parmesan.

TASTING NOTES Butterscotch and caramel, with a lactic acid tang and crunchy texture, this finishes with a bite unexpected from a cheese bearing the name Edam.

HOW TO ENJOY Excellent with aromatic white or dessert wines, it also stands up to a full-bodied red or even beer.

NEW ZEALAND Kerikeri, Northland	
Age 18–24 months	
Weight and Shape 11lb (5kg) or 22lb (10kg), round	
Size D. 9in (23cm) or 13in (33cm) H. 4in (10cm) or 4½in (11cm)	
Milk Cow	
Classification Hard	
Producer Mahoe Farmhouse Cheese	

Mahoe Vintage Gouda

The Rosevears produce cheese from August through to April using milk from their small Friesian herd. After 22 years they remain small and family-run, skilfully producing some of New Zealand's best cheese. Their Gouda is as authentic as any made under that name in the Netherlands.

TASTING NOTES Fudgy, slightly crumbly with age, but not dry, the cheese has a sweet toffee caramel richness that finishes with a bite at the end.

HOW TO ENJOY Shave over a summer salad, or include as the highlight of a lunch platter. Excellent with a sweet or peaty single-malt whisky.

NEW ZEALAND Kerikeri, Northland	
Age 18–24 months	
Weight and Shape 11lb (5kg) or 22lb (10kg), boulder	
Size D. 9in (23cm) or 13in (33cm) H. 4in (10cm) or 4½in (11cm)	
Milk Cow	
Classification Hard	
Producer Mahoe Farmhouse Cheese	

Meadowcroft Farm Goat's Curd

Golden Bay, at the top of the South Island, is the sunniest place in New Zealand and where Averill Turnbull makes her simple but sublime cheese. Her 50 goats are well looked after and carefully milked—the reason, she believes, her cheese is so good.

TASTING NOTES Whether it is plain, rolled in fresh herbs, or marinated in oil, the curd possesses a finely tuned balance of acidity and salt, and a texture that is moist and very slightly granular.

HOW TO ENJOY Perfect on crusty bread with Sauvignon Blanc or Champagne, or spooned over fresh fruit and honey.

NEW ZEALAND Golden Bay, Tasman	
Age 0–5 weeks	
Weight and Shape 7oz (200g), packet	
Size No size	
Milk Goat	
Classification Fresh	
Producer Meadowcroft Farm	

Mercer Maasdam

Maasdam is made by several of New Zealand's Dutch cheesemakers, including Albert Alfrink of Mercer Cheese. He sells it from his small shop, which is packed with hundreds of different Dutch-style cheeses.

TASTING NOTES Proprionic acid bacteria added to the milk produces the small holes in the soft, rubbery interior and a distinctive fermenting fruit sweetness that mellows out with age. With age, it is more like Emmental.

HOW TO ENJOY Excellent with cured meats, particularly ham, it melts beautifully, also making it ideal on pizza or in a fondue. Lovely with an off-dry Riesling.

NEW ZEALAND Hamilton, Waikato	
Age 4–7 months	
Weight and Shape 22lb (10kg), fat boulder	
Size D. 13in (33cm), H. 4½in (11cm)	
Milk Cow	
Classification Semi-soft	
Producer Mercer Cheese	

Meyer Vintage Gouda

Chosen as "Cheese of the Decade" at Juliet Harbutt's last New Zealand Cheese Awards in 2003, this vintage Gouda has been handmade by Dutch cheesemakers the Meyers since the 1980s. It uses a traditional recipe with calf rennet and milk from their herd.

TASTING NOTES Smooth, chewy, and caramel-sweet, with a savory tang and a sprinkling of calcium crystals. At three years, it is as dark, intense, and rock-hard as any Dutch Boerenkaas.

HOW TO ENJOY Lovely eaten in generous chunks with sourdough bread, or in a toasted sandwich with onions. Match with lighter red wines or lager.

NEW ZEALAND Hamilton, Waikato	
Age 18–24 months	
Weight and Shape 22lb (10kg), boulder	
Size D. 13in (33cm), H. 5in (12cm)	
Milk Cow	
Classification Hard	
Producer Meyer Gouda Cheese	

Mt. Eliza Red Leicester

Cheesemakers Chris and Jill Whalley started making cheese in 2007 and are the only New Zealand cheesemakers maturing hard cheeses in cloth. The Red Leicester curd is finely cut and twice-milled, to give it a uniquely authentic close texture.

TASTING NOTES Bright orange from the annatto, this cheese is dense, smooth, and slightly sweet, with a strong bite at the back of the tongue. It is earthy and deep-flavored near the rind.

HOW TO ENJOY Lovely with darker beers and real ale, it is perfect in a sandwich with raw onion or peppery watercress, and makes a good Welsh rarebit.

NEW ZEALAND Katikati, Bay of Plenty	
Age 8–10 months	
Weight and Shape 17½lb (8kg), wheel	
Size D. 9½in (24cm), H. 6in (16cm)	
Milk Cow	
Classification Hard	
Producer Mt. Eliza Cheese	

Mt Hector Kapiti

Kapiti Cheese was established in 1985 and has had a huge influence on cheesemaking in New Zealand. Mount Hector, with its *Penicillium geotrichum* and *P. candidum* molds, and pyramid shape, is decidedly French in style.

TASTING NOTES: At its best this cheese is chalky at the center and runny under the rind, and smells of hay and nuts. Slightly almondy with a sharp lemony tang, it can become very goaty and overripe if left in its wrapper too long.

HOW TO ENJOY Very versatile when young, this is great with fruit compotes, melted, or spread on a crispy baguette, accompanied by a dry white wine.

NEW ZEALAND Paraparaumu, Wellington	
Age 4–6 weeks	
Weight and Shape 4oz (120g), truncated pyramid	
Size D. 2in (5cm), H. 2½in (6cm)	
Milk Goat	
Classification Soft white	
Producer Kapiti Fine Foods	

Neudorf Richmond Red

New Zealand's first ewe's milk cheese, Neudorf Richmond Red was created by Kate Light in the late 1990s. Brian Beuke, her milk supplier, has now taken up the mantle and continues to make this excellent cheese.

TASTING NOTES At 10 months it is dense and creamy with a nutty and caramel sweetness. At 20 months it is hard and the flavor more intense, but not as sheepy and salty at Italian Pecorino.

HOW TO ENJOY Wonderful with sliced pear or quince paste, and the harder version is perfect grated on risotto or spaghetti, with a Pinot Noir or Pinot Gris.

NEW ZEALAND Upper Moutere, Nelson	
Age 10–20 months	
Weight and Shape 3lb 3oz (1.5kg), round	
Size D. 5in (13cm), H. 2½in (6cm)	
Milk Ewe	
Classification Hard	
Producer Neudorf Dairy	

Te Mata Irongate

Set up in 2005, with a viewing galley and excellent café, Te Mata Cheese makes a range of soft and blue cow's, sheep's, and goat's milk cheeses. Included among these is Irongate, based loosely on Pont l'Évêque (*see p78*).

TASTING NOTES A washed rind with white penicillium mold, it is more flavorful than most New Zealand Bries, but milder than typical washed cheeses. It is best when extra soft, russet-rinded, rich, smooth, and slightly smelly.

HOW TO ENJOY Serve with crusty bread and slices of apple and pear, or melt with fried onions. Try with apple or pear cider or even Calvados.

NEW ZEALAND Havelock North, Hawkes Bay	
Age 6–10 weeks	
Weight and Shape 3lb (1.3kg), square	
Size D. 7½in (19cm), H. 1in (3cm)	
Milk Cow	
Classification Semi-soft	
Producer Te Mata Cheese	

Te Mata Pakipaki

Hawkes Bay's hot, dry summers provide the ideal grazing for goats to produce flavorsome, aromatic milk for this Brie-style cheese and Te Mata's pyramid-shaped feta-style Mt Erin and lemony fresh goat's curd Summerlee.

TASTING NOTES Pakipaki achieves the delicate balance of fully realized goat flavors, without being too much for the developing New Zealand palate, although it can be runny, sticky, and feral when slightly overripe.

HOW TO ENJOY Use for goat's cheese tart, or serve with thin, crisp ginger biscuits. A fine match for Sauvignon Blanc or a lighter malt whisky.

NEW ZEALAND Havelock North, Hawkes Bay	
Age 8–10 weeks	
Weight and Shape 3lb (1.3kg), round	
Size D. 8½in (22cm), H. 1in (3cm)	
Milk Goat	
Classification Soft white	
Producer Te Mata Cheese	

Te Mata Port Ahuriri

One of three blue cheeses made by Te Mata from both cow's and ewe's milk, Port Ahuriri Blue distinguishes itself from the plethora of "creamy" blue cheeses available in New Zealand by not adding extra cream and allowing a full blue flavor to develop.

TASTING NOTES The strong flavor of Port Ahuriri is balanced by a salty sweet and nutty undertone. Its texture is almost fudge-like and slightly crumbly.

HOW TO ENJOY Perfect with dried fruits such as dates or figs, or with sticky dessert wines, sherry, or port, Port Ahuriri's intense flavor also makes it ideal for crumbling over salads.

NEW ZEALAND Havelock North, Hawkes Bay	
Age 6–8 months	
Weight and Shape 6½lb (3kg), round	
Size D. 8½in (22cm), H. 3½in (9cm)	
Milk Cow	
Classification Blue	
Producer Te Mata Cheese	

Waimata Camembert

Established in 1995, Rick and Carol Thorpe's Waimata Cheese Company is the largest independent cheesemaker in New Zealand, producing more than 300 tons of soft and blue cheese a year. Despite this, its large Camembert is traditionally mold-ripened and among the best of this cheese style in New Zealand.

TASTING NOTES When young, it is mild and milky, but once ripe can either develop into a light runny vanilla cream or become strong and "farmy".

HOW TO ENJOY Serve in a properly made fresh crusty baguette, ideally with a good sparkling or light white wine.

NEW ZEALAND Gisborne, East Cape	
Age 4–7 weeks	
Weight and Shape 1¾lb (800g), round	
Size D. 7½in (19cm), H. 3½in (9cm)	
Milk Cow	
Classification Soft white	
Producer Waimata Cheese Company	

Whitestone Windsor Blue

Set up in the mid 1980s by Bob Berry, Whitestone is another early pioneer of New Zealand's cheese renaissance. Windsor Blue, its flagship blue, holds true to the company's mantra: "unique as the land that created it".

TASTING NOTES The added cream gives it a taste like blue butter. Fruity and sharp when young, it becomes sweet, slightly salty, and spicy with age.

HOW TO ENJOY Spread on crackers or baguette, toss into hot pasta, or serve with pears and gingerbread for dessert. Match with a slightly sweet, spritzy white wine.

NEW ZEALAND Oamaru, Otago	
Age 3–8 months	
Weight and Shape 2lb (3.6kg), round	
Size D. 8in (21cm), H. 2in (5cm)	
Milk Cow	
Classification Blue	
Producer Whitestone Cheese	

Zany Zeus Halloumi

Mike Matsis's passion for cheese started when his Cyprus-born mother taught him to make halloumi, as her mother had done before her. Fascinated by the process, he decided to become a cheesemaker and makes authentic Mediterranean-style cheeses.

TASTING NOTES Eaten cooked, halloumi tastes deliciously salty, feels slightly squeaky like a dense mozzarella, and has a caramel sweetness from the milk sugars that caramelize on the outside.

HOW TO ENJOY When fried or barbecued on skewers, halloumi becomes crisp on the outside and melts on the inside. Serve with fruity white or red wines.

NEW ZEALAND Petone, Wellington	
Age From a few days	
Weight and Shape 9oz (250g), block	
Size L. 2½in (6cm), W. 1½in (4cm), H. 1½in (4 cm)	
Milk Cow	
Classification Fresh	
Producer Zany Zeus	

Glossary

ANNATTO
Orange-red dye, obtained from the natural pigments in the seeds of the Annatto tree (*Bixa orellana*).

BACTERIA LINENS
Formally known as *bacillus linens*, this bacteria is used to create the sticky orange rind on washed-rind cheeses.

BRINE
A strong salt solution used to seal the outside of some cheeses and prevent unwanted mold from growing.

BUTTERMILK
The slightly sour liquid left after butter has been churned.

CAROTENE
The yellow to red natural colorant that comes from grasses and is converted through the liver into Vitamin A.

CASEIN
Milk's chief and particular protein, precipitated in cheesemaking by acid development and by rennin enzyme, becoming curd.

COAGULATION
Also called curdling, this refers to the separation of the solids and liquids in milk caused by acid and enzyme activity and heat. It is the fundamental process in cheesemaking.

COOKED CHEESES
Cheeses in which the just cut curd is heated or "cooked" in the whey, rendering the curd more elastic and expelling more whey.

CURDS
The solid protein that forms when milk coagulates. This is the basis of cheese. (See also Whey.)

ESTERS
The fatty acids and glycerides in plants. Aromatic esters from flora consumed by animals give aroma and flavor to cheeses.

EYES
The small eye-shaped holes that form in the body of some cheeses during fermentation. Most are small and uniform except in the Gruyère-style cheeses, such as Emmentaler, where they are round and more often referred to as "holes".

FAT CONTENT
Fat is a carrier of flavor and feels soft and creamy in the mouth. If the fat is reduced or removed from milk, it will change its depth of flavor and texture or "mouth feel." The recipe for cheeses that have always been made with skim or low fat milk, however, have been developed to bring out the best in the milk and consumers can rarely tell they are lower in fat.

FERMENTATION
During ripening, the fat, protein, and carbohydrates in the cheese are broken down by biochemical changes with the help of temperature, humidity, bacteria, and enzymes, which affect the texture, flavor, and aroma of the ripe cheese.

FULL FAT
Indicates that the milk has not been skimmed before being turned into cheese. Most cheeses are made from full-fat milk. It should be noted, however, that the fat content of milk is only 3.8 percent for cow's milk to 16 percent for reindeer's milk, and the fat content of cheese ranges from 20–34 percent, significantly lower than most people realize.

GLOBULES
Form in which fat is present in milk. Fat globules vary in size depending on the breed of animal.

HOOP
The container into which fresh curd is packed after salting, it typically has a perforated base and sides, and an open top. (See also Mold.)

LACTATION
The period of time covering the milk production season of a cow, from calving to drying out.

LACTIC ACID
Formed by the bacterial action on lactose in milk. Within three months, the natural acidity of a cheese will kill off the remaining bacteria, leaving the enzymes to continue the ripening.

LACTIC FERMENTATION
The curdling of milk from lactose to lactic acid using only a starter culture (when rennet is not used), traditionally made by souring the previous day's milk or whey. Today, they are mostly prepared in laboratories. Also known as Lactic Cheese.

LACTOSE
Soluble sugar, specific to milk of all mammals. Converted to lactic acid by the enzyme action of some micro-organisms in the Lactic Fermentation.

MARBLING
See Veining.

MOLD
1. The container into which the fresh curd is packed after salting, it typically has a perforated base but an open top with perforations on the walls. The end is fixed. (See also Hoop.)
2. Micro-organisms belonging to the *mycota* family that grow on the outside or inside of cheeses and come from the *aspergillus*, *mucor*, and *penicillium genus*.

MOLD-RIPENED
The process by which molds on the rind of cheeses, typically white, gray-blue, and orange colored, speed up the breakdown of the curd.

ORGANIC
Cheeses produced on farms approved by an official, government scheme that adheres to the principles of organic production, such as no pesticides or chemicals on the land, in the dairy, or for the animals.

PASTA FILATA
Also known as Stretched Curd, a technique whereby curd is immersed in hot acid whey to make it elastic, then kneaded or stretched in hot water. Examples include Mozzarella and Provolone.

PASTEURIZATION
The heat treatment of raw milk for at least one minute at 163°F (73°C) to destroy any potential harmful micro-organisms. Unfortunately, it also destroys many flavor-enriching micro-organisms.

PASTE
Used in European cheeses to describe the interior of a cheese. Also known as Pâte.

PENICILLIUM CANDIDUM
A white mold with a mushroom aroma and taste that grows on soft white cheeses such as Camembert and Brie.

PIERCING
Inserting of needles into a cheese to facilitate the entry and development of blue molds.

PROCESSED CHEESE
Cheese is heated along with an emulsifying agent, oil, and water, and shaped when hot and immediately sealed in its final pack.

PROTEOLYSIS
Breakdown of proteins by enzymes, acids, alkalis or heat.

RANCID
Used as a general term for unpleasant flavors in fats.

RAW MILK
Term used to describe milk, in its natural state, not subjected to pasteurization.

RENNET
An enzyme extracted from the stomach lining of a milk-fed animal, which breaks down the solids in milk into a digestible form, helping coagulation.

RIPENING
1. (of milk) Natural maturing of milk through rising acidity before renneting, without addition of starter culture.
2. (of cheese) Continuing enzyme action of rennet and completion of bacterial action on curd, and consequent enzyme action.

SERUM
See Whey.

SILAGE
Grasses and legumes preserved by air-free storage, with limited fermentation.

SMEAR-RIPENED
A cheese whose rind is rubbed or smeared with a solution of brine and *bacillus linens*, usually with a cloth that forms a sticky orange rind.

STARTER CULTURE
Typically a combination of lactic bacterial cultures used to start transformation of lactose to lactic acid which causes the milk to curdle. Mostly used in conjunction with rennet.

TABLE CHEESE
A term used in Italy to describe a hard cheese that can be used as an eating or snacking cheese as well as in cooking, and was traditionally left on the table.

THERMIZED CHEESES
Cheeses whose curd has been heated to 130°F (54°C) in the whey—lower than pasteurization.

TURNING
The process of regularly turning a whole cheese while maturing, it ensures that the moisture in a cheese is evenly distributed and the mold grows evenly.

VAT
A container in which the milk is contained for cheesemaking.

VEGETARIAN CHEESE
Cheeses in which a non-animal alternative to rennet is used to curdle the milk, in place of the more traditional animal rennet. The difference in taste in most cheeses is barely distinguishable.

VEINING
Also known as Marbling, this refers to the streaks or lines of blue mold found in the body of all blue cheeses. The Italians use the word *erborinatura* and the French use the term *persille* (both mean "parsley") to describe the scattered veining in their traditional cheeses.

WASHED RIND
Cheeses that are washed regularly over a period of time, not just once or twice, in a brine solution, often mixed with spices or alcohol, creating a sticky orange rind.

WHEY
The liquid residue of milk after most of the solids, including the fats, have been coagulated into curd. It is sometimes referred to as Serum.

Cheese-tasting terms

The following terms are commonly used to describe the aroma, texture, and flavor of cheese:

Acidity In a cheese, like wine, this can be a positive attribute if it is not excessive—it leaves a refreshing, sometimes tingly, sensation in the mouth.

Aromatic A sensation of varied and interesting aromas—could be spicy, perfumed, herbaceous, or fruity.

Bite A distinct, sharp, intense initial flavor, usually carried through to the finish.

Bitter A characteristic taste of some cheeses; can be a positive attribute as in strong Cheddar or a fault when used to describe Brie.

Body The sensation of weight and substance in the mouth, like red wine or Port.

Dry A feeling of lack of moisture in the mouth.

Earthy An aroma of freshly tilled soil.

Elastic A firm but flexible texture that returns to its original shape after gentle pressure, often with a tearable layered texture.

Finish The aftertaste, or sensation left on the palate after the last mouthful.

Friable The tendency of a cheese to crumble into small grainy fragments.

Fruity A flavor reminiscent of both the odor and taste of fresh fruit picked at its optimum stage of ripeness, such as pears, apples, melons, and mangoes.

Grainy A texture in which barely detectable small particles can be discerned—these are usually salt or crystals of calcium lactate.

Grassy Characteristic flavor of freshly cut grass.

Green Grass A fresh, pleasantly sharp grassy flavor.

Herbaceous The leafy fragrance of wild flowers, hedges, and grasses.

Lactic The taste of slightly soured milk.

Lactose The sugar in milk that is converted to lactic acid as the milk sours.

Metallic The mold in blue cheeses can be mild and slightly fruity, reminiscent of tarragon and thyme, or when strong develops a distinct sharp mineral or metallic taint.

Moist Used in contrast to "dry", as in the texture of some cakes.

Pungent A forceful, pleasant, sometimes almost bitter flavor reminiscent of chicory, or fresh young grass.

Rubbery A bouncy springy feel and a rippable, rather than breakable, texture

Smooth An absence of any structure, like heavy cream or custard.

Soft A yielding texture like mashed potato or cheesecake.

Squeaky When curd is washed it becomes very smooth and feels shiny and "squeaky" clean.

Supple More dense than "rubbery", as it has an underlying structure.

Tangy A tart or acidic flavor that causes the mouth to pucker and tingle. Often associated with mature hard cheeses such as Cheddar.

Unctuous Fatty and greasy to English speakers but creamy, rich, and luxurious when used by some Europeans.

Velvety Thick but soft, smooth, and without structure, such as processed cheese.

Resources

If you would like to explore the cheese world further, Juliet Harbutt's website is a great resource. **www.thecheeseweb.com.** To bring a world of cheeses to your refrigerator, this choice of suppliers from around the globe is an excellent start.

USA
Artisanal
www.artisanalcheese.com
Tel: +1 877 797 1200
This mail order company ships worldwide.

Beecher's Handmade Cheese
www.beechershandmadecheese.com
1600 Pike Place, Seattle, WA 98101
Tel: +1 206 956 1964

Buzios Brazilian Store
20 West 46th Street, New York, NY
Tel: +1 212 869 6552

Central Market
www.centralmarket.com

4001 N. Lamar Blvd. Austin, TX 78756
Tel: +1 512 206-1000

5750 E. Lovers Ln. Dallas, TX 75206
Tel: +1 214 234-7000

3815 Westheimer, Houston, TX 77027
Tel: +1 713 386-1700

4821 Broadway St. San Antonio, TX 78209
Tel: +1 210 368-8600

Chelsea Market Baskets
www.chelsemarketbaskets.com
Tel: +1 888 727 7887
This is a mail order store that ships throughout the US.

The Cheese Works
www.thecheeseworks.com
Tel: +1 800 962 1220
This is a mail order store only for those in the California area.

Cowgirl Creamery
www.cowgirlcreamery.com

Ferry Plaza, 1 Ferry Building, #17, San Francisco, CA 94111
Tel: +1 415 362 9354

919 F Street, Penn Quarter, Washington, D.C. 20004
Tel: +1 202 393 6880
Di Bruno Bros.
www.dibruno.com

1730 Chestnut Street, Philadelphia, PA 19103
Tel: +1 215-665-9220

1701 JFK Blvd, Philadelphia, PA 19103
Tel: +1 215-531-5666

Fahey & Fromagerie
51 Pleasant St. Nantucket, MA 02554
Tel: +1 508 325 5644

Gourmet International
www.gourmetint.com
Tel: +1 800 875 5557
This is a mail order store that ships throughout the US.

Grace's Marketplace
www.gracesmarketplace.com

1237 Third Avenue NYC 10021
Tel: +1 212 737 0600

81 Glen Cove Road, Greenvale, Long Island, NY 11548
Tel: +1 516 621 5100

HEB
www.heb.com
Tel: +1 512 421 1170
4544 South Lamar Blvd, Austin, TX 78745

igourmet
www.igourmet.com
Tel: +1 877 446 8763
This mail order store ships throughout the US.

La Fromagerie
www.lafromagerieonline.com
1222 King Street, Alexandria, VA 22314
Tel: +1 703 879 2467

Murray's Cheese Shop
www.murrayscheese.com

254 Bleecker St. New York, NY 10014
Tel: +1 212 243.3289

43rd St. & Lexington, New York, NY 10017
Tel: +1 212 922.1540

Taste
www.tastecheese.com
1243 1/2 University Ave, San Diego, CA 92103
Tel: +1 619 683 2306

St. James Cheese Company
www.stjamescheese.com
5004 Prytania Streer, New Orleans, LA 70118
Tel: +1 504 899 4737

Trader Joe's
www. traderjoes.com

8928 Holly Ave NE, Albuquerque, NM 87122
Tel: +1 505 796 0311

5600 N Port Washington Rd, Milwaukee, WI 53217
Tel: +1 414 962 3382

3909 Hillsboro Pike, Nashville, TN 37215
Tel: +1 615 297 6560

Vermont Shepherd Farm
www.vermontshepherd.com
281 Patch Farm Road, Putney, VT 05346
Tel: +1 802 387 4473

Whole Foods
www.wholefoodsmarket.com

Ponce de Leon, 650 Ponce de Leon Ave NE, Atlanta, GA 30308
Tel: +1 404 853 1681

2693 Edmonson Rd, Cincinnati, OH 45209
Tel: +1 513 531 8015

Capitol Hill, 900 E. 11th Ave, Denver, CO 80218
Tel: +303 832 7701

Galleria, 1601 S. Brentwood Blvd, St. Louis, MO 63144
Tel: +314 968 7744

Zingerman's Deli
www.zingermansdeli.com
422 Detroit St. Ann Arbor, MI 48104
Tel: +1 734 663 3354

Zupan's Markets
www.zupans.com
3301 SE Belmont, Portland, OR
Tel: +1 503 239 3720

CANADA
Denninger's Foods of the World
www.denningers.com

699 Guelph Line Burlington, ON
Tel: +1 905-639-0510

284 King Street East Hamilton, ON
Tel: +1 905-528-8468

Jackson Square Mall, 2 King Street West,
Hamilton, ON
Tel: +1 905-525-9641

2410 Lakeshore Road Oakville, ON
Tel: +1 905-827-3717

Fromagerie Hamel
www.fromageriehamel.com
220 rue Jean-Talon Est, Montréal, QC
Tel: +1 514 272 1161

Gourmet Laurier
1042 rue Laurier ouest, Montréal, QC H2V 2K8
Tel: +1 514 274 5601

Les Amis du Fromage
www.buycheese.com

843 East Hastings Street, Vancouver, BC V6A 1R8
Tel: +1 604-253-4218

#518 Park Royal South, Vancouver, BC V7T 2W4
Tel: +1 604-925-4218

1752 West 2nd Avenue, Vancouver, BC V6J 1H6
Tel: +1 604 732 4218

Yannick Fromagerie
www.yannickfromagerie.ca
11690 rue du Salaberry (Marché de l'Ouest),
Dollard-des-Ormeaux H9B 2R8
Tel: +1 514 421 9944

UK
Barrington's Delicatessen
www.barringtonsdeli.co.uk
60 High Street, Bishops Waltham, Hampshire
SO32 1AB
Tel: +44 (0) 14 8989 6600

The Borough Cheese Company
www.boroughcheesecompany.com
At Borough Market, 8 Southwark Street SE1 1TL

The Cheeseboard,
1 Commercial Street, Harrogate, North Yorkshire
Tel: +44 (0) 14 2350 8837

The Cheeseworks
www.thecheeseworks.co.uk
5 Regent Street, Cheltenham, Gloucestershire
Tel: +44 (0) 12 4225 5022

The Cotswold Delicatessen
www.cotswolddelicatessen.co.uk
2 Middle Row, Chipping Norton OX7 5NH
Oxfordshire
Tel: +44 (0) 16 0864 2843

Harrods
www.harrods.com
87-135 Brompton Road, SW1X 7XL
Tel: +44 (0) 20 7730 1234

KäseSwiss
www.kaseswiss.co.uk
At Borough Market, 8 Southwark Street SE1 1TL
Mortimer and Bennet
www.mortimerandbennett.co.uk
33 Turnham Green Terrace, London W4 1RG
Tel: +44 (0) 20 8995 4145

Mr. Christian's
www.mrchristians.co.uk
11 Elgin Crescent, Notting Hill, London W11 2JA
Tel: +44 (0) 20 7229 0501

Neal's Yard Dairy
www.nealsyarddairy.co.uk
17 Shorts Gardens, London WC2H 9AT
Tel: +44 (0)20 7240 5700

Rick Stein's Delicatessen
www.rickstein.com
South Quay, Padstow, Cornwall PL28 8BY
Tel: +44 (0)1841 533486

Rippon Cheese Stores
www.ripponcheese.com
26 Upper Tachbrook Street, SW1V 1SW
Tel: +44 (0) 20 7931 0628/0668

Scandinavian Kitchen
www.scandikitchen.co.uk
61 Great Titchfield Street, W1W 7PP
Tel: +44 (0) 20 7580 7161

Wensleydale Cheese Shop
www.wensleydale.co.uk
Wensleydale Creamery, Gayles Lane, Hawes, North
Yorkshire
Tel: +44 (0) 19 6966 7664

ITALY
Casa del Parmigiano
www.famigliagastaldello.it
Piazza Castello, 25, 36063 Marosica, Vicenza
Tel: +39 (0) 424 75071

FRANCE
Androuët
www.androuët.com
134, rue Mouffetard - 75005 Paris
Tel: +33 (0) 1 45 87 85 05

Fauchon
www.fauchon.com
24-26 Place de la Madeleine, Paris
Tel: +33 (0) 1 70 39 38 00

Fromagerie Barthélémy (Sté)
Ad51, rue de Grenelle, 75007 Paris.
Tel: +33 (0) 1 42 22 82 24

Quatrehomme
62 Rue Sèvres, 75007 Paris
Tel: +33 (0) 1 47 34 33 45
SPAIN
Poncelet
www.poncelet.es
Calle Argensola, 27, 28004-Madrid
Tel: +34 (0) 91 308 02 21

BELGIUM
Kaasaffineurs Michel Van Tricht & zoon
www.kaasmeestervantricht.be
Fruit Hoflaan 13-15, 2600 Berchem
Tel: +32 (0) 3440 7212

THE NETHERLANDS
De Kaaskammer
Runstraat 7, Jordaan, 1016, Amsterdam
Tel: +31 (0) 20 623 3483

ISRAEL
Ran Buck's Cheese Cellar
www. gvina.co.il
81 Sokolov St. Ramat Hasharon
Tel: +972 3 547 2332

JAPAN
Fermier
www.shopping.fermier.fm
1 F Atago AS Building, 1-5-3, Atago, Minato-ku,
Tokyo 105 0002

AUSTRALIA
Rosalie Gourmet Market
www.rosaliegourmet.com.au
Rosalie Village, Paddington, Brisbane
Tel: +61 (0) 7 3876 6222

NEW ZEALAND
Canterbury Cheesemongers
www.cheesemongers.co.nz
44 Salisbury St, Christchurch, New Zealand.
Tel: +64 (0) 3 379 0075

Index

A

A Casinca 32
A Filetta 32
Abbaye de Cîteaux 30
Abbaye du Mont des Cats 30
Abbaye Notre-Dame de Belloc 30
Abbaye de la Pierre-qui-Vire 31
Abbaye de Tamié 31
Abbaye de Troisvaux 100
Abondance AOC 31
Ädelost 250
Affidélis (Plaisir au Chablis) 77
affineurs 7
Afuega'l Pitu DOP 148
Aged Fresh cheeses 8, 12–13, 24, 25
Aged Green Peppercorn Chèvre 270
Agrì di Valtorta 142
Ahumado de Pría 148
Aisy Cendré 48
Akkawi 264
Allegretto 312
Allerdale 172
Allgäuer Bergkäse 235
Allgäuer Emmental 234, 235
Almkäse 104
Alpine Lakes Creamy Bleu 306
Alsea Acre Fromage Blanc 270
L'Alt Urgell y La Cerdanya DOP 148
Altenburger Ziegenkäse PDO 234, 235
Ami du Chambertin 32
Anari 261
Ancient Heritage Scio 306
Andante Dairy Picolo 270
Angelot (Pont-l'Evêque AOC) 78
Anthotyros DOC 256, 257
AOC 8
Appalachian 271
Appel Farms Cheddar 271
Appenzeller 240
Ardi-Gasna 33
Ardrahan 219
Ardsallagh 219
Argentina 269, 321
Arômes au Gêne de Marc 33
Arzúa-Ulloa DOP 149
Ascutney Mountain Cheese 271
Ashed Tomette 272
Asiago PDO 104
Asiago d'Allevo 104
Asiago Pressato 104
Australia 326–34
Austria 234, 238–9
Avonlea Clothbound Cheddar 312
Awe Brie 272
Ayr (Vermont Ayr) 304
Azeitão DOP 167

B

Baby Blue 312
Baby Muenster (Oltermanni) 253
Bad Ax 306
Bagòss 104
Baguette Laonnaise 33
Banon
    Banon AOC 34
    Banon aux Baies Roses 34
    Banon à la Sarriette 34
    Hoja Santa 288
Barely Buzzed 272
Barkham Blue 172
Barossa Valley Washington Washrind 334
La Barre du Jour 313
Barry's Bay Cheddar 335

Bastardo del Grapa 105
Bastelicaccia 100
Bath Soft Cheese 172
Bath, Wyfe of 206
Bauernkäse (Lagundo) 143
Bauma Carrat 149
Bavaria Blu (Bavarian Blue) 21, 236
Bayerische Bierkäse (Weisslacker) 237
Bayley Hazen Blue 273
Beato de Tábara 149
Beaufort AOC 18, 19, 38–9
Beaufort d'Alpage 38
Beaufort d'Hiver 38
Beechers Flagship Reserve 306
Beenleigh Blue 173
Beenoskee 220
Beira Baxta (Castelo Branco DOP) 167
Bel Paese 119
Bela Badia 143
Belgium 226, 227–9
Bella Italia 119
Bella Milano 119
Belle Chèvre 273
Bellelay (Tête de Moine AOC) 244
Bellingham Blue 219
Bellwether Farms Crescenza 273
Benabarre 150
Benasque 150
Bergkäse (Pusteria) 144
Bergues 35
Berkswell 25, 173
Bernardo 143
Berrichon 35
Bethmale 35
Bettelmatt 105
Beyaz Peynir 261
Big Island Feta 274
Big Woods Blue 274
Bio Bleu 227
Birdwood Blue Heaven 173
Bishop Kennedy 207
Bitto DOC PDO 105
Bla Castello 247
Black-eyed Susan 174
Blacksticks Blue 174
Blanca Bianca 274
Bleu Age 307
Bleu d'Auvergne AOC 36
Bleu Bénédictin 313
Bleu des Causses AOC 36
Bleu de Chèvre 36
Bleu de Gex Haut-Jura AOC 37
Bleu Mont Cheddar 275
Bleu de Termignon 307
Bleu du Vercors-Sassenage AOC 37
Blissful Blue Buffalo 174
Blue Castello (Bla Castello) 247
Blue cheeses 8, 20–1, 25, 302
Blue Monday 207, 212
Blue Moon (Gorau Glas) 214
Blue Pearl (Perl Las) 215
Blue River Curio Bay Pecorino 335
Blue River Tussock Creek Sheep Feta 335
Blue Vinney, Dorset 178
Blythedale Farm Camembert 275
Bonde de Gâtine 40
Boulette d'Avesnes 40, 100
Boulette de Cambrai 40
Boulette de Papleux 100
Bouquetin de Portneuf 313
Bourrée 275
Bouton-de-Culotte 41
Bouyguette des Collines 41
Bra DOC PDO 107
Bra Duro 107
Bra Tenero 107
Braculina (Paglierine) 124
Branzi 107
Brazil 269, 321
Brebis du Lochois 41
Bridgewater Round 277

Brie & Brie-style
    Awe Brie 272
    Baby Blue 312
    Bath Soft Cheese 172
    Bla Castello 247
    Brie de Meaux AOC 14, 15, 46–7
    Brie de Melun AOC 15, 42
    Brie de Nangis 42
    Clava Brie 208
    Coulommiers 53
    Evansdale Farmhouse Brie 336
    Fougerus 60
    Hartwell 288
    Le Petit Chèvre Bleu 295
    Pont Gar 215
    St. Endellion 195
    Sharpham 15, 195
    Te Mata Irongate 340
    Te Mata Pakipaki 340
Brigid's Abbey 277
Brillat-Savarin 42
Brindamour (Fleur du Maquis) 59
Brindisi Fontina 307
Brique du Forez 43
Brocciu
    Brocciu AOC 43
    Brocciu Pasu 43
    Petit Nuage 324
Brossauthym 43
Bruny Island C2 328
Bruny Island Lewis 328
Bryndza PGI 260
Bubulus Bubalis Mozzarella di Bufala 277
Buchette Pont d'Yeu 44
Buffalo Blue 175
buffalo milk cheeses 6
    Blissful Blue Buffalo 174
    Buffalo Blue 175
    Pendragon 189
    Ricotta di Bufala Campana (PDO transitory list) 144
    see also Caciocavallo; Mozzarella
Burrata 107, 145

C

C2 (Bruny Island C2) 328
Le Cabanon 314
Cabécou de Rocamadour (Rocamadour AOC) 80
Caboc 210–11, 212
Cabot Clothbound 278
Cabra Rufino 151
Cabra Transmontano DOP 167
Cabrales DOP 150, 153
Cabri Ariégeois 44
Cacio Reale 119
Caciocavallo 108
    Caciocavallo Occhiato 108
    Caciocavallo Podolico 108
    Caciocavallo Silano PDO 109
    Kachokabaro 323
Cacioricotta 143
Caciotta 109
Caciotta di Pecora (Toscanello) 145
Caerphilly & Caerphilly-style 171, 204, 215, 216–17
    Caws Cenarth 215, 216
    Dragons Back 213
    Lavistown 223, 224
Cairnsmore Ewes 207
Calcagno 109
Camembert & Camembert-style 322
    Bavaria Blu (Bavarian Blue) 21, 236
    Blythedale Farm Camembert 275
    Camembert de Normandie AOC 6, 14, 15, 25, 44, 46
    Le Cendré des Prés 314
    Comfort Cream 315
    Cooleeney 221
    Farleigh Wallop 182

Little Ryding 185
St. Eadburgha 194
Tunworth 202
Waimata Camembert 341
Camerano DOP 151
Campscott 175
Canaan Labane 336
Canada 268, 312–19
Cañarejal 151
Canestrato Foggiano (Pecorino Dauno) 125
Canestrato Moliterno 106, 112
Canestrato di Pecora 143
Canestrato Pugliese PDO 112
Canestrato di Vacca 143
Cantabria DOP 152
Cantal AOC 45
Capri Lezeen 45
Capricorn Goat 14, 15, 175
Caprino Fresco 112
Caprino Stagionato 113
Carmela 307
Carnia 113
Carré de l'Est 45
Carré Saint Domnin 84
Casatella Trevigiana 113
Casciotta d'Urbino PDO 115
Caseus Helveticus (Sbrinz AOC) 241
Cashel Blue 220, 221
Casín DOP 152
Casolet 115, 134
Castellano 152
Castelmagno PDO 115
Castelo Branco DOP 167
Cathare 48
Cave Aged Marisa 278
Caws Cenarth 215, 216
Cayuse Mountain 307
Cebreiro 153
Cendré Lochois 41
Cendré de Niort 48
Le Cendré des Prés 314
Cendré de Vergy 48
Cerney Pyramid 176
Cerwyn 213
Chabichou du Poitou AOC 49, 52, 92
Chalet d'Alpage 38
Chaource AOC 15, 49
Charolais
    Charolais (France) 49
    Charolais (USA) 278
    Racotin 79
Cheddar & Cheddar-style 19, 47, 180–1, 327
    Appel Farms Cheddar 271
    Avonlea Clothbound Cheddar 312
    Barely Buzzed 272
    Barry's Bay Cheddar 335
    Beechers Flagship Reserve 306
    Bleu Mont Cheddar 275
    Cabot Clothbound 278
    Cantal AOC 45
    Daylesford Cheddar 177, 197
    5 Spoke Creamery Browning Gold 306
    Hafod 214
    Lincolnshire Poacher 185
    Mount Callan 225
    Pendragon 189
    Quickes Hard Goat 190
    R&R Cheddar 297
    Seven-Year-Old Orange Cheddar 319
Cheddar Curds 314
Cheeseboard selections 24–5
Cheesemaking,
    history & techniques 6–7
    see also specific cheeses (eg Gouda); specific types (eg Soft White cheeses)
Cheshire 176
Chevrotin des Aravis AOC 51
Chevrotin des Bauges AOC 51

Chimay
    Chimay à la Bière 227, 229
    Vieux Chimay 229
Chorherrenkäse 238
Christian IX (Danbo) 247
Ch'ti Roux 51
Cîteaux (Abbaye de Cîteaux) 30
City of Ships 279
Clacbitou 49
    Mini Clac 41
Claire de Lune 307
Clava Brie 208
Clemson Blue 279
Clochette 12, 13, 52
Coeur de Neufchâtel AOC 52
Coeur de Rollot 80
Coeur de Touraine 52
Colonel (Livarot AOC) 66
ColoRouge, MouCo 292
Comfort Cream 315
Comté AOC 56–7
Constant Bliss 279
Coolea 220
Cooleeney 221
Corleggy 221
Cornish Blue 176
Cotherstone 177
Cottage Cheese 11
Coulommiers 53
Coupole 280, 310
Crabotin 100
Cranberry Ridge Farm Chèvre 280
Crayeux de Roncq 53
Creamery Subblime 307
Crémet du Cap Blanc-Nez 100
Crémeux du Puy 53
Crescent Dairy Farmhouse 336
Crescenza 116
    Bellwether Farms Crescenza 273
Crottin 219, 225
    Bouquetin de Portneuf 313
    Crottin de Chavignol AOC 13, 35,
      54, 92
    Pine Stump Crottin 309
Crowdie 208, 210
Crozier Blue 221
Le Cru des Érables 315
Cuillin Goats 208
curds
    Cheddar Curds 314
    Meadowcroft Farm Goat's Curd
      338
    Peli Pabo 213
    Schichtkäse 237
    Te Mata Summerlee 340
Curé Nantais 54, 58
Curio Bay Pecorino (Blue River Curio
Bay Pecorino) 335
Curworthy 177
Cyprus 255, 261–3

D

Danablu 247
Danbo 247
Danish Blue (Danablu) 247
Danish Port Salut see Esrom PGI
Dauphin 54
Daylesford Cheddar 177, 197
Daylesford Creamery Penyston 189
Deauville 55
Le Délice des Appalaches 315
Délice des Cabasses 55
Délice de la Vallée 280
Denmark 246, 247–8
Denomination & Designation of
    Origin 8
Derby 194
Desmond 222
Dobbiaco 116
DOC 8
Doddington 178

Dôme de Vézelay 55
Dorset 281
Dorset Blue Vinney 178
Double Gloucester 178
    see also Snodsbury Goat
Dragons Back 213
Dragon's Breath Blue 316
Dry Jack 18, 286, 287
Duddleswell 179
Dunlop 209
Durrus 222

E

Edam & Edam-style 17, 22, 230, 232
    Mahoe Vintage Edam 337
    Mimolette 19, 68
    Tulare Cannonball 303
Eden 281
Edith (Woodside Edith) 334
Eiffel Tower (Pouligny-Saint-Pierre
    AOC) 78
Ekta Gjetost 249
Elk Mountain Tomme 308
Embruns aux Algues 58
Emmental & Emmental-style 322
    Allgäuer Bergkäse 235
    Allgäuer Emmental 234, 235
    Danbo 247
    Emmental de Savoie 58
    Emmental 19, 242–3
    Fontal 117
    Grevéost 251
    Jarlsberg 249
    Maasdam 231
    Samsø 248
England 171, 172–206
Epoisses & Epoisses-style
    Abbaye de la Pierre-qui-Vire 31
    Epoisses Affinée 64
    Epoisses de Bourgogne AOC 48,
      64–5
    Epoisses Frais 64
    Langres AOC 16, 17, 63, 86
    Palet de Bourgogne 71
    Plaisir au Chablis 77
    Soumaintrain 88
Erzincan 261
Esrom PGI 248
Evansdale Farmhouse Brie 336
Everona Piedmont 281
Évora DOP 168
Ewe's Blue 282
Exmoor Blue PGI 179
Extra Mature Smoked Gubbeen 223

F

Fairlight 179
Farleigh Wallop 182
Ferns Edge Goat Dairy Chèvre 308
Feta & Feta-style
    Beyaz Peynir 261
    Big Island Feta 274
    Blue River Tussock Creek Sheep
      Feta 335
    Bryndza PGI 260
    Feta PDO 11, 257, 258–9
    Ffetys 213
    Te Mata Mt. Erin 340
    Weisslacker 237
    Yarra Valley Dairy Persian Fetta
      334
Feuille de Dreux 58
Ffetys 213
Figuette 59
Finland 246, 253
Finlandia Cheese (Oltermanni) 253
Finn 182
Fiore Sardo PDO 116
Fium'Orbu 59

5 Spoke Creamery Browning Gold 306
Flavor-added cheeses 8, 22–3, 24, 25
Fleur-de-Lis 282
Fleur du Maquis 59
    see also Piacere
Fleur de la Terre 282
Flor de Guía 153
Flower Marie 182
Fog Lights 283
Fontal 117
Fontina
    Brindisi Fontina 307
    Fontina PDO 117
Forest Blue (Fowlers Forest Blue) 183
Formaggella del Luinese 117
Formaggio di Fossa 118
Formaggio Primo Sale 126, 129
Formaggio Ubriaco 118
Formai de Mut dell'Alta Val
    Brembana PDO 118
Forme d'Antoine 60
Fort de Béthune 101
Fouchtra 60
Fougerus 60
Fourme d'Ambert AOC 61
Fourme de Laguiole (Laguiole AOC) 63
Fourme de Montbrison AOC 61
Fowlers Forest Blue 183
France 26–101
Les Frères 283
Frisian Farms Mature Gouda 283
Fromage Blanc (Richard Thomas
    Fromage Blanc) 332
fromage fort, Pot Corse 78
Fromage Frais 11
Fromage du Pays Nantais dit du
    Curé (Curé Nantais) 54, 58
Fruité du Boulonnais 61

G

Gabriel 222
Galotiri DOC 257
Gammelost 249
Gamonedo DOP 153
Gamonedo del Valle 153
Gaperon 62
Garrotxa 156
Geitenkaas Met Kruiden 230
Germany 234–7
Gérômé (Munster AOC) 70
Gippsland Blue 328
Gjetost 249
Glebe Brethan 222
Gloucester
    Double Gloucester 178
    Single Gloucester PDO 197
    see also Snodsbury Goat
Goatzarella 284
Golden Cross 183
Golden Glen Creamery Mozzarella
308
Goldilocks 174
Gorau Glas 214
Gorgonzola & Gorgonzola-style
    Bavaria Blu (Bavarian Blue) 21,
      236
    Cornish Blue 176
    Gippsland Blue 328
    Gorgonzola DOP 20, 21, 110–11, 138
Gouda & Gouda-style 19, 22, 230,
    232–3
    Coolea 220
    Frisian Farms Mature Gouda 283
    Ilha Graciosa 168
    Kanterkaas 231
    Leidse Kaas 231
    Mahoe Vintage Gouda 337
    Meyer Vintage Gouda 338
    Mossfield Organic 224
    Nagelkaas 23, 231

Northumberland 187
Oakdale Cheese Company Gouda
    293
Old Grizzly 317
Ribblesdale Original Goat 191
São Jorge DOP 169
Steamboat Island Goat Farm
    Gouda 311
Teifi Farmhouse 218
Tilsiterkäse 253
Winchester Super Aged Gouda 305
Gour Blanc 62
Gour Noir 62
Grace 223
Graciosa (Ilha Graciosa) 168
Grana 130
Grana Padano PDO 19, 119, 138
Grand Queso 284
Gratte-Paille 62
Gravenstein Gold 284
Graviera DOC 256
Grayson 285
Great Hill Blue 285
Greece 254–9
Grevéost 251
Gruyère & Gruyère-style
    Bettelmatt 105
    Graviera DOC 256
    Gruyère AOC 19, 240, 243
    Gruyère Surchoix 285
    Heidi Farm Gruyère 330
    Herrgårdsost 251
    Pleasant Ridge Reserve 295
Gubbeen 223
Guernsey Cream 323
Gunnamatta Gold 329
Gympie Farmhouse Chèvre 329

H

Hafod 214
Halloumi 10, 11, 262–3
    Zany Zeus Halloumi 341
Handkäse 236
Hard cheeses 8, 18–19, 25
Hartwell 288
Harvest Moon 316
Harzer Käse 236
Havarti & Havarti-style
    Havarti (Havarthi) 17, 248
    Oltermanni 253
    Turunmaa 253
Healey's Pyengana 329
Heidi Farm Gruyère 330
Heidi Farm Raclette 330
Hereford Hop 22, 183
Herreño 156
Herrgårdsost 251
Hervé 227
Hobelkäse 240
Hocpustertaler (Pusteria) 144
Hoja Santa 288
Holland 226, 230–3
Holy Goat La Luna 330
Holy Goat Pandora 331
Hooligan 288
Hubbardston Blue 289
Hungary 254, 255, 260
Hushållsost 251

I

Ibérico 156
Ibores DOP 157
Icklesham 179
Idiazábal DO 23, 157
Ilha Graciosa 168
Inbar 264
Innes Button 25, 184
Iona Cromag 209
Ireland 170, 219–25

Irongate (Te Mata Irongate) 340
Ironstone Extra 331
Isis (Oxford Isis) 188
Isle of Wight Blue 184
Israel 255, 264–5
Italico 119
Italy 102–45

J

Jack see Monterey Jack
Jacks' Cheese 286
Japan 322–5
Jarlsberg 249
Jensen's Red Washed Rind 331
Jersey Shield 187
Juustoleipä 253

K

Kachokabaro 323
Kanterkaas 231
Kapiti (Mt. Hector Kapiti) 339
Karikaas Vintage Leyden 337
Kaseri DOC 256
Kashkaval 260
Kebbuck 209
Kefalotyri DOC 257
Keiems Bloempje 228
Keltic Gold 184
Kernhem 230
Ketem 13, 264
King Christian (Danbo) 247
King Island Roaring Forties 332
King Island Stormy 333
Knockdrinna Gold 223
Kunik 289

L

La Aulaga Camerano DOP 151
La Barre du Jour 313
La Luna (Holy Goat La Luna) 330
La Peral 161
la Pierre-qui-Vire (Abbaye de la Pierre-qui-Vire) 31
La Sauvagine 318
Labane 265
    Canaan Labane 336
Laguiole AOC 63
Lagundo 143
L'Alt Urgell y La Cerdanya DOP 148
Lanark Blue 212
Lancashire 185
Langres AOC 16, 17, 63, 86
Larzac 289
Latteria 119
Lavistown 223, 224
Lavort 63
Le Cabanon 314
Le Cendré des Prés 314
Le Cru des Érables 315
Le Délice des Appalaches 315
Le Paillasson de l'isle d'Orléans 317
Le Petit Chèvre Bleu 295
Le Sabot de Blanchette 318
Lebanon 255, 264
Leicester see Red Leicester
Leidse Kaas 231
    Nökkelost 250
Les Frères 283
Lewis (Bruny Island Lewis) 328
Leyden (Karikaas Vintage Leyden) 337
Liébana DOP 157
Limburger 236
    Hervé 227
Lincolnshire Poacher 185
Lingot de la Ginestarie 66
Little Ryding 185
Little Wallop 186

Livarot AOC 66
    see also Deauville
Lord of the Hundreds 186
Los Montes de Toledo 158
Losange de Saint-Paul 100
Lou Rocaillou 66
Lou Sotch 67
Lubelski 255
Lucullus 67

M

Maasdam 231
    Mercer 338
Mâconnaise AOC 67
    Bouton-de-Culotte 41
Mahoe Vintage Edam 337
Mahoe Vintage Gouda 337
Mahón DO 154–5
Mainzer 236
Maiorchino (Piacentinu Ennese) 128
Majorero DOP 158
Manchego
    Grand Queso 284
    Manchego DOC 18, 19, 162–3
Manouri 257
Marisa (Cave Aged Marisa) 278
Maroilles & Maroilles-style
    Baguette Laonnaise 33
    Boulette de Papleux 100
    Dauphin 54
    Fort de Béthune 101
    Maroilles AOC 6, 68
    Rollot 80
    Vieux-Lille 99
Marzolino 122
Mascare 101
Mascarpone 11, 122, 283
Matos St. George 290
Maytag Blue 290
Meadowcroft Farm Goat's Curd 338
Menuet 290
Mercer Maasdam 338
Meredith Blue 332
Mesost 252
Mexico 269, 320
Meyer Vintage Gouda 338
Mezzo Secco 286, 287, 291
Midcoast Teleme 308
Milleens 170, 224
Mimolette 19, 68
Mini Clac 41
Mona 291
Monastery-style see Trappist-style
Mondseer 238
Monet 291
Mont des Cats (Abbaye du Mont des Cats) 30
Mont d'Or & Mont d'Or-style
    Cabri Ariégeois 44
    Mont d'Or AOC 68
    Pechegos 73
Mont Ventoux 101
Montasio
    Montasio PDO 122
    Samish Bay Cheese Montasio 309
Monte Enebro 158
Monte Veronese PDO 123
Monterey Jack 286–7
    Dry Jack 18, 286, 287
    Mezzo Secco 286, 287, 291
    Young Jack 286, 287
Los Montes de Toledo 158
Morbier AOC 69
    see also La Barre du Jour
Mori No Cheese 323
Morlacco 123
Morn Dew 190
Morvan 69
Mossfield Organic 224
Mothais-sur-Feuille 69
MouCo ColoRouge 292

Mount Callan 225
Mt. Eliza Red Leicester 339
Mt. Erin (Te Mata Mt. Erin) 340
Mt. Hector Kapiti 339
Mt. Tam 276, 292
Mountain Top Bleu 292
Mozzarella & Mozzarella-style 10, 11, 274, 283, 288
    Bubulus Bubalis Mozzarella di Bufala 277
    Burrata 107, 145
    Goatzarella 284
    Golden Glen Creamery Mozzarella 308
    Lubelski 255
    Mozzarella di Bufala 120–1, 144
    Mozzarella Passita (Scamorza) 137
    Shaw River Buffalo Mozzarella 333
Mt. see Mount
Munster
    Munster AOC 70, 101
    St. Severin 238
Murazzano PDO 123
Murcia al Vino DOP 159
Mutschli 241
    Pleasant Valley Dairy Mutschli 309
Mysost 249
Myzithra 257

N

Nagelkaas (Nail cheese) 23, 231
Natural smoked cheeses see Smoked cheeses
Neal's Yard Creamery Finn 182
Neal's Yard Creamery Perroche 189
Neal's Yard Creamery Ragstone 191
The Netherlands 226, 230–3
Neudorf Richmond Red 339
Neufchâtel 52
New Forest Blue 186
New Zealand 327, 335–41
Nîmois 101
Nisa DOP 168
Nökkelost 250
Norsworthy 187, 190
Northumberland 187
Norway 246, 249–50
Notre-Dame de Belloc (Abbaye Notre-Dame de Belloc) 30
Nut Knowle Farm Wealden 203
Nut Knowle Farm Wealdway 204

O

Oakdale Cheese Company Gouda 293
O'Cooch 293
Ogleshield 187
Oka Classique 316
Old Grizzly 317
Old Kentucky Tome 293
Old Sarum 188
Old Smales (Old Winchester) 188
Old Winchester 188
Olivet 70
Olivet Cendré 70
Olivet au Foin 70
Olivet Poivre 70
Olmützer Quargel 236
Oltermanni 253
organic cheeses
    Baby Blue 312
    Bath Soft Cheese 172
    Birdwood Blue Heaven 173
    Bleu Mont Cheddar 275
    Campscott 175
    Le Cendré des Prés 314
    Claire de Lune 307
    Creamery Sublime 307
    Daylesford Cheddar 177, 197

Fairlight 179
Fleur de la Terre 282
Grace 223
Gunnamatta Gold 329
Holy Goat La Luna 330
Holy Goat Pandora 331
Keiems Bloempje 228
Little Ryding 185
Menuet 290
Mossfield Organic 224
Mt. Tam 292
Pas de Rouge 228
Pavé de la Ginestarie 72
Penyston 189
St. Tola Log 225
Sussex Slipcote 198
Tarentaise 300
Vaquero Blue 304
Original Blue (Point Reyes Original Blue) 309
Original Goat (Ribblesdale Original Goat) 191
Orkney 212
Ossau-Iraty AOC 70
    see also Tomme de Brebis Corse
Ossolano 124
Oštiepok PGI 260
Oszcypek 260
Ouray 308
Oxford Blue 188
Oxford Isis 188

P

Paglierine 124
Paglietta (Paglierine) 124
Le Paillasson de l'isle d'Orléans 317
Pakipaki (Te Mata Pakipaki) 340
Palermo DOP 159
Palet de Bourgogne 71
Pandora (Holy Goat Pandora) 331
Pannarello 124
Pannerone 125
Pant-Ys-Gawn 214
Parmigiano-Reggiano (Parmesan) & Parmigiano-Reggiano-style
    Dry Jack 18, 286, 287
    Mahón DO 154–5
    Parmigiano-Reggiano DOC 6, 18, 19, 130–1
    Sbrinz AOC 241
Pas de Rouge 228
Pasiego de las Garmillas 159
Passendale 228
pasta filata cheeses
    Kashkaval 260
    Ragusano PDO 133
    Stracciata 145
    Vastedda della Valle del Belice 145
    see also Caciocavallo; Mozzarella; Provolone
Pata de Mulo 160
    Monte Enebro 158
Pavé d'Auge 71
Pavé Blésois 71
Pavé de la Ginestarie 72
Pavé de Moyaux 71
Pavé du Nord 72
Pavé du Plessis 71
Pavé de Roubaix (Pavé du Nord) 72
Pavin 72
Payoyo 160
PDO 8
Peasmarsh 179
Pecan Chèvre 295
Pechegos 73
Pecorino 18
    Blue River Curio Bay Pecorino 335
    Pecorino Crotonese 125
    Pecorino Dauno 125
    Pecorino delle Crete Senesi (Pecorino di Pienza) 127

Pecorino di Filiano PDO 143
Pecorino Laticauda 144
Pecorino di Pienza 127
Pecorino Romano PDO 127
Pecorino Sardo PDO 127
Pecorino Sardo Dolce 127
Pecorino Sardo Maturo 127
Pecorino Siciliano PDO 9, 128
Pecorino Toscano PDO 128
Sardo 321
Pedrazzi's Jack Cheese 286
Pélardon AOC 73
Pélardon d'Altier 73
Pélardon d'Anduze 73
Pélardon de Cévennes 73
Peli Pabo 213
Peña Blanca de Corrales 160
Pendragon 189
Penyston 189
Pérail 73
La Peral 161
Perl Las 215
Perroche 189
Persian Fetta, Yarra Valley Dairy 334
Persillé des Aravis 101
Persillé des Grand-Bornand 101
Persillé des Thônes 101
Persillé de Tignes 50, 76
Le Petit Chèvre Bleu 295
Petit Fiancé des Pyrénées 76
Petit Frère 283
Petit Marcel 308
Petit Nuage 324
Piacentinu Ennese 128
Piacere 317
Piano Hill Ironstone Extra 331
Piave 129
Picodon AOC 76
Picón Bejes Tresviso DOP 161
Picos de Europa (Valdeón DO) 166
Picurino (Primo Sale) 126, 129
Piedmont (Everona Piedmont) 281
Pierre-qui-Vire (Abbaye de la
Pierre-qui-Vire) 31
Pierre-Robert 77
Pine Stump Crottin 309
Pithiviers 77
Plaisir au Chablis 77
Pleasant Ridge Reserve 295
Pleasant Valley Dairy Mutschli 309
Point Reyes Original Blue 309
Pondhopper 296
Pont Gar 215
Pont-l'Évêque & Pont-l'Évêque-style
Deauville 55
Pavé d'Auge 71
Penyston 189
Pont-l'Évêque AOC 78
Te Mata Irongate 340
Port Ahuriri (Te Mata Port Ahuriri)
340
Port-du-Salut style
Abbaye du Mont des Cats 30
Esrom PGI 248
Oka Classique 316
Portugal 146–7, 167–9
Posbury 190
Postel 229
Pot Corse 78
Pouligny-Saint-Pierre AOC 78, 92
Pozo Tomme 309
Prälatenkäse (Chorherrenkäse) 238
Prästost 252
Prestige 318
Pride of Bacchus 281
Primo Sale 126, 129
Provolone & Provolone-style
Kaseri DOC 256
Provolone (Italy) 129
Provolone (Japan) 324
Provolone del Monaco (PDO
transitory list) 132
Provolone Valpadana PDO 132

Provolone Valpadana Dolce 132
Provolone Valpadana Piccante
132
Puant de Lille (Vieux-Lille) 99
Pusteria 144
Pustertaler (Pusteria) 144
Puzzone 115
Puzzone di Moena 132
Pyengana (Healey's Pyengana) 329

Q

Quark
Surfing Goat Dairy Quark 300
see also Schichtkäse
Quartirolo Lombardo PDO 133
see also Salva Cremasco
Quattrofacce (Ragusano PDO) 133
Queijo Mineiro 321
Queso Anejo 320
Queso Blanco 320
Queso Blanco Pais 286
Queso de Cabra Rufino 151
Queso Fresco 320
Queso de Mano 296
Queso Nata de Cantabria DOP 152
Queso del Pais 286
Quickes Hard Goat 190

R

R&R Cheddar 297
Rachel 190
Raclette & Raclette-style
La Barre du Jour 313
Heidi Farm Raclette 330
Ogleshield 187
Raclette (Switzerland) 241
Raclette fumée 79
Raclette la moutarde 79
Raclette de Savoie 79
Raclette au vin blanc 79
Tomme de Chartreux 91
Racotin 79
Ragstone 191
Ragusano PDO 133
Ranscombe 218
Raschera PDO 133
Re-formed cheeses 22, 23
Reblochon & Reblochon-style
Abbaye de Tamié 31
Bishop Kennedy 207
Chevrotin des Aravis AOC 51
Chevrotin des Bauges AOC 51
Crémeux du Puy 53
Reblochon de Savoie AOC 51, 74–5
Red Hill Gunnamatta Gold 329
Red Leicester 191
Mt. Eliza Red Leicester 339
Red Washed Rind (Tarago River
Jensen's Red Washed Rind) 331
reindeer milk cheese 6, 246
Juustoleipä 253
Requeijão Cremosa (Catupiry) 321
Ribblesdale Original Goat 191
Richard Thomas Fromage Blanc
332
Richmond Red (Neudorf Richmond
Red) 339
Ricotta 11, 277
Ricotta Affumicata 114, 135
Ricotta di Bufala Campana (PDO
transitory list) 144
Ricotta di Pecora 135
Ricotta Romana PDO 144
Ridder 250
Rigotte de Condrieu AOC 79
Rind-flavored cheeses 22, 23
Roaring Forties 332
Robiola
Murazzano PDO 123

Robiola (Japan) 324
Robiola d'Alba 135
Robiola di Roccaverano PDO 136
Robiola della Valsassina 136
Rocaillou (Lou Rocaillou) 66
Rocamadour AOC 67, 80
Rocha Uverani (Robiola di
Roccaverano) 136
Rogue River Blue 294, 296
Rollot 80
Roncal DOP 161
Roquefort & Roquefort-style
Alpine Lakes Creamy Bleu 306
Bleu d'Auvergne AOC 36
Bleu des Causses AOC 36
Crozier Blue 221
Ewe's Blue 282
Lanark Blue 212
Maytag Blue 290
Roquefort AOC 8, 20, 21, 82–3
Turkeez 265
Rosa Camuna 134
Rosary Plain 194
Rosemary's Waltz 297
Rouelle du Tarn 80
Rove Cendré 81
Roves des Garrigues 81
R&R Cheddar 297
Rubens 229
Rustic (Sharpham Rustic) 196
Rustic Bleu Goat 309

S

Sablé de Wissant 81
Le Sabot de Blanchette 318
Sage Derby 194
Saint-Christophe 84
Saint Domnin 84
St. Eadburgha 194
St. Endellion 195
Saint Félicien 84
Saint-Florentin 85
St. Gall Extra Mature 225
Saint-Jacques 85
St. Jorge 297
Saint-Marcellin 85
see also Saint Felicien
Sainte-Maure & Sainte-Maure-style
Golden Cross 183
Ketem 264
Saint-Christophe 84
Sainte-Maure de Touraine AOC
24, 92–3
Saint-Nectaire AOC 87
Saint-Nicolas-de-la-Dalmerie 87
St. Oswald 195
St. Severin 238
St. Tola Log 13, 225
Sakura 325
Sally Jackson 298
Salva Cremasco (PDO transitory list)
136
Samish Bay Cheese Montasio 309
Samsø 248
Danbo 247
San Juaquin Gold 298
San Simón da Costa 164
Sancerrois (Berrichon) 35
Santa Agata's Nipple (Tétoun e Santa
Agata) 89
São Jorge DOP 169
see also Ilha Graciosa
Sardo 321
Sarments d'Amour 87
La Sauvagine 318
Saval 215
Sbrinz AOC 241
Scamorza 137
Scamorza Affumicata 137
Schabziger 244
Schachtelkäse (Mondseer) 238

Schichtkäse 237
Scotch (Lou Scotch) 67
Scotland 170, 207–12
Seastack 298
Selles-sur-Cher AOC 88, 92, 98
Semi-soft cheeses 8, 16–17, 24, 25
Serendipity 325
Serpa DOP 169
Serra da Estrela DOP 169
Seven-Year-Old Orange Cheddar 319
Sharpham 15, 195
Sharpham Rustic 196
Sharpham Ticklemore Goat 199
Shaw River Buffalo Mozzarella 333
Shepherd (Vermont Shepherd) 304
Shipcord 196
Shropshire Blue 196
Sierra Nevada 299
Sieur du Duplessis 319
Signal 88
Silter 144
Single Gloucester PDO 197
Slipcote (Sussex Slipcote) 198
Slovakia 254, 260
Smear-ripened cheeses 17
Smoked cheeses 22, 23
Ahumado de Pría 148
Extra Mature Smoked Gubbeen
223
Gamonedo DOP 153
Herreño 156
Idiazábal DO 23, 157
Liébana DOP 157
Oštiepok PGI 260
Palmero DOP 159
Pendragon 189
Raclette fumée 79
Ricotta Affumicata 114, 135
San Simón da Costa 164
Scamorza Affumicata 137
Smokey Blue Cheese 299
Up in Smoke 311
Smokey Blue Cheese 299
Snodsbury Goat 197
Soft Wheel 299
Soft White cheeses 8, 14–15, 25
Sora 137, 140
Soumaintrain 88
Spain 146–6
Spressa delle Giudicarie PDO 137
Spretz Tzaorì (Puzzone di Moena)
132
Squacquarone 144
Steamboat Island Goat Farm Gouda
311
Stelvio PDO 145
Stichelton 197
Stilfser (Stelvio PDO) 145
Stilton & Stilton-style
Shropshire Blue 196
Stichelton 197
Stilton PDO 20, 21, 192–3
White Stilton PDO 205
Stinking Bishop 17, 197, 198
Stony Man 281
Stormy 333
Stracchino di Gorgonzola
(Gorgonzola DOP) 20, 21, 110–11,
138
Stracciata 145
Strachìtunt 141
Strathdon Blue 212
Strzelecki Blue 333
Suffolk Gold 198
Summerlee (Te Mata Summerlee)
340
Surfing Goat Dairy Quark 300
Sussex Slipcote 198
Swaledale Goat 199
Sweden 246, 250–2
Swiss Tilsit 237
Switzerland 234, 237, 240–5

T

Taleggio
   Dorset 281
   Taleggio DOP & PDO 17, 24, 138–9
Talley Mountain Goat's Cheese 218
Talley Mountain Mature Cheese 218
Tamié (Abbaye de Tamié) 31
Tarago River Gippsland Blue 328
Tarago River Jensen's Red Washed Rind 331
Tarago River Strzelecki Blue 333
Taramundi 22, 164
Tarentais 89
Tarentaise 300
Taupinette Charentaise 89
Taupinière 300
Te Mata Irongate 340
Te Mata Mt. Erin 340
Te Mata Pakipaki 340
Te Mata Port Ahuriri 340
Te Mata Summerlee 340
Teifi Farmhouse 218
Teleme (Midcoast Teleme) 308
Telford Reserve 301
terroir 7, 8
Tête de Moine AOC 244
Tetilla DO 164
Tétoun e Santa Agata 89
Thermized cheeses 19
thistle rennet cheeses 147
   Cañarejal 151
   Castelo Branco DOP 167
   Évora DOP 168
   Flor de Guîa 153
   Nisa DOP 168
   Serpa DOP 169
   Serra da Estrela DOP 169
   Tortas Extremeñas 165
Thomasville Tomme 301
Ticklemore Beenleigh Blue 173
Ticklemore Goat 199
Tickton 199
Tilsit (Swiss Tilsit) 237
Tilsiterkäse 237
tipicità 7, 8
Tiroler Graukäse 239
Toma Piemontese PDO 141
Tome & Tomini 141
Tome des Bauges AOC 90
Tomette (Ashed Tomette) 272
Tomino di Melle 141
Tommes
   Appalachian 271
   Elk Mountain Tomme 308
   Old Kentucky Tome 293

Pozo Tomme 309
Shipcord 196
Thomasville Tomme 301
Tomme à l'Ancienne 90
Tomme de Bargkass 101
Tomme de Brebis Corse 90
Tomme Caprine des Pyrénées 91
Tomme de Chartreux 91
Tomme de Chèvre 244
Tomme de Chèvre des Charentes 91
Tomme Fleurette 244
Tomme aux Herbes 94
Tomme de Savoie 91, 94
Tomme Vaudoise 244
Tumalo Tomme 303
Tommettes
   Ashed Tomette 272
   Tommette Brebis des Alpes 94
   Tommette de Chèvre des Bauges 95
Tortas
   Cabra Rufino 151
   Cañarejal 151
   Los Montes de Toledo 158
   Torta de Barros 165
   Torta del Casar 165
   Torta la Serena 151, 165
   Tortas Extremeñas 165
Toscanello 145
Tou del Til.lers 165
Trappe de Beval 100
Trappe d'Echourgnac 95
Trappist-style 6, 16
   Abbaye de Cîteaux 30
   Abbaye de Troisvaux 100
   Chimay à la bière 227, 229
   Chorherrenkäse 238
   Losange de Saint-Paul 100
   Mondseer 238
   Oka Classique 316
   Pas de Rouge 228
   St. Severin 238
   Trappe de Beval 100
Trèfle 95
Trentingrana PDO 142
Triple Cream Wheel 301
Trois Cornes de Vendée 96
Troisvaux (Abbaye de Troisvaux) 100
Tronchón 165
Trouville 71
Truffe de Valensole 96
Tulare Cannonball 303
Tulum 261
Tumalo Tomme 303
Tunworth 202
Tupí 166
Turkeez 265
Turkey 255, 261
Turunmaa 253

Tussock Creek Sheep Feta, Blue River 335
Twig Farm Square Cheese 303
Two Faced Blue Peccato 311
Tymsboro 202

U

U Bel Fiuritu 96
U Pecurinu 97
Up in Smoke 311
USA 266–7, 270–311

V

Vache de Vashon 311
Vacherin Fribourgeois AOC 245
Vacherin Mont D'or AOC 17, 245
Valdeón DO 25, 166
Valençay
   Cerney Pyramid 176
   Valençay AOC 13, 92, 97
Valle D'Aosta Fromadzo PDO 145
Valle Maggia 245
Valtellina Casera PDO 145
Vaquero Blue 304
Vastedda della Valle del Belice (PDO transitory list) 145
Västerbottenost 252
Vaudoise 244
Venaco 97
Ventadour 99
Vermont Ayr 304
Vermont Shepherd 304
Vezzena 115, 142
Vicky's Spring Splendour 13, 319
Vieux-Boulogne 99
Vieux Chimay 229
Vieux-Lille 99
Village Green 202
Vorarlberger Bergkäse 239
Vulscombe 203

W

Wabash Cannonball 305
Waimata Camembert 341
Wales 171, 213–18
Washed-curd cheeses 19
   Healey's Pyengana 329
   Murcia al Vino DOP 159
   Norsworthy 187, 190
   see also Edam; Gouda
Washed-rind cheeses 16, 17
Washington Washrind 334
Waterloo 203

Wealden 203
Wealdway 204
Wedmore 204
Weinkäse 239
Weisslacker 237
Wensleydale 204
   Wensleydale with Cranberries 22
whey cheeses
   Anthotyros DOC 256
   Kefalatyri DOC 257
   Manouri 257
   Mesost 252
   Myzithra 257
   Petit Nuage 324
   see also Ricotta
White Nancy 205
White Stilton PDO 205
Whitehaven 205
Whitestone Windsor Blue 341
Widmers Cellars Aged Brick Cheese 311
Wild Garlic Yarg 200
Winchelsea 179
Winchester Super Aged Gouda 305
Windrush 206
Windsor Blue (Whitestone Windsor Blue) 341
Wine choices 25
   see also specific cheeses (eg Roquefort AOC); specific types (eg Soft White cheeses)
Winnemere 305
Woodside Edith 334
Woolsery English Goat 206
Wyfe of Bath 206

Y

Yama No Cheese 325
Yarg Cornish Cheese 22, 24, 200–1
Yarra Valley Dairy Persian Fetta 334
Yerba Santa Dairy Fresca 311
yogurt-based cheeses
   Canaan Labane 336
   Labane 265
Young Jack 286, 287

Z

Zamorano DO 166
Zany Zeus Halloumi 341
Zfatit 265

Contributors

FRANCE: As a native of Southern France, **Stéphane Blohorn** is the product of a Provençal education, which shows in his love of the outdoors, of animals, and of the gifts of the land. In 2005, Stéphane took over Androuët's house, and in 2006, he was inducted into the Guilde des Fromagers (France's elite cheese brotherhood). He dreams of preserving and furthering the quality and diversity of cheeses for future generations.

ITALY: Vincenzo Bozzetti began his career as a dairy master in 1960, and after nearly 40 years in the industry, he began training and teaching cheese judges for commercial trades and cheese contests. Today, he is a manager and columnist for *Il Latte*, an Italian dairy magazine. Vincenzo has written several dairy books and many articles for Italian and international dairy magazines.

SPAIN AND PORTUGAL: Monika Linton founded Brindisa, a highly respected warehouse and shop that brings Spanish food to British customers, 21 years ago. Armed with years of instruction in the language and her experiences of living with Spanish and Catalan people, she has guided the shop from its beginning, when it carried only Spanish farmhouse cheeses, into the successful business it is today.

ENGLAND: It was the award-winning cheeseboard at Leith's, where he waited tables while studying journalism, that first made **Joe Warwick** a cheerleader for British cheese. He is the founder of The World's 50 Best Restaurants Awards, the author of *Hg2 Eat London*, and a contributor of articles on restaurants, food and travel to publications including *The Observer*, *Waitrose Food Illustrated* and *Square Meal*.

Katie Jarvis's interest in cheese began at the age of eight, when she spent a year in Paris. As a supporter of artisan producers, she writes about food and reviews restaurants for *Cotswold Life* magazine, and has written two books on the Cotswolds. She is one of the judges at the British Cheese Awards.

SCOTLAND: Kevin John Broome took up a full apprenticeship in cooking and went on to achieve two Michelin stars for his cooking at both of his co-owned Channel Islands restaurants. Kevin has won many awards for his fresh, unique, and locally sourced dishes. He now lives and works in the Highlands of Scotland with his partner Liz and son Jerome.

WALES: As a food writer, food consultant, and former chef to the rich and famous, **Angela Gray** has had a lot of food experience. Her passion for food has led her to present cookery series for the BBC, write books, and participate in live cooking festivals. Angela is also course director at Wales' first food and wine school, where she teaches children and adults how to cook.

IRELAND: Dianne Curtin is a freelance food writer, stylist, broadcaster, and author with a special interest in Irish artisan food production. In 2006, she set up a weekly artisan food market, and in 2007, published her first book, *The Creators, Individuals of Irish Food*. Dianne works closely with several organizations to promote Ireland's regional produce.

BELGIUM, DENMARK, NORWAY, SWEDEN, FINLAND, GREECE, HUNGARY, SLOVAKIA, MEXICO, BRAZIL, AND ARGENTINA: Jim Davies has helped to run The Great British Cheese Festival and The British Cheese Awards. He has a passion for seasonal, high-quality, local foods, which led him to become a director of The Cotswold Brewing Company, an artisan brewery that produces fresh, additive-free lagers and wheat beer.

THE NETHERLANDS: Aad Vernooij has been working in the Information Department of the Dutch Dairy Association since 1980. He is the author of a book on the history of fine Dutch cheeses.

GERMANY, AUSTRIA, AND SWITZERLAND: Hansueli Renz was born into a life of cheese, as both his father and grandfather specialized in making soft cheese. After attending the Commerical School in Neufchâtel, he progressed from apprentice to master to expert. After working for 15 years in his own soft cheese plant, which he sold in 1987, Hansueli started a cheese shop with his wife. In 2007 he sold the shop and retired.

TURKEY, CYPRUS, LEBANON, AND ISRAEL: Cheese expert and chef **Ran Buck** studied at the French Culinary Institute and specialized in cheese at the New York Ideal Cheese Shop. Returning to Israel, Ran established two cheese importing companies and a concept cheese shop. Ran wrote *Gvinot*—the most complete and encompassing guide to cheese written in Hebrew.

Sagi Cooper started his culinary writing career in 2002. He writes for several magazines as well as online portals, including Israel's www.ynet. co.il (where he co-writes a column about cheese with Ran Buck).

USA (East Coast): Sheana Davis, creator and owner of The Epicurean Connection, is celebrating 20 years as chef, caterer, and culinary educator. She offers a range of food experiences and services while traveling between Sonoma, California, and New Orleans, Louisiana. Sheana has recently released the cheese Délice de la Vallée to the national market.

USA (West Coast): Richard Sutton's life-long love of cheese led him to work at Paxton & Whitfield in London, where he acquired much of his cheese training. In 2006, he moved to New Orleans, Louisiana, where he and his wife attended university. Together, they founded St. James Cheese Company, which supplies many of the city's restaurants and offers one of the largest selections of cheese in the southern United States.

CANADA: Gurth Pretty is the founder of www. CheeseofCanada.ca; author of *The Definitive Guide to Canadian Artisanal and Fine Cheese* (a World Gourmand Cookbook award winner); and co-author of *The Definitive Canadian Wine and Cheese Cookbook*. He is active within the Canadian cheese industry as chairman of the Ontario Cheese Society and as a member of La Société des fromages du Québec.

JAPAN: In 1986, **Rumiko Honma** established Fermier, a mostly French cheese company in Tokyo. Rumiko has always emphasized the origins of cheeses, and as such, has visited many places to see the cheeses being made. Rumiko has become one of the key figures spreading information about European culture through cheese in Japan.

Rie Hijikata began exploring cheese by studying the history, origin, making, and terroir of cheeses. That knowledge base was expanded during a stay at an organic cheesemaking farm in Switzerland. Rie now works for Fermier's import department.

AUSTRALIA: Will Studd has worked with specialist cheeses for more than three decades. After establishing delicatessens in London, he moved to Australia. Will has written several books, and he produces and presents the international TV show Cheese Slices. Following his campaign to allow the sale of raw-milk cheese in Australia, Will was made the only Ambassadeur of the Guilde des Fromagers and awarded the Ordre Mérite Agricole.

NEW ZEALAND: Martin Aspinwall started his cheese career during a one-year sabbatical from social work, which extended into several years at London's Neal's Yard Dairy. After emigrating to New Zealand, Martin and his Kiwi wife Sarah started selling cheeses at the markets in Christchurch, and in 2002, they opened Canterbury Cheesemongers, a community bakery and cheese shop.

Acknowledgments

Juliet Harbutt's Acknowledgments

Writing, editing, researching, and publishing a book like this could not be achieved without a team effort from all concerned and a genuine commitment to achieving excellence, and the author would like to thank all those directly involved, particularly the contributors and the team at Dorling Kindersley in London.

However, I would like to say a special thank you to those people who were there to encourage, feed, and cajole me when the task seemed insurmountable. Linda Slide, Sue Taylor and Casper from the Cotswold Consultancy, Katie Jarvis, freelance journalist, Jim Davis, script writer and researcher, Miles and Emily Lampson of the Kingham Plough, Diana Tietjens and Sarah Aspinwall (New Zealand), Kate Arding, Richard Sutton and Cowgirl Creamery (USA), Kevin John Broome, and Rory Stone (Scotland).

The knowledge and inspiration however for a book like this has come not only from working in the industry for nearly 30 years as a retailer, affineur, trainer, and speaker but from meeting my cheese heroes. The most influential and inspirational cheese experts of the 20th and 21st century whose common traits are a passion for cheese and a desire to share it. Patrick Rance, Pierre Androuet, James Aldridge, Eurwen Richards, Carole Faulkner, Mariano Sanchez, Eugene Burns, and all the wonderful cheesemakers who have shared their cheeses and their dreams with me.

Dorling Kindersley's Acknowledgments

Will Heap, Alex Havret, Sara Essex, Kelsie Parsons, Andrew Harris, Stephen Goodenough, Sean McDevitt, Oded Marom, and Cath Harries for photography; Danaya Bunnag, Mandy Earey, Pamela Shiels for design assistance; Amy Sutton and Todd Webb for illustrations; Dawn Bates, Siobhan O'Connor, Helena Caldon, Tarda Davison-Aitkins for editorial assistance; Jenny Faithfull for picture research; Susan Bosanko for the index; Rupert Linton and Katie Jarvis for food research and writing; Jane Ewart for art direction in Paris; Susan Varajanant for food styling in New York; François at Androuët's, Paris; Charles Martell at Dymock for allowing us to photograph the Stinking Bishop process; Rebecca Warren, Michelle Baxter, Liza Kaplan, of the New York office; Rita Costa and Cynthia Gilbert, of DK IPL; Rebecca Amarnani, Blaine Williams, Terri Moore, Gillian Morgan.

And the following for generously supplying cheese for photography: Rachael Sills at KäseSwiss, Jonas Aurell at Scandinavian Kitchen, Monika Linton at Brindisa, Rippon Cheese Stores, Neal's Yard Dairy, Harrods, Sue Cloke at Cheese at Leadenhall, Dominic at The Borough Cheese Company, Mortimer & Bennett, Valio, Rick Stein's Delicatessen, Mr. Christian's Delicatessen, Jeroboam's, Rick Stein's Delicatessen, Swara Trading International Ltd, Nigel Jefferies at Y Cwt Caws, Loraine Makowski-Heaton at Kid Me Not, Cynthia Jennings at Pant Mawr Cheeses, Kathy Biss at West Highland Dairy, Margaret Davies at Quirt Farm, Kellys Organic, Mossfield Organic Farm, Silke Croppe at Corleggy Cheese, De Kaaskammer, Poncelet, Kaasaffineurs Michel Van Tricht & zoon, FrieslandCampina Cheese & Butter; Dries Debergh at Het Hinkelspel; Adbdij van Postel; Chimay Fromages; Murray's Cheese, New York; Luigi Guffanti, Italy; Jose Luis Martin, Spain; Rainha Santa; Iberica.